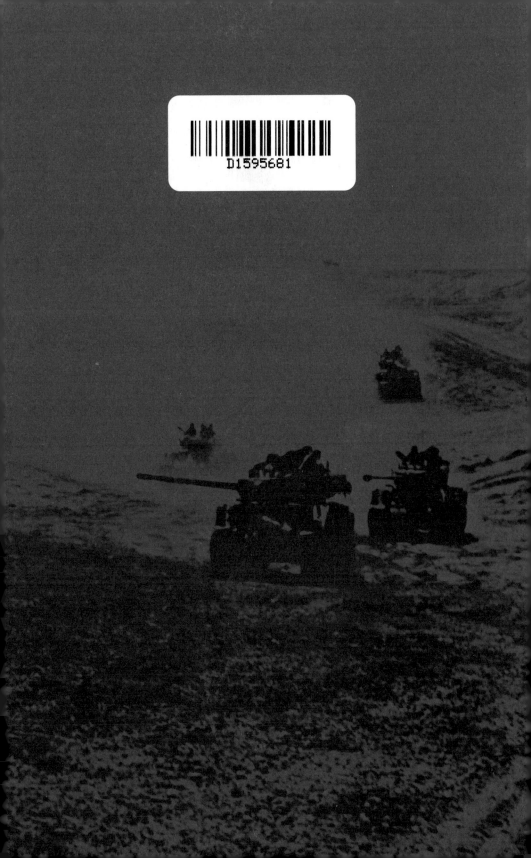

THE LONG WAR ✳

Israel and the Arabs Since 1946

THE LONG WAR

Israel and the Arabs Since 1946

By J. Bowyer Bell

Prentice-Hall, Inc., Englewood Cliffs, N. J.

Passages from *Diary of the Sinai Campaign* by Moshe Dayan have been reprinted by permission of Harper & Row, Publishers.

From *New Star in the Near East* by Kenneth W. Bilby. Copyright 1950 by Kenneth W. Bilby, reprinted by permission of Doubleday & Company, Inc.

From *The Edge of the Sword* by Netanel Lorch. Copyright © 1961 by Netanel Lorch, reprinted by permission of G. P. Putnam's Sons.

From *A Soldier With the Arabs* by Sir John Glubb. Reprinted by permission of Hodder and Stoughton Limited.

This book is dedicated to two men without whose very different contributions this book would never have been written. For my seniors:

John Bowyer Bell, senior   Charles Snowden Rockey, senior

Preface

Some years ago Albert B. Gerber of Philadelphia, in what I now suspect was an ill-advised maneuver, prodded me onto the dark and bloody ground of contemporary Middle Eastern history, leaving me there, poorly equipped, to grope my way toward this book. What has eventually evolved in the light of my serious shortcomings—no knowledge of Hebrew and less of Arabic—is not so much a conventional history of an immensely complicated era still largely beyond the reach of the skilled specialists but rather a narrative of war by various means. If it is true that war, in Karl von Clausewitz's hallowed statement, is the extension of policy by other means, then the reverse is also true and nowhere truer than in the twenty-year Israeli-Arab conflict, where no opportunity, however slight, has been neglected to maim an enemy.

Assuming, as did Cicero, that wars are undertaken so that men may live in peace without suffering wrong, then few wars have been so justified as that between the Arabs and the Israelis, for their ambitions have conflicted, forcing one to live in frustration and the other in fear. The clash of Zionist and Arab aspirations, almost more than any other contempoary issue, has been irreconcilable and, more dangerous to international stability, impossible to soften. The Arabs feel that they have been shamefully wronged by the Zionists. For twenty

years they have seized every available means, violent or not, to re-
deem their heritage in Palestine. The Israelis hold as an article of faith
their legitimacy as present and future heirs to the ancient Hebrew
kingdoms, now transformed into a modern state. For twenty years
they have employed every available resource, orthodox or not, to
secure their position. The result has been a lethal quarrel ranging from
the quiet halls of diplomacy to the sandy battlefields of Sinai and
using every possible weapon—the acid pen, the assassin's gun, lies,
truth, big battalions, raw courage, and statistical distortions. No field
is more fertile for those dedicated to analysis of violence than this
long war waged by men with different dreams.

Because truth is a seamless garment, woven from pro and con, those
objective historians foolish enough to pick among the raveled threads
run the risk of bringing down upon themselves the obloquy of the
faithful on either side. In Middle Eastern affairs the wise or the wary
have left the field largely to the committed, who, seldom hampered
by doubt, have written their versions with conviction and often with
scrupulous care. I have rushed in among the conflicting claims to
truth and contradictory dogmas hopeful that I can avoid both conversion and the insidious temptation to view the real truth as neatly
balanced between the opposing poles of belief. To remain disinterested among the dedicated is a chore for the saint, not the scholar,
but I should like to think I have been fair if harsh, honest if not wise.
I fear, however, that this goal may seem insufficient to all of those
who have shared with me their time, their knowledge, and often their
dreams. For them my book can be only a disappointment, for I have
found few men without fault, few dreams without blemish. Still, I
believe that I have struggled among the claims of faith and can only
hope to be forgiven for stating the truth as I see it.

The conventional disclaimer that those who have assisted the author
are excused from responsibility for his opinions is perhaps insufficient
in this case. I am certain that many both named and unnamed who
have helped me will not only be appalled at the result but will in fact
regret their assistance. I am, nevertheless, deeply indebted to a variety
of individuals and institutions. Over the course of the years, Mrs.
Sylvia Landress, Director, and the staff of the Zionist Archives and
Library have been more than kind and invariably helpful. Richard
Griffin, at the New York Institute of Technology Library, has always
been willing to track down books and dissertations buried in numerous

libraries scattered about the country. Our Departmental Assistant Mr. Gerald Mentor (Social Science, New York Institute of Technology) has willingly undertaken all the unpleasant tasks that are usually the lot of departmental assistants. I should also like to thank those in New York—Mr. Moshe Aumann of the Consulate General of Israel, Miss Kazam of the Arab Information Center, Dr. Izzat Tannous and his staff at the Palestine Liberation Organization Office, Mr. Joujati of the Syrian Permanent Mission to the United Nations, the staff of the United Nations Library, and a variety of aides and informants who cannot be named here.

I have long threatened not to include at this point the traditional homage to my wife, who hates both war and books about it, although she will read proof when pressed; instead I determined to write a brief eulogy to what has been for so many a second home—The New York Public Library. Beyond the lions I have invariably found a staff cooperative under stress, tolerant of the vague, kind to the scholar, and full of learning; but, unjustly, it is those millions of books that I really love, without whose cooperation *The Long War* would have taken considerably longer.

J. B. B.
New York City

Before *The Long War* could be published, the balloon had again gone up in the Middle East necessitating the inclusion of material on the latest battle. Rather than alter the book in light of the events of June 1967 and additional material, particularly on the earlier Suez crisis, I have let the text stand. I, no more than Gamal Abdel Nasser, Moshe Dayan, or anyone else, foresaw "war" in June 1967, for like most others I overestimated Arab prudence. I do think, however, that it will interest the reader, now blessed with hindsight, to examine the thrust of the book unaltered by retrospective tinkering. For the material in the "Epilogue" I am again grateful for the assistance of the Zionist Archives, and particularly to Lieutenant Colonel Y. Offer, Israeli military attaché in London, for his aid. Although unable to be very helpful, the officials of the Egyptian Section of the Pakistani Embassy in London, were most gracious.

J. B. B.
New York City

Contents

I

The Battleground*
The Long Prologue

For thousands of years before the arrival of either the Jews or the Arabs, Palestine had been a battleground on which the destinies of empires clashed and lost tribes scuffled for local advantage. The Hebrews first trickled among the arid hills in approximately the fourteenth century before Christ. Astride the Fertile Crescent, Palestine was a crossroads for commerce in the ancient world, the home of a mixture of peoples and languages, a magnet to conquest. For centuries the Hebrews struggled with the Canaanites, the Phoenicians, the Aramaeans, and the Philistines for control of the narrow littoral between the sea and the desert. In a brief era free from great aggressive empires, the Hebrews managed to carve out a kingdom of their own. In 1000 B.C. the Hebrew dominion under King David stretched from Damascus to Arabia; it was a powerful and splendid state. After King Solomon's death in 935 B.C., the kingdom split into Israel and Judea, both increasingly prey to the ambitions of strong new empires. Though alien peoples and vast armies came into Palestine to conquer or be absorbed, the Hebrews remained unassimilated and unyielding as their fortunes varied from century to century. Neither wholesale exile nor war could completely destroy the Hebrew hold on part, at least, of Palestine. Finally, the monolithic Roman Empire would no longer

1

tolerate the hard nugget of Hebrew resistance. In 63 B.C., after a three-month siege, Pompey's Roman legions breached the last ramparts of Jewish Jerusalem. The independent Judean kingdom became part of the Roman province of Syria.

Subsequent efforts to revive a Hebrew state in Palestine failed in the face of Roman power, but neither the Roman legions nor the tolerant arguments of Hellenism could accomplish the assimilation of the Jews into a pagan and immoral empire. The climax of the long effort to re-establish a Jewish state was provoked in A.D. 70, when the legions of Titus, son of the Emperor Vespasian, captured Jerusalem. Titus burned the temple and, according to his own estimate, killed 600,000 Jews. Although the Diaspora is usually dated from the destruction of the temple, many Jews still refused to give up their hopes for an independent state. In A.D. 13 a revolt under Simon Bar Kochba failed. The survivors were massacred or sold into slavery.

Bar Kochba's revolt was the last major attempt for centuries to create a Jewish state, for the revenge of the Romans was as ruthless as it was efficient. Hebrew power had been broken. The Kingdom of Solomon and David had been lost. Judea and Israel had disappeared. As hope for a Jewish state flickered and finally died, Judaism shifted its emphasis to spiritual rather than secular salvation. In the long, dark night of the Middle Ages and on through further centuries of persecution, humiliation, and even partial assimilation, the central aspiration of the Jews was to maintain their unique spiritual heritage, rather than to pursue a seemingly hopeless will-o'-the-wisp. Israel became a religious symbol rather than a practical goal. Jews might promise to meet "next year in Jerusalem," but no one actually anticipated keeping the promise.

After the scattering of all but a remnant of the Jews, the world empire of Rome in its own time gave way to the eastern empire of Byzantium. These Greeks were driven from Palestine by the fanatical legions of Islam riding out of the deserts of Arabia. In 634 these Arab horsemen struck against the Byzantine legions at Ajnodagn and in the following year drove the Greeks back as far as Damascus. Within a decade the Arabs had seized Persia, Mesopotamia, Palestine, and Egypt without sating their appetite for conquest or eroding their religious zeal. In less than a century Islamic horsemen had swept across Africa, through Spain, and into France. They reduced the

Byzantine Empire to a bastion in Anatolia. To the east, Arab armies reached into central Asia and India.

These victories, however, did not lead to a great world empire stretching from the Pyrenees to the Himalayas. Even before the tide of conquest reached its peak, dynastic and religious schisms appeared. Islam was split between the Sunni and the Shia. The Arabs were torn by the ambitions and quarrels of the Umayyad and Abbasid dynasties. Century after century constant quarrels, sudden expeditions, and big wars troubled Palestine.

In the eleventh century the Ayyubid dynasty of the legendary Saladin, still not secure from Arab rivals, faced still another competitor for Palestine. The Frankish Crusaders, allied with the Greeks, had come to reconquer the Holy Land. The Christians, thanks to surprise tactics unfamiliar to their opponents, and Arab disunity, swept to a series of victories. On July 15, 1099, the Christians stormed over the walls of Jerusalem. Their leader, Godfrey of Lorraine, became Defender of the Holy Sepulcher. The Crusaders parceled out the Holy Land, amid much acrimony, establishing miniature feudal states. Within a century their heirs had frittered away the Holy Land, leaving little but the ruins of their castles and the memory of their final defeat.

Then, in the fourteenth century, the Mamluk Empire of the Bahri, the eventual inheritor of Palestine, came under increasing pressure from the newest wave of Asians converted to Islam, the Ottoman Turks. Unlike their predecessors the Seljuk Turks, the new Turks, although converted to Islam, retained their own language and customs. When the Ottoman Selim moved south into Syria in 1507, he came as an alien though Islamic conqueror, not as a new Arab ruler. The Mamluks could not hold off the Turks. With the Turkish victory in Egypt on January 22, 1517, the era of Arab domination flickered out outside the isolated wastes of the Arabian peninsula.

Palestine no longer existed, even as a Turkish administrative district. This status was no novelty, for there had seldom been a united Palestine with recognized borders, even as part of a distant caliphate. What was new was its domination, for the first time since the short-lived Crusader states, by a non-Arab ruler. Like the Crusaders, the Seljuk Turks dominated and exploited the population without assimilating it. The Arabs, whatever their diverse backgrounds, remained

Arabs, suffering under a cruel and callous despotism. In time any alternative came to seem preferable. In the nineteenth century the Arabs welcomed with great enthusiasm occupation by the Albanian troops of Muhammad Ali, ruler of Egypt. But Muhammad Ali proved equally oppressive. In May 1834, the Arabs in Nablus and Hebron rose up against the Albanians, but it was European intervention in 1840 that finally forced Muhammad Ali to withdraw in favor of the Turks. The return of the Turks was hardly a sign of renewed strength in the Ottoman Empire, which was in fact growing both feebler and more brutal. The long decline proved irreversible, and the Ottoman Empire became the focus of increased European intervention and interference. The Russians, the new German empire, the French, and the British all had designs on the Turks. In 1908 the militant Young Turks tried to end the downward spiral but to little effect. Almost in desperation the Turkish government decided, after the outbreak of World War I, to ally itself with the Germans. Before the Turks could move, however, the Russians declared war on them on November 2, 1914, thus denying the Ottoman Empire even this last gesture of independence.

To the surprise of the Western Allies, the "sick man of Europe" was not yet moribund. The Turks, with considerable German help, fought on for four years. The British failed to force the straits at Gallipoli. The Russian front swayed back and forth. The British expedition into Mesopotamia found the going heavy. Finally, after deciding against a landing at Alexandretta, the British opted for an advance north from Egypt, protected on the land flank by an Arab uprising against the Turks. Once again Arab horsemen rode out of the desert, but this time they were allied with a Christian empire and led by a young English romantic, T. E. Lawrence. Grudgingly, the Turks withdrew from the Arabian peninsula. General E. H. H. Allenby's Egyptian Expeditionary Force pressed north, slowly forcing a Turkish withdrawal. On December 9, 1917, Major General Sir John Shea accepted the keys of Jerusalem. On the following day Allenby ceremoniously entered through the Jaffa Gate. The Turkish army was still just over the horizon, but the British, with the Arabs riding on their flank, had arrived in Jerusalem.

By the time of the long-delayed collapse of the Ottoman Empire in 1918, the fate of the Levant from Gaza to Acre had become the subject of considerable secret debate and extended negotiations. Palestine was of concern not only to the British and the Arabs but also to the French, perhaps even to the Italians, the Vatican, the Eastern Orthodox Church, and all Protestant sects. Amid the welter of promises, oral agreements, and secret treaties with both the French and the Arabs during the war, the British had in 1917 issued an unexpected and unprecedented statement—The Balfour Declaration—favoring establishment of a Jewish national homeland in Palestine, thus adding one more interested party. Although there had been Jewish communities scattered throughout the Middle East since Roman times, including a few ultra-orthodox settlements in Palestine, this British-sponsored homeland was to accommodate a new kind of Jew, the Zionist.

Although Zionism is a child of the nineteenth century, a sort of emotional Zionism, a longing for the land of David had been an integral part of the heritage of Judaism since the Diaspora. Through the centuries, a tiny trickle of Jews had returned to the land of Zion as pilgrims or settlers, but not until the first half of the nineteenth century were serious suggestions that a Jewish homeland be established in Palestine advanced. These proposals, beginning with an offer of general resettlement by Napoleon Bonaparte in 1799, gained fresh impetus during the 1880s and 1890s. The growing persecution of Jews in Russia during the reigns of Czars Alexander III and Nicholas II convinced many people that the only hope for Russian Jews lay in emigration. Simultaneously, various Zionist movements proposed emigration to a land of their own in Palestine as the only alternative to further persecution and alienation. This program, however, remained the goal of only a few. Most Jews in Eastern Europe preferred emigration to the United States or creation of a new socialist society. In Western Europe the assimilated Jew recognized no threat and therefore no need to emigrate to the wastes of the Middle East. But the Zionists persisted. In 1897 the First Zionist Congress met at Basel. It was conceived and organized by Theodor Herzl, the driving force of the movement for a national home, and marked the birth of modern Zionism. Herzl saw no solution for the homeless Jew, always an alien, always a target of the Gentile world's latent anti-Semitism, but to seek a portion of the globe large enough for a Jewish nation. Rejecting a British offer of part of East Africa, an increasing number of

Zionists had emigrated to Palestine before 1914. The Zionist organizations grew in strength and influence, even though they remained a minority in the broad spectrum of Jewish political opinion. The next major step came as a result of Great Britain's war with Turkey. Zionist spokesmen sought to convince the British government of the justice of Herzl's cause. Partially as a result of its own inclinations and surely to accomplish the Empire's own immediate ends, the British Cabinet turned a willing ear to the persuasive arguments of the British Zionist leaders, in particular Dr. Chaim Weizmann. On November 2, 1917, Foreign Minister Arthur Balfour sent Lionel, Lord Rothschild a communication expressing favor for the establishment of a "national home for the Jewish people."[1]

For nearly half a century the motives and intentions of the British leaders have been analyzed, their papers sifted for clues, their speeches scrutinized, and their private lives dissected. There has never been a consensus on their motives; vague gratitude, foolish romanticism, Machiavellian cynicism, greed, arrogant ignorance, or combinations of these and other explanations all have had proponents. Whatever the immediate aims of the British Cabinet or the members' individual motives in 1917, however, there can be no doubt that the Cabinet believed the Declaration would be to British advantage. In the tangles of decision making at a moment of severe military crisis, the harried British leaders had neither the time nor the knowledge to look too closely at a distant and undefined area, still largely occupied by enemy troops. In any case, the unknown Arabs, reduced to political impotence and economic penury for 500 years, were little more than "natives" to the British. Arab dreams and aspirations lay unrecognized and unconsidered, for even the shattering impact of total industrialized war and the virulent new nationalism of Eastern Europe had not dented the British imperial ideal. To London in 1917, the national aspirations of the Poles and Czechs may in fact have had some validity, but the Palestinian Arabs seemed a primitive people in an exotic but desolate land. Their need for tutelage was obvious. The impact of Westernized, skilled European Jews would certainly be to the Arabs' advantage, the English reasoned. Under Britain's aegis and with a Jewish example, something might be done for the underdeveloped but strategically located Holy Land. Little attention was paid to Arab political maturity or to Arab desires. Almost at once, however, in 1918, the British learned that, though Arab political maturity might still be a long way off, the Arab sheikhs (chiefs), sharifs (religious nobles), and emirs (local rulers) had very definite desires. Britain's desert allies had no intention of folding their war tents and returning to the wastelands of Arabia. Still, the dawning aspirations of the Arabs for a great new kingdom and the limited demands of the Zionists for a homeland did not necessarily appear mutually exclusive. In January 1919 Emir Faisal, aspirant to the throne of a united Arab kingdom, and Chaim Weizmann, personification of Zionism, even pledged cordial cooperation. Apparently the British were going to muddle through once again and were going to stumble onto a solution to their own advantage, even perhaps to the advantage of the Zionists and Arabs also.

After a period of negotiation and manipulation, the British and the French managed to redraw the map of the Middle East to their mutual satisfaction. There was, however, to be no great Arab kingdom but only a covey of small client states. The new League of Nations, with British and French diplomats dictating the basic terms, sanctioned the establishment of these quasi states under a mandate system that gave the divided Arabs the distant hope of independence and the immediate prospect of Anglo-French control. Emir Faisal's ambition for a great Arab state had been thwarted; it had never seemed more than a romantic dream to the jaundiced eyes of London and Paris. Faisal was exiled and humiliated, and his heirs were reduced to reigning over a barren fiefdom across the Jordan River from the new Palestine Mandate. Faisal and most of the Arabs had been foxed, but the Zionists had been rewarded. Through all the machinations, the concept of "Palestine" had remained. The area vaguely coterminous with King David's kingdom had been extended far to the south by the addition of a great triangle of the Negev Desert, with its point on the Gulf of 'Aqaba. In that area ample provision had been made for the Zionists. The League of Nations Mandate, granted in July 1922, called upon the British to place "the country under such political, administrative and economic conditions as will secure the establishment of the Jewish National Home."[2] London appeared more than willing to do so.

Confident of their special relationship with the British, the Zionists immediately sponsored immigration into the Mandate territory. They

largely ignored the possibility of Arab opposition, apparently justifiably, for until 1929 the Arab and Jewish communities lived in relative peace. One of the major reasons for this tranquillity was the
obvious failure of the Zionists to attract heavy immigration into Palestine. With Russian Jewry cut off by the communist revolution and
the reluctance of Western European Jews to emigrate, the national
homeland was off to a slow start. The failure of Zionist proselytizing
was so serious that in one year Jewish emigration from Palestine ex-
ceeded immigration. Still the course of Arab-Jewish relations was not
entirely smooth. Occasional sporadic violence occurred, but it was
hardly surprising considering the great differences between the two
communities in values, wealth, and cultural background. But, with
the rise of Jewish immigration in the late 1920s, Arab resentment
increased.[3] Jews flooded the country and created flowering agricultural colonies out of wasteland. Jews built factories and businesses.
The suburbs of western Jerusalem and Tel Aviv outside Jaffa became
new cities. On every hand the Jews flourished, daily underlining the
continuing poverty and misery of the Arabs. The British Mandate
administration became increasingly involved as a referee, struggling
with conflicting claims and endless hassles over land sales, immigration
quotas, and Jewish union policies—all the battlefields of a mixed and
competing population.

Ill equipped to fight a bureaucratic campaign within the Mandate
and suspicious of London's intentions, the Arabs grew more bitter. In
August 1929 a series of riots and demonstrations against the Jews
resulted in 472 Jewish and 268 Arab deaths. Arab frustrations had at
last erupted against the Jews on a large scale. Moderates on both sides,
however, hoped that with time would come toleration, that the Arab
population would gradually accept the Jewish community and even
benefit by its example. This hope for the slow maturing of a Jewish
homeland within Arab Palestine rested on the unstated assumption
that Jewish immigration would, despite Zionist efforts, remain relatively low.

Within a few years the entire situation had changed. The fanatical
anti-Semitic Nazi Party had grown into a major force in Germany. In
1933 Hitler took power. The threat of the German Jewish community drove the Zionists to even greater efforts. Conditions in Eastern
Europe, though not so desperate, were ominous. Immigration figures

climbed beyond the wildest dreams of the Zionists. The Arabs' resentment grew apace, more virulent because of frustration by British
power and Zionist efficiency. The British government became increasingly uneasy over rising tensions. There was even talk in the cafés of
a new jihad (holy war). On April 19, 1939, riots in Jaffa resulted in
twenty Jewish deaths. On April 20 in Nablus the Arab leaders united
to form the Arab National Committee under the presidency of the
Mufti of Jerusalem, al-Hajj Amin al-Huseini. They vowed that they
would no longer tolerate British passivity toward the Jewish flood
sweeping over their country. If nothing were done, the Arabs would
become a minority in their own land.

The situation deteriorated rapidly as random violence grew to the
proportions of revolt. Armed bands roamed the hills sniping at Jews
and British. The Jews, with the exception of a few extremists,
formally announced a policy of restraint and depended for the time
being upon British protection. On their part, the British outwaited
the ill-led and poorly prepared Arabs. A great Arab general strike
sputtered on through the late summer. By October 12, when the
Arab National Committee called off the general strike, it was clear
that the first stage of the revolt had failed utterly.[4]

This Arab revolt, which broke out again several times during the
next three years, revealed not only the extent of Arab alienation from
British policy but also the deep schisms in Arab Palestine. Divided
between country and city, competing family loyalties, and historic
grudges, the many Arab leaders despised one another. The overwhelming majority of the Arabs was, in modern terms, apolitical;
they had lived for centuries in rural poverty or squalid urban ghettos.
Restricted by a rigid class system, they were stirred to mass action
only by religious fanaticism and violent xenophobia. They remained
better material for a mob than for a sophisticated political protest or a
disciplined civil war. Their leaders had done little to rectify this impotence. The Palestinian Arab national movement had not been
founded until December 1920 in Haifa, and little progress had been
made in the ensuing years toward creating a unified and effective
organization. Endless quarrels and vendettas continued while the
masses remained sullen and explosive. The wealthy landed families
and the small urban professional class, a tiny elite, could find no
common policy but truculent opposition. The Mandate had turned

into a horror as the British scrambled to find some solution other than naked repression.

Gradually, it became clear that British policy in Palestine was shifting. London spoke more often of the onerous pro-Zionist terms of the Mandate, most of which had been written by British statesmen. With the growing threat from an aggressive Germany and Italy, the strategic importance of the Middle East became more apparent. The governments of the other Arab states had made clear their distaste for Britain's long Zionist honeymoon. The British Conservative government began to listen more intently to the pleas of the British Arabists. This virtual network of high civil servants and respected private experts, of scholars and well-placed journalists, increasingly advanced the thesis that vital British interests could best be secured by recognizing the just claims of the Arabs. Weizmann, living in London so as to exert pressure, had fewer British visitors.

The winds were indeed changing. The failure of the Munich compromise had brought war very near. On May 17, 1939, the British government issued a White Paper that had been long in the works. Jewish immigration and land purchase in Palestine were to be restricted. Worse for the Zionists, the British promised independence to a unitary Palestine, relegating the Jews to permanent minority status. Faced with a war against Germany, Britain apparently found a loyal Arab world more desirable than a grateful Jewish people. Neither legal arguments over the terms of the Mandate nor impassioned pleas for the doomed German Jews had any effect. The strategic interests of the Empire came first. On July 12 the British suspended any Jewish immigration to Palestine for the six months beginning October 1. The Arabs were to be placated and the Jews ignored. Whatever the government's expectations, the White Paper harvested only hatred. The Arabs wanted independence and the departure of the British. The White Paper might be more than they had hoped for, but it was less than they dreamed of. The Jews went underground, determined to continue immigration, even though it had to be "illegal"; they were committed to force if necessary. Efforts to arm and train the secret army, the Haganah, were stepped up. The more extreme groups, intolerant of passivity, refused to wait and prepared a campaign of violence and terror. Then, in September 1939, World War II began in Europe. The three-cornered struggle for Palestine was soon overshadowed by the global conflict.

Although the Arabs remained convinced that the British intended to frustrate their aspirations, the war in Europe produced a truce in Palestine. War demands brought prosperity to the Mandate, softening Arab hostility and postponing any open confrontation with the British or the Jews. In 1939 the Arabs were truly neutral and the Palestine Arabs more passive than most. Few Arabs could, however, appreciate the idealism of the Allied effort. Hitler's Germany was distant, and its greatest international crimes seemed to be successful aggression and anti-Semitism. To many Arabs, both efforts seemed impressive, even admirable. The obnoxious hegemony of the British and the French was an everyday humiliation, and vague pro-Arab feelers from Italy and Germany seemed to carry no threat and even some hope for change. As a result, many people scattered throughout the Middle East kept open minds about the war. Then in swift succession came the collapse of Poland, the fall of France, and the isolation of a British battered under massive air attacks. Some Arabs became less passive. The Mufti of Jerusalem, Hajj Amin, moved to Beirut, became involved in various Nazi activities, and eventually turned up in Berlin. The Vichy French administrators in Syria and Lebanon permitted expression of a variety of pro-German sentiments among the Arabs. In April 1941 Rashid Ali al-Ghailani even led an unsuccessful anti-British coup in Iraq. By February 1942, when a British defeat in North Africa seemed very near, Egyptian loyalties had become so suspect that the British, in a secret power play, forced King Faruk to install a hand-picked puppet government. But, once General Erwin Rommel had been driven back at Alamein, Arab discontent seethed more quietly. The Arabs, once again passive, watched the war recede into Europe and ultimate Allied victory become a certainty. A few, like Abdullah ibn-Husein of Transjordan, had remained steadfast allies of the British; many others had not; but most had remained quiet, waiting. Yet the British seemed almost unaware of the rippling currents of Arab disloyalty. Their diplomats encouraged discussions of unity. Their spokesmen talked in glowing terms of the Anglo-Arab future.

To the Jews the Arabs' pro-Nazi machinations, motivated by national self-interest, seemed to have had the effect of driving the British to appeasement, even admiration, whereas Jewish patience and cooperation were apparently to be unrewarded. Opposed to the same enemy as the Western Allies, the Palestine Jews, except for a tiny minority, offered to support the British war effort. The campaign against the 1939 White Paper was shelved, and the Jews pleaded for a part in the war. For some time London seemed little interested in Jewish enthusiasm. Only after several years, and then apparently reluctantly, did Britain allow the formation of a Jewish brigade. The British were still, evidently, persuaded that the future of the Middle East lay in close Anglo-Arab cooperation and mutual trust. There were no signs of English gratitude for the Jewish war effort. The situation boded ill for the Zionists in Palestine.

A small minority of Jews had always regarded the British as the greatest menace: London had betrayed the Balfour Declaration, broken the terms of the Mandate, and condemned untold thousands of Jews to death in concentration camps through its strict immigration quotas. British policy seemed to them to have gone beyond the demands of self-interest. Great Britain, hardly less than Germany, appeared truly the enemy of the Jewish people. The British had to be punished. In 1944, before the war in Europe had ended, a new secret war of terror against the British began in the Middle East. The campaign was directed by the extremist offshoots of Vladimir Jabotinsky's revisionists, who had seceded from the Zionist Organization in 1935 over his impatient policy and tactics. After various revisionist schisms two small, violently anti-British groups had emerged. The larger and more moderate, the Irgun Zvai Leumi, could claim no more than a few hundred dedicated activists in 1944. The other, the Lohmey Herut Israel (Lechi), the well-known Stern Group, had far fewer members but also far less restraint. These groups carried out a series of raids and attacks, mainly against the British.[5] They barely failed to assassinate Sir Harold MacMichael, High Commissioner for Palestine. Then, late in 1944, the Stern Group decided to carry the attacks farther afield.

On November 6 in Cairo two young Palestine Jews loitered outside the villa of Lord Moyne, British Minister of State in the Middle East. Moyne was not only the highest British official in the Middle East but also a friend of Prime Minister Winston Churchill. He was also a target for the Lechi. His black Humber drew up outside the villa, and his aide-de-camp, Captain Arthur Hughes-Onslow, climbed out and walked slowly toward the door of the villa. The driver, Lance Corporal A. T. Fuller, stepped up to open the rear door for Lord

THE BATTLEGROUND: THE LONG PROLOGUE 13

Moyne and his secretary, Miss Dorothy Osmonde. Suddenly the two Jewish boys dashed across the lawn waving revolvers. Each fired three times. Fuller fell dead. Lord Moyne sprawled on the seat of the Humber, hit three times and mortally wounded. Racing off on their bicycles, the two young men only just missed escaping. Once captured, they made no secret of who they were and why they had shot Lord Moyne. The assassination had a shattering effect on the British. In the midst of a world conflict in which every sinew was strained to achieve victory over the Nazi forces, they could scarcely credit the motives of the assassins. Churchill, if anything pro-Zionist, was horribly shocked by the death of his friend at the hands of irresponsible fanatics. Even before the defeat of the Jews' greatest enemy by British arms, the dreadful violence in Palestine had begun once again. For the Lechi the riddled body of Lord Moyne was both a symbol of retribution and a warning. To the British it seemed an incomprehensible crime.[6]

The vast majority of Palestine Jews, as well as their Zionist representatives abroad, were equally horrified by the assassination, not only because it was an inexcusable crime but also because it was a dangerously provocative act. Although eschewing terrorism, the Jews in Palestine had hardened their demands. Gradual realization of the extent of Hitler's slaughter of European Jewry persuaded even the more moderate Zionists that the only hope for the future lay in a national state rather than in an ill-defined "homeland." During the war the position of the statists within the Zionist movement had improved, and their control of the world organization had tightened. In 1942 the unofficial Zionist Biltmore program had even demanded all of Palestine for the new state. Control of the future had thus gradually shifted from Weizmann's cautious practical Zionism, slowly evolving and British-based, to David Ben-Gurion's call for a fully independent state, open to all Jews and dependent on no outside power. The day of Weizmann's leadership from London had passed. The bitterly frustrating British immigration policy under the White Paper and the helplessness of the Palestine Jews to do more than smuggle in a few "illegal" immigrants could no longer be tolerated. The British must be made to understand that the White Paper policy, a misguided abomination even at its inception, had become obsolete.

The makers of Britain's policy were unconcerned with Jewish

anxiety. After Lord Moyne's death, the British Arabists seemed more fully in control. The experts—the influential officials and the dedicated academic specialists—promoted a policy that would tie Britain's postwar position in the world to a revitalized and Anglicized Arab world. Britain, through alliance and friendship, would secure a permanent strategic advantage, not to mention access to the vast pools of Middle Eastern oil. The resources of 40 million Arabs far outweighed the friendship of a few hundred thousand Jews. In March 1945 the first step, the creation of the Arab League, was taken, with Great Britain serving as godfather. Blandly the British prepared to ignore the Jews. The French were to be edged out of Syria and Lebanon; the Americans were too far away and inexperienced to be considered a serious rival. From London a great Anglo-Arab alliance appeared a definite postwar prospect.

Although some Arabs were encouraged by British intentions in the Middle East, many had little real faith in London's promises or generosity. British friendship had once before proved a frail reed in Palestine, where in 1945 the Arabs were most vulnerable. The Zionists' repeated demands for a state and for unlimited immigration had already fallen on fertile ground in the United States. The Jews in Palestine had developed their own army, the Haganah. The Palestine Arabs had none. The Jews had viable political and economic institutions. The Arabs had none. In view of substantial world sympathy for the Jewish victims of the Nazis and their own Mufti's awkward cooperation with the Axis, the Palestine Arabs realized that they were at the mercy of powerful external forces. When the war in Europe came to an end in May 1945, the Arabs accepted the fact that the British government would be the decisive factor in their future. Even the support of the nominally independent Arab states would be ineffectual against British power.

Then, in the midst of the European peace conferences and even before the final defeat of Japan, the whole kaleidoscope of pressures, policies, and politicians was given an unexpected shake. Trusting in the admiration and affection of the victorious British, Winston Churchill called a wartime election. Amazingly, the Labour Party was swept into office after a generation in opposition. On July 27, 1945, the new government formally took office with Clement Attlee as Prime Minister and Ernest Bevin as Foreign Secretary. Pledged to carry out a social revolution at home, the Labour Party was less certain about policies abroad. In one area, however, there was ample evidence of its intentions. Knowledgeable Arabs were shattered at the election returns, for the Labour Party had for twenty-five years been a staunch supporter of Zionist aspirations. Over the years individuals, committees, and conferences had issued declarations expressing enthusiasm for the Jewish national homeland. Many Labour Party notables had been intimates of Weizmann. Now these men controlled the destiny of the Mandate. Incredibly, at the last minute, just as the Conservative government under the influence of the Arabists had proposed an Anglo-Arab alliance, victory over the Zionists had been snatched away by the British electorate.

Arab anxiety proved premature. The new government, overwhelmed with postwar problems and untutored in international affairs, had to trust the same group of pro-Arab experts in the Foreign Office, the Colonial Office, and all the other offices, bureaus, and committees staffed by the permanent Civil Service. The harsh realities of Britain's strategic needs in the Arab Middle East, as detailed by the professionals, had to take precedence over romantic affection for the Zionists and heartfelt sympathy for the plight of European Jews. Many in the Labour government realized, with sorrow, that there was indeed an Arab problem and that a pro-Zionist course would almost certainly alienate 40 million Arabs. A generation of credible Zionist explanations turned sour in several mouths. On August 25 the Colonial Office informed Weizmann that the immigration quota would remain at 1,500 per month. The Labour Party, although reluctantly in some cases, would follow the policy of the 1939 White Paper.

Once again Arab victory had been wrung from certain defeat. First, the dubious conduct of so many Arabs during the war had been forgotten; then some of the Zionists' own friends had deserted them. But, although they were publicly grateful for the British stand, the Arabs were privately humiliated by their own dependence. In any case, the Arab position in Palestine was far from secure. The new American President, Harry S Truman, continued his predecessor's policy of issuing palliative statements to both sides. In view of the potent Zionist propaganda apparatus in American and the important Jewish vote, most Arabs had their doubts about the United States.

Soviet Russia's postwar intentions in the Middle East remained unclear, but hardening Soviet demands in Europe might prove ominous. One hopeful sign was the establishment of the United Nations. The Arab states had five representatives, but no one could guess how effective the organization would be. Still, Arab prospects in 1945 appeared brighter than could have been anticipated.

The Jewish Agency in Palestine—the organization recognized by British Mandate—was appalled at the Labour government's policy. Late in September David Ben-Gurion and the Agency apparently took the decision to institute a program of active resistance. The British could not be allowed to impose their policy without protest, for a solution from London that produced only disorder and armed resistance would be no solution at all in the eyes of the world. The crisis was believed to be so serious that a secret agreement was negotiated with the Irgun. Whereas in the past the Haganah and the Agency had at times cooperated with the British to suppress the Irgun, now the extremist group's cadres were to be used. Early in October 1945 the illegal Haganah Voice of Israel radio station began broadcasting again for the first time since June 1940. The British publicly announced that the restrictions on immigration would remain. Additional British troops began to arrive in the Mandate. On the night of October 31 the Haganah and the Irgun carried out highly efficient surprise attacks on the Palestine railroad system. In one night they cut the railroad in 153 places, totally disrupting traffic. London had been warned. The Jews would achieve a reversal of policy with force if need be. They would be adamant, and they would have a state. Their need was too great to be denied.

The British had no intention of being intimidated. London ordered in an airborne division. The Mandate announced broad new policy powers to curb violence, and security measures were tightened. The Labour government, however, did not wish to force a showdown. After six years of world war, fighting Jews in the Holy Land had little popular appeal. Some thought was given to asking the United Nations to secure a breathing space, but the Soviet attitude at the Foreign Ministers' Conference earlier in October had demonstrated that it would be dangerous to give Russia any chance to interfere. Instead London decided to involve the United States, apparently on the assumption that more intimate American concern with the Palestine problem might lessen Britain's own burden as referee and give the

American government some insight into Middle Eastern questions. At worst, the Palestine Jews could be persuaded to remain quiescent during an Anglo-American investigation. And one more committee would at least allow the vacillating Labour government a respite to return to the myriad postwar problems it faced. On November 13 the formation of a joint Anglo-American committee to investigate increased Jewish immigration was announced. The effort to buy time worked. Jewish violence faded.

At the end of 1945 Jews and Arabs thus awaited once again the arrival of an outside committee. For twenty-five years there had been investigations and reports, each one shelved and none ever proposing a solution satisfactory to both the Jews and Arabs. Yet even in 1945 neither the Jews nor the Arabs saw the other as the main barrier to their ambitions. That a Jewish state cutting across Palestine could not be tolerated by the Arabs seemed less important than the next British policy statement. That 600,000 Jews could not be isolated and swallowed up in an Arab state caused less concern than the vacillations of British politics. For a generation the British had absorbed Arab attention and monitored Arab ambitions. After 1945 the destinies of the Arabs and Jews might clash increasingly in open battle, but in the meantime the British dominated the minds of both. Neither Jews nor Arabs foresaw that they were on the eve of a long war. Palestine seemed likely to remain a Mandate, rather than a battleground, for a while longer.

NOTES

1. The most extensive work on this document is Leonard Stein, *The Balfour Declaration* (London: 1961). It is worth noting that the British must have had occasional second thoughts, for the final, 1917 text included the wording "viewed with favour" instead of "accepts the principle," which were in the July 1917 draft. *Cf.* Chaim Weizmann, *Trial and Error* (New York: 1949), p. 236.

2. The most accessible source for the significant documents of this period is J. C. Hurewitz, ed. *Diplomacy of the Middle East: Vol. II. A Documentary Record 1914–1956* (Princeton: 1956).

3. John Marlowe, *The Seat of Pilate: An Account of the Palestine Mandate* (London: 1959), p. 108, gives a tidy chart of the shifts in population:

	Arabs	Jews
1920	599,000	67,000
1926	740,000	150,000
1929	794,000	156,000
1931	840,000	172,000
1933	895,000	235,000
1936	920,000	384,000
1942	1,122,000	484,000

4. The Arab revolt of 1936–1939 remains largely unchronicled, which is unfortunate, as it began as the most primitive of modern social-protest movements, based on popular affection for a bandit, and grew to include irregular warfare, a general strike, and a most successful application of anti-insurgent tactics. By and large, however, it remained a peasant uprising, despite the veneer of urban political sophistication provided by the Arab National Committee. As such it had more in common with the rising of the Andalusian Anarchists (1809's–1939) or with the Great Fear of 1789 (a peasant panic leading to irrational attacks on their lords) than it did with even the Arab revolt of 1916–1918. See Marlowe, *Rebellion in Palestine* (London: 1946).

5. There is a number of books about the Irgun and the Lechi, most of them memoirs or works of special pleading. Despite their eventual evolution into the quite legal Herut Party, the extreme revisionists' notorious reputation, both in and out of Israel, has in part prevented disinterested analysis.

6. The entire sequence of events surrounding the assassination has been brilliantly examined by Gerold Frank in *The Deed* (New York: 1963). Although Frank makes clear the very real Western abhorrence of terror as a political weapon even in a just cause, his own attitude is ambivalent; he is appalled by the deed, yet admires the doers. Cf. Leo Benjamin, *Martyrs in Cairo: The Trial of the Assassins of Lord Moyne* (New York: 1953).

2

The Mandate
Disintegrates

For many people 1946 was the first year of a peace, heralding the return to international law and order and the beginning of a unified world and a just society. The atomic bomb had apparently made war obsolete. In San Francisco the United Nations had taken the first giant step toward realizing the dream of permanent peace and stability. In an atmosphere of hope and dedication, the victors concentrated on reforming the aggressors and preparing to rebuild after ten long years of destruction. Assuredly, the tasks of salvaging the bombed-out wreckage of Europe, of establishing an ordered and democratic Asia, of providing for the homeless and the hungry had reached awesome proportions. Still, 1946 in some capitals—and in many individual hearts—was hailed as the springtime of good will, the first year of a new era.

Not all the world's people regarded 1946 as either an ending or a beginning, however. Quietly, almost unnoticed during the hectic days of war, a wave of intense nationalism had swept through the old empires and protectorates. Revolution simmered just below the surface throughout much of the world. The humiliations and frustrations of generations, coupled with the social and political upheavals of the war, had created a ferment not to be stilled by the old formulas and techniques. China hovered on the brink of full civil war. India's

19

leaders demanded instant independence, even at the risk of anarchy. In French Indochina and the Dutch East Indies secret armies and clandestine parties had formed. The conflicting ambitions of the new nationalism and the old imperial interests had already surfaced in the Arab Middle East. Although few Arabs could be certain of Allied intentions, many were determined to end the days of tutelage, manipulated governments, and imposed alliances. In the British Mandate of Palestine, where the national aspirations of the Zionists and the Arabs had been competing for a generation, 1946 heralded little but continued conflict. The previous year had been one of bitterness, frustration, and terror—a year of night raids, crumbling civil order, reprisal, and retaliation. In 1946 there was no promise of real peace in Palestine, even though there was still no real war.

In the Mandate the new year began as the old one had ended—with the threat of violence. On January 1 the British were still hunting Irgunists who had raided two police stations and an arms dump on the night of December 27, killing nine members of the British forces. Although David Ben-Gurion and his aide, Moshe Shertok, informed the new High Commissioner, Sir Alan Cunningham, that they completely disassociated the Zionist movement from the crimes, most of the British had their doubts. On Christmas Day the illegal steamer *Hanah Senes* had been secretly beached near Naharayim north of Acre. Some 200 immigrants had waded ashore and disappeared among the Yishuva, the Jews of Palestine, without a trace. By January 1 the British still had no information on where they had gone. British searches had met with open resistance so violent as to result in ninety Jewish injuries and twelve to British forces. On January 1 Bar Kochba Street in Jerusalem was rocked by an accidental explosion in a secret Jewish chemical laboratory for the manufacture of bombs and automatic weapons. On January 2 two bombs exploded, scattering leaflets announcing that the Lechi and the Irgun had been responsible for the December 27 attacks and had suffered two killed. In 1946 some Jews obviously believed that they had already waited too long for their state. There had been too many broken promises and sterile, even seemingly evil, proposals.[1] The reports for a "solution" to the Mandate's future, buried in the archives, stretched back to the beginning of the Mandate: the Haycraft Report, the Shaw Report, the Hope Simpson Report, the Passfield White Paper, the Pell Report, the Woodhead Report. Little faith could be put in any future Anglo-American committee report. Although distant diplomats might be cheered by the recess achieved through appointment of the Anglo-American committee, the Mandate officials had to confront the prospect of continually declining restraint.

During January and February every action of the Mandate administration or the government in London seemed only to antagonize one side without winning the respect of the other. In January 1946 the British navy intercepted an illegal Jewish vessel carrying 900 unauthorized immigrants. Once more the Jews were embittered at Great Britain's preventing the homeless and displaced from finding a refuge in Palestine. When on January 30 Cunningham announced that Jewish immigration could continue at 1,500 a month, the Agency considered the announcement less than a sop. The secret Immigration Bureau—created by the Agency to bring in anyone they could—redoubled its efforts. More and more often, the Haganah itself became involved in expediting clandestine immigration.[2] The Arabs, on their side, regarded the 1,500 figure, especially in view of the almost open smuggling of immigrants, as a betrayal. To the Arabs the quota system was a dangerous chink in the dike holding back untold thousands of Zionists; to the Jews it was a violation not only of common humanity but also of the intent of the Mandate. The Irgun and the Lechi struck repeatedly. On January 28 Cunningham announced severe emergency laws, specifying the death penalty for raids and even for membership in terrorist groups. On January 30, perhaps to balance the influence of the Jewish Agency, the British allowed the Mufti's cousin, Jamal al-Huseini to return to Palestine. Jamal gave no evidence of gratitude; instead his conversations were laden with references to future violence if the British did not produce an Arab Palestine.

Whereas Anglo-Arab relations remained troubled, almost all sincere British communication with the Zionists had been eroded. The Jewish Agency and the Haganah continued their secret cooperation with the Irgun and the Lechi. On February 20 the united resistance, primarily the Palmach (the striking force of the Haganah), carried out another series of raids on British facilities used to prohibit free immigration. It hit police posts, the Mount Carmel radar station, and three R.A.F. military airfields, destroying fifteen planes and causing an estimated $1 million worth of damage. More ominous still, 50,000

Jews participated in funeral ceremonies for the four Palmach men killed in the raids. In the face of such open defiance, the British stepped up their military and police activities. Endless cordons and searches, heavy patrols, passport checks, and police raids produced little concrete result. The only hopeful sign was that, in searches for Irgun and Lechi men, the Jewish population submitted quietly, whereas in raids for Palmach and Haganah men the British often met open resistance. At least Yishuv, the Palestine Jews, recognized a difference between the selective and retaliatory raids of the military arm of the Jewish Agency and the irresponsible attacks of the extremists. It was but a small crevice in the hostility of the Jews.

On April 25 the Lechi staged a surprise attack on the British 6th Airborne Division's car park in Tel Aviv. It was the division's first experience with a deliberate attack. The eight "guards" were unprepared and unarmed, and at least some were asleep. Without warning, the Lechi assault group slipped in and opened fire on them. Seven men were killed. The British officers and men regarded the attack as premeditated and unprovoked murder of innocent, helpless men. The Lechi answer that a state of war existed between Yishuv and Britain was dismissed as wild propaganda, a spurious plea for legitimacy from avowed criminals.

The local British military commander, Major General A. F. H. Cassel's immediate response was horror and disgust, understandably enough. Disastrously for British prospects, he acted on his immediate anger without serious consideration of the ultimate results. In a harsh letter to the Jewish Mayor of Tel Aviv, Cassel in effect accused all Jews of direct complicity in the attack: "There is no doubt whatsoever in my mind that many members either knew of this project or could have given some warning before it happened . . . you could produce the criminals."[3] He further held the Jews collectively responsible for all terrorist acts. A harsh curfew was imposed. Even worse was the reaction of many British soldiers. Taking matters into their own hands, they rioted in the Jewish towns of Natnayah and Be'er Tuveyah, smashing windows, breaking up furniture, and manhandling anyone encountered on the streets.

In Tel Aviv the British had blundered badly, though understandably, in response to open provocation. By treating all Jews as guilty of murder, as passive if not active terrorists, Cassel had voiced a self-fulfilling accusation. And the familiar barely restrained anti-Jewish attitude of some British troops, the crude slogans daubed on walls, the arrogant searches, the passing slurs had been replaced by open rioting. In an almost hysterical atmosphere, even a single unofficial anti-Semitic incident assumed ugly proportions. Under threat of punishment, with their complicity assumed, the Jews drew together against the enemy, the brutal British. The methods of the Irgun and the Lechi, once viewed as abominable, now seemed to many more Jews an appropriate answer to the British. Cassel had failed to divide Tel Aviv's Jewish community and had failed to isolate and degrade the extremists. Instead he had played into the hands of the violent fighters by identifying all with the few, insulting the community and assuring its enmity. His response, immediate and reflecting the British soldiers' distaste for their unpleasant task, was a grave error. It did not even please the Arabs, who demanded more stringent measures, for during 1936–1939 the British had been far harsher with them. The Jews felt persecuted. It was no wonder that the harried British boiled with frustration and bitterness.

On the diplomatic front, there was soon news, but it was equally as bad. On May 1, 1946, the Anglo-American committee made its report. After exhaustive studies in the United States, Great Britain, the capitals of the Middle East, the displaced-person camps of Europe, and Palestine; after examining expert opinion, private conversation, detailed research, and personal impressions, the members had finally produced one more plan. Trapped between Ernest Bevin's demand for a trusteeship and Harry S Truman's insistence that 100,000 Jews be allowed to immigrate into Palestine, the committee came up with an ingenious solution. The 100,000 Jewish immigrants would be allowed to enter Palestine immediately. A binational state, with one Jewish province and one Arab province, would be established in a Palestine united under a United Nations trusteeship. The report pleased no one. Truman announced his pleasure at the provision for immigrants and his doubts about the political implications of the plan. Clement Attlee pointed out that 100,000 Jews could not be admitted until the illegal Jewish armies had been disbanded and the Jewish Agency had taken a share in the suppression of terrorism.

The inquiry had failed to produce a joint Anglo-American policy and had also failed to satisfy either the Arabs or the Jews. The Arabs

turned the proposals down flat. In June the Council of the Arab
League dispatched a memorandum to Washington, denying the right
of the United States to meddle in Palestine. A memorandum to
London demanded immediate Anglo-Arab negotiations. For the first
time, the nations of the Arab Council set up a Palestine Committee.
There were rumors that the Council had drawn up an agreement on
sanctions and aid for the Palestine Arabs. On its part, the Jewish
Agency welcomed the 100,000 immigrants but insisted that there
could be no national home without a Jewish state. All the committee's
work had thus been in vain. Of course, as none of the previous reports had been acceptable to both sides, neither the Zionists nor the
Arabs had really expected this one to be acceptable anyway. Even
London's hoped-for fringe benefit of involving the United States in
Palestine had proved illusory.[4] In June 1946 conditions in both Palestine and the Foreign Office looked equally bleak.

The Arabs in Palestine, long spectators, had once again been unable
to create their own unified committee. Jamal al-Huseini, the outstanding Palestine leader, possessed neither the talent nor the prestige to
force himself upon his traditional enemies. Then on May 29, 1946, his
cousin the Mufti, Hajj Amin al-Huseini, escaped from loose protec-
tive custody in France and appeared in Cairo. The Arabs, except for
his old enemies, were delighted, and the Palestine Huseini Party demanded his immediate return there. The British were unmoved by the
demand. The League then created an Arab higher executive with the
Mufti as chairman and Jamal as vice-chairman, and the Arab world
seemed at last on the move.

Anglo-Egyptian conversations on a new treaty had stalled, and anti-
British agitation had increased in Egypt. British troops were moving
out of the former French Mandate of Syria and Lebanon. Iraq still
seemed loyal, but the mob was untrustworthy. Abdullah ibn-Husein
in Transjordan remained faithful, reassured by a British declaration to
the United Nations General Assembly that on January 17, 1946,
London would recognize his desert state's full independence. Recognition of Transjordan's independence had been only a small step. The
Arabs increasingly felt that London must be made to realize that,
only if there were proper settlement of "the Palestine question,"
would there be 40 million loyal Arabs.

The Jewish Agency was equally concerned at British vacillation.

London's willingness to consider some sort of withdrawal from Egypt could mean only that massive bases in Palestine would replace the lost enclaves in Egypt, Haifa would take the place of Alexandria, and the Negev would serve as Britain's corridor to the Suez Canal through which came vital Persian oil. All these advantages would be purchased with a pro-Arab policy at the expense of the Jews. Their answer was renewed violence to force Britain to reckon with the Zionists. On June 16, the Palmach struck all over the Mandate in a massive display of strength. Attack groups hit every rail and bridge crossing the Palestine border. The whole operation had been carefully planned and proved highly effective tactically. The prestige of the British was badly damaged—too badly—and the British army decided to retaliate heavily for its embarrassment. Although the diplomats could not find a solution, the army, provoked once too often, determined to impose at least civil order by force. Repeated searches and seizures began. The British occupied the headquarters of the Jewish Agency in Jerusalem and its Tel Aviv offices. They seized all Agency papers. Some 2,700 Jews were arrested, including all the Agency leaders the British could find. They made nearly a clean sweep, missing only Ben-Gurion and Shertok, who were in Paris. The most important leaders were trucked out to a detention camp at Latrun to broil under the summer sun and to consider the error of their ways. Strict limitations were placed on the civil liberties of those not arrested.

Some of the more moderate Jews had lost patience too. On July 1 Israel Galili, the commander of the Haganah, apparently decided to allow the Irgun to activate Operation Chick, the bombing of Jerusalem's King David Hotel; the Lechi was to attempt a similar operation against the David Brothers Building.[5] The key strike would be the former; the southwest wing of the hotel had been taken over for British military headquarters; many of the remaining offices housed the Mandate secretariat. The adjacent building had been occupied by the British Military Police and the Special Investigations Branch. The entire area had been surrounded with heavy barbed wire. There were nets to prevent random grenades. Cordoned off in this way and constantly guarded by alert military units, the King David had become the core of the British administration and a symbol of oppression to the Irgun. Attempts to attack the hotel with homemade rockets, which the British had dubbed "V3," had misfired. A frontal assault on the barbed-wire corridors, sandbagged emplacements, and the steel front doors appeared hopeless. But the Irgun had another ploy, an internal bomb placed in the basement. British security had been grossly lax in ignoring the basement, which extended unguarded under the entire hotel. But the Irgun operation had to be postponed several times nonetheless. Communications between the Irgun and the Haganah broke down. The Lechi attack stalled. Finally, the Irgun scheduled Operation Chick for July 22.

About noon on that day members of the Irgun assault unit, dressed in flowing Arab robes, wandered into the basement of the Régence Café. No one paid any attention to the "Arabs," who carried milk cans. There was no one in the café anyway but some real Arab kitchen workers. They were locked up in a side room, and the Irgun "Arabs" moved their milk cans to the area under the British wing. Each can contained 500 pounds of a TNT-gelignite mixture, guaranteed by the Irgun explosive expert Gideon (a cover name) sufficient to bring down the entire southwest wing. The milk-can bombs, carefully labeled, "Mines Do Not Touch," had just been pushed into position when a British officer wandered by. He became suspicious of the "Arabs" and moved forward to investigate. At the same time a British policeman walked in. The "Arabs" and the British opened fire simultaneously. The two British passersby fell dead. The Irgunists gathered up their own casualties and freed the Arab kitchen workers, who took off in all directions. The assault group dashed out, hopped into a truck, and drove away unmolested. In front of the hotel, a string of firecrackers went off to scare away pedestrians. Then things seemed to settle down.

Within a few minutes, at 12:10 P.M., the hotel switchboard received an incoming call warning that the hotel would explode in half an hour. Telephone calls followed immediately to the offices of the *Jerusalem Post* and to the French Consulate General opposite the hotel. Inside the King David no one could be sure that the half-hour warning was more than a hoax. There was considerable confusion. No one has ever been able to discover exactly what happened.[6] Whether orders were given to stay or to leave or not given at all, the result was that very few people left the hotel. There was not the quick evacuation that the Irgun had intended. Instead the minutes ticked by. At 12:37 P.M. Jerusalem shook with the impact of a huge explosion. The entire southwest wing of the hotel crumbled into the basement, forming a great pile of broken masonry under a billowing cloud of dust and smoke. Six stories had been sheared off the hotel and dumped into a heap, burying more than 100 men and women. More than eighty British, Arab, and Jewish lives were lost, needlessly the Irgun would say, callously the British would say.[7]

The hard British policy had borne bitter fruit. British response to the explosion was instant and predictable. Once again the Britons were disgusted and horrified, once again understandably. Once again, they blamed the entire Jewish population, as well as the Haganah, the Jewish Agency, and the extremists. After the fact, they again failed to split the united resistance at the very moment when the Haganah was having serious misgivings about the whole King David operation. Jewish opinion hovered momentarily between admiration for the exploit and horror at the deaths. Galili telephoned Menachem Begin, the Irgun leader, and urged him to announce that his group alone had planted the bomb. In France Ben-Gurion told a reporter from *France Soir* that "The Irgun is the enemy of the Jewish people. . . ."[8] The heat was on, and the Haganah and the Jewish Agency wanted out. Civilian deaths, particularly of Jews, had tarnished the success of the operation, and renewed revulsion against terror hovered over Yishuv. The British ignored the possibilities of exploiting the divisions and uncertainty.

While wide spread searches were taking place in Jerusalem, the British military commander, Lieutenant General Sir Evelyn Barker, drew up a secret order to the British army, vituperative in tone and language. In a country in which the British were surrounded by spies, informers, and agents, Barker should have anticipated that the order would fall into unfriendly hands; perhaps he did. In any case, the content of the order, which banned all Anglo-Jewish fraternization, was certain to alienate the Jews, intensify their suspicions of the British, awaken the tranquil, and embitter the tolerant:

> I am determined that they should be punished and made aware of our feelings of contempt and disgust at their behavior. . . . I understand that these measures will create difficulties for the troops, but I am certain that if my reasons are explained to them, they will

understand their duty and will punish the Jews in the manner this race dislikes the most: by hitting them in the pocket, which will demonstrate our disgust for them.[9]

There it was under the threadbare cloak of British morality: an ingrained and arrogant anti-Semitism; perfidious Albion was revealed at its worst. No matter that Barker had written in haste and anger, that the provocation had been extreme and frustration beyond bearing; the words had been written. Within twenty-four hours the Irgun information service had secured a copy. Within a week placards reproducing the order without comment had appeared on the walls.

British bumbling continued. On July 24 the government in London issued a White Paper showing the connection between the Jewish Agency and the terror campaign. The timing was incredibly clumsy: The report looked like a smear rather than a judicious analysis. No one in Palestine, either British or Jews, really believed the allegation, except, of course, those few who knew it to be true. On July 30 Cunningham announced that the British had "clear evidence" that the terrorists were in Tel Aviv, and he set in motion Operation Shark to rid the city of them. The 20,000 troops of General Cassel's 6th Airborne, backed by other units, began a massive cordon-and-search operation. In four days 100,000 Jews were "processed" at battalion level and 10,000 at brigade level; 787 were eventually detained and trucked to a detention camp at Rafa. The British did find five arms dumps, as well as explosives, illegal papers, and even forged bearer bonds. It was something concrete but not a very impressive haul for the time and effort expended; furthermore, no "terrorist" guilty of the King David explosion could be produced. The combination of Barker's order, the indiscriminate Tel Aviv searches, and the escape of the King David attack group neutralized all the British efforts.

Although it was not yet clear in London and Washington, or even in Jerusalem and Tel Aviv, the point of no return had been reached by the Palestine Jews. The only alternative left to the British administration if it insisted on refusing the minimum Zionist demands was naked force in an "obscure and repugnant campaign."[10] The British government could no longer hope to impose a solution unless it was willing to commit the army to a policy of massive repression. On the other hand, any agreement with the Jewish Agency would surely destroy hopes for an Anglo-Arab alliance and would lead just as surely to Arab violence, perhaps throughout the entire Middle East. London faced a cruel dilemma, a dilemma that most members of the government chose to ignore in the rush of other business and other crises.

With fear and force walking the streets of Tel Aviv, the scene again shifted to the diplomatic arena. On July 31 the House of Commons learned that a committee appointed after the Anglo-American Committee investigation had completed work on a compromise scheme, the Morrison-Grady Plan. Similar to the 1943 cantonization proposal of the Colonial Office—by 1946 no solution could be very novel—the Morrison-Grady Plan proposed the conversion of the Mandate into a Jewish province, an Arab province, and two neutral districts—Jerusalem and the Negev. In time the plan could lead either to a unitary binational state or to partition. During the first year of the proposed plan's operation, 100,000 Jewish immigrants would be permitted to enter Palestine. This design was actually a British rather than an Anglo-American solution, for at the direction of President Truman the United States delegates had withdrawn from the final discussions. The Plan did provide for the 100,000 immigrants Truman had demanded, but if failed to involve Washington in a Palestine solution, much less to lead to a commitment of American troops. As a formula for keeping Britain in Palestine with American support, the long Anglo-American investigation, culminating in the Morrison-Grady proposal, had proved abortive.

As a basis for negotiation with the Arabs and the Zionists, however, the result was not quite that sterile. On August 5 the Jewish Agency executives, meeting with Ben-Gurion in Paris, turned down the plan but did propose a plan of their own, based on the concept of partition. On August 12, the Arab League, meeting in Alexandria, agreed to negotiations with Great Britain, as long as the Jewish Agency and the United States government were not involved or the Morrison-Grady Plan used as a basis for discussion. Later in the month, the Palestine Higher Executive—the Arab equivalent of the Jewish Agency—agreed to negotiations if the Mufti Hajj Amin were invited to participate. At least the Arabs and Jews were willing to talk, even though not to each other and not about the results of the Anglo-American committee's labors. On September 10, therefore, the British convened a conference in London, which was attended only by delegates from the independent Arab states. The Arabs presented a plan for a unitary Arab state based on the White Paper of 1939. The British adjourned the conference without commitment or comment.

The British now could either negotiate on Arab terms, which would alienate the United States and provoke the Palestine Jews to full-scale resistance, or abandon their Arab entente in favor of a Jewish state, in the certainty that their entire Middle East position would collapse in violence and revolt. Even a realistic policy of partitioning the Mandate between Abdullah of Transjordan and the Jewish Agency would only ensure for Britain the hostility of the other Arab states and a commitment to maintain Abdullah that might grow beyond London's lessening military capacity. To members of the harassed and uncertain Cabinet, beset by staggering domestic problems and a worsening international situation, either alternative seemed grim. Like Scarlett O'Hara, they decided to "think about it tomorrow."

There were not many tomorrows left for Palestine. The situation in the Mandate certainly violated some sort of conservation-of-violence law, for no matter how chaotic Palestine became, there seemed always infinite room for escalation of conflict. In August the British again refused to allow expanded immigration and instituted a policy of transporting "illegals" to detention camps on Cyprus. For many Jews the journey to the Promised Land had been a trek through a series of barbed-wire way stations—German, American, and British— only to end, not in Palestine but in the hot and dusty compounds of Cyprus. The new immigration policy did little to allay Arab suspicions and much to antagonize further not only the hypersensitive Jews but also world opinion in general. In Palestine the uneasy alliance of the united resistance continued a sporadic cooperation through the late summer and early fall, although the misgivings of the Haganah and the Jewish Agency were growing. Then, about the time of the Anglo-Arab London conference in September, a plateau seemed to be reached. The intentions of both the Arabs and the Jews had been made clear to the British. London would have to come to some decision and bear its consequences. Momentarily a relaxation of tension occurred in the Mandate.

The British tried a local policy of dual appeasement to prolong the moment of calm. Five of Hajj Amin's exiled partisans were freed by the Colonial Office, and a general amnesty was granted to others of the Mufti's supporters. Jewish Agency leaders were released from the Lydda camp. These moves seemed to bear some fruit, for on October 29 the Haganah condemned terrorism, breaking with the Irgun and the Lechi. Yet the apparent armistice in no way diminished the demands of the Jews or of the Arabs; in fact, the reverse seemed true. While the British dithered in London and continued their searches and seizures in Palestine, both competing sides consolidated their forces for the moment of truth.

During the fall the Zionists' hands had been strengthened by attitudes expressed in the American election campaign. Both Democratic and Republican candidates had come out in favor of the proposal for 100,000 immigrants. The British could hardly ignore rising American sympathies for Zionist aspirations. In Demember the Twenty-second Zionist Congress met in Basel. The statists won a clear victory. Although still influential, Chaim Weizmann and the moderates no longer had the votes to control policy. Their policy, attuned to dependence on Great Britain and to negotiation, was discarded: Neither affection nor past history could be allowed to prevent the establishment of a Jewish state. Out of respect for Weizmann, the presidency of the Zionist Organization was left vacant as a symbol. After the conference, the resources of world Zionism were clearly in hands of the statists. If Britain could have produced a viable compromise, the moderate Zionists might have played a part, but, in any case, Zionism was now committed to immediate establishment of a state.

The Arab population in Palestine had been waiting for the violence to end, passively trusting in the diplomats of the Arab states, in the Mufti, or even in the British. Sullen, apprehensive, publicly defiant, and privately insecure, they watched from the sidelines. The submerged poor, the peasants and the tenement-bound workers, had little information and less impact on events. The spokesmen of the Arabs came from the still-disorganized elite, from self-appointed prophets and feudal tribal leaders. In fact, the only potential power base for the leadership in Palestine remained the mob, hysterical, volatile, and ephemeral. As a threat the mob was serious, but as a weapon it was hopelessly inadequate. During most of 1946 pressure on the British in behalf of the Palestinians had, as expected, come through the warnings and threats of the Arab states. Within Palestine, despite the growing urgency of the crisis, the failure of local leadership still had not been corrected. Even with the growing domination of Hajj Amin's Arab Higher Executive, the old suspicions and rivalries continued to hamper any all-Arab movement. Old family feuds, spite, pride, and habit kept the Arabs divided between the Huseinis of Hajj Amin and the Najjadah party under the influence of Abdullah of Transjordan. Each man had organized and armed a small private army, each had publicly professed a policy of driving out the British and destroying the Jews, but each hated the other. As a result, despite Hajj Amin's efforts in Egypt, there was no shadow Arab government to face the Jewish Agency; no secret army comparable to the Haganah; no silent, closely knit Arab movement waiting to achieve its ends by force if the British failed it. After a year of crisis and negotiations, there remained only isolated and sullen cabals, exiled leaders, primitive local organizations, and rival bands of irregulars.

In December violence in the Mandate took another quantum jump. Smarting under the continuing Irgun-Lechi sorties, the British announced that flogging would be introduced as a punishment. On December 27 a seventeen-year-old Irgunist, Kimchi, was given eighteen lashes. On December 29, in retaliation, the Irgun seized a British major and three noncommissioned officers in three swift snatch raids. Each was given eighteen lashes. A week later, to the delight of the Irgun and most of Yishuv, the British rescinded their flogging order. Vengeance had proved effective. On the night of December 29, however, a British cordon of the 7th Parachute Battalion shot up a speeding car trying to run a roadblock. The British mortally wounded one Jew and captured four others. Swiftly British Army Headquarters announced the capture of four "thugs" who would be tried under the emergency regulations, which specified the death penalty for terrorists. It was a grim Christmas week in the Holy Land.

Although disclaiming any responsibility for the acts of the Irgun, the Jewish Agency received considerable "fallout" benefit. To some extent the Agency could turn aside British anger and accusations by holding out clean hands while the Irgun and the Lechi kept up the pressure. The other side of the coin was that the extremists lacked restraint and even, on occasion, a sense of timing. Their attacks kept the pressure for massive British retaliation up, for it was obvious that

the British were treading a narrow line between forbearance and retaliation. Still, never for a moment could the British administrators
and army officers in Palestine or the government in London forget
that the Jews had the capacity and the will to defend their interests
by force, that the time for decision was ticking away. The year 1946
ended as it had begun—in terror, frustration, and failure.

From September to January little had changed. Nothing had been
forgotten, and nothing had been learned. There had been no break,
however slight, in the intransigence of the Jews and Arabs. On January 27, 1947, the second London conference opened but with even
dimmer prospects than that of the previous September. Although
Jamal al-Huseini appeared to represent the Palestine Arabs, the Jewish Agency continued its boycott. The United States had sent no
observer. British Foreign Secretary Bevin and Colonial Secretary
Arthur Creech-Jones were thus limited to listening to the Arab states
and Jamal al-Huseini present the old adamant demands, still backed
by the old legal, moral, and historical arguments delivered in the most
uncompromising language. Overtures to representatives of the Jewish
Agency simply proved that, in the four months since the previous
conference, the Zionists had stiffened, not relaxed, their posture.
There was simply no middle ground between the conflicting minimum demands of the Arabs and Jews. Despite all the talk, there had
not been a middle ground for years.

Finally, the British unilaterally presented their own proposal: A
British trusteeship for no more than five years if the Arabs and Jews
could agree on a unitary, binational Arab-Jewish state. Under this
plan, the population of Palestine would be granted canton self-gov-
ernment with no possibility of partition into two independent states.
The 100,000 Jewish immigrants would be admitted over a two-year
period, but the Arab population would then be allowed a voice in
determining future immigration policy. For Great Britain this solution appeared ideal, for it balanced both its own position in the
Middle East and its need not to alienate American Zionist sentiment.
Actually, it gave the Arabs more than they should have hoped for
and the Zionists less than they already had. The Jewish Agency rejected the proposal out of hand, for it would have prevented the
creation of a Jewish state open to all Jews who wished to immigrate
to Palestine. The Arabs regarded the British plan as simply another

promise of future action—a promise that limited the Arabs' right to
rule their own country. For once Arab and Jew agreed: It was a
matter of perfidious Albion again, cooing compromise and snatching
strategic advantage. After two refusals, the next move was up to
Britain. The Mandate daily slipped toward anarchy.

Palestine had become a garrison state under martial law, with a
maze of attendant regulations limiting all civil liberties in the name of
order. By January 1947 more than 80,000 regular British troops and
16,000 policemen, along with units of the Transjordanian Arab Legion, had been stationed in the Mandate. Even with one soldier or
police officer for every eighteen civilians, there had been no pacifica-
tion. Sixty huge concrete police structures—Teggart forts—were
studded throughout the Mandate, in a fashion reminiscent of the
Crusaders' castles. There were vast army and air-force camps, innumerable roadblocks, mile after mile of barbed wire. All the facilities
and resources of a modern police state were present. The British made
arrests and searches without warrants, decreed fines and forfeits of
property without judicial process; they also censored the press without explanation. The decks had been cleared for the continuing rise
of terror with the evacuation of 2,000 British civilian personnel.
Those who remained lived sealed in heavily guarded, wire-enclosed
ghetto security zones. All fraternization with Jews had been prohibited after Barker's order; in fact, only eleven British civilians still
lived outside the elaborate armed camps. In the streets army patrols
and tanks roamed back and forth ceaselessly. Heavy naval units
hovered off the coast to intercept illegal immigration ships. To everyone, inside and outside the Mandate, the situation had become intolerable.

For British purposes the real crusher was that the whole expensive
system—which tied down too many troops and ate up too many
precious pounds sterling—thus curtailing London's flexibility elsewhere—simply did not work. If an evil jinn had proposed to Bevin, to
the Colonial Office, to the British army the most fruitless of policies,
it could not have guaranteed more disastrous results than the British
had achieved on their own by 1947. Instead of dividing the Jews, the
British had united them. Instead of isolating the terrorists, the British
had isolated themselves. Cut off from local intelligence, gossip, and
old friendships, the British fumbled in the dark, dependent upon

heavy sealed tanks and barbed-wire ghettos. While the terrorist fish swam easily through the sea, 100,000 Britons sat blind and deaf in their bunkers. All around them the Jews were painstakingly creating a shadow government, smuggling in additional arms, evading or ignoring British regulations. Even the older Arabs, critical of the feeble British efforts, began to give up on their allies. They redoubled their efforts, and the two small Arab paramilitary units began to acquire uniforms and arms. Two little illegal states, one Arab and one Zionist, were being created under the half-blind eyes of the British. The entire position had become untenable. The British wanted out of Palestine. From the generals to the privates, they were sickened by their duties, revolted by the Jews, and disappointed in the Arabs. No one wanted to use naked violence; no one wanted a bloodbath. Slaughter would probably be futile, and it would certainly be immoral. Palestine, whatever the Foreign Office may have thought, did not seem worth it.

Back in Britain the London Conference was all but suspended, and the British cabinet had reached the end of its patience. Everywhere in the world "irresponsible" people carped and criticized. Everyone suspected British motives and failed to credit its principles. Even the cabinet members had grown uncertain of their own intentions. British Middle Eastern policy since 1944 had spun vast schemes. Affection for the Arab League had risen and fallen. Opinions of the possibility of using Egypt as a base had waxed and waned. A great move to establish Kenya as the pivot of power; the apparent significance of Aden, the Negev, Haifa; relations with Iran and Transjordan; and predictions of the future alignment of Syria and Lebanon all went through sea changes. By 1947 the Palestine Mandate had become an intolerable burden rather than a strategic key. Problems in Washington, in Moscow, in the Far East demanded attention, while the socialization of England itself and the very real difficulties of the domestic economy left the Labour Cabinet with little time to reflect on Palestine.

By February 1947 Britain was enduring its darkest days since the war. Although victorious in the battle against the Axis, Great Britain had almost exhausted its resources. It was no longer able to maintain its former commitments abroad. In fact, London had already indicated to the Americans that British troops would have to be pulled out of Greece. This polite ultimatum did at least lead to involvement of the United States in March, in the defense of Greece and Turkey under the Truman Doctrine. The Army was not even equal to policing the Empire; in fact, the Empire was tottering. India was on the verge of independence. The Egyptians had tired of English tutelage. All through the Asian and African satrapies, there were ominous national stirrings; secret parties plotted in Malaya and Kenya.

It was not only abroad that British government prestige was dribbling away. At home the economy was grinding to a halt as the country slumped deeper into a postwar recession. Six years of war and two of peace had brought multiple strains, endless shortages, and exhaustion of spirit. Furthermore, the British Isles were in the grip of the worst winter storm in years. Wheat imports were down and food and milk stocks in danger. On February 7 the government announced that coal supplies were critically low and imposed strict rationing of electricity. Factories began to shut down for lack of fuel and power. The horror of unemployment spread. With a full agenda of imminent and crucial decisions, in a cold and exhausted country, the Cabinet hurriedly gave up on the whole Palestine muddle.

On February 14 the British abruptly announced that they had decided to refer the problem of Palestine to the United Nations. Speaking in the House of Commons four days later, Bevin pointed out why the British had been unable to reconcile the Arabs and the Jews:

> There are in Palestine about 1,200,000 Arabs and 600,000 Jews. For the Jews, the essential point of principle is the creation of a sovereign Jewish State. For the Arabs the essential point of principle is to resist to the last the establishment of Jewish sovereignty in any part of Palestine . . . there is no prospect of resolving this conflict by any settlement negotiated between the parties. . . .[11]

What Bevin did not make clear was that Britain could not force a decision one way or the other without either alienating the United States and rupturing the essential Anglo-American alliance or alienating the Arab world and destroying Britain's precarious position in the Middle East. More humiliating, Britain had neither the will nor the resources to force a decision, even if such a move had been advantageous. Trapped in an impasse only partly of its own making, beset by crises, and indignant at endless criticism, Britain left the baby at the United Nations' door.

By that time almost no one concerned could accept any British position on Palestine at face value, particularly as, after Bevin's speech, heavily tinged with righteous indignation as it was, Colonial Secretary Creech-Jones told the House of Commons on February 25, "We are not going to the United Nations to surrender the Mandate."[12] So the British seemed divided. At the very time when Britain appeared to be withdrawing from Palestine under one "policy," some members of the government apparently wanted to continue the Mandate, perhaps after the United Nations had "failed." The Cabinet sought both to encourage United Nations intervention and to be ready for its failure, both to prepare for withdrawal and to remain. To many this ambivalence seemed a sly British maneuver to shift the responsibility for decision to the United Nations while retaining the strategic benefits of occupying Palestine. Neither the Jews nor the Arabs could believe that, after a generation of investment in a massive complex of military bases in so vital an area, Britain would opt out. The diplomats, both the cynical and the wise, could not believe that the British truly anticipated a "decision" from an organization already increasingly divided by East-West rivalry. Everyone thus remained skeptical, seeking the ulterior motive. For the Arabs and the Jews, at least, after February there would be a change, a broadening of the battlefield.

While all further negotiations were suspended until the United Nations had received formal notice of Great Britain's request, intensive analysis of Britain's newest ploy began in Palestine. Although uncertainty in London had produced contradictory policies, there was even less clarity in Palestine. The generals and civilians administering the Mandate had to make policy from day to day, from ultimatum to ultimatum. Few had any idea of the intentions of the Labour government for the obvious reason that the Labour government had no clear intentions. Policy had to be improvised in response to the continuing disorders. Each relevant department's lower reaches made their own decisions. Rarely was the Foreign Office, the Minister of State, or a chief of staff consulted. Directives from above were vague. It is no wonder that those seeking a hint to Britain's real plans were so often baffled. There was ample evidence to support practically any theory, and there were comparable counter indications for each. The only accepted certainty was that there was method in the muddle.

On April 2 Great Britain formally asked the Secretary-General of the United Nations, Trygve Lie, to call a special session of the General Assembly to consider the Palestine problem. In Palestine itself the routine rounds of provocation, suppression, and violence went on as before. Although the Haganah and the Jewish Agency were content to avoid direct action, the Irgun and the Lechi were not. Increasingly during 1947 the extremists raised the stakes, which forced the British to act in such a way as to produce still further violence. British efforts to maintain order by force, specifically the threat of executions, only produced more violent disorder. Already by April six captured Irgun "thugs" were in prison, under sentence of death and awaiting the outcome of an appeal filed in behalf of one of their number, Dov Gruner. The Irgun had already kidnapped a British officer and a civilian magistrate in retaliation for Gruner's sentence. The two Englishmen had been released only after a stay of execution had been granted—fresh evidence of the efficacy of terror. By April 14, after the denial of the appeal, the British authorities had decided that the time had come to carry out the death sentences rather than to submit to further blackmail. Four of the Irgunists, including Gruner, were secretly transferred from Jerusalem to the military fortress at Acre, where under heavy security precautions they were hanged on April 16, 1947. The Irgun immediately began to plan a retaliatory operation against the Acre prison to release the remaining Jewish prisoners. Regardless of diplomatic maneuvers, the level of violence in the Mandate had risen.

On April 28 the General Assembly special session opened at Lake Success. Reports from the Mandate created a sense of urgency and dedication among the delegates. The East-West schism had not yet fully paralyzed the United Nations or disillusioned those who saw the organization as the midwife for an era of world peace. Perhaps it was this faith in the value and possibilities of the United Nations, shared by so many of the delegates that more than anything else hampered the Arabs. For the Arab League believed that Palestine was essentially an Anglo-Arab problem, that Washington, Moscow, the Jewish Agency, and even the United Nations had neither legal nor moral rights to intervene in the destiny of an Arab nation. The Zionists, on the other hand, were eager for recognition in any forum. Their spokesmen could mingle biblical arguments, interpretations of international law, and moral considerations with every appearance of sweet reason. Substituting for Ben-Gurion (who was head of the Jewish agency and didn't want to leave Palestine) Dr. Abba Hillel Silver presented the case for the Jews with eloquence and passion:

> The Jewish people belongs in this society of nations. Surely the Jewish people is no less deserving than other peoples whose national freedom and independence have been established and whose representatives are now seated here. The Jews were your allies in the war, and joined their sacrifices to yours to achieve a common victory. The representatives of the people which gave to mankind spiritual and ethical values, inspiring human personalities and sacred texts which are your treasured possessions, and which is now rebuilding its national life in its ancient homeland will be welcomed before long by you to this noble fellowship of the United Nations.[13]

Though at the core the Zionists were as rigid as the Arabs, their posture remained flexible; their representatives understood and above all were respectful of the authority and prestige of the United Nations. By contrast the Arabs seemed negative and truculent, proposing sly maneuvers to evade inquiry.

The Arabs had equal time to present their case before the committee established to hear relevant evidence, but by that time it was clear that they were unhappy with the involvement of the United Nations, with Silver's appearance, with the apparent sympathy in some delegations for the emotional Zionist arguments. In essence the Arabs wanted an independent Arab Palestine; they argued that Palestine was in fact an Arab country, and it had a *right* to be independent. As their position was the "right" one, there could be no alternative, no compromise, no give and take. They demanded an Arab Palestine or nothing—no deals, no partial settlement, no cantons, no partition. That to grant the Zionists' aspirations would be a resuscitation of the impractical past, a violation of the right to self-determination seemed obvious to all but the muddle-headed. Henry Catton of the Arab Higher Committee outlined the Arabs' just claims and dissected the Zionist arguments:

> The Zionists claim Palestine on the grounds that at one time, more than two thousand years ago, the Jews had a kingdom in a part of it.

Were this argument to be taken as a basis for settling international issues, a dislocation of immeasurable magnitude would take place. It would mean the re-drawing of the map of the whole world. It has been said that you cannot set back the hands of the clock of history by twenty years. What should be said when an effort is made to set the clock of history back by twenty centuries in an attempt to give away a country on the ground of a transitory historical association?[14]

It was obvious that all the arguments of the Jews—the economic briefs, the use of the refugee problem, the Balfour Declaration—were specious.

For many Arabs it seemed better to be right and lose all than to compromise and gain almost all.[15] The Arabs had thus turned down the British plan in January. Despite their five delegates and their many friends or potential friends, their diplomats had alienated and antagonized many. In a world in which no issue appeared clear-cut, with justice all on one side, how could the Arabs be so uncompromising? The Jews had also made a strong case. The delegates, dedicated to compromise, looked to compromise for a solution. Almost from the first, despite Arab intransigence, general sentiment had favored some sort of investigating committee. Although opinion differed on its composition, the American preference for a neutral group of small nations, which was acceptable to the British, gained ground. The Russians seemed less interested in hampering the investigation, as many had predicted they would do, than in expediting British withdrawal from the Mandate. The result of the special session was establishment of an eleven-nation group, the United Nations Special Committee on Palestine, or UNSCOP, which was composed of delegates from Australia, Canada, Czechoslovakia, Guatemala, India, Iran, the Netherlands, Peru, Sweden, Uruguay, and Yugoslavia. The backgrounds and competence of the members of the new committee differed markedly: There were a Moslem Indian who had little international experience, two embarrassingly pro-Zionist "converts" from supposedly neutral South America, a pro-Arab Persian, and other honest and capable men whose knowledge of the Middle East was limited. Still, UNSCOP probably represented as fair a cross section of the small nations in the United Nations as was possible in 1947. The members chose Justice Emil Sandstrom of Sweden as chairman and secured the extremely valuable services of Dr. Ralph Bunche, Director-General of the Trusteeship Council, who was detached to aid the committee.

In Palestine no one, Jew, Arab, or Briton, had much confidence in the neutrality or the reasonableness of the new investigating committee, the twenty-second such committee since the beginning of the Mandate. The Jews suspected the motives of the British; the Arabs imagined an Anglo-American plot; the British administrators and army officers doubted the Committee's competence and resented its interference. Still, in time, all but the Arabs in Palestine agreed to cooperate. UNSCOP eventually did earn respect, through its vigorous efforts. On June 16 it opened hearings in Palestine. It was not an auspicious day for the beginning of efforts toward peace. On May 4, the Irgun had successfully carried out its raid against the prison at Acre. Blasting open the walls, the attack group had freed 251 prisoners, but five members of the raiding party had been captured by the British and brought to trial. A military tribunal had swiftly found them guilty of crimes that could earn them the death sentence. The British, with an elegant sense of timing, were to hand down three of the sentences on the opening day of the investigation.

The court sat in a large, grim, white building belonging to the Mandate Government. On the judge's bench was a British colonel in uniform. He conducted the hearing with dispatch and without apparent emotion. In front of him stood three young men in khaki shorts and open shirts. In a pile on the floor beside them were their leg irons. None of the three looked much like a "thug." Behind the three young men were rows of chairs filled with about thirty of their relatives. The proceedings were swift and stern. Almost before the spectators were aware of the judge's intentions, the penalty for the first prisoner was being read: "The Court sentences you to suffer death by being hanged." The colonel quickly repeated the same words for each of the other prisoners. The young men began to sing "Hatikvah," the Jewish national anthem. The other Jews in the courtroom, many of them in tears, joined in. The colonel turned and left the room, still without showing emotion.[16] As continued violence had provoked the April executions, the executions in turn had provoked the attack on Acre, and the attack had brought the June death sentences. Few believed that the cycle would be interrupted by the presence of UNSCOP. Violence had become a way of life in Palestine. The United Nations diplomats had received a proper introduction to the

Mandate: jail breaks, armed attacks, military tribunals, and death sentences.

Several members of UNSCOP were deeply shocked by conditions in Palestine, particularly the methods that the British deemed necessary to maintain the peace. This attitude was especially strong among the Latin Americans. In Latin America, the subtle difference between a political crime and a civil crime had by necessity long been recognized. Despite the British contention that the three young Irgunists were thugs and murderers, the impression the young men gave was clearly one of dedicated, if misguided, patriots. Their death sentences for political crimes did much to turn the Guatemalan representative, Jorge García-Granados, into an advocate of Jewish aspirations. "These men are fighting for their ideals as they fought for them in Europe against Hitler. They fight for their people and for their beliefs. In all conscience I cannot pass judgment upon them."[17] Although he tried to remain disinterested, García-Granados became, as others had before him, emotionally involved in the fate of Palestine.

UNSCOP collectively discussed the harsh British practices, and a majority voted to send a carefully worded resolution on the death sentences to the Mandate government. Unofficially the British were outraged at what they considered the Committee's unwarranted interference in the internal judicial affairs of the Mandate government. Officially they sent the Committee a coldly formal telegram explaining that the case was sub judice. The British may have asked the United Nations to enter Palestine, but they had no intention of allowing UNSCOP to interfere in Mandate business.

The Irgun had as little faith in UNSCOP as the British did. While the Committee members traveled throughout Palestine, meeting officially with Jewish and British representatives and on occasion unofficially with the Arabs, the Irgun prepared retaliation for the death sentences. On July 13 it seized two British sergeants and a Jewish War Department clerk, who were strolling along a street in Natanya. A car drew up, and a group of armed men bustled the three into the back seat. The car sped off and was lost to sight. The Jewish clerk proved his identity a few minutes later and was thrown, still bound, from the car into an orange grove. The car, with the two sergeants trussed up on the back seat, then vanished without a trace. The British immediately issued an ultimatum: Natanya must produce the two sergeants unharmed by 7:00 P.M. July 14. The town officials protested that they were not to blame and that they did not support the Irgun terrorist policy. The British were unmoved. The local Haganah condemned the kidnapping and made a fruitless search of the area. On the morning of July 14 the secret Irgun radio transmitter announced that the two sergeants would not be released until the sentences of the Irgun men were commuted.[18]

At 7:00 that night the British placed Natanya and twenty outlying settlements under martial law; 5,000 British troops sealed off the area from the rest of Palestine and carried out an exhaustive search. Still the hostages could not be found. Natanya was a ghost city, its streets deserted except for patrolling tanks and squads of heavily armed soldiers. All inhabitants were under house arrest. The city remained paralyzed while the searches continued. One after another, the troops brought in groups of thirty or forty Jews to be questioned. No one knew anything. The hostages could not be found. One more cordon-and-search operation had failed. This time it might cost the lives of two British soldiers. In Palestine UNSCOP was discovering not a mere historical controversy—not the quietly reasoned arguments, and neat position papers bound up with legal qualifications that were usually presented to the General Assembly—but fanaticism, vengeance, and death.

Perhaps the daily violence in the Mandate did more than the members of UNSCOP realized to persuade them of the need for partition. Without much doubt it revealed the bankruptcy of British policy. Evidence of the Mandate's failures could be seen on all sides. No one in Palestine wanted the Mandate to continue, apparently not even the British. Some inhabitants had already gone further and accepted the idea of partition. García-Granados of Guatemala and Enrique Rodríguez Fabregat of Uruguay had arranged to meet the mysterious Begin, the leader of the Irgun. By that time, Begin's meetings with transient notables must have been a source of considerable irritation to British security forces. In any case, the meeting, which the two UNSCOP members undertook in hopes of reducing tensions caused by the Irgun's kidnapping, gave Begin an opportunity to explain his refusal to release the hostages and his aspirations for a greater Jewish Palestine:

"Three of our soldiers have been unjustly condemned to death by an illegal military court. We are holding the sergeants as a guarantee against the hanging of our men. The British military courts have no right to function in Palestine. They are courts of an army of occupation. To counteract these unlawful courts we establish courts of our own. And we never execute a man without judging him first."

"But these sergeants have nothing to do with the sentencing of your men," Fabregat interrupted.

Begin shook his head. "They are soldiers of an army invading our soil. Britain must suffer the consequences if she refuses to respect the laws of war and executes our soldiers when they are prisoners of war."[19]

García-Granados later recalled his efforts to convince Begin of the impossibility of an all-Jewish Palestine, but he was probably not fully aware that he had thus tacitly accepted the need to partition Palestine into two states:

> "The views of Irgun on that (the historical right of the Jews to Palestine) are well known to us," I said. "It is useless to discuss them. We certainly cannot contemplate a solution that does not take into account Arab rights to self-government and to a free state of their own."[20]

Not all the UNSCOP members were as sure as García-Granados of the proper remedy for the situation in the Mandate.

Still another crisis brought the issues in Palestine into sharper focus, not only for UNSCOP but also for the rest of the world. During June there had been a pause in Jewish illegal immigration, perhaps for tactical, perhaps for technical, reasons. Then late on July 17, a small wooden steamer, *Exodus, 1947* (formerly an excursion ship, *President Warfield*, on the Baltimore-to-Norfolk run) steamed slowly toward the coast. Originally built for 700 passengers, it had been refitted as a floating barracks accommodating 4,500 people. All those aboard were illegal immigrants subject to deportation to Cyprus if seized by the British. Carefully trailing the steamer, invisible in the darkness, were the British cruiser *H.M.S. Ajax* and five destroyers. By dawn the next day, the thitherto insignificant coastal steamer had become the focus of attention for all those interested in the fate of the Mandate. The old steamer was carrying the largest cargo of nonquota refugees ever to sail to Palestine. It had sailed before dawn on July 11 from Toulon, France, without a pilot. There had been a fouled cable and a jarred pier; for a few minutes *Exodus* had even been aground. Almost as soon as it had cleared the port, a British destroyer had taken up a flanking position. By day British patrol planes had followed the ship's progress westward, and closer to Palestine the trailing ships had been reinforced. A swift dash to the shore seemed to have dim prospects of success, but no matter what the ultimate fate of the *Exodus* venture—success or seizure—the British were once more assured of a black eye. The crew and passengers were prepared to resist any British efforts to seize the *Exodus*. Around the desk was a maze of barbed wire, wooden fencing, and other obstacles, including a holed steam pipe hooked up to the boiler. *Exodus* tried to evade the British navy off Gaza and almost succeeded before the destroyers drew alongside. The end came just short of Palestine waters.

Soon after 3:00 on the morning of July 18, *Exodus* hove to, probably in international waters. A British boarding party came alongside but had to fight its way on board. A wild battle raged on the deck and around the wheelhouse, with the Jews defending their ship by throwing tins of food at the British. In the melee three Jews were killed, including one of the ship's officers, an American named Will Bernstein. More than 100 Jews were injured. As events reached a climax on board, the Jews in Palestine listened on their radios, for *Exodus* broadcast to Yishuv. Within minutes, the fate of the refugees was known to all. By dawn of July 18 *Exodus* was sailing slowly toward Haifa harbor under armed British escort. When the ship reached Haifa later that day Justice Sandstrom, Chairman of UNSCOP, was watching from shore.

If the incident of *Exodus* had ended on July 18, when the vessel sailed into Haifa under guard Britain's position would have been difficult enough. Few members of UNSCOP could have failed to be moved by the long agony of the "illegal" Jews: first the black night of Nazism, afterward the squalid displaced-person camps, then extinguishing of hope when their bitter odyssey was frustrated within sight of Palestine. But the *Exodus* "incident" was not over. It lasted two more months. The British government, resentful at what it believed to be undeserved criticism, decided to make an example of *Exodus*. Instead of transferring the immigrants to Cyprus, the British shipped them back to their port of embarkation in southern France. Only 130 Jews disembarked voluntarily, and the rest were escorted to displaced-person camps in the British Zone of Germany. The apparent vindictiveness of the British government and the agonized two months between the boarding battle on July 18 and the arrival of the refugees in Germany only weakened the British position as disinterested referee in Palestine. The skilled technicians of the Zionist information offices slashed British pretenses to ribbons.

UNSCOP left the Palestine Mandate on July 20; the same state of crisis and chaos existed there as when they had arrived. *Exodus* was anchored off Haifa. The three Irgun terrorists were still under sentence of death, and the two British sergeants were still held hostage. The Arabs, watching the Jewish-British conflict from the wings, still showed no inclination to modify their demands. The British remained sullen and their policy ambivalent. Everyone knew that the situation could not continue. Eventually the *Exodus* immigrants ended in Germany, the Irgunists were executed, and the British sergeants were hanged in retaliation. Yet there was always room for one more crisis, for greater violence, in Palestine. UNSCOP recognized that it must produce a solution, but, as British High Commissioner Sir Alan Cunningham pointed out, a peaceful solution seemed unlikely:

> No solution can be found which gives absolute justice to everyone. It is clear, too, that no solution can be found which will be wholly agreed to by everyone. Therefore, it seems that to a great or lesser degree whatever solution you find must be imposed.
> There must be a solution, however. Time has shown a constantly accelerated deterioration of conditions in this country. The sands are running out. The only answer is an early political solution.[21]

The Mandate had collapsed in all but name. The last hope for a solution lay with UNSCOP and ultimately with the General Assembly.

Yet, even as violence and tension in the Mandate increased by quantum jumps, even as the internationalization of the crisis progressed with the involvement of the United Nations, the Arabs and Jews within Palestine continued to view their future in terms of the immediate past. For more than a year the Arab-Zionist confrontation had been pursued not by mutual violence, despite rising tensions but by various competing efforts to persuade or force the British to impose the appropriate solution. Incredibly enough, in the struggle for the future of the Mandate the two competitors tended to ignore each other and to concentrate on their British overlord. Elsewhere in the world pundits might foretell in voices of doom a jihad, a racial massacre, a vast bloodletting; but in Palestine both sides anticipated an enforced decision that could be accepted or rejected. Neither had yet anticipated a power vacuum—certainly not as long as the British were involved—in which Jew and Arab would clash unaided and unrestrained. With the arrival of UNSCOP, the scope of any future enforced decision had been broadened. Perhaps the General Assembly could be levered one way or another, but the key remained in London with the British Cabinet. Neither Jew nor Arab felt himself master of his own fate. Energies were increasingly spent in the international forum, rather than wasted on futile conflict.

NOTES

1. The Irgun, with about 400 members, had actually begun its anti-British campaign in January 1944 and the Lechi at about the same time. The Haganah had always been reluctant to attack the British directly, and, when it did, specific symbolic targets—facilities used to prevent immigration—were chosen rather than the British in general.

2. There is a considerable literature on the "smuggling" of immigrants, which had gone on as long as there had been a British quota. See Efraim Dekel, *SHAI: The Exploits of Haganah Intelligence* (New York: 1959); Munya M. Mardor, *Strictly Illegal* (London: 1946); Leo W. Schwarz, *The Redeemers* (New York: 1953); and Bracha Habas, *The Gate Breakers* (New York: 1963).

3. Major R. D. Wilson, *Cordon and Search: With 6th Airborne in Palestine* (Aldershot: 1949), p. 47.

4. One man's odyssey through the tangles of Palestine with the Anglo-American committee is recorded in Richard Crossman, *Palestine Mission* (New York: 1947).

5. The extent of the Haganah's responsibility for the attack on the King David has never been made quite clear. Galili had a reputation as an opponent of terrorism, but in the summer of 1946 the Haganah was cooperating with the Irgun. Menachem Begin, *The Revolt* (New York: 1951), reports that Galili gave his permission for Operation Chick; the delays and breakdown in communications between the Irgun and the Haganah, however, left room for Galili to claim, perhaps justifiably, that he did not order the attack on July 22. With the passage of years, apparently, many members of the Haganah would like to forget both those periods of cooperation with the Irgun and also Haganah-British cooperation in actions against the Irgun.

6. One of the cherished anecdotes of the period, probably apocryphal, involves the supposed response of Sir John V. Shaw, Chief Secretary for Palestine, when informed by the manager of the hotel of the Irgun warning: "I am here to give orders to the Jews and not to receive orders from them." Begin, *This Is the Resistance: Palestine's Fighting Army of Liberation* (New York: n.d.), p. 13.

7. Begin, *Revolt*, pp. 212–30.

8. *Ibid.*, p. 223. Begin points out Ben-Gurion's addition that the Irgun "had always opposed me." The distaste of the Jewish Agency, particularly the Left wing, for Begin was very strong indeed. The more orthodox Zionists had been able neither to absorb nor to expel the extreme revisionists; even in the Warsaw ghetto rising, the revisionists had gone their own way, intolerant of what they considered half-measures. For a great many years in Palestine, Ben-Gurion must have felt that his Zionist cross bore Jabotinsky's name.

9. The order is quoted in full in Jon Kimche, *Seven Fallen Pillars: The Middle East Front 1945 to 1952* (New York: 1953), pp. 42–43; the specific chapter is most appropriately entitled "Government by Insult."

10. Wilson, *op. cit.*, p. 202. Independently a great many of the British involved expressed their disgust with the entire Palestine affair, often noting the similarities to the Irish "troubles" in 1918–1921. They were not alone in recognizing the parallel; for example, Avshalon Habib, one of the three young Irgunists condemned to death by the British in July 1947 underlined in his final political testament the failure of the same British tactics and techniques in Ireland. All agreed that, although the British might tolerate naked force against "natives" in Kenya or Malaya, somehow the Irish and the Jews seemed different. Their forcible repression was repugnant and would in time stain British honor.

11. *Parliamentary Debates, House of Commons*, Vol. 433 (London: 1947), col. 988.

12. *Ibid.*, col. 2007.

13. *Official Records 1st Special Session of the General Assembly*, III (Lake Success, N.Y.: 1947), 116.

14. *Ibid.*, p. 197.

15. An example of what one long-time friend of the Arabs, Sir John Bagot Glubb, in *A Soldier with the Arabs* (New York: 1957), p. 152, calls "justice though the heavens fall" is this conversation between Glubb and Taufiq Pasha, Prime Minister of Transjordan:

    I was one day explaining to him what would happen if the Jews broke through at a certain point, and how we should then have to withdraw from a neighbouring position.

    "You cannot withdraw," he said.

    "But if we do not withdraw, a large part of the army will be cut off and destroyed," I said.

    "Better to have the army destroyed than to give up part of the country to an enemy who has no right to it," retorted the Prime Minister.

    "But if the army is destroyed, the enemy will take the whole country, not only the small area from which we would otherwise have withdrawn. That surely would be much worse," I argued.

16. Jorge García-Granados, in *The Birth of Israel* (New York: 1949), pp. 50–52, gives a second-hand description of the sentencing. See Itzhak Gurion, *Triumph on the Gallows* (New York: 1950), pp. 154–64, for the political declarations of the three prisoners, which were given on June 12.

17. García-Granados, *op. cit.*, p. 59.

18. The kidnapping of the sergeants and the two-weeks crisis that culminated in their murder was, perhaps, the key event in the long campaign of terror. Although the impact on the members of UNSCOP was great, equally significant was the spread of disgust from British Palestine to London.

19. García-Granados, *op. cit.*, p. 159.

20. *Ibid.*, p. 157.

21. *Ibid.*, pp. 191–92.

3

The Struggle
Over Partition

Ever so slowly the implications of the UNSCOP investigation rippled through the Arab Middle East.
Great Britain, of course, remained the major factor, but perhaps—
just perhaps—the fate of Palestine might be largely decided by international negotiation; the techniques of pressure and promise might have
to be brought to bear on the United Nations in general and on
UNSCOP in particular. When the Committee members arrived in
Lebanon, the delegates of the Arab States again presented their standard arguments. They would never accept partition and, if necessary,
would fight to prevent it. The Lebanese Foreign Minister Hamid Bey
Franjiyyah warned that the safety of Arab Palestine was at stake and
that this peril gave the Arabs the right to oppose Zionism by every
means. A quick flight to Amman, Transjordan, to meet Abdullah, who
some members thought might be a secret moderate, revealed that
Transjordan's position was no different from that of the other
Arab states: A Jewish state could be created only by violence, and
the Arabs would oppose it by every means. On its departure from the
Middle East, UNSCOP took with it impressions not only of chaos
in the British Mandate but also of irreducible and mutually exclusive
aspirations of the Zionists and the Arabs. UNSCOP faced an issue
apparently beyond reasonable compromise.

On July 27 the committee members arrived in Geneva, the site of their final deliberations. By a vote of six to four, they decided to dispatch a subcommittee to visit the Jewish displaced-person camps in Germany and Austria. There in the shadows of the Nazi gas chambers the unaltered determination of most of the European Jews to emigrate to Palestine was fully revealed. When the subcommittee returned, the eleven delegates had privately reached a consensus on at least some vital points. First, the British Mandate was bankrupt, and Great Britain would have to withdraw. Even the Commonwealth members and the pro-British Dutch and Swedish delegates agreed. Further meetings with representatives of the British Foreign Office only confirmed suspicions about London's curious ambivalence. No one liked what the Mandate had become, and no one could fathom Britain's true intentions. Beyond ending the Mandate, there was general agreement on the need to maintain the economic unity of Palestine and to ensure the democratic structure of the new states or state. Eleven basic points were accepted unanimously; together with one other, which drew two dissenting votes, they formed the basis from which an equitable settlement had to be constructed.

The fundamental nature of UNSCOP's recommendations became immediately apparent when the Committee split over a proposal for political partition with an economic union. Clearly there was little argument on the issue of partition itself but only on the boundaries of the two proposed states.

The majority proposed a Jewish territory that would include eastern Galilee, the central coastal plain from a point south of Acre to one just north of Isdud, and the vast and barren Negev Desert. The Negev had been the key point of contention among UNSCOP members; Zionist dreams of making the desert flower had outweighed the more mundane strategic goals of the British. The Arab territory would thus consist of western Galilee, central Palestine, and the coastal plain in the far north and far south. The Jerusalem-Bethlehem area would form an international zone, to be administered by the United Nations. A two-year probationary period would begin on September 1, 1947; Great Britain would administer it either alone or jointly with one or more members of the United Nations. Jewish immigration would continue at a rate of 6,250 a month in the first two years and 5,000 a month after that. An economic union was to be the basis of a ten-year Arab-Jewish treaty.

The minority, sympathetic to Arab hopes, sought to produce an alternative plan that would attract sufficient delegate enthusiasm in the General Assembly to prevent the dismemberment of Palestine. The plan hewed more closely to Arab demands. After a three-year United Nations administration both Arab and Jewish regimes would be established within Palestine; there would be a single capital at Jerusalem. Although Jewish immigration would continue for three years, no specific figures were suggested, nor was a definite long-range immigration plan outlined. Despite the immigration provision, the minority plan essentially resembled previous Arab proposals.

The two reports, both to be submitted to the General Assembly, were completed only five minutes before the deadline at midnight August 31. The final results had come about through the deliberations of the Committee members, rather than as the result of pressures from the Arabs or the Jews, from the British, or even from the members' own governments. Not that in some cases advice had not been taken or positions considered. The Zionists had had two first-rate foreign policy advisers on hand, David Horowitz and Abba Eban. The Arabs, less certain about the whole UNSCOP affair, had been represented vaguely by an agent of the Arab Higher Committee. Various spokesmen had appeared from time to time, most significantly the British, who apparently alienated many members by their vague statements. In any case UNSCOP had done its job. The second regular session of the General Assembly was to meet in a little more than two weeks to consider the committee's two proposals. Once more, after weeks of work, there were "plans" to end the Palestine stalemate.

The reaction of the Arabs to the UNSCOP plans was immediate and predictable. The Arab League Information Office in New York warned the United Nations that acceptance of either proposal would mean violence in the Middle East. The Zionist General Council, meeting in Zurich, swiftly rejected the minority scheme of federalism but withheld final judgment on the partition plan until the General Assembly had taken action. There was little doubt, however, that the satisfaction expressed by the General Council over the partition plan meant that the Zionists would work for its adoption by the General Assembly. Elsewhere official reaction to the labors of UNSCOP was extremely cautious. British circles had not anticipated the total junking of the Mandate, but there was no immediate comment from London. In the United States there was only silence for some time.

Eventually, Secretary of State George Marshall noted that Washington gave great weight to the UNSCOP proposal. No one knew what that remark meant. The Soviet Union had no particular Middle Eastern policy other than Anglophobia. Both the Zionists and the Arabs remained hopeful without any concrete encouragement of Russian support. From August 31 until the opening of the United Nations session on September 16, there was thus confusion and uncertainty in all camps. Few nations had much interest in Palestine; fewer still had a policy, public or private.

When the delegates gathered at Lake Success, the international situation had deteriorated since their previous meeting. Tensions in the entire postwar world had been increasing throughout 1947. In Greece there was civil war, deeply involving both East and West. The unification of Korea seemed increasingly remote. In July the Soviet Union had turned down the Marshall Plan. In September the Cominform had emerged, reflecting a renewal of Russian efforts to foment international revolution. At all East-West contact points cooperation had declined and friction increased. The West had not yet fully recognized what the journalists called the "cold war," but Russia was increasingly straining the tolerance of its former allies. There was also no secret about the divergence of the American and British views on Palestine. The United Nations would thus have to decide the future of the Mandate in the context of rising East-West alienation and the failure of Anglo-American diplomats to find a common policy.

While UNSCOP was carrying out its deliberations in Geneva, the turmoil in the Mandate had continued. The Mufti's Huseini Party had tightened its grip on the Palestine Arabs and had stepped up its agitation and propaganda. Tension had reached the point at which a series of clashes between the Jews and Arabs along the Jaffa–Tel Aviv border in August had required the intervention of British forces. The hysteria in Palestine had spread to Great Britain when news of the execution of two sergeants was released. There had been public attacks on Jewish property and synagogues and a rising spiral of anti-Semitic speeches and pamphlets from the lunatic fringe of British politics. More important for the deliberations at Lake Success, there had been widespread revulsion at the whole Palestine imbroglio. Just as their undesired role as overlords had disgusted the British within the Mandate, increasingly the British public at home wanted out too. No one wanted to shoot Jews, or Arabs, for that matter, although this prospect seemed less soul searing. No one wanted pleasant young British soldiers hanged simply to maintain some vague imperial advantage. Malaya or Kenya, where natives could be shot with less compunction, might be another story; but Palestine, like Ireland thirty years before, did not seem worth the slaughter of men, Jews or Arabs, who should be and who had been friends. This disgust had its effect on the government, but at Lake Success the slow and uncertain policy metamorphosis was not apparent. Only the rising disorder in Palestine was clear to the delegates.

On September 23 the United Nations General Assembly, at the suggestion of the Secretariat submitted the Palestine question to an ad hoc committee, composed of delegates from all member nations, to allow more scope for parliamentary maneuver. The ad hoc committee met fourteen times in the next twenty-four days; it not only debated the ancient arguments but also responded to an Arab diplomatic offensive designed to scuttle the UNSCOP proposals. Recognizing that most nations and therefore most delegates had no real interest in Palestine, the diplomats from the five Arab League states had sought to formulate several motions that would sidetrack an open vote on the UNSCOP plans. As an offensive tactic, it had much to recommend it. The Arabs had few real international enemies and a good many potential friends. If they could piece together even a quick majority on an emotionally positive alternative, the UNSCOP proposals might well end where all the other proposals had ended—forgotten in dusty pigeonholes. Apparently, the ploy was a little too obvious, however. At an earlier time or in another place (London, for example), the Arabs might have gotten away with it, but at Lake Success there were just enough delegates to reject the appealing form of the Arabs' motions because of their negative intentions. When the Arabs had run out of motions, the ad hoc committee prepared to vote on the UNSCOP proposals. The Arabs' position was weakened by their failure to present an alternative that seemed reasonable. A further blow to Arab hopes came on October 13, when the Soviet delegate Semen K. Tsarapkin endorsed partition. Two days earlier the United States had also expressed support of the majority plan, as the Arabs had feared. With the Americans and Russians incredibly on the same side and without a generally acceptable alternative plan of their own, the Arabs could not muster anything near a majority. The motion in favor of the majority UNSCOP plan passed twenty-five to thirteen, with seventeen abstentions. But, though the Arabs had lost a battle, their prospects were still not hopeless, as less than a majority of the ad hoc committee had voted for the UNSCOP proposal.

Rather than going directly to a vote in the General Assembly, supporters of UNSCOP's proposals undertook further efforts to make them more generally attractive. On October 21 three new subcommittees were set up and entrusted with the task of modifying the original proposals in the light of the previous debate. Once more there was debate—new maneuvers and threadbare arguments. The committee mill grinds exceptionally slowly indeed. Actually, none of the knowledgeable delegates had much hope for the success of the committees. The major purposes of the new investigation were to allow time for a consensus to form behind the majority plan and to secure British acquiescence if not support. Even if partition were to pass, no one could tell what the British would do. Colonial Secretary Arthur Creech-Jones and the British delegate to the United Nations, Sir Alexander Cadogan, had been less than candid about British intentions, saying only that London would support no policy that was unacceptable to both Zionists and Arabs. As no such policy would ever exist, Britain's attitude remained an enigma. The subcommittees worked in the dark, their members hopeful that time would crystallize support.

As the United Nations made its tortuous way toward a final vote, the Jewish Agency increasingly accepted the possibility of partition. Almost without exception, the Jewish leaders both in Palestine and in the Zionist organizations had previously assumed that there would be no British withdrawal. Perhaps only David Ben-Gurion had foreseen at least the possibility of evacuation, although even he had not viewed it as a certainty; but once the activities of the General Assembly had accelerated, all eyes switched to Lake Success. A favorable vote on partition in the United Nations seemed likely somehow to solve everything, and more Jewish concern, more Jewish money, and more Jewish talent were channeled into New York. Lobbying in delegates' lounges and securing favorable editorials from major newspapers and glowing endorsements from the mighty were the modes of action that most Jews believed would produce the hoped-for Jewish state.

But the realists, Ben-Gurion and a few officers of the Haganah, sensed the urgency of the situation. On September 23 Creech-Jones informed the General Assembly in effect that Britain would not implement partition. If Britain would not, who would? There was no United Nations army. If the Arab states tried to prevent partition by force, who would forestall them? The Haganah was a magnificent weapon for internal war and settlement defense, but it had no heavy equipment, no airplanes, tanks, or artillery. Except for Ben-Gurion, few Jews seemed to care. Most Jews expected that the whole question would be decided at Lake Success and that the Arabs would have to accept the inevitable, even though the Secretary-General of the Arab League, Abdul Rahman Azzam Pasha, had warned the two principal Zionist advisers on foreign policy, Abba Eban and David Horowitz, that the Arabs would fight for Palestine. The bellicose Arab warnings were continual, but for most Jews the net effect was nil. The Arabs had cried wolf too long. In October Ben-Gurion ordered the Haganah to plan for a general mobilization of Jewish manpower in Palestine. The following month a secret mission left for Europe and Canada to negotiate the first large-scale Zionist purchase of arms and military equipment.

The Arabs, too, had to reconsider their position and their prospects. With the United States, however gingerly, and the Soviet Union, however callously, on record in favor of partition, the Zionists might actually round up a two-thirds vote. The Arabs' early optimism was evaporating. In September, despite the addition to the United Nations of Yemeni and Islamic Pakistani delegations, early votes on the delaying resolutions showed only patchy support for the Arabs. Their warnings had been dismissed. Although the diplomatic phase was far from over, more serious thought had to be given to the future.

The first attempt at a practical military agreement among the Arab states came at a meeting of the Arab League Political Committee in Sofar, Lebanon, on September 16. It was a typically discouraging League meeting. The Secretary-General had not even called the meeting, and neither Egypt nor Saudi Arabia favored holding it. In fact, Iraq had sent out the invitation. Because of rising popular discontent at the Iraqi government's treaty negotiations with Britain, Baghdad wanted attention diverted to its hard line on Palestine. The result was an Arab League official note to Washington and London warning that the creation of a Jewish state would inevitably bring violence with it. Reluctantly, the Arabs faced the fact that they would soon have to sort out their differences or have their threats exposed as bluffs.

Those Arab states to which the Palestinian Arabs looked for aid and comfort had the trappings of power without the substance. The Middle East was rich in colorful national flags, independent and tame monarchs, smartly uniformed armies; but the armies' strength was often illusory, though capable of mesmerizing not only the Arabs themselves but also even the British creators. Too often this façade hid foreign manipulation, economic exploitation, and subsidized politics. To one generation of Arab politicians, the achievement of independence had seemed sufficient, and the revolutionaries of yesteryear had become the pudgy oligarchs of 1947. Many of the old nationalists were barely aware of the seething discontent in the cities or the grinding poverty of the countryside. Many had become corrupt and venal. Others were tired or tamed to palace politics. Some hardly realized their own nation's weaknesses, the absence of the political and economic institutions of the modern state. Often the state was an incredible collection of anachronisms held together by customs and loyalties that had changed little in a thousand years. In the more sophisticated capitals political parties were opportunistic coteries concerned more with patronage than with principle. Ideas were the currency only of the politically emasculated left-wing intellectuals few, feeble, and without power or of the large, but clandestine Muslim Brotherhood, which was centered in Egypt, and dominated by a fanatical Islamic ideology and a romantic dedication to a just society. Labor unions were feeble and suspect. There was no educated electorate. The population often had no channel for satisfying grievances but the street, where it was manipulated by the police and politicians.

If the Arabs' freedom of political action was hampered by their political instability, their military capacity was even more limited. Nearly all the states lacked the wherewithal to make war. None had a viable, balanced economy. Manufacturing hardly existed; heavy industry was unknown. Raw materials were exploited by outsiders.

Much of the Middle East remained sunk in medieval squalor. The armies were clothed, armed, and often paid from abroad. The peasants hated to serve. The officers often saw the armies as a collection of sinecures rather than as a profession. A few young men chose military careers as a way to rise in an otherwise immobile society, but they could hardly balance off the sullen soldiers and the complacent officer corps. There was only one real Arab army, King Abdullah ibn-Husein's elite Bedouin corps, the Arab Legion, which had been recruited, trained, and led by British advisers. But the Legion, still equipped and subsidized by the British, who had a romantic fondness for the Bedouins, had never fought any action more serious than a scuffle over an oasis. Nonetheless, it was the only crack Arab force. The one comforting thought, to those easily comforted, was that the Zionists had only the underground Haganah.

More vital than their political and military problems as first-generation states were the deep fissures in the ostensibly solid rock of Pan-Arabism. The supposed coalition of 40 million Arabs directed by a united League was an illusion, as much British as Arab. What did exist was a universal and incandescent attachment to Arab unity, clouded in detail but articulate in expression. Beyond this attachment, however, the old rivalries and enmities remained embedded. It is quite impossible to delineate briefly even the major schisms in the Arab world of 1947. Each independent nation had its own ambitions, which often could be secured only at the expense of other Arabs. These national goals were complicated by dynastic rivalries, arising mostly from the aftermath of the Arab revolt during World War I. There were also long-standing regional prejudices. All the suspicions (often justified) and all the hatreds (usually reciprocated) haunted the meetings of the Arab League. On the subject of Palestine, however, all Arabs agreed at least to the proposition that the Zionists should not have a state in Palestine. All agreed that there could be only an Arab Palestine. But beneath this comforting cloak of anti-Zionism, the Arabs found little else of common interest in September.

On October 2 the Arab League met again at Aley in Lebanon. In view of the negative votes on Arab resolutions before the ad hoc committee at Lake Success, the delegates struggled to piece together a unified policy. They resolved to uphold a series of secret agreements made in June 1946 at Bludan in Syria. These agreements had included denial of economic concessions to the United States and Great Britain, withdrawal of the Arabs from any international organization, and the need to make war in Palestine if the Zionists remained. For the first time an effort was made to carry out the threat of war. The Arabs set up a military committee that included representatives of Iraq, Palestine, Lebanon, Syria, and Transjordan. A beginning was made on a joint mobilization of Arab armies on the boundaries of Palestine. The League also called for the procurement of 10,000 rifles for the Palestine Arabs, as well as efforts to acquire more fighter planes. Once again there were no decisions on specific military intervention and no significant moves toward a single command. As always, suspicion and distrust hampered cooperative effort.

Iraq, the most militant Arab state, had neither a common boundary with Palestine nor the confidence of the other Arab states. Prime Minister Mahmud Fahmi Nokrashy of Egypt openly shrank from embarking on any military adventures. Saudi Arabia, for once, agreed with the Egyptians. Lebanon, with its delicately balanced religious blocs, sought only to avoid crisis. Many Arabs regarded the bellicose Mufti Najj Amin al-Huseini of Jerusalem as a competitor rather than as a partner. When he demanded that the Arab League equip a Palestinian army under his control, Egypt supported him because King Farouk I hoped to control him, and Saudi Arabia supported him because King Abdul-Ariz ibn-Saud hated Transjordan's Abdullah. Iraq and Transjordan adamantly opposed helping the Mufti. Abdullah hated the Mufti, veiwed Farouk with distaste, and looked upon ibn-Saud with enmity As Abdullah's Arab Legion was the only effective Arab military force, his opinion of the Mufti was crucial. Abdullah's plans, however, remained mysterious, open to the most cynical suspicions. Some opponents suggested that he was sufficiently corrupt to divide Palestine with the Zionists. A trip to Transjordan by some of the delegates immediately after the conference at Aley revealed only that Abdullah would not accept a Palestine "government" with or without the Mufti nor would he help arm the Palestine Arabs. The suspicious delegates returned to their capitals to report.

As late as November the Arabs had not taken any decisive steps toward joint military action. In fact, Abdullah was evidently seeking to avoid war by compromising with the Zionists, whereas Egypt and Saudi Arabia, equally unwilling to fight, sought to compete with

Transjordan by backing the Mufti. Iraq was too distant to fight and Lebanon too weak. Syria had evaded commitment. There was no single commander, no war plan. The Arabs could do little but wait and see if their diplomats could defeat partition at Lake Success.

From October 21 to November 10 the subcommittee on Palestine partition worked on its final report. Various changes were introduced, but in essence the report was the same as the original UNSCOP majority report. The committee found it impossible to come to any sort of agreement with the British delegation. From the time that Creech-Jones had told the delegates that Great Britain would play no role in implementing any solution, including partition, that did not have the acceptance of both the Arabs and the Jews, London had grown increasingly uncooperative and its attitude increasingly enigmatic. But at last the committee decided to call upon London to end the Mandate on May 1, 1948. The subsequent transition period was reduced to two months in hopes of avoiding the chaos and violence that the British repeatedly predicted. The transfer of power to the Jews and Arabs was to be completed by July 1. Both the United States and Russia agreed to the revised partition plan and the new timetable. On November 13 Cadogan announced that the United Kingdom would not evacuate its troops until August 1 and that, as long as British troops remained, they and not the United Nations would exercise power. The committee went back to work, revising its report to incorporate the new British conditions. The major difficulty was that no one was quite sure precisely what the British wanted or to what they were objecting.

British policies were not, as Guatemala's Jorge García-Granados suggested, solely the result of "resentment and hurt pride," although these emotions played a part:

> In a word, from the moment the United Kingdom brought this problem to the United Nations, its statements have been vague and its policies tantalizing.
>
> We can only conclude that, although the United Kingdom had said that it will not oppose the partition plan, it is, in fact, opposing it. The British say they will respect the report and hand over authority to the Commission, but, in fact, they refuse to hand over anything; they will not agree to give the Commission an area in which to start work.[1]

There was ample evidence, as García-Granados noted, that Britain had become increasingly truculent within the United Nations. As the weeks passed, London seemed to be acting from a combination of pique and self-interest. Originally, Foreign Secretary Ernest Bevin and Prime Minister Clement Attlee had not foreseen that an appeal to the United Nations would lead to positive action in the latter body. At worst or perhaps even at best, they had expected the British Mandate to be sanctioned in some form by the General Assembly. During the summer of rising terrorism, which had culminated in the hanging of the two British sergeants, there had been growing sentiment for disentanglement. Then UNSCOP insistence on an end to the Mandate had been a blow to British self-esteem. By September British policy in Palestine was a graveyard of frustrated hopes and bitter disappointments. By September 1947 Britain no longer had a Palestine policy. Instead the British had only undefined interests in the Middle East and a desire to retain Arab friendship.

Increasingly, British policy had to be interpreted from the actions and statements of British officials on the spot in Cairo, in Jerusalem, or at Lake Success. They seldom said the same things or acted for the same reasons. Often, these men acted on their own from vague instruction. When the Arab League met at Aley in October, Brigadier Iltyd N. Clayton of the Cairo Residency was present, as he had been at the earlier Bludan meeting. Surely his presence implied British support for forcible Arab efforts to prevent partition, or so said the experts. Elsewhere British diplomats viewed threats of Arab violence with alarm and preached moderation. Some Cabinet members gave up hope of remaining in Palestine only reluctantly; others were delighted to do so. As other problems grew more pressing, details of Palestine policy were left to the men on the spot. A great many of these men were Arabists, who encouraged Arab aspirations in the belief that they were in Britain's own best interests. Other officials were simply soldiers or police officers performing distasteful duties with little guidance. Generally, in the Foreign Ministry, the Colonial Office, the Imperial War Staff, and the embassies sentiment ran strongly in favor of the Arabs, though its forms were various. But this open sympathy alienated many diplomats at Lake Success and all the Zionists, without fully earning the gratitude of the Arabs. In sum, no one suspected that the British were drifting on vague tides of pro-Arab sentiment without policy or program—everyone was still searching for the ulterior motive.

This hesitant but real shift of the British government to a pro-Arab policy meant that the Arabs had won the long competition with the Zionists for the "appropriate" British decision but had won too late. The struggle had shifted to the General Assembly, and Britain had abdicated its unilateral control of Palestine. Of course, with the possibility of honorable evacuation, the British no longer had to be limited by American scruples or the expense of repressing Zionist violence indefinitely. They could woo the Arabs, although secretly and haltingly, and could even oppose the Zionists by passive means rather than by frontal assault. Before the involvement of the United Nations, this British policy might have been sufficient to secure an Arab solution, but by November British sympathy, regardless of how it was expressed, was no substitute for the essential votes in the General Assembly. The Arabs and Zionists were locked in a different struggle, though for the same stakes. Britain no longer had a central role—there were other more vital actors and a different stage.

On November 19 the subcommittee on partition unanimously adopted its last report, hoping that in time Britain would give up its attempt to frustrate the progress of partition. On November 20 Cadogan again declared that Britain would be the judge in timing the termination of the Mandate and the transfer of authority to any United Nations Palestine Commission. Still, no one knew what he meant. In any case, the partition report, along with that of the subcommittee on a unitary state, was sent before the ad hoc committee of all fifty-seven member nations. If either report were adopted it would be presented before the General Assembly, where it would need a two-thirds majority of those voting to pass.

On November 24 the last subcommittee reports were presented to the General Assembly. The subcommittee on conciliation had found, as anticipated, no means to reduce the area of disagreement between the two sides. The Islamic subcommittee, as anticipated, proposed an Arab Palestine. The partition subcommittee had made certain refinements in the UNSCOP proposal on boundaries, the transition period, and implementation. They included reduction of the Jewish state from 6,000 to 5,500 square miles and removal of some of the Negev and the Arab city of Jaffa. The Mandate was to end not later than

August 1, 1948, and a United Nations commission was to administer Palestine during the transition. Although the Arabs would present their proposal as well, the actual issue at stake before the General Assembly would be the final partition plan. In the last, thirty-fourth, meeting of the ad hoc committee, only a majority vote would be needed, and partition obviously had a simple majority. Not the outcome of the first vote but the size of the Zionist and Arab blocs would be the key to the future General Assembly vote. The vote on the Arab resolution came first, and it was defeated, twenty-five to twelve. On the report for partition, the Arabs picked up one previous abstainer, and the vote was twenty-five in favor and thirteen opposed. The division, one short of a two-thirds majority, meant that the final vote was far from decided. Some votes might still be switched, however, and some of the abstainers might declare for one side or the other. The final vote was going to be very close, but at that moment the Arabs had a razor-thin edge.

Both the Arabs and the Zionists realized that the next few days would be crucial. Their experts once more scanned the roster, seeking the uncertain and the pliable. The positions of the three involved major powers—Great Britain, the United States, and Soviet Russia— had become clear earlier in November. From September on the delegates from the United Kingdom had been reiterating their determination to abstain from voting on any resolution opposed by either the Arabs or the Zionists. This abstention and such influence as the British cared to exert tended to favor the Arabs. The Soviets were opposed to the British and their Empire, suspicious of the Arab "vassal" states, and unsympathetic to Arab nationalism in general. Although traditionally anti-Zionist, Russia saw partition as the swiftest way to ease the British out of the Middle East without involving the United States more deeply in the area. Partition had a nice ring of self-determination and would likely cause further embarrassment to the British and distract the Americans. For its part, the United States government had, during September, moved cautiously toward partition. Most experts in the Departments of State and Defense had urged consideration for the strategic value of Arab friendship and for the military and commercial importance of Arab oil. President Harry S Truman and many leading members of both the government and the Democratic Party, however, had long been sympathetic to the arguments of the Zionists. Furthermore, the strictly partisan Democratic advisers had their eyes on the hallowed Jewish vote in the big cities, and viewed partition in terms of the November 1948 elections. American support for partition grew all during the General Assembly meeting so that by November Washington was not only firmly committed but also a devout advocate. Sentiment, politics, the absence of any reasonable alternative all proved stronger than cold statistics on oil reserves. But, although the positions of the Big Three had been decided by November, the same could not be said of many of the smaller nations.

The Arabs continued their lobbying. Still hampered by their own negativism, they concentrated on the Latin American delegates, among whom they had discovered pools of sympathy. Elsewhere there were many who doubted the wisdom of partition and were willing to listen to the Arab arguments. Several nations had expatriate colonies in Arab countries. Others had their own Islamic colonies or Islamic minorities. Some might be influenced by oil considerations, by the solid six-vote Arab bloc in the United Nations, or simply by the justice of the Arab cause. In contrast to the Zionists, the eloquent and sincere Arab diplomats lacked practice in the techniques of international persuasion, lacked easy access to the mass-communications media, lacked contacts equal to those the Zionists had built up through years of international lobbying. An added handicap was the atmosphere of New York City, where there were more Jews than in all of Palestine. No other American city was so pro-Zionist; in the town houses, in the newspapers and on the radio, at dinners and cocktail parties, on the streets and in the taxis the Arabs were surrounded by sympathy for the Zionist cause. The memory of the gas chambers and traditional American fondness for the underdog had converted many with little knowledge of the Middle East. Atmosphere does not necessarily swing votes, but the Arabs must have felt themselves swimming against a tide of misplaced and irresponsible sentiment manipulated by their rivals. Still, they needed only a very few votes.

The Zionists in contrast had a great deal going for them, but a two-thirds majority is always difficult to obtain and more difficult to hold onto. They had to use every gambit, every ploy learned in a generation of politics by pressure, persuasion, and conversion. They capitalized on everything from Hitler's crimes to Harry Truman's former Jewish haberdashery partner. No country was too certain or too negative to be wooed. No delegation secretary or transient diplomat was too unimportant to court. Vast pressure was applied, particularly to American public figures, often already sympathetic. Support of American friends from Robert Taft to Eleanor Roosevelt was marshaled. Twenty-seven senators, including Robert Wagner of New York, drafted a telegram in favor of partition and sent it to thirteen United Nations delegations. The committed delegations from Guatemala, Uruguay, and Czechoslovakia lobbied in the United Nations lounges. If anything, under a growing sense of urgency, the pressure of the Zionists was so intensive and so overwhelming as almost to defeat its own aims. No stone was left unturned, and some stones at least must have resented being turned so regularly. Despite everything, however, the last careful polls still left the issue in doubt.

On Wednesday, November 26, the General Assembly met to vote. Many of the wise believed that the Zionists had not yet secured their two-thirds vote. Haiti had spoken against partition in the debate. Paraguay had not instructed its delegation. Liberia was still unsure. Greece had decided to vote no. Apparently the Philippines would too. Several states might abstain, thus narrowing the affirmative majority. All during that day speakers marched to the rostrum to add their views and their arguments to the record. Finally at 5:00 P.M., with many speeches still on the agenda, the Assembly decided to postpone the actual vote until Friday, November 28, the day after the American Thanksgiving holiday. That decision left forty-eight more hours to maneuver for votes.

The Zionists shored up their position. More pressure was applied, particularly by the United States government. Antonio Vieux of Haiti, who had spoken eloquently against partition, received new instructions to vote for it. President Mañuel Roxas Y Acuña of the Philippines agreed not to oppose the wishes of Ambassador Elizalde in Washington, who had been under considerable American pressure to reverse General Carlos Rómulo's strong stand against partition. After Rómulo abruptly departed for an Atlantic voyage, the Philippine delegation received new instructions from Manila to vote yes. Belgium, the Netherlands, and New Zealand, instead of abstaining as they had been planning, reluctantly agreed to vote yes. The Paraguayan delegation received instructions to vote yes. Liberia decided to vote yes. Then, because of a revolution in Thailand, the new government in Bangkok refused to recognize the old regime's United Nations delegate, so that Thailand would be unable to vote. Despite these shifts, Zionist victory was not certain. Tension mounted at Lake Success when, on November 28, Alexandre Parodi of France requested a last-minute postponement to allow for one more effort at conciliation. Paris apparently wanted the extra twenty-four hours to show her Islamic colonies that France was doing everything possible to find some solution other than partition. Finally, the vote was scheduled for Saturday, November 29. The Zionists believed that they had the votes, including that of France, if there were no more shifts.

On Saturday the vote took only three minutes. It was a brief final reckoning, the culmination of three months of diplomatic competition in an atmosphere of rising hysteria. Afghanistan voted no, as expected. Argentina abstained, as expected. Australia voted yes, as expected. As the roll call continued, only Chile switched to abstention after a sudden change in instructions. With Yugoslavia's final abstention, it was all over. The Zionists had their majority: thirty-three yes, thirteen no, and ten absentions. Thailand was absent.

In retrospect it is all too easy to point out the Arab blunders, their missed opportunities, their intransigence. It is only just, however, to note that it is easy to urge compromise of another's principle, to urge someone else to give up half a loaf of his own bread. Surely the Arab argument had much justice. Shorn of biblical quotations, emotional references to the "final solution," and loaded statistics, the Zionist case looked no stronger, and probably somewhat weaker, than the Arab case to disinterested observers. To the Arabs the demand for an Arab Palestine seemed neither novel nor extreme; it seemed just and in accordance with international practice. That there were two competing "rights" all agreed; but that what had been the feebler, the minority, position could be chosen seemed incredible. Whittled down to basics, the Zionist position was that, given the Palestine dilemma, they would settle for half whereas the Arabs unfairly continued to demand all. It was ingenious, it was evil, and it threw the entire Arab argument into the wrong frame of reference. More devastating still, it proved effective.

The Arabs had a good cause, a true one, buttressed by all manner of argument, international law, and common sense. They can hardly be faulted for hewing to their beliefs. In point of fact, by the fall of 1947 Arab leaders could hardly do anything else. They had dinned "no, no, never" too firmly into the heads of their peoples to draw back at the last minute. Had they tried they would undoubtedly have faced the swift and inflexible justice of Arab politics, in which violent revenge is institutionalized. It was not, however, lack of either moral or physical courage among diplomats or governments that prevented a more flexible approach. On the contrary, most Arab leaders had no desire to jettison the true cause for a shoddy and dishonorable compromise urged by false friends. Rather they shared a general dedication to the truth of the proposition that Palestine was an Arab country. If other nations could not or would not see the obvious, so much the worse for them. If they insisted on voting for a plan, any plan, simply to take a "positive" step, they were foolish.[2] Although United Nations delegates might be blinded by Zionist emotionalism, guilt-ridden idealism, misguided romanticism, or simple cynicism, the Arabs could do no more than display their truth and withdraw, once more frustrated and humiliated, by the hypocrisy and ignorance of the outer world. They had fought the good fight in the lounges, in the chambers, at the legations, and in the consulates. What else could they have done, they argued—compromised their principles, sold out the Palestinians, traded Arabs lives for comforting words from distant and alien men? They could only defend the truth. They had been rejected. After the tally there was only bitterness:

. . . The Government of Saudi Arabia registers, on this historic occasion, the fact that it does not consider itself bound by the resolution adopted today by the General Assembly. Furthermore, it reserves to itself the full right to act freely in whatever way it deems fit, in accordance with the principles of right and justice.[3]

Iraq does not recognize the validity of this decision, will reserve freedom of action toward its implementation and hold those who were influential in passing it against the free conscience of mankind responsible for the consequences.[4]

Just what the consequences of the Arab diplomatic defeat were to be escaped most of the delegates. Their maneuvers had taken place in a wonderland of rosy optimism. All those who voted for partition, the United States most of all, hoped that somehow everything would work out for the best, that the Arabs would bow to the inevitable, that Britain would be cooperative, that wisdom and self-restraint would prevail. Their ears deaf to threats of war, and to British prophecies of chaos, the United Nations delegates chose what seemed to them the best course possible under the circumstances. Beyond it no one could see clearly; few tried. Surely the prestige of the United Nations, the reasonableness of the diplomats, the proven futility of war would dampen the volatile and dissuade the violent.

On November 30, the day after the partition vote at Lake Success, Arab irregulars ambushed a Jewish bus outside Jerusalem. They killed seven Jews. The diplomatic competition was over, and the armed confrontation, evaded and postponed for years, had begun. Arab threats, so long ignored, suddenly returned with a vengeance to haunt the United Nations. Amir Arslan of Syria had warned, "Let the consequences be on the heads of others, not on ours."[5] Now the Arabs of Palestine had acted. As the shaken and discredited Mandate collapsed into anarchy, Palestine finally became a battleground.

NOTES

1. Jorge García-Granados, *The Birth of Israel* (New York: 1949), p. 257.

2. The Arabs were, of course, perfectly aware of the Zionists' tactics but could do little to block them. The Lebanese delegate to the United Nations, Camille Chamoun, highly respected by his colleagues, specifically countered the "any plan is better than no plan" approach in debate before the General Assembly. Perhaps, in view of conditions in the Mandate, many delegates thought that "any plan" was better than anarchy.

3. *Official Record of the Second Session of the General Assembly*, II, (Lake Success, N.Y.: 1947), 1425.

4. *Ibid.*, p. 1427.

5. *Ibid.*

4

The Undeclared War *
The Arab Attack

On December 1 the Jews of Palestine were still swimming in a sea of euphoria. Their diplomats and their
cause had been victorious at Lake Success. What had been won, the
Jewish state, would not, of course, actually come into existence until
later, but, for the moment, the intervening months seemed unimportant. It was only with reluctance that the Jewish Agency turned
from Lake Success to analyze the immediate future within the Mandate. The ambush of seven Jews by the Palestinian Arabs indicated
that the long Anglo-Zionist struggle now had an added dimension.
Even though there was no threat of a formal Arab invasion until
the state was actually established and assuming that the British would
withdraw as promised, a new Arab rebellion directed solely against
the Jews would present the Agency and the Haganah with a severe
test. Early December, then, found the Jews growing cautious in their
optimism but still reluctant to believe that the disorganized and unprepared Arabs would challenge partition by force.

Despite the warnings of their diplomats at the United Nations, the
Arab states still had no firm plans. Although the time margin for
decision had narrowed, there was still no sense of urgency. Between
December 12 and 17 the prime ministers of the Arab League states
met in Cairo. Inter-Arab friction had grown, if anything, more

abrasive. Iraq supported immediate intervention with volunteers, insisted on arming the Palestine army, and even proposed concentrating the regular armies of Arab states on the borders of the Mandate. Iraqi General Sir Ismail Safwat Pasha, the chairman of the League's military committee, included all these proposals in his report. He estimated that the Jewish military establishment had 50,000 men, plus additional reserves backed up by artillery, armor, and even a secret air force. Although the sources of Safwat's information remained vague, his conviction that the Palestine Arabs could not defend themselves single-handedly remained firm. Safwat and Iraq insisted that the League must act. Nonetheless, unanimity of action could not yet be produced. Saudi Arabia was against both arming the Palestine Arabs and the intervention of regular Arab armies in Palestine. Egypt opposed intervention but supported sending aid to the volunteers in Palestine. The Mufti of Jerusalem, Hajj Amin al-Huseini, wanted no regular armies in Palestine. King Abdullah ibn-Husein of Transjordan wanted to use regular armies and to avoid building a volunteer force loyal to the Mufti. Lebanon was mute. Syria was vague. As always, the private ambitions of each leader hampered the action of all.

Eventually an unsatisfactory compromise was reached. The Arab states would supply the military committee with 10,000 rifles and would arrange for training and equipping 3,000 volunteers in Syria. There was to be a war chest of £1 million. Further talk in Amman between the Iraqis and Abdullah elicited a statement of approval from Abdullah. But what had been achieved at Cairo and Amman had been agreement on half-measures. If Safwat's estimate of Jewish strength were accurate, then 3,000 volunteers could obviously do no more than encourage local Arabs to undertake limited guerrilla warfare against the Jews. Alone, or even in cooperation with the Palestinian Arab paramilitary groups, they could not prevent partition. But they could be displayed as evidence of the League's intentions. The rising Jewish fear of a massive influx into the Mandate of trained Arab soldiers thus had no basis in fact. Formal invasion or even heavy infiltration still remained a threat rather than an operational plan.

Jewish fears grew all during December. The first attack on November 30 had not been the last. Early in December sniping began on the border between Arab Jaffa and Jewish Tel Aviv. At first there was no discernible plan behind the Arab attacks. They were individual enterprises without a central command, the local Arabs having simply taken matters into their own hands. Day after day Arabs picked up rifles and moved into protected sniper nests to shoot at the Jews. In an effort to stop the infiltrating snipers, the Haganah came into the open, although its defensive operations were disguised until the last minute, in order to prevent British intervention. The random sniping spread to other mixed cities, particularly Jerusalem. Reports began to come into the Jewish Agency of hit-and-run raids on the Jewish settlements isolated deep in the Arab areas of Palestine. Secondary roads through Arab areas could no longer be used safely by Jews. Jewish vehicles drew fire on main arterial routes. Gradually, still without central direction and dependent on local whim and opportunity, the attacks accelerated. When one ploy proved effective in damaging the Jews without excessive Arab casualties, it was repeated. More and more Arabs drifted into the countryside to join paramilitary groups. Others simply took off a few hours now and then to have a shot at the Jews. For the Jews events began to assume an ugly pattern. Little could be done to prevent the elusive Arabs from firing into residential districts or bushwhacking trucks on the main roads. Almost from the first the Arabs had found an ideal method of punishing the Jews without greatly risking their own necks. Many Arabs believed that, if they could inflict sufficient such punishment, partition would prove impossible. In the meantime, frustrated and embittered but no longer helpless spectators, they were finally "getting their own back."

Although the Jewish population, scattered as it was throughout the Mandate, was obviously vulnerable to Arab attacks in an irregular war, the location of the Jews also had certain advantages. The so-called "mixed cities" were often not as integrated as they at first appeared; for example, in Jerusalem the great majority of Jews was concentrated in the New City to the west. Even in the Old City there was a compact Jewish quarter. In the countryside the normal type of Jewish settlement had been the kibbutz, a communal colony usually constructed with an eye to defense. These settlements, often on ideal defensive ground with self-contained paramilitary units, were not easy targets, not even those located in Arab areas. At least, the kibbutzim that were on high ground and had trained defenders were far more secure than their positions on the map would indicate.

Consequently, the pattern of Jewish settlement, spotted throughout the countryside in self-contained units and concentrated in large urban residential areas, had certain recognizable defensive advantages.

The Arabs continued to assume that the Jews had a 50,000-man army to do the defending. The Arabs' general impression of the Haganah—and not theirs alone, for many Jews in Palestine shared it—was that of a highly organized, superbly equipped army waiting underground for the right tactical moment to emerge. The truth was quite different. There were only 400 full-time Haganah members. The Haganah's only mobile force, the Palmach, commanded by Yigal Alon, had a strength of 3,100, including women, and its full mobilization at any given time was impossible. The remainder of the Haganah, still unmobilized, amounted to about 32,000 people, divided into the H.I.S.M. (the field army) and the H.I.M. (the garrison army). These troops were really militia, trained and equipped only for guerrilla warfare and kibbutz defense. They were not really an army; in fact, the indoctrination of the Haganah, particularly the Palmach, strongly emphasized individual initiative, the irregular approach, and the equality of all ranks. The organization more often resembled that of a band of brothers, resolute, brave, and ingenious, rather than of a regiment in mufti. The Haganah simply was not, could not have been, a formal, well-balanced, authoritarian force. For its purposes, defense of the Jews and hit-and-run strikes against British installations, it had been superb. For a war of attrition against Arab irregular attacks, it might be adequate. For a real war, it was woefully unprepared. Signals, intelligence, and medical branches had been developed with great care, but there was still insufficient modern equipment. There were no aircraft except a couple of small civilian planes, no tanks, no armored transport but steel-plated trucks, few heavy mortars, no artillery, no navy other than a few motorboats. Many of the existing small arms—of various manufacture, caliber, condition, and origin—had been scattered among the kibbutzim and we were unavailable for concentrated action. In the past small arms and light automatic weapons had been sufficient for the Haganah. Some members believed that their arms, organization, and tactics were still sufficient. After all, they were backed by 1,700 members of the Jewish settlement police, and there were also the men of the Irgun and the Lechi. There were secret, small-scale arms factories, and guns and ammunition were being smuggled into the Mandate. To some Jews these resources seemed enough. To the knowing, however, the war potential of the Yishuv seemed appallingly feeble if the Arabs meant business.

David Ben-Gurion and the executive of the Jewish Agency, along with Israel Galili and his Haganah staff officers, had concluded that a massive effort would be necessary to prepare the Haganah for any eventuality. Control of Haganah strategy passed directly to Ben-Gurion, Chairman of the Jewish Agency, and a high command representative of all political factions. Operational command supposedly remained with Chief of Staff Galili, but in effect Ben-Gurion increasingly dominated both tactical and strategic decisions. The command arrangements, particularly the political high command, often proved awkward, but the prime operational difficulty was continuing British interference and the arbitrary restrictions seemingly intended to hamper Jewish defense efforts. Despite constant British activity, which declined somewhat after December 1947, the Haganah created three rural and three urban commands on geographical lines. In November Ben-Gurion had prepared a plan to integrate the HISH units into the territorial commands as mobile units rather than as part of local forces. Essentially, the hopes of both the civilian and military commanders were that the Haganah would not be called on for offensive action and that a stiff defense would deter the local Arabs during the months before the establishment of the state. By then the Haganah would be on a war footing.

In the meantime every effort was made to speed mobilization, training, and in particular accumulation of arms and ammunition. In October 1947, beside the limited matériel of the Irgun and the Lechi, the Haganah had 8,300 rifles, 3,600 sten guns, 700 light machine guns, 200 medium machine guns, 600 two-inch and 100 three-inch mortars. There was ammunition for only three days of full-scale fighting. By December Ehud Avriel had arrived in Europe with orders to purchase 10,000 rifles and 450 machine guns in particular and whatever else he could find in general. By the end of 1947 the rapidly expanding network of agents had shipped six consignments into Palestine from their base at Magenta outside Milan, by means of a variety of ruses. The total was 200 bren guns, 1,000 British army rifles, 400 (mainly 9-millimeter submachine guns, 500 revolvers of various types, and 1 million rounds of .303- and 9-millimeter ammunition. Although welcome, it was patently insufficient. Avriel would have to do far better.

The "smugglers" received an unexpected assist from the Zionist diplomats. In January Moshe Shertok began a series of protracted and delicate conversations in New York with the Russian United Nations delegate, Andrei Gromyko. Gromyko proved sympathetic, but Moscow could not become openly involved; however, these conversations led to more serious talks with the Czechs. Prague agreed to accept Avriel's portfolio of documents as sufficiently legal for secret arms sales. The Czechs seemed delighted to have payment in dollars for surplus, often obsolete, World War II arms. This equipment, of various national origins, ages, and conditions drifted west to Italy, where another veteran smuggler, Yehuda Arazi, transshipped them under a variety of guises. Elsewhere—in France, in the United States, in Germany—Zionist agents or sympathizers quietly circulated in the shadowy world of illegal arms procurement. Hidden arms dumps were ferreted out. Rumors of stashed tanks or mortars were traced. Front companies appeared and disappeared. In the United States negotiations were opened for surplus transport planes. A C-46 Curtis transport could be had for $5,000 and a Constellation for $15,000, if one had the proper credentials.[1] More extensive purchases were negotiated with the helpful Czechs. All this activity, though promising for the future, had little immediate effect in Palestine, where British security measures had reduced illegal imports to a trickle of light arms. The weeks passed, and the Haganah still had no heavy weapons and even insufficient small-arms and ammunition for defensive purposes. Meanwhile Arab attacks increased.

By January the pattern of Arab irregular warfare had become clearer. During December the Arab attacks had multiplied. On December 15, for example, a Jewish supply convoy on its way from Tel Aviv to the Children's Village at Ben Shemen had come under heavy fire. Fourteen Jews were killed. Soon an average of fifty Jews a week were being killed. The sniping in mixed cities was constant. Jewish road traffic ran a continuous risk of ambush. Movement on the edge of Jerusalem had to be limited. Traffic to The Hebrew University and the Hadassah Hospital on the slopes of Mount Scopus ran a gauntlet of rifle fire. During December one nurse was killed, and several were wounded. Thirty-nine Jewish workers were killed when the Arabs ran amok in the Haifa oil refinery. The Arabs were, at their convenience, picking off isolated Jews, cutting road traffic, harassing residential areas. They were making normal life dangerous, even impossible. The Haganah could not be everywhere at once. Defense against the Arabs could be made easier by consolidation of the Jewish population, a consolidation that in some areas had already begun informally with the withdrawal of Jews from Arab residential areas. Fearful of murder, arson, and retaliation, the Arabs in turn left the Jewish districts. The Haganah was particularly worried, however, about the breakdown of communications with the kibbutzim. Defense of these isolated settlements, thirty-three of which were outside the boundaries of the United Nations resolution, put added strains on Haganah resources, but none of the settlers wanted to evacuate, no matter how perilous their situation.

Within the councils of the Haganah and the Jewish Agency, the problem of defensive tactics against Arab guerrilla attacks took precedence over all other matters. The Haganah preferred consolidation. Ben-Gurion, whose stature and influence grew under pressure, refused. He forced a "Zionist" decision, against all military experience and massive odds. Ben-Gurion decided, and his associates, civilian and military, concurred, that every settlement would be held—the Jews would evacuate nothing. No matter how isolated a kibbutz, its settlers must hold out. They had planned to do so anyway, but now the word came from the top—no retreat, ever. Even the 1,000 Jews deep in the Negev among 100,000 Arabs would have to remain. The settlements north and south of Jerusalem, at the end of fragile lifelines passing through heavily populated Arab quarters, would not be withdrawn. It was an impossible tactical decision and had been opposed for good reason by many of the Haganah officers. The Haganah would be scattered throughout the country, protecting strategically useless settlements or guarding convoys to distant kibbutzim instead of striking back at the Arabs.

By 1948, as the crisis grew more serious, Ben-Gurion, long the dominant figure in the Zionist struggle, overshadowed all others. Since 1906, when he had first arrived in Palestine from Płońsk in Russian Poland at the age of twenty, his Zionist career had been spectacular. He had all the virtues of command: dedication, drive, integrity, pure talent, and the capacity to engender loyalty and

sacrifice. So, of course, had others. But in a community of true
believers Ben-Gurion had become pre-eminent. His craggy face
topped by a mane of white hair, his mesmeric personality—assets for
a politician—paled in importance before the almost visible faith in the
future that he exuded. Victory over odds is seldom won on faith
alone, but Yishuv accepted that he alone intuitively knew the direction of the future. Often egotistical, uncompromising, even petty, he
was in reality no messiah but a shrewd, often cautious visionary,
acutely conscious of what was possible, capable of hedging his bets,
of leaving as little to faith and hope as possible. He had seen farther
and more clearly than had any other man, and the people, expert and
ordinary, knew it. His Zionist decision on withdrawal reflected the
incorporation of both his blinding faith in the future and his clear
vision of reality.

Ben-Gurion's plan, though tactically "impossible," was still an
astute political and strategic plan. A policy of no retreat would prove
that partition was possible, despite Arab efforts to prevent it. Second, it would underline from the very beginning that for the
Jewish community there was to be no retreat. Ben-Gurion depended
almost entirely on the courage and stamina of Yishuv. The Jews
would have to stand and fight or wait and suffer. There was to be no
new exodus, no timid concentration of fleeing refugees. This time in
this place, the Jews would fight and, if need be, die for every inch of
the Promised Land, even some inches that the United Nations had not
promised.

Not only did the Jews have to contend with the Arab attacks, but
also the Haganah found its operations seriously hampered by British
interference, interference that invariably appeared to favor the Arabs.
The British refused to supply escorts for Jewish convoys, as this
action might imply their implementation of partition, but they also
refused to allow armed Jewish guards to ride the trucks. As early as
December 25, 1947, the British Palestine government had assured the
Jews that British forces would keep watch over the Tel Aviv–Jerusalem road. On the following day the Arabs had ambushed and killed
seven Jews on the British-protected road. Although Colonial Secretary Arthur Creech-Jones had insisted that the British acceptance of
partition was "not a grudging acceptance . . . we wish our authority transferred to our successor in an orderly manner,"[2] the English-

men on the spot seemed quite willing to allow the Arabs a free hand while continuing a crackdown on Jewish activities. All the Haganah wanted was to be left alone; by 1948 the only anti-British operations were those of the Lechi and the Irgun, and even they were rare. But the British insisted upon maintaining a one-sided order. Repeatedly the world and the Jews were informed that the British would run the Mandate to the last:

> Britain has made it clear that, as she could not take part in im-
> plementing the United Nations plan, it would be undesirable for the
> Commission to arrive in Palestine until a short period before the
> termination of the Mandate. For reasons of administrative efficiency
> and security the overlapping period should be comparatively brief.[3]

This attitude meant that Britain would refuse to hand over, even gradually, the administrative apparatus to the Arabs and the Jews or even to the United Nations. Only in the Jaffa–Tel Aviv area were Arab and Jewish police permitted. Britain insisted that no other emergency police were needed. On January 22, 1948, seven Jewish settlement policemen, traveling in open trucks because armored cars were prohibited, ran into an Arab ambush. All were killed and their bodies mutilated. A week later Colonel Nelson at British headquarters informed the Jews that they still could not use armored cars, as such use would arouse the Arabs. Apparently, the British intended to hamstring the Haganah and to ignore Arab attacks.

Outside the Mandate the Arabs had other evidence of Britain's sympathy and good will. In London, Nuri as-Said, Iraq's elder statesman and a long-time Anglophile, received word of the proceedings of the Arab League's Cairo and Amman meetings. On January 16, 1948, he met privately with Foreign Secretary Ernest Bevin and fully informed him of the League's intentions. Nuri's impression was that Britain clearly viewed the Arab aims with favor. Talks about weapons for the Iraqi army under terms of the new Anglo-Iraqi treaty proved most satisfactory. Obviously the British knew how the arms were to be used. Similar conversations were continuing between the British and both Saudi Arabia and Transjordan.

In Cairo Brigadier Clayton did make a delicate protest at the entry of Arab volunteers into the Mandate, but Abdul Rahman Azzam

Pasha of the League reminded him that, for the time being, volunteers were surely more desirable than regular Arab armies invading the Mandate. The British agreed. General Sir Gordon MacMillan in Jerusalem was ordered to avoid interfering with the volunteers if possible.

So far the volunteers had taken no real action. A motley collection of local Arabs and a few transients had organized an attack of sorts on the two northernmost Jewish settlements, Dan and Kfar Szold. On January 9 two bands totaling 150 men rushed the settlements, but the clumsy attack bogged down. Eventually the British arrived and shooed them off. The volunteers who were massing farther to the south in the Arab triangle were quite upset by the unauthorized attack. They were not ready to move yet. Those Arabs, the 1st Yarmuk Battalion, were to form the basis of the volunteer Arab Liberation Army. Their commander would be Fawzi el-Kaukji, rumored to be a Kurd or a Turk, who was extremely popular in ultranationalist circles. An avid follower of the Mufti, he had participated without notable success in the Arab revolt of 1936–1939 in the Nablus district. During W.W. II he had taken part in the pro-Axis coup in Iraq and had been wounded in the face. After that he had wandered in obscurity. Now his force of irregulars, along with a few Syrian army officers and soldiers, was to be the largest in Palestine. During the last two weeks of January, 2,000 armed Arabs moved into Palestine. Kaukji's army had, or at least some of his men had, uniforms: plain khaki tunics and slacks with striking white and red head cloths and black headbands. They had a mishmash of arms, mostly obsolete rifles, but Kaukji had wangled some old French 105- and 75-millimeter artillery pieces from the Syrian army on some sort of extended loan. There were no quartermaster corps, no administrative apparatus, no intelligence or signals, not even a medical unit other than two or three orderlies supplied with quinine and purgatives. The only transport consisted of hired trucks. In fact, the Arab Liberation Army could be called an "army" only by redefining the term.

Actually, what Kaukji had was a collection of several thousand eager but untrained and poorly armed men decked out with military titles and head cloths. General John Bagot Glubb, British commander of the Arab Legion, was appalled. He had pointed out to the Arab leaders the time and effort that building a real "army" would require but no one had wanted to face facts:

In December 1947, recruitment of irregulars was started in Syria and a motley force was collected under the title "Arab Liberation Army." [The interpreter in Arab Legion headquarters rather ineptly translated their Arabic title as "The Salvation Army."] To those with even the slightest knowledge of the immense labour, organization, training and equipment necessary to build up an army, the idea that a mob of bandits and enthusiasts could, in three or four weeks, be made into an army was ludicrous in the extreme. But the Arab governments were utterly ignorant of military matters, and had never waged a war of their own.[4]

Glubb may have been a bit harsh, as the volunteers were not proposing to fight a formal war. Still, a guerrilla army cannot learn the techniques of irregular war overnight, nor can it operate without tight discipline and considerable personal sacrifice. The volunteers, of all sorts and conditions—the greedy, the dedicated, the drifters—knew little of any kind of war and nothing of discipline; they had volunteered for victories, not for sacrifices. Their officers were no better. Yet several thousand armed enthusiasts, bandits or no, could play havoc with Jewish communications and settlements.

On January 21, despite the warnings of the Jewish Agency, the British somehow missed the arrival of the 2nd Yarmuk Battalion, 800 armed Syrian volunteers under the command of Adib Shishekli. They had crossed over the Allenby Bridge from Transjordan without incident and had moved into prepared camps in the Samarian hills, twenty miles from British headquarters. They were followed by the Kadisya and Husein Battalions. The British ignored the whole affair. General MacMillan had arranged a secret agreement with Kaukji, which allowed the Arab Liberation Army to remain in Palestine as long as it was quiet. Strangely enough, the Jews also had a secret "agreement" with Kaukji along somewhat similar lines. Kaukji had no intention of doing all the fighting himself, to the advantage of his political opponents, who were legion. The Arab Liberation Army would wait for the appropriate moment to descend on the Jews.

Although Kaukji's Arab Liberation Army was the largest force in Palestine, the volunteer movement, as could be expected, was hampered by divided councils. The groups favoring the Mufti, the Huseini, refused to cooperate with his foes. Arab League commanders feuded with the Mufti's commanders. In Jaffa, for example, there were two commanders giving often conflicting orders to the Arab volunteers. Regularly the various Arab states played one Palestine "army" off against another, refusing arms to one group in order to put them in the hands of a favored faction. There were all kinds of ancient prejudices and suspicions even among groups within the same army. The Druzes, the Syrian "Lions of Aleppo," the Yugoslavian Muslims, the Egyptians, and the Iraqis found that they had little in common except their hatred of the Zionists. No one knew the exact number of armed volunteers sitting about on the hills or wandering in the Arab quarters, least of all their self-proclaimed leaders. A reasonable guess is that they numbered between 6,000 and 8,000 men. As they slipped into the Mandate, many volunteers informally took part in sniping at the Jews, but during January the local Palestinians did most of the fighting.

On January 5 the Haganah attacked the headquarters of the Najada, a local paramilitary group, deep in the Arab quarter of Katamon in Jerusalem. The Arabs attacked kibbutzim in the Judean mountains, in western Galilee, and in the Negev. A heavy attack under the command of Abdel Kader hit Kfar Etzion south of Jerusalem. Kader had been less than subtle in his tactics, and the attack was a fiasco, with an estimated 150 Arabs dead and a similar number wounded, but the Jews had been badly shaken, and their supplies and ammunition were spent. On January 17 a unit of thirty-five HISH and Palmach men, mostly Hebrew University students, rushed on foot through little-used mountain passes to reinforce Kfar Etzion. The local Arabs discovered them and surrounded the column, calling up more and more irregulars to revenge their earlier losses. All the Jews were killed. The Jews of Jerusalem were deeply shocked; almost everyone knew at least one of the young men or his parents. The fact that the Haganah was carrying out an increasing number of retaliatory raids on "guilty" Arab villages did little to comfort the friends and relatives of the slain. On January 24 the Haganah went into action near Kastel above the Jerusalem–Tel Aviv road to clear out the snipers and break up the roadblock to Jewish transport. Forty Arabs and ten Jews died. The British finally intervened by firing on the Jews. By February, even discounting the full participation of the Arab volunteers, the Mandate had declined into chaos. Civil order, except directly under British guns, had dissolved as the Arabs pushed the attack with increasing boldness. The casualties mounted. From

December 1 to February 1 869 people were killed and about 2,000 wounded according to the official British figures.

During February the Arab pressure increased. The pattern was the same as in December and January: attacks on transport, on kibbutzim, on residential areas. Jewish communications were faltering. The Tel Aviv–Jerusalem road was a death trap. Shortages became commonplace, particularly for the 100,000 Jews in Jerusalem. The Haganah's resources were stretched over a series of defensive operations and retaliatory raids. Ammunition was going, and no arms were arriving in quantity from Europe. The British seemed willing, in some cases eager, for the collapse of order. General MacMillan had allowed the Arab volunteers to enter while his British troops restricted the Haganah and continued the searches and seizures. The violence so often predicted by the British at Lake Success now actually threatened; but the chaotic conditions seemed a direct result of Britain's policies, which allowed the Arabs to attack while London issued pious proclamations of neutrality.

Despite all evidence to the contrary, Britain insisted that its policies could still work. Bevin seemed to believe that the Palestine question was not yet settled.[5] There have been suggestions that he hoped that partition would fail and that Britain, as the Arabs' friend, would benefit accordingly. In any case Bevin was determined to hang on until May 15 and to keep his options open. On February 18 Britain once again refused to allow the United Nations Commission to enter the Mandate before May 1, on the grounds that such entry might bring about Arab demonstrations. Creech-Jones continued to refuse United Nations requests that a Palestinian port be opened for Jewish immigration, insisting that, because of British influence, the Arabs had shown considerable restraint but that with an open port this restraint would collapse.* To the Jewish Agency, it seemed as if Britain intended to use its control of the Mandate to ensure that the Arabs, not the diplomats at Lake Success, would determine the final solution to the Palestine problem.

Subsequent theories about British motives for allowing the Mandate to collapse into anarchy assume that a plot was afoot either to

---

* As early as December 12, 1947, Bevin had refused to designate such a port, warning of Arab violence. This refusal was perhaps the greatest British contribution to the Arab cause.

remain in the Mandate or to allow an Arab victory. Either eventuality would, of course, have had certain advantages for Great Britain; but once more British policy was merely drifting. The army wanted out with as few casualties as possible. The Foreign Office wanted to retain the friendship of the Arabs. The Colonial Office hated to see a generation of British effort, experience, and expense go down the drain. The result looked suspiciously like an anti-Zionist policy, which in effect, of course, it was.

The depth of anti-Zionist, even anti-Jewish, feeling in the British army also became clear during February. The long Anglo-Zionist struggle, waged in secret and with terror, had eroded most of whatever neutrality the British forces possessed, embittering both officers and men who had sought for years to show restraint against hit-and-run attacks. From being anti-Irgun the army generally became anti-Zionist and, by February 1948, more often than not anti-Semitic. Rational reluctance to be ambushed and kidnapped had given way to emotional, unreasoning hatred of all Jews.[6] Some merely watched with vicarious glee as the Arabs turned the tables on the Jews. Others, their self-restraint exhausted, took matters into their own hands. For them provocation had gone on too long without retaliation.

On February 1 an explosion destroyed the building of the Jewish *Palestine Post* in Jerusalem. Government inquiries produced no result, but investigation by the Jewish Agency revealed that British police personnel were guilty. No action was taken. On February 12 four Haganah men were arrested in Jerusalem by an army patrol and then turned loose in the Arab quarter of the Old City near St. Stephen's Gate. Three hours later their mutilated bodies were discovered. The British investigation found only that the sergeant major of the patrol had been guilty of an error of judgment. No further action was taken. On February 22 an explosion in Ben Yehuda Street, the main shopping center of the Jewish New City, wrecked several buildings, killed 52 people, and injured more than 100. The British investigation produced no results, but the Jewish Agency once again found that British police personnel had been involved. On February 29 British troops disarmed the members of a Jewish outpost on the Jaffa–Tel Aviv border and turned them over to an Arab mob. Nine were killed on the spot. From December 1 to April 3, however, British casualties were 430, most as a result of Jewish action. Some soldiers did resort to violence, but they were actually very few. Yet it was cold comfort to the Jewish Agency that few armies could have shown as much restraint under such continual provocation. To many Jews, the British army seemed ready to aid the Arabs unofficially but actively.

In February the Arab Liberation Army, concentrated around Tubas, undertook its first formal operation. Although Kaukji was not particularly anxious to risk his army, the activists insisted; on February 15 he therefore undertook a hastily prepared attack on the Jewish religious settlement of Tirat Zevi. Kaukji did not even bother to truck in his artillery; apparently the mere appearance of the Arabs was deemed sufficient. The 500 members of the Arab army, supported by local irregulars, made a frontal assault on the settlement. The Jews mowed them down and signalled for help, but the Arabs had already had enough. By the time the British arrived, they were on their way back to their camps. They had lost twelve killed and thirty-six wounded but none of their enthusiasm. For Kaukji the attack was a victory, even though only one Jew had been killed and two wounded. The Arab capacity to ignore the unpleasant and to rely on the word instead of the completed deed came to his aid. The attack on Tirat Zevi was transformed into a victory. And, in fact, although Kaukji had not achieved a real victory, the Arab attacks in general seemed well on the way to destroying the vitality of the Yishuv.

One most astute observer had considerable doubt about the eventual success of the Arab irregulars. King Abdullah of Transjordan had great respect for the recuperative powers and adaptability of the Zionists. In his view the Arab volunteers were picadors wounding the Zionist bull so that his own Arab Legion could finish it off. From the moment the partition resolution had been passed at Lake Success, Abdullah had intended to enter Palestine on the day of Britain's departure and to occupy all of Palestine contiguous with the Transjordanian frontier—in particular, Jerusalem. It was obvious to Abdullah that a successful Arab Palestine could not exist within the jigsaw division proposed under partition and with the absence of any local Arab political institutions. Even if such a state were possible, its leader would be his ancient enemy, the Mufti. Abdullah thus hoped for a swift, bloodless coup that would leave him in possession of central Palestine, which would be the basis of a new Kingdom of Jordan with its capital at Jerusalem. He was willing to allow the establishment of a Jewish state; the Arab Legion was probably not strong enough to prevent it. He did not miss the possibility that the Jewish state might ultimately be considerably smaller than that foreseen in the partition plan, but he recognized that total victory over the Jews was a chimera. His views were heresy, however, secret heresy but heresy nevertheless.

Although Transjordan continued to participate in Arab League meetings and Transjordanians howled for Jewish blood, Abdullah's real intentions remained hidden. On February 2 the League met again in Cairo to hear General Sir Ismail Safwat Pasha plead once more for united military action. All present listened sympathetically, but none responded. In the meantime Abdullah kept open contacts with the Jewish Agency and continued negotiations with the British. Late in February Jordanian Prime Minister Tewfic Abdul Huda met with Bevin; General John Bagot Glubb was present as translator. When he revealed Abdullah's plans, Bevin replied, "It seems the obvious thing to do."[7] With British agreement, or at least toleration, Abdullah believed that he had an excellent chance to secure the major part of Arab Palestine.

Then the Iraqi government, long tottering, suddenly collapsed before the anger of mobs at the terms of the Anglo-Iraqi Treaty, which had been signed at Portsmouth on February 15. For some while Abdullah's Iraqi competitor would be removed from the Palestinian scene. In addition, Mahmud Fahmi Nokrashy of Egypt still wanted no military adventures. The Syrians had only one weak infantry division and serious misgivings. The other Arab states were too distant or too small to determine events. The way seemed open for Abdullah to move in on the heels of the Arab Liberation Army. Perhaps as a consolation prize, Egypt could have some of the desert to the south and the Syrians some of the hills to the north, but the rich center, including Jerusalem, the jewel in the crown, would be Abdullah's. That possibility had hardly escaped his bitterly jealous but militarily ineffectual rivals. In Cairo, in Damascus, in Baghdad, they watched the campaigns of the Arab volunteers and irregulars in Palestine, hoping against hope that invasion would ba unnecessary, that somehow Abdullah would be foiled.

By March the British were giving every indication of withdrawing, an eventuality that neither the Arab states nor the Jewish Agency had ever fully accepted. On March 5 the first 1,800 troops left Haifa for Liverpool. Two days later another 2,000 sailed. One by one the British strong points were dismantled and evacuated. British equipment was shipped out, sold, or destroyed. Records were destroyed. Administrative functions abruptly ended. Neither the Arabs nor the Jews could yet be truly certain that withdrawal would continue, but, in the meantime, as the British slowly released their grip on the Mandate, the Arab-Jewish conflict could continue more openly.

By March the Arabs had accumulated sufficient armed volunteers to undertake full-scale assaults. Although their forces were little more than armed mobs in the eyes of British officers, irregular warfare was the Arabs' best hope of preventing partition. In a highly complicated situation, still controlled by the British, the volunteers could operate with partial tolerance, whereas a formal Arab invasion would certainly create unfortunate international complications. Continuing irregular warfare would hide the schisms in the Arab world and encourage the Palestinians. What remained uncertain was its potential effect. The volunteers' problems were obvious: lack of training, of modern arms, of auxiliary services, of discipline, and of central direction. Their potential, however, was great, for they could operate in the sanctuary of the Arab areas, free to strike when and where they pleased, limited only by the scruples of the British and the resilience of the Jews. In three months both the local bands and volunteers had probed the Jews' strength, seeking the easy kills and the vulnerable points. In three months they had cut up the Mandate and isolated pockets of Jews. They had partially besieged the mixed cities. They had created an atmosphere of uncertainty and gloom in the Yishuv, alarmed distant diplomats, and inspired the local Arabs. For little bands of amateurs, their accomplishments had been impressive.

Early in March the campaign accelerated. Kaukji's Arab Liberation Army began a heavy attack on Magdi'el and Kfar Saba on the coastal plain. But attacks against the seemingly vulnerable kibbutzim never went well for the Arabs. The Jews' paramilitary training, their concrete buildings, and the dogged refusal of civilians to panic inevitably turned the settlements into small fortresses. Yet, knowing the Jews' limited personnel and ammunition, the Arabs kept on taking disproportionate casualties, hoping for a collapse that never came. At Magdi'el and Kfar Saba they whacked away on and off for more than a week before withdrawing. On March 11 the Jerusalem Arabs made a successful bomb attack on the Jewish Agency headquarters. The explosion killed eleven Jews and dealt one more heavy blow to morale in Jerusalem. West of the city, the Arabs swarmed down on Hartuv but failed to push the assault through. In the Negev near Nitzanim, they struck again, losing twenty killed to only four Jewish deaths. Everywhere the tempo of attack increased, though not its success. Ben-Gurion's Zionist policy of no retreat had made such attacks inevitable, but, as he had hoped, the Jews were holding their own. What frightened them was the growing realization that the Arabs controlled all the lines of communication. Not only the desert tracks and mountain lanes but also the major arterial roads were closed. What the Arab irregulars could not manage by frontal assaults might well be accomplished at far less cost by cutting the Jewish supply lines.

Jerusalem held the key. There the 100,000 Jews had gradually come to realize that they were under siege. For months there had been sniping and bombing, looting and arson, ambushes, streetfighting, and terror raids. These attacks could be tolerated because the Haganah gave as well as received, but it could not keep open the road to Tel Aviv. This vital highway ran southeast from Tel Aviv across the coastal plain, then twisted through the Judean mountains— through narrow passes and steep ravines below Arab hilltop villages— until the craggy mountains gave way to the rolling hills of the western suburbs of the New City. For the Jews of Jerusalem, the sixty-five kilometers of the Tel Aviv road became a daily preoccupation. The Arab irregulars in the villages of Bab el-Wad and Kastel grew bolder, regularly interrupting all traffic. The slender link with the coast had become the major artery through which Jerusalem's food supplies had to flow. Although the railway remained open, it was vulnerable to British interference and Arab sabotage, and the Jews could not depend on it. The shipment of agricultural goods from the outlying Arab areas had dribbled to a halt. Local Jewish supplies were hopelessly inadequate. Only the trucks from Tel Aviv could bring in the necessary tons of supplies needed daily. In February only two convoys of gray buses and khaki trucks, plated with homemade armor and "illegally" escorted by Haganah men, were able to break through the blockade. Without food, fuel, and water, Jewish Jerusalem could last only a few weeks.

Dependent, in turn, upon Jerusalem for their supplies were the outlying settlements cut off by the intervening Arab districts. To reach Nebi Yaakov to the north or the Kfar Etzion bloc to the south meant a running gun battle and often disaster for the Jews. General Blubb later described what he and General MacMillan saw when they stumbled onto one of these road battles. The Arabs had blocked the road at Safad, ambushing a Jewish convoy on its way to Nebi Yaquob. The Arabs claimed that on the previous day a Jewish convoy had run over and killed a little girl and then kept going, but the fact that a convoy was Jewish usually was sufficient cause for attack. By the time Glubb and MacMillan arrived, at least two Jewish trucks had been destroyed and their drivers killed, but a homemade Jewish armored car was still firing.

> When we rounded the bend in the road, we saw a large Jewish armoured car halted in the middle of the village street. The street was wide, and the houses on each side had small gardens in front of them. The houses and garden were full of Arabs firing their rifles at the armoured car. Every now and then, the muzzle of an automatic was thrust through a loophole in the side of the armoured car and fired a few bursts at the Arabs, and was then withdrawn. There were obviously living Jews inside the armoured car, but we could not tell how many. The noise of the firing was deafening.[8]

General MacMillan managed to bring up British troops, and assisted by General Glubb he persuaded the Arabs to stop firing in return for yielding the armored car and its contents. The British troops then surrounded the car and persuaded the few Jews still alive to abandon it while they had a chance.

> At last the Jews ventured to open a crack of the door. The sight of the Household Cavalry sergeant reassured them. One by one we got them out, passing them between us into the British vehicle. Two could hop. Several were dead. It was difficult to see whether some were dead or alive. Their clothes were torn, they were little more than a heap of lacerated meat. It was like a butcher's shop— so much torn flesh and pools of blood. Dragging, carrying, pushing, and covering them with our bodies, we thrust them into the British vehicles, which drove off. I called our soldiers over to one side. I waved to the villagers—"It's all yours," I shouted.[9]

On a smaller or larger scale, such "incidents" during the battle of the roads were repeated again and again. Usually the British were reluctant to intervene, seeing no reason to incur further casualties and Arab displeasure.

Jewish efforts to ram convoys through had not proved very successful, whether the British intervened or not. The Arabs had all the advantages, including safety from counterattack. The Jews had to trust to luck and speed, knowing the unappealing odds if the convoys were halted. By March neither speed nor luck worked anymore. There were too many Jews in Jerusalem to depend on the erratic arrival of a few trucks. By March there were no meat, no eggs, no milk, no vegetables. There were a minimal bread ration, little cooking fuel, and less gasoline. Jerusalem seemed to be withering on the vine, isolated and forgotten by the Haganah and the Jewish Agency.

Actually the fate of Jerusalem remained foremost in Ben-Gurion's mind; far from being forgotten it was a constant preoccupation. Ben-Gurion, like Abdullah, considered Jerusalem the ultimate prize. Secretly he hoped that the Holy City would be the capital of the new state. In any case, the Tel Aviv–Jerusalem axis was vital for the future. Ben-Gurion might have bowed to internationalization if the Arabs had accepted partition, but, as they had chosen force, he was unwavering in his intention to secure the city. In December he had ordered Dov Joseph and Mrs. Golda Meir to head a Jerusalem emergency committee to prepare for a siege. For months Joseph had struggled to hoard supplies, to build secret water cisterns, to organize medical and civil-defense services. By March he had worked wonders but not miracles. The situation was bleak. The kibbutzim to the north and south were isolated. The Jewish quarter in the Old City lived under the unpredictable protection of the British. In the New City thirst and hunger were never far away. The Arab irregulars seemed to hover on the brink of victory.

The impact of the Arab attacks had had far-reaching effects in the United States. Obviously, the Mandate had fallen into the hands of roving bands, self-appointed police, irregulars, and secret armies. The prospect of partition had released a spiraling conflict completely unanticipated by the optimistic delegates at Lake Success. Long before March many of those responsible for the partition resolution were having sober second thoughts. The United States government still contained officials who thought that alienation of the Arabs was unwise and partition unenforceable. Other Americans believed that the only thing created by the November resolution had been a vacuum. Despite genuine good will, the United States had been partially responsible for opening a chamber of horrors. The result was that American policy gyrated back and forth from unqualified support of partition to hesitation, delay, and compromise, as the experts scrambled for a formula to prevent war. On March 19 Warren Austin, the United States delegate to the United Nations, suggested that, in view of the increasing disorder in the Mandate, partition be postponed and a temporary trusteeship instituted. What the Arabs had not yet won on the battlefields of irregular warfare might be granted by the United States' informal efforts.

But compromise of any kind was a futile dream. Despite diplomatic efforts that would continue to the last minute, the Jews and the Arabs were determined to seek their own separate destinies. The Arabs had no interest in another trusteeship when victory seemed imminent. The Jews were appalled at the very suggestion. Having expected so much from the United Nations, they now felt that they had received little. From December on the respect of the Yishuv for the United Nations disintegrated bit by bit. "Increasingly one feels cheated when one thinks of the U.N."[10] More important than Arab or Zionist distaste for a vague trusteeship was the opposition of the Soviet Union. Moscow howled down the idea of trusteeship, accusing Washington of undermining the United Nations and advocating colonialism. The British showed no interest in staying. No one showed any interest in squandering lives and money by replacing the British. So, during the latter part of March, the inconclusive discussions dragged on day after day. The very suggestion of a renewed trusteeship at Lake Success demonstrated to the Jewish Agency just how crucial the next months would be. Old friends and old enemies both doubted the capacity of the Jews to survive.

On March 24 a convoy ran into a mined section along the Tel Aviv–Jerusalem road and turned back, but thirteen trucks were lost. On March 25 an eighty-vehicle convoy, stretching for two miles and protected by homemade armored cars, finally pushed through, but heavy Arab fire killed five Jews and wounded nine. On the same day the Arabs smashed a convoy to Ataroth, killing fourteen Jews. On

March 27 1,000 Arabs under Abdel Kader ambushed, near Nebi Daniel, a convoy on its way back to Jerusalem from Kfar Etzion. Within a few minutes, the Arabs destroyed most of the trucks and blocked the road both ahead and behind the convoy. Still under heavy fire, the convoy commander positioned his remaining armored vehicles to make three sides of a square, using a ruined wall for the fourth. Hedgehogged in an all-around dug-in defense were 200 Jews; they were surrounded by a mob of armed Arabs whose friends and neighbors, attracted by the sound of firing, began showing up with rifles.

There was no possibility of relief, for there were no Jewish settlements nearer than Jerusalem, and the British refused to aid unauthorized convoys. All day the Arabs pounded away at the little stockade of riddled vehicles. The firing continued that night and into the next day. The disorganized Arabs could not push through any of their clumsy charges, and the Jews had no chance of breaking free. The Jewish commander salvaged a portable radio transmitter and called for—incredibly—air support. For the first time the Jewish "air force" intervened in a battle. The air support consisted of one Piper Cub dropping hand grenades. As the Piper Cub, nicknamed *Zipora*, "bird," kept in air-to-ground contact with the besieged convoy, the conversation could be picked up by radios in the Jerusalem area. Sitting safely in Jerusalem, listeners followed the fighting. Obviously the support of *Zipora* was militarily ineffectual. By dawn the next day the situation of the Jews was desperate. Ammunition was low, and the Arabs were massing for a final charge. Finally, the British decided to intervene. They arranged for safe conduct of the Jews into Jerusalem and turned over the Jews' weapons and armored cars to the Arabs. In a day and a half 135 Arabs and 12 Jews had been killed, but the Jews had lost almost the entire Jerusalem fleet of armored trucks. It was also the last convoy to make it through to the Etzion bloc, now totally isolated and without hope of supplies. The whole Jewish position in Jerusalem looked perilous.

It was clear to all that a turning point had been reached. The Arab irregulars had paralyzed the Yishuv. Everywhere the Haganah had been successful in defense as the volunteers' clumsy attacks broke before their fire, yet everywhere the Arabs had appeared to attack again. No kibbutz had fallen, no matter how heavy or prolonged the attacks. Yet the defensive successes of the Haganah had all been in vain because the roads had been closed anyway. Frontal assaults by the volunteers were unnecessary in a war of attrition with all the geographical and tactical advantages on the side of the Arabs. All qualified observers agreed that the Jews had bought it. In London Field Marshall Bernard Montgomery foresaw total victory as soon as the Arab armies intervened; in Palestine General MacMillan agreed. The Arabs in Palestine did not even think that they would have to wait for the regular Arab armies. Ben-Gurion argreed. Unless the links among Jewish communities could be reforged, hopes for a Jewish state would die before the Mandate ended. The time for the Haganah to go over to the offensive, to clear out the Arabs' secure areas, and to destroy the roadblocks had come much too soon. The next round of the undeclared war was the Jews' attack.

NOTES

1. An excellent account of the secret campaign to secure an air force can be found in Colonel Benjamin Kagan, *Combat Secret pour Israël* (Loos-lez-Lille: 1963). Jewish efforts did not end with modified transport but extended to the acquisition of heavy four-engine B-17 bombers. The Irgun, too, had agents scrambling about in the international arms market; see Doris Katz, *The Lady Was a Terrorist* (New York: 1953), pp. 115–34.

2. *Parliamentary Debates, House of Commons*, Vol. 445 (London) col. 1212.

3. *Ibid.*, col. 1213.

4. Sir John Bagot Glubb, *A Soldier with the Arabs* (New York: 1957), p. 79.

5. Although from December through March Bevin's speeches in Commons were filled with references to the British intention to withdraw, the Jews simply doubted his word.

6. In his book *New Star in the Near East* (New York: 1950), pp. 13–4, the Middle East correspondent for *The New York Herald Tribune*,

Kenneth Bilby, reports a conversation with a young British major in the Arab Legion:

One night my wife and I invited a young Legion major and a British correspondent to our room in the Philadelphia Hotel at Amman. There had been several rounds of drinks when the conversation turned to Middle East politics, an inevitable subject in that part of the world. Tears suddenly sprouted in the major's eyes and he gripped his martini glass until his fingers were white.

"My wife and two boys are coming here to live with me soon," he said slowly. "I intend to teach my sons to grow up hating Jews the way I do. I want to spend the rest of my life killing Jews. I'll fight them, and I'll fight anyone who helps them. Anyone who does is my enemy."

With his last word, the martini glass shattered under the pressure of his fingers. A jagged edge cut a deep gash in his wrist. We were too stunned to move. Tears continued coursing down his cheeks, and he rubbed his wrist along the wall, coating it with large smears of blood. It was several minutes before my wife could calm him enough to cover the slash with bandages.

7. Glubb, *Soldier with the Arabs*, pp. 63, 66.

8. *Ibid.*, p. 75.

9. *Ibid.*, p. 77.

10. Harry Levin, *I Saw the Battle of Jerusalem* (New York: 1950), p. 51.

5

The Undeclared War＊
The Jews Attack

B oth David Ben-Gurion and Israel Galili had prepared
to take offensive action to secure the future state once
the British had withdrawn, but neither had anticipated the piecemeal deterioration of the Mandate or a staged British evacuation.
Dalet, an overall plan, had been prepared under the assumption
that offensive operations would begin when the Haganah was safe
from British intervention. Dalet (it was named for the fourth letter
of the Hebrew alphabet and superseded three earlier plans that had
been discarded) called for the defense of the future state and the
settlements outside the United Nations boundaries by seizure of the
strategic Arab heights to open the way to Jerusalem and to occupy
the vacuum areas left by the departing British. Such operations would
require full mobilization, long opposed by many civilian leaders, and
a considerable influx of modern weapons. Everyone had hoped
during March that the Haganah would be able to open a way
into Jerusalem without major action. Instead the city was more
tightly sealed off than ever. On March 21 David Shaltiel, the Jerusalem area commander, reported to the High Command that not
only could he take no offensive action but also that "Our forces
are hardly sufficient for defensive warfare."[1]
On March 31 Ben-Gurion took the first step to achieve the pre-

conditions for success of Dalet. He made contact with the arms agents in Prague, where increasingly close cooperation with the Czechs had continued. (By March the Zionist agents had negotiated the purchase of several Dakota DC-3 transport planes and had secured permission to use the Zatec airdrome near Prague.) Ben-Gurion wanted an immediate arms shipment flown into the Mandate. The agents in Prague jammed a Dakota with rifles and German machine guns. On the night of April 1 the Dakota landed near Tel Aviv at Beit Darass airfield, only recently evacuated by the British. The arms were quickly unloaded and distributed. The Dakota took off before dawn, leaving no evidence for the British investigators who came the next day, attracted by rumors of strange planes landing at night on an abandoned airfield. The 100 Spandau machine guns and the several thousand rifles would permit activation of Dalet; furthermore, the Haganah's High Command knew that an illegal arms ship was due momentarily. When the ship slipped through on April 3, the arms, still in their original packing, were rushed to Haganah troops in a transit camp near Tel Aviv, cleaned, and tried out at once—for by then Dalet was underway.

On the day of April 1 the High Command had met to discuss the first operation of Dalet, the lifting of the Jerusalem siege. Ben-Gurion had insisted on an immediate attack. At first the Haganah command could find only 400 men. Ben-Gurion insisted that, regardless of difficulties, the attack required 1,500 armed troops. He promised the arms, then in transit on the Dakota, and the Haganah scraped up the men. The action would take place with a battalion three times the size of any previous Haganah force. Not only would the entire mobile reserve be needed, but also it would be necessary to drain off men from elsewhere. Not all the Haganah commanders believed that the city was worth the risk, but Ben-Gurion was obsessed with Jerusalem. If Jerusalem held, the Arabs could not concentrate their forces against the Jewish coastal enclave. If Jerusalem held, the policy of no retreat would be vindicated. If Jerusalem held, all might still be won. If the city fell, the Arabs could move on to Tel Aviv. Jerusalem, the cornerstone of victory, became a fixation. By force of character and by reason, Ben-Gurion carried the Haganah with him.

The proposed offensive to relieve the 100,000 Jews in Jerusalem was designated Operation Nahshon after Nahshon Ben Aminadav, the man who had first jumped into the Red Sea when Moses ordered the fleeing Hebrews to cross the water. The Haganah planned to seize the Arab strong points above the Jerusalem-Tel Aviv highway with 1,500 troops organized along normal army lines, supported by auxiliary services but without artillery. The operation would consist of a two-pronged advance, one column moving west from Jerusalem to attack the Arab village of Kastel, the other column attacking east from Hulda to clear the Bab el-Wad area. Once a free corridor had been opened, several huge convoys of trucks were to be rammed through to Jerusalem. Immediately before Nahshon began, the Haganah carried out an attack on the volunteers at Hassan Salame's Druze headquarters. A bomb demolished the building and most of Salame's staff, but Salame himself escaped. On April 4 a Haganah sortie surprised the Arabs at Kastel, supposedly safe on their 2,500-foot peak. The Arabs, driven off in the first rush, made an appeal for help and hurriedly launched a counterattack.

On April 6 Nahshon formally got underway with the attacks at the two ends of the corridor. Neither was a complete success, but a sufficient number of heights were taken to risk running a convoy. The convoy left Hulda at midnight and crept along the winding highway, reaching Jerusalem ten hours later. Meanwhile, word reverberated through Arab Jerusalem that the Jews had attacked. Abdel Kader, who was conferring in Damascus, hurried back to take personal control of operations. By then the most vicious fighting had developed around the outskirts of Kastel. The Arabs had driven out the Palmach unit but in turn had been forced to give up the village. When Kader arrived, he concentrated all his men for another counterattack. Arabs from the neighboring villages of Bet Safaf, Malkieh, Ein Karen, and Deir Yassin rushed up to join Kader. For two days the Arabs counterattacked again and again. One after another the outlying Jewish positions fell. The Palmach forces in Kastel obstinately held onto the village itself, keeping open the eastern end of the highway. By April 9 the Arabs had forced the Palmach back into the narrow streets of the village. With no relief in sight, the Jews decided to abandon Kastel.

A few minutes before the final withdrawal, with the Arabs under the impression that it had already taken place, a Palmach machine gunner mistook three Arabs walking casually down the middle of the main street for Jewish reinforcements. At the last minute he realized his mistake, opened fire, and killed all three instantly. One of them was Abdel Kader, the only competent Arab military leader in the

Jerusalem area and the only one with any kind of personal following. He would be replaced by Émile Ghoury, a Christian Arab who had attended The American University at Beirut; but Kader proved irreplaceable. The Jews withdrew before they discovered their victim's identity. It was a difficult retreat, with the Palmach commanders covering their men as they scrambled back under Arab fire. As a result, only one section leader escaped. Kastel was in Arab hands, and, despite Kader's death, the Jerusalem Arabs were delighted. Their joy was short-lived; for without Abdel Kader, the Arabs quarreled among themselves, and many of the villagers turned around and went home. The other Arabs withdrew from Kastel after only twenty-four hours, making no continuing effort to defend it. A new Haganah attack force simply moved in and found it unoccupied. The Jerusalem highway was clear in the east.

On April 9 the Irgun and the Lechi opened an independent attack against the Arab village of Deir Yassin, apparently with little or no liaison with the Haganah commanders of Nahshon.[2] The village had been known for its unwillingness to allow the Arab irregulars to be garrisoned there, and its site had no great strategic value. The Irgun, however, decided to take it. In accordance with Irgun custom, the village was warned. Apparently, the Irgun assumed that the villagers would not resist when the Jews showed up; but some Arabs did fire on the attack group. The capture of the village soon degenerated from a walk-in-and-mop-up operation into a brutal massacre. More than 200 civilians, including women and children, were shot down. The Arabs claimed that 254 had been slaughtered and that their bodies had been left scattered on the streets or thrown down the village well. A few captives were brought back into Jerusalem blindfolded in open trucks. In the afternoon the trucks drove slowly down King George Avenue displaying the stunned Arabs. The Jewish Agency and the Haganah were horrified and repelled by the news of the massacre. The Agency issued a statement expressing horror and regret and took the unusual step of cabling the release to Abdullah. The Arabs, however, did not believe that the responsibility ended with the Irgun. To them, all Jews were guilty.

More significant than Jewish guilt was rising Arab fear. Kastel had been lost and Kader killed. General Sir Ismail Safwat Pasha, Inspector General of the Arab volunteer armies, insisted that the Arabs "have extracted themselves from the areas besieged by the Jews."[3] This statement meant retreat. At the other end of the corridor, around Bab el-Wad, things had not gone much better. Although the Jews had not been successful everywhere, the Haganah had opened a way into the New City. Three huge convoys followed the first on April 12, 17, and 20. By the time the last convoy set out, the Arabs had regrouped. A smaller Haganah operation, Harel, begun on April 15, had not succeeded in clearing the highway around Latrun, and this last convoy of more than 300 vehicles ran into an ambush. The Arabs shot up many of the trucks, their burnt-out hulks joining other rusting and riddled wrecks beside the highway. Still, the major part of the convoy broke through. The siege of Jerusalem had been lifted, even though only temporarily. Jewish morale was very high. The Jews no longer felt cut off and forgotten. Ben-Gurion himself had ridden in on the last convoy. The Jerusalem Arabs recognized the tipping of the scales, and their early optimism turned to apprehension. More disturbing news would soon arrive from the north.

With the Haganah reserve tied down in the Tel Aviv-Jerusalem corridor, Kaukji decided that the time had come for the Arab Liberation Army to achieve an independent victory, the long-sought capture of a kibbutz. He chose Mishmar Ha'emek, a strategic settlement at the gateway to the coastal plain near Haifa and the Jezeel Valley. On paper the operation looked good. Kaukji had 1,000 volunteers and six French 75-millimeter artillery pieces. Surprise was on his side, and he had no fear that the Jews would bring up reserves. On April 4 the Arab Liberation Army struck. Following this first artillery barrage of the war, which shattered the settlement, the Arabs charged. The Jews opened up with small-arms fire and one machine gun. The Arabs reached the settlement fence, hesitated, and fell back. They had counted on the artillery barrage to smash any resistance, which it very nearly had, and were horribly disappointed at the heavy Jewish fire. The Arabs were most reluctant to make a second attack and milled about uncertainly. Kaukji had to wait until the following morning to renew his assault. In the meantime, he kept up an irregular bombardment. The Jews had only one two-inch mortar with which to reply and could only sit out the bombardment, fearful that another massive charge would swamp them. The artillery fire eventually attracted the attention of the British 3rd Hussars. They then carried on desultory negotiations with one of Kaukji's deputies and withdrew. The next day the Arabs renewed the artillery barrage. It made a great deal of noise and encouraged the Arabs no end, but no one had much will for another frontal assault. Once more the shelling attracted the British. Lieutenant Colonel Peel arranged a twenty-four-hour truce on April 7 to allow the Jews to evacuate the women and children from the kibbutz. The Arabs were delirious with joy at their "victory." But the Jews succeeded in bringing up Haganah reinforcements and the following day turned down Peel's offer to extend the truce. Kaukji reopened his bombardment. During the day the shelling and the heavy Arab fire wore down the Jews. Kaukji still did not care to ram his skittish volunteers into the settlement defenses. On April 9, he intensified the shelling, and the defenders in Mishmar Ha'emek braced for the last attack. It never came. Kaukji decided to cut his losses and withdrew.

On April 14 the second round began at Mishmar Ha'emek, as the Arabs cautiously slipped back into the area. This time Kaukji was more discrete. He ordered his 1,000 men to infiltrate the heights above the settlement. The maneuver may have seemed sly to the Arabs, but the Jews had anticipated it; furthermore, the Haganah was intimately familiar with the terrain, an old training ground. The Jews were entrenched in the Arab rear. The Arabs, concentrating on the prize of Mishmar Ha'emek and not on their exposed flanks, crept past. At a range of 300 yards, the Palmach opened up a withering fire. Kaukji's attack collapsed. The Arab Liberation Army retreated all the way back to the main camp near Tubas. The local Arab villagers, shocked at their desertion, fled. Kaukji's independent victory had turned into a disastrous defeat but a defeat that he refused to recognize. He told foreign correspondents that the whole attack had been a wild success. When asked how long it would take the Arab Liberation Army to sweep the Jews into the sea, he had a ready answer: "I took Mishmar in ninety minutes, so, all you have to do is to find out how many other Jewish settlements there are and multiply them by ninety."[4] Kaukji may even have believed himself, but his army did not. As an effective military instrument, it had been severely damaged.

When Kaukji ran into trouble at Mishmar Ha'emek, he had been forced, humiliating as it was, to call for aid from Shakhib Wahab's Druze battalion. To take pressure off Kaukji, Wahab launched a typical Arab assault on the kibbutz Ramat Yohanan—in broad daylight the Druzes rushed directly into Jewish small-arms fire. The

Arabs lost heart and retreated. They, like Kaukji's army, had failed and in failing had collapsed as an effective force. On April 18 the Haganah captured Tiberias. The Arabs, fearful and uncertain, fled.[5] The tide had turned. The Arab volunteer forces had been shattered twice. Kader had been killed. Wahab's staff had also been killed. Jerusalem's larders had been restocked. The Arab leaders in Palestine were desperate. The Arab Liberation Army even telegraphed to Abdullah for reinforcements, a request that must have given him considerable satisfaction. The Arabs had been forced to recognize that, without outside help, they faced disaster. Any formal Arab invasion, however, would have to wait until the end of the Mandate on May 15. Much could happen in a month.

The British were slow to react to the Arab predicament. In fact, Bevin and Montgomery were not even aware that there was a predicament. The friendly British within the Mandate did what they could and sometimes what they were ordered to do by London. Rather than release control of the Mandate in all areas on a single date, the British army had decided to move out by stages. This method would reduce chaos and last-minute casualties and would have the added benefit of permitting the local Arabs to move in behind the British. The usual practice was to inform the local Arab military leaders in advance of the British withdrawal, so that an orderly exchange could take place. If it seemed convenient or advantageous, the Arabs were even allowed to move in before the British army withdrew. On occasion this policy was frustrated by the Haganah intelligence, but usually the local Arabs had first crack at the evacuated areas. This advantage now seemed jeopardized because of the Haganah's increasing effectiveness. Even with British assistance, the Arabs were hard-pressed. The units of the Arab Legion stationed in the Mandate did all that they believed was possible. Individual British commanders leaned over backward, but the military weakness of the volunteers increasingly left Arab areas vulnerable.

In Haifa, the major Palestinian port and the terminal of the great oil pipelines, Major General H. C. Stockwell, the British army commander, decided that there was no further point in holding onto the whole city. Evacuation of his troops to the port area would keep open British lines of communication without subjecting his men to the risk of being caught in any future fighting in the city. Haifa had a population of 80,000 Jews and 70,000 Arabs, but as usual they lived in segregated residential districts. The Arabs lived in the Old City close to the port, whereas the Jewish districts were above them on Hadar Harcarmel, or Mount Carmel. The Haifa Arabs had other disadvantages. The original organizer of the Haifa Arab National Guard, which had 350 members (half of them only part-time), had been killed on March 17. Yunis Naffa, a sanitary inspector, had taken over temporarily, but on March 28 he had been replaced by Captain Amin Izzedin, a Lebanese Druze who had served in the Transjordan Frontier Force. Izzedin brought in a platoon of thirty or forty men to reinforce the Arab position in Haifa and immediately began to prepare for the showdown. The results were not too impressive. There were not enough arms and by April only about 500 armed Arabs. The civil-defense organizations remained rudimentary. Nothing could be done to compensate for Jewish tactical advantage of possession of the heights above the Old City. Local notables preferred to take extended trips to Beirut or Cairo. Efforts to abtain real assistance from the Arab League or the Mufti resulted only in frustration. In contrast, the Jews had a highly effective shadow government and an experienced Haganah unit under Moshe Carmel and Mordechai Makleff. They had carefully planned that, as soon as the British moved out, they would seize the city, in Operation Misparayim ("scissors") from what they estimated would be a superior Arab force under Izzedin.

On April 21 General Stockwell decided to pull the 6th Airborne Division out of the increasingly tense city. He assumed that the Haganah, with 4,000 men, would be able to take Haifa, although he bet a bottle of whiskey that it would take them a week. The order of events remains murky,* but apparently orders went out to the British to withdraw sometime during the morning of April 21. Stockwell had

* The precise times, the intentions of individuals, and the exact order of events would be of only minor historical interest if it were not for the fact that the Haifa exodus has subsequently assumed major importance in the placing of responsibility for the Arab refugees. For a considerable time Zionist writers denied that the British had informed Carmel rather than Izzedin of the withdrawal. It now appears, however, that Stockwell did just that. See Walid Khalidi, "The Fall of Haifa," *Middle East Forum*, 25, No. 10 (December 1959), 22–32, who outlines the historiography of the crisis, most of which took place in the articles and letter columns of editor Jon Kimche's *Jewish Observer and Middle East Review*.

invited Izzedin to visit his headquarters on Stella Maris Road at 11:30 that morning. But, at that time, Stockwell apparently did not tell him that British troops were already withdrawing, for Izzedin immediately left for Damascus, thereby cutting Arab-British communications. But by that time Moshe Carmel had been informed that the British were pulling out. He activated Misparayim.

One blade of the scissors crossed the bridge over Wadi Rushmiyal on the evening of April 21, but soon after midnight the Arabs, reacting swiftly, pinned down the attack group in a stone building close to the bridge. All efforts to reinforce the building from across the bridge failed. At daybreak the column was finally relieved, but by then the other Jewish attacks had succeeded. Sweeping into the unprepared Arab quarter, the Jews sliced the Old City into three parts. Divided, surrounded, without leaders, the Arabs found their position deteriorating rapidly. The high level of Jewish fire, the Jewish radio and sound trucks blaring warnings, the crescendo of general sound frightened the Arabs. In panic the civilians began fleeing toward the port. By morning on April 22 resistance in Haifa had almost collapsed. The Arab population was in the grips of hysteria.

General Stockwell offered to mediate in negotiating for the surrender of the remaining Arab forces. An emergency Arab committee had already been in contact with Stockwell early in the morning to protest British withdrawal and to demand British intervention. At about 10:00 A.M. the committee met with him, but he refused to intervene and instead suggested acceptance of Carmel's truce terms: the surrender of all Arab weapons, an immediate curfew, and Haganah control of the city. The Arabs were aghast but helpless. They left Stockwell to attend a meeting in an atmosphere of gloom, foreboding, and contention. At about 4:00 in the afternoon the committee reluctantly left to meet with the Jews at the town hall. Efforts to make contact with the Syrian government had failed. No reinforcements were to be expected. At the town hall, Shabetai Levy, Haifa's Jewish mayor, explained the terms of surrender again. There was to be no negotiation. Stockwell urged, "If you don't sign this truce I shall not be responsible if three or four hundred more are killed by tomorrow."* After a long recess, the Arab committee re-

* Khalidi, *op. cit.,* p. 131.

turned. It had no choice. The port was filling up with fleeing refugees, the Old City was shattered, the wounded and dead were everywhere. Yet the Arabs proudly refused to sign any agreement with the Jews. Instead they had decided to evacuate all the Arab population and asked only for British transport. Neither the entreaties of Levy nor of General Stockwell could sway the five self-appointed delegates. The Arabs would leave.

Since as early as December 1947, a gradual exodus of individual Arabs from the Mandate had been underway. The first refugees, the wealthy and the wise, had left early after making satisfactory preparations, intending to wait out the troubles in Egypt or Lebanon. Many of these local notables were the potential leaders of the Arab community, so that often the Arab population, without direction from above and without institutions of their own, were left at the mercy of rumor, anxiety, and fear. As long as the Arab irregular war was going well, these fears had been minimal. As the fighting continued, however, Arab civilians had begun to flee from the mixed areas. There is little doubt that the vast majority of the Arabs, rich and poor, firmly believed the promises of the Arab League and the ultranationalists: The Jews would be swept into the sea. Nonetheless, the early refugees hoped to avoid both fighting and compromising their own future by accepting, even temporarily, Jewish control. There were even rumors that the Arab League or the Mufti approved of such a course, although there is ample evidence that they did not.* With the beginning of the Haganah offensive in April, however, the Arabs in Palestine, regardless of their leaders' intentions or the confusion of the moment, fled because they were afraid of the Jews. There had been a massacre at Deir Yassin, and there could be another at Tiberias or Haifa; they left their homes and businesses to save their lives.

Although not the first such flight, the Arab evacuation of Haifa became the prototype of the subsequent Arab exodus from all parts

---

* There has long been argument about the existence of an order from the Arab Higher Committee. The Arabs deny it, pointing out that no text, not even a paraphrase, has ever been produced. The Israelis insist that its existence was common knowledge among the Arabs in 1948. The importance of such an order now would be to weaken greatly the present Arab claim that the refugees were driven out by the Jews.

of Palestine controlled by the Jews. At Haifa, at least, the Jews claimed they did everything they could to prevent the Arabs from leaving after the surrender, and this claim was confirmed by the British District Superintendent of Police. But, huddled on the edge of the shattered Arab Old City, defeated and defenseless, the Arabs were having none of it. By the end of April, more than 60,000 Arabs had left Haifa. Many Arabs have accused the Jews of encouraging evacuations in Palestine, of using the disaster at Deir Yassin as a club to drive out the Arabs, thus removing any future minority problem and opening the land to new Jewish immigrants. But that was surely not the case in Haifa, although, as the war continued and bitterness and uncertainty grew, there is no doubt that the Jews gave up any effort to retain their future Arab citizens. They began to regard the exodus as beneficial; certainly it solved the purely military problem of a possible Arab fifth column. Soon military commanders began to think it essential to cleanse certain Arab districts to prevent guerrilla warfare behind their own troops when facing the regular Arab armies. In May, Yigal Alon in Galilee spread rumors and urged flight employing Jewish mukhtars (mayors) who had contacts with the local Arabs.* In some areas, the result was the capture of key points without a shot being fired. Not only did the Arab exodus eliminate many military problems; it also eventually simplified the new Jewish state's development by removing a large, potentially rebellious minority and by freeing for confiscation all the Arab lands and assets. If the Jewish Agency and the Haganah actually had, with Machiavellian cleverness, encouraged Arab emigration, had plotted coldly and immorally the massacre at Deir Yassin, had used at all times and all places threats and terror the results could not have been more impressive.

Later there were many who, as they examined the results, could believe only that in fact the Jewish Agency had acted deliberately.

---

* Khalidi, in "Plan Dalet: The Zionist Blueprint for the Conquest of Palestine," *Middle Eastern Forum*, 37, No. 9 (November 1961), 22–8, takes pleasure in quoting Yigal Alon, *Ha Sepher Ha*, 286; but, of course, he does not give much weight to the military necessity for Alon's actions, which made possible the capture without fighting of the areas around Hule. In May 1948 the Jews would have had to be omniscient to foresee the ultimate Arab-refugee problem, but there is evidence that they did partially instigate the Arab flight whether or not they expected an eventual return.

The Jews replied with some justice that the Arabs had been ordered by their own leaders to flee, that Deir Yassin had horrified most of them as well, and that the Jews were not to blame for the Arab exodus. In either case, the Arabs, prey to rumor, poorly advised, uncertain, and above all frightened, did leave. In rising numbers, they fled to Jordan, to Lebanon, to the Gaza areas. They collected in filthy, makeshift shanties and tattered tents. They huddled in caves and tar-paper shacks, starving, diseased, hungry, the flotsam of war. Trapped in desperation and defeat, their numbers mounted. The thousands of Arabs from Haifa were only the first installment of those who would eventually suffer misery in exile waiting for the time when they could return in safety. That time, of course, has never come. The refugees' fears of massacre, largely unjustified, led them to abandon Palestine. Although the Jews are partially responsible for playing on those fears, it must be remembered that the structure of Palestinian Arab society was too feeble to ensure its own protection in the face of spreading terror. Arab pride and Arab confidence collapsed before vague threats. This deep humiliation only made the bitterness greater.

The Arabs were not alone in their frustration and humiliation. The British, too, had remained confident of ultimate Arab success. Even the warnings of early April had been dismissed, but the rapid series of Haganah successes during the month shattered London's complacency. On April 22 Bevin met with Prime Minister Clement Attlee at No. 10 Downing Street. The Arab newspapers had reported the massacre of 23,000 Arabs in Haifa while Stockwell stood by. Attlee summoned Montgomery, who found Bevin extremely agitated. Further meetings took place, and on April 23 Creech-Jones told the special session of the General Assembly that Britain believed that the United Nations must accept something less than partition. Apparently Britain favored the most drastic reduction of the proposed Jewish state. Such a proposal at the very moment when Arab resistance in Palestine appeared to have collapsed seemed arrogant and curiously ill timed. The United Nations delegations did not seem much interested. The Arabs, however, wanted more than a diplomatic gesture at Lake Success; they were, in fact, desperate.

That is, all were desperate but Abdullah, who had watched events take what seemed to him their predestined course. On March 17 his delegate to the Arab League conference had announced that Trans-jordan would reserve its freedom of action concerning Palestine. On April 10 the League had met again in Cairo for twelve days of talks. General Safwat had gloomily reviewed the defeats and suggested that the time had come for the regular armies to enter Palestine. The Transjordanian delegation immediately announced that the Arab Legion would enter Palestine as soon as the Mandate terminated. On April 12 King Faruk told the delegates that the occupation of Palestine by an outside Arab army must be only temporary and that Palestine must eventually be returned to the Palestinians. Abdullah ordered his delegation to make it clear that Palestine and Transjordan were one country. His point was clearly made. There was nothing much the jealous Egyptians and Syrians could do.

On April 30 the League met again, in Amman. The League Political Committee had concluded that it would be sufficient for the Arab armies simply to move into Arab Palestine, that no fighting would be necessary, and that the major powers would force the Jews to accept Arab terms. It was an appealing course, although it bore no relation to reality and no one believed in it. The Egyptians were still reluctant actually to risk their army. Abdullah had no such qualms. He still hoped to march in and annex Arab Palestine without a full and final showdown with the Jews, who would be allowed to keep a somewhat shrunken territory. He still hoped that the Syrians, Iraqis, and Egyptians would be helpless to interfere. He wanted a nice, quick, and advantageous partition. Of course, the rapid successes of the Jews did complicate his project. Unless that tendency were reversed, there might be no Arab Palestine left to annex.

The Haganah commanders would hardly have credited the depths of Arab pessimism—they had too many problems of their own. With the end of the Mandate only a few weeks off and the intervention of the Arab armies becoming a certainty, the Yishuv was still far from prepared for invasion. Every effort was made to secure the strategic points, whether in Arab hands or not, and to link up the kibbutzim. Even though the Arab volunteer movement was disintegrating, the lack of armed and mobile Jewish troops made every operation a desperate affair, its success dependent on will rather than on numbers and matériel. The Haganah was spread too thin; the Palmach could be in only so many places. One of the essential areas was eastern Galilee along the Sea of Galilee and up along the Syrian frontier to Lebanon. Alon, the Palmach commander, wanted to prepare Galilee for the Arab invasion by capturing key Arab positions and opening the roads to traffic. But he simply did not have the men to do the job. Similar problems existed in the northern Negev and in the coastal plane. Alon nevertheless proposed Operation Yiftach to consolidate eastern Galilee. He intended not only to avoid reinforcing any settlement under attack but also to strip most of the kibbutzim of what men and arms they did have to supply his own attacks. The settlers were understandably upset, but Alon pointed out that, without Yiftach, the regular Arab armies would wipe them out anyway.

One of the prime aims of Yiftach was to clear a way through to Safad, where the Jewish quarter had been under siege for months. Safad, on the slopes of a hill overlooking the Sea of Galilee, occupied a strategic military position dominating the main roads of central Galilee. For the Jews it also had considerable historic importance as one of the main strong points of Flavius Josephus' revolt against the Roman Empire and later as the center of Jewish medieval mysticism. Its historical and spiritual value in 1948 was hardly of prime concern, however; it was the 3,000-foot hill commanding the surrounding Galilean countryside that attracted Alon. Relief of the hard-pressed Jewish quarter would be a bonus.

At the top of the hill was a large plateau overgrown with bushes, formerly the site of a medieval fortress. The town spread below this plateau. The Jewish quarter, 150 feet down the slope, constituted one-fourth of Safad. The entire town was dominated by the ruined fortress above and by one of the huge concrete-and-steel Teggart fortresses farther away on the slope of Mount Canaan. The Safad fortress was the second largest in Palestine, impenetrable to anything but heavy explosives. Within the city itself, below the ruin, the two key structures were the heavy municipal police station and the Arab-occupied Shalva House. In 1948 there were 12,000 Arabs and 1,500 Jews living in Safad. Many of the Jews were elderly descendants of the first Zionist settlers in Palestine. For the most part the Jews were unarmed and unprepared to defend their quarter. Even if they had been prepared, the odds would have been against them: All the surrounding hills, except Mount Canaan, were in Arab hands, and the only nearby kibbutz was Ein Zeitim, which could barely defend itself. Apparently, only the presence of the Irish Guards, 1st Battalion, prevented an open Arab attack. As elsewhere, despite their handicaps, the Jews of Safad had held on, thus giving Alon a friendly pivot for Yiftach.

The British were doubtful of Jewish defense capabilities. The Irish Guards estimated that the Jews were living on borrowed time, that the quarter would be overrun within two hours of the batallion's withdrawal. The British commander was under orders to hand over all the commanding positions, including the police station and the Teggart fortress to the local Arabs. Orders to evacuate would be the signal for a combined attack and massacre by the Arab Liberation Army, which hovered offstage, and local irregulars. Until the last minute British officers sought to persuade the Jews to give up both Safad and the Ein Zeitim kibbutz before it was too late. The twenty-five-year-old local Haganah commander, Maiberg, was a sabra, a Jew born in Palestine. Although he understood the military "impossibility" of defending Safad, he fully accepted the logic of Ben-Gurion's Zionist decision. There was no place to which to retreat, Safad was home, and therefore the defense of Safad was the only remaining possibility. Such a defense could not be impossible, only difficult. The British failed to grasp Maiberg's logic and foresaw disaster.

The Arabs, barely restrained by the British, had already begun to attack the Jewish quarter. Moving up to within a few feet of the Jewish areas, the Arabs blew up houses along the edges, fired down exposed streets, and sniped away at random day and night. The Jews had little with which to return the fire. There were some firearms and three two-inch mortars. On April 14 a Palmach platoon infiltrated Arab picket lines and slipped into the city. The arrival of these rather limited reinforcements did revive the sinking hopes of the Safad Jews. Work on fortifications was speeded up, continuing during Passover, for the rabbis viewed it not as labor but as religious activity. A feeling of unity and confidence spread through the quarter. The men of the Palmach unit received free shoeshines, soft drinks, and haircuts. Other civilians were undertaking more practical preparations.

Chaim Maiberg, a descendant of the original immigrants of the 1880's and father of Safad's Haganah commander, had been turning his Central Hotel into a citadel of sorts. For some time he had been constructing fortifications in the dead of night—a series of brick-and-concrete pillboxes on the hotel roof. During the day the British regularly discovered them and insisted upon their demolition. During the afternoon Maiberg would tear them down, and then during the night he would rebuild them. While British attention was focused on the appearing and disappearing pillboxes, the elder Maiberg constructed a series of peculiar devices. Arthur Koestler later reported that one of these brick structures looked curiously like a Parisian urinal.[6] These strange half-walls, brick "urinals," bridges, and sudden tunnels eventually revealed themselves as units in a fortified communications and supply line, leading from the Central Hotel to the center of the quarter, and protected from all the Arab firing lines. But Maiberg was not satisfied with his secret corridor and disappearing pillboxes. Jewish boys suddenly began digging an "irrigation canal" between the hotel and the fortress above. The British decided that it was not a trench as it was open to fire from above; nor did it seem to be a tank trap, as it would have been difficult to maneuver a tank into it. What Maiberg actually had in mind was a barrier against rolling bombs from above, but this possibility did not occur to the British. By the middle of April Maiberg and the Central Hotel were ready. Elsewhere in the Jewish quarter similar activity had increased preparedness.

On April 16, around noon, Haganah scouts reported that Adib Shishekli of the Arab Liberation Army and Sidi Qadura, the local chief of police, occupied the police station with a platoon of twenty Arabs. At the same time a British infantry patrol, supported by armored cars, penned a detachment of Haganah infantry on Mount Canaan until Iraqi volunteers could occupy the Teggart fortress. By 3:00 in the afternoon, the last British troops had pulled out of Safad. Even before that, the Arabs had begun firing into the Jewish quarter from the police station. Other Arab detachments occupied the plateau 150 feet above the city. As the British had warned, all the strategic positions were in Arab hands. The Jews reacted promptly. Jacob Edrei hurriedly raised a flagpole on the roof of the Central Hotel, ran up the blue-and-white flag, and popped out of sight before the Arab snipers could pick him off. The battle for Safad was underway.

By that time the Arabs in general were cautious about frontal assaults. Most saw no reason to risk death in a bloody charge when a war of attrition was safer and just as certain. So, protected on the heights, the Arabs poured withering fire into the Jewish quarter day after day. The Jewish defense was concentrated in the area around the Central Hotel, the Commercial Center, and the Technical School. For three weeks the Arabs fired into the buildings, dropped mortar shells on them, and rolled explosives against them. The Technical School finally collapsed under the mortar fire. The Arabs had nearly completed a 100-yard tunnel from under the foundations of the Commercial Center. Their plan to eliminate the second center of Jewish resistance with a massive underground mine was forestalled only by the accidental malfunction of a Jewish mortar shell, which landed exactly on the extreme point of the tunnel. The Arabs assumed that the Jews had discovered the tunnel and abandoned the project. Efforts to roll barrels of dynamite against the Central Hotel were frustrated by Maiberg's "irrigation ditch." The Arabs were not discouraged. They had all the tactical marbles and plenty of time to use them.

Their lack of urgency and their limited knowledge of other Jewish operations created a sense of isolated complacency. Little attention was paid to the possibility of a Jewish relief force. On April 28 they did not react quickly to the British withdrawal from the police fortress at Rosh Pina and the nearby army camp. Alon immediately seized both. The back door to Safad was open. Alon cleared a corridor to the Jewish quarter and began moving in supplies and reinforcements. Then, at the worst possible moment for the overcommitted Jews, an independent unit of the Arab Liberation Army attacked the small kibbutz of Ramat Naphtali. The settlers, under Arab artillery fire, pleaded for reinforcements. If Alon agreed, he would have to give up his Safad attack; if he did not, Ramot Naphtali had little chance. Alon refused either to send reinforcements or to allow the settlers to withdraw. To make his point, he informed the settlers that a detachment of the Palmach had been given orders to shoot any Jews evacuating the area. The Arabs hammered away all day, reducing Ramat Naphtali to rubble. The next day they renewed the assault. Finally, when pressure eased elsewhere, a Palmach battalion cleared the route from the Sea of Galilee to Rosh Pina, outflanking the Arabs attacking Ramat Naphtali. The Arabs withdrew, easing the situation for all the kibbutzim along the Syrian border and allowing Alon to concentrate on Safad.

His first attack was up toward the plateau. After some early gains, the main effort bogged down. The attack was called off. The Arabs responded by calling up the artillery used at Ramat Naphtali and bombarding the Jewish quarter. The civilians all but gave up. To them it appeared as if the Palmach had failed and the city would be reduced. Alon turned down a request for civilian evacuation. On May 10 the Jews struck at all three Arab strongholds. The police station proved to be the most difficult to crack. Ten sappers were hit before the walls were breached, and then because of a rainstorm the wet TNT would not ignite. The attack commander was killed trying to clear the first floor. The Arabs grudgingly retreated upward. Even long after daylight a dozen Arabs still held out on the roof, hopelessly isolated but unwilling to surrender. The assault on Shalva House also ran into trouble. Bitter room-to-room fighting in the pitch dark took its toll. Abraham Licht, the assault commander, was killed when one of the Jewish soldiers snapped on a flashlight at the wrong moment. Arabs rushing down the stairway riddled Licht with bullets, but the Jews did go on to take the building. By morning Safad was in Jewish hands. Disheartened, the Iraqis, in cooperation with the Arab Liberation Army, withdrew from the Teggart fortress without a fight. Operation Yiftach had succeeded. Eastern Galilee had been consolidated for defense.

Elsewhere, similar Dalet operations had been undertaken. Late in April and early in May the Haganah seized a few key villages in the Negev, opening up a road to the isolated kibbutzim. Later, on May 12, Operation Barak, culminating in the capture of the strategic city of Breir, cleared the inland Julis–Breir road and scattered the local Arab irregulars and civilians into the Hebron hills. On the coast between Haifa and Lebanon, the Haganah moved north to take "Napoleon Hill" east of Acre and the city itself two days later. Acre, which had defied Napoleon in 1799, fell to a scratch force led by a commander who had spent months in the military prison there for engaging in illegal military training.

The Haganah commanders had prepared operation Chametz to seize Jaffa, which, though a mixed city, represented an Arab enclave in the Jewish coastal bloc. The city, however, was not then a threat and could be occupied swiftly once the British had fully withdrawn. But the Irgun, still operating independently, had organized a major surprise attack on Jaffa on April 25 before the British were completely withdrawn. Several hundred Irgun troops, supported by mortars, hit the only defended quarter of the city and soon bogged down before a stubborn Arab defense. The Haganah began cooperating with the Irgun attack. On April 27 the Irgun broke through to the beach, cutting off the Manshiya quarter. By then the situation in the city had deteriorated. Many Jews were looting the captured areas. Firing was continual. The Arab civilians had panicked. General MacMillan then decided to move into the city in order to protect his evacuation route from the large British army camp at Sarafand. British artillery began shelling Tel Aviv, and a British air strike for no tactical reason hit the city's Bat Yam quarter. MacMillan had made his point. The Jews negotiated a temporary truce in Jaffa but continued to clear the areas north and south of the city. On April 29 Kaukji managed to send in a few of his volunteers; but the Arabs had lost heart. Order in Jaffa collapsed. In London the War Office took the Arab defeat as a deliberate affront. General MacMillan was ordered to "Recapture Jaffa, and hand it back to the Arabs." But MacMillan believed that London's intervention was "quite unrealistic."[7] A fight with the Jews at the last minute would be both bloody and pointless; in any case, the inevitable Arab exodus was underway, and both civilian and military leadership had dissolved. On May 11 an emergency Arab committee began negotiations, which ended two days later in the surrender of the city. Only 3,000 of the 70,000 Arab residents remained in Jaffa—the rest withdrew, with MacMillan's aid, to Jordan.

Operation Dalet had gone well everywhere. Not all its operations had been victories, but a sufficient number of strategic heights had been secured to re-establish Jewish communications. The Haganah had cleared large areas not only of armed irregulars but also of Arab civilians. Often operations had been nip-and-tuck affairs, in which a few men one way or the other had made the difference, but the élan of the Haganah and Palmach, coupled with the morale of the kibbutzim settlers, had outweighed initial Arab advantages. As encouraging as the results of Dalet were, Ben-Gurion was far from satisfied. Jerusalem, capture of which had become an *idée fixe* for the Jews, remained vulnerable to the Arab irregulars and wide open to more formal invasion. Despite early successes along the corridor, all local Jerusalem news had been bad. On April 13 a convoy of professors, doctors, and hospital personnel on the way to the Mount Scopus complex had run into an ambush in the Arab quarter of Sheikh Jarrach. The British would not intervene, and after a seven-hour battle the Arabs had finished off the convoy. On April 15 Mount Scopus had been cut off, and convoys to the Jewish potash works at the Dead Sea had ceased. On April 18 the Arabs had seized Augusta Victoria Hospital on Mount Scopus. The Nebi Yaakov kibbutz could be reached only at night by small patrols. Contact with the Etzion bloc of kibbutzim to the south depended solely on the erratic flights of small planes. Ben-Gurion, who had ridden in with the huge April 20 convoy, had spent a week in the city conferring with the local commanders. Until Ben-Gurion could bring in the Harel Brigade as reinforcements, Colonel David Shaltiel simply would not have enough men to maintain communications with the isolated Jewish areas. Now, however, Ben-Gurion decided that something had to be done to consolidate Jerusalem.

It had been a difficult decision to use the limited Jewish resources in the Jerusalem area rather than to reopen the corridor that had closed behind the April 20 convoy. The plight of the Jews isolated in the Old City and in the outlying kibbutzim had outweighed the need for fresh supplies. Operation Jebusi, called after the original name for Jerusalem, would link the scattered Jewish areas by means of a three-pronged attack. One attack, on Nebi Samuel, the Arab village on the highest crest of the Judean mountains, would open a way to the north. A second would clear the Sheikh Jarrach quarter and open a corridor to Mount Scopus. The third would consolidate the Mekor Hayim area by the occupation of the Arab quarter of Katamon. Overall direction was to be under Itzhak Sadeh, with David Shaltiel commanding the Etzioni Brigade in Jerusalem and Itzhak Rabin commanding the Harel Brigade in the foothills.

The operation began on April 26 and met with only partial success. In the attack on Nebi Samuel, the company commander, Poża, ran into an ambush and was mortally wounded; thirty-three men were killed. Reinforcements could not fight their way through the Arabs and the British. The attack had to be called off. The Sheikh Jarrach operation went much better, but once again the British intervened. Brigadier Jones informed Sadeh that the quarter was on the British evacuation route and that the Jews would have to withdraw. Sadeh refused. The British moved a battalion of infantry forward under an artillery bombardment. Sadeh reluctantly withdrew after Jones promised to turn over the quarter when the British left. The attack on Katamon alone succeeded, although even then success came only after heavy fighting with Iraqi volunteers. The Haganah occupied not only Katamon but also the Greek quarters and several adjacent areas beyond the scope of Jebusi's objectives.

While the fighting in the corridor continued, day-to-day life for the Jews of Jerusalem remained the same: grim, nerve-racking, and uncertain. In Amman the Prime Minister reportedly told the Transjordanian parliament that Arab resistance in Palestine had collapsed, "but you don't feel it in Jerusalem."[8] The convoys had done little to alleviate the shortages of everything; even for water people had to stand in line for hours. The erratic shelling and firing had become normal household noises. As often happens with sieges, the sense of isolation had been very great. Far away in Galilee or in the Negev, there might have been victories, but in Jerusalem the Haganah seemed barely able to hold on. The fate of the Jews in the Old City had been a constant source of anxiety to everyone. The future of the Etzion bloc to the south directly on the key highway linking Jerusalem with Hebron, Beersheba, and Egypt would be bleak and brief if the Arabs could ever organize a full-scale attack. The primary threat was a full-scale attack by the Arab Legion, the Egyptians, or the Iraqis. If the existence of Jerusalem's Jewish community had been precarious under the disorganized forays by ill-armed irregulars, what chance would the city have against the modern Arab armies? There was, however, neither defeatism nor despondence but only a sense of dedication, a dedication that some feared might be insufficient: Jerusalem could become another Masada, the besieged Jewish fortress taken by the Romans in A.D. 73, which had been doomed from the start.

The news from Kfar Etzion had all been bad. On May 2 the Haganah command had ordered the defenders to close the Jerusalem–Hebron road to Arab traffic. The Jews reinforced the Russian monastery that was close to the road and on the following day cut up an Arab convoy. General Sir John Bagot Glubb regarded the highway as the vital link with his Arab Legion units in Hebron, and he could not allow the Etzion bloc to cut off the Arab South without retaliation. The highway was also necessary for withdrawal of the Legion to Transjordan upon the termination of the Mandate. The Legion was to leave Palestine one day as a British unit and to return the next to attack Jerusalem as an Arab army.

On May 4 the Arab Legion, escorted by British tanks and accompanied by a horde of local villagers, attacked the Russian monastery. This first official Legion action did not go well. The Arabs broke into the monastery but were driven out, and the Legion pulled back. But for the Jews the successful defense was a disaster. They lost twelve killed and twenty-eight wounded and used up irreplaceable ammunition. On May 12 the Legion began a full-scale attack. The Jews simply did not have the firepower to stop it. By noon the Legion had cut the roadblock in half, seized the airstrip, and put an end to united Jewish defense. By evening the monastery had fallen. Only eight wounded Jews of the original thirty-two defenders escaped alive. The next day Legion armor penetrated Kfar Etzion and forced the few remaining Jewish residents to surrender. A Legion officer lined up the fifteen survivors for a photograph. Suddenly a local Arab lifted his submachine gun and mowed down the entire row before the Legion officer could stop him. Only four Jews escaped alive from Kfar Etzion. Elsewhere in the bloc, the situation was equally hopeless. To prevent a massacre, the Red Cross managed to negotiate a surrender agreement on the morning of May 14. The wounded were shipped to Hebron and the rest to Bethlehem. At last the Kfar Etzion bloc had fallen. At last the Arabs had their kibbutz victory. But, significantly, it had taken the intervention of the Arab Legion. In Jerusalem the local Arabs were jubilant; they had a victory after six weeks of disappointment. As soon as the real Arab armies showed up, they were certain, the tide would turn again, and, as promised, the Jews would be swept into the sea.

The focus of the Jewish offensive switched over to the Jerusalem corridor, with Operation Maccabi on the night of May 7–8. Yitzhak Rabin's Harel Brigade attacked the Arab village of Bet Machzir in the Judean hills. The Arabs held on, supported by artillery until May 11. To the west, at the other end of the corridor, the Givati Brigade then opened an attack on Kaukji's Arab Liberation Army around Deir Ayub-Latrun, to clear a way through to Bab el-Wad. An attempt to ram an armored convoy through without holding Deir Ayub and Latrun collapsed in bloody failure. As the last days of the Mandate passed, Givati repeatedly hit Kaukji's positions, protected not only by his own borrowed artillery but also by an assisting British artillery unit. By May 15 the Givati Brigade had badly mauled the Arabs but had not captured the two key points. Then, on the night of May 15, Kaukji suddenly withdrew, apparently under the impression that he was to be replaced by invading Arab armies.

For the first time the Tel Aviv-Jerusalem corridor was open and all the heights secure. In the growing confusion on the eve of the promised Arab invasion, no Jewish convoy had been prepared. A makeshift string of forty trucks rushed through the gap, but, before more could reach Jerusalem, the corridor was closed again. Then the Haganah Chief of Operations Yigal Yadin telegraphed Ben-Gurion that he would have to take the Givati Brigade out of Latrun and Haganah Chief of Operations Yigal Yadin telegraphed Ben-Gurion reluctantly accepted Yadin's argument. Two days later the Arabs moved back in, and Jerusalem was again cut off.

By the middle of May, however, individual defeats could not seriously shake Jewish determination. Ben-Gurion's emotional Zionist decision had become an article of faith. The Haganah continued plans to occupy all the key British security zones at the moment that the British army moved out. Rushed as they were, the British in some cases could only invite the Arabs onstage as they withdrew. In most places there was a race between the Haganah and the Arabs to seize and hold as much territory as possible, while attempting to expel the other side from its newly won areas. The British were reluctant to toss up their last security areas for grabs. They had hoped that some sort of truce could be arranged for the Holy City—at least an armistice that would prevent heavy fighting among the shrines. All efforts to achieve an effective armistice for the city failed. The United Nations, neutral consuls, the Mandate government, and the British army each failed to persuade both sides simultaneously that such a truce might be to their advantage. Neither the Jews nor the Arabs seemed greatly concerned about last-minute British anxiety to protect Jerusalem from potential devastation.

As the British began the final withdrawal, the Etzioni Brigade immediately began Operation Pitchfork, to secure the evacuated zones in and around Jerusalem. The Arabs, still excited over the battle at the Etzion bloc, had made only rudimentary plans. Consequently, Etzioni managed, in the last few days of the Mandate, to take over most of the vital areas: "Bevingrad," the central barbed-wire British administrative area; the Russian compound district; the King David Hotel; the railroad station; and the Monastery of Notre Dame. The local Arabs, however, were not too concerned—the real war was about to start, and they would be rescued by real armies. In Cairo Abdul Rahman Azzam Pasha was announcing to the Egyptian press the future of the Jews: "This will be a war of extermination and a momentous mission which will be spoken of like the Mongol massacres and the Crusades."[9] The Arab masses accepted his prediction. The major results of the undeclared war actually had been a rude shock to Arab leaders, but most news from Palestine had been filtered through the fine sieve of Arab optimism. Soon, they rejoiced, a great wave of Arabs would sweep into Palestine.

Ben-Gurion and the Haganah commanders, though hardly sanguine, were reasonably confident that, given additional arms, the Yishuv could be defended and the new state maintained. Operation Dalet had worked about as anticipated, except in the Jerusalem corridor. The successes of the last six weeks were attributable to the spirit of the elite Palmach and Haganah. These men had total confidence in one another, in their cause, and in their destiny. For the Arabs they had cold contempt. There are military advantages in arrogance, in despising the capacity of an enemy, that are surely as great as professional respect or awed admiration. Overweening pride may, of course, lead to overconfidence and disaster, but the Haganah's analysis, partly emotional, partly realistic, had proved accurate. The Arabs had fought well here and there, particularly in defense, but generally they had shown themselves to be ill equipped in adversity, unimaginative, and prone to panic. The Arabs of the formal armies, even the Legion, would not be different in kind, only in the quality of their equipment. Galili, Sadeh, Alon, Yadin, and the old elite, given the resources Ben-Gurion anticipated, believed that they could defend the new state.

NOTES

1. Jon Kimche and David Kimche, *Both Sides of the Hill: Britain and the Palestine War* (London: 1960), p. 133.

2. The whole Deir Yassin affair, like most Irgun operations, is cloaked in controversy. What does seem to be accepted by Jewish opinion is that, provoked or not, the massacre was a spontaneous act. The Arabs are inclined to regard the attack as an integral part of Operation Nahshon. In any case, they claim, again with some evidence, that the Irgon used Deir Yassin to frighten the Arabs into flight. See Walid Khalidi, "The Fall of Haifa," *Middle East Forum*, 35 No. 10 (December 1959), p. 29.

3. Harry Levin, *I Saw the Battle of Jerusalem* (New York: 1950), p. 80.

4. Alec Kirkbride, *A Crackle of Thorns* (London: 1956), p. 157.

5. Levin, *op. cit.*, p. 81, noted the Tiberias exodus in his diary on April 16 with the comment: "I wonder what's behind it. It can't be just fear of the Jews." It is safe to say that the immediate Jewish impression was the same. The reason, discovered in ex post facto analysis, was that someone had ordered them to flee; this explanation came in time to be accepted as dogma by most Israelis.

6. Arthur Koestler, *Promise and Fulfillment: Palestine 1917–1949* (New York: 1949), pp. 208–215.

7. Kimche and Kimche, *Both Sides of the Hill*, p. 113.

8. Levin, *Battle of Jerusalem*, p. 127.

9. *Ibid.*, p. 165.

6

The Four-Week War

May 14, 1948, the last day of the Mandate, dawned bright and clear. At precisely 8:00 in the morning High Commissioner Sir Alan Cunningham emerged from the solid Government House in Jerusalem to review an honor guard of the Highland Light Infantry. After a brief speech Cunningham climbed into his black, bullet-proof Daimler to the sound of the Highlanders' bagpipes playing a Scottish funeral dirge. With an armed escort the Daimler wound its way toward the Kadandia airport in the northern suburbs, as heavy firing broke out all over Jerusalem. By 1:00 the last Union Jack in the city had been lowered, and the last British battalion had marched off. Cunningham flew to Haifa, where there was a brief farewell meeting with Jewish Mayor Shabetai Levy, and a few Moslem, Christian, and Jewish officials. At the dock there was another honor guard. The Irish Guards played "God Save the King." Cunningham climbed into a small motorlaunch, which would transfer him to the aircraft carrier *H.M.S. Ocean.* There he would remain, in Palestinian waters, until midnight and the formal end of the Mandate. No one in Palestine seemed to pay much attention to the British evacuation, for so long the source of analysis and speculation. "They shuffle out in darkness and chaos almost unnoticed."[1] By the time the former High Commissioner had sailed for Malta, on the cruiser

H.M.S. Euryalus, just after midnight, the State of Israel had been proclaimed, and the Arab armies were on the move.

The Jewish Agency had decided to declare the independence of the new state on Friday, May 14, at 4:00 in the afternoon, eight hours before official termination of the Mandate, for the rabbis would allow no official business to be transacted on the Sabbath, which began at sundown. Preparations for the state had gone on for months: Departments had been created, organized, and staffed; a flag, postage stamps, and currency had been designed; civil servants had been recruited; typewriters with Hebrew characters had been unearthed; a diplomatic corps had been established. On May 12 "Israel" had formally been chosen as the name of the new state. On May 13 invitations had been sent out for the ceremony at which the new state was to be declared. At the appointed hour on Friday afternoon, in the Tel Aviv Museum under Theodor Herzl's portrait, David Ben-Gurion rapped his gavel, and the jam-packed audience rose to sing the "Hatikvah," Ben-Gurion quietly read the Declaration of Independence, which began at the beginning—"The Land of Israel was the birthplace of the Jewish people"—and ended nearly 2,000 years later with the establishment of the Jewish state:

> With trust in Almighty God, we set our hand to this Declaration, at this Session of the Provisional State Council, on the soil of the Homeland, in the city of Tel Aviv, on this Sabbath eve, the fifth of Iyar, 5708, the fourteenth day of May, 1948.[2]

During the second week in May, as the last hours of the Mandate had passed, the United Nations Political Committee had seized on proposals for a truce and the appointment of a mediator for Palestine. For months formulas had been devised, debated, and discarded. No one wanted to see war in Palestine, but no one had been able to uncover a method for preventing it. Debate at Lake Success had grown increasingly meaningless in relation to conditions within Palestine. Finally, only seventy-five minutes before the end of the Mandate, the General Assembly met to vote on the final two proposals. At six minutes before the deadline, which was to be 6:00 in the evening New York time, the debate ended. Before a vote could be called, time had run out. Israel had been established. Eleven minutes later, in a surprise move, President Harry S Truman announced United States recognition of the new State of Israel:

> This Government has been informed that a Jewish State has been proclaimed in Palestine, and recognition has been requested by the provisional government thereof. The United States recognizes the provisional government as the *de facto* authority of the new State of Israel.[3]

In the diplomatic realm, despite maneuvers within the United Nations, Israel existed as a fact and was recognized by Washington; but the fate of the new state and of the Yishuv would be determined in Palestine, not in the corridors at Lake Success or in foreign ministries around the world. The Jews had increasingly cast a cold eye on the world of diplomacy, for the workings of the diplomats seemed inadequate and irresponsible. Israel would have to depend on the resources of the Yishuv to meet the Arab challenge.

At the Red House in Tel Aviv, Ben-Gurion and the Haganah commanders once again reviewed the woefully inadequate military resources of the new state. With proper armament Ben-Gurion and Yigal Yadin were certain that the state could be defended; without it the future looked bleak. Actually, substantial consignments could be anticipated in the immediate future. In Czechoslovakia, Jewish agents had negotiated the purchase of ten Messerschmitt 109 fighters; elsewhere transport planes, even American four-engined B-17 bombers, had been secured, and some were already en route to Israel. Operation Balak, to fly in supplies was set, and on May 16 the first two transports arrived. The British had released an Israeli arms vessel, ostensibly carrying a cargo of onions, after a cursory inspection, which was inhibited by the onions' odor. More ships were on the way, and so were carefully recruited specialists and volunteers. On paper things still looked bad. The air force had only light planes. The navy was limited to motorboats. There were just one or two British tanks and only four old 65-millimeter guns. There were, however, enough light arms, rifles, Sten guns, and machine guns for the Haganah's current state of mobilization. The local arms industry had been turning out more Sten guns, piats, antitank rifles, grenades, and mines, but the real lack was in heavy equipment.[4]

Furthermore, although Ben-Gurion recognized that the Haganah included the cream of the country's military talents, he doubted that Israel could any longer depend solely on the old fighting methods. In a full-scale war he wanted to incorporate the native Jews and the new immigrants into a professional army led by men familiar with regular warfare, traditional formations, and conventional chains of command. The Palmach and Haganah commanders, well aware of Ben-Gurion's view, resisted change as much from attachment to the ideology of their elite and revolutionary formations as for military reasons. On May 2 Ben-Gurion had informed Israel Galili, his own candidate for commander of the Haganah, that the old three-man High Command, with its balanced political representation, was no longer needed. In effect, Ben-Gurion would command the Haganah and, as all knew, would bring in as senior commanders men who had served with the Allied armies in World War II to replace the old Palestinian commanders. The Haganah had been shocked at the tone of Ben-Gurion's announcement and had opposed the innovation. First, Zvi Ayalon and then Yigal Yadin had refused to accept the new position as Deputy Commander under Ben-Gurion, who then had second thoughts. On May 9 Ben-Gurion and Galili had issued a joint statement rescinding the new plan. Galili had returned to his post as Operational Commander of the three-man High Command.[5] When Ben-Gurion and his commanders met at Red House in Tel Aviv to wait out the hours before the Arabs could invade the Mandate, the disagreement had thus been patched up. For the next weeks at least, Israel would have to depend primarily on Galili's Haganah to meet what the Israelis assumed would be a massive and coordinated Arab invasion.

Despite accelerating mobilization and training, the Haganah still had only about 35,000 effective men on May 15, although there were additional paramilitary forces. There would also be an increase of volunteers, many of them trained, from Europe and America; an influx of Jews currently interned on Cyprus; and additional immigration, but the Haganah would have to make do for perhaps several weeks with the exhausted troops already on hand. These men had been incorporated into nine territorial brigades: the Yiftah under Yigal Alon, the Golani under Moshe Montag, and the Carmeli under Moshe Carmel in the north; the Alexandroni under Dan Even and the Kiryati under Michael Ben-Gal in the center; the Givati under Shimon Avidan and the Hanegev under Nahum Sarig in the south;

the Etzioni under David Shaltiel in Jerusalem; the Harel under Yosef Tabenkin in the corridor. These brigades, all under strength, varied considerably in numbers, armament, training, and competence; but, most important, seldom could their full complement, be used as a striking force. Both individually and collectively, however, they were first-rate troops, dedicated, resourceful, and determined. They had fought over the country, knew the possibilities of the terrain, and could react swiftly and effectively. Although the Haganah had suffered serious losses during the undeclared war, the atmosphere of the equalitarian elite had not been diluted.

Although Ben-Gurion had command problems in May, Arab difficulties were catastrophic. The final Arab invasion plans had been completed at the headquarters of Iraqi General Taha Hashemi in Damascus and accepted by the Arab League Political Committee. Iraqi General Nur ad-Din Mahmoud was to be invested with the title Commander of the Regular and Irregular Forces for the Saving of Palestine. He would direct a coordinated attack by the armies of Egypt, Transjordan, Iraq, Syria, and Lebanon, geared to seize the city of Haifa by a combination of a northern pincers and a southern blocking maneuver. The Lebanese army would move south along the coast. The Syrians would move into central Palestine to link up, at Afuleh, with an Iraqi army and the Arab Legion moving north. A second Iraqi army would move into Palestine from Haharayim and advance toward Afuleh. The Egyptian army, advancing on Tel Aviv from the south, would divert Jewish forces from the pincers closing on Haifa. This plan, with Haifa, Mediterranean outlet for the oil pipelines, as the keystone, had obvious advantages for Syria and Iraq and at the same time would allow the Egyptians to occupy much of the south. Militarily it was a sound plan, based on the maximum use of both terrain and available forces, but no Arab state was about to judge any joint plan on a tactical basis. To complicate matters, neither the Syrian nor the Egyptian cabinet had as yet composed itself for war. General Taha Hashemi had been forced to ignore this unpleasant fact and to anticipate their reluctant consent. More serious was the attitude of King Abdullah ibn-Husein of Transjordan, whose Arab Legion would bear the brunt of the invasion.

On May 13 Abdullah made his position abundantly clear. He informed the League's Political Committee that, not only did he want to be supreme commander but also he wanted sweeping changes in the invasion plans drawn up by the Iraqis. Abdullah was not interested in Haifa or pincers movements. He wanted Jerusalem: The their armies would be chopped up. Not to act at all would be to give the Jewish settlements in the Jordan Valley; the Legion would seize Jerusalem. Instead of an elegant pincers movement on Afuleh, the Syrian-Iraqi forces would make a frontal assault on a well-defended Jewish district. Instead of a free-wheeling Legion strike, General John Bagot Glubb of the Legion would have to take Jerusalem by direct attack. It was obvious to all the Arab states that Abdullah was not interested in overall military success or in their own aspirations but only in his ambition to be King of Jerusalem. Equally obvious was the fact that they could not prevent him. Acting independently, their armies would be chopped up. Not to act at all would be to give Abdullah a free hand to annex peacefully what he wanted. The nerve center of the Arab world, in Damascus, was stricken by panic, as rival leaders sought an alternative. President Kuwatly of Syria telephoned Abdullah immediately and insisted that the Syrian army could not switch objectives and still be effective. Abdullah did not seem concerned. Reluctantly, Kuwatly agreed to order the Syrians south to Samakh. The Iraqis would cooperate. Abdullah could be commander. The Iraqis and Syrians did not want to be maneuvered out of the invasion altogether.

No doubt Abdullah would have preferred to act unilaterally, avoiding not only an Arab-Israeli war but even any war at all. In November he had revealed to representatives of the Jewish Agency his intention of annexing the Arab areas of Palestine. The Jews had regarded such a move as no business of the Agency. Then the undeclared war forced Abdullah's hand. On May 10 he made a last-ditch effort to find a compromise with the Jews. Golda Meir, disguised as an Arab woman, and Ezra Danin had met with Abdullah in Amman to explore the last, fragile possibilities. Abdullah explained that his unilateral annexation would no longer do, that now the entire Arab world had become deeply involved. "I was then alone but now I am one among five. I have no alternative and I cannot act otherwise."[6] In other words, unless the Jewish Agency accepted a one-year moratorium on establishing the Jewish state, the Legion would invade. Abdullah suggested an Arab-Jewish state under his crown.

Mrs. Meir and Danin, who had known of his proposals in advance, had come not to bargain over the existence of Israel but rather to keep open the lines of communication for the future. The conversations were aimed not so much at preventing a war both sides now accepted as inevitable as at preparing for the subsequent peace. As always cordial, charming, and infinitely polite, Abdullah openly indicated that he had no desire for war but that events had forced his hand:

> I am very sorry. I deplore the coming bloodshed and destruction. Let us hope we shall meet again and will not sever our relations. If you find it necessary to meet me during the actual fighting, do not hesitate and come to see me. I shall always be glad to have such a meeting.[7]

If the Arab volunteers had done nothing more, they had provoked the Jews to carry out Dalet. This operation in turn had created such hysteria and humiliation in the Arab world that a joint invasion had become inevitable, in order to prevent a Transjordanian coup. Reluctantly, Abdullah discarded his hopes for annexation without war, but he still had no intention of waging a jihad. The Legion would fight a limited campaign to achieve Abdullah's ambitions.

That the Legion would fight was accepted by everyone in the Arab world. That Syria and Iraq would be dragged along as auxiliaries no one had realized until the last minute. In Egypt the Cabinet was desperately trying to evade a similar fate. The Egyptian army command, in a rare instance of self-analysis, revealed that Egypt was incapable of fighting a modern war or, in fact, any war. Early in May Minister of Defense General Haidar refused even to consider intervention. "We shall never even contemplate entering an official war. We are not mad. We shall allow our men and officers to volunteer for service in Palestine, and we shall give them weapons, but no more."[8]

Prime Minister Mahmud Fahmi Nokrashy's cabinet was fully united behind Haidar's view. No military preparations had been made. The Egyptian army in Sinai remained on a peace footing, trained if at all for barracks drill and ceremonial parades. Then King Faruk independently decided that his prestige demanded Egyptian participation. Faruk knew or cared nothing about military "matters" but a great deal about his image and competition with his Arab rivals. He informed Nokrashy of his intentions. On May 12, only three days before the end of the British Mandate, Nokrashy undertook to summon the parliament to a secret session to authorize intervention. Nokrashy was unaware that, even before he himself had been told, Faruk had already ordered the invasion. When General Muawi, commander of the Egyptian army in Sinai, rushed to Cairo to insist that his forces were not fit for battle, Nokrashy, filled with his own doubts, had to reassure him that there would not be a real war, that there would be little fighting, that the United Nations would intervene, that the Egyptians were making a gesture, not a campaign. Muawi had no alternative but to march. "We have our orders. Our duty is to carry them out, not to question them."[9] The fact is that every Egyptian leader except Faruk did question them. On the other hand, the Egyptian population, so long accustomed to sugar coating that they were unaware of the pills underneath, assumed that the army would sweep victoriously through Palestine.

The Egyptian invasion force, the army "unready to fight," numbered only 10,000 men and was divided into three battalions supported by the British-trained and -equipped air force. Actually, the Egyptians were better armed than General Haidar had indicated. In contrast to the Israelis, Muawi and his deputy, Colonel Mohammed Neguib, had armor, artillery, and command of the air. What they did not have was any tactical experience or officers and men familiar with the nature of war. The hierarchy of the Egyptian army was lazy, occasionally corrupt, dedicated to formalities and prestige. Many officers of all grades were inept, trained on blackboards and not on terrain. Logistics were weak, and liaison among artillery, armor, infantry, and air was faulty at best. The private soldiers, poorly trained, had little capacity to act independently or to endure unexpected reverses. They, like many of their officers, were gripped by emotional enthusiasm for a campaign that they did not know how to fight.

Much the same could be said of the armies of Syria, Iraq, and Lebanon. Both Syria and Iraq intended to commit forces of 3,000 men each, supported by air, armor, and artillery. The Iraqis had the better equipment but also long lines of communication and supply to maintain. The Syrians, without a historical British connection, had to depend upon former French military stocks. The Lebanese planned vaguely to move in a 1,000-man force to cooperate with stagglers from the Arab Liberation Army in Galilee, but Beirut's army was more a mobile police force or a civil guard than a fighting force. In addition, there were still several thousand volunteers scattered about Arab Palestine and in the border areas, but most of them were a liability, except on garrison duty. Only Abdullah's Arab Legion of 4,500 well-trained and highly motivated men could be considered a first-rate force. The Legion was balanced, well-officered (many officers had been seconded from the British army), and most important, imbued with a professional esprit de corps. General John Bagot Glubb worried about the lack of ammunition and reserves but not about the Legion's fighting ability. The grand total of the Arab invasion forces came to about 25,000 men. The long-heralded invasion was hardly going to be a massive holy war waged by 40 million Arabs.

Few in the Arab world knew or cared. The vast majority of the civilians and regular soldiers assumed that the united Arab armies would face a Jewish civilian rabble. As Arab jounalists and orators had long promised, the Jews would be swept into the sea, for the Arab cause was just and the armies determined. Within a few days the Arabs would be in Haifa, Tel Aviv, and Jerusalem. Together with this magnificent overconfidence, however, there existed in some significant quarters the deepest pessimism. Haidar and Muawi had no illusions about sweeping north to Tel Aviv in a few hours. General Glubb was deeply concerned about Abdullah's order to seize Jerusalem, for the Legion could not afford the heavy casualties that city fighting might entail. The pessimism of the Arab generals was based mainly on knowledge of their own weakness and a fantastic overestimation of Israeli strength. Glubb assumed, for example, that the Israelis had 65,000 well-armed troops, including 20,000 men who had served in the Polish and Russian armies. Other Arab sources reported that the Jews had 80,000–100,000 troops under arms, as well as stocks of tanks and airplanes. A persistant rumor floating about the Arab capitals was that the Jews had built an atomic bomb. The Arabs were to invade Palestine with the masses and the soldiers expecting an immediate victory and most of the generals and prime ministers hoping only to avoid disaster.

The strategic appreciations of both the Jews and Arabs in May

1948 were thus considerably out of line with the realities. There was neither a coordinated, slick, modern Arab invasion force of five professional armies nor a great, well-armed Haganah. Despite all the subsequent myth making on both sides, the war was fought between two very small armies of nearly equal size, each with counterbalancing strategic and tactical assets. The Arabs were far better equipped. The Israelis had nothing except their ingenuity to match the Arabs' tanks, guns, and planes, however ineptly used. The Arabs, furthermore, could move through the friendly Arab areas and strike when and where they pleased. On their part, the Israelis had all the tangible and intangible assets for defense. In retrospect it is clear that the Arabs simply did not have sufficient men to attack the fiercely defended Israeli strong points. Their equipment could not fully compensate for poor training and Israeli determination. For a solid victory their only real hope would have been a failure of nerve on the part of the Israelis after some initial reverses. The response of the Yishuv during the undeclared war made this hope a faint one at best. On May 15, whatever the fears of Ben-Gurion in the Red House in Tel Aviv, the best the Arabs could hope for was to punish the Jews with air power and artillery, to secure certain local gains, and to strain, perhaps severely, the resources of Israel.

The four-week war was not, then, a struggle between David and Goliath but a series of disorganized clashes between gravely understrength units, seldom of even regimental size. There were no front lines in the conventional sense; there were only Arab and Jewish areas dominated by key roads or hilltops. Around the vital kibbutzim or police fortresses, the limited resources of both sides came together in engagements that seldom could last more than a few days without bleeding away the attacker's strength. There were too many targets and too many demands to allow much switching about of units. Without reserves or hope of reinforcements, all that either side could do was to hit and hope. The result was dozens of independent battles seemingly without pattern or plan. Beside these chaotic campaigns, the constant possibility of international intervention constantly hampered planning. Neither side could be certain of the responses of the major powers, particularly Great Britain, or of the intentions of the United Nations. The war had to be fought with one eye on the fragmentary fronts and the other on the quarreling diplomats. Increasingly, it became clear that the United Nations might force an imposed truce, which complicated tactical decisions by creating an uncertain time limit to the war. Few conflicts have been as limited by minimal military resources, by the threat of international interference, by diplomatic considerations, by general confusion and uncertainty.

Despite the obstacles, real and imagined, the Arabs did invade. The war, a real war, in spite of its pocket size, began at 5:00 on the morning of May 15, when three Egyptian Spitfires swept in from the sea unspotted by the almost nonexistent Tel Aviv air-defense system. The flight swung around and made one bombing run over the airfield at about 1,000 feet. Later three more Spitfires flew low over the city. A single Israeli machine gunner on the roof of the power station near the airport opened fire and miraculously brought down an Egyptian plane. The other two flew on and disappeared over the Mediterranean. The next day the Egyptians came back, and there were Iraqi airstrikes in the north. The Legion was reported moving into the Jerusalem area, the Iraqis and Syrians were active on the northeast border, the Lebanese were probing central Galilee, and the Egyptians were moving north. From Tel Aviv the Arabs appeared to be attacking in the north and south to divert the Israelis while the Legion struck a decisive blow in the center. Actually, the Arabs were not at all sure what they were doing. Abdullah's veto of the invasion plan had thrown the entire Arab war effort out of gear. The Arab Liberation Army had simply pulled back from its strategic positions in central Palestine and Jerusalem. Glubb later claimed that the confusion was so great that the Israelis could have walked into much of Arab Palestine. Galili and Yadin, of course, simply did not have the troops with which to challenge the Arabs. The Israelis could only wait to react to the main Arab threat.

The battles in each area were largely fought independently of the war elsewhere. The Israelis fought that way because they lacked mobile reserves and the Arabs because of their internal differences. In the North, the Israeli High Command felt more secure than in any other areas. Moshe Montag's 1st Haganah Brigade, the Golani; Yigal Alon's Palmach Yiftach Brigade; and Moshe Carmel's 2nd Haganah Brigade, the Carmeli, were perhaps the best Israeli troops available; furthermore, the Arab invasion forces in the North were considered less dangerous than the Arab Legion or the Egyptian army. The Israelis had to defend a great U-shaped territory facing north. One leg, on the coast, had been occupied during the first days of the war, and the Lebanese showed no interest in moving into it. The second, secured in the undeclared war and dotted with some of the oldest kibbutzim, ran along the Syrian-Jordan border. Between the two legs lay central Galilee, protected from Jewish invasion only by the scattered Arab volunteers. To achieve a victory in the North, the Arabs would have to break through the eastern leg. To prevent the Lebanese from filtering down into central Galilee and hitting the settlements from the rear or cutting the base of the U, Moshe Carmel intended to seal off the Lebanese frontier at the Malkieh Gate.

The Arabs saw the situation in the north much as the Israelis did. The Syrians intended to strike across the Jordan River south of the Sea of Galilee and through the rich Jewish settlements in the Judean Valley, in order to cut the eastern leg at the base. The Iraqi army would move into Palestine farther south, drive through the Israeli border defenses, and turn north into the Arab-triangle area of central Palestine: Jenin-Tulkarm-Nablus. If all went well, the Syrians would unite there in the Afuleh area with the Iraqis and the Lebanese and the volunteers moving south; they would then mass for the final plunge toward the coast and Haifa.[10] Liaison among the Arab forces was vague; for example, there was no tactical communication between the Syrian attack on Samakh at the Sea of Galilee and the Iraqi attack at Gesher six miles to the south. The Lebanese proved timid and the volunteers useless. From the first, in all sectors, things did not go as anticipated.

Along the Lebanese border, the Yiftach Brigade had begun operations three days before the formal invasion to seal off the Malkieh Gate by capturing the towns of Malkieh and Kadesh and the Nebi Yusha police fortress to the south. Alon decided to bypass Nebi Yusha and sent Dan Laner with the 1st Palmach Battalion to invest the two towns from the rear, while the 3rd Palmach Battalion raided the Lebanese frontier area.[11] Laner captured the two towns as planned but ran directly into the Lebanese and volunteer invasion force of about 3,000 troops, backed up with artillery and armor. He extracted his men only after forty-eight hours of hard fighting. Outnumbered six to one, short of food and water, lightly armed and without artillery support, Laner's battalion fought a first-rate withdrawal action despite heavy casualties. The Lebanese had reopened the Malkieh Gate but were reluctant to enter. The 3rd Palmach Battalion raid across the border on May 15-16 had added to Lebanese uncertainty. Laner's withdrawal had inflicted heavy losses. The next night the Israelis captured Nebi Yusha after the Lebanese, under attack by Piper Cubs drooping incendiary bombs, fled north. The Lebanese in Malkieh dug in to await a frontal assault. Instead Alon sent an armored column, driving with dim lights, from the Marara settlement across the Lebanese frontier and then inside the boundary toward the rear of Malkieh. Lebanese attention was diverted by a feint near Nebi Yusha, a maneuver intended to make more noise than progress. After ten miles the Israeli column ran into the Arab reinforcements moving up toward the border. The Israelis knocked out two armored cars and four troop trucks. The Arab column disintegrated. The first units of the Yiftach Brigade swept into Malkieh from the north, and the confused and demoralized Lebanese hurriedly withdrew. The Lebanese frontier had been sealed and the U transformed into a hollow square. Not until June 6, after weeks of quiet and the gradual withdrawal of the Israeli garrisons, did the Arabs try again. Then, a mixed force of Syrians, Lebanese, and Arab Liberation Army volunteers moved south. Only the Lebanese pushed the attack and secured the village of Kadesh, opening a way into Galilee. The Liberation Army took the opportunity to filter down into central Galilee.

While the Yiftach Brigade struggled to seal off Galilee, the Israelis in the eastern leg of the U struggled against a far more serious Syrian challenge than they had anticipated. On the night of May 15 the Syrians moved a long column of trucks, a few tanks, and some artillery down along the eastern shore of the Sea of Galilee toward the Jordan. Arab planes strafed the Jordan Valley settlements. The area of the Syrian attack contained some of the most famous Jewish settlements in Palestine, scattered on both sides of the Jordan River to Samakh at the sea's southern tip. Vehicle headlights remained fully on, for apparently the Syrians believed that surprise would be unnecessary. Well before dawn on May 16 the Syrians opened an artillery bombardment on Ein Gev, the only Israeli settlement on the eastern shore of the lake, and on Masada and Sha'ar Hagolan east of the Jordan. Arab planes strafed the Jordan Valley settlements. The area of the Syrian attack contained some of the most famous Jewish settlements in Palestine, scattered on both sides of the Jordan River to the east and west of the Samakh–Naharayim highway. Ein Gev, on the far shore of Galilee, and Masada and Sha'ar Hagolan, on the eastern shore of the Jordan River, were tempting targets, almost completely isolated from the other Jordan Valley kibbutzim. On the western shore were the two Kinnerets and the two Deganias, four Zionist showplaces, all to the west of the road from Samakh to Naharayim. Not only were the kibbutzim rich prizes in themselves, but also, once they had been seized, the way into central Galilee would be open. Apparently the Syrians planned to move across the Jordan River and to concentrate their efforts on the key police fortress at Samakh. Once this fortress had been taken, the Syrian armor could sweep on up the western shore of the lake. The kibbutzim had nothing much with which to stop the Syrian armored cars and French Renault tanks. When the Degania-Kinneret bloc had fallen, the other isolated settlements could be picked off while the main Syrian thrust moved into Galilee.

The major Syrian attack, preceded by an artillery bombardment, began on May 16. Syrian infantry moved into a collection of buildings just south of Samakh, but Israeli reinforcements arrived in time to prevent the enemy from breaching the town's perimeter defenses in one continuous thrust. In the meantime, a second Syrian column hit Sha'ar Hagolan and Masada to secure the force's rear. Lightly defended with only one recently acquired 20-millimeter gun, the Israelis were hard-pressed. Losses were heavy, but the Syrians were forced to pull back from the fences and retrench. The Israelis had no reinforcements to bring up. They ran endless circles of truck convoys, created "tank parks" by running all the settlement tractors at once, and harassed the Syrians with motor-launch raids. The Syrians were not greatly impressed. On May 18 they launched the decisive attack on Samakh. Thirty armored vehicles moved slowly forward in a wide arc, followed by infantry. Well-placed shells kept down Israeli fire. With no antitank weapons the Israelis did not stand much of a chance. The Syrians broke into the police station but only after all forty-two defenders had been killed. The armored cars were in the streets before all the Israelis could get out of the town. Those who did escape stumbled under heavy fire to the nearest settlements. Samakh was in Syrian hands. That same night Masada and Sha'ar Hagolan had to be evacuated. Syrian artillery and armor continued to shell the remaining kibbutzim during the night. Shock and gloom settled over both eastern Galilee and Tel Aviv. The Syrians were proving to be a more serious threat than anyone had assumed.

If the Syrians were successful in smashing into the Degania-Kinneret bloc on May 19, the whole northeast sector might collapse, but by May 19 nearly every Israeli sector had in fact reached a crisis. Every brigade, except the Carmeli in western Galilee, which occupied an ostensibly Arab area, was heavily engaged, and each commander feared that without reinforcements his sector would collapse. Ben-Gurion could not help Alon, not even with encouraging words: "There are not enough guns, not enough planes; men are lacking on all fronts. The situation is very severe in the Negev, is difficult in Jerusalem, in Upper Galilee. The whole country is a front line. We cannot send reinforcements."[12] Ben-Gurion did send the brilliant and experienced Moshe Dayan with orders to hold Dagania at all cost. Dayan brought along two elderly artillery pieces, 65-millimeter guns, and a homemade flamethrower. The major antitank weapon would have to be Molotov cocktails thrown at a range of a few yards. As Yigal Yadin noted, "a grievous risk, but it is the only way."[13] Meanwhile, on the night of May 18 the Israelis carried out a raid on a large supply dump across the Jordan River from Mishmar Hayarden. The resulting chain explosion could be heard for miles, and Alon hoped that it would delay any Syrian activity north of the lake.* The prospects for the Dagania-Kinneret area still remained dim.

At 4:30 on the morning of May 20 the Syrians began their attack on Degania A and Degania B. Once again the Syrians depended on their armor to win the day. The Renault tanks and the armored cars moved up to plaster Dagania A, but the infantry hung back. The Israelis were shelled out of their fortifications but were able to take

---

* A curious side advantage came to the Israelis as a result of the monster explosion. The Heibi Arabs, a small Bedouin tribe on the west bank of the Jordan, were decidedly impressed and came over to the Israelis. They formed the Pal-Heib Company, an exotic group led by a veteran member of the Palmach in full Bedouin garb, riding a white stallion and followed by a mounted bodyguard.

cover in the communications trenches. The Syrian infantry, depending heavily on armor, retreated from the continuing Israeli fire. There were no Israeli mines or antitank weapons, and the Syrian armor broke through the outer fence and moved in toward the inner fence. One armored car was disabled by a 20-millimeter gun, and finally a tank was stopped when a Molotov cocktail hit its caterpillar tread. One tank broke the final fence and rumbled along the edge of a slit trench inside the settlement. Two Molotov cocktails smashed against it, and the tank burst into flames.[14] The Syrian armor milled around uncertainly and then began to pull out. The infantry still had not come up to support it. The loss of six vehicles had disheartened the hesitant infantry and doomed the attack.

After this failure the Syrians moved on to Degania B. Once again the armor battered the visible bunkers and pillboxes, forcing the Israelis into slit trenches. This time, however, the Syrian infantry remained right behind the armor. One assault faltered within thirty yards of the trenches. A second was repulsed by accurate machine-gun fire directed at the slits of the armored cars. As the Syrians withdrew, Dayan's two artillery pieces suddenly opened fire. The Syrians broke off the attack. That night they withdrew from Samakh, and four days later they razed Masada and Sha'ar Hagolan. Once their attack on the Deganias had failed, however, the Syrians seemed uncertain what to do next. The weight of iron from their armor and artillery had proved insufficient, and the poorly trained infantry showed no willingness to dash into the heavy Israeli fire. Rather than sit in Samakh, the Syrians decided to pull out and try elsewhere, this time without any grandiose hopes of pushing into Galilee.

While the Syrians reorganized their forces, time began to run out; a United Nations truce appeared imminent. The Syrians decided to seek tangible local advantage by seizing a few wedges in the area of the vital headwaters of the Jordan. The British had carefully excluded the Syrians from contact with the Jordan River and the Sea of Galilee when they had arranged the boundaries of the Mandate, but a victory or two might strengthen the long-standing Syrian claim and would certainly add to Syrian prestige and position at any future bargaining table. On June 7 the Syrians launched a carefully planned and this time secretly prepared assault across the Jordan at the settlement of Mishmar Hayarden, defended by the newly created Oded Brigade. The first attack failed, and the Oded Brigade asked for reinforcements. On June 10 before the Carmeli Brigade could be moved into position, the Syrians captured all three fords at Mishmar Hayarden and dug in bridgeheads north and south of the settlement. By noon Mishmar Hayarden had been invested on all sides. Communication with the Israeli command broke down. The defense was cut up, and the last pockets of resistance were taken late in the afternoon. Similar assaults on Ramat Naphtali at the western end of the finger and Ein Gev on the eastern shore failed, although at Ein Gev the Syrians actually broke into the settlement before being forced to withdraw. Despite a United Nations truce, supposedly effective on the morning of June 11, the Syrians continued to press their local attacks in the area [until the afternoon of June 12] but without much success. At least, however, Damascus could claim that some advantage had been gained in its invasion for its forces occupied the Mishmar Hayarden bridgehead in an area granted to Israel under the partition plan. The Israelis found the loss of Mishmar Hayarden distressing, but it did not threaten the security of Israel. Eastern Galilee was safe, with only a single small bridgehead in Syrian hands.

Events in the third sector of the North, the Iraqi front, had developed similarly to those at Samakha: a hopeful Arab blitz, a sullen withdrawal, and a shift of emphasis to local targets. Another phase was added, however, for the Israelis managed to organize a substantial counterattack. On May 15 the Iraqi army crossed the Jordan River about six miles south of the Syrian striking force. The Iraqis, with 3,000 troops and light armor, planned a two-pronged assault on Gesher from the north and south, timed to coincide with their occupation of the old crusader fortress of Belvoir on the heights of nearby Kaukat al Hawa. The Israelis had anticipated the Arab maneuver and had moved troops into Belvoir. When the Arabs arrived on May 16, they sat down to breakfast halfway up the 1,200-foot rise. They also sat down in the middle of an Israeli ambush. The Iraqis fled down the hill, leaving dozens of dead and considerable equipment behind them.

At Gesher they fared somewhat better. On May 16 their heavy frontal assault was driven back after having mauled the Israelis. The next day the Arabs hit again with armor-and-infantry attacks from north and south. This time the Iraqi infantry reached the walls of the

Gesher police fortress and blew open the main gate. Following an armored car, the infantry rushed into the courtyard, only to be raked with heavy fire. The armored car, hit by a Molotov cocktail, blew up. The Iraqis had to withdraw to their two bridgeheads. On May 22 the Israelis moved to break the stalemate by sending down the two 65-millimeter artillery pieces from the Dagania defense. Had there been spotters in the Belvoir fortress, and had the guns been equipped with sights, the artillery fire could have been extremely accurate. Instead the Israelis were extremely lucky, which is nearly as good. One of the first shells hit an Iraqi gasoline truck, which produced a spectacular explosion. On May 23 the Iraqis withdrew across the Jordan. As with the Syrians, the first blitz attack had not come off.

Glubb and Abdullah were most anxious for the Iraqis to move into the Arab-triangle area, in order to release the Legion forces for the Jerusalem sector. With the attack at Gesher stalled, the Iraqi high command agreed to Glubb's request and ordered its expeditionary force to cross the Jordan farther south, where there were no Jewish settlements. On May 24 the Iraqis arrived in Nablus. Almost immediately, an urgent plea arrived from the Legion front. The Israelis had launched a heavy attack near Latrun, and Glubb wanted the Iraqis to relieve some of the pressure on the central front. During the next three days the Iraqis carried out a series of limited probing patrols toward the Mediterranean. On May 28 they captured Geulim near Tulkarm and attacked Kfar Javits. On May 29, they attacked Kfar Jonah and Ein Vered, both close to the road from Tulkarm to Natanya on the coast. These hesitant attacks failed, and the Alexandroni Brigade recaptured Geulim and repelled a series of Iraqi counterattacks. On May 30 the Iraqis attacked farther south and captured the important Rosh Haayin pumping station. None of these attacks was a major operation, none drew off Israelis from the central front, but Iraqi aggressiveness worried the Israelis. With interior lines of communications inside the triangle area, a variety of offensive possibilities was open to the Iraqi high command. Hard-pressed as they were, the Israelis decided to respond.

Carmel would go over to the offensive in the triangle area and would attack Jenin in the area south of Afuleh. This action would limit the freedom of the Iraqis in the triangle, forcing them to fight on ground chosen by Carmel instead of surprising the Israelis elsewhere.

Unfortunately for the Israelis, Carmel's intelligence was confused about the location and strength of the Arab troops; furthermore, the operation was planned with haste and without sufficient coordination. Although most of the Israeli reactions to Arab advances were make-do operations, the attack on Jenin suffered more than most from vagueness of purpose. Stage one was to be a Golani Brigade offensive against the ancient strongholds of Megiddo and Lajun in the Gilboa Hills to protect the flank of the main thrust. Once Lajun and Megiddo had fallen, the Carmeli Brigade would move southeast from Afuleh, clear the rest of the Gilboa Hills, and move on to Jenin. The Alexandroni Brigade was to create a diversion by attacking the triangle from the west and simultaneously recapturing Rosh Haayin. The Carmeli Brigade commanders, rushing to prepare their own attack, remained uncertain of the scope of the Alexandroni operation. Their own attack would be the largest Israeli offensive in the northern sector. There would even be limited air and artillery support. Still, it was a shoestring affair, uncoordinated with the Alexandroni attack, and directed against the core of Arab Palestine. Tel Aviv was convinced, however, that the Arabs could no longer be allowed freedom of movement within the triangle—an offensive, even one haphazardly prepared, was essential.

The first stage, carried out by the Golani Brigade, was delayed for twenty-four hours by a breakdown in supplies, but the Israelis captured Megiddo on the night of May 30. Then began a mad dash to reach Lajun before the Iraqis did. Israeli armor, consisting of a captured Renault tank and some homemade armor-plated trucks, rushed into Lajun and overpowered the small Arab garrison before the Iraqi armored cars could arrive. All day on May 31 the Iraqis counterattacked unsuccessfully. With Megiddo and Lajun secure, the Carmeli Brigade could begin its assault on Jenin, stage two. All went smoothly. The Gilboa Hills were cleared with little resistance from the local Arabs. Makleff, leading the Carmeli's attack, moved his men down either side of the road to Jenin. By June 3 three battalions had reached the hills overlooking Jenin from both sides and the rear. At that point the fall of Jenin seemed assured, but before Makleff could make his move, unexpected Iraqi reinforcements began moving north. On June 4 a disturbing report reached the Haganah command from the Carmeli Brigade:

The attack on Jenin develops according to plan. Already we occupy the strongholds on either side of the road dominating the city. Our forces also hold the hills to the north of the city. Enemy resist severely with all arms, including guns. The battle continues. It is imperative that a diversionary attack be undertaken by Alexandroni, to prevent reinforcements from being sent to this sector.[15]

By noon the next day an Iraqi reinforcement column was reported moving north. Arab artillery and mortar fire increased. Iraqi planes strafed the front lines. A shell landed on the forward Israeli headquarters, killing all the officers. Communications with the attack commander and the advance points became sporadic. Some withdrawal began, on the basis of misunderstood orders. Soon the entire Israeli operation teetered on the edge of failure. Casualties had been heavy during the unordered and unplanned retreat. Heat and lack of water were reducing the offensive capacity of the remaining troops. The whole affair, which had begun so hopefully, seemed doomed.

In order to rectify the situation, Makleff decided to send a reserve "armored" column straight into Jenin. The column, four civilian buses each carrying an infantry platoon, simply drove into the city unmolested. Jenin was empty. The Iraqi troops were concentrating on capturing the heights around the town—once they had succeeded, they would look right down upon Makleff's four platoons. Makleff believed that the Jenin operation could not succeed unless the Alexandroni Brigade was preparing to launch a full-scale offensive against the triangle. At 11:00 that night he revealed his difficulties to Tel Aviv:

> It is impossible to hold Jenin as a lone wedge in the triangle. All enemy forces there will be hurled against it. If you plan to attack Tulkarm and to capture it soon, it would seem to me that we ought to hold Jenin at any price. However, if there is no intention to attack the triangle at any other point, it may be preferable to abandon Jenin before we suffer additional casualties.[16]

In less than an hour word came that no attack on Tulkarm would be forthcoming. At midnight the Israelis began withdrawing, and before dawn the Iraqis were in Jenin. Makleff had been asked to bite off more than he could chew. There had been too many unexpected

Iraqis and no real help from the Alexandroni; probably none had been planned. In the last days before the truce, the Israelis on the northern front settled down to a series of limited probes to keep the Iraqis off balance.

In the northern sector the four-week war had proved a greater trial than Tel Aviv had anticipated, but the eventual results had been satisfactory. In many cases the margin had seemed very, very narrow—a Molotov cocktail at Degania or the "lucky" artillery shell at Gesher. The North, however, had been held, and at Jenin the Haganah had even gone over to the offensive. As for the Arabs, the popular hope for a mad dash to the coast had proved to be illusory. There had been some compensations in the local successes scored by the Syrians and Lebanese in the last days before the truce and the successful Iraqi defense at Jenin. Both the Arabs and the Israelis were exhausted by the futile attacks and cliff-hanging defenses. Obviously, however, a second round would be forthcoming in the North. There were four Arab armies in various stages of disarray still inside northern Palestine. If the governments in Damascus, Baghdad, and Beirut could act swiftly, the fragile Israeli margin of safety might still be eroded.

The military situation in the South, on the Egyptian front, had been equally critical for Israel, but the nature of the crisis was different. Much of south Palestine was barren desert, crossed only by occasional transient Bedouins. Nearly three-quarters of the Negev, the area south of Beersheba, was without roads or permanent residents, either Arab or Jewish. Military operations or even nominal occupation in the far south was almost impossible, so that most of the fighting was in the northern areas, where the scattered Jewish kibbutzim were in a position to restrict Egyptian motor traffic along the main arterial roads. The key objectives of both sides remained the roads and trails. Control of the highways brought with it control of the South. Even if the Egyptians penetrated far to the north, to the suburbs of Tel Aviv, they could not maintain their front without control of the roads. The Egyptian invasion thus proceeded cautiously, forgoing a sudden dash for Tel Aviv in favor of a slow, staged advance. The Egyptian front commander, Major General Muawi's second-in-command, Colonel Neguib, would lead the main column along the coast road from the Egyptian base at El 'Arîsh north through Gaza and Isdud toward Tel Aviv. For all but the last twenty miles, the Egyptians would be moving through Arab areas, dotted with occasional kibbutzim. A second smaller force under Lieutenant General Abdal-Aziz would advance north east on the inland road to Beersheba, through the Hebron hills, and would link up with the Arab Legion south of Jerusalem. Both Muawi and Neguib were reluctant dragons, doubting their army's capacity and impressed by the recent Israeli successes. On May 10, five days before the Arabs invasion, the Muslim Brotherhood's irregulars had been thrown back from the key settlement of Kfar Darom, despite numerical superiority and artillery support. Muawi decided that he would not rush north until Kfar Darom had been reduced, a more reasonable goal than a blitz up the coast.

The Israelis anticipated just this kind of armored drive north, a drive that they felt incapable of stopping. The Givati Brigade under Shimon Avidan had been in action for months, replacements were poorly trained, and the five battalions were scattered in seventeen defensive positions. Avidan had no fluid reserve, no prospect of reinforcements, no armor, and no air support. The Hanegev Brigade under Nahum Sarig was based farther to the south in the Negev under orders to defend the isolated kibbutzim. Sarig had little hope of taking offensive action to harass the Egyptian inland advance, and cooperation with the Givati Brigade would have been difficult. Avidan knew he would have to depend on the 1,800 "bayonets" of the 4,800-man Givati Brigade to halt the Egyptian coastal advance without aid from Sarig in the south or from Tel Aviv, where Ben-Gal's Kiryati Brigade had fewer than 1,000 men. Actually, Avidan's position was not as perilous as he assumed. There was almost a numerical parity between his forces and the Egyptian column led by Neguib. Neguib had 2,500 men concentrated in the spearhead, but he assumed that the Israelis had twice that number. The Egyptians did, of course, have armor, ten tanks, and some artillery. Avidan could not match them, but the Egyptians did not know it. Avidan was thus not as badly outnumbered as he supposed, although his troops were dispersed and the Egyptians concentrated, but he was certainly outgunned.

On May 15 the Egyptians cautiously opened their attacks on Kfar Daron and Nirim. The assault on Nirim collapsed the moment the

Egyptian armor ran into an Israeli ruse, signs announcing, in English: "Caution! Mines!" The Egyptians were content to devastate the settlement with an artillery bombardment the next day. At Kfar Darom the Egyptian armor pulled back under Israeli fire and left the infantry in the open. Instead of renewing the attack, the Egyptians again limited themselves to an artillery bombardment. Vague grumblings could be heard from the junior officers, but Muawi decided to bypass the two settlements and to move directly north; he could not, however, move very far. The next Israeli settlement, Yad Mordechai, was situated right on the highway north of Gaza. The Egyptians could not bypass it without losing road contact with their base at El 'Arîsh.

The Egyptians spent most of the morning of May 19 bombarding a pillbox south of Yad Mordechai. After three hours the Israelis pulled back. The Egyptians tried to penetrate at their rear but failed. The next day the Egyptians tried four times to break the Israeli perimeter without success. Egyptian morale was shaken. Inside Yad Mordechai the Israelis were equally shaken. Despite the arrival of reinforcements on the night of May 20, the future appeared bleak. Ammunition and supplies were short, and still worse the wounded were without medical assistance. For two days the Egyptians shelled the settlement regularly. By May 22 the reports reaching Tel Aviv from Yad Mordechai were desperate.

> The men's morale is sinking; they approach exhaustion. There is fear of another Kfar Etzion. The settlement must be reinforced or abandoned. It is vital that women and wounded be evacuated immediately. . . . The enemy shells heavily; dugouts and ditches have been destroyed. There is no room for the wounded; no water. Exhaustion . . . What does GHQ have in mind? If no help is forthcoming, we will break out tonight and evacuate. We are no longer able to defend the settlement on account of the heavy casualties and the large number of wounded.[17]

On May 23 the Egyptians attacked, and Egyptian armor penetrated the perimeter. Only the arrival of a relief unit of commandos from the Hanegev Brigade stabilized the situation. Just before dawn on May 24 the Israelis escaped through the Egyptian lines, leaving ruined Yad Mordechai empty.

Despite their considerable losses, the Egyptian commanders regarded Yad Mordechai as a tactical victory, for the coastal road had been cleared. In Cairo the newspapers were filled with reports of Egyptian victories and the capture of Gaza, Beersheba, and Hebron, all Arab-held cities to begin with. Army officers and men in Egypt were less elated, for there were whispers of "a political campaign,"[18] with the soldiers to be sacrificed for the politicians' ambitions. Everyone could see that there had been no proper preparations, no real plans except those that the Cairo papers had published before the army marched, no decent medical arrangements, not even regular food supplies. Many of the commanders proved less than competent in their first real war. Still, by the end of May Neguib's column had moved up the coast to occupy Isdud. The inland column had a walk-on part and linked up with the Arab Legion on May 22. The connecting roads between Majdal on the coast and Hebron had been occupied and a series of strong points constructed to dominate the main highway. In effect, the Egyptians had already secured King Faruk's basic objectives: control of the south and a counter balance to Abdullah's Legion.

The five days gained at Yad Mordechai allowed the Israelis to concentrate most of the Givati Brigade in a line across the coastal highway. Until May 30 these troops had been in action on the central front, but Israeli scouts had reported a seemingly endless stream of tanks, trucks, and armored cars, perhaps 1,500 vehicles, in the Egyptian column moving north. On May 29 the Egyptian column passed through Ashdod and stopped at the south end of the Ashdod Bridge two miles north of the city. Sappers from the Givati Brigade had blown the bridge, and Neguib now had to wait for his engineers to repair it; in any case, he was increasingly fearful of an Israeli counterattack. And, in fact, at the very moment that the vanguard of the Egyptian force drew up to the ruined bridge, the Israelis were preparing a surprise for Neguib. Mechanics were hastily assembling the first four Messerschmitt 109 fighters which had been flown into Israel crated inside a Dakota transport. Although the first sorties had been planned against the Egyptian air base at El 'Arîsh, the Israeli High Command decided to hit the long, stalled Egyptian column. The air strike came as a complete surprise to the Egyptians, although they reacted promptly, bringing down one Israeli plane and damaging another. Most important, Neguib's growing suspicions were confirmed:

Not only were there well-armed 4,000 Zionists facing him across the bridge, but also the Jews had heavy equipment to commit. The Egyptians began to dig in alongside the highway; the slow advance on the north was halted.

On the night of May 29 Israeli 65-millimeter guns began shelling the road, and Givati units carried out pinprick raids. Finally, after false starts, the long-awaited Israeli attack began at nightfall on June 2. The two-pronged operation ran into trouble. The main Israeli force walked into heavy Egyptian fire, and the second prong took too long plowing through sand dunes near the sea to be of much help. The Israelis were bitterly disappointed at their failure to nip off the vulnerable column, but unknowingly they had changed the whole nature of the Egyptian posture. Thenceforth, the Egyptians would go on the defensive.

> Although that attack was repulsed, the enemy was able to attain at least one objective: the pinning down of the Egyptian army to its positions in Ashdod. It will not be an exaggeration to state, that the Jewish attack against Ashdod was the turning point in the Egyptian-Israeli struggle, since from that moment on the Egyptian High Command was compelled to change its plans. Instead of continuing its pursuit after the Zionist gangs, the Egyptian High Command now decided to content itself with the isolation of the Negev from the rest of the country.[19]

In fact, the Egyptian High Command had never wanted to pursue the "Zionist gangs" into the mouth of a trap. The Egyptian army had not wanted to fight Faruk's war at all, but, given its positions on June 3, the commanders believed that they could hold much of the South. The Egyptians therefore concentrated on taking the key Israeli settlements dominating the network of lateral roads.

The first target was Negba, a threat to traffic on the Majdal-Bet Gubrin road. By this time, aware of the Israeli lack of antitank weapons, the Egyptians decided to depend on their armor to smash the Israeli defenses. The Egyptians sent in seven armored vehicles. One tank was hit before the settlement perimeter. Another, after crashing the fence, rolled to within fifteen feet of the Israeli defense positions before being hit by two Molotov cocktails. In flames the tank began to withdraw just as two others ran over land mines outside the fence. Suddenly a mobile Israeli jeep patrol appeared on the Egyptian flank and opened light machine-gun fire on the armor. The Egyptians broke off the attack. Four tanks and two half-tracks had been damaged, and the infantry had been unable to move close enough to Negba to be effective. The second Egyptian attack, against Nitzanim, which had been bypassed by the coastal column, proved more successful. At 6:00 the morning of June 7, after a night-long artillery barrage, the Egyptian infantry hit. It was forced back. More artillery and air strikes softened up Nitzanim. At 11:00 a second attack began, with the support of tanks, and by noon it had penetrated the settlement. Although fighting continued until 4:00 in the afternoon, when the Israelis surrendered. Nitzanim was already lost when the tanks began grinding across the trenches at noon. Before the Egyptians could continue their piecemeal elimination of the settlements in the Negev, however, the tide shifted. The Egyptians had taken too long with Negba and Nitzanim without keeping up their pressure elsewhere. The column at Isdud had been quiescent. The Egyptians had dug in along the roads and waited. The sorely pressed Israelis had been given a breathing space in which to assemble a mobile force.

The last days before the expected truce were used by the Israelis to break the Egyptian line along the Majdal–Faluja–Hebron road and also to secure positions overlooking the Ashdod column. Once again the problem was scraping together enough men to undertake a series of independent operations. On the night of June 6 an Israeli attack on Isdud failed, but Hill 69 near Nitzanim was occupied. On the night of June 9 an attack on Nitzanim from Hill 69 failed, and on the following day the Egyptians captured the hill. Operations to break through the lateral highway line were only slightly more successful, but the cross fire from the Egyptian-held Iraq-Suedan police fortress became too great, and the Israeli advance units, which had penetrated most of the outlying defenses, were compelled to withdraw. An unexpected Israeli attack on Bir Asluj by the Negev Brigade cut the El 'Auja-Beersheba road; but the Egyptian engineers, protected by a screen of infantry, opened an alternative track, bypassing Bir Asluj and frustrating the one Israeli success of the last days of the campaign in the South.

The war in the South had gone much as had the operations in the North, with the invasion forces occupying the Arab areas, failing to penetrate deeply into Israel, and then repelling counterattacks. In the South, however, the Egyptians, with their command of the highways, controlled great areas of Arab Palestine. All that Faruk could reasonably have hoped for had been secured. Abdullah had been frustrated, and Cairo was in an excellent bargaining position. To add to this gain, the Israeli settlements in the Negev were in a precarious position. From Tel Aviv the danger was apparent, but Ben-Gurion and Galili had feared for the security of Tel Aviv itself. To them the loss of some kibbutzim, though heartrending, did not change the fact that the Egyptian threat to Israel had been turned back, the point of the lance blunted at Isdud. In the South both sides, though fearing disaster, had achieved a stalemate.

For Ben-Gurion and his major military opponent, Abdullah, the focal point of the war was in the center, around Jerusalem. In a real sense the operations in the North and South were sideshows. As long as the Yiftach or Givati Brigade could defend Israel without draining off reserves from the center, Ben-Gurion was satisfied. As long as the Syrians or the Egyptians diverted Israeli troops, Abdullah was content. Both continued to believe that whoever won Jerusalem would also have won the war. Just how the battle for Jerusalem was to be won was somewhat less certain for their military commanders. General Glubb hoped right up to the last minute that some sort of truce could be arranged in the city, making it unnecessary to commit the Arab Legion to street fighting. He wanted to use the Legion in the triangle area, where its armor and experience would be most effective, but finally Abdullah informed him that the Legion would be used in Jerusalem. There was a major snag, however, in that the Arab Liberation Army had packed up and gone back to Syria, leaving not only the Jerusalem corridor open but also much of the triangle undefended. After the Legion crossed the Allenby Bridge on May 15, much of its strength had to be drained off to occupy the vacuum areas. Even before the battle for Jerusalem began, therefore, the Legion had been whittled down well below what Glubb believed to be necessary to defeat the Haganah. On his side of the city, Shaltiel was even more pessimistic. The Tel Aviv road was still closed. The Jewish quarter in the Old City was still isolated. The Kfar Etzion bloc had been lost. On May 17 the Israelis, under Legion pressure, evacuated Nebi Yaakov and Ataroth to the north and gave up Bet

Haavara and the potash works at the northern tip of the Dead Sea, evacuating the settlers by boat south to Sodom. With no outposts, the Israelis found their defense perimeter moved to the edge of the New City. Neither Shaltiel nor Glubb faced the battle for Jerusalem with assurance.

Glubb's plan of attack was to move down from the Legion positions north of the city and to occupy the Sheikh Jarrach crossroads, which the British, as promised, had returned to the Jews. This move would isolate the Israeli complex on Mount Scopus and at the same time would allow the Legion to move into Jerusalem through the Damascus Gate. A second attack, reinforced by Egyptian units moving up from Hebron in the south, would overrun Ramat Rahel, a strategic kibbutz dominating the southern suburbs of the New City. Additional Legion troops would be sent into the Old City to help the locals and volunteers to mop up the Jewish quarter. Shaltiel did not have any plan of battle. His troops, exhausted by the undeclared war, could not take independent action but could only respond to the Legion attacks.

At 3:45 on the morning of May 19 the Arab Legion opened the attack on Sheikh Jarrach with one company of infantry, a squadron of armored cars, four six-pound antitank guns, and four three-inch mortars. Artillery support consisted of four twenty-five pounders. Glubb rightly believed that this force was dangerously small to drive into the city from the north. He was depending on a combination of luck, gall, and the spirit of the Legion. His luck came swiftly. The Irgun had been assigned the Sheikh Jarrach quarter, but by May 19 it had done little to prepare defensive positions. The Legion barreled through, seized the Palestine Police School, and cleared the rest of the quarter by 7:30 in the morning. By 2:00 in the afternoon, Legion patrols were near the Damascus Gate. One force attacked the Jewish quarter of northern Jerusalem, and a second tried to force its way past the Mandlebaum houses up the Street of the Prophet toward the center of the city. The fighting in the northern suburbs continued for several days with little Arab progress until Glubb broke off the attempt, in view of his mounting casualties. The major Legion effort was the thrust into Jerusalem itself.

The southern prong of the Arab attack was at first successful. On May 21 a heavy artillery bombardment smashed into Ramat Rahel, flattening the outlying positions and cutting off communications with the New City. The settlers' morale was shattered by the heavy artillery barrage. All Shaltiel had with which to answer the Arab fire were a few Davidkas, homemade mortars that made an incredible noise but did very little damage. At Ramat Rahel itself the Israelis had nothing but light arms. The Arab bombardment continued on May 22 while Arab volunteers and Egyptians occupied a hill overlooking the kibbutz. The Jews pulled out. The Arabs were wild with joy, particularly the irregulars, who ran up the Egyptian flag and began looting the settlement. The irregulars were still busily engaged in gobbling down barbecued chickens when HISH troops recaptured Ramat Rahel later that night. The Arabs mounted their own counterattack and retook the kibbutz. Harel Brigade reinforcements and Etzioni units fought their way back into the settlement, but the ruins of Ramat Rahel were to change hands three more times before the Haganah was finally successful in holding it. The seesaw struggle over Ramat Rahel meant that there would be no pincer moving up from the south to help out Glubb in the north. The Legion would have to press on alone.

On May 23 at noon Glubb opened his attack on the Convent of Notre Dame de France, which overlooked much of the Old City and was only a half-mile from the center of the Jewish New City. While his antitank guns and mortars zeroed in on Notre Dame, the Legion troops, led by armored cars, moved slowly through the narrow streets parallel with the walls of the Old City. A single Molotov cocktail hit the lead armored car, setting it afire. The rest of the armor could not get around the flaming wreck blocking the narrow street and pulled back. As Glubb had feared, his armor was vulnerable in the streets; he would have to depend on the infantry. The Arabs kept up their assaults all through the afternoon and evening. At one point they reached a point within fifteen yards of the main building of the convent. Finally, at 7:00 on the morning of May 24, Legion troops broke into the grounds of Notre Dame; they clung to their position all during the day in the face of heavy fire. Ten Legionnaires actually got inside one of the buildings but were forced to withdraw. At 5:00 in the afternoon Glubb gave it up. With his superiority in equipment neutralized by unsuitable fighting conditions, his infantry was being drained away far too rapidly.

Of the 200 infantry who had set out to attack Notre Dame on May
23rd, nearly half were either killed or were stretcher cases—the
walking wounded as usual remained in the line. 4 Company had
lost all its officers and N.C.O.s except one. At five o'clock on the
afternoon of May 24th, the attack was abandoned.[20]

To take a strongly held building without armor and without close
artillery support and using only 200 men required more than gall or
luck. Glubb needed a miracle. When none came, he had the sense to
pull out of a situation that he had suspected from the start was
hopeless. Abdullah, however, was to have one victory in Jerusalem.

The Jewish quarter of the Old City had seemed a ripe plum ready
for picking from the moment that the British pulled out. Cut off from
the rest of Jewish Palestine since December 1947, the 1,700 Jews
remaining of the original 2,500 had little hope of holding out against
thousands of Arab irregulars backed up by the Legion. Many of the
Jews were elderly, and a substantial percentage belonged to the "old
Yishuv," Jews who had been living in Jerusalem for generations,
dedicating their lives to the study of the Torah. The active defenders
consisted of two HISH platoons of the Haganah and units of the
Irgun. As soon as the British left, the Arabs struck at the Jewish
position around the Zion Gate, the probable route of any relief force
from the New City. After taking the gate, the Arabs began squeezing
the perimeter, occupying one ruined house after another. By May 16
the defenders feared that the position was hopeless. They informed
Shaltiel that, without reinforcements, they could not hold out. His
reaction was to insist that they hold out at all costs. Trapped among
the helpless civilians, who were being regularly shelled and who
endured constant rifle and machine-gun fire, without proper arms and
with little ammunition, the defenders felt abandoned. The Jewish
quarter was not a kibbutz; its defenders were not a Palmach unit but
only a handful of exhausted men defending frightened old men,
women, and children. By the following day only 100 square yards of
the quarter remained in Jewish hands. Much of that area was covered
with rubble. The Arabs were moving closer to Misgav Ladach, the
only hospital in the Jewish area and the site of the command post.
The firing seemed to build up to a crescendo under the heavy pall of
smoke hanging over the Old City.

Shaltiel, recognizing that time was short, prepared an operation to break into the quarter to bring out the survivors or to reinforce them. One section of the Harel Brigade was to capture Mount Zion in order to reach the Old City by way of the Zion Gate, while four platoons of the Etzioni Brigade were to concentrate at the old commercial center and then to storm the Jaffa Gate. The Etzioni attack, hampered by administrative difficulties and faulty liaison with the Harel, had been anticipated by the Arabs. All the Israeli sappers were killed or wounded before they could reach the gate, and the operation collapsed into efforts to remove the wounded from the open square. The Harel operation, benefiting from the diversion created by the Etzioni, moved down from Mount Zion, which it had taken the previous night, and blew the Zion Gate at 3:25 A.M. on May 19. Taking advantage of the thunderous explosion, the assault platoon rushed through into the Jewish quarter. The siege had been lifted. A temporary supply line immediately began operating, sending in rifles, Sten guns, and ammunition. But no reinforcements appeared to hold the Zion Gate. The assault platoon would be unable to hold off an Arab attack at dawn. Just before light, the gate was given up, and the quarter was again isolated. Although eighty-seven troops and additional supplies had been left behind, the chance to threaten the whole Arab position in the Old City had been abandoned.

During the next days Israeli attempts to break through the Zion Gate a second time failed. The Arabs would wait until the Israelis entered the gate and then spray them with machine-gun fire, turning the narrow entrance into a death trap. Inside the Jewish quarter conditions, if possible, grew worse. The houses had crumbled to rubble. An organized defense proved impossible. To prevent a massacre of the civilians, the few remaining defenders, dazed, exhausted, and mostly wounded, decided to surrender. On the morning of May 28 two ancient rabbis hobbled out of the ruins to negotiate the details with officers of the Arab Legion. At 3:25 that afternoon it was over at last; the Jewish quarter, a rubble of smashed buildings, charred wood, and ruined temples, had surrendered. The handful of defenders were taken away as prisoners of war, and the old men, women, and children were sent to the New City. Abdullah had secured at least half his precious Jerusalem by expelling the Israelis from the Old City, Sheikh Jarrach, and Mount Scopus; but there was to be no more fighting in the city—it cost too many Legion lives.

The shift in emphasis by the Legion was not immediately apparent to the beleaguered Jews in the New City. All the news had been bad for weeks: Kfar Etzion, Nebi Yaakov and Atarot lost, the Old City lost, Mount Scopus lost. The Arab artillery pounded away day after day, taking a rising toll of civilian lives, crushing suburban houses, and pitting streets. Food supplies were nearly gone. Water was distributed by trucks. There was no electricity, no gasoline, and no newspapers. All that the civilians could do was wait, carrying out a feeble pretense of everyday activities while the fighting rumbled on to the north, to the south, and to the east on the edge of the New City. The military situation was not much better. The Haganah was exhausted. Ammunition was scarce. A few bits and pieces—like a daily handful of mortar shells—could be flown in by Piper Cubs, but the mini-airlift could not hope to alleviate the battle losses. Shaltiel had a difficult time establishing effective liaison with the Palmach troops in the Judean Hills, and his relations with the Irgun and the Lechi were poor at best. The Irgun continued to act independently and would not reveal its operational strength to Shaltiel. The most important factor was not Shaltiel's command structure but his dwindling supply of ammunition and supplies. Even if the Legion no longer intended to butt its way into the New City, its stranglehold on the heights above the Tel Aviv–Jerusalem highway could still win for Abdullah the remaining half of the city.

Ben-Gurion was determined, despite the obstacles, to open a way into Jerusalem. The Legion's hold on the corridor would have to be broken, no matter what the cost. He ordered an attack on the Arab position at Latrun, where the Legion's 4th Regiment held a mountain spur commanding traffic on the western stretch of the highway. Ben-Gurion wanted no delays and no excuses. If there were no troops, then they would have to be found. Yadin knew that any such operation was almost hopeless, but Ben-Gurion would accept no alternatives. Jerusalem had to be saved, and Yadin had to find a way to save it. Units of the Alexandroni could be used but would be insufficient. On May 22 Yadin created the 7th Brigade out of untrained recent immigrants. Their arms were still at sea, but their attack was scheduled for May 24, with or without arms. Yadin did manage to wangle a twenty-four-hour delay while he patched together the new Brigade. The whole operation was makeshift, held together only by Ben-Gurion's overriding determination that the attack must take place.

At 2:00 in the morning on May 25, still without support weapons, the hastily assembled troops moved out of Hulda toward Latrun to obey Yadin's orders: "Attack at all cost."[21] At the last minute half-tracks, machine guns, and mortars began arriving at Hulda directly from Tel Aviv, where they had been unloaded a few hours before. With these supplies moving into Hulda from Tel Aviv and the buses loaded with the 7th Brigade moving out of Hulda toward Latrun, the Arabs listening to the noise and watching the headlights only six miles away could not help knowing what was coming. Hastily organized, inexperienced, unfamiliar with the ground, unaware that they faced the prepared and professional Legion rather than a surprised scattering of Arab volunteers, the 7th Brigade never had a chance. The attack was made in broad daylight, and accurate Arab fire quickly scattered the Israelis. The 7th Brigade swiftly disintegrated into bands of retreating men. The Alexandroni forces were mauled. The remainder of the day was spent in extricating pinned-down pockets of men and evacuating the dead and wounded. Ben-Gurion's desperate ploy had been a costly disaster.

The Legion reacted swiftly to the Israeli attack by strengthening its hold on the highway. The Legion seized a high hill farther to the east, where the British had erected a radar tower. All the Israeli efforts to retake Radar Hill from the Legion failed, but at least the Arabs were prevented from moving closer to the highway. This fact was small consolation because the Legion's position at Latrun effectively closed the highway in any case. Although Ben-Gurion realized the demoralizing effect of the defeat at Latrun, particularly on new troops, he insisted that the Legion hold must be broken. Obviously the attack on Radar meant that Glubb and Abdullah were equally aware of the meaning of the corridor. Ben-Gurion sent experienced reinforcements to the 7th Brigade and nominated a single commander for the front, Colonel David Marcus. "Mickey" Marcus, who had already led a series of commando raids against the Egyptians, was an American, a graduate of West Point who had served on General Eisenhower's staff in Europe. Though he could not have professional soldiers, at least Ben-Gurion was going to make sure of professional commanders. Despite Marcus' hurried arrival and the additional troops borrowed from the Givati, the second assault on Latrun would also have to be a makeshift operation.

The second attack, on May 31, was to be slightly more subtle, moving in from two directions rather than as another frontal assault. The main effort, led by armored cars, started directly from the Israeli position toward the police station, the key stronghold of the Legion. A second force of Givati troops moved out of Beit Susin on the flank to the rear of Latrun. Although this force reached Deir Ayub without opposition, heavy Arab fire then hit the troops, and unwilling to take heavy casualties, they pulled back. For awhile the armored column, unaware of the Givati's withdrawals, was more successful. Unfortunately, it soon left its infantry support behind. The Israeli armor managed to break into the courtyard of the police station. Then everything went wrong. The demolition team was hit by an Arab shell before it could breach the walls of the police station. The infantry would not advance into the heavy Arab fire. The armored cars, isolated inside the courtyard, had to withdraw under fire. The attack was abandoned. Marcus cabled Yadin: "I was there and saw the battle. Plan good. Artillery good. Armor excellent. Infantry disgraceful."[22] The second battle of Latrun was over. The newly created 7th Brigade had been badly mauled; 137 of its men had been killed between May 24 and May 31. Glubb was delighted with the Legion, assuming even heavier Israeli casualties. Ben-Gurion, however, was not as dissatisfied as were some of the Haganah commanders, for he believed that the Legion's offensive capacity had been badly eroded.

Although the Haganah planned one more operation to take Latrun, the action had to be postponed when the participating Givati Battalion was shifted back to the Egyptian front at the end of May. More important, the capture of Latrun became less a life-and-death matter for Jerusalem when in June an alternative route into the New City was discovered. Three Harel soldiers had found that they could walk through the Judean Mountains down to the coastal plain parallel to the regular highway. The bypass was a combination of paths, ruts, and rough ground, but it looked hopeful. On June 1 a company from the Harel followed the trail, and later a jeep ground its way over the new route to see if it could be used by vehicular traffic. Only a few hundred yards of the path just east of Feb Susi, where there was a steep 400-foot rise, proved impassable. The High Command immediately decided to turn the dirt path into a passable road. Five hundred workers labored day and night, under sporadic artillery fire, to transform the ruts into a little Burma Road. Almost from the first, troops and mule-train convoys began moving into Jerusalem. Eventually the Burma Road was open to trucks, except for the one steep spot where the vehicles had to be hauled up the rise. With the opening of the new road, the siege of Jerusalem was broken.

Despite the Burma Road, Ben-Gurion continued to insist that the capture of Latrun was essential. Once more, on June 9, the Israelis attacked from the rear but had to withdraw from the captured positions. The next night there was a variety of delays and misunderstandings, culminating in one Israeli battalion's attacking another Israeli battalion in a position recently occupied by Arabs. On June 10 the Arab Legion counterattacked, captured the settlement of Gezer, and for some time endangered the Israeli position at Hulda, the Haganah base for the entire area. Finally, the Israelis launched their own counterattack and captured Gezer just before time ran out and the United Nations truce became effective at 10:00 in the morning of June 11. One of the last casualties on the Jerusalem front was the sector commander. A little before 4:00 in the morning, Colonel Marcus, wrapped in a blanket, had gone outside the perimeter fence of his headquarters at Abu Ghosh. On his return, he was challenged by a sentry in Hebrew. Marcus replied in English. The sentry fired one warning shot and then shot Marcus in the chest. The whole Latrun sector seemed to have been dogged with disasters from the first. Israel's only offensive potential had been committed there and then mauled by the Legion. Marcus had been killed. On the surface, little had been accomplished.

In fact, much the same could be said for the entire central front. The pattern of conflict, though it was not apparent at the time either to the Arabs or to the Israelis, had been similar to that in the North and the South: an Arab advance through Arab areas, blunting of their offensive momentum after some local successes, and then unsuccessful Israeli counterattacks wearing away Arab strength but not capturing much ground. The Arabs in the center had done as well as could have been expected in view of their limitations. With insufficient troops, there was simply not much hope of overrunning the Israelis. Glubb's 200 troops never had much chance pushing into the New City, no matter how beleaguered the ill-armed Jews in Notre Dame might have felt. The Arab infantry had proved feeble in assaulting prepared positions though more effective in defense. Arab armor, if not downright timid, had at least been poorly used; primarily the Arabs did not know how to carry out a balanced attack. Still they had done better than the prime ministers and generals had anticipated. On their side of the hill, the Israelis were convinced that they had turned back an overwhelming challenge from five modern Arab armies heavily supported by all the weapons of contemporary warfare. Everywhere the issue had been in doubt. Nearly everywhere the defense had been successful even though often only by narrow margins. On June 11 both sides, strained and exhausted, were stalled as much by their own lack of resources as by the United Nations truce. The four weeks of war ended in a stalemate.

NOTES

1. Harry Levin, *I Saw the Battle of Jerusalem* (New York: 1950), p. 150.

2. The Declaration of the Establishment of the State of Israel was published in the *Official Gazette*, No. 1 (May 14, 1948). Zeev Sharef, in *Three Days* (Garden City, N.Y.: 1962) gives a detailed account of the hectic efforts to create a functioning government in the midst of the undeclared war.

3. Walter Eytan, *The First Ten Years* (New York: 1958), p. 11. See Harry S Truman, *Memoirs*, 2 (New York: 1956), p. 193: "I was told that to some of the career men of the State Department this announcement came as a surprise. It should not have been if these men had faithfully supported my policy."

4. As with most aspects of the Arab-Israel conflict, there is considerable confusion over just how well armed the Israelis were. David Ben-Gurion, in "The Hagana on the Eve," *Jewish Observer and Middle East Review*, 14, No. 12 (March 19, 1965), pp. 15–18, gives a list for April 1947: 10,073 rifles, 1,900 submachine guns, 186 machine guns, 672 two-inch mortars, and 96 three-inch mortars. These figures are probably the lowest possible and may not include some arms belonging to the Irgun or the Jewish settlement police. For example, before May 15, an arms ship had

brought in 4,500 rifles, 200 machine guns, and 20 antiaircraft guns. Walid Khalidi, in "Plan Dalet: the Zionist Blueprint for the Conquest of Palestine," *Middle East Forum* 37, No 9 (November 1961), pp. 22–8, is critical of what could be called "the David myth": "The arms at the disposal of these forces was much in excess of what may be superficially gathered from Zionist sources." What no one can deny, however, is that the Israelis had no armor and no artillery except the homemade variety. This lack, not the lack of rifles, was their real weakness.

5. Jon Kimche and David Kimche, *Both Sides of the Hill* (London: 1960), pp. 146–9. After the scuffle over appointing Galili, Ben-Gurion, despite the retention of the old command structure, became in reality commander in chief, Yigal Yadin as Director of Military Operations evolved into the dominant Haganah figure, and Galili declined in influence

6. Sharef, *op. cit.*, p. 74.

7. *Ibid.*, p. 75.

8. The quotation is from a statement made by Mohammed Hassein Haykal, the editor of the Cairo Weekly *Ahar Sa'ah* in 1953 and quoted by Dov Joseph, *The Faithful City: The Siege of Jerusalem, 1948* (New York: 1960), pp. 207–8.

9. Kimche and Kimche, *Both Sides of the Hill*, p. 154.

10. There is an all but irresistible urge to outline in detail the intentions of the various Arab armies, their likely battle plans, tactical goals, and ultimate objectives. Just what the various armies really intended, in the North and elsewhere, is vague. Perhaps, the Syrians really did intend to break through the leg, link up with the other Arabs, and drive toward Haifa. Mostly, however, the Arabs were playing it by ear. Generally historians have attributed more order to the Arabs' plans than actually existed, in order to make tidier history.

11. One of the new volunteers from abroad, the American Mickey Marcus, watched the departure of the 1st Battalion. Kimche and Kimche, *Both Sides of the Hill*, p. 152.

13. *Ibid.*, p. 152.

14. The names and careers of many of the individuals who threw specific Molotov cocktails are known and generally give some insight into the nature of Israeli morale. At Degania, for example, the first was thrown by Shalom Hochbaum, who had spent five years in thirteen different

concentration and displaced-person camps, including Belsen; the second was thrown by Yehuda Sprung, a former student of law at the University of Cracow. Neither had ever seen a tank before.

15. Lorch, *Edge of the Sword*, p. 174.

16. *Ibid.*, p. 175.

17. *Ibid.*, p. 208.

18. Gamal Abdel Nasser, *The Truth About the Palestine War* (Cairo: 1956), pp. 10, 14. It is interesting that neither Colonel Neguib nor his principle staff officer Abdel Hakim Amer was blamed for the Egyptian difficulties. Major Amer, Nasser's friend, in time became Egyptian Commander in Chief and Neguib was the figurehead of the Free Officers' revolution. The tendency in 1948 and later was to place the blame in Cairo not in Palestine; the army's humiliation was considered the fault of the politicians, not of the soldiers.

19. Lorch, *Edge of the Sword*, p. 219.

20. Sir John Bagot Glubb, *A Soldier with the Arabs* (New York: 1957), pp. 124–5.

21. Kimche and Kimche, *Both Sides of the Hill*, p. 190.

22. Marcus believed that the prime reason for the failure of the second attack on Latrun was the failure of 52nd Battalion of the Givati Brigade to push its encircling attack after losing only two men. *See* Ted Berkman, *Cast a Giant Shadow* (Garden City, N.Y.: 1962), pp. 277–8. Most if not all of the old Haganah commanders had no enthusiasm for a second attack, despite additional troops and support weapons and despite Marcus' battle plan. Avidan apparently suggested that the 52nd Battalion should not take excessive casualties in a pointless attack. This attitude was partially the result of the friends-and-neighbors composition of the old Haganah units in which every loss was a personal one, although the 52nd had many new recruits. Whether or not the attack could have suceeded is, of course, problematical, but the reaction of Marcus and Ben-Gurion to the individualism of the old Haganah commanders was intense. Both were determined to introduce a new professionalism and to end the band-of-brothers spirit that had up to then been so valuable.

7

The Four-Week Truce

When the British withdrew from Palestine on May 14, the Special Session of the General Assembly was unable to do more than create the position of Mediator for Palestine. The Mediator's responsibilities were to secure a cease-fire and then to negotiate a formal truce and a peaceful solution. After the Arabs invaded, the United States, on May 17, insisted that a breach of the peace had taken place and that the Security Council should order an immediate cease-fire. The British, by then openly backing the Arabs in the expectation of an Israeli setback that would enable London to recoup its prestige, had no corresponding sense of urgency. The world newspapers announced daily in screaming black headlines Arab victories in Gaza and Hebron, in Jerusalem, in the North. In London, at least, the impression remained that the Arabs were about to crunch the Israelis. On May 18 the British delegate to the United Nations, Sir Alexander Cadogan, expressed doubt that there had been either aggression or a breach of the peace. On May 19 Cadogan did, however, support the appointment of the Mediator. On May 22 Count Folke Bernadotte, President of the Swedish Red Cross, formally accepted the United Nations appointment as Mediator empowered to seek a truce and a solution. Bernadotte, who was not a Middle East expert, would have to rely almost

159

entirely on moral blackmail to achieve a truce and on more ingenuity than anyone had previously shown to find a compromise. In effect, a dedicated representative of a neutral small power had been thrown into the Middle Eastern lions' den.

At Lake Success on May 22, the United States again asked that sanctions be applied to force a cease-fire. Again Cadogan demurred. As long as the Arabs were doing well, Great Britain was willing to dawdle. The result of the deliberations at the United Nations was a request for a cease-fire, which was forwarded to the Arabs and Israelis. On the following day, May 23, the Israelis accepted a truce to begin within thirty-six hours, provided that the Arabs would do the same. The Syrian delegation asked for an additional forty-eight-hour delay. The Arabs wanted time to consider the proposal, but the prospects for Arab acceptance were hardly glowing. On May 23 Abdullah declared that "My troops did not enter Palestine in order to stop the war to no purpose."[1] The Arab consultations went on for days with no discernible results while the fighting in Palestine continued. The Legion was in Jerusalem, the Egyptians were in the Negev, the Syrians and Iraqis were in Galilee. The Arabs felt no need for haste.

Bernadotte had already left Sweden to seek peace through his own personal efforts. On May 25 he conferred in Paris with the British chargé d'affaires, Ashley Clarke. There he learned that Britain had no intention of acting against the Arabs or of supporting the American resolution that the Arab invasion was a breach of the United Nations Charter. Bernadotte also met with Dr. Nahum Goldman, Vice-President of the Jewish Agency, to hear the Israeli views for the first time. On May 28 Bernadotte arrived in Cairo with an excellent idea of the problems he faced, particularly in relation to British aspirations. In fact, he had decided that the best course was to explore the practical means of implementing the United Nations partition resolution. For aspects of the Palestine problem as of May 1948 rather than to seek Bernadotte, as for the British, the partition resolution had lost much of its validity as a basis for solution. He wanted to incorporate practicalities into his proposal. The difficulty was the number of "practicalities" that seemed to exist in the Middle East.

   To sum up, one might say that in putting forward any proposal for the solution of the Palestine problem one must bear in mind the aspirations of the Jews, the political difficulties and differences of opinion of the Arab leaders, the strategic interests of Great Britain, the financial commitments of the United States and the Soviet Union, the outcome of the war, and finally the authority and prestige of the United Nations.[2]

Any final solution, however, would have to wait for a cease-fire, and no cease-fire seemed forthcoming.

On May 29 the Security Council passed another cease-fire resolution. The Israelis accepted. The impression was that the Arabs had accepted as well. The cease-fire was to begin on June 3, but instead the fighting continued without pause. Then, during the next week, the tide of battle began to shift. Three weeks of war had mauled the Arab armies, depleted their stocks of matériel, and strained their soldiers to the point of exhaustion. The Arab drives had lost momentum, and increasingly the Israelis were taking the offensive. At Lake Success pressure for peace mounted. In the Middle East Bernadotte pulled out all the stops to obtain a cease-fire. While prolonged exchanges were still going on between Bernadotte and the combatants, without final agreement on the details of the cease-fire, the Mediator fixed June 7 at noon as the truce deadline. Eventually, he had to push the date back to 6:00 A.M. June 11 because of continuing snags in establishing the terms of the truce. Each side wanted to conduct one more military operation and was reluctant to accept the Mediator's restrictions. Finally, on June 9 the Israelis and Arabs agreed to a twenty-eight-day cease-fire.

On the morning of June 11 the long-awaited United Nations truce began everywhere but on the Syrian front. On the following day the fighting around Mishmar Hayarden also dwindled away, and for the first time in 1948 peace came to Palestine. The twenty-eight-day cease-fire was the only visible result of months of negotiation and discussion at Lake Success. For six months and long before the British withdrawal, it had been obvious to diplomats that partition was not going to proceed peacefully, but neither before May 15 nor after the outbreak of the Arab-Israeli war had anyone put forth an acceptable compromise, a reasonable alternative to violence. Reluctantly, the diplomats at Lake Success had to accept the fact that no nation capable of doing so wanted the responsibility of imposing a forced solution on Palestine. The British were getting out as fast as possible and quietly shifting their support to the Arab states. The Americans, barely aware of their new international responsibilities, showed little enthusiasm for deeper involvement in the Middle East; in any case, despite his professional advisers' distaste, President Harry S Truman seemed to be following a pro-Israeli policy. The Soviet Union, suspicious both of the impact of Zionism on its own Jews and of the British-supported Arab "puppets," seemed interested only in compounding the confusion at the expense of the West. The small nations had neither the resources nor the interest to intervene, and there was no international peace-keeping force. Incapable of either devising a peaceful compromise or of preventing open war, the United Nations had sought instead, after May 15, to impose a truce in order to allow still further negotiations.

Bernadotte's truce was a document designed not simply to end the fighting but also to freeze the military status quo. A truce commission, composed of consular officials from the United States, Belgium, and France, who had served on the fruitless Jerusalem Truce Commission, a brief three-power attempt to secure a truce in Jerusalem, would supervise the cease-fire. The Commission had neither the staff (ultimately seventy members) nor the resources to enforce all the intricate restrictions necessary, but Bernadotte had to use what was on hand. More important, both the Israelis and the Arabs had made clear their serious reservations about the cease-fire. The Israelis had already observed that immigration would, of course, continue, although Bernadotte had insisted that there be no mobilization or training of new immigrants. The Israelis had also informed Bernadotte that Jerusalem would be supplied from territory gained during the fighting, despite the Mediator's intention that essential supplies in the city should not be substantially greater at the end of the truce than at the beginning. Israel had no intention of giving up the Burma Road or of cutting off the influx of new citizens. The Arabs, too, made qualifications. The most important stipulation was that, unless Palestine became an Arab state with restricted Jewish immigration, the war would be renewed. With a skeleton staff to enforce a truce that both sides publicly interpreted to suit themselves, Bernadotte had been able to no more than end the fighting for twenty-eight days. After six months of diplomatic failure, it was accomplishment enough for a beginning.

While Bernadotte undertook steps to extend the lull, to find common ground for discussion, and to flesh out a compromise plan, both the Arabs and the Israelis began extensive preparations for the second round of war. Neither had the slightest intention of abiding by the limitations of the cease-fire agreement, as to do so would be to ensure subsequent defeat. Bernadotte could not enforce his truce, and neither side had any illusions about the good faith of the other. The four weeks of fighting, ending in an exhausted stalemate, had persuaded neither that a negotiated settlement was feasible. Neither was willing to compromise its irreducible aspirations. Even acceptance of the truce had brought howls of indignation from many quarters. In Israel the Irgun and the Lechi considered the cease-fire a shameful unconditional surrender. Even many citizens loyal to David Ben-Gurion's provisional government believed that the truce terms were pro-Arab. This attitude was particularly strong in Jerusalem, where the Truce Commission seemed to enforce the freeze with considerable rigidity. The Arab populations, fed newspaper reports of victories and shielded from the slightest hint of reality, could not understand why their governments had allowed total victory to be snatched away at the last moment. Arab armies were in Jerusalem, outside Tel Aviv, massed in Galilee. Many Arabs in the Middle East thus saw the truce as a swindle and a danger to their cause.

Those closer to the seats of power or simply to the front lines knew that, militarily at least, the truce had been essential. Both sides were close to exhaustion by June 11. The "victorious" Arabs had lost not only their offensive capacity but also perhaps their ability to defend Arab Palestine. This analysis by the military, who demanded massive reinforcements, had helped to persuade the Arab politicians to accept the truce. The Israelis had all along been more accommodating in accepting the proposed cease-fires, out of diplomatic necessity, but the final truce on June 11 had been accepted with alacrity for purely military reasons. The Haganah had fought to a standstill. Moshe Carmel regarded the truce as "dew from heaven."[3] Bernadotte may have been under the impression that the truce was a first step toward conciliation, but the Arabs and Israelis knew better. In four weeks no final military decision had been possible, for neither side had had the necessary resources to gain victory. But both sides were hopeful that those resources could be acquired during the next four weeks. A solution could be achieved only by force. The supervisory work of the United Nations Truce Commission seemed therefore largely a farce, an irritant that required extra effort to subvert or evade. The Commission could do little but go through the motions of supervision while Bernadotte sought the elusive diplomatic compromise.

The Israelis simply did not believe that any peaceful compromise could possibly be forthcoming. If Bernadotte or the United Nations could come up with an acceptable plan, then Ben-Gurion would be delighted, but after forty years it was obvious that such a plan existed only in the realm of diplomatic theory. If Bernadotte could persuade the Arabs to accept an extended cease-fire, then Ben-Gurion would have to accept it, albeit reluctantly; but that the Arabs would be willing to postpone fulfillment of their cherished aspirations seemed quite unlikely. As had been the case for months, Ben-Gurion's energies continued to be directed toward waging the war. The previous month had been harrowing. The Haganah urgently needed to be rested, reinforced, and refitted. Ben-Gurion was also convinced that broad reforms in the nature and structure of the army were long overdue. Finally, the dangerous independence of the Irgun and the Lechi had to be curbed. Israel could not return to war with private armies and independent brigades any more than with handmade artillery and patched Piper Cubs.

When the brigade commanders met on June 11 in Tel Aviv to review the previous four weeks, summation of the past, rather than plans for the future, dominated the conference. But their depressing reports revealed the magnitude of the preparations necessary for the second round. All the commanders were exhausted by the continuous fighting. Their men had suffered heavy casualties. Their tactical successes had been overshadowed by their failures. The army was exhausted, its resources in men and matériel all but spent. The Harel Brigade had lost 220 killed and 617 wounded, leaving only 200 effective troops. Shlomo Shamir's new 7th Brigade had been badly bloodied at Latrun. The story was the same for the other brigades. Everywhere ammunition had been expended beyond any reserve margin. There had been all kinds of errors. Mobilization had often been chaotic. Men had fought without proper clothing, without leave, without assurance that their families would be supported or even safe. On the tactical level there had been serious problems.

Brigade cooperation had been poor in the Jerusalem sector, at Gezer, at Jenin. In Jerusalem the civilians were unhappy with Shaltiel, unhappy at the loss of the Old City, unhappy with the lax control over looting. The battles at Latrun had been mismanaged. Many doubted their necessity. Each brigade commander insisted that he needed huge transfusions of men and equipment, that his men had to rest. Above all, they wanted heavy equipment, if not tanks at the very least antitank guns. Still battle-shocked and drained by cliff-hanging engagements with makeshift weapons, the commanders argued that only a major miracle could prepare Israel for a second round.

Ben-Gurion assured them that, unlikely as it seemed, the miracle was in the making. Within the month the Israeli army would go through a metamorphosis and would emerge almost unrecognizable. The days of the Molotov cocktail, the sightless 65-millimeter guns, the sandwich-plated armored trucks would be over; the army would be almost tripled in size and equipped with weapons comparable to those of the Arabs. The long-promised, almost mythical heavy equipment was already pouring into Israel. Although in four weeks the army would have 60,000 men, the striking change would be in new equipment rather than in increased numbers. Artillery almost equal to that of the Legion's twenty-five pounders would be available. Armored cars, jeeps, and real tanks would give the army a vastly greater striking potential. There would be more than enough rifles and light machine guns and a great increase in heavy mortars and antitank weapons. One of the most impressive changes would be in the air force. Ever since April 23, when the first contract for ten Messerschmitt 109s had been signed with the Czechs, Israeli agents had been hyperactive. Even during the four-week war, some of the new planes had arrived, but during the truce the buildup would continue, culminating in a B-17 raid on Cairo on July 14, when Flying Fortresses would carry out their first mission on the way to Israel and before their crews even set foot on Israeli soil. Brigadier Chaim Ladkin was commander of this new air force, with its varied collection of military aircraft. An Israeli navy, under Commander Mordechai Limon, had actually scrounged real ships, including two corvettes. Meanwhile, other agents were still working, purchasing artillery and gasoline in Mexico or smuggling ammunition out of

Hawaii. The trickle of April and May would grow to a flood by July.

Of all the "smuggling" activities, Operation Pirate most clearly revealed the extent of the Israeli secret-intelligence network, one of the new state's greatest assets. In 1948 the Czechs were playing no favorites. Early in the year Prague had sold a Syrian delegation, led by Major Fuad Mardam, $11 million worth of arms, including 8,000 rifles, 10 million bullets and grenades, and explosives. This purchase would provide sufficient light arms to double the size of the Arab Liberation Army. The arms had been loaded on a Danube River boat, which had carried them to the port of Bratislava. At that point agents of the Haganah had caught up with the shipment and had bribed the port officials to delay its passage. Eventually, despite constant harassment, Mardam had finally moved the arms to an Adriatic port near Fiume. But before he could have all the arms loaded onto the chartered *Lino*, an Italian steamer, Yugoslavian Jews had switched many of the rifles with useless ones. When the *Lino* finally sailed, Major Mardam ran into a storm and was forced to stop over in the Italian port of Bari. A Haganah plane, which had been trailing the steamer, reported the change in course to the commander of Operation Pirate. Soon after the *Lino* docked, a Palmach frogman attached a limpet mine. The explosion blew a hole in the vessel and it settled down onto the shallow bed of Bari harbor.

Mardam refused to give up. He salvaged much of the Syrian shipment, including the rifles, but he had considerable difficulty in chartering another vessel. Italian ship owners had already seen the *Lino* blow up and sink, and "discreet" warnings from Haganah agents lessened any enthusiasm for making a quick profit from the Syrians. Finally, Mardam persuaded the captain of the *Algiro* to take his arms. At long last on August 20, when the *Algiro* sailed for Beirut, Mardam could assume that his mission had been accomplished.[4] But he was premature. On board the *Algiro* were two engineers, both Israeli agents of Operation Pirate. As soon as the *Algiro* reached international waters, the "engineers" found an excuse to stop the engines. Almost at once a small fishing boat came alongside with two "Syrian officers," supposedly detailed by Damascus to escort the shipment to Syria. The Italian captain accepted their credentials and allowed them on board. Once more the *Algiro* got underway. The "Syrian" members of the Palmach set up a radio and began broadcasting in a strange language, accepted as Arabic by the Italian captain but actually Hebrew instructions to the Israeli navy. A few days later, near the Dodecanese Islands, two Israeli ships appeared alongside. The arms and crew were transferred, and the *Algiro* was sunk.

Operation Pirate, considering the obstacles, was one of the most effective operations of the war. Significantly it used to advantage the extensive network of Israeli agents, their contacts, and their capacity to carry out operations that called upon the talents of underwater-demolition experts, illicit patrol planes, and East European friends. Similar operations would produce permanent networks and contacts throughout the world. Even in its infancy, Israeli intelligence and covert operations were impressive. In the years ahead, the Israelis developed one of the finest intelligence operations in the world, overshadowed only by the vast resources of a few major powers. In the summer of 1948, however, the main preoccupation of Israeli intelligence outside of the Middle East remained arms operations. On June 11 in Tel Aviv the Israeli commanders who had fought the war with their hands and their determination could hardly imagine the changes such operations would produce in their army.

Not only their equipment but even the very nature of the Haganah would change. On May 28 the new army of the state had been established—the Israel Defense Force, or Zahal—but the old Haganah brigades had continued to fight until the truce. The Zahal was to be greatly expanded by new mobilization and immigrant recruits. The Control of Man Power Ordinance had called up all men between the ages of seventeen and fifty-five. All settlement males between eighteen and thirty-six were to be either in the Zahal or engaged in agricultural labor. All seventeen-year-olds were called up for two months' training. Soon all men thirty-six to forty-two would be called up for labor. Truce or no, immigration continued, and there was a steady stream of recruits from abroad, known as the gahal. The most important immigrants were the mahal, military volunteers already trained and experienced in World War II. Eventually foreign recruits came from fifty-two countries and constituted 18 percent of the Zahal. The influx meant that formations that had often reached only fractions of their paper sizes could be brought up to strength. The new 7th and Oded Brigades could be filled out. A Palmach armored brigade was organized. Schools for N.C.O.s, training programs for auxiliary services, even a military-police program were established overnight. On June 1 a naval academy was opened. Mahal men flooded into the new Israeli air force. With the old restrictions of the British and the daily attacks of the Arabs no longer factors, the Zahal began to absorb, arm, and train men at a hectic pace. The Haganah commanders, so pessimistic at the onset of the truce, soon found themselves surrounded by new men and new arms.

Ben-Gurion had never seriously doubted that the transformation in size and equipment would take place. What he continued to doubt was that the Zahal would prove effective without comparable changes in the command structure. The old equalitarian elite would have to go. The failures, which he attributed directly to the free-wheeling habits of the Palmach and the Haganah, could not be repeated. As a first step, he forced through [over the anguished opposition of the Palmach] a series of measures to professionalize the Zahal. There were to be standard uniforms, standard insignia for officers, differences in pay, officers' messes, and even regular military police. The days of the independent Palmach were clearly numbered. With great reluctance, the Palmach and the Haganah swallowed these changes, but the real crisis came on the issue of command. Ben-Gurion was determined to ease out Israel Galili, nominally head of the general staff, and Yaakov Dori, Galili's chief of staff; the responsibilities and powers of both men had become increasingly ambiguous as Ben-Gurion had continued to dominate tactical planning. Ben-Gurion also wanted to replace many of the brigade commanders with British-trained officers. Even the old commanders agreed that the army structure had become chaotic and that the old organizational table would have to go, but few of the Haganah commanders believed that Ben-Gurion's ideas or his selections were desirable.

Ben-Gurion went ahead with his reorganization. He wanted the country divided into three fronts, rather than into the previous brigade areas. He informed the general staff that he intended to appoint Mordechai Makleff to command the Center and Shlomo Shamir to command the South. Neither was an experienced old-line commander. Opposition was led by Yigal Yadin, who headed the Operational Planning Section under Deputy Chief of Staff Zvi Ayalon. Yadin agreed to the three-front concept, but he wanted Yigal Alon, the Palmach commander, appointed in the South and Shimon Avidan

in the Center. More than simply a conflict over promotions and personalities, the disagreement between Ben-Gurion and Yadin covered
the entire course of the four-week war and proposals for the second
round. Yadin and the Haganah believed that it was Ben-Gurion's
impatience that had wrecked the Latrun operation and that his *idée
fixe* about Jerusalem should no longer dominate Israeli strategy. During the increasingly bitter arguments over priorities and personalities,
Ben-Gurion demanded Yadin's obedience, even to the extent of
threatening a court-martial. Yadin immediately resigned. The entire
general staff followed his example. Ben-Gurion refused to accept the
resignations, and the general staff refused to withdraw them.

In an effort to settle the command crisis, a ministerial committee
was established to investigate the problem. Day after day passed without a recommendation while the "resigned" general staff continued
the work of building up the Zahal. The major handicap was that no
specific preparation could be made for future Israeli offensives until
the Zahal had a single commander, either Galili, Yadin, or Ben-
Gurion himself. Someone had to make the ultimate decisions. Finally,
on the morning of July 7, the committee submitted a report that,
stripped of qualifications, strongly supported Galili as Director General of the Army at the expense of Ben-Gurion as Defense Minister.
That same evening Ben-Gurion replied with a letter criticizing the
committee's findings and, in effect, threatening to resign: "In order to
save the valuable time of the Government, I ask you to lay aside the
proposals for the organization of the Ministry of Defense—if the
intention is to have a Ministry of Defense of which I shall be the
head."[5]

The committee realized that it had gone too far. However irritating
and dictatorial Ben-Gurion had been and would continue to be, Israel
could not get along without him. Then Ben-Gurion sent along a
suggestion that a "new" committee, whose duties would be vague,
might be acceptable. Yadin and Ayalon agreed to accept the orders of
the government, that is, to "unresign." Ben-Gurion and Yadin
worked out a compromise on the commanders. There would be no
central-front commander, but Yadin won Alon for the Lydda operation, a choice that proved wise, and Ben-Gurion had his way on
almost everything else. Above all, the Zahal was to evolve into a
conventional army.

Ben-Gurion was also interested in creating a unified command in a somewhat different, if equally delicate, area. For years the relations between the Jewish Agency and the Haganah on one hand and the Irgun and the Lechi on the other had been abrasive. To Ben-Gurion the politics, personalities, methods, and attitudes of the extremists were anathema. The Jewish Agency, mainly dominated by men of the Left, deplored the Irgun's arbitrary use of terror and the rhetoric of fascism. And their arrogant claim to be the vanguard of Zionism irritated the other Zionists. The Irgun often complained that the Jewish Agency had carried moderation to the point of treason. The Irgun could not forget that in the past the Haganah had cooperated with the British to eliminate the Irgun. During the undeclared war, the mutual antagonism had hardly lessened. The Haganah commanders regarded the Deir Yassin massacre with disgust and the capacities of the Irgun with contempt. The Irgun suspected that Ben-Gurion would sell out for half a loaf or less if anyone offered him the chance. Still an agreement had been negotiated that incorporated the Irgun units into the Zahal as independent formations everywhere but in Jerusalem. After May 15 Ben-Gurion believed that there was no longer any need or even any excuse for the existence of an Irgun army. Willing as he was to risk the displeasure of the cherished Palmach in his program of unity, he was more than willing—he was eager and determined—to erase the Irgun as an independent military factor in Israel. While the Irgun was cooperating with the Zahal but not consolidated with it, Ben-Gurion could not be satisfied, but he had been forced to bide his time.

During the truce, the opportunity to eliminate the Irgun as a separate military force finally occurred. Ben-Gurion was quick to seize it and was strongly supported by both the government and the Zahal. On June 11 a former 4,000-ton LST, renamed the *Altalena*, sailed from Port de Bouc near Marseilles for Haifa. The *Altalena* was an Irgun arms ship, laden with the fruits of secret purchases in Europe by Irgun agents. On board were hundreds of Irgun-recruited volunteers and 5,000 rifles, as well as machine guns, antitank weapons, and ammunition. Under the command of Abraham Stavsky, long a most controversial Palestinian figure,[6] the *Altalena* sailed before negotiations had been completed between the Irgun and the Israeli government to determine the fate of the cargo. The Irgun leaders insisted that 20 percent of the arms should go to Jerusalem and the remainder to the Irgun battalions in the Zahal, which they claimed had not been properly armed. The Irgun had purchased, assembled, and shipped the arms, and with some justification its leaders believed that they should largely determine their destination. Ben-Gurion decided that the new state could not compromise its sovereignty with dissidents. It was not only a question of prestige; there was also no point in allowing the enemy of tomorrow to be armed today. Still, the government agreed to a compromise. Twenty percent of the arms could go to Jerusalem, but the remainder would be given directly to the Zahal. It is doubtful that the government expected the Irgun to accept. On June 17 negotiations broke down. On Sunday, June 20, the *Altalena* arrived off the beach at Kfar Vitkin, twenty miles north of Tel Aviv.

During the night most of the volunteers disembarked, carrying with them some of the arms, but, when dawn came, the Irgun found that the beach had been surrounded by Zahal troops, backed up by artillery and armored cars. Offshore the navy's two corvettes were closing in on the anchored *Altalena*. Ben-Gurion had allowed the Irgun to sail into a showdown. As neither the Irgun nor the government wanted the crisis to develop into a violent one, long hours of confused and often vitriolic negotiations began. Neither side would back down. Tempers flared. Suddenly, on the afternoon of June 21, firing began. The *Altalena* hurriedly sailed south along the coast to Tel Aviv, chased by the corvettes. Stavsky rammed the *Altalena* directly onto the beach just opposite the Kaete Dan Hotel, headquarters of the United Nations Truce Commission. Apparently Stavsky hoped that the remaining arms could be unloaded under the eyes of all Tel Aviv. Ben-Gurion would not want to risk using force in front of witnesses. But Ben-Gurion could not allow the authority of the government to be undermined, particularly in the presence of the United Nations and the foreign press. If the Irgun wanted to force his hand, he would reply with force, despite the agony of civil strife or the army's need for the arms on board the *Altalena*. Zahal troops from the Tel Aviv area were rushed to the beach. Heavy machine-gun posts and artillery emplacements were thrown up.

At dawn an Irgun motor launch left the *Altalena* and established a tiny beachhead on the shore. A second motorboat started toward the beach. A Zahal machine gun opened fire, perhaps as a warning. The motor launch zigzagged wildly. Confused firing broke out all along the beach. Zahal artillery tossed a shell alongside the *Altalena,* again perhaps as a warning, but the next shell crashed into the *Altalena.* Unbelievably, Jew was fighting Jew while the civilian population, the United Nations officials, and foreign correspondents stood on the verandas, terraces, and rooftops watching. The *Altalena* was afire. Stavsky had been killed. Irgun troops on shore, bolstered by the survivors brought off the ship on surfboards, were massing in the Manshieh quarter between Tel Aviv and Jaffa. Tel Aviv could hardly believe that a civil war had begun. That night Yigal Yadin and Foreign Minister Moshe Sharett met with the foreign press to review the situation. The Irgun still controlled part of the beach and the Manshiya quarter. Sharett told the press that the government would not back down.

> The existence of the state is at stake. We are facing an internal crisis and we are determined to see it through. The state will not tolerate political and military anarchy resulting from the action of rebellious dissidents. The Jewish people are badly in need of arms, but it is better to see them go up in flames than into the hands of those who are ready to turn them against the state. We must uphold the sovereignty of the state and its capacity to honor international obligations.[7]

After a confused and uncertain night, the Irgun decided not to resist. Tel Aviv, however, remained in a state of unbearable tension. Even those who supported Ben-Gurion thought that the loss of forty Jewish lives had been too great a price to pay for unity. Although Ben-Gurion felt unable to dissolve the Irgun units in the Zahal, restrictive measures were carried out. The government pursued a policy of arrests and internments. As a dissident force the Irgun had been smashed. Although the price Ben-Gurion had paid was high, he did not think it was too high to allow Israel to face the second round "under a single authority and with an Army united."[8]

The Arabs also had their problems in creating a single authority and a united army, even though the problems did not lead to open fighting. Although the Arab public and to some extent the politicians were under the impression that the truce had saved the Jews, the military commanders on the front knew that their armies needed more arms and men for the second round. Only the Syrian army had shown any reluctance to accept the truce. Elsewhere the Arabs needed the pause as much as the Israelis did. General Sir John Bagot Glubb's Arab Legion had been under heavy pressure and in the midst of the fighting had lost all the seconded British officers and N.C.O.s, who were recalled by London. By June his ammunition stocks had dwindled and his lack of reserves had begun to hurt. The Egyptians and Iraqis both needed refitting and additional trained units. What was most needed, however, was a unified war plan. General Salih Said al-Jabouri, the Iraqi Chief of Staff, reported that the Arab lack of success was a direct result of the lack of a unified command. The nominal commander, King Abdullah ibn-Husein of Transjordan, had controlled only the Legion. All other units had acted independently, although the Iraqis had reluctantly moved into the triangle at Abdullah's request. To succeed in the second round, a real battle plan was as essential as were more men and equipment.

Although General Al-Jabouri was undoubtedly correct, in that a major factor in the limited success of the Arabs had been disunity, there were other factors that he chose to ignore. In some Arab capitals there had been all along a lack of enthusiasm for the Palestine adventure and everywhere serious neglect in preparing for the invasion. Few Arabs had cared to admit that their vaunted military resources were in fact so sparse. Even fewer had done much to rectify the situation. After the war had begun, Lebanese participation was little better than nominal. The Egyptians were exceptionally cautious. The Iraqis in the triangle did little but react to Israeli pressure. Arab control of the air was wasted. Nowhere had the better-equipped Arab armies proved a match for the Israelis. There had been successful defenses at Latrun and Jenin, and the Syrians had held onto their wedge in Galilee, but at best the Arabs could claim only a draw. If the Israelis showed even minimal recuperative powers, the Arabs would have to make a far greater effort of their own to maintain the balance. There would have to be changes in command, in commitment, in attitude, if the Arabs were not to court disaster.

Many Arabs believed that these changes could be made, that in July the Arabs could go into the second round with the forces and the élan that they should have had in May. No one except Abdullah seemed to realize that in July the Israelis were not going to be as feeble as they had been in May. Conditions had changed, and the

Arabs had not responded to the change. No one was more aware than Abdullah of the Israeli shift. The Legion, the main—really the only—prop of his regime, had suffered far too many casualties. Glubb's men had done a marvelous job. There had been many casualties but few taken prisoner. Although the British officers had gone, the Legion had retained its fighting capacity. But there were no reserves. The tide of Arab refugees had created chaotic conditions around Jerusalem and in Transjordan. Abdullah could see no reason for a second round, which could not benefit him and might lose him all that the Legion had won. Even to absorb the areas he had occupied would be a difficult task. There was little practical chance of increasing his hold on Palestine, and almost certainly his Legion would be the Israelis' prime target. Abdullah wanted no second round; it would be bad for Transjordan and bad for the Arabs.

On June 27 Abdullah visited Cairo in order to persuade King Faruk and Prime Minister Mahmud Fahmi Nokrashy that a lengthy delay was necessary in order to re-equip the Legion and to set up a unified command with an acceptable operational plan. In effect he wanted Nokrashy to call off the war. He was even willing to offer the supreme command to the Egyptians. Nokrashy was at first sympathetic, but he procrastinated. Unlike Abdullah, he could not act independently of all the dangerous forces and personalities of Cairo politics: the mob, the King, the Muslim Brotherhood, the army, and his own party. He showed little interest in Abdullah's ammunition problem despite the fact that the Egyptians had seized Legion supplies that were being shipped through Suez. Abdullah was not permitted to visit Egyptian army headquarters, as King Faruk himself had not yet done so. Ultimately, Abdullah achieved nothing in Cairo. Nokrashy became, if anything, more adamant. Abdullah even met with his ancient rival, the Mufti of Jerusalem, Hajj Amin al-Huseini, with no result. On June 27 he flew to see his dynastic rival, King ibn-Saud of Saudi Arabia. Again he could arouse no interest in postponement. Unlike Transjordan, Saudi Arabia had nothing to lose by a second round. Abdullah flew on to Baghdad to see the Regent. He was told that Iraq intended to renew the fighting after the termination of the truce—Iraqi reinforcements were already on the way to the triangle in Palestine. When the Arab League finally met in Cairo for a decision, Transjordan stood alone.

For their own reasons the other states would go to war. The Lebanese were fearful of isolating themselves from the Arab world. Syria had hopes of establishing another wedge across the Jordan. Egypt would fight as much to spite Abdullah as to protect the Palestinian Arabs. Iraq saw domestic political advantages in a popular foreign war. Transjordan, one among five, had to vote for a second round. Abdullah knew that an assassin probably awaited him if he deserted the Palestine Arabs. There was still no unity of command and no prospect for cooperation. Even if all the fervent promises to increase the Arab armies were fulfilled, Abdullah would still expect the worst. If the full weight of the Israelis came down on the Legion, he could expect little help from his brother Arabs.

The Arabs had made extensive efforts to strengthen their invasion forces. Baghdad had increased the number of Iraqi troops in Palestine to about 15,000 men, supplied by eleven large convoys. Eventually some of this new ammunition was turned over to the Arab Legion, easing Glubb's supply problem. The Arab Liberation Army was integrated into the Lebanese command. By July, Fawzi el-Kaukji had only about 2,000 troops left, after the loss of the Iraqi volunteers, who had joined their own country's forces; in addition, many of the local irregulars had drifted home. The Egyptian army had been increased to 18,000 men, practically all Cairo's military capacity. Syria had carried on extensive recruitment, but the motorized brigade on the Galilee frontier was really the entire Syrian army. In Egypt and Iraq British equipment was still arriving under treaty agreements and being shipped on to Palestine. The Iraqi and Egyptian air forces continued to draw replacement parts from the R.A.F. depots. Although their equipment would not be up to European standards at the end of the truce, the Arabs would still be slightly better off than the Israelis would. They would have 40,000–45,000 men in the field. In contrast to their position on May 15, however, the Arabs had declined in strength relative to Israel; if Arab intelligence reports were to be believed, in May the Israelis had had 60,000 well-equipped men in the Haganah. As in May there was no unified operational plan, yet the kings and politicians did not seem unduly concerned about this problem. Nearly all of them expected great things. The second round was to finish off the Israelis.

While the buildup continued on both sides of the cease-fire line,

Bernadotte worked desperately to prevent the second round that the Arabs desired and the Israelis anticipated. The Truce Commission had found that its activities were mere formalities earning the distrust of both sides, who evaded the restrictions in any case. In Jerusalem the Israelis viewed with a jaundiced eye attempts to freeze the status quo at the time of the cease-fire. The new rules seemed beyond the competence of the Commission to enforce and intended to maintain the New City on a starvation basis. Arab violations went unpunished. The Israeli military governor, Dov Joseph, harassed by the endless crises of the long siege, eventually lost all faith in the United Nations Commission.

> In the last analysis it boiled down to the point of view of the Truce Commission, and one regrettably had to recognize the fact that this body in practice showed partiality toward the Arab side and allowed them in effect to dictate the course the commission should follow. The Arabs for their part did everything in their power to slow down and hold up our supplies, and the pedantic attitude of the U.N. helped them.[9]

The Arabs too had little faith in the Truce Commission, which seemed incapable of preventing Israeli immigration and arms shipments; besides, most Arabs still seethed over the United Nations vote on partition. The Truce Commission thus could not prevent the Iraqi convoys, the arrival of Israeli arms consignments, the convoys over the Burma road to Jerusalem, or the arrival of Egyptian reinforcements in the Negev. The effort to freeze the military situation was far beyond the capacity of the Commission. The failure damaged the very United Nations prestige that Bernadotte wanted to protect. He had to accept the facts that the truce had not worked as he had planned and that it probably could not be extended unless he could come up with an attractive alternative to war.

On June 27 the Mediator presented his long-awaited solution as a general basis of discussion. Bernadotte had based his plan on what he found to be the most important realities: the existence of Israel, the effectiveness of the Arab Legion, and the interests of Great Britain. But his solution had little to offer anyone; each side wanted something and, more important, believed that it could seize what it wanted. July 1948 was certainly not a golden moment for solution by diplomacy and negotiation. The Arabs were incapable of recognizing any point of view but their own. The Israelis had no intention of accepting less than they had won by force of arms. Amid wartime hysteria and without a decisive military conclusion, no one was able to give serious attention to one more plan whipped up in a couple of weeks by a rank outsider.

In his efforts to adapt a solution to the realities, Bernadotte had interpreted curiously the events of the four-week war. He suggested a federated state of Israel and Transjordan, which the former would never have accepted and the latter's Arab allies would never have permitted. This federated state would have allowed unlimited immigration for two years, and then the United Nations would have proposed a final solution of free or limited immigration. But no Arab would countenance Jewish immigration, and no Israeli would agree to limit it. Finally, the Arab refugees would be repatriated; Bernadotte's was the first such proposal in an endless stream. His boundary proposals were equally ill advised. Israel would lose the Negev and Jerusalem and gain western Galilee. The rest would go to Transjordan. But the other Arab states had entered the war to prevent the establishment of just such a greater Transjordan. Israel in four weeks had successfully defended Jerusalem, had long since occupied western Galilee, and had retained a hold on the Negev. Yet, under Bernadotte's plan, it would have had to relinquish the boundaries granted in the United Nations partition resolution and give up Jerusalem. The boundary adjustments could thus have pleased no one but Abdullah. The federated state could be acceptable only to Abdullah.

As far as the Arab states and Israel could see, the prime beneficiaries of the Bernadotte plan would be the British and their ally Abdullah—both to be given what they had been unable to secure either by diplomacy or by war. Egypt would gain nothing under the new plan; in fact, Cairo would have to evacuate the South and turn it over to the British-sponsored Abdullah. Syria would have to give up its wedge in Galilee and face the threat of absorption into Abdullah's new kingdom. Lebanon would receive nothing. Iraq would end up only with a strong rival in the new Jordan. Everyone would have to give up not only his aspirations but also his hard-won gains. Everyone would face a strong and ambitious Abdullah preaching unity on his terms. The Arab League, with Abdullah concurring, rejected the plan.

The Israelis were equally negative: The partition resolution was to be discarded, Israeli military victories were to be ignored, Arab aggression was to remain unchastised, even the state was to be federated. On July 6 Israel rejected the Mediator's plan. Rarely had one proposed solution antagonized so many.

When his suggestions for discussion were rejected, Bernadotte attempted to gain an extension of the truce. The Arabs were not interested. There was to be an Arab Palestine or war, a position that left little room for compromise. On July 8 the Mediator reluctantly instructed the Truce Commission to abandon its posts. On the same day, twenty-eight hours early, the impatient Egyptians could wait no longer. They jumped the gun and simultaneously attacked several kibbutzim. The second round had begun. Bernadotte had never really had a chance. The Arabs could not accept the existence of Israel. Equally important, they could see no reason not to consolidate their local gains. Yet they reopened the war woefully unprepared to confront the immeasurably strengthened Zahal. In the second round the Israelis would at last have the reserves and equipment to fight major offensive operations. On their side of the front lines, the Arabs had sufficient troops only to continue the same piecemeal war as before but without even their former clear superiority in armor, artillery, and aircraft. Despite Abdullah's warnings that the Arabs could not fight a real war, the governments in Cairo, Damascus, and Baghdad were determined to take the risk, to ignore the obstacles, to fight.

What Abdullah only vaguely understood and even the Israelis did not fully realize was that the entire balance of power in the Middle East had shifted. In May the Arab Middle East of 40 million faithful had managed to put into the field an army barely superior to that of the Israelis. In July, even by scraping the bottom of the barrel and doubling their commitments, the Arabs could not match Israel. By late summer Israel would have the military capacity not only to clear Palestine but also to smash the Arab states singly or collectively. This strength even the pessimistic Abdullah could not yet fully appreciate. The withdrawal of the British, still far from complete, from full control of the Middle East had left a military vacuum that could not be filled by the paper armies of the Arabs. When they opted for a second round, they risked the prestige and pretensions of all 40 million Arabs. The assumption that, although they perhaps could not win, they certainly could not lose was disastrous. The second round was a giant step toward a future that few could foresee in the summer of 1948. Nothing was more typical of the old Arab world than the decision for war in July. In ten short days that old Arab world would receive the first of a series of shocks that would utterly change the Middle East and the mind of the Arab.

NOTES

1. Dov Joseph, *The Faithful City: The Siege of Jerusalem, 1948* (New York: 1960), p. 212.

2. Count Folke Bernadotte, *To Jerusalem* (London: 1951), pp. 114–5.

3. Jon Kimche and David Kimche, *Both Sides of the Hill: Britain and the Palestine War* (London: 1960), p. 200.

4. After the war, Mardam was condemned to death by a Syrian court for selling arms to the Zionists but freed when the government was overthrown by Colonel Husny Zaim. *Ibid.*, p. 206.

5. *Ibid.*, p. 213.

6. Stavsky had been tried, convicted, and sentenced for the murder of Dr. Chaim Arlosoroff of the Jewish Agency's Political Department in 1933. He was later acquitted on appeal. The case was a *cause célèbre* in the Jewish Agency–Revisionist struggle.

7. Kenneth W. Bilby, *New Star in the Near East* (Garden City, N.Y.: 1950), p. 123.

8. David Ben-Gurion, *Rebirth and Destiny of Israel* (New York: 1954), p. 260.

9. Joseph, *Faithful City*, p. 237.

Prime Minister Levi Eshkol inspecting trainees. (Israel Office of Information Research Department)

Secretary-General U Thant conferring with President Gamal Abdel Nasser, 1967. (United Nations)

8

The Ten-Day War

When Count Folke Bernadotte's truce ended abruptly on July 8, the Arabs and the Israelis had in common one basic assumption, that the fighting during the second round would be conclusive. That the United Nations would seek to end the conflict was obvious, but that such international pressure would be immediately effective was doubtful. Bernadotte's only answer to the renewed war was an invitation to the belligerents to meet with him on Rhodes. No one showed any interest in such a meeting. When the Egyptians attacked on July 8, it seemed clear that the United Nations and Bernadotte would have to wait until one side or the other had forced a decision by military means. Any future cease-fire would result only from the collapse of the Arab effort, for the Israelis could afford to accept a truce. The Arabs, on the other hand, had made it abundantly clear that, unless they could win an Arab Palestine, they would continue the war, assuming, of course, that David Ben-Gurion and the Zahal recognized Arab intransigence, but they also assumed that Arab pride and United Nations uncertainty would allow the Israelis sufficient time to inflict such a defeat.

Israeli plans for the second round centered on the destruction of the most impressive opponent, the Arab Legion, in a battle that would clear the Jerusalem corridor and open up a variety of offensive options. Although the Zahal commanders still did not agree that the Jerusalem corridor deserved such precedence, they did agree with Ben-Gurion that the prime target should be the Legion. [A fully successful operation against the Legion would split the Arabs reducing the Syrian and Egyptian positions to peripheral wedges easily cleared.] The main thrust was thus to be in the Center, where Yigal Alon planned to use an indirect approach, rather than the frontal assault originally suggested by Yigal Yadin. With nearly a division at his disposal Alon planned to pinch off the Lydda-Er Ramle area northwest of Latrun. He could then press directly west toward Ramallah, outflanking the Legion at Latrun and breaking through the central Arab front. Alon's attack would require a substantial portion of the Israeli offensive capacity, but it would by no means be the only offensive. In the North, the Israelis decided to erase the Syrian bridgehead at Mishmar Hayarden. Although this operation was purportedly adopted because the Syrians were the most dangerous force in the sector, at least as important was the desire to remove the Arabs from Israeli territory, as defined in the partition resolution. Given time, a second operation would hit Fawzi el-Kaukji's Arab Liberation Army, the weakest and most vulnerable opponent. No operations were prepared against either the Lebanese or the Iraqis. In the South the prime objective was still to cut the lateral Majdal-Hebron highway and to open a safe path into the northern Negev. If all went well, the second round would clear the Arabs from all but a few pockets in Palestine; the Arabs would then be forced to accept the existence of Israel and to sue for peace.

The Arab armies had no such grandiose plans. No real consideration had been given to a cooperative venture; no two armies had made joint plans. Those Arabs who anticipated a smashing offensive to drive the Zionist gangs into the sea were a long way from the front. None of the armies had prepared more than the most limited of local operations. The Lebanese intended to sit out the second round. The Arab Legion, fearing just the sort of offensive that Alon had in mind, anticipated only defensive operations and a withdrawal from its more exposed positions. The Syrians were concentrating on their one wedge. Kaukji hoped somehow to capture a kibbutz and to reap the resulting prestige. The Iraqis were apparently open to opportunity, but, despite the large number of Iraqi troops concentrated in the triangle, their commanders had little enthusiasm for another Jenin.

Only the Egyptians had any firm offensive intentions, and these intentions were actually strategically defensive in that Muawi was eager only to eliminate the previously bypassed Israeli settlements and to broaden his east-west blocking position. Although the avowed Arab aim of creating an Arab Palestine by force of arms was trumpeted in the journals and on the radios of the Middle East, there was no evidence along the front that it was accepted there. The Arab armies planned only to pick up bits and pieces of territory.

To seize the main Israeli objective in the north, the Syrian bridgehead at Mishmar Hayarden, Moshe Carmel had prepared an elaborate textbook attack, which included deep investing maneuvers to cut off the Syrian wedge from the rear and to avoid a frontal assault. One arm of a pincers was to cross Lake Hule by boat on the first night and to take the Syrian police station near the Dardara settlement. This move would cut the one supply route to the Syrian bridgehead. A second force would establish a ford on the Jordan, allowing the Israeli engineers to construct a pontoon bridge across the river. The 2nd Infantry Battalion would cross over and complete the envelopment. The two remaining battalions would hold static positions to tie down the Syrians in Mishmar Hayarden. On paper it was an ideal operation, but the Syrians had apparently already read the paper. Although the police station fell as scheduled on the night of July 9, little else went well. When the engineers slipped up to begin work on the pontoon bridge, the Syrians dropped a previously ranged artillery barrage on them. In the darkness and confusion the engineers could not put up the bridge. The result was a tedious, chaotic infantry crossing that ate up four hours. Carmel finally decided to break off the fording operation, and the 2nd Battalion then dug in on both sides of the ford. One thrust of the pincers had been halted. Carmel's timetable had come apart. During the night information arrived that the Syrians would attack at dawn. Still, the police station had been taken and the Syrian positions whittled down to Mishmar Hayarden and one other stronghold to the west.

Reacting swiftly to the Israeli challenge, the Syrians dealt a heavy counterblow, supported by armored cars and tanks. As the Israeli air force was engaged elsewhere, the Syrians also had air supremacy. In their first thrust they recaptured several of the strongpoints lost the night before and then pressed in on the ford, threatening to cut off the Israelis still entrenched on the far bank. There was nothing for

Carmel to do but pull them back from the eastern bank of the ford in broad daylight under heavy Syrian fire. Those who could swam across, but the wounded had to be left behind. The Syrians pushed on north before losing momentum late in the day. On the same afternoon the Israelis also pulled back from the police station into Dardara. The Syrians followed up with an attack but wasted three hours shelling an unfortified hill above the settlement. When the main Syrian assault came, the Israelis had already ranged their mortars and heavy machine guns on the Syrian line of attack. Cut up by the Israeli fire, the Syrians ran into the settlement mine fields and pulled back.

On the following day Carmel found that, far from sweeping around Mishmar Hayarden in an elegant envelopment, he had been drawn into a pounding struggle to protect the main north-south highway in eastern Galilee.[1] For two days the Syrians and Israelis yielded and retook ground in bloody fighting. Then on the night of July 13 the Carmeli Brigade made one more attempt to overrun the Syrian bridgehead with an attack from the south through an area that had been fairly quiet. But again the Syrians seemed to have read the same paper, and the Israelis ran into strongly fortified positions. The attack collapsed. Carmel had lost all his mobility, and his brigade had been sucked into a succession of futile attacks and counterattacks on fortified positions reminiscent of World War I trench warfare. The Syrians had not collapsed, nor had they lacked the will to carry out repeated counterattacks. Once more operations in the North had not been the expected walkover. After July 14 both sides settled down, and neither tried seriously to break the stalemate. The Syrians limited themselves to occasional tank sorties, whereas the only new Israeli operation consisted of a raid on Mishmar Hayarden by a B-17. The center of operations in the North had shifted elsewhere.

While the Carmeli Brigade was tied up by the Syrians, the Iraqi army and Kaukji's Arab Liberation Army had gone into action. The Iraqis, augmented by local volunteers, began to push north from Jenin. The Golani Brigade gave up the villages south of the Gilboan hills in the Valley of Dothan, preferring to set up a secure line in the hills farther north. The Zahal commanders were glad to see the Iraqis tied up in a slow, tactically pointless operation, even though it did mean giving up the territory won in the earlier Jenin operation. Once the Iraqis reached the hills, however, their offensive spirit disappeared. Farther north Kaukji had carefully selected an isolated kibbutz for his one big operation. Sejera, at the tip of a small Jewish wedge, poking into Arab-held central Galilee looked ideal. On paper Kaukji's attack seemed to be an effort to threaten the Israeli route south to Tiberias, but in reality Kaukji simply wanted a victory, and Sejera was already surrounded by Arab territory on three sides.

In the previous six months Kaukji had apparently learned nothing and forgotten everything. His army, fleshed out by the local mob, made a daylight rush on the settlement. The Israelis' heavy fire drove the Arab wave back. At night the defenders laid mines and carried out a series of commando raids. These operations were carried on with impunity, for the Arabs as usual did not want to fight in the dark. The next day the frontal assaults began again, plowing into heavy Israeli machine-gun fire and stumbling over the mines laid the previous night. Arab casualties began to pile up. On July 12, Kaukji, supported by artillery dropping shrapnel bursts over the settlement, launched an unsuccessful attack from three directions. On July 14, supported as well by air strikes, the Arabs attacked eight times. At one point Arab armored vehicles reached the entrance of the colony before pulling back in the face of heavy mortar fire. Throughout Kaukji's attention remained riveted on his immediate objective, oblivious to any possible Israeli reaction elsewhere.

The Israeli reaction was Operation Dekel, an attack on Nazareth from the west that would outflank Kaukji's positions around Sejera. As Kaukji did not consider himself bound by any action taken by the United Nations,[2] limited fighting had taken place along the western finger of Galilee throughout the truce. As it had become apparent that the Lebanese did not pose a threat to the western finger, the Zahal had been moving inland and occupying a series of Arab villages in the foothills of central Galilee. On July 11 three large anti-Arab Druze villages had asked to be captured. Kaukji's only response had been two half-hearted attacks opposite Naharayim and Acre. With Kaukji heavily committed at Sejera, Operation Dekel could be well underway before he could recognize the direction of the attack or the implied threat to his position at Sejera. Under the command of Chaim Laskov and Brigadier Ben Dunkelman, who had been a Canadian armored-corps commander in World War II, the Israeli attack would be a straight dash by four battalions from the west into Nazareth, evading any fighting that might divert the flow of the operation.

On the morning of July 14 Zahal units captured Shfar Ann, an ancient hilltop village on the road to Nazareth. At the same time units of the Golani Brigade moved north and took the Arab village of Ma-alul, lifting the long siege of Kfar Hahoresh west of Nazareth. On the night of July 15 the settlers from Kfar Hahoresh joined up with the Golani in a fifteen-mile dash to the Arab hill village of Zipori. By 6:00 in the morning, they had taken Zipori, and the way to Nazareth lay open. Arab civilians could be seen fleeing the neighboring villages, a sure harbinger of Israeli success. Laskov began the move into the city. At 5:15 P.M., after pushing aside ineffectual local resistance, his armored column ran into the Arab mobile reserve of eight armored cars. An Israeli half-track carrying a 20-millimeter gun knocked off six of the Arab vehicles one after another, which smashed the last resistance. In an hour the Arab notables remaining in Nazareth arrived at Zahal field headquarters to surrender the city.

Laskov had pulled off an elegant operation. Keeping to the main line of attack, he had swept into Nazareth, indirectly levering Kaukji out of southern Galilee. As Kaukji withdrew northward, another string of Arab villages fell to the Israelis. The Arab Liberation Army began to come apart again. Kaukji would soon take a long leave of absence. The Arabs left were little more than an embittered collection of armed refugees hiding out in the hills to the north, living off a sullen countryside.

Operation Dekel had gone beautifully for the Israelis. After the unexpectedly brief ten days of fighting, they were revealed as the clear winners in the North, though not by a massive margin. The Arab Liberation Army had collapsed. The Lebanese were still quiet. But, although the Syrians had been badly battered, they had kept their wedge. In contrast to the Israeli gains around Nazareth and the Arab villages not previously cleared near Haifa, only the Iraqis could claim any gains, and those gains had been more in the nature of tactical gifts. In fact, considering the number of Iraqi troops and the possibilities open to them, their lack of action in the triangle was curious. Perhaps, the Iraqis believed that they had plenty of time, but the evidence suggests that they had no intention of launching any operation that would draw an Israeli reaction.

In the South both sides once again concentrated on the lateral highway. During the cease-fire the United Nations Truce Commission had been unsuccessful in persuading the Egyptians to grant the Israelis use of the north-south roads. The Egyptians would not allow the Israelis to supply Kfar Darom, thereby forcing its evacuation on the night of July 7. Shimon Avidan realized only too well that Kfar Darom's fate could easily be shared by the remainder of the Negev settlements unless he could break through the Egyptian center. The Egyptians had not waited for Avidan to move, and before any Israeli operations could be undertaken he would have to respond to the Egyptian surprise attack of July 8, in which the Egyptians seized a line of strong points, upsetting the original timing of Avidan's offensive. The Negev Brigade had been forced to give up Kaukaba and withdraw south toward Huleikat. To the north of the highway, the Egyptians had occupied Hill 113 and a position near Bet Daras. An Egyptian Sudanese surprise attack on Bet Daras had faltered and then collapsed under its own artillery fire.[3] Following through, the Israelis forced the Egyptians out of their position near Bet Daras but not out of Hill 113. Avidan decided that he would have to advance his timetable and attack before the Egyptians could consolidate their early gains.

On the night of July 8, the Givati Brigade moved south to occupy the main villages and hills along the highway. The Negev Brigade moved north to attack the Iraq-Suedan police station, the "Monster on the Hill." If the two brigades could link up at Iraq Suedan, the corridor into the Negev would be secure. Equally important, if the attacks could be exploited the Egyptians could be split into two long and vulnerable fingers on the coast and on the weakly held inland road to Jerusalem. The Givati attack went well, taking all targets: the villages of Iraq Suedan, Bet Affa, and Ibdis, but only eighteen Israelis were left to make the attack that breached the last Egyptian position at Ibdis. The Egyptians did not wait to count their attackers, however, but fled shouting, "The Jew has come." The night attack by the Negev Brigade on the Monster on the Hill did not go as well. The Israelis were late in arriving outside the fortress, and, as soon as they had cut the first perimeter wire, the Egyptians opened fire. By the time that the Israelis had cut the next four fences dawn was near. The advance troops, still under heavy fire, had to pull back. The Givati then had to give up the village of Iraq Suedan, which was directly under the police fortress. While the Iraq Suedan attack was breaking down, another Zahal force mopped up the area north of the highway against only scattered opposition, as thousands of local Arabs began to leave. Clearing the north side of the highway, however, did not compensate for the failure to take the Monster on the Hill.

At dawn the Egyptians responded with an attack centered on Negba. Moving in two encircling columns, the Egyptians hoped not only to recoup what they had lost but also to force the Israelis well back from the road. One column succeeded in overrunning Bet Affa, but the Egyptian infantry would not continue the advance into the Ibdis outpost. Egyptian armor moved up and fired directly into Ibdis until an Israeli 65-millimeter antitank gun made a direct hit on one tank. The Egyptians then withdrew. The next morning they opened a heavy artillery barrage and attacked Ibdis again, but by noon the attack had been broken off. The flanking operation through Ibdis to the east and Julis to the west had not worked out. But there was still Negba. On July 12, the Egyptians put a heavy barrage down on both Ibdis and Julis, as well as on Negba. Egyptian aircraft dove to the attack of Negba. At 11:00 in the morning, the Egyptian infantry moved in from east and west. The first surge came within fifty yards of the perimeter fence. During the afternoon a second attack reached the inner fence but failed to overrun the settlement. During the next three days the Egyptians concentrated on occupying strategic spots around Negba but made no further major attacks. Their momentum was spent.[4]

Avidan, realizing that time was running out and that the Egyptians had settled in, decided to repeat the north-south attack. On the night of July 17, operations began against the two small villages of Hatta and Kharatya and the key point, Bet Affa, which had been heavily fortified by the Egyptians. The attack on Bet Affa failed, but the two smaller villages fell to the Israelis, which meant that Avidan at last controlled a strip of the east-west highway. The anticipated Egyptian counterattacks the following morning could not dislodge the Israelis. Before the Egyptians could launch a third attack, a new truce came into effect, at 7:00 in the evening of July 18. The Israelis still controlled their strip of the highway, but their gain did not prove as great as they had hoped. The Egyptians quickly occupied a series of hills facing Kharatya and built an alternate road. The block was thus reconstructed, and what had been an Israeli gate into the Negev at

Kharatya became simply a wedge pointed at the new Egyptian positions. Basically the situation in the South had not changed.

Avidan was convinced that to clear the lateral highway would require a major commitment. He reported to Tel Aviv on the problem of using limited operations against the Egyptian army.

> There is no small or partial solution for the problem of the Negev; in order to force a way to the Negev a corridor of strongholds had to be created, its width depending upon the point of breach, which in turn will necessitate very considerable forces to protect it against the danger of renewed disruption.[5]

This effort, of course, was not the only way to free the Negev, for if the entire Egyptian army were to be defeated there would be no need to defend a corridor against disruption. In July 1948, however, Avidan could not undertake operations on so impressive a scale. The idea of a major offensive operation in the South had as yet attracted little serious attention. Avidan had been forced to make do. The ten days had brought not even a partial solution for the Israelis in the South. The Egyptians still blocked the way to the Negev.

Although operations in the North and the South had been limited by the drain of troops and equipment to the Center, David Shaltiel, commander at Jerusalem, the main focus of Ben-Gurion's war plans faced a similar problem. The general staff had decided that Shaltiel should be able to seize several objectives in the Jerusalem sector without any direct cooperation with Alon's major offensive. Some thought must have been given to the fact that, if Alon's attack went well, operations in Jerusalem might prove unnecessary. Encouraged by the supplies coming in on the Burma Road, however, Shaltiel estimated that he could carry out his operations in a few days. He saw no need to hurry. The main thrust would be elsewhere along the Lydda-Er Ramle bulge. There Alon hoped to outflank and gobble up Lydda and Er Ramle and then to smash on into Ramallah, which would cut off the Legion in Latrun to the south. The Legion would have to fall back perhaps beyond Jerusalem, leaving open a wide corridor into the city. To the north the Iraqis would be outflanked, and to the south a wedge could be driven between the Legion and the Egyptians south of Jerusalem on the Beersheba road. Once the

Legion had broken, the entire Arab position, excluding a few pockets, would simply come apart.

Alon's attack on the Lydda-Er Ramle sector was to be a pincers movement, one arm moving down from the north and the other up from the south, while a diversionary frontal attack was made from the direction of Tel Aviv. Hopefully, the Legion would not anticipate an attack in the area and would react too slowly to prevent envelopment. On the night of July 9 a battalion of the Yiftach Brigade jumped off in the south and captured a series of villages. By evening of the next day, Gimzu behind Er Ramle had been taken, and the point was probing Lydda. The northern force under the "Old Man," Itzhak Sadeh, consisted of the 82nd Armored Battalion and two infantry battalions from the Kiryati and Alexandroni Brigades. They moved out on the morning of July 10, encountering only sporadic opposition. The Alexandroni Battalion quickly captured Wilhelma, a former German settlement named for Wilhelm II. The Arabs gave up the Lydda airport after less than an hour of resistance. Sadeh's 82nd Armored Battalion ran into trouble, however, near the village of Deir Tarif in the hills behind Lydda. Although Glubb was unwilling to try to hold the Lydda-Ramle bulge, he recognized the Zahal offensive as a serious threat to this flank. He had ordered the 1st Regiment with its armor to the road junction at Beit Nabala near Deir Tarif in front of Sadeh's column. Sadeh was forced to pull his armor out of Deir Tarif. The northern pincer had been stopped.

With Sadeh's armored battalion tied down, Moshe Dayan's mobile commando group bypassed Deir Tarif and drove south to Ben Shemen. As Dayan moved south, he received a hurried call from the Yiftach Brigade for armor support from Sadeh's 82nd Battalion. The Yiftach had entered Lydda without its own armor, but Dayan knew that Sadeh could not break free from the Legion's 1st Regiment in time to help. He decided to make a wild, motorized cavalry charge, using his jeeps as tanks, from Ben Shemen directly into Lydda, hoping to scatter the Arabs. Led by a captured Legion armored car firing a two-pounder, Dayan's column moved toward Lydda. When the Arabs began withdrawing under the fire of the two-pounder, Dayan took his jeeps in after them.

That was the crucial moment. To follow in the footsteps of the escapees:

The main road was blocked, and the unit moved along a side track, which fortunately, had not been mined. Soon afterward we penetrated through the line of positions. The column moved slowly, in line, along the narrow track. Barricades were breached from time to time. Firing went on at full speed. The jeeps, whose only armor were their weapons, their light machine guns, shot at windows, at fences, at sandbag positions. The cactus fence was cut by machine guns, as if with a sickle. We increased our speed and left the positions behind us. From the junction at the entrance of Lydda, the column continued south toward Ramle, and entered that city under a hail of fire. . . . The visit to Ramle was exceedingly brief. The unit had been badly hit. . . .[6]

Dayan drew back to Ben Shemen. The whole operation had cost nine dead and seventeen wounded. The raid lasted only forty-seven minutes, but in Lydda and Er Ramle the Arabs were left confused and uncertain. Their position had been breached—Israeli armor had destroyed their cohesiveness. Their nerves were gone.

Exploiting the Arab shock, Yiftach infantry moved into Lydda and cleared the city by nightfall without armor or artillery. The next morning, however, a Legion patrol penetrated the city. Many of the local Arabs snatched up arms again, turning instantly from passive civilians to eager volunteers. Once again Yiftach troops were in a tricky position. For a moment it looked as if they were all going to be prisoners of their prisoners, but the Legion patrol withdrew, and the Arab civilian-soldiers surrendered. On July 11 only the Arabs in the police fortress between Lydda and Er Ramle still held out, but the next day Yiftach units found that the fortress had been deserted during the night. On the same day Rosh Haayin to the north was recaptured from the Iraqis. Alon's first stage had gone as planned. The next twenty-four hours were spent methodically regrouping for the next stage.

By the evening of July 12 the Israeli general staff realized that it had committed a serious error in ignoring the deliberations at the United Nations. Once the news of Israeli victories had reached the sensitive ears of the British, there was an immediate and serious shift of policy. Suddenly the British felt a great sense of urgency, as well they might, for the Arab Legion seemed to be on the run. Demands for an instant cease-fire began. Instead of having unlimited time to carry out his operations in the Center in careful, well-prepared steps and to slice up the Legion like salami, Alon was now forced to bite off as much as he could in the short time remaining. To complicate his tactical dispositions, no one either in Tel Aviv or at Lake Success had a clue to exactly how much time did remain before the inevitable truce. The general staff jettisoned the thrust through to Ramallah and decided to settle for Latrun and the water pipeline from Rosh Haayin into Jerusalem. This capture would not shatter the whole Arab position in Palestine, but it would secure Jerusalem. Glubb too was aware of the time limit on Israeli operations, and he anticipated the Latrun attack. If the Legion could hold the Latrun wedge long enough for a truce to be effected, then Glubb's position, despite the loss of Lydda and Er Ramle, would still be secure. Latrun would remain the key, but the prime factor would be time. The last operations of the second round were conducted in a race against the erratic United Nations clock.

On the night of July 14 the Yiftach and Kiryati Brigades carried out operations to secure further positions along the road from Latrun to Ramallah; but the main blow was to be a flanking movement elsewhere. Alon's battle plan called for an attack on the hills dominating the road into Latrun from Ramallah. When the Harel Brigade launched the attack on the night of July 14, Alon immediately discovered that Glubb had foreseen the battle developing in this way and had moved another Legion battalion into the Latrun area and built his own Burma Road to permit armor to move up without using the vulnerable Ramallah road. Despite Glubb's preparations, however, one Harel company seized its objectives; the second company ran directly into superior Legion force. Then the sudden appearance of Legion armor where none was supposed to exist proved decisive. Both companies pulled back. [Alon's intentions had been too obvious, and the Legion had reacted.] On July 15 the Arabs attacked a Yiftach battalion dug in on a key hill near the village of Budrus. The Israelis held out for six hours but gave up the hill and Budrus soon after sunset.

On the following night the Yiftach seized a position allowing them to harass Legion traffic on the Ramallah road. The Legion launched a series of fierce counterattacks. Alon's loop, established piecemeal, was beginning to tighten. On July 17 both sides prepared for the final twenty-four hours. Glubb knew that, as time ran out, Alon would make one last effort, but the Legion was fully committed to keeping the loop from closing. Alon hoped that the Arab counterattacks would reduce Arab capacity to react to an unexpected direct frontal assault on Latrun.

The final battle at Latrun began at 6:00 in the evening with an Israeli armor thrust against the police station. Alon sent in five British Cromwell tanks supported by bren-gun carriers and armored trucks. Once the armor had reached the police station, the infantry would follow. But Alon had bad luck. The lead Cromwell's gun jammed, and the tank commander turned back to remove the shell casing from the barrel. The other tanks assumed that attack had been called off and moved back. The Legion was delighted. Glubb believed that the accurate fire of a single six pounder from the police station had forced the Israelis back. In any case, the infantry could not attack after the tanks had failed. There was no time to sort out the operation that night, and by the next day the new cease-fire had gone into effect. The Legion still held Latrun, and the highway to Jerusalem still had not been cleared, but Alon had occupied the important Lydda-Er Ramle bulge and mauled the Arab Legion for ten days. King Abdullah ibn-Husein's prized army had narrowly been saved by the United Nations bell.

In Jerusalem Shaltiel had also been slow to react to developments in the United Nations. He had been confident that he could carry out his operations, but he had left practical preparations until very late. Then he had too many targets and not enough time. His three major objectives were the Sheikh Jarrach quarter, the Old City, and the Tel Aviv–Jerusalem railway. It was an overambitious program, considering the peculiar difficulties in mounting operations in Jerusalem with limited forces, very limited matériel, and poor liaison. On the night of July 9 the Oded Brigade began an operation in the south to capture the villages of Malha and Ein Karen as a base for the joint action with the Harel on the west, aimed at capturing the railway. The fighting was limited, but the Egyptian air force did carry out the first air raid on Jerusalem in history. By July 14 it was obvious that a truce was in prospect and might even be enforced in Jerusalem earlier than elsewhere in Palestine. Shaltiel immediately decided to secure at least some of his targets. At that point the Arab Legion suddenly renewed the attacks from the north, seizing the Mandlebaum buildings and some houses south of the Damascus Gate. The Israelis were forced to react. Their counterattacks recaptured some of the houses, but, more important than a few local gains, the Arabs had thrown out of gear Shaltiel's plan to attack the Old City with the Etzioni Brigade.

On July 16 Ben-Gurion informed Shaltiel that the truce would be imposed in Jerusalem just before 6:00 the next morning. Shaltiel had less than twenty-four hours. Yadin ordered Shaltiel to try to take both Sheikh Jarrach and the Old City. If there were no time for both operations, Yadin wanted Shaltiel to give up driving a wedge into the Old City and to concentrate on Sheikh Jarrach. Shaltiel, apparently on his own hook, decided that his only chance for success was Operation Kedem, the capture of the Old City by two frontal attacks on the New Gate and the Zion Gate. That night the Irgun force managed to advance a few yards into the Old City through the New Gate but could not capture the Collège des Frères, its first objective, before dawn. The Irgun had to retreat. The other attack did no better. Preceded by an artillery barrage, with Davidka mortar fire and machine-gun support, HISH units tried to break through the Zion Gate. Sappers set up explosives beside the four-foot-thick walls of the Old City, and the charge was detonated with a tremendous roar. The wall was hardly scratched. Operation Kedem was a last-minute failure. Although bitter fighting continued around the Mandlebaum houses for two more days, the situation at the beginning of the second cease-fire on July 19 was essentially the same as it had been on July 9.

On a large-scale map the changes after the ten days of fighting do not seem very impressive. The Israelis had picked up a slice of central Galilee and had fattened up the Jerusalem salient. The Iraqi and Egyptians had picked up bits and pieces. The Israelis had had much the best of it, but the vital change wrought by the ten days was not the rather limited exchange of real estate. Alon's offensive had convinced Abdullah once and for all that the Legion could not stand up to the Zahal. If it were to try, Abdullah would lose his army and his throne. He could no longer allow the Legion to be chopped up in the name of Arab unity. Abdullah wanted out of the Palestine invasion, keeping what he could salvage, but most definitely out. The other Arab states were not so impressed with the Zahal. Their armies had faced only minor and limited assaults and had often done well. They had been sent into Palestine to achieve something and had not at least lost anything during the ten days. The Syrians still had Mishmar Hayarden. The Lebanese held central Galilee. The Iraqis held the triangle. The Egyptians had the Negev. All, along with the Mufti of Jerusalem, Hajj Amin al-Huseini, had the satisfaction of seeing Abdullah thwarted and his prized Legion battered. Only the Arab refugees had nothing, which was unfortunate but not vital. Everywhere the Arabs recognized that the second round had not gone too well, but they believed that there would be other chances.

For the Israelis the second round had not gone as planned either, but the main reason was that only ten days had been allowed them in which to crush the Arabs. The second truce did not convince Tel Aviv any more than it did Cairo or Damascus that the war had ended. There were too many loose ends to be tidied up. Alon's offensive had crippled the Legion. And, as the Arabs seemed determined to risk their armies further despite the evidence of Lydda-Er Ramle, Ben-Gurion saw no reason not to take advantage of their recklessness. After the ten days, the Israelis knew that the balance had shifted heavily in their favor. The Arabs, except for Abdullah, refused to see it, refused to give up their aspirations and their bits and pieces of Palestinian real estate. Not until they were actually crushed in the field could the Arabs accept the proof that they could lose.

NOTES

1. Edgar O'Ballance, in the *Arab-Israeli War 1948* (London: 1956), argues that the Mishmar Hayarden operation was too ambitious and based on the fallacious expectation that the Syrians would retreat. He notes that the Syrian counterattack was prompt and well controlled and had the advantage of good coordination among the different arms. It might be added that it is likely that the counterattack had originally been prepared during the truce, as a straight forward attack; in any case, the Israeli Operation Barosh left much to be desired.

2. Kaukji's ambiguous legal position gave him the impression that he could evade United Nations resolutions, but such evasion also put him outside

United Nations protection. Very early, Bernadotte had decided that, if the Arab states would not be responsible for him, then the Israelis had a right to operate against him. See Count Folke Bernadotte, *To Jerusalem* (London: 1951), p. 125. In their own time, the Israelis picked up Bernadotte's hint.

3. According to Netanel Lorch in *The Edge of the Sword* (New York: 1961), p. 302, the major reason for the failure of the attack was that Matityahu Baruchin, a Tel Aviv clerk in command of the second outpost, threw four grenades back at the Sudanese. Gamal Abdel Nasser, in *The Truth About the Palestine War* (Cairo: 1956), p. 23, claims that the Sudanese had taken Bet Daras and then gave the wrong signal, bringing down their own artillery.

4. During the Negba battle, Nasser was hit in the chest but apparently with only a metal cartridge rather than the bullet.

5. Lorch, *Edge of the Sword*, p. 311.

6. *Ibid.*, p. 285.

9

The Second Truce *
Limited War

The renewed truce brought not peace but illicit war, open violence, and intense frustration. No one but King Abdullah ibn-Husein had wanted a cease-fire, and no one but Abdullah benefited by it. The Israelis lost their opportunity to secure their state, thanks to the swift British intervention at Lake Success. The United Nations showed neither the interest nor the capacity to punish the Arab aggression, and to enforce the terms of the partition resolution. Instead there was only an ineffectual imposed truce, which protected the Arab armies without safeguarding Israel. The Arab press howled again that the Jews had been saved by a trick, a United Nations conspiracy. The Arab commanders and politicians suspected that the truce was little more than a British expedient to protect Abdullah or else a product of Zionist diplomacy. In ten days neither Israelis nor Arabs could find any new basis for a solution. The truncated second round had solved nothing, nor would the renewed pause do so. Once again the United Nations Truce Commission could do little but keep track of the spiralling truce violations. Once again the diplomats could do little but discuss compromises that no one would accept. Increasingly, only the threat of substantial United Nations sanctions prevented full-scale military operations. Increasingly, the truce became a façade hiding a limited war.

In the Negev, out of sight of the Truce Commission, the Israelis and Egyptians continued operations, although on a slightly more limited scale. Truce or no, the South could not even be considered a quiet sector comparable to Jerusalem. Both sides were anxious to tidy up loose ends. The Egyptians took a particularly firm line on how the truce should be interpreted. On August 18 the United Nations Chief of Staff, General Aage Lundstrom, decided that the Israelis could move supplies across the east-west highway in alternating six-hour periods. The Egyptians ignored the order and fired on the passing Israeli convoys. In response to the continued blockade, Yigal Alon, the new front commander in the South, activated Operation Avak to replace the exhausted Negev Brigade with the refitted Yiftach Brigade by means of a secret airlift. Alon set up his headquarters at Gedera, near the main axis running into the Negev and close to the important Israeli airfield at Akir. On August 22 the first transport plane landed in the Negev. By the end of the operation, more than 400 round-trip flights had been made, bringing in 2,000 tons of equipment and nearly 2,000 troops. Operation Avak not only bolstered the existing defenses of the Negev but also created an effective brigade to use in an offensive against the Egyptians. Both Alon and Yigal Yadin were determined that the Egyptians would not be allowed a grip on the South. The Egyptians, unaware of Operation Avak, continued hacking at the Israelis, digging in deeply, spreading mine fields, unwinding miles of barbed wire, and moving in reinforcements.

The Egyptians were not alone in rushing preparations for the final collapse of the truce, but as always Arab preparations were bedeviled by quarreling and recriminations. The ten days had produced none of the benefits expected by the optimists. As no one would credit the setbacks to Israeli superiority, each Arab state sought the cause of failure among its allies. Transjordan was accused of withdrawing from Lydda and Er Ramle without fighting, Lebanon of avoiding battle, Egypt of refusing to cooperate, the Iraqis of doing nothing. Treason was suspected and duplicity assumed. No one but Abdullah recognized the fact that the initiative had passed to Israel. No one had ever trusted Abdullah, and many hated him. Now his caution was dismissed, as only an invitation to further defeat. Many Arabs still believed that a military solution could be achieved. All the Arab armies were therefore reinforced again and partially re-equipped. The

Arab Liberation Army was reorganized and tied into the Syrian and Lebanese command. Reinforcements were sent into Palestine by Egypt, Iraq, and Syria. The Arab Legion's strength was boosted to 10,000 men, but the average interval between enlistment and assignment to front-line duty was only fifteen days. In any case the other Arabs no longer believed that they could depend on the Legion. By the end of August, Jamal Huseini could report, somewhat inaccurately, that in Palestine there were 20,000 Iraqi troops, 10,000 Syrian and Lebanese, 3,000 soldiers of the Arab Liberation Army—now commanded by Colonel Aref Bey Shukeir—and 10,000 Arab irregulars. With all these troops, plus 15,000 Egyptians and the Legion, the Arabs, it was claimed, would be able to crush the Zionist gangs. Actually, by straining their resources, calling in the most distant volunteers, patching together every bit of equipment, cannibalizing obsolete aircraft, and borrowing from the British, the Arabs by the end of the summer had approximately 55,000 adequately equipped troops committed to Palestine. Yet the reinforced and re-equipped Arabs still had not reached the Israeli troop levels of early July. The aggressive optimists, ignoring as always the dissensions and limitations, eagerly anticipated the next and "final" round.

On their side of the truce line, the Israelis continued preparations with growing confidence in their military capacity. By fall the Zahal had grown to nearly 80,000 troops, with all kinds of arms and equipment, still of mixed issue but quite comparable to those of the Arabs. In September thirty surplus United States tanks were to arrive and in October fifty jeeps from Antwerp, which were to be armed with mounted light machine guns; they would serve as mobile raiders. The patchwork Zahal organization was divided into uniformed brigade and front organizations. The auxiliary services were consolidated and streamlined. The inefficient, self-proclaimed experts were weeded out and the skilled volunteers more rationally employed. As the weeks of the phony truce stretched out, the Zahal was honed for the next operations. Increasingly, David Ben-Gurion and the general staff grew impatient with the truce without peace, the cease-fire with firing.

In view of the continuing Arab refusal to consider peace or even a sincere cease-fire, Ben-Gurion began to look for an opportunity to use the modern army that he had sought for so long. When the Arabs

blew up the Latrun pumping station on August 12, he had the excuse
he needed. The general staff and the brigade commanders had been
preparing a variety of offensive operations. The Zahal was ready. The
Arabs were still wrangling and divided. The truce had been broken.
Ben-Gurion's governmental colleagues were not as enthusiastic. A
majority of the government, including his own Mapai Party, opposed
an attack on Jerusalem and the Hebron hills. The international situation was tricky. Some Israelis believed that a military victory in
August might lead to a diplomatic defeat. Ben-Gurion had to shelve
his offensive, but his desire for a final military solution remained. The
tension all along the Arab Legion front was high. The situation in
Jerusalem was explosive. Rumors of a proposed Arab offensive on
September 15 were released to the foreign correspondents by "informed Israelis." On September 15 it was "learned" that the attack
had been postponed until September 21. Observers in Jerusalem were
sure that preparations for the next round were underway.

On September 17 Count Folke Bernadotte flew into Jerusalem
from Damascus to dampen the smoldering crisis. The Arab Legion
believed the situation in Jerusalem so explosive that the Mediator
either should postpone visiting the city or accept an armored escort.
Bernadotte refused to listen and ordered his car into Jerusalem, crossing over to the New City for lunch at the Y.M.C.A. with United
Nations observers. After lunch the Mediator's convoy of three cars
drove to Government House, which was under consideration as the
location for United Nations headquarters in Palestine. Everything
had gone well. There had been no incidents. The truce line had been
quiet. After inspecting Government House, the United Nations party
drove back through the Katamon quarter. The lead driver halted the
convoy because an Israeli army jeep had been parked across the road.
Because the four men in the jeep wore Zahal uniforms, the drivers
and the United Nations people thought that they had run into an
official Israeli checkpoint. Three of the uniformed men climbed out
and began walking down the row of cars, one on one side and two on
the other. They reached Bernadotte's car, the last in line, and stopped.
Bernadotte and his aide, French Colonel André Pierre Sérot, assumed
that the Israelis were about to ask for their passes.

Without warning, one man thrust his Schmeisser automatic pistol
through the window and fired a long burst at point-blank range. He

jumped back and fired a few shots into the car's radiator. The two men on the other side riddled the tires and radiators of the three United Nations cars. Then they rushed back and leaped into the jeep, which disappeared around the corner. The assassin escaped across country. Count Bernadotte was dead, hit six times. Colonel Sérot was dead, hit seventeen times. The next day the Lechi appeared to accept responsibility for the murder, although there was some evidence that it had been an individual act of terrorism. All that could be discovered was that the jeep had been stolen from the United Nations and repainted. The assassins could not be found.[1] Regardless of who had been specifically guilty, few doubted that Israel would be held responsible.

The world was horrified at the pointless murder of the dedicated Bernadotte. Private opinion in Israel, where everyone was glutted with terror and immune to violence, was less sensitive. Many had regarded the Mediator as a tool of the British, an enemy of Israel. Both the Mediator and the United Nations had long been viewed with considerable skepticism. To people in the midst of war and hardened to the sudden deaths of friends, the loss of an apparent enemy seemed of little consequence. There was thus little nationwide outcry at the assassination but only a deep and very real concern over the possible consequences. Fear of international retaliation rather than horror at the murder was the prevailing emotion. No one had wanted Bernadotte killed, and the official response of the Israeli government was immediate and proper. Ben-Gurion arrested hundreds of suspects and outlawed the Lechi. The Irgun units in Jerusalem were dissolved. An extensive investigation began. But public interest soon faded, the American Dr. Ralph Bunche took over as Acting Mediator, and things continued much as before.

One significant change had occurred as a result of Bernadotte's intervention in the truce situation. Ben-Gurion insisted that the Mediator's final proposals could not stand unchallenged. The Bernadotte Report (circulated after his death) gave the Negev to the Arabs, Galilee to Israel, and Jerusalem to no one. All Bernadotte's suggested boundaries were based on the existing military frontiers. The only alternative that Ben-Gurion could see to accepting this United Nations compromise would be to change the existing situation by renewing hostilities. If the United Nations were presented with a fait accompli, then the chances were that the new Zahal conquests could be retained. Ben-Gurion decided to break the truce before the cease-fire lines could be frozen into international boundaries.

As always, Ben-Gurion believed that the war would be won on the central front. He thus proposed an offensive against the Arab Legion in the Judean hills. Yadin, however, argued that the Negev deserved priority. With the Burma Road, Jerusalem was secure, whereas the Negev settlements remained isolated. The Israeli troops and settlers in the Negev were exhausted, short of arms and ammunition, and still vastly outnumbered. Operation Avak had not redressed the balance. Ben-Gurion could see the point; furthermore, Yadin had discovered a satisfactory "legal" means of renewing the war in the South. Because Egyptian refusals to allow Israeli convoys into the Negev were in violation of the United Nations truce, Yadin thought that a satisfactory incident could be created by attempting to push a convoy past the Egyptian roadblock while truce observers were present. Given a reasonable pretext for war and aware of the precarious Israeli claim on the Negev, Ben-Gurion agreed to consider an operation to smash the Egyptian east-west bloc and to re-establish Israel's hold on the northern Negev. Ben-Gurion would then be able to negotiate from a position of strength, possession being nine points of the law.

Yadin had long considered the Egyptian army, rather than the Legion, the most dangerous Arab force. He preferred a concentrated operation to erase the Egyptians. His front commander, Alon, however, preferred to combine the effort to break into the Negev with a second attack to the north through Hebron and Bethlehem to Jerusalem. Yadin feared that Alon's proposal would fail to achieve both ends, for there might not be time to take two difficult targets. With Alon's assistance, Yadin therefore prepared Operation Ten Plagues, an offensive aimed solely at the Negev offensive.

On October 5 the Egyptians, unwilling to allow sleeping Israelis to lie, bombed a number of Negev settlements and dropped artillery barrages on Israeli strong points. On October 6 Operation Ten Plagues was set. Continuing Egyptian aggression had forced the issue. The Egyptians expanded their operations, attacking the Hirbet-Mahaz complex near both the Mishmar Hanegev road and the major Israeli airstrip at Ruhama before breaking off after seven assaults. By then the defending Yiftach Brigade had inflicted sufficient losses to impair the usefulness of the Egyptian battalions for the immediate future. The Egyptians had simply weakened themselves and confirmed Yadin's argument that the South was the critical front.

As the reports of the battle at Hirbet-Mahaz sifted into Zahal headquarters at Tel Aviv, discussions of Ten Plagues continued. The last obstacle was Alon's request for the 8th Brigade; Yadin insisted that the 8th Brigade must remain in reserve. Without it Alon would still have nearly 15,000 troops with armor and air support. Operation Ten Plagues, renamed Yoav for security reasons, would be a far cry from the hurried shoestring offensives launched by decimated groups six months before.

Yadin's Yoav battle plan was based on the theory of the indirect approach, as devised and elaborated by the British military historian, B. H. Liddell Hart, tutor of a whole generation of commanders: "The true aim is not so much to seek battle as to seek a strategic situation so advantageous that if it does not of itself produce a decision, its continuation by battle is sure to achieve this".[2] Yadin's plan was to cut the Egyptians' communications, forcing them either to retreat or to defend their existing positions, which could be turned into isolated pockets. Avoiding a frontal assault, Yadin proposed to cut off supply lines, block routes of retreat, and strike at administrative centers. All these operations were to be flexible, the forces fluid, and the possibilities for exploitation numerous. The Egyptians would not be offered battle as such but rather would be faced with dangerous alternatives for action.

The Egyptian army had dug in solidly in a static defense. Its positions resembled an H, with one leg up the coast to Isdud and the other, less strongly defended, up the inland highway from El 'Auja all the way to Jerusalem; the east-west highway provided the cross axis. This key strip had been fortified with interlocking firing ranges, barbed-wire entanglements, mine fields, and tank traps. With no mobile reserves, the Egyptians were tied down to brittle defensive positions that were mutually dependent. A break in one place would endanger the entire H. Yadin intended to cut the key east-west line with a series of wedges that would simultaneously destroy Egyptian communications and threaten lines of retreat. Yadin later quoted Napoleon in support of his preparations: "The whole secret of the art of war lies in the ability to become master of the lines of communications."[3] In the Negev, where communications could be maintained only over a few main roads, Yadin would have an ideal opportunity to apply his theories of war.

Specifically, his major concentration would be against the axis from the north. Operations within the southern Negev were planned only as raids and diversions to keep the Egyptians off balance. The main wedges would be driven from the north by the Givati Brigade. At the same time the Yiftach Brigade would concentrate on driving a wedge westward to the sea at Bet Hanun between Gaza and Majdal, cutting off the Egyptian column along the Mediterranean coast. If all went well, the Egyptians would have to choose between retreating or remaining in isolated pockets.

On October 15 all Alon's forces were at their jumping-off point. All that remained was to establish the legitimacy of the attack. At noon the Israelis informed the United Nations Truce Supervision headquarters that a convoy was on its way from Haratiya to the Negev. As expected, the Egyptians opened artillery fire on the convoy. They had officially broken the truce and had unwittingly signaled the start of Operation Yoav. The break was followed by heavy and totally unexpected Israeli air strikes on the Egyptian air bases in Sinai and the Negev. Although the Egyptian air force was by no means destroyed on the ground, the raids did seriously damage its immediate effectiveness and its morale. All during Yoav the Israeli air force controlled the sky over the Negev.

On the evening of October 15, the Negev commandos carried out extensive hit-and-run raids on Egyptian positions. Yiftach units secured a wedge near Bet Hanun 600 yards from the coast. The Givati Brigade forced a similar wedge through, near the lateral highway. The balloon was up, and the Egyptians had to respond to a dozen jabs, each of which could turn out to be a pinprick or the main thrust. Alon had planned his major thrust through the lateral axis at Iraq-el-Manshiya. Indirectly, the breakthrough there would endanger the entire Egyptian position along the lateral road. Coupled with the problems created by the wedge at Bet Hanun and the Negev raids, these actions would confront the Egyptians with some very unpleasant decisions.

On the morning of October 16, after forty minutes of artillery preparation, Alon gave the orders for the major breakthrough. The tank battalion began to roll forward to join the infantry assault battalion. At first all went well. Soon observers reported Arabs fleeing from the village of Iraq-el-Manshiya. Then the Israeli tanks were hit, ran out of ammunition, or lost contact with the infantry. The first assault company withdrew and passed the second, on its way forward, creating considerable confusion. Egypt's best service, the artillery, opened a heavy barrage on the Israeli infantry. The bursting shells were brutally effective. An attack to recoup the situation collapsed. Only fifty infantrymen managed to retreat to the starting line. The major thrust had been turned back.

Alon faced unpalatable alternatives. He had either to continue his efforts at Iraq-el-Manshiya or within a few hours to seek an alternative approach. Repeated attacks against the alerted Egyptians at Iraq-el-Manshiya could gobble up his men with no results, but a shift in mid-battle would risk vast confusion. Alon broke off his attack. Within a few hours he had completed plans for a direct attack west of the Faluja crossroads to occupy the hills overlooking the road junction. That evening Israeli units continued to carry out raids, while additional wedges were driven through Egyptian positions. At 10:30 the Israeli assault platoons hit Hills 113 and 100, to the west of Faluja. By midnight they had secured both positions, and a third attack had captured the junction. The Egyptians' passage over the lateral highway had been blocked.

At first light the Egyptians counterattacked. Despite heavy armor and artillery support, they failed to retake the crossroads. Their other positions in the immediate area were therefore untenable and had to be evacuated but the Egyptian position at Huleikat prevented the Israelis from using the north-south road into the Negev. As long as Huleikat held out, Alon's offensive would be thwarted. An effort by the Yiftach Brigade to overrun the Egyptians from the rear failed. Alon realized that the turning point had come. He had wedges all along the line, and the Egyptian command was clearly in a turmoil; but without a complete breakthrough of the lateral axis, all the Israeli operations would have been in vain. The only solution was a frontal assault on Huleikat. Failure there would mean that Operation Yoav, despite its indirect approach, its subtle wedges, its alternative avenues of approach, had also failed in its primary task—to open the Negev.

Alon persuaded first Yadin and then his two front commanders,

Itzhak Sadeh and Shimon Avidan, that a direct assault was the only solution. Not only the tactical but also the political situation demanded the attack. On October 19 the Security Council, meeting at Lake Success, had adopted a proposal for a cease-fire; the implications were obvious. Once again the campaign had to be conducted in a race against an uncertain deadline. On the night of October 20 Alon began his assault, led by Yaacov Prulov's 52nd Battalion of the Givati Brigade, on the six interlocking Egyptian positions at Huleikat.[4] After a fierce battle, the hills to the north were overrun. The Egyptians soon pulled out of Huleikat, but a simultaneous Israeli assault on the Iraq Suedan police station, the Monster on the Hill, failed for the fifth time. The sixth attack, on the next night, came very close, but the assault platoon was badly decimated, and only one man, platoon leader Peres, actually entered the fortress. The Monster remained in Egyptian hands, but it had become the core around which a pocket was forming. The Egyptians around Faluja were cut off from the coast in the west. Retreat toward Hebron might still be possible, but the risks of stringing the army out along the highway between the Israeli brigades to the north and south were great. In one night the lateral axis had become a trap. Alon, however, had no time to slam the door on the Faluja pocket; he wanted to exploit his breakthrough farther south.

On October 20 Nahum Sarig's Negev Brigade began to prepare a sudden blitz attack on Beersheba. On the night of October 21 the hastily assembled striking force concentrated at Mishmar Hanegev. At 4:00 in the morning, the main body moved toward Beersheba, and two mobile columns set out to cut the road north and south of the city. Unaware that the Negev was open, the Egyptian commander at Beersheba was stunned by the sudden appearance of Israeli units. The Israelis secured the New Quarter of Beersheba during the night. The Egyptian response had been feeble and uncertain. Unaware of the size of the Israeli force, the Egyptians began to crumble at dawn, when Israeli reinforcements arrived. At 8:00 in the morning a single Israeli gun opened fire on the police station. After firing four rounds, the Egyptians surrendered. The inland Egyptian finger had been cut, isolating the Egyptians to the north in the Hebron hills. The southern half of the finger had become a road leading from Egypt nowhere.

Much the same fate befell the coastal finger. When the Yiftach

Brigade cut the coastal road at Bet Hanun, the Egyptians at Majdal and Isdud were trapped. Egyptian engineers quickly devised a temporary road over the sand dunes and extracted most of their troops before forward units of the Yiftach realized what had happened. But crowning Egyptian disaster came when the infant Israeli navy attacked and sank the *Emir Faruk*, the flagship of the small Egyptian navy, in a sea battle lasting only a few minutes. Operation Yoav had also opened up a tempting possibility to the north along the southern edge of the Tel Aviv-Jerusalem corridor.

At staff headquarters in Tel Aviv Ben-Gurion and Yadin decided that an attack on the Egyptian positions in the Hebron hills, if pursued swiftly and decisively, could clear all Arab Palestine south of Jerusalem. The operation would be delicate because of the presence of Arab Legion forces in the Jerusalem area. No one wanted to bring Transjordan into the fighting. To avoid this consequence, Yadin depended on speed and surprise, hoping to occupy the loosely held Egyptian positions before the Legion could react. On the night of October 18, the Harel Brigade moved into the Hebron hills against scanty resistance. Obstructed only by occasional shots from the fleeing Arabs, the Harel Brigade moved south and east toward Bethlehem and Hebron. The next night, October 19, front commander Zvi Ayalon ordered Moshe Dayan to secure Bethlehem within forty-eight hours for another truce was in prospect. At that moment there was nothing in front of Dayan, but suddenly the Legion came into the picture. Abdullah and Glubb had realized that, without prompt action on their part, the Israelis would occupy everything south of Jerusalem to the Jericho line, thus outflanking the Legion. Abdullah informed Israel unofficially that he would consider entering into negotiations for an armistice if the Zahal refrained from attacking Legion troops. Simultaneously, he rushed token detachments south toward Bethlehem and Hebron to occupy "officially" as much as possible.

The result was a race between the Legion and Dayan to control the area. Dayan's troubles began immediately. Delays and confusion ate up the night. The Israelis did capture the last stretch of the railway line into Jerusalem, but the key heights at Beit Jala overlooking Bethlehem remained in Arab hands. By the next afternoon Legion troops had occupied Beit Jala. Dayan's attack had to be cancelled.[5]

Farther south, the Harel Brigade continued to occupy areas that had been nominally under Egyptian control. By October 22 advance units of the Harel had moved to within seven miles of Bethlehem; but on that day the truce was reimposed.

Although Abba Eban, the Israeli observer at Lake Success, had tried to delay United Nations action until Alon could complete his operation, the Security Council insisted on a cease-fire, which had little real effect on mopping-up operations in the South. The Harel Brigade continued to occupy vacuum areas, and other Israeli units took Isdud, Hill 69, and Majdal in the coastal finger. On October 27, after two days of fighting, the Zahal took the Gubrin police fortress. On October 28 Kubieba and Lahish surrendered. The major loose ends had been tidied up. The Egyptians had been sealed off in the two northern fragments of the H, and 2,500 men had also surrendered in the Faluja pocket.

The collapse of the Egyptians was one more traumatic shock to the Arab states. Even before Yoav, inter-Arab relations had been deteriorating. The newspapers and orators grew vituperative about betrayals and sellouts. In September a National Palestine Council met in Egyptian-held Gaza and created an Arab Palestinian government, and on October 1 the Mufti of Jerusalem, Hajj Amin al-Huseini, was elected President. Egypt, Syria, Lebanon, and Iraq recognized the Mufti, but everyone knew that his government, propped up by the Egyptians, had no authority and engendered no loyalty among the Arab people. The entire affair was an Egyptian maneuver to thwart Abdullah's ambition to annex central Palestine. Abdullah refused to recognize the Mufti and organized annexation sentiment within Palestine. When Israel opened Yoav, the last vestiges of Arab unity were already being frittered away.

The Arab Joint General Command hurriedly met in Amman to work out a joint response to the Israeli attack. When the meeting opened, no one could bring himself to speak. For five minutes the delegates sat in gloomy silence. Finally, Abdullah suggested that perhaps Nokrashy might have something to say. He did not. "God, I have come to listen, not to talk."[6] The meeting immediately collapsed into recriminations. Nokrashy refused to accept the news that Beersheba had fallen. He attacked Transjordan. No one had a constructive suggestion. The following day Nokrashy had to admit that

Beersheba had been lost and that the Egyptian position was desperate. Still no one had a constructive suggestion. Eventually Glubb and Abdullah came up with a proposal to rescue the Egyptians in the Faluja pocket, Operation Damascus.

In Cairo there were grave doubts about Operation Damascus. In the Faluja pocket itself the Sudanese commander, Sayid Taha, had misgivings about the practical aspects. At El 'Arîsh headquarters the British liaison officer Lockett declared, "It is impossible to place reliance on the diversionary actions which are intended to engage the Jews."[7] The new Egyptian commander, General Fuad Sadeq, suspected a trap; he feared that Abdullah and Glubb were not to be trusted. In fact, he claimed, the Jews probably knew about the plan. Sadeq ordered Taha to "reject the plan and drive out the mercenary Lockett. Defend your posts to the last bullet and to the last soldier as befitting of Egyptian soldiers."[*] Discussions ran down, and the Faluja pocket was abandoned to its fate. With the air still heavy with recriminations and betrayals, the Arabs suffered one more shock from an unexpected quarter. In a masterpiece of mistiming, the Arab Liberation Army renewed offensive operations in the North on October 22, the day on which the new truce was imposed in the South. After the ten-day war the Arab Liberation Army had again been rebuilt. There had been no notable increase in armaments, but it still had French 75-millimeter guns. An effort to control the volunteers more tightly had been implemented by seconding Aref Bey Shukeir from the Lebanese army to keep a checkrein on Fawziel-Kaukji. But, with his 3,000-man army rested and reinforced and the Israelis busy in the Negev, Kaukji could not be restrained. As an objective, he had selected Manara, a small, isolated kibbutz almost on the Lebanese border and seven miles from the nearest Israeli settlement at Nebi Yusha. Kaukji would have in his favor an isolated target, surprise, and numerical superiority. On October 22 his first attack swamped the unprepared outpost to the north of Manara.

---

* Jon Kimche and David Kimche, *Both Sides of the Hill: Britain and the Palestine War* (London: 1960), pp. 254–5. The Israelis, by monitoring open Arab radio communications, had, in fact, learned of the plan. Later, at the Rhodes armistice talks, Yadin let this fact "slip," thus doing his part to further Arab disunity, for the Egyptians were then convinced that Abdullah had been selling them out.

Kaukji was correct in assuming that the attention of the Israelis was not focused on the North. The Arab Liberation Army was simply not regarded as a sufficient threat, even though its occasional raids had violated the truce. When Kaukji hit Manara, however, he opened the door to reappraisal. An "unofficial" Arab army outside international law, unencumbered by government control, and securely based in the Galilee hills menaced the security of all the Israeli settlements in the North. Kaukji had thus escalated his attacks to the point at which Israeli retaliation was certain. Ben-Gurion and Yadin expected the occupation of central Galilee to be relatively easy. If, as had happened in the Negev, the other Arab states remained quiet, the operation was well worth the risk in view of the small investment necessary and the high rewards for success. They decided not to respond directly to Kaukji's attack on Manara but to institute a major offensive, Operation Hiram, to clear all Galilee.

While preparations for Hiram were begun, the fighting for Manara continued. Israeli counterattacks to recapture the lost outpost failed. An effort to reinforce the settlement by means of a reconnaissance column of jeeps and half-tracks from Nebi Yusha was stopped when the Israelis ran into heavy Arab fire. The ambushed vehicles had to be abandoned, and the dismounted Israelis pulled back to Nebi Yusha. Manara remained cut off on three sides. Kaukji moved some of his Arabs down into the valley to harass traffic moving along the last road link with Manara. This time, Kaukji thought, it would be difficult for the Israelis to surprise him with a counterattack through the rough terrain. Operation Hiram, however, was not going to be a direct response to Kaukji's provocation.

Moshe Carmel intended to cut off all of Galilee, using four brigades. The 7th Brigade and the Oded Brigade would move into northern Galilee from the east and west, respectively and would link up at Sasa. This move would cut off from other Arab armies all but a strip running east and west along the Lebanon border. Once the junction had been made at Sasa, one column would move west to the sea, rolling up any resistance in the border strip, and the second would move north into the eastern finger of Galilee clearing the area between Lebanon and Syria. Meanwhile in southern Galilee the Golani Brigade would undertake probing actions to divert Kaukji's attention from the main pincers. The Carmeli Brigade would continue operations in the Manara area to tie down as many of Kaukji's troops as possible. The major consideration was speed. If the junction at Sasa could be secured swiftly, Arab resistance could be expected to collapse. The less time given either the Arab states or the United Nations to respond, the more chance there would be for a quick and relatively painless victory.

On October 29 the Israeli air force opened operations with strikes on Arab concentrations throughout Galilee. Artillery mounted on trucks moved along the front lines dropping shells on the Arab positions. Swift raids and diversionary fire fights began in the south. Not until zero hour on the night of October 28 did Kaukji receive a hint that he was facing a major attack. Even then he was unaware of Carmel's specific intentions; he realized only that a full-scale Israeli operation had been launched.

The attack from Safad by the 7th Brigade caught the Arabs by surprise. The brigade followed its timetable with no great difficulty, taking Safsaf and Meron. There was little resistance. The 7th Brigade then assaulted Jish, which was held by units of the Arab Liberation Army and a recently arrived Syrian battalion. The Syrians were unfamiliar with the terrain and unprepared for a heavy attack. The 7th Brigade rolled over them, and the defense collapsed. The Israelis cut up the Syrian battalion, killing 200 men. That afternoon the Arabs evacuated Mount Jarmark, the highest mountain in Palestine, and continued to fall back on Sasa. Their counterattacks were weak, and their artillery fire ineffective.

In the west the Oded Brigade's attack had not fared as well. An assault on Tarshiha broke down. The main Oded column ran into a carefully prepared, complex mine field, which held it up until daylight. A flanking attack by pro-Israeli Druze troops had gone as planned, but the Druzes had to be pulled back when the main thrust stalled. By the evening of October 29 Carmel's western pincer had nothing to show but casualties. Kaukji, instead of sending troops to reinforce the south, withdrew his units to the north. The original plan of Hiram became inoperative.

Carmel responded to the changing situation by ordering the eastern force to move on through Sasa and to link up with the Oded Brigade in front of Tarshiha. The diversionary attack by the Golani Brigade in the south would be escalated into a full-fledged advance. By dawn on October 29 it was obvious that any Israeli attack from any direction would be successful. The Arab forces no longer had the capacity to respond to the Israeli advance, except by withdrawing. The Oded troops took Tarshiha after an artillery barrage. The Arabs had moved out to the north, along a dirt track. The last remnants of the Arab formations in the Oded sector eventually crossed into Lebanon and out of the war. The Arabs left in the south, in what was becoming the Galilee pocket, continued to drift north all during the day. That evening the Arabs held out against Golani attacks just long enough for the majority of the troops to be extracted from the closing trap. The next day the Oded and 7th Brigades met at Sasa.

As planned, the Oded began moving along the border of Lebanon toward the sea. There was no opposition. The 7th Brigade moved in the other direction and turned north. There was no opposition. When the vanguard reached Manara, Kaukji had already gone. In a series of swift advances at the tip of the eastern finger the Carmeli troops drove the Arabs over the border and occupied fourteen villages inside Lebanon. In sixty hours, Operation Hiram had destroyed the Arab Liberation Army, occupied all of Galilee, and seized a strip of Lebanon. The Arabs had lost 400 killed, including the 200 Syrians at Jish. Israeli casualties were negligible: nine dead. The war in the North was over.

While the Zahal continued mopping up in the South and settling into Galilee, the diplomats took over. From the onset of Yoav Acting Mediator Ralph Bunche had sought a resumption of the truce. The Security Council's resolution calling for a renewed cease-fire had been accepted formally, and technically at least there was a cease-fire in the Negev after October 22. There could be no doubt, however, that operations in the South, coupled with the sixty-hour blitz in the North, had completely transformed the Palestine situation. The British were determined to use diplomacy to force the Israelis to give up their gains. By November 4 the British had persuaded a majority of the Security Council to vote for an Israeli withdrawal to the original truce lines. The resolution with attached deadline simply ignored the Palestine situation.

Ben-Gurion and the Israeli government had no intention of bowing to the British maneuver to rob them of their gains at the bargaining table. The Israelis simply could not afford to give back to the Arabs what they had taken on the battlefield without endangering the security of Israel. To ask them to do so would result only in a disastrous showdown that might damage the prestige of the United Nations and lead to the most violent complications. Ralph Bunche, more attuned to the realities, made every effort to find a satisfactory solution. On November 17, as the critical deadline for compliance approached, Bunche suggested a possible formula to Eban. Israel was to withdraw all the mobile forces in the Negev but not the garrisons. In that way Israel could both stay and withdraw. It was an ingenious idea. Israel promptly accepted. Bunche immediately announced that this acceptance satisfied the Security Council resolution. The British were outraged. London had wanted the Israelis out of the Negev, their successes annulled. Instead Bunche's formula had in effect recognized the occupation as legal. Both the Egyptian army and the British diplomats had failed to protect the Negev, and Arab Galilee had been lost as well.

Even while the diplomats were carrying on their deliberations, Israeli operations in the Negev had quietly and effectively continued. Alon tightened the loop around Faluja, occupied positions in the Hebron area, and re-established communications with the isolated settlements in the Negev. On November 9 he launched another major attack on Iraq-Suedan. Preceded by a massive artillery bombardment and supported by tanks, the assault force reached the walls at about 4:00 in the afternoon. A wall had been breached by sappers, and the infantry moved through for the final attack. The last charge was not needed. The Egyptians, dazed by the artillery attack, stumbled out to surrender. The Monster on the Hill had fallen. The Faluja pocket had been reduced by half. The commander of the pocket. Taha the Black Tiger, had no hope of escape. Alon sent in a delegation led by Yeruham Cohen to seek the pocket's surrender. Cohen met one of Taha's staff officers, Gamal Abdel Nasser, and arranged a meeting the next day. At that time Alon, introduced as Yesha'ya Bergstein, for security reasons tried to persuade Taha to surrender, insisting that Egypt's real enemy was the British. Taha recognized the gravity of his situation and may have agreed with Alon's analysis of Anglo-Egyptian relations, but he refused to surrender: "But one thing I shall be able to save: the honor of the Egyptian Army."[8] Taha had decided to hold out. Supplied by secret camel convoys and occasional air drops, Taha and the Egyptians hung on and did indeed "save the honor of the Egyptian army." The Faluja pocket never surrendered.

The area of the pocket offered no tactical advantage to either the Egyptians or the Israelis. Elsewhere the advantages gained by Yoav continued to be exploited. A unit of the Negev Brigade moved across the Judean desert and re-established contact with Sodom, isolated since May 18. Farther south the Golani Brigade established a defensive line that narrowed the Egyptian coastal finger. Operation Assaf began on December 5 with the capture of Shu'ut. By the next day all major targets had been secured, clearing the Northern Negev but the Egyptians launched a major counterattack. For a while Egyptian armor threatened to outflank the new Israeli positions, but the one infantry attack failed, and the Egyptians withdrew. The next day the Israelis hit the Egyptians while they were concentrating for another counterattack; the Egyptians dispersed and gave up their attacks.

Despite Alon's victory in the South and Carmel's victory in Galilee, there had still been no final military solution. Israel was immeasurably stronger than it had been at the end of the ten-day war, but there were international restrictions on using the new strength. Only Bunche's formula had prevented a first-rate crisis over the Security Council resolution. Although Abdullah had been putting out feelers for a permanent armistice to replace the fragile cease-fire, he could not take the lead in admitting defeat and recognizing Israel. Syria was content with the bridgehead at Mishmar Hayarden and saw no need to take the initiative. Lebanon, though anxious for Israel to evacuate the villages lost during Hiram, did not want to take the first step. Iraq had no common border with Palestine and felt no sense of urgency. Even Egypt, despite its defeat in October and the gradual deterioration of its military position, would not consider armistice discussions. No Arab leader felt sufficiently secure to explain the true military situation to his people. Unable to admit defeat and unable to continue the war, the Arabs were in a dilemma. So, for that matter, were the Israelis, who had the power to inflict more defeats on the Arabs but, fearful of international repercussions, were reluctant to renew the war. At the United Nations diplomats could force a cease-fire with threats of sanctions, but they could not impose peace.

NOTES

1. Eye witness reports of the assassination are included in a series of addenda at the end of Count Folke Bernadotte, *To Jerusalem* (London: 1951).

2. B. H. Liddell Hart, *Strategy* (New York: 1955), p. 339. Yadin in his brief discussion of Operation *Ten Plagues*, published in *Bamachaneh* (September 1949), quotes this definition; in turn, Liddell Hart incorporated Yadin's article in *Strategy*, Appendix II, pp. 386–391.

3. From Yadin's article. Liddell Hart, *Strategy*, p. 387.

4. Yaacov Prulov's successful attack with the 52nd Battalion went far to compensate for his earlier failure to attack at Latrun. There had even been talk then of a court-martial.

5. In the inevitable retrospective replay of the war, the failure of Dayan to secure Bethlehem looms large. Ben-Gurion was quoted in the General Zionist daily, *Haboker*, to the effect that, had Dayan been commander, Israel would have had better frontiers. Yadin retaliated by noting the failure of Dayan to take Bethlehem when it was wide open. Essentially the problem was not Dayan's slow progress but Ben-Gurion's own decision not to engage the Arab Legion. See Jon Kimche's articles in the *Jewish Observer and Middle East Review*, Vol. 13, No. 11 (March 13, 1964), and Vol. 8, No. 12 (March 20, 1959).

6. Ibn ul Hussein Abdallāh, *My Memoirs Completed* (Washington, D.C.: 1954), p. 26.

7. Kimche and David Kimche, *Both Sides of the Hill: Britain and the Palestine War* (London: 1960), p. 254.

8. Yeruham Cohen, "The Secret Negev Talks," *Jewish Observer and Middle East Review*, 2, No. 9 (February 13, 1953), 6–8. See also Gamal Abdel Nasser, *The Truth About the Palestine War* (Cairo: 1956), p. 72. For reasons none too clear, the Black Tiger was posted to a minor position at Asyût in Upper Egypt after the war. Nasser later claimed, during the Suez crisis of 1956 that he himself had made the "honor" speech and not Taha.

10

The Second Truce*
Campaign for an Armistice

The failure of Operation Yoav to force a final solution became clear when the Egyptian government informed Bunche that it opposed any armistice negotiations. Despite its recent military humiliation, Egypt refused to negotiate; the government, perhaps even the throne, could not risk an admission of defeat. While Egypt refused to negotiate the other Arab governments would not take the initiative, even though King Abdullah ibn-Husein was obviously anxious for agreement. During November secret informal discussions had been carried on and had ultimately led to the signing by Colonel Abdullah el-Tell and Lieutenant Colonel Mashe Dayan a "sincere cease-fire" for Jerusalem on December 1. Furthermore, Abdullah could not act alone without risking the security of his state, now crowded with embittered Arab refugees.

The Israelis decided once again to force the issue, through one more offensive operation, designed to give the Egyptians the alternatives of accepting total military defeat or of opening armistice talks. A secondary benefit of such an attack would be the complete occupation of the Negev, which would give Israel access to Asia through the Gulf of 'Aqaba. The Israelis would risk varying degrees of international repercussion, but Ben-Gurion wanted to end the debilitating strain of no war and no peace. The diplomats were obviously aware that the responsibility for the continued strife lay not in Tel Aviv but in Cairo.

On December 10, four days after Operation Assaf had ended the fighting in the Negev, Yigal Yadin completed plans for Operation Ayin. Again he and Yigal Alon planned to use the indirect approach, tying down the Egyptian army with a heavy attack south of Gaza while sweeping around the entire Egyptian position inland and coming out through Sinai to drive north to the army base at El 'Arîsh. Once Alon's spearhead had touched the sea, the entire Egyptian army would be cut off. The Egyptian positions were still wide open to such a swift and flexible attack. The mass of Egyptian military power was dug into static defenses along the seacoast, immobile and dependent on fragile supply lines. Alon and Yadin doubted that the Egyptians could respond to the swift shifts of Ayin.

Alon would have five brigades for Ayin, but one, the Alexandroni, would be tied down at the Faluja pocket. The Golani would first attack Hill 86 south of Gaza and would drive a wedge toward the sea. While the Egyptians were thus diverted, the armored brigade, beefed up with a battalion from the Harel, and the Negev Brigade would sweep up from Beersheba to El 'Auja. Alon finally devised a method to keep the armor hidden until the last minute with an assist from the Roman Empire. Scouts from the Negev Brigade discovered an old Roman road from Beersheba to El 'Auja, which bypassed the Egyptian roadblocks on the modern highway. The trouble was that no one had done much resurfacing on the road during the previous 2,000 years. Israeli engineers finally decided that, with emergency repairs, the road would take armor, but that the last seven miles to El 'Auja would have to be left in the condition in which they had been found. Alon decided to take the risk and send his armor over the old track, for the armor could bypass the roadblocks while the Negev Brigade moved behind, clearing the road leisurely.

At last, on the afternoon of December 22, after further delay Ayin began with a massive Israeli artillery barrage. All afternoon the Israeli artillery shelled along the entire Gaza strip, shifting targets to divert attention from the Golani's diversionary attack on Hill 86 but keeping Egyptian eyes focused on the coast. As soon as darkness came, the Golani assault battalion moved out. They managed to creep to within 150 yards of their objective before the Egyptians discovered them.

By then it was too late, and the Golani took the hill in one quick rush. The Israelis had to hang on to the hill until reinforcements with heavy weapons could be moved up. For a while luck appeared to be with them. None of the Egyptian counterattacks during the night was pushed very hard, but no support arrived.

At dawn the Israelis had to face the Egyptians with only four piats and some captured mortars. Egyptian armor began circling the hill. All morning the tanks fired into the Israeli positions, but only one moved up to the perimeter. The Israelis knocked it out with a piat. While the tanks were milling about, the Egyptian infantry moved up behind a cactus fence 150 yards away and started shooting. The Israelis' situation deteriorated rapidly. Rain began falling in the early afternoon, jamming many of the Israeli weapons not already ruined by the sand. Ammunition was running out. Then four Egyptian half-tracks rumbled around the cactus fence and toward the perimeter, opening up with flamethrowers. At the last minute, the Golani drove them off, using hand grenades. Rather than wait for the inevitable, one company launched its own attack but ran directly into a heavy Egyptian armor unit moving up the hill. The Israelis pulled back. Further defense of the hill would be suicidal, and the Golani withdrew entirely. The Egyptians believed that they had won an impressive victory: "The Jewish objective in capturing this hill was obvious; to isolate and to destroy the garrison of Gaza and so to repeat the tragedy of Faluja."[1] Although Alon would have been delighted at such results of the Golani attack on Hill 85, his real objective of the opening gambit had already been won.

To the south and east of Faluja all was quiet. But the quiet was ominous and Israeli disinterest a carefully constructed illusion. On Saturday morning, December 25, the armored brigade moved out along the Roman road, and that evening the Negev Brigade began its successful attack on the Bir T'mil positions on the Beersheba-El 'Auja road. The "French Commando" ad hoc force, led by a Christian volunteer, who was celebrating Christmas in decidedly curious circumstances, captured Hill 13 and by mistake temporarily occupied Hill 14 as well. The Egyptians responded with a series of heavy counterattacks. Although isolated, the French Commandos held onto Hill 13 until just before dawn. When the first light came on December 26, the Egyptians could be seen dancing about in glee on the peak of the hill. Their joy proved premature. Soon after dawn the Negev commando battalion launched the main attack in several columns. The Egyptian strength fell apart. By 9:00 the Israelis were moving on toward El 'Auja.

The armored brigade's end run over the Roman road did not go as smoothly. Creeping along, the brigade fell nine hours behind schedule. By then the Negev Brigade's attack on T'mil-Mishrefe and an air strike on El 'Auja on the morning of December 26 had destroyed hope for a surprise attack. In order to regain the lost time, the armored brigade launched a frontal assault on El 'Auja but could not penetrate the well-prepared defenses. The Egyptians attempted to rush a column down to El 'Auja from Rafa. The Harel Brigade, still in the process of setting up roadblocks, had scattered some land mines. The Egyptians drove on through the land mines until they ran up against the last block. There the Harel held them off. By nightfall on December 26 El 'Auja was cut off from the north.

From Alon's point of view the overall situation was still not too promising. The Israeli armored brigade was deployed to defend itself, regardless of the fate of El 'Auja, but Alon did not want his armor stalled in front of the town. To open up the battle, the brigade had to turn the corner at El 'Auja and quickly, so that the Egyptians could not respond soon enough to limit the Israelis tactical gains. The Israelis were not interested in sweeping the Egyptians back to the border but only in cutting off their army.

On the other side of the hill, the Egyptians were even more worried: A heavy armored force had suddenly appeared out of the impassable desert and had cut El 'Auja off from Rafa. No one had a clue to the fate of the fortified hills along the Beersheba road. The Israelis were probing along the side of the Gaza strip. Without central guidance, each local commander had to react independently to pressures that he could not assess.

At El 'Auja the Egyptian defenses were still intact but wavering. Israeli armor moved around the town and attacked from the rear along the Abu Agueila-El 'Auja highway on December 26. With the roads from both Abu Agueila and Rafa cut and reports of another force moving against them over the Beersheba highway, the besieged Egyptians lost hope. Soon after 8:00 in the morning, the Israelis occupied the major part of El 'Auja and at 2:00 in the afternoon the

Negev Brigade arrived, after clearing the Beersheba road. The Egyptians defending the road had either surrendered or fled into the desert. But within a few days those escapees who could stumbled back to the road to surrender.

With the arrival of the Negev Brigade, the first phase of Operation Ayin was completed. The corner had been turned even though it had taken longer than expected. There was now a real chance that the war could be won in a week. The Egyptians had very little in front of the Israelis at El 'Auja. In order to prevent the Egyptians from shifting forces from the Gaza area, Alon ordered the Golani Brigade to carry out another attack on Daribet-esh-Sheikh, meanwhile, to the south of Hill 86. From El 'Auja the Negev Brigade, supported by a tank battalion, moved out toward Abu Aguella and the most important highway junction in the Sinai Peninsula. At 4:00 on the afternoon of December 28 the Negev Brigade ran into an Egyptian position about six miles from Abu Agueila, which held it up until evening, but by midnight the remaining resistance had evaporated. At dawn Israeli scouts drove into Abu Agueila to report the Egyptians moving out toward El 'Arîsh.

As he had anticipated, Alon now had two choices. He could mount a full-scale attack either on El 'Arîsh or on Rafa, which was closer to the Gaza strip. Either move would force the Egyptian army to move out of Palestine or to accept encirclement. Although farther from the main Egyptian concentrations, El 'Arîsh was preferable for attack, as more defenders could be sealed off there at less cost. As Israeli armor began probing toward El 'Arîsh on December 29, a light mobile column struck fifty miles deep into Sinai and raided the Egyptian airstrip at Bir Hama. The only Egyptian defense force left in Sinai was the air force, which did strike ineffectually at the Negev Brigade commando battalion rolling north toward El 'Arîsh.

The commandos kept on driving through the desert and pulled up at the airport twelve miles south of El 'Arîsh at 3:00 in the afternoon. The commando battalions began evacuating the captured Egyptian aircraft and several "dummy planes." The tank battalion edged north to Bir Lafham and dislodged a hastily dug-in defense block. Although by that time Alon's forces were scattered and exhausted, the Egyptian position at El 'Arîsh appeared bleak. None of the troops tied down in the Gaza strip had been shifted. There was no hope of reinforcements from Egypt. The morale of the troops had plummeted. Only a disastrous attack on the Faluja pocket by the Alexandroni Brigade, one of the worst Israeli defeats of the war, had marred an uninterrupted series of Israeli victories. Standing on a sand dune three miles south of El 'Arîsh on the evening of December 29, Alon believed that the fates of the town, of the Egyptian army, and of the war in the South had already been determined.

But he was wrong. On December 29 the Security Council had passed another cease-fire resolution, which required withdrawal to the positions held before the hostilities. This time the British were determined that the Israelis not be given an opportunity to "interpret" the resolution or to "delay" its implementation. The British government immediately sent an ultimatum to Tel Aviv demanding immediate acceptance of the resolution. If Israel refused, Great Britain, under the terms of the Anglo-Egyptian Treaty of 1936, would employ British troops to force acceptance. The British ultimatum was motivated by the desire not only to salvage the Egyptian army but also to persuade Cairo that the 1936 treaty, which permitted British troops in the Suez Canal Zone, should not be abrogated. The ultimatum, legal or not, placed Israel in a dangerous position. If Britain did intervene, all that had been gained during a year of war might be lost. International sympathy for the Israeli offensive had been slight, and even the United States appeared opposed to Israeli efforts. Prime Minister David Ben-Gurion decided that he could not risk an open break and perhaps war with Great Britain. As the key factor seemed to be the presence of Israeli troops inside Egypt, he ordered Alon to evacuate Egypt within twenty-four hours.

Alon, isolated in Sinai, was stunned. He flew directly to Tel Aviv in an attempt to have the order rescinded. Yadin at once informed him of the British ultimatum and the unfavorable international developments. Alon was not sufficiently impressed. Yadin explained that, although he too was willing to risk the operation, Ben-Gurion had already refused. Alon met with Foreign Minister Moshe Sharett and tried to persuade him to allow at least time to destroy El 'Arîsh before withdrawing. Sharett believed that this move would bring the British into the war. Alon then suggested an alternative: All the Israeli units would remain in the desert four days so that the Egyptians would weaken the Gaza area to reinforce El 'Arîsh, and he would then attack the strip. Sharett telephoned Ben-Gurion in Tiberias, but the latter reluctantly refused. Instead, he agreed that Alon could use the El 'Auja-Rafah road, most of which was inside Egypt, to launch an attack on Rafa, which was on the international boundary. The Gaza strip could still be turned into the Gaza pocket.

Ben-Gurion indicated to Alon that this alternative was the best one left, militarily far less desirable but diplomatically feasible. Alon had to accept the fact that international pressure would dictate his tactics. Despite the handicaps of limited time to concentrate and deploy, he would have to pull out of Egypt on the brink of victory and attack an alerted Rafa. At 10:00 in the evening of December 31 the official withdrawal orders reached the Negev Brigade's headquarters. At least by then, both Alon and Ben-Gurion knew that the other Arab states could be discounted. A meeting among the military commanders of Iraq, Egypt, and Transjordan had been held after the opening of Operation Ayat, but there had been no concrete results. The Egyptians had pleaded for a joint Iraqi-Legion attack to divert Israeli troops from the southern front, but they were told that such an attack would have to be in division strength, which did not exist, and would have to include Syrian and Lebanese units, which would not cooperate. In effect, the Egyptians were told no. All Alon had to worry about therefore was the Egyptian defense at Rafa.

That the military position of the Egyptian army was growing rapidly hopeless was apparent not only to the other Arab leaders and to the British but also for the first time to the Egyptian public. During November rumors of the Egyptian army's failures had begun to seep back to Cairo. Soldiers on leave told their friends of the bungling and omissions. Gossip began. After the prepared diet of magnificent victories and romantic heroes offered by the Cairo press, the disillusionment with Faruk and the government of Mahmud Fahmi Nokrashy was intense. Criticism and unrest mushroomed. Nokrashy sought stabilization by neutralizing the main critics of the government, the Muslim Brotherhood. At the end of November the General Secretary and several important members of the organization were "detained." But disorders grew worse, and wanton terror began to spread. Huge mobs demonstrated in Cairo. December was an uninterrupted crisis. Nokrashy outlawed the Muslim Brotherhood, but before he could supervise its destruction he was assassinated, on December 28. Egypt seemed on the verge not only of losing its army but also of sliding into anarchy. One more shock might topple the entire establishment.

With chaos in Cairo and Sinai near collapse, it was little wonder that Egypt's Arab neighbors saw no reason to take risks to aid a lost cause. King Abdullah ibn-Husein, in something less than a disinterested gesture, suggested that the Egyptian forces still in position in the Hebron hills might be evacuated and used as reinforcements while Legion troops took over their positions. His suggestion was obviously motivated by a desire to extend Transjordan's control of Arab Palestine rather than by a feeling of Arab brotherhood. Regardless of the course of military events, the struggle for shrinking Arab Palestine was continuing. On December 3 the Transjordanian parliament had passed a resolution in favor of the unification of Arab Palestine and Transjordan. No mention was made of the Mufti of Jerusalem, Hajj Amin al-Huseini, and his Palestine government. On December 13 the parliament accepted the necessary constitutional changes. Egypt had barely had time to be enraged before the Israelis attacked. It had protested violently, supported by Saudi Arabia and Syria. Iraq, as mediator, had persuaded Abdullah to delay unification, but he hardly forgot Cairo's efforts to thwart his desires. His offer to occupy the Hebron area was a subtle revenge. Egypt was about to sink, and Abdullah intended to salvage much of the debris.

General Fuad Sadeq, the Egyptian commander, was well aware that his ship was going under. There was no hope of effective Arab intervention, no possibility of reinforcement from Egypt, no real chance of British intervention. Before the United Nations could enforce the truce resolution of December 29, the Israelis would strike again. All that he believed he could do was to wait for the inevitable attack. Despite the fact that the Egyptians anticipated an attack, the Israelis were relatively confident that they could drive the final wedge to the sea at Rafa. Alon planned a joint assault from east and west. In the east the Golani Brigade would move out of the western Negev, cut the Rafa-Gaza highway, and occupy the hills southeast of Rafa. The Harel Brigade would attack from the direction of El 'Auja, cut the Rafa-El 'Arîsh highway to the west, and occupy the road junction and hills to the south of Rafa. In a wide semicircle the two brigades would continue a coordinated advance on the Egyptian positions around the town. With the armored and Negev brigades in reserve for the final thrust, Alon would have sufficient force to roll through to the sea, even if the Egyptians proved tougher than anticipated. On January 3,1948, the attack began.

The new Egyptian government, appointed by Faruk after Nokrashy's assassination, was in a state of near panic. Cairo was filled with rumors that Faruk's personal airplane stood by to fly him to the Suez Canal Zone and that the British army was prepared to occupy the city in case of civil war. By January 6, 1949, it was obvious to the government that Alon's wedge had all but reached the coast. The Egyptian army's luck had run out. Its surrender would surely bring down the government and probably drag Egypt into anarchy. On January 6 the Egyptian government announced that it was willing to open armistice discussions at the Mediator Ralph Bunche's headquarters on Rhodes. At 2:00 in the afternoon of January 7, a cease-fire became effective on the southern front. Even without final victory, Alon's Ayin had achieved its purpose, to bring Egypt to the peace table.

But, in the final hours of fighting, the British again intervened and threatened all that had been gained. Five British fighters from the Suez Canal Zone circled over the battle, supposedly in a reconnaissance flight to determine whether or not the Israelis had withdrawn from Egyptian territory. When the planes strayed over the Negev, the Israeli air force engaged them, assuming that they were Egyptian. All five were shot down near Nirim. The British were enraged. Twelve hours later they had reinforced their base at 'Aqaba in Transjordan, demanded compensation for the planes, and insisted upon the withdrawal of all Israeli troops from Egyptian territory. The British ultimatum would lever the Israelis out several key positions and off the El 'Auja-Rafa road. Egypt, quick to see an opening, immediately announced that acceptance of armistice talks was conditional on Israeli withdrawal. Time might actually have been on the side of Tel Aviv. The United States government had taken a dim view of the British demands. In Britain itself there was considerable public opposition to Foreign Minister Ernest Bevin's having risked the lives of R.A.F. pilots in a pointless flight over a war zone. Ben-Gurion, however, decided that too much was at stake to give the British an excuse to intervene. He overruled Alon and ordered withdrawal. At long last, armistice talk could begin.

On January 12 the Israeli and Egyptian delegations arrived in Rhodes to begin closed sessions with Bunche at the Hôtel des Roses. At first the Egyptians were suspicious and reluctant to meet with Bunche while the Israelis were present. This attitude did not last long, however; Bunche proved to be an ideal mediator, practical, patient, and capable of devising a satisfactory formula to break almost any deadlock. Bunche simply would not give anyone, on Rhodes or off, an opportunity to frustrate the discussions. He was less interested in the ambitions of the major powers than had been Bernadotte. The major difficulty during the negotiations resulted from the continuing ignorance of the Egyptian public of the extent of Israel's offensive success. The Egyptian government believed that it must have some tangible gain in the armistice agreement to prove that the Egyptian army still occupied a large part of Palestine. The first Egyptian proposal was that an Egyptian military governor of Beersheba be appointed, although his headquarters could be in Gaza or Cairo. Israel had no intention of creating a situation that might allow an Egyptian claim on the Negev or of allowing an Egyptian "military governor" within Israeli territory.

The Israeli delegation, headed by Walter Eytan, persuaded the Egyptians that their request was absurd. The Egyptians then suggested a governor of Bir Asluj, a tiny village on the Beersheba-El 'Auja road. Again the Israelis refused. Finally the Egyptians suggested as their last alternative a governor for El 'Auja, a collection of four mud buildings near the international boundary but still inside Palestine. The Israeli delegation refused. The negotiations were deadlocked. Bunche recognized the Egyptian need for a face-saving clause. Without it the talks might fail, no matter what the ultimate consequences for Cairo. The Egyptians needed "evidence" that the Israeli offensive had not driven their army out of everything but the Gaza strip. Bunche finally persuaded the Israelis to compromise on a demilitarized zone around El 'Auja, to be under the control of a Mixed Armistice Commission. Eytan claims that he was never sure whether the Egyptians had tricked Israel into the demilitarized zone by shrewd negotiations or whether the Bunche compromise was really essential. In any case, with the "military governor" problem solved, final agreement was swiftly negotiated.

On February 24, 1949, the two delegations signed the Israeli-Egyptian Armistice Agreement. With one or two minor exceptions, Israel retained the territory occupied during Ayin and received the Faluja pocket, which was gradually evacuated by the Egyptians. The Gaza strip continued under the control of the Egyptian army. The armistice line, based on the military situation on January 7, was "not to be construed in any sense as political or territorial boundary."[2] Although the agreement did contain a clause that allowed either party to appeal to the Secretary-General of the United Nations for revision at the end of a year, no one at Rhodes foresaw that there would be any real need for such a revision. Once similar agreements had been signed with the other Arab states (Transjordan and Lebanon had already intimated that they would like to join the discussions at Rhodes), a permanent peace treaty would have to be negotiated.

On February 28 the Transjordanian delegation arrived in Rhodes. It had been assumed that Abdullah was the most anxious to secure an armistice and a return to normal relations, but the Israelis soon sensed that his delegation did not have the authority to act. Ben-Gurion suspected that Abdullah was stalling. Intelligence reports arrived that Iraqi troops were about to withdraw from Palestine, and were allowing the Arab Legion to occupy their positions. Abdullah too had obviously noted that the military lines had become the armistice lines. His tactics opened another opportunity for Israel to renew the war. A final victory, so often forestalled, over the Arab Legion might still be achieved with no more than temporary diplomatic protests. Ben-Gurion and Yadin began to work on Operation Shin-Tav-Shin to occupy the Arab triangle and central Palestine up to the Jordan River

Even before operational plans had been completed, however, everyone began to have second thoughts. The third offensive might just be the straw that would break the patient United Nations' back. After all, whether Abdullah stalled or not, peace did seem on the way. Great Britain might be more aggressive in defense of its longtime supporter Abdullah. Then too, a fully successful operation, even if it were tolerated at Lake Success and in London, would either bring vast numbers of Arabs into Israel or create hundreds of thousands of new Arab refugees on the border. Either result would endanger the future security of Israel nearly as much as would an Arab-controlled central Palestine. Ben-Gurion decided that Shin-Tav-Shin might bring more problems than accomplishments; nevertheless, he insisted that preparations continue.

Instead of using Shin-Tav-Shin as a military bludgeon, he decided to use it as a diplomatic lever. Israeli preparations became increasingly overt. Yadin saw that news of Shin-Tav-Shin leaked to Abdullah. At that point an informal communication passed through the Legion's military governor in Jerusalem, Colonel el-Tell, informing Abdullah that, if Iraqi troops evacuated their positions, Israel would feel free to occupy the area. Abdullah could not be sure whether or not it was a bluff, but he was in no position to call it by renewing the war. General Sir John Bagot Glubb estimated that, even with the additional Iraqi troops, the Arabs would have only 30,000 men, whereas Israel had four or five times that number. As Israel and Transjordan continued to play diplomatic poker, the Israeli delegation on Rhodes suddenly begin to show very little interest in constructive discussion. On March 7 Abdullah discovered that once more the Arabs had been outflanked.

With the approval of Ben-Gurion and the government, the Israeli general staff did undertake one last offensive, Operation Uvda, an extremely curious military operation that involved no fighting. Uvda was designed to secure effective control, through a bloodless take-over, of all the southern Negev included in the partition resolution. Neither the diplomats nor the generals had paid much attention to this uninhabited desert. The Egyptians had given up any claim at Rhodes. Transjordan, however, had token Legion units on the Gulf of 'Aqaba and a police post at Um Resh Resh. At Rhodes Abdullah could and probably would claim that the area was "occupied" by the Legion. To complicate matters, Bevin had already informed Parliament that Transjordan occupied the southern Negev. Alon and Yaakov Dori had decided that the best approach was to bypass potential diplomatic complications by sending two mobile columns down to Elath on the Gulf of 'Aqaba without opening hostilities.

Israeli reconnaissance during late February and the first week of March had discovered a site thirty-five miles north of Elath where an airstrip could be constructed. From the proposed strip at Sde Abraham, a tortuous and all but impassable trail twisted down to Elath. On March 5 units of the Negev Brigade, accompanied by a working party left Beersheba to construct the strip. First following the road to

El 'Auja, they branched off into the desert. It was a brutal trek. The column took three hours to cover one four-mile section. The spearhead finally arrived at Sde Abraham on the afternoon of March 6. At 6:00 in the evening, the first two commando planes landed. On March 7 the column on the eastern side of the Negev triangle moved out from the oasis at Ein Hussub, where the Elath-Sodom and Beersheba-Sodom caravan trails crossed. Later that evening the advance jeeps reached Ein Webe, fifteen miles farther south. The Legion quickly reported the move to Amman. Abdullah now understood the reason for the sudden delay at Rhodes.

The arrival of the Israeli column was a shock. The Legion had been aware of unusual Israeli activity in the southern Negev, but the continuing talks at Rhodes had lulled suspicions. On March 7, as soon as Israel's intentions became clear, the Transjordanian government ordered its delegation to appeal to the Mediator:

> Inform Dr. Bunche as follows. Considerable force of Jewish jeeps and armoured cars supported by aircraft crossed our lines morning seventh March one kilo west of Bir ibn Auda. Situations will be extremely delicate unless Israel stops active military operations during negotiations.[3]

As far as Transjordan was concerned, the situation was indeed delicate. If the Legion attempted to prevent the Israeli columns from occupying Elath, Tel Aviv could claim that Transjordan was renewing hostilities in an effort to prevent Israel from occupying what the United Nations had allotted to it under the partition resolution. With Shin-Tav-Shin hanging fire, this new incident might be just what the wily Ben-Gurion wanted. As Abdullah and Glubb feared that renewed hostilities would mean total disaster—the loss of all Arab Palestine—the Legion could not be allowed to defend the Negev. In any case, the Israelis had sufficient strength in the Negev to brush aside the Legion outposts. The protest to Bunche proved futile. On March 9 the eastern Israeli column continued its advance toward a Legion post in the foothills of Mount Ketura forty miles north of the Gulf of 'Aqaba. When the Israelis arrived the next morning, the Legion had withdrawn into Transjordan. Neither Glubb nor the local commander was willing to risk useless resistance. At 3:00 in the afternoon on March 10, the first scouts of the Golani Brigade reached the sea at Elath. Soon the men from Sde Abraham joined them. Far to the north, the Alexandroni Brigade had occupied Ein Gedi on the shore of the Dead Sea. Abdullah had lost any tenuous claim to the Negev.

Israeli pressure to achieve an armistice continued with the buildup of Shin-Tav-Shin. Israeli Foreign Minister Sharett informed Bunche officially that Israel would feel free to occupy Iraqi-held Palestine if there were a withdrawal. Even though another "sincere" cease-fire was signed on Rhodes on March 11, by Israel and Jordan, the Iraqi evacuation presented Israel with one more excuse to renew the war against Abdullah. No one could be sure what Ben-Gurion had in mind. Abdullah managed to persuade the Iraqis to remain a few days after the scheduled evacuation date of March 13. Then he made contact with Moshe Dayan through Colonel el-Tell's direct telephone line. The time had come to talk seriously. Abdullah proposed a secret meeting at his winter palace at Shune near the Dead Sea.

Abdullah greeted the Israel delegation politely and with no preamble began reviewing the situation. Within a few minutes it was clear that Abdullah was not speaking to the Israelis but to his own ministers, accusing them of errors of judgment and blaming them for the war. After his analysis Abdullah invited the Israelis in to dinner, where he relaxed and chatted informally, at one point discussing Islamic poetry with Yadin. After dinner Abdullah retired, and Fawzi el-Mulki and Colonel el-Tell directed the conversation to more immediate problems. Essentially Israel wanted some particular advantages out of the Iraqi withdrawal, whereas the Transjordanians needed a genuine armistice but wanted to give up as little as possible in return. The discussions, which lasted for nearly a week, pivoted on the Israeli request for the strategic hill positions occupied by the Iraqi army along the Israeli perimeter. As Iraq had formally designated Transjordan as its plenipotentiary at Rhodes, where the secret agreement would be ratified, Abdullah could negotiate on these positions. Although the Transjordanians could not call the Israeli bluff, they did manage to persuade the Israeli delegation to modify its demands at the last minute.

When Colonel el-Tell finally accepted the fact that the Israelis would not compromise, he agreed to draw the final cease-fire line.

Standing before a large painting of the Battle of Trafalgar, el-Tell picked up a cigarette box and drew a tentative boundary on the back. The Israelis appeared content. Fawzi el-Mulki arrived at that moment and found that el-Tell's hasty line would give Israel not only the hilltops but also the villages. He insisted that the villages could not be given up. The government had already been embarrassed by the Legion failure to defend Lydda and Er Ramle. The population, particularly the refugees, would never accept another "sellout." Before the stalemate could be renewed, Brigadier Coaker of the Arab Legion, along with Yadin and Harkabi of Israel, redrew the line to give the villages back. Abdullah approved. Both delegations signed the agreement at 3:00 in the morning.

Moshe Dayan and the Arab delegate, Jundi, flew the agreement to Rhodes. Miraculously, the next morning there was a break in the long stalemate. Bunche received the Israeli-Jordanian agreement, supposedly negotiated at Rhodes. The agreement, patterned on the Egyptian armistice, was limited to cease-fire conditions and military boundaries. The other outstanding issues were assigned to a special committee, to meet during the eventual permanent peace negotiations. On April 3, 1949, the formal armistice agreement was signed. Lebanon had already signed an armistice on March 23 at Rosh Hanikra on its frontier with Israel. Iraq had withdrawn its troops and designated Transjordan as plenipotentiary. The few hundred Saudi Arabian troops in Palestine had been detached from the Egyptian army and evacuated. Only Syria remained officially at war. Two days after the Transjordanian agreement, on April 5, 1949, talks began with Syria in no man's land near Mahanayim. As it still had control of Mishmar Hayarden, Syria was in a strong bargaining position, particularly in view of the other four agreements, which had reduced the odds that Israel would renew the war at the last minute. Syria hoped to gain control of the headwaters of the Jordan by insisting that the international boundary should run east of the waterline rather than west, as specified in the Anglo-French Agreement of 1923. Israel insisted on the old line and the immediate evacuation of Mishmar Hayarden. The talks made no progress, dragging on and on.

While the protracted negotiations with Syria continued, life in Israel gradually returned to something like "normal." Many members of the Zahal were demobilized. More immigrants flooded into the new state. Despite the war, by the end of 1948 102,000 new immigrants had arrived. On January 11, 1949, the British had released the last "illegal" immigrants from Cyprus to join the steady stream from Europe, Africa, and Asia. The old agricultural colonies had been revived and repaired, and even during the fighting new ones had been founded. More were planned. New industries to absorb the new work force were on the drawing boards. On January 20, 1949, the United States Import-Export Bank had granted a $100 million development loan. There was talk of an Israeli airline, of making the Negev bloom, of tapping the waters of the Jordan, of expanding the Hebrew University. Many people—and not only the new immigrants —could not fully accept the wonder of Israeli postage stamps, Israeli currency, an Israeli parliament (the Knesset). One of the greatest satisfactions had been rapid international recognition of the new state, evidence that other nations accepted the reality of what for so many Jews still seemed a dream.

From the moment of President Truman's immediate recognition, there had been a stream of diplomatic recognitions, from Guatemala to the Soviet Union. By March 1 forty-five nations had tendered official recognition, and within a month the figure rose to fifty-three. Although the Security Council had rejected Israel's first request for membership in the United Nations on December 17, 1948, because of the necessity for clarifying the situation, on March 3, 1949, the Security Council reversed itself by a vote of nine to one; Egypt voted no, and Great Britain abstained. On May 11, almost exactly a year after the declaration of the new state on the eve of the Arab invasion, the General Assembly approved the Security Council recommendation that Israel be admitted to the United Nations. Independence had been won; the state created, with Dr. Chaim Weizmann as President; and peace assured by the armistice agreements.

The one last agreement, with Syria, proved very difficult to achieve, however. Despite the efforts of General Will Riley of the United Nations Truce Supervision Organization and Dr. Bunche, negotiations were broken off entirely on May 17. After a month Bunche found a satisfactory compromise. Where the existing military frontier followed the Mandate boundary, it would be the armistice line; where it did not, an armistice line would be drawn halfway between the military frontier and the Mandate boundary; furthermore, the area would be between the two demilitarized zones. The Israelis would stay where they were and the Syrians would withdraw. This armistice line was "not to be interpreted as having any relation whatsoever to ultimate territorial arrangements affecting the two Parties."[4] Although negotiations continued to drag on for weeks, a basis for a satisfactory settlement had been found. On July 20, 1949, Syria and Israel signed the formal agreement, leaving disposition of the disputed territory for a final settlement. The agreement attracted little attention, for efforts to secure a final settlement were already underway under the auspices of the Conciliation Commission for Palestine, which had been created by a General Assembly resolution of December 11, 1948. Still, on July 20, 1949, the war was officially over and an effective armistice assured.

The Israelis hopefully and the Arabs reluctantly expected final treaties to come out of the Commission's negotiations. The last act in the drama of the Israel-Arab war appeared to be drawing to a close. Within Israel there was little time for reflection, for analysis of the factors behind victory. The Zahal commanders, to be sure, reviewed their operations and dissected their moves, but, for most Israelis, it was enough that their cause had been just and their army successful. The one lesson learned was that Israel's security would thenceforth depend mainly on the power and will of the Israelis. The United Nations and all its agencies had as often been a hindrance as a prop to Israeli ambitions. Even the United States had faltered. The most effective weapon had been a discreet application of military power to the Arab jugular, backed up by a diplomatic holding operation. The existence of Israel, swept clean of Arabs and extended beyond the partition boundaries, seemed clear evidence of the capacity of the new state to protect itself against the squabbling Arabs and the machinations of the great powers.

Although the Israelis turned swiftly from the war to building their state, the Arabs could neither forget the war nor accept their defeat. The humiliation to Arab pretensions, to Arab pride was too great to be borne. Some leaders, like Mahmud Fahmi Nokrashy, had already paid the price for failure. Others in positions of power looked at their colleagues or their rivals to place the guilt. For some the "prime causes of the disaster were the British."[5] Most early Arab self-analysis was dominated by recriminations: The city people of Palestine had been indifferent to the Legion; the Egyptian army had mistrusted the local Arabs and had had no front-line experience; the local leaders at Haifa had fled; the Galileean villagers had deserted to the Jews.[6] There would be an occasional broader negative: The truce had been a mistake, or the lack of military coordination had been a factor. In a few quarters the lessons of the Palestine war were read as a condemnation of the Arab world, its lack of unity, its poor regimes, its hopeless masses, but policies to rectify the situation remained tantalizingly vague. The best course seemed to most Arabs to be to deny the defeat and to ignore its consequences.

The Palestine war had far-reaching consequences, whether or not many Arabs were ready to face them. The stability of the Arab regimes had been severely and permanently undermined. Careers had been compromised and governments discredited. Even Abdullah, the wisest of the lot, had gained only a quarter of the loaf he had hoped for and with it hundreds of thousands of hostile new subjects. The comfortable world of the men who had run the Middle East for a generation had begun to crumble. Thousands of bitter young men swore never to suffer another such humiliation from the Jews, from the British, from their monarchs, from anyone. Hundreds of thousands of bitter and violent refugees huddled in wretched camps swearing vengeance on someone. Millions of barely literate Arabs felt a loss, a betrayal they hardly understood. The old system of paid politicians, British advisers, and treaty agreements had proved inadequate. A new generation, bred on ultranationalism, considered British hegemony insupportable. One by one, Britain's old friends were to go, exiled, assassinated, imprisoned. The process took longer than many Arab nationalists expected but less time than Britain believed possible. In the place of the British, the Arabs sought new friends. In 1949 the Arabs out of power could not see far into the future, but they were certain, in fact determined, that it would not repeat the past.

Elsewhere the ramifications of the Palestine war brought agonizing reappraisals. The British were forced to recognize that neither their formal neutrality during the last days of the Mandate nor their championing of the Arabs afterward had brought stability to the Middle East or strategic benefits to London. Increasingly harassed by the complex problems of the East-West confrontation, the Labour government still could not give sufficient time to rethinking its policy in the Middle East. In Washington the same zigzag between support for Israel and practical considerations continued. Primarily, however, both Washington and London wanted a tranquil Middle East, open to democratic guidance and economic development. In 1949 no one could tell, and few even had the time to ask, whether or not the existence of Israel would be an asset to the West. Even the Soviet Union showed no avid desire to become more deeply involved in the Middle East, having more promising crises to tend to in Europe and Asia. That the basic stability of the Arab world had been utterly shaken, opening innumerable choices and uncertainties, gradually came to be accepted by some reluctantly and by others with delight. In 1949, however, the expectations of the world's diplomats, as well as of the Israelis and the Arabs themselves, was that some kind of satisfactory settlement would be hammered out by the Conciliation Commission.

NOTES

1. Netanel Lorch, *The Edge of the Sword* (New York: 1961), p. 412.

2. *Official Records of the Security Council*, 4th year (1949), Special Supplement 3.

3. Sir John Bagot Glubb, *A Soldier with the Arabs* (New York: 1957), pp. 229–230.

4. *Official Records of the Security Council*, 4th year (1949), Special Supplement 2.

5. Musa Alami, "The Lessons of Palestine," *Middle East Journal*, 3, No. 4 (October 1949), 373.

6. One of the few relatively unpolemical volumes on the Arab reaction to the Palestine War is *Be' enei Oyev* (*Through the Eyes of the Enemy*) (Tel Aviv: 1955), which include the memoirs of an Arab clerk at Haifa, a leader of the Muslim volunteers on the Egyptian front, and a captain

in the Arab Legion. There criticisms are echoed elsewhere. The intellectuals found the cause of defeat in the political systems and sought an alternative Arab ideology for the modern world. Young army officers like Gamal Abdel Nasser were sure at first at least, that the fault lay with the corrupt governments making political wars at home rather than with the army in particular and the Arab world in general. Those in power blamed one another. The rationalization of defeat came to form the basis of ideas on which the next generation would be brought up. In contrast, the Israelis believed that they had won because they had the advantages of qualitative training, education, and moral superiority, whereas the Egyptians had an archaic social system and a largely feudal army. See "Israel Commander Answers Neguib," *Jewish Observer and Middle East Review*, 1. No. 26.

II

The Violent Peace*
Conflict by Attrition

L ong before the Syrian armistice of July 20, 1949, there
had been ample evidence that the ultimate peace
treaties were going to be difficult to negotiate. The further realization that the armistice agreements would not necessarily lead to
permanent peace came more slowly, for war without open fighting
was a relatively novel concept. The shooting war between Israel and
the Arabs had itself been a novel war. It had been fought in spurts,
interrupted by international directives, limited by political considerations, and restircted by great-power intervention. Seldom had a
military conflict been so hedged about by directives, ultimatums,
agreements, recommendations, plans, and protocols. Even for the
cynical and the defiant, there was still little reason during the summer
of 1949 to suppose that the barrage of international directives and resolutions would not lead to a final settlement. The instrument of
negotiation was the Conciliation Commission for Palestine, established
on December 11, 1948, by the United Nations General Assembly.

The Commission proceeded with considerable deliberation, arriving in Jerusalem on January 24, 1949, for the traditional tour of the
capitals. In February discussions began. In March the Commission
moved on to Beirut to meet with the delegates of the four belligerent
Arab states, Syria, Lebanon, Transjordan, and Egypt. By that time

237

serious doubts had been created in some quarters about the competence and prospects of the Commission.

A wide range of experts, including Mediator Ralph Bunche, had strongly advised against meeting with the Arab states as a bloc. In contrast to Bunche's interpretation of his instructions, the Commission decided that the "two parties" meant the Arab states on one hand and Israel on the other. As the only true Arab unity was expressed in hatred of Israel, whatever individual moderation and restraint existed in secret was discarded in public polemics. Unable to assume in public any other than a negative attitude, the Arabs were encouraged to do so by the Commission's apparent acceptance of their united intransigence as natural. Other disquieting differences between the armistice talks and the conciliation efforts developed rapidly. Unlike the Mediator, who was responsible solely and directly to the United Nations, the three members of the Commission were not international civil servants but national appointees from France, Turkey, and the United States. Consequently, the Commission members almost inevitably were inclined to consider first the policies of their own governments, rather than concentrating solely on writing an effective treaty. The members also showed a greater interest in personal publicity than Bunche had done, a greater concern with reporting openly and at length to the United Nations than Bunche had found wise, and a greater capacity to accept Arab delays and evasions at face value than Bunche had demonstrated.

When the Commission moved to Lausanne, Switzerland, in April, Arab unity in dissent continued. When the Israelis arrived on April 27, they found the arrangements quite different from those at Rhodes. The Arab delegations were lodged at the Lausanne Palace at one end of town and the Israeli delegation, along with the Commission and the Mediator, on the other side of town at the Beau Rivage by the lake at Ouchy. There would thus be no opportunity for informal contacts. Furthermore, the Arabs immediately announced that they would not sit at the same table with the Israeli delegation, and the Commission decided to accept this refusal. There would not be an opportunity even for formal contacts.

Not only the housing arrangements and procedures were different from those on Rhodes; so was the general atmosphere. Almost at once, each member of the Commission began to express the views of his government. The Turks were fearful of Russia in 1949 and therefore not averse to an alliance with the Arabs. The French showed great sympathy for the views of Syria. The Americans, still unable to decide where their interests lay, gave early indications that they [in order to pose as the Arabs' friend], intended to pressure the Israelis into early concessions. The immediate result of so much private lobbying was to turn the conference into a diplomatic farce. Although technically the activities of the Commission could be termed "negotiations," they were in reality limited to transferring messages from one immovable delegation to another. The Arabs, as often as not encouraged by the supposedly disinterested commissioners, did not refuse to negotiate. They simply refused any agenda or program that might lead to serious negotiations.

The Arabs' position seemed to be that they should be bribed by Israeli concessions to open serious negotiations, which could then be concluded by more extensive concessions. Washington apparently agreed. In April Mark Ethridge, the American delegate, supported an Arab demand that, before any discussion of a general settlement, the refugee problem be settled. As long as Israel refused to allow the nearly 1 million refugees back into Palestine, the Arabs refused to consider a final peace treaty. Beside supporting this stand, the United States State Department went further and in April insisted that any boundary settlement must be based on the partition plan. The Israelis were suspicious, fearing that one unilateral concession would lead to another without satisfying the Arabs. To concede all the disputed points in order to negotiate on the same points seemed most unrealistic. The Israelis did reluctantly offer a plan for the immediate reunion of Arab refugees with their families in Israel, but both the Arabs and the Americans seemed to view this offer as a miserly sop. Negotiations were deadlocked. Week after week, negative notes passed from one end of Lausanne to the other as the impasse continued.

The Israelis, who took the conference most seriously, were aware that the Arab unity was superficial. Even before the conference, there had been no general Arab agreement on boundaries, on Jerusalem, even on the refugees. Several of the Arab states, however, had shown sincere interest in moving from the armistice to a final treaty. In Lausanne the Israelis held ultra-secret meetings with individual Arab spokesmen, who were most insistent that the other Arab delegations learn nothing of the meetings. These secret conversations proved no more fruitful than did the official proceedings. Wedded to public negativism, permitted by the Commission to continue that policy, encouraged by the efforts on their behalf among the major powers, the Arabs could safely refuse to compromise or to concede anything. Desperate for some positive results, the Commission drew up an innocuous protocol, which included a map of Palestine based on the November 1947 partition resolution, as a basis for discussion. Even though the protocol in no way restricted future positions or even limited the existing ones, the Commission believed that it was a forward step. The Arabs refused to sign it in the presence of the Israeli delegation, so on May 14 it had to be signed at two separate meetings. Although the Arabs would later claim that Israel had recognized the partition boundaries, the document meant nothing. The protocol was little more than a symbol of the lack of progress.

The American State Department took a hand by pressing its concession policy on Israel. On May 29 Washington sent a strong note in President Harry S Truman's name to Prime Minister David Ben-Gurion, insisting on Israeli concessions. Ben-Gurion rejected the note. Truman, who was often out of touch with the intentions of the State Department, showed no further interest in "his" proposal. Then the State Department produced the McGhee Plan, which tied the refugee problem to a vast Middle Eastern economic-development scheme. Israel would allow 100,000 refugees to be repatriated, and the remainder would be resettled elsewhere as an integral part of a United States-sponsored and -supported development plan; Israel, however, would have to give up Galilee and the Negev, in return for the Gaza strip. Israel rejected the plan. In Lausanne the Israelis presented their own proposals for settlements with Egypt, Lebanon, and Jordan. In turn, the Arabs produced a counterproposal. With Bunche alone common ground might have been found, but with the Commission also present no serious effort was made. Talks dragged on until an adjournment on July 1. When the conference reopened on July 19 there had actually been a compromise on procedure so that discussions could begin with the refugee problem as part of a general settlement.

On August 3 Israel offered to receive 100,000 refugees. This offer should have been the first and greatest step toward hard bargaining, but Washington expressed dissatisfaction with its size. Nor did the Commission seem impressed with the Israeli concession. On August 15 the Arabs rejected the offer as insufficient. The Commission then sent a mission to investigate the refugee problem in detail. It was the first step on the road to nowhere.

Stalled over the refugees, the Commission turned to boundary problems. The Israelis declared, in effect, that they intended to keep what had been included in the armistice agreements. The Arabs collectively claimed 12,000 of the 17,000 square kilometers controlled by Israel. On September 19, 1949, the Commission gave up. After several other desultory conferences, it reported to the General Assembly two years later, in November 1951, that it had failed.

That the Commission had proved unsuccessful came as a great disappointment to the Israelis, who had believed with considerable reason that there was sufficient Arab sentiment for a final settlement. Their personal contacts with the Arabs had been good. Their experience with Bunche had been encouraging. Then the constant self-seeking intervention of other powers and the bungling of the Commission had allowed the opportunity to slip away. The future remained vague. Israel was not yet convinced that separate treaties were impossible, but a great deal of time had been lost at Lausanne. The Arabs were equally uncertain about future negotiations. Even in the fall of 1949 both the Arabs and the Israelis assumed that a state of no war and no peace would not be allowed to continue. There were too many urgent problems: the Arab refugees, the arbitrary frontiers based only on immediate military necessities, the demilitarized zones, the proposed Arab free port on the Israeli Mediterranean coast, Egyptian-Jordan access through the Negev, and the status of Jerusalem. Some sort of lasting agreement was essential.

Of all the Arab leaders King Abdullah ibn-Husein of Transjordan was still the one with the most to gain from an agreement with Israel. The Arab Legion held half of Jerusalem and much of central Palestine, and Abdullah had already taken the necessary preparatory steps for annexation. He knew that Great Britain sympathized with his ambition to create a Kingdom of Jordan, although perhaps not with his choice of Jerusalem as the capital. He knew what the reaction would be in other Arab countries and planned to ignore it, but he did not know what the Israelis would do. He might gain much from a formal treaty, for he assumed that Ben-Gurion would be even more anxious for a treaty and he himself might therefore hope for some significant concessions. These concessions would in turn help to placate the vast numbers of discontented and embittered Palestinian Arabs, many of them refugees, on the west bank of the Jordan. If the refugees were left without hope for the future, his regime could never be stable, but, if he could win substantial concessions for them and for himself, they and the west-bank Arabs might regard him as a savior instead of as a scapegoat. Confident of his skills and his analysis, Abdullah decided to risk the certain ire of his Arab peers and the possible misunderstanding of his subjects.[1] He renewed his secret contacts with the Israelis.

But Abdullah misjudged the Israelis. Tel Aviv was not at first particularly interested in an agreement with Transjordan, hoping instead to play off the Syrians and Egyptians against Abdullah. An early agreement with him would have alienated the other Arab states and precluded a general settlement; furthermore, the Israelis still hoped that an agreement with Egypt might even force Abdullah out of the west bank and make possible establishment there of a weak, miniature Arab buffer state. But these Israeli hopes had gradually to be abandoned. The course of the discussions at Lausanne had revealed that any immediate agreement with Egypt was unlikely. Still Israel responded to Abdullah's feelers only reluctantly, for there were many other complications.

Abdullah was confident of his staying power and his bargaining position. His first demands were access to the Mediterranean through Beersheba and Gaza, the return of the Arab quarters of Jerusalem, passage along the Jerusalem-Bethlehem road, and a free port in Haifa. In return he offered Israel access to the potash works on the north shore of the Dead Sea and a free port on the Gulf of 'Aqaba, which implied that at least some of the southern Negev would be returned to Transjordan. On paper it looked as if Abdullah thought that the Arab Legion had won the Palestine war. The Israelis rejected the proposals. In the meantime, rumors of the secret talks had leaked into the Arab press. Egypt retaliated by drumming up support in the United Nations for the immediate internationalization of Jerusalem. In December 1949 the Egyptian ploy succeeded. Backed by the new Asian-Arab bloc, the Vatican, and the votes of the Latin American states, the resolution was adopted by the General Assembly. The resolution had a revitalizing effect on Israel-Transjordan discussions.

As both Abdullah and Ben-Gurion were determined to retain their positions in Jerusalem, the resolution was an added spur to an agreement that would present the United Nations with the fait accompli of a formally divided Jerusalem. Abdullah proposed a settlement limited to Jerusalem that would restore the Arab quarter without compensating Israel. Once again Israel refused. Two weeks later, giving up on his hard demands, Abdullah presented another plan, limited to a five-year nonaggression pact. Intensive discussions led to a formal treaty. For five years the frontiers would remain unchanged while various committees worked on outstanding problems, but there would be normal trade and travel, a free-port zone in Haifa for Transjordan, and mutual access to the holy places in Jerusalem. It was the closest to a negotiated settlement that the Israelis had come in a year of talking. Although Israeli Foreign Ministry officials were content, other Israelis were not. There were a great many risks in signing the agreement. The Soviet Union had warned Israel that Abdullah was Britain's puppet and Russia's enemy. Israel needed Soviet diplomatic support and trade. On their part the Israelis, like the Russians, remained suspicious of Abdullah's British ties. Ben-Gurion and Yigal Yadin, the new Israeli Chief of Staff, pointed out the military disadvantages of a frozen border. Others noted that the treaty would mean giving up all Israeli claims to the rest of Palestine. Despite hesitations and doubts, the Cabinet finally decided to accept the treaty. In March the draft treaty was initialed by both delegations. Now Abdullah would have to sell it to the Arabs.

In March 1950 the atmosphere in the Middle East was hardly conducive to peaceful negotiation. Rumors of the extended Israeli-Transjordanian talks had been reported all over the Arab world. The press had revealed, often accurately, the direction of the supposedly secret negotiations. The other Arab states, still fearful of Abdullah, had been righteously indignant, but the full force of their opposition had been muted by the lack of positive results. Once the draft treaty had been initialed, however, the storm broke over Abdullah's head. Threats and accusations, both official and unofficial, poured into Amman. Syria threatened to close its Transjordanian border. The Arab radio stations and newspapers dripped venom. Transjordan faced a cabinet crisis. The population on the west bank seethed. On March 25, 1950, the Arab League met in Cairo to castigate Abdullah. The time had come to expel the heretic.

When the League met in Cairo, Egypt and Saudi Arabia opened bitter attacks on Abdullah. Egypt, which still supported the phantom government of the Mufti Hajj Amin al-Huseini in the Gaza strip, wanted Abdullah excommunicated, thrown out of the League. King ibn-Saud concurred, continuing his opposition to anything that might benefit Abdullah and his support of any maneuver that might harm him. But, with the help of Tewfik as-Saudi of Iraq and the representative of Yemen, the Transjordanian delegation managed to sidetrack Egypt's expulsion campaign. In return Transjordan had to vote for a resolution affirming that the Arab states were in Palestine as trustees and for a second resolution prohibiting separate agreements with Israel.

Abdullah, however, was still in the game, for League meetings had never greatly influenced his plans. Cairo had voted a resolution, but Cairo could hardly enforce it against a united Jordan. He hoped that the impending elections in Transjordan would vindicate his policy; then he could again ignore Egypt. Instead, the elections killed his draft treaty. The electorate supported candidates favoring Abdullah's ambitions to annex the west bank but not his intention to make peace with the Zionists. Knowing that the British, who were then involved in a dispute with Egypt over the presence of British troops in the Suez Canal Zone, would not rush to his aid,[2] Abdullah did what he could. On April 24 he annexed all of Arab Palestine occupied by the Legion. Great Britain gave immediate de facto recognition to the annexation. Abdullah had his Kingdom of Jordan. As he had anticipated, the League dithered but did nothing.

The population of Jordan had spoken clearly against any deal with the Zionists; that aspect of Abdullah's program had therefore to be postponed. The problem of Jerusalem had been solved for Abdullah by the annexation. The Israelis had already moved the Knesset, their new parliament, to Jerusalem for the first session in February, and the government ministeries soon began moving into the city. But other problems remained. There was only the armistice agreement to regularize Jordan-Israel relations. Although informal contacts between the two states continued, no results were forthcoming. During 1951 the last hopes for a permanent treaty faded in both Jordan and Isreal. Having already antagonized all the Arab world outside Jordan, Abdullah was too wise to risk again antagonizing his own subjects, who clearly would regard any settlement with Israel as treasonous. Abdullah's subjects were no longer mainly the loyal Bedouins of the old Arab world but instead the bitter, dispossessed Palestinian Arabs. They cared little for the practical policies of the shrewd old desert emir. They wanted revenge, not reconciliation.

Then, July 20, 1951, on the steps of the Mosque of Omar, an assassin struck down Abdullah as a traitor to Arab unity. The assassins were, according to Jordanian reports, directed by relatives of the Mufti, but Abdulla el-Tell was charged as an accessory and condemned to death in absentia. El-Tell, who denied the charge, had been a favorite of Abdullah, who had secured his promotion to lieutenant colonel; he had commanded a battalion in the siege of the Jewish quarter of Jerusalem. Later he became Governor of Jerusalem, but he resigned and accepted an Egyptian sinecure in January 1950. In Egypt he took a strong pro-Egyptian line against Abdullah. Gratitude has never been a major factor in Arab politics. Although ambition and greed motivated the assassins, who had no ideas and no program, the lesson was not lost on potential Arab moderates elsewhere. The price of conciliation would be death.

For a year everyone had cried for peace, yet still there was no peace. On the other hand, there was no war either. What existed was a temporary truce based on the four general armistice agreements, extended indefinitely. The armistice agreements had been intended only as a most transitory stage on the way to a formal settlement, but, through a fortunate combination of Bunche's skill and general acceptance of the need for a final treaty, they were far more inclusive than a simple cease-fire would have been. These four agreements were permanent, in that they implicitly recognized the signers' rights to exist and to develop. They were thus actually little treaties, ending the fighting but not resolving the basic issues. The cease-fire was to be maintained by both the United Nations Truce Supervision Organization and the new Mixed Armistice Commission, with recourse to the Security Council and, perhaps, event to the General Assembly. All this elaborate machinery had been envisioned as temporary, so that both the Mixed Armistice Commission and the Truce Organization anticipated their own imminent dissolution. Instead, with the failure of the Conciliation Commission and the fading hopes for separate treaties, the "temporary" machinery became permanent. Arab-Israeli relations had entered what was euphemistically called the "armistice regime."

The armistice period evolved unevenly into what would pass as normality in the Middle East: an unwanted Israel, developing in isolation, hampered by Arab hatred and fear. As the last hopes for formal peace sputtered out in 1950, the exaltation of the Israelis during the challenging days of invasion and war turned into the daily strain of creating a viable state. The elation and excitement over postage stamps and naval victories was dissipated under the tide of immigration, the demands of industrialization, the worrisome balance of payments, the income tax, and the rigid austerity measures. Israel was to be open to all Jews, but only through fantastic efforts could an economy capable of absorbing the influx be created. Even the problems facing the diplomats paled before those created by the flood of new citizens demanding, in a dozen tongues, jobs and homes and help.

The very reason for the existence of Israel was to provide a homeland for the Jews; yet, obviously, not all Jews could, even if they had wanted to, move to Israel, a small checkerboard of arid land, ragged mountains, and barren deserts. Even if miraculously obtained water could make the deserts bloom, Israel would still be unable to feed a population of millions. Even with massive injections of capital, Israeli industry could never absorb so many millions of Jews, trained or untrained. Although the Zionists, albeit at times reluctantly, accepted the fact that Israel could never contain all the world's Jews, they took as an article of faith that all who wanted to immigrate must be encouraged. Some talked of a population of 2 million in a decade, particularly those who had little idea of the practical integration of such a number into a functioning state. In 1948–1949 the immediate arrival of already-waiting immigrants brought 340,895 new citizens into Israel. This influx included a substantial portion of the long-denied Jewry of Europe, but it also included immigrants from Africa and Asia, where local anti-Zionist tensions had threatened Jewish communities. This huge number was not unexpected. Continuing but declining immigration from Europe had been predicted. By 1954 the reservoirs of European immigrants had been sufficiently exhausted, so that in that year only 981 arrived in Israel. What had not been fully anticipated, however, had been the burgeoning immigration from Africa and Asia.

These African and Asian Jews were neither Zionists nor Westernized, but had fled the Islamic countries from fear of persecution. Their skills, their social structure, their world outlook had more in common with those of ghetto Arabs than with those of the East European founders of Israel. Isolated from the outside world for centuries, they had maintained only their Judaism. Suddenly overnight, as often from necessity as from choice, they were thrown into a booming, ultramodern socialist state. First from one area and then from another—in fear of persecution or to fulfill biblical prediction— they came. When one pocket had been drained, another was found elsewhere. The Asian influx sank from 102,668 in 1951 to 1,221 in 1955, but African immigration rose to 32,549 in 1955 and 45,263 the following year. All these frightened and bewildered people had to be dragged into the twentieth century, fed, housed, taught Hebrew, trained, employed. The aged and crippled from Europe had also to be comforted and maintained. The cost, though hardly incalculable, could not be met by the resources of the fledgling state.

This gap between the available resources and the demands of the growing population dominated government thinking. A vast amount of money had to be poured into basic construction—roads, schools, apartments, sewers—that could not pay immediate dividends. Even to keep pace with the continuing immigration was impossible. To some extent, the deficit was made up by large development loans and the efforts of Zionist charities and bond drives. More important was the heavy infusion of private Jewish capital into Israeli industry. Undoubtedly the most significant "invisible" economic asset was the international Zionist movement. Nowhere was this factor more important than in the United States, where, as previous immigrant groups had done in earlier generations, the Zionists called on the resources of American Jewry to bolster the economy of the new state. There were regular and highly successful bond drives, steady investment by individuals, charity campaigns, special loans, exchange scholarships, educational programs, and recruitment of skilled emigrants. American Jews, even those who were not potential emigrants, were deeply devoted to Israel and most willing to contribute to its security. To the Arabs, it seemed as if the Zionists had converted America, for there were many Jews who were prominent in the mass media, publishing, and politics; at times it appeared that the entire American entertainment industry was a Zionist front group. The outward sign of this enthusiasm for Israel was the flow of hard currency by various routes into the new state, permitting a level of long-term investment far higher than the domestic economy alone would have allowed. The success of Israel, the blooming desert, thus depended substantially on American gold, a fact that the Arabs noted. The American contribution, along with those of other national Zionist groups, could not, however, alone or even in conjunction with United States government assistance, meet Israeli demands. Israel continued to live beyond its means.

Still, by 1952 not even the harshest austerity measures could prevent Israel from tottering on the edge of bankruptcy. The New Economic Plan was the last hope, and the economists expected only that it would postpone the inevitable economic ruin. Then, at its lowest ebb, the Israeli economy was rescued by the German reparations agreement, which guaranteed $715 million in goods over a fourteen-year period. Although the economy had been salvaged by the reparations agreement, there was no immediate economic miracle, only a lessening of tension and a gradual improvement.

To anyone visiting Israel regularly, the improvement seemed far from gradual; Israelis untrained in economics, though aware of the irritating shortages, individual sacrifices, ruinous taxes, and official pessimism, could see change everywhere. Far from allowing the weight of the Oriental immigration to drag down their aspirations or their standards, their attitude was the reverse. The African or Asian immigrant had to be Zionized, inspired, trained, motivated, imbued with democracy, and given a share in the future. To a surprising extent this effort succeeded. Everyone, from former German lawyers to illiterate Yemenite children, learned Hebrew. Nearly everyone found a productive occupation, a home of sorts, and a place in society.[3] Strains there were and inequalities and failures but not as a result of negligence. Tel Aviv grew like a great blot along the coast, turning the shore highway into a long, sprawling metropolis. The new city was transformed into a modern capital. Everywhere there were new industries, new buildings, wider roads, new forests, new kibbutzim, new projects. Whatever else Israel was, it was hardly dull. The country was in the constant grip of change. The exuberant nationalism and pioneering spirit of the country could not be dulled, at least at first, by either cold statistics or the lack of living comforts. Looking around them, most Israelis, despite the galloping population graphs and the balance-of-payments problem, could see progress daily. Although far from out of the woods of financial difficulties, they had left behind the worst thickets in the first five years. Although the state remained largely dependent on loans and reparations, much of the money had been carefully invested in the future. Not yet a land of milk and honey, Israel was nonetheless flourishing.

To the Arabs Israel's existence was sufficiently galling; that it should flourish was insupportable. When the possibility of an enforced settlement diminished during the fall of 1949, the Arabs, at first almost imperceptibly, moved toward a policy of war by other than military means in order to isolate, harass, and hamper Israel. When this tentative approach met no strong opposition in the international community nor any firm pressure for renewed direct negotiations, the Arabs created the actual machinery of limited war, a war by blockade, boycott, political pressure, propaganda, and border violence. The Arabs' legal rationale, which Egypt would later offer almost as an aside, was that a state of war still existed between Israel and the Arab states, despite the general armistice agreements. Only by the most sophistic use of the loopholes of international law and by pointedly ignoring the provisions of the armistice agreements, could the Egyptians defend the legality of their continuing "war!" The weaknesses of the Arab defense were immaterial, for no one but Israel seemed particularly concerned. As long as the situation did not get too far out of hand, most nations tolerated or at best evaded Arab regulations intended to destroy Israel by a campaign of attrition. Within a year of the failure of the conciliation talks, the Arabs had pieced together their program of war by nonmilitary means.

Reluctantly accepting that an overt military attack would be frustrated in the near future, the Arabs discovered that, in the absence of a formal treaty with Israel, a variety of most promising options remained open. There was no difficulty in sealing the Israeli frontier, which could be squeezed from time to time by irregular border warfare, nor in isolating Israel from the Arab world diplomatically and economically. If the isolation could be extended to the new Asian powers, to other Islamic states, to those powers that needed the oil and bases of the Middle East, then the future of Israel would be bleak indeed. The Arabs believed, with some justification, that time was on their side. Their combined population was twenty times as large as that of Israel, their potential resources were immense, their future was promising. The Arabs could harass Israel for years while building their own strength and awaiting a shift in the international climate that would ensure military victory in the final round. After all, as Arab diplomats were prone to point out regularly, the Crusaders had come, established alien states, existed on overseas subsidies, and then departed. The Seljuk Turks had come and gone. The Ottoman Turks and the British and the French had come and gone. Only the Arabs remained. Even Israel's momentary military superiority appeared a feeble prop, in view of the far more impressive backing of the Crusader states by Christendom or of the Palestine Mandate by the British Empire. The Arabs therefore decided to use any means short of open war to limit the growth and erode the strength of the imposed and alien Zionist state.

One of the least costly and most frustrating Arab maneuvers was the diplomatic quarantine. The entire border, except for a tiny crevice at Rosh Hanikra, Lebanon, open mainly to foreign diplomats, and the Mandlebaum Gate in Jerusalem, which was limited to non-Jews entering the city, remained tightly closed. Anyone crossing the border risked death on both sides of the line. No Israeli passport was accepted in any Arab state, and some states extended this ban to any passport held by a Jew. No person was allowed into any Arab state whose passport bore an Israeli visa, which meant that at times neutral travelers had to resort to carrying two passports, in some cases even three, in order to travel in the Middle East. Continuing efforts were made to prevent non-Arabic nations from establishing diplomatic relations with Israel. This policy was particularly effective with the new generation of nations, which were easily persuaded that Israel was an imperialistic puppet rather than an emerging nation similar to themselves. Many nations had substantial Islamic minorities and others had expatriate colonies within the Arab world. These states were cool to Israeli overtures. At the Bandung Conference of Afro-

Asian states in 1955, the Arabs managed to have Israel barred though not condemned by resolution.

In the wider world of international diplomacy, the Arabs treated the Israelis as pariahs. No Israeli was allowed access to the Middle East regional offices of international agencies, like the World Health Organization or the Food and Agricultural Organization. Only with great reluctance would any Arab delegate participate in any agency at any level with an Israeli. Diplomatic cocktail parties and international receptions became the scenes of delicate social maneuvers to avoid accidental confrontations between Arabs and Israelis. Even in international sports competition, the Arabs refused to play with the Israelis. Although often petty, the diplomatic isolation did bring the Arabs certain benefits. Many doors that might have been open to Israel remained closed; many potential friends found other outlets for their sympathy. At the United Nations, in Paris, and in Washington the Arab policy was little more than an irritant to everyone, but in the Middle East it separated Israel from Asia with a wall of nonrecognition that took years to breach.

More damaging than the diplomatic quarantine was the Arab economic boycott. During 1949 there had been some trade, carried on through middlemen, between Israel and Arabs more dedicated to profit than to politics. The Arab states did not devise a formal policy of no trade with the Zionists, but individually the government disapproved. During January 1950, however, the Arab League officially drew up a formal boycott to prohibit any form of cooperation between the Arab states and Israel, including trade, shipping, and cultural relations. There remained sufficient loopholes for the greedy so that in 1951 a central boycott office was established in Damascus, with national branches. One by one, the Arab states enacted stiff controls with harsh penalties for violators. Their lead was followed by the small states of the Persian Gulf and several new African Islamic nations: Libya, Tunisia, and Morocco. Concerted efforts were made to persuade non-Islamic nations to recognize the boycott, but Israel's major customers, the United States and Great Britain, ignored the request. In fact, Israeli-Russian trade increased substantially until the change in Soviet policy in 1955.

Shifting their emphasis, the Arabs pressured individual concerns to accept the boycott through the threat of blacklisting or expulsion from the Arab market. Many major air and maritime companies were dissuaded from serving Israel. No plane that had touched down at the Lydda or Haifa air terminals could fly over an Arab state, much less land at an Arab terminal. No flights to Asia could originate in Israel, and no Europe-Israel-Asia route could be established. Israel soon became a minor side stop, rather than an international cross-roads. Not until 1956 did Air France set up a dogleg route via Turkey to Teheran. It was more difficult for the Arabs to persuade private firms that branches in Israel or even business with Israel would bar them from the Arab Middle East. Veiled threats met with varying success, depending both on the attitudes of the individual concerns and their governments and on the potential loss the Arabs might face in enforcing the boycott. The final step was to extend the provisions of the boycott to include firms controlled or directed by Jews, a step that was seldom effective and brought with it far stronger international criticism of the boycott than had any other measure.

The impact of the boycott is difficult to judge.[4] At first, the Israelis and many others considered it little more than ineffectual petulance that would wear thin. Even the threat of a break in diplomatic relations failed to prevent Germany from signing the vital reparations agreements. Many private concerns seemed quite able to ignore the boycott without penalty. Although far from total even in the Arab world, the boycott did not wear thin. The trade patterns and production balances of the Middle East changed. Palestine had been both a consumer of agricultural produce and a major exchange area with the large port at Haifa; for example, Iraqi oil passed through Syria in pipelines to be refined in and shipped from Haifa. All this activity disappeared. The pipeline was idle. Jordan had to transship through Syria to Beirut, to the immense advantage of the latter. New markets had to be found for Arab agricultural and commercial production. In turn, the Israelis were cut off from their traditional markets and their traditional suppliers. Israel was forced at great expense to increase its own agricultural sector and simultaneously to import from more distant suppliers. All this change, however, had advantages, as well as disadvantages, for both sides. In the Arab world the burden of the boycott was shared unevenly and proved to be of considerable advantage to Syrian and Lebanese merchants. Undoubtedly, Israeli losses were great, although no one is sure of the specific figure. Most important was the economic quarantine from the rest of the Middle

East. But the imposed isolation did drive the Israelis to create a far more extensive and ultimately profitable agricultural sector than they might otherwise have done. Israeli industry, relying on the technological skills of the new immigrants and limited in raw materials, developed different products and different markets than it would have if the underdeveloped Arab areas had been open to exploitation. The boycott drove the Israelis at great expense to measures that might, in the long run, be advantageous, even though, in the short run, they strained the economy.

Regardless of the cost to themselves of the boycott, the Arabs regarded the economic isolation of Israel as a net gain, for it prevented the economic and financial domination of the Middle East by the more advanced Israeli economy. That the boycott penalized certain Arab states and certain businesses and that it unduly hampered large sectors of the Arab economy had to be accepted as the price of harm done to Israel. That the boycott stimulated Israel to rapid investment and heavy development to meet the Arab challenge had to be ignored. The Arabs knew that the boycott caused severe Israeli losses, hampered and strained Israeli economic development, and above all had prevented Israeli integration into the economic life of the Middle East. Israeli aspirations to be an Asian state had been thwarted.

Probably even more damaging to the infant Israeli economy was the Egyptian blockade. Not unexpectedly, during the Palestine war Egypt had closed the Suez Canal to shipping destined for Israel. After the armistice agreement, this ban had not been lifted. Israel appealed to the Mixed Armistice Commission, the first step in a long, involved dispute on the scope of the armistice agreement, the competence of various United Nations agencies, and the general legality of Egypt's novel interpretation of belligerent rights in time of peace. Long before any final decision, on February 6, 1950, an Egyptian royal decree closed the canal to Israeli "war contraband," a most extensive list, and created penalties for violators, including a blacklist. Subsequently other provisions were added to close the loopholes. Soon the ships of "neutrals" like Greece and Italy were being halted and the "contraband cargoes" confiscated. Increasingly, shipping companies showed reluctance to accept Israeli charters or to risk transporting consignments to Israel.

The Egyptian position was that a state of war still existed and that an armistice did not prohibit a country from exercising certain rights of war. Whether or not even a state of war made Egypt's blockade legal was dubious, for under the terms of the Suez Convention traffic could not be interrupted even in wartime; furthermore, the United Nations Charter and the Arab-Israeli armistice agreements made no provision for the kind of belligerent rights Egypt claimed to be exercising. On July 11, 1951, Israel formally complained to the Security Council. Sentiment in the Council was definitely against the blockade, but efforts to persuade the Egyptians to modify their position were unavailing. After a long discussion, the Security Council adopted, on September 1, 1951, a resolution asking Egypt to end the restriction on international shipping through the Suez Canal. For a while the Egyptians did ease their restrictions, and during much of 1952 and 1953 detentions were rare as the new Egyptian government seemed willing to consider a rapprochement. In November and December 1953, however, new restrictions were imposed and detentions again rose. It was hardly coincidental that Israel had just begun trade negotiations with India and Pakistan, in an attempt to circumvent the Arab quarantine. Early in 1954 Israel again brought the Canal issue before the Security Council. On March 20 the Soviet Union, which was slowly shifting its Middle Eastern posture, vetoed a resolution calling on Egypt to end the blockade. Six months later on September 28 the Egyptians seized the Israeli ship *Bat Galim* as it attempted to pass through the Canal in a test of Egyptian policy. On October 14 Israel again complained to the Security Council. The Council meetings on January 4 and 13, 1955, produced no result. The Suez blockade continued, protected by the Russian veto.

Israel's only other route to Asia, through the Gulf of 'Aqaba, had also been blocked by Egyptian action. It had been intended that the tiny Israeli settlement of Elath at the southern tip of the Negev would play a great part in the eventual development of Israel. There were plans for an oil pipeline to carry Persian oil north to the Haifa refinery, which had been cut off from Iraqi oil. David Ben-Gurion particularly wanted to see Elath evolve into a major port linking Israel to Asia and opening up the southern Negev. In the early years of the state, little serious attention could be paid to either Elath or the southern Negev. Port facilities were at best primitive, and connections with the rest of the country almost nonexistent. Still Elath was an integral part of plans to make the desert flourish and to tie Israel to the East. But Israeli access to the Indian Ocean through the long, shallow Gulf of 'Aqaba was vulnerable, for the only navigable channel at the southern end of the Gulf was just three miles from the Egyptian coast. Off the tip of the Sinai Peninsula in the Strait of Tiran are two bleak, uninhabited islands, Senafir and Tiran; ships must navigate between them and Sharm-el-Sheikh on the Sinai side.

In 1949, with the permission of Saudi Arabia, Egypt fortified Tiran and constructed an extensive military complex at Sharm-el-Sheikh. Although at first Egypt announced that there would be no interference with shipping in the Gulf of 'Aqaba, the blockade was soon in force there as well as in Suez. Incidents in the gulf were relatively few, as traffic was slight, but all shipping to Elath, regardless of nationality, was turned back or detained. Elath remained shut off from the sea by unilateral Egyptian action, a situation that the Israelis could not continue to tolerate indefinitely. In the legal maze of the Suez issue, tangled as it was in fine arguments, major-power interests, and United Nations uncertainty, Israel had little hope of forcing the Egyptians to change their policy. Yet Ben-Gurion was convinced that the stranglehold on the Gulf of 'Aqaba could not be allowed to continue and to deny Israel access to Asia. After his return to the government, Ben-Gurion announced, in September 1955, that he wanted the gulf open to Israeli shipping within a year, by negotiation or if necessary by force.

Although the closing of the Gulf of 'Aqaba was a relatively minor matter, restricting only a potential, the Suez blockade severely damaged the developing Israeli economy. No one could accurately estimate the direct and indirect losses resulting from the blockade, but they were great, probably far greater than those caused by the boycott and without the compensating stimulation of Israeli development.[5] For the Arabs, the Suez blockade had the further advantage of demanding no sacrifices. With no cost to the Arabs, Israel had been denied both the raw materials essential to create a viable industrial complex and the Asian markets to dispose of their produce. More than any other aspect of the war of attrition, the blockade crippled Israeli development.

During the years from 1949 to 1956, the most abrasive Israeli-Arab confrontation was not in the economic sphere but along the armistice borders. The agreements had, for the most part, simply frozen the positions controlled by the opposing military forces and had not been intended to establish international boundaries. Once the Arab states had adopted a policy of belligerency without war, however, the cease-fire lines became the de facto boundaries. Drawn on a large-scale map by men interested in immediate military advantages, the boundaries made no concession to civilian needs. They cut off villages from their fields and fields from their wells. Almost nowhere was the line clearly marked. At once, local Arabs began to filter across the artificial boundary to reclaim their possessions, abandoned in what had become Israel. Some attempted to work their old fields on the wrong side of the line. Although these early border violators were innocent of military intent, the combination of thousands of bitter refugees camped across the cease-fire line and the opportunities for irregular guerrilla intrusions created an ominous situation for Israel. Determined to prevent incidents by sealing the border against infiltrators, innocent or not, the Israelis pursued a tough policy. Soon there was an increasing cycle of infiltration, incidents, reprisals, and raids.

The border war, which continued spasmodically all along the cease-fire line year in and year out, was the result of three kinds of Arab intrusion: individual, organized local, and national. Particularly in the beginning, border crossing was an individual affair, undertaken for private profit or, on rare occasions, for personal vengeance. Bedouin tribes wandered at will, unaware of red lines on a map, Arab peasants crept back to steal the produce of their stolen fields, or old volunteers took their rifles across in the night to have a go at the Zionists. The Israelis met these infiltrations with force. Increasingly, as United Nations supervision of the borders deteriorated, the Arabs organized raids across the line. These local raids were often tolerated and sometimes actually organized by lower-echelon Arab officials or the local police. Seldom, however, were such raids directed from Amman or Cairo as instruments of national policy. Humiliated and frustrated, the border Arabs, particularly the refugees, simply wanted to strike back at the Zionists. What Arab could blame them? What official could prevent them without risking heresy? Murder, theft, and arson became patriotic duties, privately undertaken. The national governments could claim innocence, although their claims were tarnished by obvious approval of the raids. Complicity was difficult to prove even when the raiders' tracks led back to police posts; so the Israelis assumed that all raids were the responsibility of the Arab states and retaliated with night raids. On occasion, however, border warfare really was carried out for reasons of national policy, although it was always disguised as defensive reactions to Israeli provocations or retaliation for Israeli raids. For example, the Syrian army might openly attack Israelis working in a disputed demilitarized zone, or Egyptian artillery might fire on Israelis for allegedly violating the armistice agreement. A more aggressive form of border warfare was deployment of armed raiding parties inside Israel to spread terror. Often these attacks did not even originate in the sponsors' territory. These deep penetrations, mainly Egyptian, were not part of the routine border tensions or armistice disputes but were barely disguised offensive thrusts to make life in Israel a hell.

By and large, world opinion regarded the border war as a one-sided affair in which the Israelis were defending their small state from numerous and unprovoked attacks from the Arab states. But such was not always the case. Between 1949 and 1956 Israel pursued an uncompromising border policy. When the cease-fire came in 1949, Israel, surrounded by enemies, had accepted the doctrine that force, although it might not ease tensions, would best ensure the future. The old policy of self-restraint, Havlagah, had died a lingering death during the last years of the Mandate. Increasingly during the undeclared war, Haganah policy had evolved from retaliatory raids against specific targets to broader punitive attacks on Arabs in general. Force was met by greater force, unofficial violence by official retaliation. Along the border there was more than adequate provocation for an Israeli policy of calculated reprisals. In an era when aggression in any form, no matter how deeply provoked, has become an international sin, Israel managed to create for itself the image of a small state penetrated by terrorists in the night. That this image was often just is undeniable, but that Israel followed a similar terrorist policy is equally undeniable. The Israelis, in fact, seldom denied their raids but only pleaded provocation that the international community could not prevent. The Israeli effort to intimidate Syria, Jordan, and Egypt by striking back hard, regardless of the immediate responsibility for specific border violations, was at times escalated into irregular warfare on some other issue. Syria might be punished for signing a military pact or Egypt for a shift away from rapprochement. There were, furthermore, certain advantages to Israel in the endless tension: international sympathy, a militant and vigilant civilian population, an army experienced in night fighting, continuing identification and concern among the Jewish communities abroad. These concerns were undoubtedly secondary, however. Even the most aggressive Israeli would have preferred a quiet border if it had been possible. In fact, the whole raison d'être of the reprisals was to end the Arab attacks. No one wanted to pay the price of the border war: terror, insecurity, civilian deaths. The Arabs, however, could not or would not stabilize the border, and, as long as the Arabs tolerated a border war, the Israelis intended that it was the Arabs who would be on the defensive.

Not all Israel's frontiers were equally dangerous, for each adjoining Arab state presented a slightly different problem. The quietest frontier was in the North between Lebanon and Israel, where incidents tended to be limited to the traditional small-scale smuggling. Once the war had ended, Lebanon, wanting no further involvement in Palestine, quarantined the refugees and carefully patrolled the border. The Syrian border proved more troublesome. The crux of the Syrian-Israeli conflict was control of the headwaters of the Jordan River. Bunche's compromise had created a demilitarized zone but had also left a variety of problems. Israel claimed that, although the zones were demilitarized, it had the right to carry out reclamation, water, and power projects within them. Syria denied this claim and even attempted to limit Israel's control over Lake Tiberias (the Sea of Galilee), which was completely outside Syria's boundaries, though often by a matter of only a few yards.

The first major disagreement between Israel and Syria involved Israeli efforts to drain the Hule swamps by running a canal through the demilitarized zone. The various United Nations peace-keeping agencies proved ineffectual, merely antagonizing both sides. Both the Syrians and the Israelis were willing to take more stringent measures against each other. On April 5, 1951, the Israelis bombed Syrian positions for an hour, openly violating the cease-fire in retaliation for the murder of seven Israeli policemen but also intending to bludgeon Syria into a more cooperative attitude. While the Security Council mulled over the Israeli violation, heavy fighting broke out around the demilitarized zone north of Lake Tiberias; despite a United Nations cease-fire order the conflict lasted twelve days. Generally the Israelis believed that the United Nations and its Middle Eastern agencies had proved ineffective in preventing Syrian intrusions. Six weeks later the United Nations finally produced a resolution on the whole Hule affair, but it did little more than recognize the status quo.

Another crisis erupted over Israeli construction at B'nat Ya'acov, which was carried on in defiance of a United Nations restraining order. This time American pressure forced the termination of Israeli construction but did not settle the basic issue. Once more the United Nations seized on the problem and once more without positive results. At Lake Tiberias Syrian efforts either to protect Arab fishermen using the waters by custom or to limit Israeli fishing boats resulted in a series of explosive crises. The raids and counterraids culminated in December 1955 with a heavy Israeli attack northeast of the lake, which resulted in the death of fifty Syrians. Israel claimed that Syria had provoked the attack. Syria claimed to be the victim of aggression. In January 1956 the United Nations condemned Israel. Some observers believed that the size of the Israeli retaliation was disproportionate to the provocation and that Israel had escalated the border war in order to express forcibly Tel Aviv's opposition to the Egyptian-Syrian Mutual Defense Pact.

Rather than remaining limited to Syrian harassment of Israeli economic development or Israeli attempts to exploit the demilitarized zones, the border conflict developed into an instrument of national policy. If Syria chose to make common cause with the other Arab states to threaten a new war, Israel could meet threats of force with real force. But the Syrians could hardly reorder their foreign policy under overt Israeli pressure. Damascus began to tolerate, if not to support, guerrilla operations against Israel by Egyptian-trained commando raiders based on Syrian territory.

Although almost all border incidents between Syria and Israel involved direct intervention of the Syrian army or its agencies, in Jordan a vastly different problem existed. The Syrian border war at least was limited by the relatively short and well-defined Syrian boundary with Israel. But the cease-fire line between Israel and Jordan twisted, largely unmarked, through central Palestine; it was crowded with Arab refugees who were constantly tempted to infiltrate. The number of incidents was huge. From June 1949 until

October 1954, for example, Israel claimed that Jordan had violated the armistice agreement 1,612 times; Jordan claimed 1,348 Israeli violations. The Mixed Armistice Commission verified that 34 of 124 Israelis killed were Jordan's responsibility and that 127 of 266 Jordanians killed were Israel's responsibility. These authorized statistics of violence are substantial for a theoretically peaceful frontier.

In 1949 the vague armistice line and the unorganized Arab population made a sealed border almost impossible to maintain with Jordan's limited resources. At first the government made little effort. Whether or not the raids from Jordan were officially sanctioned, Israel invariably held the Jordanian government responsible. The Israelis could see little purpose in distinguishing between an "unofficial" Arab violator who had killed an Israeli civilian and an official agent of Jordan. Increasingly between 1949 and 1956, Jordan made an effort to prevent border violations, in order to prevent heavy Israeli retaliatory raids. The shaky government in Amman could not admit that Jordan was unable to respond to the provocation of the Israeli raids and, therefore, preferred to close the border. Eventually, therefore, in vindication of the tough Israeli policy, individual violations and locally organized raids tapered off. Beginning in 1955, however, Jordan was troubled by raids from its territory but directed from other Arab states, usually Egypt; these raiding parties could kill Jews with impunity, for Israeli reprisals would be directed against Jordan. At times, on the other hand, Jordanian efforts to prevent these terrorist raids were less than sincere and resulted in further retaliation.

The most notorious reprisal raid by Israel occurred on the night of October 14, 1953, against the Jordanian village of Qibiya. The United Nations Mixed Armistice Commission reported that at least half a battalion had attacked the village at night with automatic weapons, grenades, and explosives, destroying forty-one houses and a school. The most shocking news was the casualty list: forty-two dead and fifteen wounded, including women and children. Opinion outside the Middle East was profoundly shocked. Israel, hoping to intimidate Jordan, made no attempt to deny the attack but insisted that continued Arab provocation had forced it to act and that Jordan, by failing to close the border, had been responsible for Israel's action. Later defenders of the Qibiya operation pointed out that in 1953 fifty-seven Israelis had been killed along the borders but that after Qibiya the number dropped to thirty-four in 1954 and eleven in 1955.[6] To some degree, however, Israel was swayed by "opinion," and future raids concentrated on military or police targets or obviously guilty irregular hideouts.

The situation along the Egyptian border combined elements of both the clash over demilitarized zones and the dispute over irregular infiltration. There were 120,000 wretched Arab refugees crammed into the narrow Gaza strip, administered by the Egyptian military government. An equal number of original inhabitants were in, if anything, more desperate straits, as they were not eligible for United Nations aid. Almost none of these Arabs saw a future for himself or his children as long as Israel continued to exist. The Arabs' frustration and hatred, fanned by extremists in the camps, made raids into Israel seem a patriotic duty, as well as the only possible means of vengeance against the Zionists who had stolen their land. At first, the Egyptian army seemed most cooperative in limiting Arab intrusion, but the combination of Israel's firm border policy, the unwarranted Israeli expulsion of a harmless Bedouin tribe from the Negev, and the general deterioration of Egyptian-Israeli relations eroded this restraint. Soon Egypt surveillance proved sufficiently lax to allow marauding bands to enter Israel, setting off the usual cycle of raids and reprisals. In the demilitarized zone around El 'Auja, the same conflict of pride and self-interest occurred that had occurred farther north. But, whereas tensions along the Jordanian frontier did decline slightly, the reverse was true in the South.

For a time after Egypt's Free Officers' coup in July 1952, there was real hope in Tel Aviv that a serious reconciliation might be achieved. Tension declined markedly, and all sorts of diplomatic overtures began. But by 1954 these efforts at rapprochement had begun to peter out. The tight border suddenly opened to infiltrators bent on terror raids. There was considerable evidence that many of the infiltrators had received some sort of commando training by the Egyptians in the Gaza strip. The intrusions continued throughout 1954 but in varying intensity, apparently related both to local conditions and to a broader Egyptian policy that leaned toward conciliation rather than terror. But the *Bat Galim* incident at Suez and the Cairo show trial of several Jews accused of spying for Israel aggravated relations. The executions of the Israelis, despite the absence of any conclusive evidence against them, became a cause célèbre in Israel.[7] In the Negev Egyptian terror and sabotage raids increased, often penetrating far into Israel. Tel Aviv claimed that the Egyptian army was training and directing the fedayeen bands. Late in February fedayeen bands penetrated as far as Tel Aviv. On February 28, 1955, Israel, as expected, carried out a raid on the Gaza strip, killing thirty-eight and wounding thirty-one Egyptians. As the new Egyptian Premier, Gamal Abdel Nasser, increasingly adopted a posture of aggressive grandeur and the role of prophet of the new Arab nationalism, the already bad border situation continued to deteriorate. Efforts by the United Nations to ameliorate the situation failed. On August 31 the Israelis struck in a heavy raid against a military outpost at Khan Yunis in the Gaza strip, not only retaliating against the Egyptian fedayeen but also protesting Egyptian-Czechoslovakian arms negotiations. On the same day the Cairo radio officially announced the existence of the fedayeen, which had been one of the Middle East's worst-kept secrets. In this deteriorating situation, the Mixed Armistice Commission proved helpless, incapable of doing more than keeping track of casualties and making fruitless pleas for moderation.

Despite great idealism, tempered by skill, labor, and dedication to peace among a great many men, the United Nations had proved singularly inept in the Arab-Israeli conflict; more often than not it was reduced to keeping statistics in the deadly quarrel. Dr. Ralph Bunche, largely owing to his own special talents, had succeeded in achieving the general armistice agreements by evading the various pitfalls of Middle Eastern diplomacy: irrational pride, governmental instability, outside interference, international irresponsibility, and encrusted suspicion. But the Conciliation Commission for Palestine eschewed his example and ignored his techniques—and stumbled into almost every pitfall. Its efforts to conciliate resulted only in growing antagonism, as restraints on Arab unilateral obstructionism eroded week by week.

In the only serious negotiations for a final settlement, those between Jordan and Israel, the one contribution by the United Nations had been its opposition to joint annexation of Jerusalem. The resolution to internationalize the city, really the result of a sly ploy by Egypt with a less than commendable assist from the Vatican, (which some people believed was willing that the Holy City should be controlled by anyone but the Jews), actually did inadvertently produce the impetus for the Israeli-Jordanian nonaggression treaty. In Paris between September 15 and November 19, 1951, the Conciliation Commission had again renewed efforts to discover a reasonable solution; but by then there were no longer any factors compelling the Arabs to consider a settlement. The proposals of the Commission to Jordan, Egypt, Lebanon, and Israel did not prove useful even as a basis for discussions.

The next year Israel did unilaterally attempt two compromise measures by offering on July 1 to take responsibility for 19,000 Arab refugees and on October 9 to release blocked Arab-refugee accounts in Israeli banks. These gestures brought no reciprocal action from the Arabs, nor could any practical observer in Tel Aviv or New York have anticipated that they would. The Arabs were by then firmly committed to a war of attrition, and no Arab monarch, minister, or spokesman could have safely taken a public step toward conciliation. Within the Arab world there was simply no longer any recognized reason for settlement, and there was a massive catalogue of excellent reasons to continue a policy of nonrecognition, blockade, and boycott to isolate Israel. Now and again there were tentative feelers or hints at moderation, but all proved abortive; certainly few originated in the United Nations. At the end of 1952, during the General Assembly debate on the Palestine question, Mexico proposed a resolution calling for Arab-Israeli negotiations. The Arab states opposed the resolution because the refugee question had not been settled on their terms. Thanks to a curious combination of the Arab bloc and the Latin American states, prodded by the Vatican, the resolution failed to receive the necessary two-thirds vote for passage in the General Assembly. Twenty-one nations voted against the negotiations, and fifteen abstained. For Israel any resemblance between the United Nations of 1952 and the ideal of an independent moral force for world peace had evaporated. For all its high-minded servants, the United Nations had become the forum for self-interested forces and partisan pressures, dedicated not to peace but to national interests.

As Mediator, Bunche had actually mediated, but, as conciliator, the United Nations frittered away much of its moral capital. Not only had there been no real conciliation, but also most suggested solutions had been motivated by national interests predicated on Israeli sacrifice. The Truce Supervision Organization had rapidly evolved into a group of mere observers, able to watch the violations without preventing them. The Arabs made every effort to limit the scope of the Mixed Armistice Commission, to evade the general clauses of the armistice agreement, even to emasculate the United Nations agencies. Israel, at first hopeful about the Truce Organization and the armistice commissions, soon grew cynical at their feeble responses, at their narrow interpretations of their roles, at their passive neutrality, which often operated to the advantage of the Arabs. Neither side wanted a disinterested referee but only an advocate.

To a large extent none of this negative atmosphere was the fault of either the United Nations agencies or their staff.[8] The armistice agreements had been intended a step toward peace, not as a permanent means of monitoring Arab-Israeli contacts. With no hope for peace, the agencies were hampered, evaded, ignored, manipulated, and suspected by both sides. Even the most competent and dedicated men in the United Nations were forced to recognize the inadequacy of the system and to accept the agencies' limited potential for easing the conflict. All continued their work, on the quite proper assumption that without some buffer, some court of appeal, the situation would get entirely out of hand. At a higher level in the United Nations, pursuit of national interests prevailed, effectively crippling conciliation. Therefore, neither the men on the spot nor those in the Security Council and the General Assembly could do more than provide a forum for expressing frustrations. In time the repeated failures of the United Nations to take positive action in the Middle East on any level produced, particularly in Israel, even greater frustration.

The singularly bleak scorecard of the United Nations was certainly not the result of lack of trying among its dedicated officials. The one massive rock on which all efforts broke was the refugee problem. Literally no one, Israeli or Arab, could accept the permanence of the refugee problem. That 1 million Arabs would be allowed to eke out marginal existences in the limbo of jerry-built camps maintained by charity year after year was not even contemplated in 1949 or 1950. The Arabs insisted and continue to insist to this day that Israel must receive all who want to return. They scorned Israel's offers to accept some and to compensate the remainder. The Palestinian refugees in Jordan did become citizens of the kingdom, but it could not absorb them economically. In Egypt they remained wards of the United Nations, penned in the Gaza strip. The Lebanese, precariously balanced between Christian and Muslim Arabs, viewed absorption as potentially disastrous. Syria and Iraq, despite much unsettled land, did not want to weaken the refugees' case for repatriation in Israel by bringing them into their own countries. So it went; the Arabs would not take the refugees because they were Israel's responsibility, and Israel could not afford to absorb all the embittered and potentially subversive Arabs. Its offer to accept a token 100,000 refugees was spurned.

Increasingly, the refugees fell prey to extreme ideas; filled with hatred and despair, they were out of touch with the reality of Israel and remembered only Arab Palestine. Repatriation as second-class citizens in an alien state, which they would barely recognize, was not their dream. Repatriation literally meant to them the redemption of Palestine. So, on the edge of starvation, unproductive and helpless, they lived with a dangerous dream. Every effort to find a solution, even a first small step toward a solution, failed. Plans and proposals, official and private, scholarly and emotional, were legion. Always with "right" on their side, the Arabs refused to consider any compromise. Always there was a limit to the compromise Israel could offer without in turn compromising its own security. In 1956, nearly seven years after the original flight, a solution for the refugees had come no closer. A new generation was growing up within the bleak and crowded camps, its horizon limited by hatred and frustration.

In only one area—and that, oddly enough, a sensitive one—did any of the dozens of conciliatory efforts come close to bearing fruit. In an area where water means life, the potential of the Jordan-Litani River system had long been recognized but not exploited. To develop the system fully, four states—Lebanon, Syria, Jordan, and Israel—would have to cooperate. Although such cooperation would be to their mutual benefit, there seemed no reason to suppose that the problem of water would be more susceptible to solution than any of the others had been. In 1953 United States Secretary of State John Foster Dulles became interested, while visiting the Middle East, in the idea of a Jordan Valley Authority. Although the United Nations Relief and Works Agency had been investigating the possibility, direct negotiations were handed over to the American Special Ambassador Eric

Johnston. Strangely enough, despite the obvious deterioration of Arab-Israeli relations in 1953 and 1954, sincere negotiations continued unimpeded. Restricted largely to technical personnel, the meetings foresaw a nonpolitical agreement, largely limiting any Israeli-Arab contact, that would produce the maximum amount of water, to be equitably divided among the four nations.

The ultimate Johnston plan was an apparently satisfactory solution to all the areas of contention: providing for exclusion of the Litani, a storage site on the Yarmuk River, and equitable division of the water. Not until June 1954 was the plan made public in the Arab world, and not until the summer of 1955 was an effort made to secure its adoption. Because the plan would benefit Israel as well as the Arab states, there was general opposition in the Arab world. The summer of 1955 was a crisis summer. Egyptian-Israeli relations were particularly poor. In October the Arab League met to consider the Johnston plan. Rather than rejecting it outright as expected, the League simply put it aside pending further study. Johnston had come as close as anyone to creating common ground between the Israelis and the Arabs. His success was partially owing to the purely technical level of the talks, the unusual secrecy surrounding them, and the obvious advantages to be gained from the detailed analysis of the water issue, even if no unified plan were forthcoming.

Once the Johnston plan had been shelved, Israel, Jordan, and Syria went ahead with individual programs to develop the Jordan basin. Israel, desperately in need of irrigation water, began large-scale planning and construction. The Arabs countered with their own uncoordinated plans. Without any legal framework for controlling the distribution of the water, the various projects simply provided additional grounds for conflict. Progress, particularly by Israel, had not been sufficient by 1956 to reach a trouble point, but even then the Arabs were complaining that the Israelis, using their more advanced technology, intended to steal the waters of the Jordan. Despite the efforts of the United Nations and the United States State Department, Israeli-Arab relations therefore seemed to grow worse.

This permanent antagonism often seemed to be the only unalterable factor in the Middle East as the Arab world evolved in a series of interal convulsions and external pressures. It took some time for the major powers to recognize that the British withdrawal from Palestine had done much to shake the area's imposed stability. In Egypt all shades of political opinion insisted on British evacuation of the enclave in the Suez Canal Zone. The British sought, through repeated overt displays of friendship, to postpone or evade withdrawal. The Egyptians retaliated with violence. In Jordan after Abdullah's assassination, the growing influence of the Palestinian refugees, who blamed Britain for their exile, weakened the already feeble foundations of the regime, which was nonetheless kept solvent by subsidies from London. In Syria few politicians and generals, whatever their other differences, had any desire to see waning French influence replaced by British. In Iraq Britain's old friend, the perennial Premier Nuri as-Said continued the Anglo-Iraqi alliance, despite mutterings from the extremists. But, although the invisible government did not work as well as it had before 1948, Great Britain still exerted immense influence, only partially usurped by American inroads in Saudi Arabia and Iran and French ambitions in Lebanon and Syria. Although the interests and aspirations of the three Western powers often conflicted in detail, their broad goals for the Middle East were relatively uniform. On May 24, 1950, without consultation or negotiation with the parties involved, the three nations issued the Tripartite Declaration banning an arms race in the Middle East and promising action to prevent forcible violations of existing armistice boundaries. The "Concert of the West" wanted and intended to ensure a stable Middle East, to protect its own strategic and economic interests.

The Middle East, however, was inherently unstable. But none of the internal political struggles or revolts had as great an effect on the evolution of the Middle East as did the long-delayed impact of East-West tensions. The stiffening of the Cold War in Europe after the Berlin blockade and in Asia during the Korean stalemate focused the attention of both the United States and Soviet Russia on the newly emerging states of Asia, where former European rulers were on the way out, voluntarily or not. Although the Soviet Union had never shown any great interest in the Arab Middle East, Dulles decided to contain potential Soviet expansion there by means of a formal military alliance. His first attempt to tie Turkey and Egypt to Britain and the United States failed, but the thin end of the wedge had penetrated the Middle East.[9] The inchoate Arab inclination to escape Western hegemony as expressed in the Tripartite Declaration accelerated into a full-fledged policy.

In Egypt as elsewhere in the Middle East there was a growing sympathy for the policy of nonalignment championed by the East Asians, which could lead to a third force. By October 1954 the Free Officers in Egypt had already achieved a major goal in the signing of an Anglo-Egyptian agreement for the evacuation of British troops from Suez. Nasser, who had replaced the figurehead leader of the coup, Colonel Mohammed Neguib, as Premier suspected that the rewards for extending his maneuvers to the East-West arena would be even greater. In any case, he had no desire to see British influence in Egypt replaced by the American hegemony. His abortive efforts to purchase Western arms convinced him further that any proposed Western alignment came with hidden strings on Egyptian sovereignty. Increasingly during 1954 and 1955 Nasser spoke for Arab nationalism unfettered by imperialism, a point of view in open opposition to that of the Arab regimes tied by treaties to Great Britain.

While still seeking to maintain intimate relations with Nasser, Dulles turned to an alternative scheme, the northern-tier pact. This alliance would cordon off Russia from the south by including the border states in an alliance with Britain and the United States, but Dulles also included Iraq, not a border state, in his proposal. The inclusion of Iraq as the only Arab state in an overtly anti-Russian alliance would involve the Middle East directly for the first time in the East-West competition. On February 24, 1955, despite vociferous Egyptian criticism, Iraq and Turkey signed a mutual-defense treaty against communist aggression in the Middle East, the first step toward the Baghdad Pact. Nasser, the spokesman for the new neutralism, regarded himself as directly challenged. Egypt's efforts to lead the Arabs out of Western bondage had been subverted by Iraq.

Russia, challenged by the Baghdad Pact and, with its options limited elsewhere, took a new look at the possibilities of the Middle East. In Egypt Nasser certainly could not be considered one of the shopworn generation of British puppet nationalists nor could several of the radical socialists of the Baathist movement in Syria—nor could a wide variety of very different young orators preaching redemption, revolution, and social justice elsewhere in the Arab world. There was by 1955 a new strain in Arab politics—not yet dominant but already articulate, devoutly revolutionary, committed to nonalignment, suspicious of the West, imbued with rudimentary doctrines of change and social justice, and tolerant of communism. In view of growing American involvement in the Middle East, in particular the Baghdad

Pact maneuver, Russia considered that the satisfactory status quo had been destroyed. Obviously there was an opportunity for penetration. In Cairo Nasser too saw that, if the Russians were present, the Western lid on arms and resulting control of Middle Eastern stability could be subverted. By 1955 the hegemony of the West began to crack.

In April Nasser flew to the Bandung Conference of Afro-Asian powers, where he learned firsthand of the rewards of nonalignment. The power and prestige for which Egypt had hungered so long could be had by bargaining in the new world of neutrals. Among U Nu, Chou En-lai, Sukarno, and Jawaharlal Nehru, Nasser at last found his place. At the suggestion of Chou En-lai, Nasser, on his return, began exploring the possibilities of obtaining arms from Russia. In May Daniel Semenovich Solod, the Soviet Ambassador in Cairo, offered Nasser an arms deal through Czechoslovakia. In July Dimitri Shepilov, editor of *Pravda,* arrived for more detailed discussions. Word began to seep out that the Russian bear had gotten in among the Arab goats. On September 27 Nasser announced an agreement with Czechoslovakia to exchange cotton for arms. The good old days were gone. The Tripartite Declaration was dead. The British were being edged out as the Americans and Russians began a struggle for control through pacts, loans, doctrines, diplomacy, and other forms of pressure. The Arabs sought to snatch what they could without forfeiting their newly discovered independence of action.

The position of Israel in this struggle was curious. Once the Russians had decided to woo the Arabs, Israel could look forward to having a major power as an enemy and articulate spokesman for the Arabs. British coldness had been bad enough, but now Soviet Russia had jettisoned its tentative support of Israel and was preaching an anti-Israel sermon indistinguishable from that of Nasser. Furthermore, in their competition with Moscow, the Americans found Israel something of an embarrassment. Although the Americans had no intention of turning against Israel for the sake of expedience, they also did not intend to assume the role of Israel's ever-present protector. On October 11, two weeks after the Egyptian arms deal, the United States refused an Israeli request to match the Soviet arms. To the Arabs' unconcealed delight, Israel was in the unenviable position of watching helplessly while East and West armed their Arab "allies."

In the competition for Arab friends, only one major power showed no enthusiasm for the Arabs. France alone, increasingly involved in a costly and bloody war against Arab nationalists in Algeria, turned a sympathetic ear to Israel's difficulties. The French government's concern for Israel was, of course, dictated more by self-interest than by ideological sympathy for little, democratic, and socialist Israel. Egypt was not only Israel's major enemy but also the Algerians' major supplier and supporter. The tentative early French-Israeli contacts of 1954 grew stronger during 1955, as the Israelis grew more concerned at their inability to maintain parity in armaments with the Arab states. The intrusion of the Cold War, which shattered the arms embargo and wrecked the Tripartite Declaration of 1950, was thus to some extent offset for the Israelis by their budding friendship with the French. But in Tel Aviv there could be no denying the fact that the balance of power in the Middle East was shifting to Israel's disadvantage.

These changes in the Arab Middle East had, in the years immediately after the Palestine war, been imperceptible. The Arab governments, as might have been expected, had been inundated by well-documented charges from their citizens of corruption, incompetence, and negligence. Mahmud Fahmi Nokrashy had been assassinated even before the end of the fighting. The Syrian government had been overthrown in a coup in 1949. Abdullah, increasingly alienated from his new Palestinian subjects, hung on until 1951. Once vengeance had been accomplished, the Arabs seemed to settle down to historic and dynastic rivalries; but behind the apparent continuity, the ferment of revolution continued. The humiliations of the Palestinian war had gone too deep for many of the young and idealistic to settle back into the worn grooves of corrupt politics and traditional alignments. Much of the Arabs' political energy was concentrated not on Israel but on the causes of Arab defeat and on programs for an Arab renascence. The Arab war of attrition thus played a peripheral role in Arab domestic politics, for revenge, it was believed, could come only at the price of reform.

The most important step on the Arabs' road to dignity came in 1952 in Egypt, where the shared discontents and aspirations of a generation of young officers flowered into conspiracy. These officers, mostly graduates of the military academy in the period 1936–39—the first groups to be admitted without social restrictions—provided, under the leadership of Lieutenant Colonel Nasser, the prototype for a new kind of military participation in the political development of new nations. Disgusted with their decadent monarch, humiliated by the patronage of Great Britain, ashamed of Israel's victory, which they attributed to civilian incompetence, the officers were determined to restore Egypt to a position of dignity and respect. Between July 23 and 26 the Egyptian Society of Free Officers deposed the corrupt King Faruk and established a new regime under the figurehead Neguib, the former commander in Palestine. The officers, dedicated to revitalizing Egypt, brought a breath of fresh air into the fetid atmosphere of Arab politics. Their advent on the scene introduced an element of practical sanity into the verbiage and rhetoric typical of politics in the Middle East; for, though they lacked governing experience, dogma or doctrine, and even a coherent program, they brought with them into power the ideal of an Arab renascence coupled with the goal of social justice.

In Israel the coup was viewed with unalloyed delight, for with practical and reasonable men who recognized the realities of the twentieth century some sort of rapprochement might be possible. The medieval xenophobia of the emirs seemed past. Colonel Nasser, with whom the Israelis had had contact during the war, had seemed more than rational. The other officers had shown considerable restraint in issuing the traditional denunciations of Israel. In fact, Neguib, Nasser, and company seemed mainly interested, not in crusades for glory, but in honest programs to enact neglected reforms. In August Ben-Gurion assured the new Egyptian government of Israel's friendship. His overture led to the long-sought negotiations. In March 1953 Israel agreed to Egyptian proposals as a basis for discussion. Border incidents declined, and in the summer of 1953 an agreement on shipping was reached. In December the old militant Ben-Gurion resigned as Premier; he was replaced by Moshe Sharett. Sincere and firm contacts continued. In August 1954 Israel made some unilateral conciliatory moves; but by then the climate had begun to change.

In April Colonel Nasser had replaced the front man Neguib as Premier. The removal of the older, more conservative man did not take place without some turmoil. Nasser concentrated immediately on levering the British out of the Canal Zone, neglecting to some extent the lagging internal reforms. The increasing involvement of the Middle East in the East-West conflict began to reveal a variety of options to Nasser at a time of some domestic difficulty. There no longer seemed any specific advantage in an agreement with Israel; in fact, considering the uneasiness at home, it seemed increasingly risky. Cairo began to sound more and more aggressive. The turning point had been reached. Whether or not the Egyptians had ever been sincere was immaterial, for the thrust of Arab opinion was opposed to conciliation. Any rapprochement would require compelling justification, and in 1954 there was almost none.

By late 1954 Nasser was rapidly evolving into the messiah of the new Arab nationalism, which left no room for a Jewish state. Although more often based on emotion than on practice or program, Nasser's expressed aspirations had immediate appeal to the Arabs. His goals—a pan-Arab state stretching from the Atlantic to the Indian Ocean, a renascence of the Arab peoples, a respected place in great-power politics thanks to an effective army, a socialist revolution—gained currency throughout the Middle East. Nasser was not yet regarded as the new prophet, but his prophesies had begun to convert the young, the ambitious, the discontented. His ideas, clouded by passion and violence of expression, found fertile ground even in the countries with traditional regimes, whose rulers were appalled at his rising influence. As a result a new crack began to appear in the already leaky vessel of Arab unity; added to the old religious, ethnic, dynastic, and geographical rivalries was the disruptive current of revolutionary Nasserism. At last, the Arab world had an articulate seer, a man who seemed able to put a halt to decadence and to build a great new society. Although at home Nasser still had serious problems with the more conservative Egyptians, who hated to see the mature Neguib replaced and were suspicious of Nasser's references to socialism; with the Muslim Brotherhood, which doubted his Islamic orthodoxy; and with the forcibly retired politicians, in the broader Arab world his star climbed.

After 1954 Nasser devoted himself to the expansion of his ideology at the expense of Western hegemony, the traditional regimes, and the State of Israel. In the case of Israel, Cairo not only broke off the secret talks but also turned immediately to more intensive border warfare. This campaign was to give the leadership of the Palestine liberation movement to Egypt, rather than to ineffectual militants elsewhere. The execution in December of several Jews on spying charges seemed intended as a direct provocation to Israel. Then came the terror raids, reaching even to Tel Aviv, and the Israeli retaliation raid on the Gaza strip two weeks after Ben-Gurion had returned to the government as Minister of Defense. In less than a year Nasser had reintroduced border warfare, this time on a far more serious scale, and had closed the Suez Canal without hope of even an informal agreement. He had opened up the Middle East to East-West competition, which could only harm Israel. He had, in fact, revitalized the Arab Middle East, to Israel's immense disadvantage. Although Nasser's rise had further strained Arab unity, alienating the monarchs and frightening the conservatives, Israel could not depend on this internal disarray for protection. As always, Israel would have to rely on its own resources and its policy of forcible retaliation for provocative acts.

During 1955 the possibility that another round of the Arab-Israeli war might be fought had to be seriously considered. The recurring crises in the Middle East had increased in number and scope. The Egyptian terror campaign along the border was almost insupportable. British frustration, French vengefulness, Cold War politics, and Egyptian ambitions had all played their parts in the growing tensions, but the last straw was an Arab-Czech arms deal in September. But the arrival of Soviet-bloc arms did not immediately upset the precarious military balance. In the fall of 1956 even this massive injection of heavy equipment could not automatically produce an effective Egyptian army. Despite Nasser's efforts to improve morale and training, to bring pride and competence to a new Egyptian army, many of the old faults remained uncorrected. First-class weapons, manned by reluctant peasants and ill-trained officers, could not alone bring victory. Ambitious officers infected with the political virus, the creeping plague of Arab armies, might have toppled governments, but they had seldom won battles. Impressive as the new equipment, the giant Soviet T-34 tanks and the MIG-15 jets, were on parade, they had not yet transformed the armed forces. The fact remained, however, that without modern equipment of its own Israel's Zahal might soon have to face a revitalized and re-equipped Egyptian army that even dedicated troops could not withstand.

It was not only the Israelis who were impressed with Nasser's arms pact. It, more than any previous single act, made Nasser the acknowledged leader of the Middle East. He alone had redressed the balance in the Middle East, harassed the old Western imperialists, and overnight turned Egypt into a power to be reckoned with in New York and London and most particularly in Tel Aviv. The prophet of grandeur was accepted as a hero in his own country and throughout the Middle East. Millions hung on his every word. In October Syria and Egypt signed a mutual-defense treaty. Long wracked by coups, abortive revolutions, and feeble parliaments ineffectually snarled, Syria, the key to domination of the Middle East, had hitched itself to Nasser's bandwagon. Even Saudi Arabia and Yemen, despite their monarchical governments, seemed impressed. On April 21, 1956, both signed a five-year trilateral military alliance with Egypt. The ring seemed to be closing around Israel. Washington and London, despite Nasser's avid anti-imperialism, apparently still thought appeasement and toleration were the proper Western response. In the summer of 1956, six years after the last armistice agreement had been signed by Syria, a permanent peace with the Arabs seemed even more distant. Despite their differences, despite the Iraqi-Egyptian rivalry, despite the deep distrust that Nasser still engendered in some quarters, the Arab world was on the march. Nasser's heavy tanks rumbled down Cairo's streets. In thousands of village cafés, Nasser's predictions of victory and vengeance over the Zionists came in loud and clear on the radio night after night. Inside the borders of Israel, the fedayeen unleashed by Nasser crept through the night. In the halls of diplomacy, Nasser's opinions were sought and his friendship bought.

In Israel for the first time there were those who began to feel that time, long boastfully claimed by the Arabs as an asset, might indeed be working against Israel. As 1956 passed, everything seemed to be going Nasser's way. His path was littered with successes. The last British troops were withdrawn from the Suez Canal Zone on June 12. On June 23 Nasser was elected President of Egypt by the impressive total of 99.9 percent of the votes. Each day that passed the Egyptian army, trained by Russian technicians, grew more proficient. Shipments of military supplies continued to arrive. Even the growing coolness of the United States toward Nasser was viewed with equanimity in Cairo as a symbol of an anticolonialist policy well waged.

Israel's security, so dearly bought in 1948–1949 and so arrogantly maintained, was dribbling away. After six years the swords of Israel's enemies were brighter than ever, their determination to secure vengeance greater than ever. To a nation isolated and surrounded by implacable foes, straining to develop despite the blockade and the boycott, the escalating Egyptian threat was intolerable. No nation can live forever under the threat of destruction without seeking the death of the potential destroyer.

By 1956 Israel had exhausted the avenues to a modus vivendi with the Arabs. The United Nations had proved unable to protect it on any level. The General Assembly and the Security Council had become mere forums for special pleading and national interests. The truce supervision was a farce. Nasser's fedayeen moved through Israel, crossing the borders not only from Gaza but also from Jordan and Syria as well. No place was secure. Many Israelis lived in the expectation of sudden, unprovoked attacks out of the dark. The major powers, with the exception of France, were rushing to woo Nasser. The predictable British had shown every willingness to placate Nasser with a "solution" at Israel's expense. At his Guildhall speech on November 9, 1955, Prime Minister Sir Anthony Eden had, after secret Anglo-Egyptian talks, "spontaneously" proposed a peace based on the cession to Egypt of the Negev. The Russians obviously knew the ultimate purpose of the Czech arms being shipped into the Middle East. So did the United States, but no help of much importance came from either Moscow or Washington. None of the traditional forms of diplomacy had brought any benefit to Israel. The United Nations had failed to guarantee its security; the Concert of the West and the Soviet bloc were dealing with its enemies. Unilateral compromises by Israel had proved barren. Contacts with Nasser in 1952–1953 had led nowhere. Even the harsh policy of retaliation on the borders was near bankruptcy. Partially effective against Syria and more so against Jordan, it was useless against Egypt, isolated beyond Sinai. The war of attrition had proved eminently successful for the Arabs.

Growing isolation, harsh austerity intensified by the boycott, the shrill voice of Arab vengeance, and above all insecurity created by the fedayeen raids had placed Israel in a state of siege. The Arab war of attrition had eroded Israeli tolerance to the zero point. Israel's economy had been disrupted. Its army had been refused equipment. Its people's lives had been lost in terrorist raids. Its security, its very existence as a state, was threatened. Living in a closed atmosphere of threats and provocations, enclosed in a garrison state, the Israelis had by 1956 reached a point of decision. The Arab war of attrition had been almost too effective, for it had driven the Israelis into a position in which their only alternative seemed to be massive retaliation. In the summer of 1956, despite Nasser's aggressive posture, the balance of power had not yet shifted in Egypt's favor. Israel was determined that this shift should not occur, for then the war of attrition would become overnight a war of extermination.

NOTES

1. The United States Ambassador to Israel at that time, James G. McDonald, reports in *My Mission in Israel* (New York: 1951), p. 212, that he had been informed by the Israelis of Abdullah's confidence:

   A month before the UN voted to insist upon internationalization, Abdullah had reiterated a desire to achieve permanent peace with Israel. He was said to be contemptuous of the stalling and obstructive attitude of the other Arab States, who were jealous of his occupation of Arab Palestine and determined to prevent any agreement between him and Israel. . . .

2. Although Earl Berger, in *The Covenant and the Sword: Arab-Israeli Relations 1948–1956* (London: 1963), p. 48, suggests that Britain was eager for an Israeli-Jordanian settlement, there is room for doubt, especially when Anglo-Egyptian relations worsened after 1949. Cf. Major General Moshe Dayan, *Diary of the Sinai Campaign* (New York: 1966), pp. 20–21:

   I will remember what King Abdullah of Jordan told me not long before he was murdered. He said he was prepared to reach an agreement with us, but the British representative Kirkbride [Sir Alexander Kirkbride, British Minister in Amman] was opposed to it, for he felt that this would harm the friendly relations between Britain and Egypt. Unfortunately Kirkbride's own book, *A Crackle of Thorns* (London: 1956), though entertaining, is not too enlightening.

3. The far-reaching impact of the Oriental immigration had not been fully appreciated before 1956; ethnic problems created completely unforeseen

social and political reactions within Israel. What was recognized was the need for assimilation. In a totally unexpected way, Israel was becoming an Eastern state but not, as the old Zionists had anticipated, by assimilation into the Middle East.

4. Berger, *The Covenant and the Sword*, p. 163, notes Abba Eban's 1950 statement to the Security Council that Israel's loss as a result of the blockade ran to tens of millions of pounds.

5. *Ibid.*, p. 151. Berger quotes various estimates of the direct and indirect costs of both the blockade and the boycott, ranging from $50 million to more than $100 million.

6. Moshe Dayan, "Israel's Border and Security Problems," *Foreign Affairs*, 33 (January 1955), 250–67; Moshe Brilliant, "Israel's Policy of Reprisals," *Harper's* (March 1955), pp. 68–72. Cf. Lieutenant General John B. Glubb, "Violence on the Jordan-Israel Border," *Foreign Affairs*, 32 (July 1954), 552–62. That the Israeli policy "worked" is difficult to dispute, and that a policy of toleration might have been effective is hard to prove; but the cost of the Israeli policy, effective or not, was high for all concerned.

7. This case was to evolve into one of the great Israeli domestic scandals, the "Lavon Affair," which involved personal rivalries and governmental procedures more than Israeli-Egyptian relations. See Jon Kimche, "The Lavon Affair: 1954–1964, *"Jewish Observer and Middle East Review*, 13 No. 51, 11–14; Kimche offers a brief introduction to an affair about which there is still no consensus, as the reaction to Haggai Eshed's study of the affair in 1965 reveals.

8. There is surely no more trying international office than that of United Nations Truce Observer. Several of the former observers have written of their trials and tribulations, revealing in passing the strain on their idealism caused by the suspicious protagonists. See Commander E. H. Hutchinson, *Violent Truce: A Military Observer Looks at the Arab-Israeli Conflict 1951–1955* (New York: 1956). Hutchinson is an American who came away less than enchanted with the Israelis. The best book, by one of the more outstanding observers, is Lieutenant General E. L. M. Burns' *Between Arab and Israeli* (Toronto: 1962).

9. Secretary Dulles has been accused, among other things, of opening up the Middle East through the introduction of sterile military pacts based solely on anticommunism. Although there is no doubt that Russia reacted strongly to the Baghdad Pact, in retrospect the lag in the Soviet reaction is far more impressive. See Walter Z. Laqueur, *The Soviet Union and the Middle East* (New York: 1959).

12

Prologue to War ∗
The Suez Crisis

The unexpected arrival of Gamal Abdel Nasser on the Egyptian stage, replacing Mohammed Neguib as Premier in April 1954, had not struck many as representing any significant shift in Egyptian policy. During the rest of the year, there was continuing international enthusiasm for the new, responsible generation of Egyptian leaders. The major concern in Cairo, dominating all else, was the negotiations with Great Britain, which were successfully concluded on July 27, 1954; Sir Anthony Eden informed the House of Commons that an agreement to evacuate British troops had been reached with Egypt. Even with the agreement, the stability of the Nasser regime under internal pressures was by no means secure. The conservatives, the old Wafd Party politicians, and the Muslem Brotherhood cared little either for Nasser or for his program. In fact, on October 26 the Brotherhood attempted to assassinate the Premier. Nasser seemed to have sufficient domestic problems to prohibit foreign adventures. Even in 1954, however, there were indications that Nasser might be considering a new course, a more militant anti-imperialism. During the winter of 1954–1955 Nasser and the Revolutionary Council began to consider the options open to them in the international sphere. An aggressive policy abroad aimed at seizing the leadership of the Arab world might divert domestic opposition.

279

In order to achieve for Egypt a new, grand role on the world stage, Nasser haltingly developed a new, militant philosophy based on traditional Arab nationalism, suspicion of imperialism, and hatred of Zionism but integrated into the context of emerging socialist neutrals on the international scene.[1] The British had been levered out, with the blessing and assistance of the United States, but a traditional alignment with the new American imperialism offered little interest. The Russians were still a distant and little-known factor, though potentially useful. The new nations of Asia offered tremendous ideological attractions but little substance. Israel, the traditional enemy, had continued to show sincere interest in rapprochement, but there were more advantages to keeping Israel as an enemy than to accepting it as a friend. To convert the Arabs of the old regimes, Nasser would have to be not only the ultra anti-imperialist but also the ultimate enemy of the Zionists.

During the winter of 1954–1955, Egypt thus began to shift to a hard line against Israel, putting the alleged Jewish spies on public trial and condemning two to death, loosening surveillance on the border, and turning a cold eye to the latest peace feelers. The not-unexpected result of the freer border was the Israeli Gaza raid on February 28, a direct response to renewed Egyptian terror attacks. In October 1955 Nasser claimed that it was at that particular moment, on February 28, that Egypt had adopted into the new policy, which led directly to the Czech arms deal: "February 28, 1955, was the turning-point. This disaster was the alarm bell. We at once started to examine the significance of peace and the balance of power in the area."[2]

Salah Salem, Minister of National Guidance, reported that, at the time of the Gaza raid, Egypt had only six serviceable military aircraft, tank ammunition for one hour, and sixty tanks, all needing major repairs, whereas the artillery was in deplorable condition and the infantry short of small arms. It hardly needed the Gaza raid, however, to expose Egyptian military needs, nor would the raid have made an eventual rapprochement impossible if Cairo had been interested in one.

At the same time that Nasser and the Revolutionary Council were drifting away from Israel they became increasingly attracted to the new neutralism. John Foster Dulles' Baghdad Pact had been turned down. The Egyptians increasingly spoke out against a Western alignment. The Iraqi-Turkish Pact of February 24 was therefore accepted as a direct challenge to Egyptian influence and prestige. In response to Iraq's defection, Syria, Saudi Arabia, and Egypt signed on March 6 a pact that created a joint command under Egyptian Minister of War Abdel Hakim Amer. Saudi Arabia was hardly an Egyptian ideological ally, but the two nations had a mutual enemy in Iraq. A week later Britain joined the Baghdad Pact, thus furthering the polarization of the Middle East.

February and March brought no irrevocable change in Egyptian policy. Both Washington and London regarded agreement with Cairo as quite possible and certainly desirable. Contacts between the Egyptians and the British area specialist Evelyn Shuckburgh continued, in connection with the prospects for Egypt's joining a Western pact. Washington, in response to Nasser's opposition to the Baghdad Pact, began to show signs of doubting the wisdom of the United States' own participation. In Israel discussions continued on whether a hard or soft line would be most effective in stabilizing Israeli-Egyptian relations. In Jerusalem, where even the doves have talons, there was no sentiment for appeasement; but Premier Moshe Sharett argued that excessive provocation was unwise. Then in April Nasser flew to Bandung, to be seduced by the prospects of nonalignment and the possibilities of Soviet-bloc arms.

After Nasser's return from the heady atmosphere of Bandung, the uncertain but perceptible shift to the new posture accelerated. In May Soviet Ambassador Daniel Solod brought news of a possible exchange of Egyptian rice and cotton for arms and of Soviet interest in the Aswan high-dam project. In June Egypt requested arms from the United States and Britain though probably without any real expectation of a positive response. The West was still bent on maintaining the arms freeze. When the request was rejected, however, Nasser had actual evidence that only the East sympathized with Cairo's need. When Dimitri Shepilov arrived in Cairo during July to tie up the loose ends, Nasser committed Egypt to the new policy, but the commitment was not irrevocable, nor was total alienation from the West inevitable. In August Secretary Dulles proposed a new solution to the Israeli-Egyptian confrontation, a solution tied to the Jordan River plan and based on the 1947 partition resolution. Cairo was unmoved. Talks, based on a British proposal, had continued between Shuckburgh and Egyptian Foreign Minister Mahmoud Fawzi during much of 1955, but Cairo had mainly been content to listen. Nasser was thus keeping open all his lines, although he could hardly have been hopeful of the results of the Anglo-American efforts.

On September 27 Nasser made public the Czech arms pact. In October the Egyptian-Israeli border truce, accepted on September 4 four days after the Israeli attack on Khan Yunis, collapsed in the usual cycle of raids and retaliations. The fedayeen began extensive operations from the Gaza strip and bases in Jordan, Syria, and Lebanon. Egypt's militant policy toward the Zionists had moved into high gear. On October 11 the Arab League, under Egyptian leadership, deferred decision on the Johnston Plan for the Jordan River. The American initiative to negotiate stability in the Middle East had failed. On October 20 Egypt and Syria signed a mutual-defense treaty that brought Damascus firmly into the Nasser camp. On November 9 Eden's carefully prepared Guildhall proposals for an Israeli-Egyptian settlement failed to evolve as planned, leaving both Nasser and Eden bitter. In Washington Dulles had not given up hope, despite Nasser's accumulating antagonism. On December 13 he told Congress that the United States preferred a peaceful compromise in the Middle East. On December 16 the United States and Britain tentatively offered to lend money for the Aswan high-dam project. Although during 1955 the entire direction of Nasser's new policies had been away from the West toward neutralism, there had been no final break, just as there had been no firm beginning.

Still an irrevocable break with the West remained a constant possibility. Late in February British Foreign Secretary Selwyn Lloyd arrived in Cairo, hopeful of arriving at an understanding with Nasser. On March 1, in conference with Nasser, Lloyd emphasized that, despite the Arab shift away from the West and the decline in British influence, at least "we still have Glubb and the Legion."[3] It must have been with great pleasure that Nasser informed Lloyd that King Hussein of Jordan had just dismissed Sir John Bagot Glubb as Chief of Staff of the Arab Legion. Although Nasser assured Lloyd that he had not manipulated Glubb's dismissal, there could be no doubt that he was delighted with the sudden collapse of Britain's Jordanian position. Lloyd returned to London convinced that Nasser was an irresponsible, charismatic dictator, dedicated to destroying British influence in the Middle East even at the expense of stability in the area. On March 14 French Foreign Minister Christian Pineau arrived in Cairo to make one more attempt to normalize Franco-Egyptian relations, which were troubled by Nasser's support of the Algerian rebels. Although mutual promises were exchanged, Pineau returned to France with the impression that Nasser could not be trusted, an impression that rapidly proved correct. Egyptian aid and comfort to the Algerians increased. Pineau's effort was a political fiasco, a failure at appeasement.

Reluctantly, the West began to give up on Nasser; the final break came over an issue generally obscured by the excitement over the arms pact, Glubb's dismissal, and the Algerian war. None of the diplomats had paid much attention to the Aswan dam, which had become one of Nasser's most cherished projects. Not only would it make possible an increase of 2 million acres of arable land, but also its very size would compare favorably with the grand monuments of the pharaohs. On February 9, 1956, the International Bank agreed to lend the Egyptian government $200 million, conditional upon a United States loan of $56 million and a British loan of $14 million, as well as upon an Egyptian commitment of $700 million. In the growing coolness between Washington and Cairo, Dulles had informed the Egyptian ambassador in Washington that there should be no side deals; in other words, the Russians should not be invited to participate. Nasser made no reply. On April 1 he announced that he had not rejected a Soviet offer. Prospects for the American loan did not look good.

In the meantime, the United States had moved closer to signing the Baghdad Pact; military liaison was set up on April 19. The Egyptians, Saudi Arabians, and Yemenis signed a military alliance two days later. In April Nasser mortgaged $200 million worth of unplanted cotton for more Soviet-bloc arms. He did not seem interested in budgeting for the Aswan dam. On May 6 an agreement to coordinate the armies of Jordan and Egypt was signed. The division of the Middle East had accelerated, and Iraq was becoming increasingly isolated. Western leaders took an increasingly jaundiced view of Nasser's new line.

The growing reliance of Egypt on Soviet support finally became too much for the long-suffering Republican administration in Washington. Lloyd had returned to London convinced that Nasser was a menace. Pineau soon after his return from Cairo accepted Nasser's duplicity. In Washington Nasser's militant stance might be excused, but his involvement with world communism could not. In 1956 Washington tended to view the world through red-colored glasses, and Nasser came through deep pink. Dulles concluded from the combination of Soviet arms and Nasser's neutralist diplomacy that Egypt would not in any way fulfill his hopes for orientation toward the West. On May 16 Egypt recognized the archdevil Red China. There no longer seemed any reason why the United States should invest $56 million in a nation whose international and domestic policies appeared to be evolving in a direction detrimental to American interests. Dulles was also reasonably sure that, if the United States canceled the loan offer, Russia would not be willing to step in with the necessary funds.

The Egyptians were perfectly aware of American opinion. In June the Egyptian embassy in Washington reported to Cairo that the loan offer was probably no longer good. Eugene Black of the International Bank gave the Egyptians the same assessment and reminded them that the Bank's loan offer was conditional upon the Anglo-American loans. Nasser apparently believed that Russia would be unable to refuse him help without dissipating new Soviet prestige in the Middle East. Early in July the Egyptians decided to ask formally for the American loan. They had little to lose by trying. On July 12 Nasser left Cairo for Belgrade to begin discussions with Marshal Tito and Jawaharlal Nehru, further evidence of his new independence of action. On July 17 the Egyptian Ambassador in Washington, Ahmed Hussein, formally requested the loan.

Hussein had to wait two days for the American answer. On July 19, 1956, the United States, pointing out the apparent unwillingness of Egypt to budget for the Aswan dam, withdrew the offer of the loan. The tenor of the note was a calculated insult to the Egyptians. On July 20 Great Britain followed suit with a curt refusal. Three days later the International Bank canceled the basic $200 million loan. As Dulles had anticipated, Russian Foreign Minister Shepilov announced on July 21 that the Soviet Union had no immediate intention of financing the project.[4] There would be no Aswan high dam. The West had pointedly underlined the penalties for Egypt's flirtation with the East. Nasser had not, however, walked into the situation blind.

During the first half of 1956 the withdrawal of Western support had been anticipated in Cairo; in fact, Nasser had seen an opportunity to use the final refusal of loans as the rationale for another long-considered step, nationalization of the Suez Canal Company. As early as 1954 nationalization had been considered. On December 15 Egypt had made financial and operational demands on the Suez Canal Company. But not until June 1956, when the last British troops had been evacuated, was there any real chance for swift and painless nationalization. By then the international balance in the Middle East had shifted, thanks to the advent of the Russians. With their behind-the-scenes support, both nationalization and the Aswan dam project could be carried through. The Anglo-American refusal of loans because of Western distaste for Egyptian independence would create the proper emotional climate. In June Nasser began meetings with Dr. Mustapha Hefinaoui, an expert on the practicalities of nationalizing the Canal Company. On his flight back from Belgrade with Nehru, Nasser discussed the possibility but gave the Indian Premier no hint of his final decision.

On July 26, the fourth anniversary of the Free Officers revolution, Nasser spoke to a huge crowd in Liberation Square, Alexandria. After an account of the negotiations with Britain and the United States, he switched to the Suez Canal. There were repeated references to its builder, Ferdinand de Lesseps. Then Nasser dropped his carefully prepared bombshell. The Suez Canal Company was being nationalized. Future revenues were to go for the construction of the Aswan dam. Acting on the code signal "de Lesseps," the Egyptians had already taken over the Canal Company. Egypt had reacted to the challenge of the West; the Egyptians had their revenge. That night a tumultuous wave of enthusiasm for the nationalization swept through the Middle East on the wings of Cairo's Voice of the Arabs radio. Once more Nasser had bested the imperialists, the political manipulators in the West.

The immediate reaction in Britain was equally tumultuous and nearly as emotional. In London Eden received the news while dining with Iraqi Premier Nuri as-Said and King Faisal II. Both the Iraqis and the British recognized the danger.[5] As word spread in London, the British overlooked the almost traditional nationalization, in no way novel, of a foreign company and demanded immediate revenge.

The actual status of the Suez Canal Company and Egypt's control of the Suez Canal were lost sight of in dissertations on one-man control of the vital lifeline linking the Commonwealth, on the new fascist challenge to Middle Eastern law and order, on the sanctity of international agreements. In the six years since the Palestine war, British domination of the Middle East had been repeatedly undermined by the Egyptians. The Canal Zone had been evacuated. Hussein had dismissed Glubb. Egyptian agents throughout the Middle East had been conniving for total British withdrawal. But, although the Empire was not what it had been, this affront proved too much. Eden, expressing much of British sentiment, was determined that Nasser could not be allowed "to steal" the Suez Canal and with it the last of Britain's prestige in the Arab world. Recalling the disastrous results of appeasement in the 1930s, Eden decided that the time had come to take a stand. Because of Nasser's unilateral seizure, without negotiation, of an international waterway, he felt confident that he would have both right and world opinion on his side.

On July 27 Eden informed the House of Commons that Britain had already begun consultations with other nations. The other nation most intimately concerned was France, less because of traditional French attachment to the Suez Canal than because of increasing French distaste for Nasser's support of the Algerian rebels. In Paris the last tattered hopes for an understanding with Nasser had evaporated soon after Pineau's return from Cairo in March. The nationalization immediately opened up the delightful prospect of smashing Nasser in a righteous cause. The bitter, brutal Algerian war, so little understood among France's supposed friends and so often opposed at home, had created deep frustration and bitterness. The French army and more militant civilians had increasingly felt themselves misunderstood; they believed that their efforts were being hampered by their own allies and that their campaign was being subverted by Arab "neutrals" led by Nasser, who was shielded by distance and diplomatic immunity. Guy Mollet's government wanted to strike and to strike at once. The British did not seem averse to force, but early word from Washington revealed only modest anguish over Nasser's coup.

When Pineau and Eden met for emergency tripartite talks with the American Robert Murphy, there was no doubt that Washington was concerned at Nasser's action but hesitant over any immediate overt action. This attitude was not positive enough for Pineau and Eden. Almost from the first moment the Western alliance showed signs of disarray. Even on July 29, as tripartite talks were in progress, French Admiral Nomy met with British military chiefs to take inventory of Anglo-French military resources available for military action. It soon became clear that some negotiations would have to be conducted. An immediate expedition was out of the question. The British military establishment was woefully unprepared for any serious Egyptian adventure, and even the French would need some time. The golden opportunity for instant gunboat diplomacy had to be forgone. The good old days when one could simply drop a few shells on the natives had passed; the natives had signed arms pacts for jet fighters, and British shells were a casualty of the balance-of-payments crisis. Temporarily at least the British and French would have to confine protest to the diplomatic stage, perhaps to drumming up American support, while a joint staff prepared a military expedition.

In Israel the Suez bombshell burst in an atmosphere of growing anxiety over Egypt's threat. Once the Czech arms deal had gone through, Israel had begun to live on a ticking bomb. Although the fedayeen raids from Gaza slackened from time to time, the Egyptians showed no inclination to cancel their plans for a jihad against the Zionists. And the sporadic deep penetrations of the fedayeen rasped Israeli nerves. At high levels, the rapid deployment of Soviet arms on Israel's border intensified the growing anxiety and uncertainty. Unless Nasser's potential aggression could be curbed, Israel would have to continue to live in the shadow of guns. The policy of retaliatory attacks had, if anything, simply aggravated the situation without bringing relief; further Egyptian threats and provocations were the main result. Alone, Israel could only consider a preventive war. The United Nations could do little. In January and April Secretary-General Dag Hammarskjöld had visited the Middle East and returned to New York more irritated with the Israeli attitude than sympathetic to Israeli fears.[6] The British and Americans, despite Nasser's actions, had paid little attention to Israel's problems. The Suez crisis, however, opened up the possibility of a preventive campaign against Nasser by the British and French or even by the Israelis with Anglo-French blessing. Although the attitude of the British remained enigmatic, the

Israelis knew that in France they had a potential ally, for in secret France had already expressed friendship for Israel in a practical way.[7]

Franco-Israeli cooperation had begun in that most delicate of all areas, atomic development. In 1949 French Professor Perrin discovered that Israeli Professor Dostrovski had developed a process for creating heavy water. Franco-Israeli scientific contacts continued. At the beginning of 1953 France acquired the process under the terms of a secret accord that opened many French nuclear installations to Israeli scientists. By that time Franco-Israeli contacts had been made in many areas. The first steps for a general accord had been taken by three young Israeli diplomats in Paris—Divon, Avni, and Sheloush—who met privately in a little café in the Bois de Boulogne to formulate a program of cooperation in commercial, scientific, and military affairs. At the time France appeared an unlikely friend. The French Foreign Ministry on the Quai d'Orsay had been traditionally pro-Arab, and France still hoped for a special position in Syria and for a continuing presence in North Africa. Israel did have certain unique advantages. The French Left retained pro-Jewish sympathies from the days of the Dreyfus affair, an affection for Israel's socialist economy, and bonds from the wartime anti-Nazi struggle. On the Right, as French-Arab relations deteriorated, there was sympathy for Israel's Arab problems. The army remembered both the Jewish Brigade in W.W. II and Jewish members of the resistance. Above all, the French remembered the Warsaw Ghetto and the gas chambers. The vital factor, however, was the impact of worsening Franco-Arab relations.

The most productive early contacts were between Moshe Dayan and General Guillaume in connection with Israel's problems in acquiring arms. But, although the French were sympathetic with Dayan in his difficulties, there was no real change in French policy. Cultural exchanges and Israeli naval visits took place in 1953, and Israeli intimacy with the complex and invisible power structure in France was growing. The most important big step, however, was the arrival in April 1953 of Pierre-Eugène Gilbert as the second French Ambassador to Israel. The Israeli Foreign Ministry had just been moved to Jerusalem in an atmosphere of rising confidence, and the Israelis found Gilbert's enthusiastic friendship most refreshing. A longer, closer look was taken at potentials for a French alliance. In Paris the

Israelis found more doors open. Dayan made several trips, which resulted in the most productive discussions with General Guillaume. Many influential individuals, particularly among the military, were predisposed to listen to the Israelis with sympathy. France was discovering Israel, recalling wartime associations and old friendships. The private talks culminated in a public reception for Dayan on his official visit to Paris during August 1954. In November 1954 the Algerians began their war of independence. Later in the year France accepted an Israeli order for the purchase of Ouragan and Mystère-2 jet fighters. Although there were certain obvious problems for Israel in a French alignment—not the least of which was the traditional instability of the French Cabinet—the Israelis decided in 1954 to depend on the French connection. When Diomède Catroux, French Secretary of State for Air, signed the accord on the fighter-plane sale, Israel had taken a giant step forward. Premier Pierre Mendes-France was sympathetic, but Israeli contacts with the generals and the permanent officials were equally important.

When David Ben-Gurion replaced Lavon as Minister of Defense, he quickly took up the suggestions of the Director-General, Shimon Peres, that French contacts be exploited. Although Edgar Faure replaced Mendes-France in February 1955, the Israelis continued to find additional friends in Paris. Peres arrived there with another and far more extensive shopping list and was welcomed by General Koenig, the new Minister of Defense. Later Dayan, along with Tolkovski of the Israel air force, arrived to follow up Peres' lead. The Israelis quickly found two valuable friends in Minister of the Interior Maurice Bourges-Maunory and his *chef de cabinet*, Abel Thomas. Both had been antagonized by Egyptian friendship for the Algerian rebels. Although there were those in the French government, particularly in the Foreign Ministry, who had not given up attempts to persuade Nasser to soften his militant stand, to French hawks such overtures smacked of appeasement. The latter fully sympathized with Israel's tough reprisal policy and did what they could for the Israelis. In 1955 General Koenig refused to allow the sale of tanks to Egypt if Israel was to be denied. After considerable wrangling between the Quai d'Orsay and the Ministry of Defense, he won his point; in fact, after his intervention, only a much-reduced shipment was sent off to Nasser. Despite all this sympathy, however, the French alignment had so far produced more contacts than military hardware. The Egyptian-Czech arms deal in September changed that.

Dayan, followed by Peres, arrived in Paris not only to explain the significance of the deal for Israel but also to reveal the extent of Nasser's cooperation with the Algerian rebels. On October 25 Prime Minister Moshe Sharett arrived. Although General Koenig had departed, his successor in the new Mollet government, General Billottee, was equally sympathetic. The Defense Ministry, however, had difficulty in acting independently of the Quai d'Orsay and had to consider the restrictions of the Tripartite Declaration and American policy. Still, arrangements were made for the shipment of twelve more Ouragans and twelve of the new Mystère-4 fighters. It was a start but not much more. On November 2 Ben-Gurion took over the office of Prime Minister while remaining as Minister of Defense. Israel stepped up efforts to acquire French arms, but there were still more hurdles. The Quai d'Orsay had not given up on conciliation with Cairo.

In January 1956 the French came up with their own Middle East solution. In March Pineau made his pilgrimage to Cairo. The Israelis had to wait out the French maneuvers. By April everyone had lost patience with Nasser. At the April North Atlantic Treaty Organization meeting the French read out a list of matériel to be sold to Israel. On April 12, eight Mystère-4s were finally delivered to Israel; the other four were to follow. This deal was aboveboard and within the scope of the Tripartite Declaration. But Israeli Ambassador to France Jacob Tsur and Peres, renewing contacts with Mollet, presented another list. On May 7 the Americans and the British agreed to limited French sales. Late in June or early in July Ben-Gurion arrived to talk with Mollet, impressing upon him Israel's perilous situation, threatened by the vast influx of Soviet arms into Egypt. In July France delivered the last Mystères committed to NATO, easing restrictions on future French sales. When Nasser nationalized the Suez Canal Company on July 26, the Israelis thus jumped at the chance to play their French card. The French were equally eager to begin the game.

On July 27 Peres arrived in Paris with new shopping lists. The round of visits and discussions began anew. The Israelis wanted a great deal more than the old limited quotas had allowed. The French thought that the time was ripe for substantial sales. Bourgès-Maunory conferred with Chief of Staff General Paul Ely, Admiral Pierre d'Escadre Barjot, and Abel Thomas. The result was that France agreed to supply Israel with sufficient arms, beyond the Tripartite Declaration restrictions. There would have to be some fudging the books and secret "illegal" shipments, but the French saw too many advantages to balk at a little dishonest bookkeeping. As early as June 1955 Peres had in passing mentioned the possibility of an Israeli attack on Egypt to Bourgès-Maunory. Obviously, ever since the arms deal in September 1955 the Israelis had been bruiting about the possibility of a preventive war. Franco-Israeli contacts had revealed precisely the direction of Israeli thinking. On October 22, 1955, Ben-Gurion had called Dayan home to review security problems and to plan an attack to clear the Gulf of 'Aqaba. By the summer of 1956 there had been no lessening of tension in the Middle East; in fact, in April Egypt had contracted for even more arms. The discussions in Paris early in August thus signaled that the possibility of an Israeli attack on Egypt had evolved into a probability. These discussions, primarily involving the secret arms sale, were narrowly limited to French military personnel, the top men at the Defense Ministry, one or two special friends of Israel, and Mollet. There were still no long range plans but only an intimate exchange of confidences. There were too many loose ends for anyone to be very definite. The French had embarked on a variety of diplomatic gambits to end the Suez crisis peacefully. They were also involved with the British in secret preparations for a Suez expedition.

Anglo-French relations were the major concern in Paris, but the Israelis were not neglected. By August conversations with Abel Thomas and Louis Mangin—a political advisor to the French Defense Minister—had brought an understanding of the possibilities. In the meantime, serious shipments of military supplies to Israel began so that Israel would be able to play an appropriate role if necessary. Heavy artillery and French AMX tanks were shipped. The first small crevice in the arms embargo had opened wider. There was not yet a flood to equal the wave of Soviet arms pouring into Egypt, but the breach had been made. Through the back door, the Israelis had quietly become advantageously involved in the turmoil and furor of the Suez crisis.

The French, as they had feared, had become increasingly enmeshed in intricate negotiations that were to some extent essential because of military considerations. On August 1 Dulles arrived in London for three-power talks. Although the Secretary of State took a legalistic approach and seemed to think that negotiations would be sufficient, Eden and Mollet were encouraged that the United States had not altogether discounted the possibility of joint military action. But by then the French had already presented the British with a list of units ready for a Suez expedition. The British had alerted certain army units as early as July 31. The British and French fleets had begun to assemble. French troops in Algeria were ordered to prepare to move out. On August 2 Britain called up the army reserves. British Canberra jet bombers flew from Britain to Malta. Neither the British nor the French made any effort to conceal the military buildup while they continued their diplomatic campaign. Dulles had made it clear during the three-power talks that Washington was not going to be rushed. Pineau had insisted that France wanted urgent and decisive action. Dulles, however, persuaded Eden and Pineau that the best move would be to summon an international conference of canal users. Given the chaotic state of their war preparations, the British and French could do little but agree.

On August 5 Great Britain invited twenty-four nations to confer in London on the status of the Suez Canal. On August 12 Egypt refused to attend, but all the others except Greece accepted the invitation. The conference opened on August 16. By August 22 a majority agreement had been reached on all points. The final declaration guaranteed Egyptian sovereign rights and a fair return on the use of the canal but insisted on international control. It included a suggestion for negotiations leading to a new Suez convention. Eighteen nations agreed to the London declaration as it stood, but four, including the Soviet Union, preferred an international advisory board with no powers of control. On August 23 the declaration was published, and Australian Prime Minister Robert Menzies was appointed chairman of a five-nation committee to convey the proposals to the Egyptian government. On September 3 Menzies arrived in Cairo. On September 9, after a week of futile discussions, Nasser rejected the London declaration. His counterproposals did not satisfy either Britain or France. Apparently there was no longer an alternative to force; even an appeal to the Security Council would have been hamstrung by Russia's veto.

During the last week of August Secretary Dulles expressed strong doubts about the success of an appeal to the Security Council. Instead he suggested, while Menzies was still in Cairo, that a canal users' association might manage the canal. The British and French had been skeptical, but no sooner had the Menzies mission failed than they found themselves involved in Dulles' newest proposal. Increasingly, Dulles and the Americans seemed to be slipping into meaningless verbiage. In September the United States informed Eden that Washington had rejected the use of force. Eisenhower suggested that the British separate the Canal question from their general Middle Eastern policy. This suggestion meant that the United States would accept a narrow "legal" solution to the nationalization of the Canal, would not be interested in disciplining Nasser as a menace to international peace, and would not approve and might oppose the use of force by Britain and France. The Western allies were drifting on separate courses.

A narrow solution, even if possible, would have been most unsatisfactory to Eden and Mollet, who had begun to talk as if Nasser were a new Benito Mussolini or Adolf Hitler. Both wanted to establish a new balance in the Arab world either by smashing Nasser or by at least humiliating him diplomatically. They would reluctantly accept a fair settlement, but in six weeks none had been forthcoming. The French had grown increasingly restive during the sterile interchange of diplomatic notes and had also developed grave doubts about the ponderous progress of British military preparations. In Britain a vocal segment of the Conservative Party—the "Suez Group"—was also unhappy with the unproductive discussions. Dulles' proposed users' association did not appear to offer a very hopeful approach, but Eden and Mollet decided to take up the American initiative and at the same time to appeal to the United Nations for action, thus taking the last peaceful course open to them. There was little evidence that the Egyptians had any sincere intentions to negotiate a resolution to the conflict, and there were ample indications that Cairo intended to delay until a "settlement" could be secured on its own terms. Both Eden and Mollet wanted more than merely a piece of paper.

The alternative to a settlement achieved by mutual agreement, the Anglo-French expeditionary force, had been hampered by problems resulting partly from the decay of the British military potential. The British found their artillery in Germany, their paratroop battalions untrained, their landing craft in mothballs, their armor division in

Libya without tanks or transport, their specialists demobilized. The militant French, more willing to risk a sudden attack, had reluctantly accepted a delay to allow the British to ready their contribution. Then, too, the entire British expedition strategy irritated the French. The British seemed to be re-enacting D-Day, planning a vast armada that would lie off the Egyptian coast for six days of air bombardment and then disgorge a huge force on Alexandria. The French did not envision the expedition that way. They had no respect for the Egyptian army (trained by the British) and saw no reason for such elaborate preparations. Their troops had fought in Indochina, their equipment had been refined in recent wars, and their commanders wanted to go in and knock Nasser over and get out. The British, whose contribution was diplomatically essential, won the argument.

Under the direction of Antony Head, the British Minister of War, a combined operations headquarters was set up in London, with branches in Paris, Malta, and Cyprus. The expedition was dubbed "Operation Hamilcar" and later "Musketeer." The joint commander would be General Sir Charles Keightley, with French Vice-Admiral d'Escarde Barjot as his deputy. To collect, arm, train, and deploy 80,000 men took even longer than the French had feared. Finally on September 10 the 80,000 Anglo-French troops were concentrated on Cyprus and Malta. Keightley planned to be ready on September 15; even then it would take another week for the troopships to reach Egypt.

By mid-September the diplomatic situation had, as cynics had expected, shown no signs of improvement. As soon as Nasser turned down the London resolutions, Mollet and Pineau arrived in London to urge an immediate expedition against the Canal Zone. But the British believed that they still had other cards to play. On September 11 the pilots of the Suez Canal Company resigned, with the backing of the British and French. The maneuver to block the canal traffic and to prove Egyptian inefficiency backfired. Volunteer pilots arrived from Eastern Europe, to find that long experience on the Canal was unnecessary. On September 16 forty-two ships passed through the Canal, more than the previous daily average. By that time, the British had been persuaded that a descent on the Canal by an Anglo-French force was preferable to an assault on Alexandria, assuming, as nearly everyone did, that Nasser continued to refuse to accept a reasonable diplomatic solution.

The French proposal for an attack on Suez had evolved at least partially out of the growing intimacy with Irsael. Increasingly through September the Israelis seemed genuinely interested in a preventive attack on Egypt in the near future. The Israelis apparently believed that, unless there was an attack on Sinai, the Egyptians would soon use the Soviet arms to attack them. During September the French were embarked on two parallel policies. On one hand, they were aiding the Israelis to achieve military parity with the Egyptians so that a lightening offensive would be possible when local and international conditions were favorable. On the other hand, they were trying to stiffen British determination to use force and in a place where it would complement an Israeli campaign. The two policies were, however, completely compartmentalized. The British Cabinet, vaguely aware of French interest in Israel, had no clue to the extent of the collaboration. The Israelis knew of Operation Musketeer, but the French showed considerable reticence about details. The British and Israelis could learn little from each other. Anglo-Israeli relations, often cool, were distant during the fall of 1956 and destined to deteriorate. So Franco-Israeli discussions went forward in complete isolation from Anglo-French diplomatic moves and work on Musketeer.

After the Menzies failure, the French made it clear to the Israelis that the prospects for diplomacy were not promising. About September 14 the Israelis began talking seriously about an attack on Egypt but still without any definite commitment. The French continued shipping arms to Israel beyond the NATO quotas. The arrival of tanks, artillery, and antitank weapons after years of postponements and evasions made a profound impression on the Israelis. On September 23 Ben-Gurion informed the Mapai Party that "Israel at last has one true ally."[8] All during the month there was a steady round of meetings, visits, and conversations in Paris. Peres was almost constantly on the move between Israel and France. Dayan and Israeli staff officers were in and out of Paris. On September 26 Operation Musketeer was at last ready, with Suez as the target. The time had come for a final understanding with Israel.

On September 29 Peres and Dayan were back in Paris with their final shopping list. On October 1 Dayan, with officers of the Israeli military attaché's staff met with French Chief of Staff General Ély, Louis Mangin, political advisor of Bourgès-Maunory, General Maurice Challe, General Martin, Colonel Simon, and a French naval officer. Ély agreed to Dayan's shopping list, despite French commitments in Algeria. The French were concerned about the military potential of the Israelis as reflected in the shopping list; even then, Dayan had not asked for too much for fear of frightening off the French. He briefed Ély on the estimated scope of an Israeli campaign into Sinai: "I added my conviction that even with the equipment we had—or rather despite the equipment that we did not have—we could, if war broke out between us and Egypt, defeat their Army and capture the Sinai Peninsula within a fortnight."[9] The French took his word for it. The date was set for October 20, conditional on Israeli Cabinet approval. The French militants had done as much as they could. The Israelis would be ready to go on October 20. Musketeer was ready to go into Suez. A final decision would have to wait on the Security Council meeting, for the diplomatic effort, though faltering, was not yet dead.

Discussions in the Security Council ground on for ten days in early October. Eventually the Security Council unanimously passed a resolution containing six principles for settling the Suez question, as proposed by Britain and France. The second part of the resolution, requesting Egypt to negotiate on the basis of the six proposals while the users' association received the tolls, was vetoed by Russia. The British and French agreed that the six principles were then meaningless. Egypt still controlled the Canal and collected the tolls. Nasser could procrastinate indefinitely, delaying negotiations as long as he controlled the Canal. Many members of the United Nations did not agree with this pessimistic view. They anticipated continued discussions based on the Security Council resolution. A "compromise" proposed by Nehru or Krishna Menon would more than likely be written in Nasserine script. In any case, the prospect of more months of sterile negotiation was too much to be borne. Eden and Mollet agreed that all practical avenues of diplomacy had been closed. All Dulles' ingenious schemes had dwindled away in discussion; the Americans seemed willing to appease Nasser, to allow American pilots to work for the nationalized company, to pay tolls to Egypt, to ignore Egyptian aggression. Russia controlled the Security Council. The new nations, far from disapproving of Nasser, admired him. Finally, the Egyptians had grown smug, confident that their "theft" was secure. The time had come to act.

On October 16 Eden and Foreign Minister Selwyn Lloyd flew to Paris. That evening they met with Mollet and Pineau at the official home of the Premier, the Hôtel Matignon. Mollet and Pineau sat under a portrait of Cardinal Richelieu. Eden and Lloyd sat beneath a tapestry on which Don Quixote tilted at windmills. It is to be assumed that the French arranged the seating. During much of the five-hour conference only the four leaders were present, without interpreters or advisers, a rare diplomatic occurrence. According to Eden, the three major topics under discussion were the direction of negotiations on the Canal in view of the Security Council decision, the possibilities for a users' association, and finally developments in the Middle East "and, in particular, the growing menace of hostility by Egypt against Israel."[10] All agreed that the Security Council had reached a dead end. All agreed that the users' association would be only a façade, legitimizing Egyptian nationalization. On the final topic, discussions were far more fruitful.

By October 10 some British staff officers and Lloyd himself had become aware of the extent of Franco-Israeli collaboration. Lloyd had informed Eden of what might be brewing. Eden reputedly had not been impressed: "What, Israel to attack Egypt? Don't be stupid."[11] In any case, on October 15 General Maurice Challe had flown to London to explain Franco-Israeli relations in greater detail. At the October 16 meeting, the British suddenly saw the light. Mollet and Pineau suggested that, if a conflict developed between Israel and Egypt in Sinai, Britain and France could intervene to protect the Canal. Such intervention would undoubtedly be opposed by Nasser, justifying the use of Musketeer to occupy the Suez Canal Zone. Such a humiliating military defeat would spell the end of Nasserism and probably of Nasser as well. Acting in the name of international peace, intervening only to separate Israel and Egypt and to ensure the operation of the Canal, the Anglo-French team could recoup some of the moral capital frittered away during the endless diplomatic discussions. The proposals may have been couched in such a manner that Eden did not have to be "officially" informed that conflict was now assured, but unofficially the British were delighted to rush down the French garden path.

The immediate result was a wrench in British Middle Eastern policy, which had been totally unrelated to Israel's needs. During the fall of 1956 the British Foreign Office had once more been attempting to tidy up the Middle East to Britain's advantage. The danger spot had been Jordan, which had been moving closer to Nasser's net ever since the dismissal of Glubb. The possibility of seeking stability by supporting an Iraqi absorption of feeble Jordan had attracted the Foreign Office. But Nuri as-Said had his doubts. Jordanian elections were scheduled for October 21, and the British suggested that Iraq at least send in troops to bolster King Hussein. Nuri as-Said made the offer, but King Hussein was not receptive, preferring to risk losing the election rather than to use the Iraqis. Rumors of possible Iraqi troops in Jordan, however, had violent repercussions in Israel. On the night of October 10 the Israelis carried out a night raid on the Jordan police fort at Kalkiliah. The heavy fighting lasted all night and immediately attracted international attention. Although the Israelis claimed that the attack on Kalkiliah was in retaliation for fedayeen raids tolerated by Hussein, the British did not see it that way. On October 11 the British chargé d'affaires in Tel Aviv, Peter Westlake, told Ben-Gurion that an Iraqi division would enter Jordan and that, if Israel reacted, Britain would intervene. Israel's new Foreign Minister, Golda Meir, replied that Iraqi intervention would destroy the precarious Middle Eastern balance and that Israel might have to react. The British warned that, if Jordan were attacked, Britain would come into the war against Israel under the terms of the Anglo-Jordanian Treaty of 1948 and the Tripartite Declaration of 1950.

The Israeli government expressed anxiety and astonishment at the British attitude, as well it might. Seldom had Middle Eastern politics seemed more like a chapter from *Alice in Wonderland*. Israel, with French assistance, was preparing a secret blitz against British's enemy, Nasser. This attack would be used as an excuse for mounting Operation Musketeer against Nasser, which would make Britain an ally of Israel. Yet, by dabbling in Jordanian politics against the wishes of both Hussein and Nuri as-Said, the British had come perilously close to an open rupture with Israel, which could lead to war before the Sinai offensive. The meeting at the Hôtel Matignon cleared the foggy glass of British diplomacy. Eden and Lloyd shifted gears.

Back in London they called off the dogs in Jordan. The Iraqis did not move in, to Hussein's relief, and on October 21 the pro-Nasserites won the Jordanian elections, to Britain's disgust. On October 17 Ben-Gurion pointed out to the Knesset that the main threat to Israel came from Nasser. After several bobbles and a near fumble, everyone finally had his signals straight—or nearly straight. In Britain the decks were cleared for action. Antony Head replaced Sir Walter Monckton as Minister of Defense, to push through Musketeer. By that time the original date of the Israeli attack had been moved back from October 20 for several reasons, not the least of which was growing concern in Israel at the need for air cover. It was Ben-Gurion's turn to hesitate. He wanted a personal meeting with Mollet. An Israeli attack, parallel to but not incorporated in Operation Musketeer, would involve at least two major risks. First, the new Egyptian air force might bomb Israeli cities, killing thousands of civilians. Second, Musketeer might never get underway at all, which would leave Israel holding the bag and Egypt controlling the air. Ben-Gurion wanted a French air umbrella and some reassurance of support.

At dawn on October 22 a passenger aircraft with Israeli markings landed at Villa Coublay southwest of Paris. The Israelis' old friend Louis Mangin was on hand to welcome Peres, Dayan, and Ben-Gurion. What with Ben-Gurion's halo of white hair and Old Testament profile and Dayan's black eye patch, a more conspicuous secret delegation is difficult to imagine. Mangin shepherded them into two cars. They were driven to a small villa in the suburb of Sèvres. The France to which they came was even more militant as a result of the events of the past week. The Algerian war seemed to go from bad to worse. On October 18 the French had intercepted the Egyptian ship *Athos*, used to train Algerian rebels, and had found it filled with arms and documents. Nasser's duplicitous soldier's oath to Pineau in March still left a nasty taste. On October 23, when Mollet and Pineau arrived at Sèvres they were eager for action and sympathetic to Ben-Gurion's fears. By noon the French had agreed to supply further air and naval cover. French warships, theoretically patrolling for further Algerian arms ships, would move to the Israeli coast immediately. Further Mystères would be flown into Israel by regular French pilots to provide air cover over Israel. That afternoon Lloyd and Patrick Dean flew in from London for their last and most detailed briefing.

The British believed that the Sinai attack would be most opportune, but they had different problems from those of the French. The British needed the continuing friendship of the Anglophile Arabs and did not want to be accused of collusion with the Zionists. If the

Israelis "independently" threatened the Canal by an attack through Sinai the British would have the best of both worlds. They could join the French in protecting the Canal from the Israelis. As Nasser would obviously resist, the British and French could then wipe out the Egyptian air force on the ground, eliminating the one threat to a successful Israeli offensive. Britain intended to remain disinterested in any Israeli-Egyptian confrontation and to act only as an umpire, refusing to defend Israel in the United Nations. This approach the Israeli delegation found reasonable.

The result was the so-called "Treaty of Sèvres," signed by Dean, Pineau, and Ben-Gurion, which set out the terms of the military cooperation from October 29 to November 6. Israel would in effect make war against Egypt in concert with France, and France would also participate in Operation Musketeer with the British. Anglo-Israeli cooperation would be limited to prior information on operations with no tactical liaison. Ben-Gurion had his reassurance and the French airplanes. He flew home on October 25 content. Israel mobilized the next day, but the British reacted too slowly to suit the French. Abel Thomas flew to London on October 27 to urge the British to allow the Musketeer ships to sail immediately. The British ordered Keightley to advance his D-Day by seven days. The French were still concerned about Musketeer's timetable, but it was too late to do much about it.

In Israel on October 25 Ben-Gurion announced his approval of the Sinai campaign, to begin at dusk on October 29, 1956, under "the assumption the British and French forces are going to take action against Egypt" on October 31.[12] That "something" was going on somewhere in connection with the Suez crisis had begun to leak out. After October 16 the British and French closed off the normal flow of military and intelligence information to Washington. In Paris American agents began to pick up hints. In Washington, caught up in the Presidential campaign, reports drifted in from intelligence sources that Israel and France might attack Egypt sometime after Election Day, November 6. In London and Paris American diplomats' questions were fobbed off by former close associates. Something was definitely brewing, but apparently the Americans thought that they had until after the November elections to head off the British and French. Then on October 18 events in Hungary suddenly gobbled up not only most of the headlines but also much of the attention of the Americans, already busy with the elections. By October 23 the Hungarians were fighting in the streets, and the world's eyes were riveted on Budapest.

The major problem in the Middle East in October seemed to be the Israel-Jordan border rather than Suez. The Iraqi-British-Israeli exchanges had appeared dangerous. On October 21 the pro-Nasser candidates had swept into office in Jordan, apparently threatening even King Hussein's throne. On October 23 Egypt, Syria, and Jordan integrated their armies under the Egyptian Commander in Chief. This move was obviously a grave threat to Israel, seemingly on the point of invading Jordan. On October 25 and 26 the American military attaché in Israel reported that mobilization was underway. On October 27 the British again informed Golda Meir that an Israeli attack on Jordan would result in British intervention. On the same day President Eisenhower sent Ben-Gurion a letter expressing his anxiety over mobilization and the crisis with Jordan. On October 28 the American Ambassador to Israel, Edward B. Lawson, reported total mobilization. Fearful of American interference, Ben-Gurion had already telegraphed Mollet for reassurance that the paper signed at Sèvres was still good. Mollet replied that it was. On October 29 Eisenhower sent Ben-Gurion a second letter pressing his concern at mobilization, as the Iraqi troops had not crossed into Jordan. If nothing else, the British Foreign Office's Iraqi gambit had diverted attention from Egypt. The Israelis, on the eve of the Sinai operation, ignored Eisenhower's note. Israeli mobilization along Jordan's border continued.

Moshe Dayan could not, of course, be absolutely certain that he would ever receive the signal to activate his Operation Kadesh, but almost all the last-minute hesitations had evaporated. Dayan, who had served as chief of the general staff since 1953, was almost as dashing as his operational plan. His black eye patch, a souvenir of the British campaign in Syria; his exploits as a jeep-commando leader in 1948; his aggressive speeches and total self-confidence were well known in Israel. He was a most visible and highly articulate general, but, his public image aside, the army trusted him. There was a faith within the army that, with Dayan in control, little could go seriously wrong. If the Zahal was a band of brothers, then Dayan was surely the biggest brother, sure, confident, skilled, and daring. As much as any man since 1948, he had molded the Zahal into a streamlined weapon, and, more than any other man except Ben-Gurion, he had come to personify determination to achieve victory.

Everything had gone almost as planned. French Mystère jets had arrived on Israeli strips. French Nord Atlas transports, based on Cyprus, were ready to parachute supplies to the Israeli columns moving through Sinai. The French fleet was in the eastern Mediterranean. On October 27 a shipment of 200 French 6 x 6 trucks arrived, ensuring mobility for the Israeli army, which was too dependent on civilian transport. On October 28 a substantial percentage of the 100,000 men needed had answered the call-up. On October 29 the concentration along the Jordan border, intended to mislead the Egyptians among others, had been completed. Then at 3:20 in the afternoon sixteen Dakota transports took off, each carrying a paratroop company. Until the very last minute many of the military commanders had expected the whole thing to be called off. At 3:30 the Dakotas were out of sight. Operation Kadesh, the capture of Sinai, had begun.

NOTES

1. The most concise if not always an illuminating explanation of Nasser's philosophy may be found in his *The Philosophy of Revolution* (Washington, D.C.: 1955), but generally his appeal is emotional rather than programmatic. He is an orator not an ideologue other than being a visionary.

2. Erskine B. Childers, *The Road to Suez* (London: 1962), p. 125.

3. Terence Robertson, *Crisis: The Inside Story of the Suez Conspiracy* (New York: 1965), p. 46.

4. The tale of Russian support for the Aswan dam is still fogged by the hectic spate of Egyptian assurances and Russian denials during July. As early as May 6 Ambassador Solod had offered Russian help for the dam, but not until the Anglo-American refusal did this offer really become firm. It is possible that Nasser was not taking too great a gamble when

he assumed that the Russians would come through with support, which in their own good time they did.

5. According to legend, Nuri as-Said told Eden that Britain should go in at once, go in alone, and go in all the way. Obviously the British were incapable of taking the Iraqi's advice.

6. Robertson, *Crisis*, p. 103, quotes Lester Pearson of Canada on Hammarskjöld's attitude toward the Israelis in October: "It appeared that, despite public statements to the contrary, Hammarskjöld was 'bitterly angry because the Israelis did not co-operate with him during his last mission to the Middle East.' "

7. The intricate Franco-Israeli relations are best documented in Michael Bar-Zohar, *Suez Ultra-Secret* (Paris: 1964), which is somewhat mistitled. There is quite a collection of works purporting to give the exact chronology of the various secret contacts in 1956, based on a wide variety of sources, usually unofficial leaks or personal interviews. By and large, the major actors have not revealed privately or publicly the "secrets" of Suez, despite their memoirs and interviews. Any chronology, and still more the actual agendas, is therefore still tentative.

8. Herman Finer, *Dulles Over Suez* (Chicago: 1964), p. 329.

9. Major General Moshe Dayan, *Diary of the Sinai Campaign* (New York: 1966), p. 31.

10. Anthony Eden, *Memoirs: Full Circle* (Boston: 1960), p. 569.

11. Finer, *Dulles Over Suez*, p. 319.

12. Although Ben-Gurion told the general staff of his intentions to go through with the Sinai campaign on October 25, he did not reveal his intentions to the multi party Cabinet until October 27 or to the opposition until October 29; even then he excluded the Communists. The French and British followed much the same procedure. The British particularly had problems with lukewarm spirits within the Conservative Party and the prospect of icy opposition from the Labour Party.

13

The Sinai War

Moshe Dayan's Operation Kadesh had to allow for a wide variety of military and diplomatic contingencies that had little to do with orthodox tactical considerations. At the same time that he was creating a "threat" to the Suez Canal, thus opening the door to Anglo-French intervention, he had also to act circumspectly, so that the Egyptians would not commit their air force. As the Suez Canal was on the other side of the Sinai Peninsula from his jumping-off point, this necessity created certain difficulties. Then, too, no one in Israel could be sure what the international response would be, except that eventually there would be an enforced cease-fire. Just how "eventually" was difficult to estimate, but Dayan had to cut his originally planned three-week campaign down so that he could already be tying up loose ends when and if the Anglo-French invasion of Egypt began. Finally, Israel had to enter Sinai in such a way that the entire operation could be called off at any of its successive stages if the international situation developed unexpectedly. The prospects for a united Arab attack in support of Egypt could, it was concluded from past experience, be largely dismissed, despite the October tripartite military pact. Even if Syria or Jordan did risk an attack, the Israelis expected that, at worst, the brigades protecting the border would be tied down in a couple of standard battles. From all these considerations, Dayan had evolved less a detailed operational plan than an anticipated series of fluid movements along east-west axes, with one or two novel gimmicks added. Dayan had to gamble that Israeli speed and daring would compensate for the obvious tactical drawbacks.

The first stage of Kadesh carried the indirect approach to the point of absurdity. On the first night at dusk Dayan planned to drop a battalion of paratroops near Mitla Pass, only 20 miles from the Suez Canal and 180 miles overland from the Israeli border. The other battalions of the brigade were expected to move along the southern axis and to link up with the paratroops within twenty-four to thirty-six hours. At one stroke the Israelis would "threaten" the Canal, thus setting in motion the Anglo-French expedition to eliminate the Egyptian air force and at the same time confusing the Egyptians. With a brigade loose in the wilds of central Sinai and paratroops at Mitla, the Egyptian command would have to decide, first, whether or not the Israelis were serious and, if they decided affirmatively, what their own reaction should be. Previous Israeli experience had been that Egyptian reaction time was slow, but, if things turned sour in Sinai or on the international scene, the whole brigade could hopefully be jerked back out and Kadesh passed off as a retaliatory raid. The most obvious tactical risk was in sending armor scooting across Sinai without control of the air. Dayan hoped that the weight of the Israeli air force, freed from air defense at home, coupled with just enough Egyptian reticence, would give him most of the daylight hours.

The second stage was only slightly more orthodox. After a pause of twenty-four hours, during which the village of Kusseima was to be taken, an Israeli force of three brigades would move out of the Negev and push west on a line through Kusseima, the Abu Agueila defenses, and Bir Gafgafa toward Ismailia on the Canal. It was hoped that this dashing about in the south would confuse the Egyptians and that, by the time the second stage was well underway, events elsewhere would have further distracted them. The major risk was in stretching the Israeli armor along the Ismailia highway, with the northern flank unprotected. The heart of Dayan's plan was simply the hope that, if he kept the ball in the air long enough, the Egyptians would drop it.

The final major stage of Kadesh was comparatively straightforward. Dayan planned a battle in the North reminiscent of Yigal Yadin's Operation Ayin, a swift hook into Rafa that would cut the

Egyptian coastal strip in half. The initial battle, a standard attack on Rafa, would be followed by an armored dash down the El 'Arish road toward the Canal. Once Rafa had fallen, another brigade would clean out the all-but-indefensible Gaza strip. After the battle for Rafa, the strategy along the coast would be a matter of exploiting the collapsing Egyptian defenses. Approximately when the last Egyptians were being cleared out of northern Sinai, the final operation would begin far to the south at the tip of the Gulf of 'Aqaba. As soon as the first results of stage one had been achieved, a brigade would move down the uninhabited and untracked eastern shore of Sinai toward Sharm-el-Sheikh. As there was no road to speak of and there were several ideal ambush points, Dayan had to assume that the Egyptians would wait for him at Sharm-el-Sheikh. Even if this column could not make it, another descent could be made along the western coast, where there was a road of sorts, by the paratroops at Mitla or by another band of paratroops dropped farther down the coast. By then, whether the Anglo-French invasion took place or not, if things had gone as planned, the Egyptians would be paralyzed and incapable of response.

In a week or so Kadesh would be completed. The operation, with the support of France and the toleration of Britain, would allow Israel to inflict a crushing defeat on the Egyptian army, wiping out Nasser's prestige and underlining the futility of Arab aggression. The nature of Kadesh was to secure a total victory, rather than to destroy the Egyptian army or even to capture its new Russian equipment.

> We did not want to kill a lot of Egyptians. There are forty million Arabs, so what's the use of killing five thousand, ten thousand, fifteen thousand of them. It was not even vital to destroy or take their equipment. They could always get more from Russia. What mattered was their defeat.[1]

A second defeat in eight years, it was hoped, would bring one or two more specific benefits: the elimination of the fedayeen menace at Gaza and the unplugging of the Gulf of 'Aqaba at Sharm-el-Sheikh. The major objective of Kadesh, however, remained the humiliation of the Egyptian army, the one great hope for Arab revenge.

The unstated premise of Kadesh was that the Israelis would be facing a second-rate army incapable of mobility or tactical flexibility.

Many of the assigned objectives, which seemed either impossible or too ambitious were, in Dayan's thinking, reasonable goals. He assumed that, in many cases, the major obstacle to swift Israeli advance would be the terrain rather than the Egyptian army. Logistics would be a matter of keeping on or catching up. On paper the gravest risk remained the Egyptian air force, which—again on paper—was capable of hitting both the Sinai columns and Israeli cities. Even with the additional French airplanes and a French air umbrella over Israel, the operations in Sinai would be acutely vulnerable. Israeli intelligence assumed that a substantial portion of the Egyptian jets would be inoperative and that the others would be flown by inexperienced and second-rate pilots. The poor quality of Egyptian maintenance under battle conditions should cut down the sorties flown. The superiority of Egyptian armor and artillery was judged less a problem. Dayan believed that good men in second-rate tanks could best second-rate men in good tanks. In view of the Egyptian tactical deployment in late October, even accepting the possibility of reinforcements moving in from across the Canal, Dayan thought that in about two days he would have maneuvered into positions that would prohibit a successful Egyptian defense.

The Egyptian army that Dayan proposed to distract and to destroy had, according to Cairo, been transformed into the vanguard of the revolution. After the July coup in 1952 one of the prime objectives of the Free Officers had been to revitalize the army, to eliminate corruption and attract dedicated personnel. The army was to be an elite institution, the foundation of the state, and a symbol of the new Egypt. As the nature and effectiveness of an army are closely related to the total structure of the nation, four years had proved too brief a time to revolutionize Egyptian society and with it the army. Consequently, many of the faults of the old royal army remained. One of the most difficult to eradicate was class division and antagonism between officers and men, which inhibited trust and largely made a truly national army impossible. A patina of revolutionary Arab socialism was not enough to erase generations of prejudices and customs. Another difficulty was the continuing organization and training of the army along orthodox Western lines, a policy inherited from the British and still substantially unchanged, without sufficient recognition of peculiarly Egyptian conditions and limitations. An additional and unforeseen result of the army's new, dominant position in the country had been the dependence of the government on army officers for administrators, which resulted in a considerable talent drain. Despite the problems, inherited and imposed, the Egyptians had made a concerted effort to rehabilitate the army.

First, the prestige of the armed forces was built up. Salaries were raised, a merit system for promotions instituted, and special training fostered. Despite recruitment problems, the army increased in size. Modern equipment was imported. Private German experts and advisers were employed. The most visible change came with the arrival of Soviet and Czech equipment. Soviet technicians had worked overtime to accelerate the absorption of the huge transfusions of matériel, but it took time to incorporate the arms into standard operational practice. The general level of technological training was low at best. Both operation and maintenance of complex and delicate equipment proved difficult. Egyptian pilots, for example, had never been outstanding, and their mastery of the new MIGs left much to be desired. Much of the heavy equipment was often inoperative. The artillery, always the best Egyptian arm, had done somewhat better. By the fall of 1956 the total mobilized strength of the army was more than 100,000 men, equipped with first-rate arms but deficient in training and experience. The Egyptian air force had about 200 fighters and 70 bombers, but it was in a low state of readiness. The small navy, with somewhat higher morale, had four destroyers and various auxiliary vessels, and submarines were on the way from Poland. In Middle Eastern terms the Egyptian military force was impressive but, despite the government's efforts, more for its matériel than for its ability to wage war.

The Egyptian deployment in Sinai had not been seriously related to the prospects of a major Israeli offensive; in fact, it was a matter more of prestige than of preparedness for war. The German advisers had urged that the most effective disposition would be in a north-south line in the middle of Sinai, where a natural line of obstacles, sand dunes, and rugged hills create a ready-made defense line. The Israelis would have to push aside a screen force on the frontier and then move nearly 100 miles in the open, with lengthening supply lines, before reaching the Egyptian defense line. The Egyptians, however, were interested not in defense but only in offense. Nasser wanted his new army to loom large on the Israeli border. So, instead of a secure line deep in Sinai, the Egyptian command deployed the bulk of the

army in Sinai along the El 'Arîsh–Rafa–Gaza area on the coast. Farther south the central axis was fortified around Abu Agueila close to
the frontier, with only weak screening forces opposite the southern
Negev. At Sharm-el-Sheikh, relatively protected by its geographical
isolation, fortifications were constructed but not fully manned. The
Egyptian dispositions for an offensive were less than perfect, but for
defense against a surprise Israeli attack they were disastrously inadequate. Tied down to static coastal hedgehogs at the end of a long and
vulnerable supply line, the Egyptian army was like a mailed fist on an
exposed and feeble arm. Once Israeli armor was loose in Sinai, the
Egyptians would have to come out of their fortified pockets or wait
to be cut off. Rushing in reinforcements, particularly armor, would
change the nature of the campaign but would not compensate for
original immobility.

After the Suez crisis broke and the Anglo-French combination
began the Cyprus buildup, Egyptian Sinai Commander General Ali
Ali Amer faced an additional problem. Nasser and General Amer
decided to pull some of the troops out of Sinai, just in case the British
and French did attack. This move left General Amer with a few more
than 30,000 troops and, still worse, with an impression that the main
threat would not be to Sinai. Both Nasser and his Commander in
Chief were distracted by the Anglo-French preparations, by the
Jordanian situation, and by the new tripartite Arab pact. On October
23 General Amer flew to Jordan to sign the pact. Then he and his
senior officers went on to participate in an extended round of conferences in Jordan and Syria. To complicate matters, the transport
bringing the Egyptian officers back from Damascus was shot down
on the eve of Kadesh, removing at one stroke most of the Egyptian
senior commanders.[2] Amer, who had taken a different plan back to
Cairo, escaped. On October 29, therefore, the Sinai command had too
few troops, a disoriented high command, vulnerable positions, and no
hint of danger. On September 3 General Hakim Amer had announced that "The Egyptian Army is prepared to the smallest detail."[3] The evidence of Sinai is against him.

By 3:30 A.M. on October 29 the Israeli Dakotas, escorted by two
layers of jet fighters weaving a high-altitude pattern, were skimming
along 500 feet over Sinai. At their objective, a monument to Colonel

A. C. Palmer, a former governor of Sinai, and known to the Israelis as "Parker's Monument," the Dakotas pulled up to 1,500 feet, and the paratroopers jumped. When they landed, they found that they had suffered two broken legs and eleven sprained ankles and had been dropped three miles from target—par for the course. By 7:30 they had reached their assigned positions and had dug in on a small hill near a fork in the road one mile from the eastern approaches of the Mitla Pass. During the drop there had been a few wild shots, possibly from Bedouins or a road gang, but scouts encountered only two Egyptian vehicles. Meanwhile, the Dakotas had returned to Israel to report the drop and the lack of Egyptian air interference. Five minutes after touchdown David Ben-Gurion's private secretary brought him the news. Ben-Gurion, who was sick in bed with a high temperature, then read himself to sleep with a book on the intellect of primitive man. There would be no fresh news until dawn. By then the remainder of the paratroop brigade should be well on the way to link up at the monument.

The 202nd Paratroop Brigade under Colonel Ariel Sharon crossed into Sinai almost on schedule an hour before the drop. Its concentration and advance had been hectic. The expected French G.M.C. 6x6 trucks did not arrive until the last minutes, and then only 46 of the promised 153 appeared. By then Sharon had lost four hours in waiting. He finally reduced his strength, eliminated some artillery and all noncombat units, except for one bulldozer, and moved out. He had to cover sixty miles across the Negev, from his deployment area on the Jordanian border to the Egyptian frontier. Two hours were saved by refueling in motion, so that his point crossed the border at 4:00 in the afternoon, after nine hours on the road. A good many vehicles did not make it that far, and only seven of the original thirteen tanks were left.

Sharon intended his advance guard to knock over the first two Egyptian defensive positions, Kuntilla and Themed, and then to bypass the larger Egyptian base at Nakhl. When the advance guard reached the drop zone, the main body of the column would take Nakhl and then follow the vanguard to the drop zone. The reunited 202nd would then establish a defensive position east of Mitla and wait to see what Dayan and the Egyptians did next. Because he had pared down his brigade at the very start and would have to drop off two companies to hold Nakhl and Themed, Sharon's brigade would not be at full strength at Mitla. The main goal, however, was to barrel through to the drop zone in twenty-four hours.

The first objective, Kuntilla, was a tiny mud village on a mesa protected by two stone watchtowers similar to the Teggart fortresses built in Palestine. Rushing in with the sun at their backs, the Israelis knocked out the towers and seized the town. The wild charge lasted only a few minutes. The Egyptians had already fled. When Sharon turned around to find the rest of his column, the road was empty. By then fifty vehicles were stuck in the sand, including all the advance guard's artillery. The rest of the column was blocked behind them. If he had not decided at the last minute to take the bulldozer, the brigade might have remained stuck tight in the desert for days. Uncertain of what was going on behind him, Sharon decided to start rolling again, in hopes that the column would catch up before he needed it. At the last minute, a gasoline truck arrived at Kuntilla, removing temporarily one more worry. There would be enough fuel to get him to Themed, hopefully before it could be reinforced. Sharon moved out again.

At 3:45 Tuesday morning, the advance guard hit Themed. There had been more attrition along the way. There were only four tanks left, and one promptly turned over before the attack could be organized. Sharon again intended to use his vehicles as if they were cavalry, driving through the Egyptian positions without pausing to mop up. The key to the defense was to the west, where the brigade would have to drive through a notch in the cliffside. Sharon decided to create smoke and stir up dust and then to rush straight up the road on the assumption that it was unmined. If one vehicle were hit on the narrow road, then the entire column would be blocked, but, unless the column attacked, it would definitely be blocked, and Sharon wanted to keep up his momentum. At dawn, with the sun behind it, the armor deployed, fired, dropped a smoke screen, reconcentrated, and suddenly drove up and over the cliff road. As soon as their perimeter was breached, the Egyptians ran, leaving fifty dead and eleven wounded. Sharon lost four killed and six wounded. Themed had fallen, but the brigade was running behind the time schedule. The advance guard was exhausted, and the rest of the brigade was strung out for ten or twelve miles.

Despite the fact that he had been on his feet for fifty-two hours and that his men were nodding, Sharon wanted to push on the forty or so miles to Nakhl. The quicker his group arrived there, the less resistance there would be. Then six Egyptian MIGs swung in low over the horizon and made three passes at the brigade. Sharon decided to wait; the strike had sapped his troops' last reserves of energy. The move to Nakhl would have to be postoned until the main body of the brigade caught up with the vanguard, in about three hours. A second air strike, by four Egyptian Vampires, reinforced his decision to wait. Then the paratroop battalion at Mitla reported that the Egyptians had shelled its perimeter and that Egyptian aircraft had attacked twice. Their second piece of intelligence was more ominous: A large column of Egyptian troops was moving east from Suez toward Mitla Pass. Time had almost run out, and Sharon gave the order to move on with the force on hand. He called for an air strike to substitute for his missing artillery. The pared-down forces rolled out of Themed at 12:45 P.M.

By 4:30 Sharon was within 1,500 yards of Nakhl, but still nothing went right. The Israeli planes could not find the village to soften it up. Sharon had to ask the circling planes to try to hit the Egyptian column reported moving toward the paratroopers. Then, suddenly, one of his long-lost artillery batteries straggled up. As it was opening fire on the village, another battery showed up and joined the barrage. The advance guard drove into the Egyptian position with another cavalry charge. The Egyptians broke and ran. Sharon's column, spread out for ten miles, had created a dust cloud thirty-five miles long. The sight of thirty-five miles of Israeli armor moving down on them had produced galloping panic among the Egyptians. Sharon took Nakhl without losing a man. The road to the paratroopers was open.

Sharon was only three hours' driving time from the drop zone, but every mile he had so far covered had made the brigade that much more vulnerable to the Egyptian armor in the north. The nearest Israeli armor was Uri Ben-Ari's 7th Armored Brigade at Kusseima, which was not only a long way back, close to the border, but was also no help in blocking the Egyptian tanks supposedly stationed around Bir Gafgafa and Bir Hama to the north. There was not much that Sharon could do about Egyptian armor but worry. He detailed two more rifle companies to defend Nakhl, and the brigade, or what was left of it, pushed off at 7:30. Ninety minutes later at Mitla the paratroops sighted the lights of Sharon's column creeping toward them across the desert. Two-thirds of the brigade's vehicles were scattered along the road all the way back across the border. When Sharon drove up to the perimeter at 10:30 P.M., he commanded little more than his own leading party.

At the temporary entrance to the all-around defense was a newly painted sign:

Stop!
International Boundary!
Show Your Passports!

Sharon called a conference of his commanders. As he prepared to speak, he glanced at the officers sitting in front of him. They were all asleep. Instead of complaining, he too collapsed into a heavy sleep. At dawn he was awakened when a 600-pound bundle crunched to earth three feet from his head. The Israeli air force was dropping supplies. The conference was resumed. He learned the details of the two Egyptian air attacks on Tuesday morning. After the attacks, fifteen Egyptian vehicles had come through the Mitla Pass and stopped two miles from the fork in the road. The Egyptians had set up mortars, but before they could do any damage Israeli Ouragan jets had hit the concentration. The Egyptians pulled back. The paratroopers had then had little more to do than wait for the rest of the 202nd to appear.

By Tuesday night the Israelis anticipated some reaction to their operations. The Egyptians knew of the airdrop and the wild dash across Sinai by the rest of the 202nd Brigade. Closer to the international border, the Israelis had taken Ras en-Nakdeb to prepare for the descent on Sharm-el-Sheikh, and farther north Kusseima had fallen, thus opening the route to the central axis. The early operations had clearly come as a surprise. Jordan was still moving additional troops into defensive positions along the border. The Iraqi buildup on the Jordan border had reached division strength. The Egyptians were quick to respond and had alerted all army, navy, and air-force units as soon as it was clear that there was deep Israeli penetration. The

Egyptian army in Sinai had been ordered to concentrate and maintain its vigilance. Cairo ordered the 1st Brigade to move to El 'Arîsh as reinforcements and sent the 2nd Brigade toward the drop zone at Mitla. The 1st Armored Brigade team moved into Sinai along the central axis. Then on Tuesday evening came the Anglo-French ultimatum to Egypt and Israel. Obviously Nasser and Abdel Hakim Amer would have other problems as well.

One unexpected Israeli problem arose when it was learned that the anticipated Anglo-French attacks on the Egyptian airdromes would be delayed. The 202nd at Mitla would thus be most vulnerable, for the brigades moving along the central axis had passed the point of no return and needed air support even more. Ben-Gurion wanted to evacuate Mitla, but Dayan persuaded him that the risk was not as great as it appeared on paper. They did agree that the 202nd should stay where it was, dug in and alert, until the time for the move south toward Sharm-el-Sheikh. At 4:30 Wednesday morning, a battalion of the 202nd, under Major Mordechai Gur, was already moving at top speed a mile down the road toward the pass, keeping up the momentum. Gur received a one-word order from the high command, through Sharon: "Stop." No sooner had the battalion pulled up than four Egyptian Vampire jets appeared, but before they could hit the brigade two Israeli Meteors hopped them. Two Vampires were shot down overhead, and a third crashed and burned on the way back to Suez. Sharon found his position too small and too open. He wanted to move closer to the pass. He was granted permission, as long as he did not become involved in any big battles. For Dayan Mitla had become a sideshow.

The 202nd did not want to be in a sideshow. Sharon wangled permission to send a reconnaissance column into Mitla Pass. The "reconnaissance column" was beefed up with a third rifle company, three tanks, and a battery of heavy mortars; it was really a strong combat team, under Major Gur. Almost as soon as the point, under Lieutenant Arieh Crespi, entered the pass, the Israeli vehicles came under fire. Gur, in the third vehicle about 300 yards behind Crespi, ordered him to keep going. All during the previous day, daring had paid off with luck. This time it did not. Crespi's half-track was knocked out, and so was the next one in line. Gur's AMX light tank stalled in front of a wreck. His crew was forced to dash for cover in some nearby rifle pits. The rest of the column suddenly rushed past into the pass, leaving Gur in a gully. The greatly sought fluidity of action had degenerated into confused dashing all over the pass. The column was split and communications broken; two half-tracks were knocked out and their crews trapped; Crespi was dead. Gur had driven straight into a trap set by the 5th and 6th Battalions of the Egyptian 2nd Brigade. The 202nd's last cavalry charge had ended in an ambush.

But Gur re-established communications, collected his column, knocked out the Egyptian half-track pinning down the trapped Israelis, and began shelling the clifftops with the AMX's gun. The situation began to look up. Although his men could not clear the sides of the defile because of heavy Egyptian fire, Gur believed that his column was in a position to stick it out or to withdraw. Sharon, back at brigade headquarters, knew almost nothing of Gur's problems. Finally the 2nd Battalion, under Lieutenant Colonel Aaron David, moved on foot up the side of the defile along the clifftop until it saw Gur's column. David flashed word to Sharon that Gur's transport was wrecked and scattered for three miles along the pass, with the Egyptians dug in on both cliff walls. David tried to move down on the Egyptians from above, but the latter resisted stubbornly. Sharon held up further operations until dark; then the 2nd Battalion moved along the clifftop from west to east, while two companies moved along the road and attacked uphill. The Egyptians held on, and their positions had to be taken one at a time. It took two hours to clear out the Egyptians. The whole "reconnaissance" had cost the brigade 34 men killed and 102 wounded.[4] Dayan, understandably, was more than annoyed:

This bloody capture of the Heitan defile at Mitla might have been justified if the task of the brigade was to reach Suez and was prevented from doing so by the Egyptian force entrenched against her. But in the present circumstances, when our aim is to proceed southwards to capture Sharm el-Sheikh and not to get any nearer to Suez, there was no vital need to attack the Egyptian unit defending the approaches to the Canal. The valour, daring and fighting spirit of the paratroop commanders are qualities which should be applauded and encouraged, but this battle was not essential. Moreover, after capturing the Pass, the paratroopers continued to base themselves near the Parker Memorial. The Pass was therefore attacked, captured and abandoned.[5]

After the Mitla battle, the 202nd sat back to wait, as ordered, for the time to move south. The fighting along the southern axis was over.

Dayan had much the same kind of problem on the central axis. On Tuesday, October 30, D-Day plus 1, Colonel Josef Harpaz's 4th Infantry Brigade had moved into Sinai as scheduled and had captured Kusseima—but not fast enough to suit the southern-front commander or the commander of the 7th Armored Brigade. Both believed that an additional twenty-four hour delay, as prescribed in Dayan's staged operational plan, was foolish. On their own hook they sent the 7th Armored on its next stage a full day early. As a heritage from the Haganah ethos, Israeli commanders assume an operational independence that in more orthodox armies would lead directly to courts-martial. Often the results excuse the original disobedience; occasionally, as at Mitla, they do not. Dayan flew into southern headquarters to see what could be done. As the former commander of a jeep-commando unit in the Lydda-Er Ramle operation, he was intimate with the value of independent action, but the commitment of heavy armor and consequent risk of Egyptian air attack were a gamble that he would have preferred not to take. It had, however, been taken for him. The 7th Armored was already grinding toward the Egyptian defensive positions at Umm Gataf in a great cloud of dust. Dayan let it alone.

The immediate objectives of the brigades operating on the central axis were the Egyptian positions around Abu Agueila, three heavily fortified sand ridges east of the village. To the north was a great sand sea, and on the south and west were barren mountains cut only by the narrow and easily defended Dyka Pass. Decision on the final method of attack had been postponed even after Harpaz's brigade had moved into Egyptian territory. Dayan had suggested several lines of approach, but success in the operations would rest on the initiative of the local commanders, as they responded to battle conditions. Defeat of the fortified hedgehogs at Abu Agueila would open up the central axis and produce a new line into Mitla. The solution appeared on the first day. Ben-Ari took a task force from the 7th Armor to within 800 yards of the first hedgehog at Umm Gataf. All the approaches were flat and open, and Ben-Ari had permission to push the attack with his full brigade only if he did not risk mauling his armor. He gave up hope of barreling through to Abu Agueila and pulled back.

A second reconnaissance team, sent to check out the Dyka Pass, had better luck. When the Israelis arrived at the southern end of the defile, Egyptian sappers blew the bridge and took off north on camels. The Israelis followed, struggling across the blown bridge and across two ditchblocks. There were no Egyptians defending the defile, and the Israelis came out on the road in back of the hedgehogs. Ben-Ari immediately requested permission to move the entire 7th Armored through Dyka Pass to the rear of the Egyptians. One combat team would plow over the miserable road in the pass and move out directly down the highway to Bir Hasne on a desert road leading southwest to Mitla. An armor combat team, including a battalion of Sherman tanks commanded by Lieutenant Colonel Avraham Adan—a small, bubbling man—would move up the pass and attack Abu Agueila, although without the necessary tank reserve. When the village fell, the rest of the brigade would move through the pass, leapfrog Adan, and hit the first hedgehog ridge. Then Bren, with his Shermans, would pass through and attack the middle ridge. From the east the 10th Brigade and the 37th Armored would hit Umm Gataf breaking the hold on access to the central axis. Dayan gave his permission, and Ben-Avi's armor moved through the pass and began probing toward Bir Hassna and Jebel Livni.

At dawn on October 31 Adan's combat team reached the Ismailia-Abu Agueila road. Without waiting to make a battle plan, Adan took his armor straight down the road toward the village. As he roared ahead, he could see the Egyptian vehicles in Abu Agueila turning around, trying to return to the crossroads to the east so that they could retreat north to El 'Arîsh. By the time Adan's lead vehicles were within 200 yards of the nearest house, the Egyptian artillery fire from the nearest fortified ridge, the Ruafa Dam, was raining down all around the column. Ahead, Egyptians were opening up with bazookas from the village. One Sherman took a direct hit and spun out. The attack slowed down. Adan, replacing a reluctant commander with his own operations officer, Lieutenant Abramovitch, ordered a sweep behind the Egyptian position. While Abramovitch successfully carried out the attack, Adan's two platoons charged into the village; they had secured the position by 7:00 in the morning.

The Egyptian artillery kept up a heavy fire on the village and the exposed column. Adan took his men down to the crossroads and set up a defensive perimeter, protected on the northeast by the sand dunes and shielded from the road by four sand hills. There his combat team could block the road and wait for the Shermans to come up. Then Adan received word that there would be no second task force to leapfrog his men and no Shermans. Ben-Ari had switched the second force to the west and was holding the Shermans as a reserve at the north end of the pass. Adan was to sit tight. The Egyptians began disorganized counterattacks directly into Israeli guns. In the first hours forty-one Egyptian vehicles were knocked out, but others kept coming. Finally, some heavy Egyptian armor showed up. Fifteen Russian-made T-34 tanks rolled in on the El 'Arîsh road from the north and parked 2,000 yards away. From the east ten tank destroyers and several weapons carriers moved into range. Adan did not regard himself as trapped, for he had fourteen good tanks and an excellent defensive position, but he was unhappy that he could not have the Shermans up to take advantage of the situation. All afternoon the tanks to the north and the armor to the east kept up a sporadic fire. The Egyptian batteries on the sand ridge joined in. Conserving ammunition for the attack on the ridge, Adan did not reply. He had received word that his Shermans would be released for the attack at sunset. He would wait until then; in any case, the Egyptians showed no inclination to attack, using their armor only as artillery.

Adan's attack began with an artillery barrage on the T-34s on the El 'Arîsh road. The T-34s milled around, then pulled back. Egyptian fire from the ridge slackened. Adan used the pause to move his troops into position. The lull ended as soon as the Egyptians realized that the Israelis were about to attack. Israeli artillery switched from the T-34s to the Egyptian artillery on the ridge. The T-34s sneaked forward a little and opened fire again. But the Israeli tanks at the crossroads opened up on the T-34s, driving them north again. By that time it was dark, and the Shermans finally started out, without clear landmarks. The tanks passed the first strong point but turned too soon and headed directly toward the ridge, instead of moving behind it as

Adan had planned. The Sherman commander was soon calling for infantry support. He had lost seven tanks. The armored infantry, still jumpy about the T-34s behind it, moved up to support the battered Shermans. Then Adan sent in the tanks from the crossroads. From then on the confusion increased rapidly.

The Shermans finally reached the ridge and began knocking out the Egyptian artillery positions. The Egyptians loaded up in half-tracks and retreated north just as the Israeli armored infantry moved toward them along the slopes. The second wave of Israeli tanks arrived. The lead units milled around on top of the burning Egyptian positions, successful but totally disorganized. Unable to straighten out the confused units on the captured ridge, Adan finally called them all back to the road. At 11:00 p.m. Adan had almost no ammunition or gasoline left, nine of his tanks were scattered derelicts on the ridge, and his men were close to exhaustion. Apparently the Egyptians were just as exhausted for there was no immediate counterattack. At 2:00 in the morning, an Israeli supply column arrived, solving some of Adan's problems. One tank company moved up the El 'Arîsh road looking for the T-34s. The armored infantry cleaned out the Egyptians who had filtered back onto the ridge. By then, however, any opportunity for further action had been lost because of the failure of the Israeli attack from the east. Adan dug in and waited, salvaging and repairing his Shermans.

On the other side of the hedghogs, Dayan had lost patience with the commanders of the 10th Brigade and the 37th Armored. Once the Dyka Pass had opened up, Dayan had wanted the hedgehogs cleared out. Ben-Ari's armor, operating in central Sinai, had only the inadequate Kusseima-Dyka supply line. Dayan pressured the commanders to hurry, insisting that the hedgehog had to be eliminated. On the night of October 31 the attempt was made. The 10th Brigade had already attempted a hesitant daylight attack on Umm Gataf. At night the two-pronged attack got lost and wandered about. One team failed to find its objective; the other did not push its attack. At 4:00 in the morning, November 1, the 37th Armored tried to drive directly into the Egyptian position, with headlights blazing and without waiting for support tanks. The brigade was mauled and had to pull back. Umm Gataf remained in Egyptian hands, blocking the central axis. Dayan thought that the whole affair had been bungled:

I gave the order to attack Um Katef at the earliest possible moment. On the face of it, the order was carried out. But Um Katef was not captured. Southern Command had all the force necessary to undertake this engagement successfully—infantry, armour, artillery and so on. But the required military action was not executed. The attack did not follow a sound operational plan which would give full battle expression to the entire strength allocated for this operation.[6]

But by the time things were sorted out on November 1, the hedgehog position was becoming less vital.

While the fighting continued at Abu Agueila and Umm Gataf, Ben-Ari's armor had been moving through central Sinai, opening up the central axis. On Tuesday morning, October 30, one task force captured Bir Hassna; but Ben-Ari's major preoccupation was the location of the Egyptian 1st Armored Brigade team, supposedly moving eastward from Bir Hama on the Ismailia-Abu Agueila highway. Ben-Ari spent most of the day arranging an ambush before he learned that he need not have bothered. The Israeli air force had found the Egyptian column at Bir Gafgafa and had chopped it up. Hit again and again, the 1st Armored had lost its cohesion. During the afternoon the Israelis moved through Bir Hama, the major Egyptian air base in Sinai, without meeting any resistance and set up camp ten miles west. The major problem, the one worrying Dayan most, was the tenuous supply line through the Dyka Pass. At dawn on Wednesday, October 31, the task force moved westward, hitting the rear guard of the retreating Egyptians, capturing eight T-34s, and destroying three others. Finally, as feared, Ben-Ari ran out of gasoline. His armor had to sit on the highway five hours, until midnight, when a supply truck arrived.

The Egyptians were in no position to take advantage of the stalled Israeli column. The hedgehog had become a pocket. The mobile armor of the 1st Armored Brigade had been cut up by the Israeli air force. And to the north, early on the morning of November 1, the attack against Rafah had begun. At dawn on Thursday, Ben-Ari learned that Egyptian armor was moving south from Bir Gafgafa, down the Wadi el Hegayib toward Mitla. Ben-Ari moved his own armor through Bir Hassna to the southern exit of the wadi, in order to meet the Egyptians. Once again Ben-Ari was frustrated. The Egyptians decided to call off the foray down the wadi. Ben-Ari moved his Shermans up the wadi and at the same time moved more armor west on the Ismailia highway, in order to cut off the Egyptian tanks at Bir Gafgafa the next day. When Ben-Ari's thirty-five Shermans and AMXs moved in on Bir Gafgafa at dawn on November 2, the Israelis found that the Egyptians were already running for Suez sixty miles away. Nasser had ordered a general withdrawal from Sinai. Within an hour, the lead AMXs made contact with the Egyptian rear guard. For the next fifty miles, Ben-Ari's point fought a high-speed, hit-and-run battle, trying to gobble up the tail end of the Egyptian column. Finally, short of the canal, Ben-Ari stopped his armor.

Back at the hedgehogs, the Egyptians had decided to pull out. Although the ridge to the west had been lost to Adan's task force, the Egyptians had repelled the Israeli attacks from the east and appeared capable of continuing their defense for some time. A growing problem had been water, normally trucked into Abu Agueila. On Thursday night, November 1, the Egyptian commander told his troops that it was every man for himself. Although their position was pressed on three sides by the Israelis, he suggested that they slip out of the hedgehog on the north and make their way across the sand sea to El 'Arish fifty-two miles away. It was an insane plan. The fifty-two miles of sand were impassable to any man but a mounted Bedouin. Each step in loose sand is exhausting. Even a brief distance at night with sufficient water is a dangerous undertaking. A fifty-two-mile march, much of the time in the blazing sun with limited water, was a slow and peculiarly painful method of suicide. Few of the Egyptian soldiers knew anything about the desert. But they slipped out and began plodding north.

At dawn tanks of the 37th Armored probed the hedgehog and found no one. Enthusiastically they raced ahead over the last ridge directly on top of the startled 7th Armored. At 1,100 yards the 7th Brigade's tanks opened up on the 37th Brigade and knocked out eight tanks in five minutes before the error was discovered. Then, too late, Israelis on both sides of the hedgehog realized that the Egyptians had pulled out. Israeli light planes followed the Egyptian tracks into the sand sea. The air observers watched the final escape into death from box seats, unable to help the Egyptians. No airplane could land on the sand. No vehicle could move on its surface. By the time that the first Israeli Piper Cubs were circling above, the Egyptians had long passed the point of no return. They staggered forward, stumbling and falling. Some did not rise again, but others kept on. At the edge of the slowly dying column Bedouins moved, stealing from the dead and killing the stragglers for loot. By nightfall all but a few of the Egyptians were dead of thirst or heat exhaustion. Of the 2,500 to 3,000 Egyptians defending the hedgehog, only 700 were captured. The desert claimed the rest. It was a brutal end to operations on the central axis.

The front commander in the North, Brigadier-General Chaim Laskov, had been given responsibility for the most orthodox part of Operation Kadesh, the attack on Rafa. Actually the battle developed as a frontal assault on the maze of fortified hills south of Rafa protecting the Egyptian army camps. On the south the position was protected by the desert and several heavy mine fields. To the north were the sea and additional positions in the Gaza strip. The hills, low-lying mounds covered with orchards, hedges, and cacti, dominated the landscape. Each of the eighteen hills had been fortified; artillery and machine guns had been placed with supporting lines of fire and protection by wire and mines. The Egyptians had scattered in the strongest positions Archer antitank destroyers, 24-pounders, and new Czech 105-millimeter short-barrel recoilless guns. The positions were manned by the 5th Infantry Brigade, reinforced by two additional battalions. Almost from the opening of Kadesh, the Egyptians had assumed that the Israelis would attack the Rafa complex, so there was no real possibility for surprise, mobility, or daring, the strongest points of Israeli planning.

Laskov had the 27th Armored Brigade and the 1st Infantry Brigade for his attack, with the 11th Brigade held back to clear the Gaza strip. Although his attack force would be less than convention required, his greatest lack was sufficient artillery support, a deficit for which he hoped to compensate with air and naval support. The only novelty would be to stage the infantry forward into the area, infiltrating rather than charging. Once the battle began, the result would be a whole series of independent attacks on each of the hills. Laskov hoped to have the whole area cleared soon after dawn, so that his armor could take off down the El 'Arîsh road. To the north Colonel Haim Barlev's 27th Brigade would clear the two hills southeast of Rafa, numbered 34 and 36. Barlev hoped to hold much of his armor in reserve for the dash down the coast. In the center two battalions of Colonel Benjamin Givli's 1st Brigade were to move on Hills 25 and 25a and then on to those closer to the El 'Arîsh road. The most difficult task was that of the final two battalions of 1st Brigade: to penetrate the mine field, capture Hill 5 in the rear, and then turn north behind the Egyptian positions to assault the three hills dominating the crossroads on the far western perimeter. The lead battalion would remain there until Barlev moved in from the north. Then Barlev's reserve, one company of low-hulled AMX tanks and one of half-track infantry, could start the drive for El 'Arîsh. The first moves would be made in the south, to penetrate the mine field, followed by the air-sea bombardment and then the general attacks.

On Tuesday night, October 30, engineers from Givli's brigade cut three gaps, each nine yards wide, through the two Egyptian mine fields. By nightfall the next day, the lead battalion had been secretly moved forward. The lead companies followed the paths through the mine field with little trouble. Even the final company, on half-tracks, had no problems. The Egyptians, using searchlights to illuminate the whole sector south of Rafa, did not open up with artillery while the Israelis were in the corridor. Nevertheless, once the Israelis were past the danger point, their attack did not go well; the infantry bumbled about looking for particular objectives. Finally, the objectives were reported captured without resistance. The only losses had been two killed and eight wounded by Egyptian artillery before the mine field had been crossed. The next stage (under the direction of Lieutenant Colonel Meir Pilavski), was the leapfrog attack by a beefed-up infantry battalion, which had the support of twelve Super-Shermans.

At 11:30 P.M. Pilavski received permission to move. At the same time the Egyptian searchlights found the gaps in the mine field. Pilavski took off as soon as the alternating six-minute Egyptian artillery bombardment slackened around midnight. But the Egyptians opened up again, hitting the second half-track, which spun onto a mine and exploded. The next vehicle swerved to avoid the smashed half-track and hit another mine. Egyptian artillery fire continued to fall around the stretched-out column. To find a way around the burning half-tracks, Pilavski's men had to prod the ground for forty minutes while the Egyptian fire continued. Fortunately for the Israelis, the Egyptians were using high-explosive rounds and the bursts were largely confined by the sand. When the route had been checked out, one company of half-tracks swung around the block and on through the field. Two Shermans followed but moved so cautiously that thirty more minutes were lost. The third Sherman exploded another mine as it crept past the block. The fourth Sherman swung out to avoid the flaming wreck and ran over still another mine. Behind it a command car burst into flames. The original two-vehicle block had become a mass of burning hulks stretching thirty feet wide and fifty feet deep. Pilavski's column, cut in two by the flames, began to attract heavy Egyptian artillery fire. Instead of barreling through to the crossroads, sirens blowing and lights ablaze, Pilavski realized that he might not be able to make it there at all.

Pilavski asked Givli to help him out or to let him pull back. Givli insisted that the attack must go on. The battle had begun, all units were engaged, and the end sweep was vital. Givli suggested, not too helpfully, that Pilavski could always walk. Somehow Pilavski did not think that an eight-mile hike through soft sand would do the brigade much good. Instead, he began to extract his column. Moving to the right of the block, his pioneer troops probed a narrow track through the mine field. Pilavski's half-track was the first one through, right on the pioneers' heels, but the Egyptian artillery hit fifteen men during the first passage. It was almost dawn when the last tank rolled slowly through the narrow gap. Then the rifle platoons, dug in to wait for the armor, had to be loaded. But, after the agony of lying in the sand listening to the Egyptian artillery for hours, morale soared. In twenty minutes Hill 5 was overrun. Pilavski jettisoned any hope of a neat, staggered assault on the crossroads and decided to bull through at top speed.

Moving at high speed toward Hills 8 and 10 south of the crossroads, Pilavski decided to hit Hill 10 with both his Shermans and half-tracks. At the last minute he noticed that fire from Hill 8 seemed weaker. On the spot he switched his half-tracks and jeeps to Hill 8. The Egyptians pulled out. On Hill 10 the Egyptians did not even wait for the Shermans. Pilavski then drove straight across the El 'Arish highway in a three-pronged attack on Hill 12. He lost one tank to a mine. The Egyptians lost thirty killed, twenty-eight wounded, forty taken prisoner, and the hill itself. At 9:00 in the morning, Pilavski reported the capture of the hills and crossroads. It was a case of first to start and last to finish.

The rest of the attack force had also had its problems. The long-anticipated naval bombardment proved less than effective. The air support to soften up the Egyptians was worse. The planes flew in, dropped flares directly over the Israeli forces, and proceeded to follow up the flares with bombs. The planes were called off. All the air-naval support had produced was a long delay. Givli's 1st Brigade soon discovered that one hill looked like another in the dark. The infantry blundered about looking for targets. One company finally identified its objective, Hill 29, only because the Egyptians intensified their fire at the last moment. The most dangerous blunder was when a Nahal company broke through into the perimeter of Hill 25 at the same time that another company attacked the hill from a different side. The two companies then joined to take Hill 25. Barlev's 27th Brigade had even more serious problems. Just as the attack moved off, two companies of mobile infantry were hit by a precision artillery barrage. Within a few minutes they lost eleven killed and eighty-eight wounded. The attack stalled.

Barlev decided to hold onto his AMXs a little longer. He sent six Shermans on a right hook to the rear of Hills 34 and 36. If the hills fell, the Shermans could move on to the Egyptian rear to help out Givli's infantry. At that point things began to go better. The two infantry companies, supposedly in a bad way in front of Hills 34 and 36, had regrouped. Captain Ben Eli decided to go ahead with his fifty-nine survivors. As the Shermans and half-track infantry came up, the other company joined Eli's attack on Hill 36. When the first Israelis were just inside the perimeter, two Israeli jets appeared and hit the hilltop with napalm and rockets. One jet came in so low that its own rocket explosions destroyed it, although the pilot parachuted to safety. Seconds after the air strike Eli overran the hill. The Shermans swerved to attack Hill 34 and were suddenly joined by the AMXs. Barlev had decided to go in with all his armor. Unless Rafa could be cleared, there could be no dash to El 'Arîsh. The two armor teams hit the hill together. The infantry hopped out of the AMXs and mopped

up. By 6:30 A.M. Hill 34 had fallen. Barlev switched his armor to help
out Givli's infantry. Moving up with the advancing infantry, the
AMXs joined the assault as it developed.

Within twenty minutes the attack force had overrun the last major
Egyptian hill position. By 7:30 the Rafa complex was an occupied
shambles. The armor began moving through the fleeing Egyptians to
link up with Pilavski at the crossroads. Right along with it went Chief
of Staff Dayan, who had been overseeing the battle at close range. His
presence must have had some inhibiting effects on the battle commanders as he watched over their shoulders all night. At 9:30 the first
AMXs reached the crossroads below Hill 12. There was a great
reunion scene, and the battle for Rafa was over.

Barlev, with Dayan still tagging along, could then turn his attention to the next stage, the drive to El 'Arîsh and on along the coast to
the Suez Canal. All morning the AMXs and Pilavski's Super-Shermans moved down the highway. At the first Egyptian defensive position, Sheikh-Zuwedi, the Israelis found that the posted battalion had
already withdrawn. At about noon on November 1 Cairo had sent
out a general withdrawal order, excluding Gaza and the garrison at
Sharm-el-Sheikh. The terms were vague and open, apparently, to
broad local interpretation. The result, as should have been expected,
was chaos. Units took off without warning, without reference to the
existing tactical situation, without waiting to inform anyone. If a
general evacuation order had gone out much earlier, immediately
after the Anglo-French ultimatum, there would have been a far better
chance to withdraw in an orderly fashion, maintaining cohesion for a
defense against the anticipated landing. By November 1, however,
with little hope of air support, the disorganized columns were extremely vulnerable to air strikes and armored pursuit. It was a case of
being ordered to run when sitting was called for and to sit when
running was preferable. By dawn on November 1 Cairo should have
been aware that disaster loomed in Sinai and that wholesale flight
would be no solution but only an invitation to slaughter and shame.
By evening the Sinai defense had turned into a shambles, for once
withdrawal began the army had turned into a mob.

When the Israelis reached the next defensive position at El-Jerardi,
an Egyptian company with artillery and antitank support opened up
on them. The leading AMX tanks knocked out four antitank guns

and then ran out of ammunition. Barlev sent in his Shermans, and the Egyptian artillery knocked out two of them. With no ammunition and very little fuel, the AMXs made one last tentative pass at El-Jerardi. But the Egyptians decided that they had done enough and rolled out down the highway. Barlev left the AMXs and pushed on with the remaining Shermans. As he drew closer to El 'Arîsh Barlev had to keep the Shermans on the road because of the high sand dunes on both sides. With Egyptian artillery fire hitting the road, the Shermans tried plowing through the sand in second gear. About four miles from El 'Arîsh, the Israelis pulled up for the night. All evening Israeli forces continued backing up behind the Shermans. The AMXs arrived, as did nine more Shermans, a battery of 25-pounders, and a mobile infantry battalion. At midnight the tanks moved up a mile or so. At dawn the Egyptians opened an artillery barrage that lasted just three minutes. An Israeli air strike burned out the batteries with a napalm attack. At 6:00 the column entered El 'Arîsh.

Even before Barlev's armor reached El 'Arîsh, an Israeli scout plane had reported a long column of Egyptian vehicles fleeing westward. Barlev asked for an air strike on the column and moved his armor through the city. One combat team occupied the city and its airport. The rest of the armor moved out along the road to Suez. After ten miles, it was halted, not by Egyptian resistance but by the rich windfall of vehicles abandoned by Egyptian troops when the Israeli jets strafed the fleeing column. They began drifting back from the dunes to the road just as the 27th Brigade arrived, thousands of them, walking right into the bag. Even more impressive, within a few minutes Barlev had captured 385 vehicles, including 40 Russian T-34 tanks. The 27th Brigade had more Egyptian armor and more prisoners than it knew what to do with. Barlev used his Shermans to move the prisoners back to El 'Arîsh. The AMXs continued the blitz down the coastal road. At 5:00 on Thursday afternoon, the advance guard passed through Rumani, twenty miles east of the Canal. In twelve hours Barlev's point had covered eighty miles and had reached a point within sight of the Suez Canal, at approximately the same moment as did Ben-Ari's tanks on the central axis.

Behind the column of AMXs the major Egyptian force in Sinai surrendered or swarmed uncaptured in the desert. The roadsides were littered with Egyptian equipment, from heavy tanks to boots. In El

'Arîsh the situation was incredible. Egyptians wandered about looking for captors and dinner. Egyptian trucks and half-tracks sat on the
roads, in some cases with motors still running. The Egyptians had
pulled out so quickly that men were left untended on operating
tables. In El 'Arîsh alone there were twenty-seven Shermans and
three T-34s that had been left behind in the flight. Some Egyptians
did not even realize what had happened. At one point a jeep load of
Egyptian officers arrived at an Israeli fueling station, asking for gas in
order to retreat.

Once the complex at Rafa was broken open, the Egyptian forces to
the north in the Gaza strip were in a hopeless position. During the
first days of the fighting, Colonel Aaron Doron's 11th Brigade had sat
on the border, rounding up the increasingly active fedayeen, who
were more interested in getting out of Gaza than in raiding Israel.
Finally, at midnight on November 1 Doron received orders to move
into the strip the next morning, Friday. Doron did not anticipate a
long campaign. The Egyptians knew that Rafa had fallen. To his
surprise, the first two hill positions outside Gaza resisted, but, after
Israeli bombardment and an infantry attack, the Egyptians pulled
back into Gaza. Doron's armor enthusiastically followed on the heels
of the retreating Egyptians. Although he managed to hold up the
infantry trucks, the armor and half-tracks, scenting instant victory,
tore into the main square of Gaza and circled. Within minutes the
armor had created a massive traffic jam. Nothing moved. For several
hours the brigade's armor was stuck tight in the middle of Egyptian-
occupied Gaza. The Egyptian tanks moved around on the outskirts
of the square, often within sight of the Israelis but not anxious to start
a fight. The Egyptian commander, Brigadier General Mahmed Fuad
e-Dagawi could not decide whether to fight or to surrender. The first
would be pointless and the second humiliating.

Eventually Lieutenant Colonel R. S. Baynard of the United States
Army, the only member of the Mixed Armistice Commission remaining in the Gaza strip, persuaded Dagawi to capitulate. At 1:30 P.M.
the white flag went up. Doron did not hear about it until an hour
later. He had spent the morning extricating his armor from the square
and concentrating it near the north-south highway. He eventually
accepted the surrender. An Israeli police force under a military
governor showed up and moved into the city. By that time many

Egyptian soldiers had discarded their uniforms and become "civilians." As at El 'Arîsh, most of the military stores and equipment were untouched, but all the camel dung and fodder had been burned. Although Dagawi had supposedly surrendered the entire strip, the commander of the Palestinian 8th Division, Major General Yussef Abdullah Agrudi, decided, as ordered by Cairo, to hold out at Khan Yunis with Lieutenant Colonel Lutfi el-Burini's 86th Palestinian Brigade "to the very end." Doron had to spend most of the night forcing the position. By 8:30 Agrudi was willing to talk, but he was not too impressed with the Israelis, "a band of robbers," and he was impressed with what his own troops might do if he surrendered. Eventually, however, Doron persuaded him, and Khan Yunis surrendered to the "robbers," although one nearby platoon held on until a Mustang air strike hit it at noon. Doron had lost ten killed and sixty-three wounded in occupying the Gaza strip, which was defended by 7,000 Egyptians. The battle of Fafa had cut the heart out of any Egyptian defense. Itching for a fight, the 11th Brigade had found the most dangerous obstacle in its campaign to be a traffic jam.

The most extraordinary phase of the Sinai campaign was the overland march to the southern tip of the peninsula; in fact, the potential obstacles were so great that Dayan hedged and prepared a second descent down the western side of the peninsula. The overland march was handed to Colonel Avraham Yoffe's 9th Brigade, formed mainly of older reservists. Originally the 9th Brigade had been assigned to follow the 202nd across the southern axis, but forty hours before the 202nd was to move the 9th received orders to move down the peninsula. Colonel Yoffe, a 230-pound bear of a man, was given full authority to determine the brigade's route. To prevent Arab observers in Jordan from noting the direction of his departure, he decided to avoid the main highway from Beersheba to Elath and instead to follow the 202nd as far as Kuntilla. He would then turn south and make for Ras en-Nakeb, the Egyptian frontier post at the head of the Gulf of 'Aqaba. The route would be longer, but the brigade could move into southern Sinai unobserved.

The first stage of the march to Ras en-Nakeb at least was certain, but once the column began moving farther south luck would largely determine the column's fate. The wastelands of the southern Sinai are crossed by no roads and few trails. There is no water and in daytime no shade. It is a land of sharp peaks, impassable ridges, dry washes, sand seas, and boulder-strewn slopes. The few existing maps of the area are based mainly on wishful thinking. On the map were two huge zigzag trails, but Yoffe, unable to tell whether or not they were passable, decided to take a direct route, unmarked by any dotted lines on the map. To a very real extent, Yoffe would be leading an exploring expedition as well as a military force through some of the most beautiful and least hospitable country in the world.

In order to keep to his timetable—three days to make 240 miles— he scaled down the brigade, discarding some transport and his AMXs, as well as the artillery. The final column would have 104 6 × 6 trucks, 32 command cars and weapons carriers, 14 half-tracks, 34 jeeps, and 2 Piper Cubs to tie together the column. Eliminating the noncombatants lowered his brigade strength to 1,701 men: two infantry battalions, one artillery battery, one heavy mortar battalion, a reconnaissance unit, and an antiaircraft troop—almost all spears and no spear carriers. Even pared down, the column would have to stretch out an incredible distance. The advance guard would be twenty miles ahead of the second serial, with the third and fourth serials maintaining intervals of several miles. The miles of road between the four serials would hopefully serve as a cushion when the vehicles stalled, as they inevitably would. Even if the advance guard ran into heavy fire, the column could in time build up behind it. Yoffe was more concerned with breakdowns than with Egyptian roadblocks.

Although the brigade would carry food for five days, water in eighteen tankers, and fuel for 375 miles, Yoffe also had an extra supply margin of sorts. Five LCMs, sea landing craft intended to carry light tanks, had been moved by rail from Haifa early on the morning of October 27. They had arrived in Beersheba safely, although several protruding houses had to be torn down along the route. From Beersheba to Elath they had been moved at night on the huge trucks used to haul phosphates from the Dead Sea works. On October 29 the LCMs were afloat at Elath, creating an Israeli navy in the Gulf of 'Aqaba. Assuming that the 9th did get through to Sharm-el-Sheikh without supply problems, the LCMs would actually land light tanks to support the final attack beside putting a landing party ashore on Tiran Island.

At dawn on Wednesday, October 31, the brigade moved out. The

202nd had already passed through Kuntilla, and a two-company task force of the 9th had taken the Egyptian post at Ras en-Nakeb. The brigade's advance through the two towns would be a "problem march" through the desert, rather than a thrust into enemy territory. Within two hours Yoffe discovered that avoiding the Beersheba-Elath highway had been a mistake. The 202nd had ruined the road to Kuntilla, churning up the surface with armor and forcing the 9th to move even more slowly than marching infantry. It took eighteen long, hard hours of plowing through knee-deep dust to reach Kuntilla. The road from there to Ras en-Nakeb was only slightly better. Even before the 9th reached the starting line, the men were exhausted. Fortunately, at that point Dayan postponed the attack for twenty-four hours. He did not want the column spread out and vulnerable to Egyptian air attack, which could not be discounted until the delay Anglo-French air strikes began. The pause gave the brigade time to recover from the long desert march.

At 4:00 in the morning on Friday, November 2, Dayan called Yoffe on a direct telephone line and ordered the 9th to move out. By noon the brigade had reached Ein-el-Furtaga twelve miles inland from the Gulf of 'Aqaba and one-third of the way from Elath to Sharm-el-Sheikh. The ground was fair, and the temperature hovered around 86 degrees Fahrenheit. All in all, it was an impressive beginning, but soon after Ein-el-Furtaga the way led uphill, and more and more boulders began to appear. The trucks and command cars had to be manhandled over much of the track. Even so, by nightfall the brigade had advanced six more miles, and it kept going painfully during the night. The column struggled along in the dark at three miles an hour until it finally stalled. The advance guard, under the command of Lieutenant Arik Nachamkain, a one-eyed veteran of the 1948 campaign, had been probing for a shortcut. Instead of a short cut, Nachamkain and Yoffe ran into an apparently impassable block.

> . . . We were pointed upward toward a divide at thirty-five hundred feet. Confronting us, blocking us, was a natural phenomenon— a great sand formation which covered both sides of the divide so that the ridge looked snow-capped.
>
> There were no dunes. Save for great ripples, the face of this sea was fairly smooth. How deep the sand was piled, there was no telling. But the field extended eight miles. Loaded as we were, the way was forbidden.[7]

The brigade took ten hours to cross eight miles of sand hicles struggled ahead, using four times the normal rate of fv own words, Yoffe's "brilliant gas calculations have been hell."[8] He radioed for two LCMs to bring gasoline to the coastal village of Dahab, halfway down the Gulf of 'Aqaba, where hopefully he would arrive the next day. Dayan had grown increasingly concerned about the 9th's prospects for making it through. Yoffe, as feared, was dropping behind the optimistic three-day timetable. Unexpectedly, for a time it had appeared that it would not matter, for air-intelligence reports that the Egyptians were evacuating Sharm-el-Sheikh had been received.

Dayan decided to prepare for all eventualities. Two companies of the 202nd paratroopers would be dropped, one at Tor two-thirds of the way down the western coast from Mitla and one at the tip near Sharm-el-Sheikh. While the transports were in the air, fresh intelligence came in that the Egyptians were not evacuating Sharm-el-Sheikh after all and that the paratroop company would be dropping into a trap. A Meteor jet barely headed the transports off and shepherded them back to drop the company at Tor. There an airlift brought in one battalion of the 12th Infantry Brigade. Units of the 202nd began to move south from Milta. On the following day, November 3, the paratroopers were to move toward Sharm-el-Sheikh, although it was doubtful that they could manage the operation alone if the Egyptians proved stubborn. Still, the 9th, stuck in the Sinai sand, no longer would have to carry the whole burden.

While Yoffe was still levering his vehicles over the sand sea, Nachamkain's advance guard drove into Dahab at noon. Unfortunately Nachamkain was too sanguine about the possibility of resistance and drove into an ambush of ten camel-mounted scouts. He lost three killed and six wounded but did wipe out the Egyptian squad. Unfortunately for the 9th, the Egyptians had a radio, and hopes for a surprise attack were no longer too bright. Nachamkain left his wounded behind with a first-aid man and continued south without waiting for the LCMs to arrive. While Yoffe was refueling, the ubiquitous Dayan flew overhead checking out the terrain. It looked lousy for vehicles and fine for ambushes.

Yoffe moved out on another shortcut south of Dahab. This time a mile-long stretch of boulders had to be cleared by the sappers. After five and a half hours the way was opened just before 2:00 Sunday morning, November 4. A half-hour later the point ran into some Egyptians, but it was too dark for the latter to do more than fire at the noise of Yoffe's vehicles. The advance guard splashed some fire around and pulled back. Yoffe decided that his men were too exhausted to fight and ordered the column to rest until dawn. At 3:00 in the morning, Dayan radioed Yoffe that speed was still essential. International repercussions had been far more menacing than anticipated, and Dayan and Ben-Gurion wanted to wind up the operation in a rush. Yoffe assured Dayan that he could finish the business the next day.

At dawn on Sunday, November 4, the 9th found that the Egyptians had given up their ambush. The column rolled on to within sight of Ras Natsrani, the heavily fortified Egyptian base commanding the narrow channel between Tiran Island and the Sinai coast. The fortress, a half-circle of concrete bunkers and trenches protected by wire entanglements and mine fields, contained the emplacements for the naval guns that guarded the strait. The Egyptian commander, Lieutenant Colonel Khana Neguib, when he learned of the progress of the 9th Brigade, faced no unusual tactical problem, for Ras Natsrani was equipped for defense against paratroops or a landing from the sea. The Israelis could be assumed to have armor, which would make defense more difficult, but the main Egyptian problem was insufficient troops. Rather than hold Ras Natsrani, which had superior fortifications, Neguib pulled all his men back to Sharm-el-Sheikh, which had an airstrip and a dock. Yoffe, not pausing to fool with Ras Natsrani, rushed on south toward Sharm-el-Sheikh, on a paved road for the first time.

Yoffe's brigade captured the first position at Tzafrat el-Al with no trouble. Mustangs softened it up, and the Israelis rushed in to find it empty. The Egyptians around the core in Sharm-el–Sheikh opened a heavy fire on the Israelis, whose point pulled back to mull things over. Yoffe decided to go in with a night attack at midnight, without waiting for the air force to soften up the Egyptians. Two charges were made, but the Israelis could not penetrate the mine fields. Egyptian machine-gun fire was heavy, and one Israeli company lost fourteen men. At 4:20 the attack was called off, and the Israelis moved two miles north, out of range, to wait for dawn. At a little after 5:00, mounted in jeeps and half-tracks and supported by mortars and air power, the 9th went in again. By 9:30 all the Egyptian posts had been steamrollered, and Neguib had surrendered. At the same time the paratroop force moving south from Tor had hooked around the tip of Sinai and taken the outlying positions south of Sharm-el-Sheikh. The battle was over.

Yoffe had lost ten killed and thirty-three wounded during the attack; the Egyptians had lost 200 killed and 200 wounded. When questioned about the battle, Lieutenant Colonel Neguib suggested that Yoffe's success had three causes: the Israeli air strikes, the lack of Egyptian artillery, and "point three—my men were no good." The officers had not been too effective either. The area commander had spent the three hours of the battle dressing and watching his batman pack his bags. He wanted to be fully prepared for captivity.

While the fighting continued, Dayan made an effort to catch up with the action. He landed at Tor but found no light plane waiting to fly him down to the paratroops. Dayan and his aide whipped up a make-do column of one command car and a couple of dubious trucks and took off south along the coast road. Dayan climbed up on the back of one of the vehicles to keep his eye on the Egyptian stragglers wandering north as the little convoy rumbled south.

> The whole picture—though it was the middle of the day—had a nightmarish quality. The scorching desert sun blazed without pity. One could see the heat haze rising from the melting surface of the tarred road. The Egyptian troops in khaki fatigues merged with the sandy landscape and only at the last moment did they spring into sight amidst the dunes. There is no doubt that they knew we were Israeli soldiers, but they neither fired at us nor did they seek to hide from us. They simply let us pass by, their faces a study of feebleness and exhaustion. The wounded among them dragged one foot after the other with difficulty, and some who were on the road did not even bother to move aside to let our vehicles pass. We had to move round them.[9]

When Dayan reached Sharm-el-Sheikh, the Sinai war was already over. Nasser's army had become a collection of exhausted men straggling back out of the desert. His T-34s were in Israeli tank parks. His MIGs were burning hulks on shattered airfields. Even one of his destroyers, the *Ibrahim el-Awal*, was docked in Haifa after surrendering at sea. On the following day, November 5, the long awaited Anglo-French invasion to finish off the tottering regime was to begin. The Israelis had a sweeping victory in one week's war. They had also neutralized the Gaza strip and had a military governor in occupation. They had unplugged the Gulf of 'Aqaba—the 9th Brigade had reported the spiked guns at Ras-Natsrani. In seven days Kadesh at a cost of 172 Israelis killed and 817 wounded, had rearranged the Middle East in Israel's favor. Not all had gone smoothly. There had been errors, wasted lives, mistakes in judgment, and narrow escapes, but victory puts a smooth patina over the pockmarks of war. Dayan's assumption that the Egyptian army on all levels still could not make war had been abundantly vindicated. Nasser's splendid new army, the main prop of Arab hopes for eventual military victory over Israel, had proved a feeble reed, splintering under Arab dreams of vengeance. Yet war may be waged with weapons other than tanks, as the Israelis knew too well, and Nasser was still in power in Cairo on November 5, still capable of recouping his prestige by words if not deeds. His voice might yet prove mightier than Dayan's sword.

NOTES

1. Robert Henriques, *100 Hours to Suez* (New York: 1957), pp. 47–8.

2. A minimum of attention has been focused on the loss of this Egyptian aircraft, possibly because of the flurry of subsequent events and also, perhaps, a traditional reluctance on the Israelis' part to discuss intelligence matters. Regardless of the cause of the crash, the loss was one that Egypt could ill afford; although there is no real reason to suppose that the presence of additional senior officers would have made any fundamental difference in Sinai.

3. Merry Bromberger and Serge Bromberger, *Secrets of Suez* (London: 1957), p. 190.

4. As in most wars, casualty figures are only estimates. In the case of the Egyptians, the Israelis kept no real count, and the Egyptians have been silent. Various sources give various figures for Israeli losses. There is even

a difference on one occasion in the figures in the text of Moshe Dayan's *Diary of the Sinai Campaign* (New York: 1966) and in his appendix on casualties.

5. *Ibid.*, pp. 101–2.

6. *Ibid.*, p. 120.

7. S. L. A. Marshall, *Sinai Victory* (New York: 1958), p. 215.

8. *Ibid.*, pp. 216–7.

9. Dayan, *Diary*, pp. 189–90.

14

The Sinai Settlement

Almost from the first the international response to the unfolding Middle Eastern crisis had been far more intense than had been anticipated. On the morning of October 30, as the first stage of the Sinai invasion unfolded in relative secrecy, the initial reaction had been one of shock and surprise. An Israeli attack on Egypt had not been foreseen, particularly in view of the Jordan crisis; in any event, world attention had been focused on the drama of Hungary. In Washington the instant reaction was that, on the eve of a Presidential election and in the midst of an Eastern European breakthrough, the Israelis had chosen a most inopportune time to rock the boat. Elsewhere uncertainty about the scope and purpose of the Israeli attack momentarily delayed violent repercussions outside the Arab bloc. If, as still appeared possible, the venture were only one more retaliatory raid, then the situation, though delicate, would not be dangerous. The Arab states pledged solidarity with Egypt and vilified Israel, but these reactions were to be expected.

Of most immediate concern was the inclusion of the words "Suez Canal" in the first Israeli military communiqué. A Sinai raid was one thing, but a Suez crisis was something else again. Very nasty suspicions began to be noised about concerning Anglo-French collusion.

Then at 4:30 London time on October 30 the true scope of the new crisis became clear. The British and French released their ultimatums to the Egyptians and Israelis, demanding immediate withdrawal—the Israelis to ten miles east and the Egyptians to ten miles west of the canal. To speed things up, the ultimatums had a twelve-hour time limit. Just when many thought that diplomacy would devise a solution to the Suez crisis or at lease postpone a showdown, Britain and France had pushed to the brink of war.

The acknowledged rationale of the ultimatums—to protect the Canal and to prevent a Middle Eastern war—fooled no one. From the scanty information available it was apparent that much of the Egyptian army remained in Sinai east of the Canal and that the ultimatums must have been prepared in anticipation of the Israeli invasion's creation of a casus belli. The apparent hypocrisy of the supposedly disinterested Anglo-French ultimatum to Egypt, the logical assumption of tripartite collusion, and the unexpected return to imperialist gunboat policies all enraged a substantial portion of world opinion, particularly in the new nations, already hypersensitive to colonialism. Equally important, the United States government believed that its erstwhile allies, the British and French, had somehow swindled it by secretly preparing aggression while pretending to negotiate in good faith. Secretary of State John Foster Dulles and President Dwight D. Eisenhower immediately seized the lead in international efforts to prohibit Anglo-French aggression and to force an Israeli withdrawal. The intensity of American opposition to the Suez expedition had not been anticipated in London and Paris.

Swiftly, before the ultimatums had expired, the United States went directly to the Security Council, at 11:00 in the morning, with a resolution calling for an immediate cease-fire. The American Ambassador to the United Nations, Henry Cabot Lodge, forced through a vote. Both Russia and the United States approved the resolution, but France and Britain used their vetos for the first time. A second resolution, proposed by the Soviet Union and supported by the United States, met the same fate. Then the twelve-hour limit expired. Israel accepted the Anglo-French conditions; Egypt did not. On the morning of October 31 Prime Minister Anthony Eden admitted before the House of Commons that a state of armed conflict with Egypt existed. In Paris concern about the timetable had heightened. Operation Musketeer, was moving too slowly and the Americans too quickly.

View of Israeli Kibbutzim from Syrian Golan Highlands. Heavy artillery emplaced upon the overlooking mountains used to threaten the settlements below.

Israeli "artillery" in the Negev, 1949. (Israel Office of Information Research Department)

King Hussein of Jordan and General Sir John Glubb, Commander of the Arab Legion. (Arab Information Center)

Israeli armor maneuvering during the attack on Rafa, June 1967.

Original picture of the Officers Club explosion in Palestine. One of the saboteurs, injured in the bombing, is being carried away by British, March 3, 1947.

Mounted scouts with the Arab Volunteer Armies rendezvous at a training camp in southern Syria. They are escorting a truck convoy of Arab volunteers on their way to new headquarters in Palestine, 1948.

Evacuation of Civilians: Any kind of vehicle that could move was brought into use by Arabs fleeing Haifa. Here is one of them on the way to the Port, 1948.

Dr. Chaim Weizmann replying to the speeches of welcome at the conference room in the Jewish Agency, where distinguished guests gathered to greet him, December 2, 1948.

Jewish-Arab Conflict, 1947-1949. Barbed wire has been placed in the streets to prevent movement of mobs and artillery. (Zionist Archives and Library)

General Abdul Khader Bey El Husseini, chief of Palestine volunteer Arabs, inspecting Arab Commandos in commando uniform at Nablus before they went into action against Jewish installations, January 19, 1948. (Zionist Archives and Library)

The *Exodus 1947* in Haifa Harbor. (Zionist Archives and Library)

Soldier waiting for snipers in one of the ruins of the 1948 skirmishes.

Count Folke Bernadotte (left) and aide, in discussion with a Jewish liaison officer, Jerusalem, 1948.

Ben-Gurion and Dayan in Sinai, 1956. (Courtesy of the Israeli government)

Attack on Upper Tawafili. (Courtesy of the Israeli government)

In New York a way around the Security Council was found when the Yugoslavian delegate proposed using a new "uniting for peace" procedure that would hand the problem over to the General Assembly. As expected, Britain and France voted against the motion, but the Council insisted that the matter was procedural and not subject to a veto. The General Assembly could take charge of the mounting crisis. On the night of October 31 British and French planes began their strikes on Egyptian airfields. On November 1 Nasser spoke to the Egyptians:

> We shall fight bitterly and not surrender in the defense of the dignity of Egypt, in the defense of the freedom of Egypt, in the defense of the honor of Egypt. . . .
> We shall fight in a bitter struggle; we shall fight from village to village, from house to house; for each one of you, countrymen, is a soldier in the armed forces to defend our dignity, to defend our honor, to defend our freedoms.[1]

Open war had come to the Middle East.

In New York the United States inspired hectic efforts to rush a cease-fire resolution through the General Assembly. The Soviet Union, [delighted to have a new crisis to divert attention from the Hungarian revolution,] violently attacked the imperialist aggression. The Asian and African states, more concerned with colonialism than with East Europe, clamored for action. Without a single source of firm support (even the old Commonwealth countries showed no enthusiasm for the adventure), the Anglo-French invasion faced almost insurmountable international obstacles. The General Assembly was almost certain to pass a resolution excommunicating Britain and France if they continued with Musketeer. There might be United Nations sanctions, United States pressure, and Soviet threats. Anglo-French freedom of action was rapidly being curtailed. In Sinai the Israelis, quick to sense international currents, accelerated Kadesh.

On November 1 the General Assembly took up the American resolution. In the midst of great haste, wild rumors, and the unfolding Hungarian disaster, the resolution came to a vote early on the morning of November 2. There were sixty-four affirmative votes, five negative votes, and six abstentions. Only New Zealand and Australia voted with Britain, France, and Israel. The surprising Canadian abstention was a result of Lester B. Pearson's desire for a positive resolution that would not simply condemn the attack on Egypt but would also provide means for a solution—a United Nations Emergency Force to move into the combat zone. In the meantime, however, the British and French would have to answer the resolution for a cease-fire.

By the following day, November 3, Israeli forces had all but cleared Sinai. Kadesh had been nearly completed, but Musketeer was bogged down in the preparatory stage, with the landing convoy still well offshore. The French were urging instant action on Eden. In New York desperate efforts to find a solution—before the British and French could strike—were continuing. The Assembly met in an atmosphere of heavy crisis. Imre Nagy announced in Budapest that Soviet troops had attacked Hungary. Communist China was reported to have enlisted volunteers for Egypt. No one could really estimate the probable Russian response to the attack on Moscow's protégé in the Middle East. Russian newspapers were vituperative, but in New York the Soviet diplomats had been content to follow the Americans' lead. With the invasion fleet at sea, Russia might grow more militant. For the first time since World War II, the delegates felt themselves tottering on the brink of an atomic cataclysm. The meeting ran over into the early hours of Sunday, November 4, when the United Nations Emergency Force was created by a vote of fifty-seven to zero, with nineteen abstentions. Trapped by their own voiced "reason" for Musketeer, the British and French could hardly oppose an international effort to carry out their own purposes; besides, the vote came too quickly. Thanks to Pearson's frantic backstage negotiations, the Emergency Force provide a way out for Britain and France. For Israel, having completed the conquest of Sinai, there was no longer any purpose in opposing a cease-fire. During the last minutes of the debate, the Israeli delegate announced that his country would agree to an immediate cease-fire if similar agreement were forthcoming from the Egyptians. In the hysteria of a war scare, the Israeli concession was not fully understood except by the British and French. One more public excuse for Musketeer was gone.

In London the moment of decision had arrived. Musketeer's ponderous schedule had allowed the United Nations to mobilize rapidly enough not only to demand an end to the expedition before it began but also to present the British and French with reasonable solution in the form of the United Nations Emergency Force. The avowed aims of the expedition could be fulfilled without further violence. Israel had already agreed to an immediate cease-fire, removing the need for an Anglo-French force to separate the combatants. The Emergency Force would remove the need for an Anglo-French presence to protect the Canal. Gamal Abdel Nasser, however, would remain— bigger and stronger than before and triumphant in the frustration of the imperialists. The French, more militant than ever, urged an instant paratroop drop. The British did not think that a last-minute drop could be arranged. Eden and his war cabinet agreed with the French that Nasser had to go, but pressures had begun to build up within the Conservative Party and the country at large.

To shore up the deteriorating Anglo-French pretense of intervention to maintain peace, Paris quickly agreed to seek a reversal of the Israeli cease-fire position. If Israel were still fighting the Egyptians, then, naturally, Musketeer, which was on the spot, could step in and separate the combatants while the Emergency Force was still on paper. Israel was rapidly discovering the risks of being a casus belli for Musketeer. After the General Assembly resolution had passed, an indication of just how determined the Americans were to secure a settlement was revealed to the Israelis in Washington on November 4. In a "private" approach to Reuben Shiloah of the Israeli Embassy, the Americans indicated that, unless Israel withdrew from Sinai, there would be not only United Nations sanctions, perhaps even expulsion, but also American sanctions, perhaps even limitations on private aid to Israel. There was not much else that the United States government could threaten short of naked force. At about the same time that the United States was revealing the penalties for continued aggression, David Ben-Gurion reluctantly came to the conclusion that, in the interest of the French alliance, Israel would reinterpret its cease-fire declaration. Ben-Gurion, particularly bitter at the British delays that had brought on the diplomatic crisis, informed the French that Israel would evade the terms of the United Nations resolution. On November 4 the Israeli statement accepting a cease-fire was publicly interpreted as meaning only that a de facto cease-fire existed, which was certainly the case except at Sharm-el-Sheikh.

Antoine Pineau and Bourgès-Maunory flew to London for the final conferences. The French were worried but determined. In Britain, they discovered the strains and pressures on Eden had become almost insurmountable. The Labour Party was up in arms howling down Conservative aggression. Some Conservatives believed that the Emergency Force would be an acceptable way out. Commonwealth support had not been forthcoming. India was even contemplating withdrawal from the Commonwealth. Nonetheless the French were relieved that Eden continued to agree that he was being offered only a paper solution that would actually buttress the villain Nasser, rather than destroying him. Musketeer would continue. There would be a drop of paratroopers on Monday, November 5. The new rationale for intervention would be the need to end hostilities, to remove the obstacles in the Suez Canal, and to force Israeli withdrawal from Sinai. The formula could hardly stand up under close scrutiny. The continuing hostilities were a direct result of French intervention with the Israelis to continue the war "officially," even though Kadesh had been completed. The obstacles in the Canal existed as a direct result of the Anglo-French air attacks, which had triggered the sinking block ships by the Egyptians. The withdrawal of Israel from Sinai was a novel addition, as the Israelis were there in the first place with British toleration and French support. Its inclusion in the Anglo-French declaration was a curious reward for Ben-Gurion's agreement to risk international censure by refusing to accept the cease-fire resolution. The details, however, were not important. The result was that Musketeer would continue, despite grave risks. Eden's broadcast speech to the nation revealed his decision:

> Our passionate love of peace and our intense loathing of war have often held us back from using force, even at times when we knew in our heads, if not in our hearts, that its use was in the interests of peace. And I believe with all my heart and my head that this is a time for action effective and swift.[2]

International reaction was swift. On November 5 Soviet Premier Nikolai Bulganin dispatched harsh notes to Britain, France, and Israel, demanding an immediate end to the adventure. His notes to the British and French implied the possibility of Soviet military intervention with rockets and atomic weapons. His note to Israel was vehement:

The Government of Israel is criminally and irresponsibly playing with the fate of peace and with the fate of its own people. It is sowing hatred of the State of Israel among the Eastern people, which cannot but leave its impression on the future of Israel and which puts a question mark against the very existence of Israel as a State. Vitally interested in the maintenance of peace and the preservation of tranquillity in the Middle East, the Soviet Government is at this moment taking steps to put an end to the war and to restrain the aggressors.[3]

Premier David Ben-Gurion and the Cabinet suddenly found that the escalating Suez crisis, in which Israel was now caught up, had created a situation that, according to Moscow, threatened the "very existence of Israel as a State." The Arabs had never been able to make good on such threats, but Russia had the capacity to do so. The question was whether the Bulganin note was a bluff, a warning, or even an ultimatum.

In Washington a galloping war scare began. Bulganin had also sent a cable to the President of the Security Council, requesting an immediate meeting to discuss the new aggression and outlining a resolution demanding a cease-fire within twelve hours under threat of United Nations members' giving "military and other assistance to the republic of Egypt."[4] There were rumors that 100 MIG fighters had landed in Syria, that Soviet planes were flying over Turkey, that there were submarines in the Mediterranean, that Russian volunteers were hovering just out of sight. On the afternoon of the same day, November 5, British and French paratroopers dropped into Port Said. Finally, the irrevocable step was taken. The point of the Musketeer expedition at last made contact with the Egyptians.

The pressure for a cease-fire became almost unbearable. Wanton aggression had seemed bad enough, but aggression risking atomic war was worse. The rising crescendo of frustrated indignation from Asia and Africa had drowned out not only any Anglo-French pretense at legality but also discussions of Russian suppression of the Hungarian revolt. The Soviet Union, covering its tracks in Eastern Europe, was winning friends and influencing people in the new nations. The Soviet Union, firmly anticolonialist, had even gone so far as to hint at possible use of atomic and ballistic missiles in such a good cause. The Americans were gravely concerned. Perhaps the Russian move was merely a bluff, but it had certainly created a dangerous confrontation. The British and French were concerned but thought that some risks could be taken: The Africans and Asians could be ignored, even in the United Nations, for a time. The Soviet note could be treated as a warning rather than as an ultimatum, in order to gain time. The United States, on the other hand, possessed a far more potent means of instant discipline: It could threaten the British pound.

Private financiers, assuming that the pound would have to be devalued, had acted accordingly. Great blocks of pound sterling were being sold in New York. The pound was sagging in relation to the dollar. The Bank of England was forced to buy blocks of £1 million. Harold MacMillan, Chancellor of the Exchequer, insisted that the Bank of England would have to have $1 billion and soon. On November 6 Eden found that a loan from the International Monetary Fund would be contingent on a cease-fire. Eden could ignore the pleas of the moralists, of his false friends and recent foes. He could call the Russian bluff. But he could not deny the bankers. The stability of the pound was more important than smashing Nasser. Eden, by November 6 a desperately sick man, began to crack.[5]

Premier Guy Mollet and his French colleagues knew, even before Eden telephoned, that the end had come. There was nothing they could say to persuade him to change his mind:

> I am cornered! I can't hang on. I'm being deserted by everybody. My loyal associate Nutting has resigned as Minister of State. I can't even rely on unanimity among the Conservatives. The Archbishop of Canterbury, the Church, the oil businessmen, everybody is against me! The Commonwealth threatens to break up. Nehru says he will break the ties. Canada, Australia are no longer following us in our policy. I cannot be the gravedigger of the Crown. And then, I want you to understand, really understand, Eisenhower phoned me. I can't go it alone without the United States. It would be the first time in the history of England. . . . No, it is not possible.[6]

Mollet wanted just a little more time. The expedition had landed and had already pushed through the port area. Columns were moving down the Canal. It would soon be over. Mollet was desperate; a day more would give the Anglo-French forces the Canal. Eden finally reluctantly agreed to delay the cease-fire until midnight November 6, but that was all.

The French were still determined to salvage the operation on their own if need be. But almost at once they discovered that they could not go it alone at once. The operations were too intimately combined under British leadership at every level to allow instant separation. Hurried consultation with the Israelis began, to see if Moshe Dayan could help out. During Operation Musketeer, Anglo-French plans had developed quite distinctly from Kadesh; contact among the three nations had been at other points. In fact the British units of Musketeer had been so "unorchestrated" that, at one point, Israeli planes attacked the destroyer *H.M.S. Crane.* Suddenly, the French wanted immediate, though secret, Israeli help. Dayan had a couple of novel suggestions, but the French could not take him up on them. There simply was not time. Frustrated by Eden's decision and by seeing victory at Suez lost by a few hours, the French government agreed to act in accord with the British. The Suez adventure would end at midnight.

On November 7 Ben-Gurion proudly reviewed before the Knesset the course of Kadesh, the great victory over the Egyptians, and the presence of the Israeli army in liberated Sinai. He implied that the Israelis had come to stay in Sinai.[7] Although Musketeer had been abortive, Kadesh had not. But the potential fruits of victory, which seemed so close on November 7, could not be savored. The concert of nations feared that a cease-fire would be insufficient. The United Nations, the United States, and the Soviet Union were determined that the aggressors must withdraw. There were to be no conditions, although the British and French assumed that recognition of their right to set conditions had been included in the cease-fire. There could be no Israeli occupation of Sinai. On the same day as his Knesset speech, Ben-Gurion received a harsh note from President Eisenhower threatening the end of friendly cooperation unless Israel withdrew from Sinai. The powers had decided that there were to be no gains from aggression, no matter how provoked, and no advantages from war, no matter how justified. Israel would have to switch from an aggressive military offensive to a tenacious diplomatic defense.

On November 8 the Israeli holding action began. Foreign Minister Golda Meir sent a letter to Secretary-General Dag Hammarskjöld informing him that Israel would withdraw from Sinai on the arrival of the Emergency Force; but she included a request that the United

Nations call on Egypt to renounce its war policy, its boycott, its blockade, its fedayeen raids, and its refusal to enter into negotiations with Israel. On the same day Ben-Gurion noted that Israel would, of course, withdraw from Sinai, but he too tried to keep consideration of the Kadesh operation firmly in the context of the long-term Egyptian-Israeli confrontation. Kadesh should not be isolated and condemned as aggression without reference to Egyptian provocation. To do so would be to return to the previous bloody stalemate, the same desperate Egyptian threat that Kadesh had been designed to remove. The Israelis were determined that Kadesh should produce security from Egyptian aggression.

What, if anything, Israel would salvage from its military success was of little importance to the community of nations. After the cease-fire on November 7, the major effort in the United Nations was to force on Britain and France an immediate unconditional evacuation. Both in Paris and in London there was growing disappointment at the reaction to the self-imposed cease-fire. Washington still showed no interest in Britain's financial straits. Egypt, as soon as the menace of invasion had been dispelled, went back to its old blackmailing ways. Nasser would not allow the Canal to be cleared until the aggressors had withdrawn. Nasser could not accept Emergency Force troops from the Commonwealth; Egypt seized on the Soviet Union's idea of demanding reparations from the British and French for war damage, although all Anglo-French property had already been confiscated. On November 15 Bulganin again sent hostile notes to Israel and France, threatening the dispatch of volunteers. Washington, for its part, was imposing unofficial oil and credit sanctions, damaging not only the British and French economies but also the European economy in general.

By November 20 there was 700 United Nations Emergency Force troops, under General E. L. M. Burns, in Egypt and 3,000 more on the way. The British and French sat tight in Port Said. American Secretary of the Treasury George M. Humphrey informed R. A. Butler, who was acting for Eden, that there would be no help for the pound until after British withdrawal. On November 22 Butler informed the House of Commons that withdrawal was about to begin, and the next day certain British, French, and Israeli units were withdrawn. But this token step did not satisfy anyone. In New York

Indian Ambassador to the United Nations Krishna Menon introduced a resolution demanding immediate evacuation. At the General Assembly meeting on November 24 he urged a snap vote, only to be interrupted by a sudden moderating Belgian amendment. The amendment lost, however. The United States abstained, a tremendous blow to its former allies. There was to be no charity for aggressors. Menon's original resolution then swept to victory with American support. Washington had not relented; it had made sure that there would be no American oil to replace that cut off by the blocking of the canal and no American money to stabilize the pound.

Although in all outside efforts to pry the aggressors out of Egypt, Israel was included among the aggressors, the main efforts were directed against Britain and France. The Israelis stayed quiet; their diplomats continued to remind any faintly friendly ear of Egyptian provocation while the army was busy removing captured Soviet equipment from Sinai. As long as the United States was determined to force evacuation, there was no hope of long delay. The French hung on as long as they could, in order, as Pineau pointed out, to give the Israelis an added margin.

> During the months of November and December we had to face at the United Nations pressures of every kind in order to force us to evacuate Port Said and the canal. We sought to gain time. We sought to gain time not because of procedure, such as phasing our withdrawal with United Nations arrival, but because time was needed to permit the Israelis to rid the Sinai of all arms deposited there, and to take them back to Israel. From our positions we were able to protect the operations of the Israelis, and this was well worth the trouble, even if it became increasingly hard to justify.[8]

The British, little concerned about Israel's problems, had hoped to establish some face-saving preconditions, but further delay might have been disastrous. The government in London was in chaos, rent by resignations and recriminations. Eden was in Jamaica recuperating from the agonizing physical strain. The Labour Party was in full cry after the guilty men of Suez. There was no oil, the pound was still in danger, and the British were international pariahs.

On December 3 the British and French announced a phased withdrawal, as the United Nations Emergency Force moved in. On

December 4 the pound was stabilized. On December 8 the Soviet news agency, Tass, announced that no Soviet volunteers would be necessary. On December 22 the last British troops left Port Said.

For Britain and France, the Suez adventure had finished, with no gains and fantastic losses. For Israel the diplomatic battle to secure some advantage from Kadesh had scarcely begun. Although Britain and France had had vital interests at stake in the Suez affair, the actual security of the State of Israel was involved in Sinai. The Israeli government intended to hold out for real guarantees against future Egyptian aggression.

Once the major aggressors had been driven out, the Arab world turned on the Zionists, still immovable in Sinai. The Syrians refused to allow repairs on the Iraqi oil pipeline, blown up during the Suez invasion. The Egyptians refused to allow the canal to be cleared of the forty-seven blocking ships, sunk almost entirely by the Egyptians. In the United Nations Hammarskjöld and most of the delegates regarded Israel as a culprit that must not be allowed to profit by aggression. Washington, eager for Arab friendship, agreed. Russia, defender of Arab interests, agreed. Great Britain, once disengaged from Musketeer, shifted back to a pro-Arab policy to win back old friends and to patch together its tattered Middle Eastern influence. To scratch up Arab support, London added British pressure for Israeli withdrawal. Only France remained faithful. The Israelis, however, seemed quite willing to suffer the castigation of the United Nations, to bear the scorn and vilification of the moralists, to wait out the traditional opposition of the British Foreign Office, Arab hostility, and Soviet-bloc censure.

The key to Israeli policy lay in Washington. To achieve security from Egyptian aggression, Israel could forgo the admiration of the diplomats and suffer the indignation of the rigidly ethical; but Israel was a "remittance state," dependent on loans, grants, and donations. If the United States government became sufficiently exasperated, all public and private assistance could be cut off. Within weeks Israel's economy would be crippled, and within a year the population would be reduced to a level of mere subsistence. Ben-Gurion hoped that the situation would not deteriorate so far, for he believed that, if Israel held out long enough, the legitimacy of its case against Egypt would gradually emerge from the clouds of Suez oratory. Although Eisenhower and Dulles might bluster and threaten, Israel could not be intimidated except by force, financial or military, Ben-Gurion did not believe that, in the long run, the crunch would occur. Israel had too many American friends. Something could be salvaged from Sinai beyond the memory of victory, originally regarded as sufficient in itself. In time, if Israel could wait it out, Washington would give a little, and even the stern Hammarskjöld might shift a bit.

In December there were no signs of anyone's giving or shifting. The Eisenhower administration, re-elected with a resounding mandate, began to consider in more detail the post–Suez Middle East. As always the experts put on their pink-colored glasses and saw mainly the Soviet presence in Egypt and Syria. The moral bankruptcy of the British position in the area was noted. The conclusion was that the Middle East lay open to Soviet penetration and that the United States must step in quickly to prevent disaster. Out of the State Department came the foundations of the Eisenhower Doctrine, the offer of military aid to any country or group of countries threatened by internal or external communism. Assuming that "communism" was the major Middle Eastern issue and that United States policy over Suez had won Arab admiration, the State Department plugged for a pro-Arab policy to fill the vacuum left by the British. To create a pro-Western power to counterbalance Nasser, in his view a villain though a wronged villain, John Foster Dulles looked first to King ibn-Saud of Saudi Arabia, where the United States had commercial and military interests. Hopefully, the British might, in time, pick up the pieces of Nuri as-Said's Iraq; in the meantime it was the duty of the United States to stabilize the Middle East. After January, with the Eisenhower Doctrine before Congress and American diplomats tying together the frayed ends of Western influence in the Middle East, Israel's presence in Sinai was a vast embarrassment to Washington. The Arabs had long considered Israel an American puppet state; now they saw no reason why Eisenhower could not order Ben-Gurion to leave Sinai. Washington believed that Israeli intransigence threatened vital American interests in the area and, furthermore, was morally indefensible. Israel, more concerned with its own vital interests, gave ground grudgingly.

On January 8 the Israeli army pulled back west of a line from Abu Ageila–Kusseima–Sharm-el-Sheikh. By January 15 El 'Arîsh had been evacuated. In both instances the small United Nations Emergency Force moved in behind the departing Israelis and just ahead of the Egyptian army. Still the staged withdrawal was too slow to please the United Nations. The Egyptians knew that the maddeningly slow pace made it possible for the Israelis to strip Sinai. The latter took with them all the bright new Soviet equipment. They left behind only desolation—the military fortifications and emplacements destroyed, the roads broken up and pushed into the desert, the buildings leveled, the gun pits filled in, the plumbing ruined. More important to Nasser was the continuing threat to his prestige posed by the very presence of Zionists inside Egypt.

In New York on January 17 one more resolution demanding instant withdrawal passed by the impressive margin of seventy-four to two; only France was still voting with Israel. The Israelis seemed undismayed. They still asked what the United Nations intended to do about the blockade, the boycott, the fedayeen, the Egypt declaration of a continuing state of war. Few people listened, and no one had answers. On January 22 Israel evacuated all of Sinai but the Gaza strip, home of the fedayeen, and Sharm-el-Sheikh, seat of the 'Aqaba blockade. On January 23 Ben-Gurion announced that, without guarantees, the Israelis would withdraw no farther.

On January 29, 1957, ibn-Saud, destined by Dulles to be the kingpin of the anticommunist Arab front, arrived in Washington. It was hardly coincidental that just then American pressure on Israel increased. But oblique American threats seemed to have no effect. United Nations resolutions had no effect. Ben-Gurion and his Cabinet were simply not going to do what Dulles, Hammarskjöld, or Nasser wanted. On February 3 the Israeli Cabinet again insisted that, without guarantees, there would be no withdrawal. Israeli diplomats continued to hammer away at the provocations that Israel had faced and the guilt of the Arabs in their undeclared war of terror and boycott. Soon, the Israelis hoped, the universal moral condemnation of aggression would ebb in the light of the actual proportions of the Egyptian provocation. On no official level was the Israeli hope realized. But, unofficially, old American friends began to speak up for Israel. The double standard of international morality was noted: Russia had not been punished for Hungary, but Israel was to be punished for Sinai. Ever so slightly that most mysterious of institutions, American public opinion, shifted in Israel's favor.

On February 3 President Eisenhower sent Ben-Gurion a letter pointing out that Israel's failure to withdraw had created continuing tensions in the Middle East. The letter hinted at possible sanctions against Israel. On February 8 Ben-Gurion pointed out the significance of the occupation of Sharm-el-Sheikh in relation to the former Egyptian blockade and of the Gaza strip to the fedayeen; he indicated Israel did not contemplate annexation but wanted a guarantee of security related to these two zones. Israel did have a case, but the Americans wanted the Canal open and the Arabs tranquil. Neither result seemed likely unless Israel withdrew unconditionally. Dulles met secretly with the Israeli Ambassador to Washington, Abba Eban, and prepared an *aide-mémoire* recognizing that the Gulf of 'Aqaba was considered international water by the United States and favoring the presence of the United Nations Emergency Force in the Gaza strip.

It was progress for the Israelis, but the *aide-mémoire* did note that the United States would support United Nations sanctions. During February the United States position seemed to shift a little farther daily, under domestic and international pressures, from uncompromising insistence on withdrawal to understanding of Israel's problems, but participants in the discussions remained insistent on withdrawal before guarantees. On February 18 Eban left for Israel to report to Ben-Gurion, who continued to support no withdrawal without firm guarantees.

On February 21 Ben-Gurion learned of the American position firsthand from Eban. There was no point in delay, for Eban believed that there was no possibility of a sudden American shift. On February 22 six nations introduced a sanctions resolution at the United Nations. Neither Hammarskjöld nor the General Assembly had shown any modification of views after three months. Washington was growing increasingly uneasy at Russia's militant stand on evacuation and the ensuing prestige created for communism in the Middle East. Washington would support sanctions.

The time had come for Israel to salvage what it could from capitulation. Eban returned to Washington to try to secure some of the firm commitments implied in the *aide-mémoire*. Dulles agreed to several points, like sending an American ship through 'Aqaba, but suggested that some areas were the province of the United Nations. Hammarskjöld, however, was unyielding. Eventually a plan was devised that provided for international maritime backing for Israeli access to the Gulf of 'Aqaba. The best that Eban could arrange for the Gaza strip was tacit American support for United Nations control but no public declaration before evacuation. Israel would have to withdraw without conditions, although with the promise of future support. Ben-Gurion reluctantly agreed to evacuation.

On March 1 Golda Meir read before the General Assembly a speech carefully drafted by the Israeli and American experts, which supported the 'Aqaba agreement and the United Nations presence in Gaza. Despite Afro-Asian grumbling, the United States was content. On March 4 Ben-Gurion gave the withdrawal order. On March 5 he told the Knesset that this withdrawal was based on the promise of United Nations presence in the Gaza strip. But the United Nations Emergency force did move into Gaza as planned. On March 13 an Egyptian civil administrator arrived in Gaza. On March 18 Golda Meir asked Dulles if the arrival of an Egyptian military staff conflicted with the understanding negotiated during February. Dulles did not seem especially concerned. The Israelis, however, were concerned. Although the presence of the Emergency Force might inhibit future fedayeen raids, the presence of the Egyptians once more created a threat.

Despite the meager results of the five-month campaign to secure concrete advantage from Kadesh, the Sinai war had not been in vain for Israel. The original purpose of the attack had been to inflict a military defeat on the Egyptians so severe as to destroy Arab hopes for one more round to destroy the Zionists. Although Nasser had, with consummate skill, thrown a cloud of rhetoric over Sinai, harping only on the diplomatic humiliation of the Anglo-French expedition, Arab military leaders were quite conscious of the gap between Egyptian military capacity and Egyptian aspirations. Dayan had made his point: Egypt alone or the Arabs united had no hope of a military victory in the foreseeable future. The secondary objectives of Kadesh—opening 'Aqaba and putting an end to terrorism—had largely been achieved.

On April 7 the United States transport *Kern Hills* sailed past the United Nations Emergency Force camp at Sharm-el-Sheikh and on up the Gulf of 'Aqaba. Elath had become an Asian port, an opening to the East. Within months the southern Negev and Elath became a boom area. In the Gaza strip the Emergency Force acted as a restraint on any Egyptian hope of reintroducing official *fedayeen* raids. Incidents there were, but *fedayeen* penetration there was not. Elsewhere, negotiations in Washington and New York to end the Suez blockade continued, but without any immediate results.

Kadesh had thus largely achieved the original objectives of October 1956. The swiftness of victory had, however, created far-reaching expectations for some Israelis: the annexation of Sinai, the end of Nasser, final peace. On November 5 none of these goals had seemed farfetched, but the collapse of Musketeer by November 7 and the immediate international isolation had swiftly dissipated the immediate aura of victory. Nasser, far from collapsing, had emerged with renewed prestige in the Middle East, his military losses in Sinai obscured by his diplomatic victory over the aggressors. Kadesh, far from leading to permanent peace, had only intensified Arab antagonism. That the more grandiose aspirations had been frustrated obscured the fact that the major objective—a military victory over the new Egypt—had been achieved. The Arabs also ignored the implications of the victory in their delight at the humiliation of Britain and France. Nasser, through his understanding of the nature of the international community in 1956, had parlayed disaster into an incredible victory. The new nations, their power emanating from moral righteousness, had flocked to his cause. The Russians had contributed just enough tension to intimidate the aggressors. The United States had temporarily become his most determined advocate. Suez became the great Armageddon, in which the ranks of the obsolete Western colonialists had been arrayed against the rightful aspirations of the emerging nations. The wave of the future, personified in Nasser, had triumphed, sweeping away the old gunboats, the resident advisers, the old treaties, the old spheres of influence. Nasser's prestige, already high in 1956, was so over-powering after Suez that even his oldest and bitterest rivals had to bend.

To the Arabs, Suez required no explanations. But the success of Kadesh presented another problem. An important facet of Nasser's campaign to snatch moral victory from actual defeat might be called "Sinai explained," although, of course, no real effort was made to "explain" the unacknowledged defeat to the Arab masses. For the Arabs Kadesh was the least interesting part of the tripartite invasion.

In any case there had been no defeat; the Arabs believed that the Egyptian army had been withdrawn to meet the Anglo-French invasion just as the air force had been flown to safety in Saudi Arabia. The Israelis were in Sinai only because the Egyptians had been busy meeting the greater challenge. This reasoning was quite sufficient for most Arabs.

Nasser could hardly admit that the original deployment of troops, ordered from on high against expert advice, had been dangerous. Nor could he acknowledge that his new army had not fought well, except in static defense positions that should rather have been bases for fluid operations. Instead, Egypt denied the occurrence of an Israeli victory by denying that there had really been a Sinai campaign. There could have been no *real* Israeli victory because the Egyptian army had already been ordered to withdraw at noon on November 1. In reality, however, an Israeli victory would have been assured even if the Egyptians had been free to commit their remaining reinforcements. There is no reason to assume that additional Egyptian forces would have been any more effective than the 1st Armored Brigade, which wandered about ineffectually near Bir Gafgafa before the Israeli air force cut it up; the 2nd Brigade, which was bloodied at Mitla; or the 1st Brigade, which walked into the bag at 'El Arîsh. Certainly, if the Egyptians had felt free to commit their total forces, the campaign would have lasted slightly longer, but the outcome could hardly have been different.

There was also the argument that, had the Egyptians activated their air force, Kadesh would have collapsed. During the October 30–November 1 period, where the force was actually in use, the Egyptians flew too few sorties and seldom pushed either air encounters or close ground strikes. Except for one strike during the fighting at Mitla Pass, the Egyptian air force did little damage to the Israeli columns. In fact the Egyptian air force proved so ineffectual that subsequent Israeli commentators announced that Israel had won the Sinai war alone and had not needed the help of the French air umbrella. The fact was that the Egyptians had simply not learned how to use their new airplanes.

Sinai rapidly faded into the background for Nasser as he exploited his new prestige, and Israel became temporarily less important than Egyptian hegemony in the Arab world. After the raucous and vitriolic diplomatic campaign for evacuation of Sinai, the Israeli-Arab confrontation quietly slipped into the familiar ruts. The uneasy frontiers remained, always a temptation to the Arabs and a danger to the Israelis. The boycott office of the Arab League continued to operate with varying effectiveness. The newly reopened Suez Canal was still not open to Israeli shipping. The diplomatic boycott continued. Arab hostility, enlivened by regular vocal attacks on aggressive Israel, the alien bastion of Western imperialism, never ceased. Once more the Israelis and the Arabs began a long, uneasy truce, a violent armistice with no peace and no war.

NOTES

1. Nasser's speech was published in *Al Ahram* on November 2 and is translated in a most interesting collection of facsimile reproductions of the world's press on that day: Wilbur Schramm, ed., *One Day in the World's Press* (Stanford, Calif.: 1959), p. 87.

2. A. J. Barker, *Suez: The Seven Day War* (New York: 1965), p. 95.

3. Major General Moshe Dayan, *Diary of the Sinai Campaign* (New York: 1966), pp. 184. Dayan notes (p. 186) the Soviet delay in developing this hard line: "Who knows whether this Sinai Campaign would have been launched if the Russian messages had been sent to Britain, France and Israel before the 29th of October?"
The texts of all notes are included in U.S. Department of State, *United States Policy in the Middle East, September 1956 to June 1957* (Washington, D.C.: 1957).

4. *United Nations Documents* S/3736.

5. Seldom have the participants in an international crisis been so dogged by poor health. President Eisenhower was in and out of Walter Reed Hospital for checkups. Dulles suffered an attack of cramps, the onset of his fatal cancer. Eden spent the last weeks before Musketeer's collapse on the edge of a total physical breakdown. Ben-Gurion, during the early days of Kadesh, was in bed with the flu.

6. Herman Finer, *Dulles Over Suez* (Chicago: 1965), p. 429, draws on J.-R. Tournoux, *Secrets d'Etat* (Paris: 1960), p. 37, for the quote and adds that the general content was confirmed in a lecture by Maurice Schumann on February 4, 1957. Terence Robertson, *Crisis: The Inside Story of the Suez Conspiracy* (New York: 1965), p. 264, quotes a similar but less dramatic version without any source. Finer's translation undoubtedly contains the gist of the conversation, even if not the exact words.

7. Ben-Gurion's speech to the Knesset furnished further ammunition, if any was actually needed, to Arabs perpetually fearful of future Israeli aggression. See Fayez A. Sayegh; *The Arab-Israeli Conflict* (New York: 1964), p. 60.

   Ben-Gurion's statement, and the selection of the words "free" and "liberated," also the use of Hebrew expressions for centuries-old Arabic names, leaves no doubt that the Israelis then planned to expand so as to include the whole of the Sinai Peninsula and the Gaza Strip. The fact that conditions in the world then prevented the Israelis from keeping what they went out to get, does not preclude the possibility that they will try again in the future.

8. Robertson, *Crisis*, pp. 296–7.

15

The Long Truce

As the Sinai crisis faded into the recent past, the Arabs temporarily moved the Zionist problem down on their agenda and turned instead to watch the meteoric rise of Gamal Abdel Nasser. He was the talk of the bazaars and cafés, the embodiment of the Arab dream. His picture was in every shop, his name in every mouth. Egyptian pretensions to hegemony in the Middle East could hardly be denied. Egypt's opponents were confounded. Little seemed to stand in the way of Nasser's ambitions. The presence of the Eisenhower Doctrine in the Middle East could give only secret comfort to rulers fearful of the mobs tuned into the Cairo radio. With allies everywhere, with the backing of Soviet Russia and the friendship of the new neutrals, Nasser's path seemed clear.

The first challenge therefore came as a shock. In April 1957 King Hussein of Jordan turned out his pro-Nasser government and soon thereafter accepted an American subsidy. Along with King Abdul-Aziz ibn-Saud of Saudi Arabia, who had accepted Washington's blandishments, Hussein presented Nasser with an unexpected ideological challenge. The old monarchs had some life left yet. Along Syria's border with Turkey, tensions reached the heights of a genuine war scare in the fall of 1957. From Cairo it appeared that the Americans and the Turks were about to overthrow the Syrian Republic. In

Iraq King Faisal II and Nuri as-Said had returned to their old ways. The Middle East, open to Nasser's control in December 1956, had slipped back into its traditional rivalries.

The chaotic internal politics of Syria gave Nasser a most promising opening. The pro-Nasser Socialist Baath Party, fearful of losing control of the government to the Syrian Communist Party turned to Cairo for help. The Baath leaders pleaded with Nasser to permit a union of Egypt and Syria, a step toward a united Arab republic. Nasser, although he recognized some if not all the risks of a hasty union, decided to take the chance. On February 1, 1958, Damascus and Cairo jointly proclaimed the United Arab Republic. The union inherited not only the vast disarray of Syrian political opinion with its bitter undercover conflicts but also potential conflicts between very different Syrian and Egyptian economic and social institutions. The average Arab, however, was wild with delight at the prospect of an accelerating unity, which would lead to a vast new state stretching from the Indus to the Atlantic. One monarch, the Imam of Yemen, was sufficiently impressed temporarily to tie his medieval kingdom briefly to the new Arab Republic; a third star was added to the new flag. Rumors flew that Nasser had a pocketful of such stars. On February 14, 1958, in an effort to counterbalance the United Arab Republic, Jordan and Iraq agreed to form a federation under King Faisal. The new Arab Union, born in the wake of Nasser's coup, made little impression; it seemed merely a merger of monarchs fearful of the future.

In Lebanon the impact of Nasserism, along with a domestic political crisis, threatened to destroy the republic. On May 12, 1958, a limited rebellion began in Beirut; the government attributed it to agitation by agents of the United Arab Republic. In the ensuing muddle of charges and countercharges, the United States took an increasingly intimate interest in preventing another Nasserite coup, which might open the door to Soviet penetration. The Lebanese government, frightened at the rapid political decay, accepted United States support. A marine-corps expeditionary force of 5,000 men landed. Britain at the same time sent detachments of troops into Jordan to prop up Hussein. The Arabs were not as invulnerable to major-power penetration as they had assumed. The complex Lebanese crisis continued, but the government managed to weather the rebellion and to produce a Levantine compromise while Arab attention was distracted by a more exciting event.

At almost the same time that American marines were landing on the beach outside Beirut, the officers of Iraq's army revolted. On July 14, 1958, they killed King Faisal and Nuri as-Said, replacing the monarch with a junta led by Abdul Karim el-Kassim as Premier. The advent of el-Kassim marked the end of the brief Arab Union with Jordan and apparently heralded another success for Nasserism. The Iraqi officers in 1958, like the Egyptians in 1952, swept out the monarchy, calling for extensive reforms to rid the country of corruption. The Iraqis, like the Egyptians, professed faith in Arab unity. Immediately, if briefly, Nasser's picture decorated walls all over Baghdad. Then, swiftly, the revelation came: There was an alternative revolutionary road to Arab unity; it led not to Cairo but to Baghdad. El-Kassim offered the Arabs the "true" route to the future, in opposition to Nasser's faulty and egotistical path. Soon the two revolutionary regimes clashed in open ideological battle. Nasser's quarrel with el-Kassim was desperately important, for el-Kassim's revolutionary alternative was a heresy, more threatening than the corrupt old ideas of the reactionary monarchs. The tattered fabric of Arab unity was rent again.

Nasser was forced to reconsider Egypt's position. Jordan had been lost, Saudi Arabia lost, Iraq won and lost. Lebanon had been occupied by the Americans. Egypt's relations with the other Arab states had never been worse. The new Islamic states of Sudan and Tunisia opposed his ambitions. Only Syria, the northern province of the United Arab Republic remained. Ominously, the United States marines had shown the extent of the American commitment in the Middle East. The Syrian Baathists had demonstrated the dangers of depending solely on the Russians and local communist cadres. Although Defense Minister Amer had visited Moscow during the Lebanese crisis in July and Russia had finally agreed in October to finance the Aswan High Dam, Nasser decided to shift a bit. He attacked the errors of the Syrian Communist Party, thus irritating the Russians. Anti-Western tirades trailed off. Washington, responding to Nasser's overtures, decided that more could be obtained from him with honey than with gall. Economic assistance was proffered and accepted.

Nasser's new moderation did not extend to his relations with Iraq;

rather, the reverse was true. Covert though unsuccessful rebellion in Iraq was fostered by Egypt. Public censure of Baghdad was regularly broadcast from Cairo and answered in kind. Nasser's attacks on el-Kassim's revolutionary regime did not prohibit Egyptian attacks on the reactionary kings. El-Kassim, however, remained the prime villain. In 1961, when Iraq claimed the oil-rich sheikhdom of Kuwait, Nasser surprisingly found himself supporting a monarchy with a British treaty agreement, in opposition to a revolutionary republican regime.

In September 1961 Nasser's ambitions took a severe body blow in the withdrawal of Syria from the United Arab Republic. Although not unforeseen, the secession of Damascus was a severe disappointment. Nasser's reaction—peaceful acceptance of the withdrawal and graceful admission of Egyptian errors—helped to soften the blow to his prestige.

Then in 1962 things looked up a bit for Nasser. His friend Ahmed Ben Bella became Premier of Algeria. In September Nasser's support of the Free Yemen Movement finally paid dividends in the overthrow of the monarchy and the establishment of a republic. Nasser immediately rushed support to the new government, still threatened by unruly tribes in the hills. It was the first open step in what was to become a fearful drain on Egyptian resources. The tribal leaders refused to accept the new republican government and began a guerrilla campaign in the mountains to the north. Egypt's military commitment in Yemen had jumped to 20,000 men by the end of 1962. Instead of a swift coup and a comfortable protégé, Nasser found his army tied down in a nasty little war. At least he was not alone, for his ideological rivals in Iraq were fighting a similar war against the Kurds. The Syrians were enmeshed in a series of frustrated coups. The cause of Arab unity had never seemed more hopeless, nor the prospects for rapid economic development worse.

Then everything changed once again. On February 8, 1963, the Iraqi Baathist Party overthrew the el-Kassim regime, which had grown increasingly tyrannical. One month later on March 8 the Syrian Baathist Party, with army support, turned out the feeble government in Damascus. In one month the potential for a tripartite Arab revolutionary republic suddenly existed. Both the Iraqi and Syrian Baathist parties supported immediate unity. The road to an expanded union lay open. Finally, on April 14, after eight tripartite meetings in Cairo, the details were settled, and a referendum on the merger was proposed.

On April 17, amid great public enthusiasm and private misgivings, the union statement was released to the press. The meetings had revealed that Nasser wanted union only on his own terms, whereas the Syrians and Iraqis were worried about the fate of the Baathist Parties. The Israelis were concerned and requested reassurances from Washington. Then, almost as soon as the Syrians had returned to Damascus, public doubts began to be expressed. By May a Baathist propaganda war against the Syrian Nasserists was in full stride. Iraq joined the attack, which gradually shifted to criticism of Egypt. On June 22 Nasser spoke against the Baathists. Tripartite union was dead. In July the Iraqis and Syrians tried on their own for union. Then on November 8 President Abdel al-Salam Arif lost patience with the quarreling Baathists and took over direction of the Iraqi government.

Although 1962 had seemed a vintage year for Arab disaster—with the Yemeni and Kurdish wars, Syrian-Egyptian recriminations over the failure of the United Arab Republic, the harangues between Nasser and el-Kassim, and the hostility of the traditional monarchs toward the new republics—1963 was worse. The swift changes in Iraq and Syria produced not union but fresh quarreling. Syria was opposed to both Nasser and Arif, as well as to the governments of Lebanon, Morocco, and Jordan. In Yemen Egypt was fighting Arabs backed by Jordan and Saudi Arabia. The Iraqis could neither defeat the Kurds nor achieve compromise with them. To compound everyone's difficulties, the Israelis were about to begin their diversion of the Jordan River, despite years of Arab threats. Syria threatened a war against Israel, which could not be won but which demanded some sort of unified Arab support.

Once again, as in 1958, Nasser decided to ease out of the vice of adamant opposition. On the issue of Israel alone, all the Arabs could unite. In the fall of 1963 Nasser began tentative moves, which led in December to a call for an Arab summit conference on the issue of Israel's diversion of the Jordan. The result was a highly salutary opening for an era of good feeling, which actually held up under severe strains for two years.

In January 1964 in Cairo the Arabs took a series of positive measures against Israel, none of which threatened to lead immediately to war, which Nasser pointed out could not yet be won. Most important, blame for inaction was spread about evenly so that Syria could not seize militant leadership. The first firm steps toward a negotiated solution of the Yemeni war were taken by the Egyptians and the Saudis. Elsewhere Egyptian relations, even with the conservative monarchs and their radical rivals, greatly improved. Many of the underlying strains remained, but there was in Cairo in 1964 an atmosphere of good will, only slightly tempered by past bitterness.

During the next two years, bit by bit, the good will disintegrated under pressure from the same old conflicts. In February 1966 Nasser attacked his conservative rivals for a variety of heresies, not the least of which was an effort to create a bloc of traditional states to counterbalance the revolutionary republics. In April, disappointed in the Yemeni negotiations, Nasser threatened to keep his 70,000 troops in place to back up his republican protégés. In July he again attacked the reactionaries, Hussein of Jordan and Faisal of Saudi Arabia. The new hard line did not, however, return the Middle East to the schismatic situation of 1963. During the summer efforts seemed underway to draw closer to Iraq and perhaps to Syria, thus creating an uneasy partnership of revolutionary regimes. In August there were reports of an agreement on Yemen. The wounds in the Arab body politic, hastily stitched up in Cairo in 1964, had not yet completely reopened.

The ten years after Suez brought, not unity among the Arabs, but only bitter quarrels, which led to open war in Yemen. The period, however, did show an immense gain for Arab ambitions in the gradual elimination of control by the great powers. After the crisis year of 1958, which had brought American intervention in Lebanon, it was no longer possible for the great powers to dictate Middle Eastern affairs. The power of Russia and the United States, even of Great Britain, remained great. Huge investments by both East and West greatly influenced Arab economic development, military status, and independence of action, but they could no longer dictate policy. Russia had to tolerate, at one time or another and in one country or another, harsh campaigns against domestic communists. In 1963 Moscow actually threatened to withdraw military aid to Iraq if the suppression of the Kurds continued. Baghdad ignored Moscow without penalty. The United States, accepting Nasser's regime, had to tolerate his ambitions and his extravagances, rather than to allow Egypt to rely solely on Soviet support. American aid to Egypt had brought little concrete benefit to the United States, to the disgust of many members of Congress. By 1966 it was impossible to assume that even an impending $150 million American development loan could force Nasser to conform to American desires. The British presence in the Middle East was fast fading; South Arabia was already under pressure from terrorist parties supported from Cairo. East of Suez Great Britain seemed destined, like France, to become a distant force, with historical associations and contemporary economic interests but little control.

If the Arabs in the Middle East are to have a glorious future, then the human and physical sources of power have to be developed more rapidly. If 60 million Arabs are to realize their dream of a renascence that will earn them a seat at the table of the mighty, then the economic and social structure of the Middle East must be transformed. Whether this transformation is brought about by traditional monarchs with revolutionary means, by revolutionary republics through orthodox private investment, by both, or by an unforeseen approach has for a decade been a source of severe ideological conflict, but that it must be brought about is recognized by all.

The development of the Arab Middle East has been hampered by political instability reflected in shifting alliances and antagonisms, as much as by any other factor. The record of coups and revolutions is depressing, the list of assassinations appalling, the number of fallen governments astronomical. In Iraq between 1958 and 1965 there were thirty-nine known military plots; two successful coups, both accompanied by brutal massacres; and ultimate fragmentation of most political organizations into quarreling factions. In Syria since 1949 there have been eight successful coups and five unsuccessful revolts. Even the idealistic Baathists have largely destroyed themselves, leaving only the military to run the country. In Jordan Hussein has managed a precarious existence, constantly threatened by Palestinian unrest, Nasserist plots, and other treason. Even in Egypt there have been two serious Muslim Brotherhood attempts to assassinate Nasser; the latest, in 1965, involved nearly 400 conspirators. To create a viable economy in an atmosphere threatening sudden violence is an imposing task.

Despite the political turmoil, giant steps have been taken in the last decade to raise the Middle East out of its medieval economy. Foreign investment, the oil wealth of the Persian Gulf, and national sacrifices have made a considerable dent on the age-old routine of barter economy, Bedouin tribes, subsistence agriculture, and reliance on the Koran as the sole guide to human endeavor.[1] There have been elaborate and impressive development schemes, from the great Aswan Dam in Egypt to a brand-new system of public schools in Kuwait. Too much capital has been funneled into the arms race, including well over $1 billion of credit obtained from Russia, or into prestigious but unproductive showcase projects, but much has also been accomplished. Perhaps the greatest difficulty is that, despite rapid growth, the mushrooming population catches up with and outdistances the impact of each new improvement. No problem in the Arab world is more troublesome than population control, but, given the historic sanctity of the Arab family, social planning for birth control faces an uncertain future. Without population control, all the incredible efforts of the past decade may prove futile.

In ten years their enormous progress, with its dramatic and visible results, has been the pride of the Arabs. Much, perhaps most, remains to be done. There has been insufficient development of the vital human resources: The illiteracy rate is too high and the number of trained technicians too low. Too great a portion of Arab agriculture has been untouched by modern methods, condemning the peasants to a life not unlike that of their grandparents. Too great a portion of Arab industry is ill planned and ill suited to the competitive world markets. But the errors and omissions are not what strikes the Arab eye; rather, it sees only the triumphs and successes. Arab cities are no longer mud ghettos and arrogant villas, for today there are new skyscrapers and new apartment projects as well. Although much Arab newspaper space is devoted to conflicts and coups, most Arabs are more intimately concerned with the impact of the new economy on their personal aspirations.

Despite the substantial Arab development, in the years after Kadesh the economic contrast between Israel and the Arab Middle East has grown more pronounced. In its first decade as a welfare state, Israel absorbed, sustained, housed, and provided advanced services for 900,000 new citizens. The continuing integration of vast numbers of

Jews is the major and most impressive accomplishment of the state, as it was intended to be. By 1966 the problems of integration the Afro-Asian Jews were being faced with less optimism but with more realism. A swift course in Hebrew and low-skilled jobs could not eradicate customs that are centuries old, but increasingly the multi-faceted techniques of modern social work have been applied to recalcitrant Jews, Westernizing as well as Zionizing them. The Israeli population explosion has differed markedly from that of the Arabs in that the new citizens have tended to strengthen rather than to weaken the economic institutions of the state.

The majority of the new citizens have not, as myth would have it, entered the kibbutzim; in fact, by 1961 the population of the various kibbutzim had slipped to 4 percent of the total population and seemed likely to drop even lower. Most of Israel's citizens, well over 80 percent, live in the sprawling urban areas. Although there have been hundreds of new agricultural settlements, an increase in irrigated land, and a rise in agricultural production, the future of the economy clearly lies in the development of industries competitive on the world market. At the same time, a substantial investment must be made for schools and housing that bring no immediate return. The symbols of the new growth—the pipeline to the Negev opened in 1964, the state forests, the new universities, the housing developments, the new museum—are the result of a fantastic investment in the future far beyond the present or even immediately foreseeable resources of the state.

Israel has been overdependent from the first on foreign funds to redress the lopsided balance of trade. Despite the outward signs of progress, the Israeli economy as constituted was and is most precarious. For nearly twenty years Israel has lived beyond its means. Imports normally run two and a half to three times higher than exports, a drain not balanced by services. The deficit was for a while corrected by aid from the United States government, world Jewry, and German reparations. But after 1963 none of these sources could be tapped at the previous rate. In 1962 German reparations tapered off and were not fully replaced by contributions from private German citizens. Many of the original Israel bonds began falling due. And the United States government started to cut economic assistance.

The Israelis are faced with the necessity of reducing internal consumption and cutting investment or finding new sources of funds. Much of the investment so far has been both wise and profitable, but Israel faces severe challenges in the future. A great deal of the land of Israel is hopelessly arid, and all available sources of water have been tapped. The prospects for desalinization on a large scale are still distant. Israeli industry is hampered by the shortage of mineral deposits, the difficulties of importing raw materials for processing, and restricted markets. A most hopeful source of income is tourism, carefully exploited by the Israelis, but even the predicted increase in tourism will not go very far toward reducing the deficit. Israel thus remains a remittance state, dependent upon declining foreign contributions even for the existing standard of living. Measured by any set of economic indexes, the prospects for Israel are bleak, but the Israelis, even the economists, have relied successfully too often on faith rather than on facts to be unwarrantedly pessimistic now. The state has gone forward, despite the dangers in the deficit, confident of eventual solvency. If worse comes to worst, Israel can always rely on miracles, a technique that has in the past often proved fruitful for the Zionists, to the confusion of their enemies.

Just as the Arabs have expended most of their time and energy on their own affairs, the Israelis have been only occasionally distracted from their development by sporadic flashes of Arab hostility. Israel has been insulated from the rest of the Middle East. The old round of quarrels and threats has continued, often reflexively. The Israelis have been far more conscious than the Arabs of these confrontations, for the Arab armies continuously threaten the vulnerable Israeli border. But the Israelis have found other friends, other markets, other alliances that they might not have sought and won had they not been cut off from the Arab Middle East. Israeli technicians have moved into Africa, Asia, and even Latin America. Particularly in Africa, the emerging nations offer markets for Israel's often overpriced industrial goods and diplomatic support in the world's forums.

Israeli relations with Washington have been more strained than could have been anticipated in the halcyon days of the Truman administration. The Israelis were forced to come to terms with the Republicans, less susceptible to domestic Zionist political pressure and more concerned with converting the Arabs to the Eisenhower Doctrine. The results were not always felicitous from the Israeli point of view, in that Washington did not respond automatically to Israel's fears and desires. Relations, however, never again reached the icy depths of the post-Sinai period, and generally the Americans could be counted on in the last resort; for example, President John F. Kennedy promised Ben-Gurion that Israel would receive American support against aggression. When the Arab tripartite unity talks had apparently succeeded in 1963, Israel again needed reassurances. American willingness to make arms sales to keep Israel on a parity with the Arabs was almost as much as the Israelis could reasonably expect. Actually, although the new weapons were vital to Israel's security, continuing generous American economic tranfusions were even more essential. In 1966, despite indications that Israel might eventually be phased out of all economic-assistance programs, relations with Washington remained close.

The same could not be said about relations with the Soviet Union. After Moscow's decision to plunge into the Middle East on the side of the radical Arab regimes, Israel could count on a major enemy. The Soviet Union harassed the Israelis at every turn, supported the Arabs diplomatically at the United Nations, and dubbed Israel an imperialist pawn. Obviously Moscow knew that arms deals with the Arabs created a dangerous threat to Israel's security, and obviously Moscow did not care about Israel's security or Middle Eastern stability. The Israeli response to Soviet pressure had to be unnaturally restrained. Inside the Soviet Union were 3 million Jews, potential Israeli citizens if Moscow should ever permit emigration. Although for years the Israelis had to suffer the Russians' hostility in relative silence, the "great thaw" after Stalin opened opportunities in the rest of Eastern Europe. Some emigration was permitted, although relatively few Jews were left. Israeli trade delegations found an increasing welcome in the smaller East European countries, sufficient so that Egyptian students complained that they were forced to purchase Zionist rather than Arab citrus fruit in Hungary. Russia, however, remained firmly pro-Arab.

Although Israel had its difficulties, both economic and diplomatic, during the decade after Sinai, the basic threat to the state, Arab intransigence, remained unchanged. Elsewhere Israel might appear as a progressive, socialist state struggling for social justice and a small place in the sun, but in the Arab Middle East, Israel was not regarded as a state but as an alien intruder, supported by the imperialists, and dedicated to aggression.

> Zionism is a colonialist movement in its inception, aggressive and expansionist in its goals, racist and segregationist in its configurations and fascist in its means and aims. Israel in its capacity as the spearhead of this destructive movement and the pillar for colonialism is a permanent source of tension and turmoil in the Middle East in particular and to the international community in general.[2]

Here were the facts about Israel that the Arabs believed were being callously ignored by millions of well-meaning people the world over who had been misled by propaganda. Here was the Zionist Israel that the Arabs were pledged to destroy, and neither the setback in Sinai nor the intervening decade had weakened their resolve by 1966. Ten years, even twenty years are but a tick of the Middle Eastern clock. The time of reckoning would come, if not soon, at least eventually. From 1957 until 1963 the hectic pace of Arab events, the collapse of governments, the ebb and flow of unity efforts, generally distracted Arab interest from the Palestine problem but never interrupted the oft-repeated promises of vengeance.

In 1963 some of these promises came due, requiring payment in the form of action. The Israelis had gone ahead with plans to divert the waters of the Jordan to the Negev. For years the Arabs had warned that the first drop of water out of the pipeline would be sufficient as a casus belli. The Syrians, after the failure of tripartite unity, insisted on war as much to shame Nasser as to intimidate the Israelis. As early as June 1962 Nasser had told a group of representatives from the Gaza strip that liberation of Palestine was a matter for the coming years. Deeply involved in Yemen and at odds with practically every Arab government, Nasser was aware that Egypt simply did not have the resources to consider war; nor could its prestige survive doing nothing in the face of Syrian militance. On December 17 the Egyptian weekly, *Rose al-Yusuf*, published an article noting both that "the United Arab Republic will not let itself be pushed into a battle with Israel before the attainment of unity among all the Arab countries" and that "the UAR knows how and when it will eliminate Israel, and it knows itself to be capable of shouldering this burden by itself."[3] But this realistic weighing of Arab capacities drew howls of indignation.

In December Nasser drove the wedge in farther with an important speech outlining the new direction of Egyptian policies.

> In order to confront Israel, which put a challenge to us last week, and whose Chief of Staff stood up and said, "We shall divert the water against the will of the Arabs, and let the Arabs do what they can," a meeting between the Arab Kings and Heads of State must take place as soon as possible, regardless of the strifes and conflicts between them. . . . We will sit and talk seriously at the meetings, and it will be no shame if we come out and say that we cannot today use force. . . . For I would lead you to disaster if I were to proclaim that I would fight at a time when I was unable to do so. I would not lead my country to disaster and would not gamble with its destiny.[4]

As Nasser intended, the speech led directly to the Arab summit. Syrian bellicosity was neutralized. Palestinian Arab frustration was given an outlet in the creation of the Palestine Liberation Organization, which was to have a military arm to train the refugees for eventual return. Schemes for diverting the tributaries of the Jordan in Syria, Lebanon, and Jordan were undertaken. A joint military-defense command was established under Egyptian leadership. The period from 1963 to 1966 was an era of suspicious good feeling among the Arab states. Most Arab leaders agreed with Nasser that it was not the time to attack Israel.

The Baathist regime in Syria was avowedly far more militant than were its peers. Damascus scorned the old monarchies, had harsh words for the Nasserists, and even quarreled with the Iraqi revolutionaries. Damascus insisted on action. Syria began preparations to divert the vital Jordan tributaries; it also pushed a tough border policy, encouraging the formation of secret commando units among the Palestinian Arabs. Despite Nasser's moderation, Syrian-Israeli relations, always tense, had deteriorated dangerously by 1966.

By then the strains of maintaining tranquility were beginning to tell on Nasser. The conservative monarchs were going their own way. The Yemen affair dragged on, despite some Egyptian concessions. The Syrians were being difficult. In February King Faisal of

Saudi Arabia was being widely criticized and threatened with the continuing presence of Egyptian troops in Yemen. In June the conservative regimes were excommunicated, barred from the eventual conquest of Palestine: "Arab reactionary elements cannot march with progressive forces even if the road leads to the liberation of Palestine."[5] In July King Hussein of Jordan was again castigated for failure to support the Palestine Liberation Organization. In the same speech Nasser, for the first time in two years, attacked the West. The United States was also accused of reducing funds to the refugees in order to liquidate the problem. By the summer of 1966 Nasser seemed to be returning to a hard line.

In two decades of almost unbroken Arab-Israeli hostility, most "events" have resulted from "conditioned reflexes" and have been limited not by self-discipline but by outside restraints. The structure of the existing international system, despite the shifts in East-West rivalry; the advent of even more new nations; and the apparent victory of economic change over stagnation, have not allowed either the Israelis or the Arabs to follow independent policies in relation to each other. Although the confrontation has expanded to farther fields, it has also been diffused; however, in the Middle East the same hard-core issues remain frozen into set patterns. The traditional Israeli reaction to programs of unity, particularly those that might include Jordan, is almost instinctive. The Arab determination to seal off Israel, creating a barren garrison state, is a matter of faith not of mere policy.

Of all the areas of conflict, the most violent and most dangerous has remained the border war. After the reverberations of the Sinai campaign had quieted, the greatest single change along the Israel border was the end of the fedayeen raids. At least citizens no longer felt a daily threat as they went their normal rounds, as they had felt it in 1956. Israel was still in many ways a garrison state besieged by frustrated Arabs, but the end of the fedayeen raids eased the pressure considerably, although it did not eliminate border clashes.

As in the past, the Lebanese frontier caused little anxiety. Only in November 1965, when the Syrian sponsored El Fatah terrorist group carried out raids through Lebanese territory, did the Israelis feel called upon to retaliate against the border villages. The Egyptian frontier also settled into reasonable tranquillity, with only sporadic infiltrations past the United Nations Emergency Force. The lengthy Jordanian frontier remained troublesome. There was a serious outbreak of fighting in Jerusalem in 1961, for example, but the real danger came from the illicit terrorist groups in Jordan. As usual, the Israelis held the Jordanians responsible for their frontier. As usual the Jordanians, trapped between the dangers of Israeli retaliation and of rebellion by Palestinian Arabs denied vengeance, did the best they could, which was sufficient to prevent a major confrontation. The real tension after 1956 came along the forty-seven-mile boundary with Syria.

The apparent crux of the Israeli-Syrian conflict was the 100-square-mile demilitarized zone, but in a broader sense the real problem was the tenuous Israeli hold on the Jordan River. Israeli determination not only to exploit the demilitarized zone but also to tap the Jordan River despite Arab and occasional United Nations opposition enraged the Syrians. Increasingly the border incidents were not isolated local clashes but genuine battles in a potentially lethal struggle. After the collapse of the United Arab Republic in September 1961, tensions increased markedly.

On March 8, 1962, Syrian artillery fired on an Israeli patrol boat in the Sea of Galilee. On March 15 three Israeli police boats came under Syrian fire. The provocation was sufficient to produce the habitual Israeli response. Ben-Gurion, after consulting almost exclusively with his military commanders, ordered a massive military retaliation. On the night of March 16 an Israeli attack from Ein Gev hit Syrian positions around the villages of Nugeib and al-Kursi. On April 9, 1962, the Security Council voted a resolution condemning the Israelis. The Syrians were delighted. On April 10 the Knesset voted seventy-six to three to reject categorically the Security Council resolution. The Israelis were infuriated that only Israeli retaliation had been condemned without reference to continual Syrian provocation.

The first new approach to the Syrian border tension came in August 1963, when Israel approached the Security Council for redress for the murder of two Israeli farmers. The United States and Great Britain introduced a resolution that implied Syrian guilt. The Soviet Union vetoed it. The Israelis had additional evidence of the futility of dependence on the United Nations. By 1963 the water issue was becoming very serious indeed, as Israeli diversion work continued. The proposed plant at Tiberias, completely within Israel, could take more water than had been assigned under the Johnston Plan. Repeatedly the Arabs warned that the diversion project would lead to war. The Israelis replied that the water would begin to be pumped into the 108-inch pipeline to the Negev late in 1964. In June 1961 the Arab League Defense Council had discussed the problem and had reputedly produced a secret plan, but neither Jordan nor Syria had been satisfied. In 1962, although Jordan development plans continued, the key Arab water project was the Syrian diversion of the Hasbani and Baniyas rivers. In 1963 the Syrians began minor preliminary work, thus for the first time challenging Israel's control of the Jordan.

On March 8, 1963, the Baathist Party and some military commanders toppled the Syrian government, the fourth and most ineffectual cabinet since the collapse of the United Arab Republic. The new government was dedicated to the cause of Arab Palestine and determined to replace the previous floundering border policy with a hard line.

> The Syrian Arab Republic considers that the liberation of Palestine is a fundamental, national objective which can be realized but through a revolutionary method resting on giving an outlet to the energy of the Arab people, whether it is political, economic, or military, combining and concentrating it for the realization of this objective, including giving a chance to the people of Palestine to organize themselves in complete freedom and mobilize their revolutionary energy in order to participate in the battle of liberation. The Syrian Arab Republic has an obligation to offer every kind of support and aid to the people of Palestine for the realization of this objective.[6]

While the Syrians were encouraging the Palestinian Arabs to organize and to act, the border with Israel rapidly took on the aspect of a front. The local Syrian farmers were moved out of the frontier villages, and the army moved in. A heavily fortified cordon was developed: Tanks were embedded in concrete, deeper emplacements dug, and additional wire strung. Although the Syrian positions were essentially defensive, designed to prevent the traditional Israeli lightning retaliation or to blunt any future mass attack, the opportunity to harass Israeli development projects was golden.

The Syrian offensive took a more subtle form. Sometime in 1964 Palestinian Arabs in Syria formed the activist paramilitary organization, El Fatah, to reclaim Palestine by violence. From its headquarters in Damascus, El Fatah recruited and trained Arabs eager to strike out at the Zionists. Although officially Syria did not recognize the secret organization, Israeli intelligence, insisted with considerable evidence, that Syrian sympathy extended as well to arming, training, and maintaining El Fatah units in Syria. From January to March 1965, according to El Fatah statements, seven sabotage raids were carried out. In general, little damage was done, but the potential for damage existed, and Israeli retaliation raids had little effect. In September and October 1965 El Fatah raided from Jordan and in November from Lebanon. Between February and August 1966 the Israelis reported ninety-six shooting incidents along the border. Five Israelis were killed and twenty-four wounded.

In July 1966 the combination of Syrian threats to divert the waters of the Jordan, Syrian support of the El Fatah raids, and continual Syrian harassment culminated in a spectacular new Israeli approach to retaliation. On July 14 Israeli jets, protected by a fighter umbrella, attacked earth-moving equipment at the Baniyas River diversion project. When four Syrian MIG-21s showed up, the Israeli Mirage-III fighters attacked and shot down one of them. The air attack apparently caught the Syrians by surprise. Damascus promptly appealed to the Security Council. On July 16 Syrian Premier Dr. Yussef Zayen stated that Syria was determined to wage a war of liberation to regain Arab rights in Palestine: "We shall teach Israel a lesson she will never forget."[7] The aggressive Syrian posture was noted in New York, where the Security Council met on the Israeli-Arab problem for the 214th time. In view of Syrian provocations and sabotage, the Council declined to censure Israel.

Although both sides were cautioned by the Security Council to avoid violence, the frontier war erupted again in August. Apparently Syrian soldiers opened fire on an Israeli patrol boat on the Sea of Galilee; in any case, firing began during the night of August 15. The Israelis sent in additional patrol boats. The Syrians then retaliated by sending in their MIGs. The Israelis scrambled into their own planes. The Israelis had not expected such rapid escalation; in fact, they had rushed a boatload of newsmen and photographers to report on the original incident. The observers had to be hurriedly evacuated when the MIGs struck. Machine-gun fire from an Israeli boat brought down a MIG-17 and an Israeli Mirage-III shot down another MIG-21 over Syria. Israeli Vautour tactical bombers worked over the Syrian positions along the coast. The Syrians described the MIG attack as a punishment operation. More ominously, Damascus indicated that Syria would no longer rely on diplomacy but would in the future rely on an offensive rather than a defensive strategy.

It was apparent that the Syrian government could no longer count on the United Nations to condemn Israeli retaliation. Without such condemnation to show Syrians that the Damascus government was effectively dealing with Israel, the only alternative was to respond to retaliation with further retaliation, a perilous cycle in view of Syrian military weakness. Syrian policy remained vague, however, and Damascus at times even showed, if not moderation, at least tentative gestures toward toleration. Just three weeks before the July outbreaks, Syria had completed a prisoner exchange long sought by the Israelis. In the summer of 1966 the forty-seven miles of twisting frontier between determined Israel and aggressive Syria held the potential for violence.

On the economic front there was considerable though still very limited easing of tension after Sinai. The Gulf of 'Aqaba remained open, and one additional effort was made to open the Suez Canal to Israeli shipments. In the opinions of most international legal experts there was no doubt that Israel had an all but unassailable case; the Egyptians were, however, largely unmoved by legal technicalities. In 1957 Dag Hammarskjöld conducted strenuous negotiations with the Egyptians, which finally produced an unwritten agreement. The Egyptians would allow passage for Israeli cargoes in non-Israeli ships. About forty such non-Israeli ships passed through the Canal before early 1959, when Egypt abrogated the agreement. On May 22, 1959, the *Inge Toft*, flying a Danish flag but carrying an Israeli cargo bound for Asia, was halted by the Egyptians at Port Said. Laborious separate discussions between Hammarskjöld and the Egyptians and Hammarskjöld and the Israelis produced another formula. In December the Greek *Astypalea*, bound for Djibouti, arrived at Port Said to test the new formula. The Egyptians stopped the *Astypalea*. After 1959 the Canal remained closed to Israel, and the blockade was back in effect. Public and private efforts in the United States, including the picketing of the Egyptian ship *Cleopatra* in New York harbor by the Seafarers International Union in April 1960, produced no visible results.

On the other hand, the Arab boycott, still directed by the Arab League Boycott of Israel Office in Damascus, ran into increasing problems in the 1960s. Although still effective in the Arab Middle East, it was resisted both by other governments uneasy at extra-legal pressure on their own nationals and by private concerns irritated at limitations on their profit-making privileges. In the United States on June 25, 1965, the Williams-Javits law was enacted; it amended the United States Export Control Act to express opposition to boycotts imposed by foreign countries against other countries. In 1965 the Israelis took an offensive step, warning seven foreign companies that they would have to do business openly in Israel, rather than through third parties, or not at all. The threat of a counterboycott persuaded the seven to trade openly in Israel.

After 1957 the Arabs' continued efforts to quarantine Israel diplomatically gradually ran into difficulties. For the most part the campaign had to be redirected toward the increasing number of newly independent nations, particularly in Africa. At Bandung Nasser and the Arab diplomats had easily barred Israel and secured a resolution friendly to Arab Palestinian aspirations, but that had been before Suez. In 1957 again the Arabs saw no reason why Israel could not be isolated from the nonaligned nations. The Arabs, however, did not recognize that their quarrel had little or no relevance to the Burmese or the Nigerians. Other Islamic nations, like Turkey and Iran, had long since established normal relations with Israel. Distant nations were even less likely to be excited about the Palestinian problem. To a large extent early Arab successes were the result of Afro-Asian ignorance of Israel and undifferentiated friendship for the Arabs. Once the Zionists began competing for the friendship of the new nations, the Arabs could no longer rest on their easily gained laurels.

In April 1958, at the Accra Conference of Independent African States, the Arabs did manage to win passage for a resolution urging a just solution to the Palestine problem. The high point of Arab success came at the Casablanca Conference of Heads of African States in 1961, when the most radical of the new states passed a resolution condemning Israel in no uncertain terms:

. . . Notes with indignation that Israel has always taken the side of the imperialists each time an important position had to be taken concerning vital problems about Africa, notably Algeria, the Congo, and the nuclear tests in Africa, and the Conference, therefore, denounces Israel as an instrument in the service of Imperialism and neo-colonialism not only in the Middle East but also in Africa and Asia.[8]

Israeli aid and commercial overtures to the new nations were attacked by Arab spokesmen as imperialism in Zionist clothing. Soviet writers joined the chorus: In October 1961 V. Nikolayev, writing in Moscow's *International Affairs*, strongly condemned Israel's African programs. But the repeated Soviet-Arab warnings fell on increasingly deaf ears.

By the end of 1961 the tides of nonalignment were shifting. The most revolutionary and radical nations did not always reap the benefits of Western aid. Nasser's ambitions in Africa gave pause to some. Self-interest began to demand more productive policies than mere friendship with the Arab bloc. Outside the Islamic states of North Africa, the Arab campaign faltered. The major reason was the arrival of the Israelis on the African scene without the predicted horns and tails and with a variety of techniques and programs that sounded most attractive to small states fearful of the dangers of too close association with the superpowers.

In the first burst of diplomatic activity after the establishment of the Jewish state in 1948, Israeli diplomats had sought only recognition. For example, Burma voted against Israel's entry into the United Nations in May 1949 but was persuaded to recognize the new state in December 1949. Thereafter relations were generally proper but unproductive. In 1952 a Burmese delegation headed by U Kyaw Nyein "accidentally" stopped in Israel during a European tour. In January 1953 Moshe Sharett attended the First Asian Socialist Conference. Generally, the Asian states remained distant and cool; for example, India did not establish diplomatic relations with Israel until September 1956. But gradually the advantages of cultivating the new nations became clear to the Israelis.

The most obvious area for penetration was Black Africa, burgeoning with new states and new leaders but facing the same development problems that Israel had faced. As early as 1953 Israel had opened a consulate at Accra; it was raised to embassy status when the Gold Coast became independent Ghana. Increasingly, Israel followed up diplomatic ties with a variety of exported development programs, often more suited to the African situation than were more elaborate Western or Soviet schemes. And the Africans felt no humiliation in accepting the assistance of another small new nation. By 1963 the impact had been sufficiently impressive so that the non-Islamic states of Africa refused to curtail their mutually profitable relations with Israel solely to accommodate Arab prejudices. At the Addis Ababa Conference of African Chiefs of State in May 1963, to which President Ahmadou Ahidjo of Cameroon flew directly from a state visit to Israel, Nasser learned that the old days of automatic support for the Arabs had definitely gone. For most Africans Israel had become a friend sympathetic to their aspirations and familiar with their difficulties; in turn they had come to know far more about Israel, from firsthand experience, than the Arabs knew. The Negro presidents bluntly informed Nasser that the Palestine problem must be excluded from the agenda:

> We are friendly with Israel. You are not. That is your business, but do not inject a personal note into Addis. If you do, you will split Africa in two. You will carry white (Arab) Africa and we will carry black Africa. We would never forgive you for splitting Africa this way.[9]

Israel's African commitments continued to accelerate. Of particular interest to the Africans were the Nahal program for army-established agricultural settlements and the Gadna program to establish a paramilitary youth corps. Not only had the Israelis evolved several exportable techniques but also their experts brought not political domination but experience with an austere pioneer society. By 1965 Israel had 600 experts working in Africa, and there were 1,200 African students studying in Israel. In 1966 Israeli Premier Levi Eshkol made a three-week tour through seven African states to visit the highly publicized Israeli projects. A new window had been opened by the supposedly quarantined Israelis. The effect could be noted at international conferences, at the United Nations, and even in the growing commitment of Egypt in Africa to counterbalance the Israeli effort. At a relatively small cost, the Israelis were reaping rich dividends: "If we had not made the effort to work with these African states there is no doubt that they would have been hostile or at best indifferent to us."[10]

Another area that had long been indifferent to Israel was Latin America. Only the control by Jews of half the Holy City had produced much interest and only then as a result of Vatican concern. Outside Argentina the Latin American Jewish population was small. Still, three hours after Premier Eshkol had returned from his African tour, President Zalman Shazar left Lydda airport for state visits to four Latin American states, underlining the new Israeli presence in Latin America. Although less extensive than the African commitment, Israeli technical cooperation missions were in nine Latin American countries, as well as Jamaica and Trinidad in the Caribbean. Since 1961 more than 1,500 Latin American students have studied in Israel. Although the Gadna program was equally as popular as in Africa, the Lachish system of planting a core urban center to service a cluster of surrounding agricultural communities attracted the most extensive interest when developed in Venezuela. Israel's specific gains in Latin America are less apparent than in Africa, but the broadening of Israel's horizons can only be beneficial to Israel. The Arabs have few comparable successes with which to combat the new Israeli showcase developments in Latin America.

The old Arab quarantine, already crumbling outside the Middle East in 1956, has endured a decade of breaches. The credo of Zionist imperialism, an article of faith for the Arabs, has attracted few devotees.

Though there were rapid changes in Israel's diplomatic posture after 1957, there was no sign of any shift on that most vexatious of all its problems, the existence of over 1 million Arab refugees on its borders. For eighteen years the refugees had remained bitter hostages in the Arab-Israeli conflict, forever dreaming of return. The ten years after Sinai saw their share of recommendations on the refugees but, as in the years before, not even a tiny step toward solution; in fact by 1966 the refugee issue had grown more complex and more dangerous.

The refugee population instead of gradually declining through absorption into the Arab world has instead increased steadily. By 1962 the total recognized as refugees and receiving aid from the United Nations Relief and Works Agency had climbed from an original 700,000 to 1,083,691; by 1965 it had reached 1,173,701. Although many experts argue that the United Nations figures are inaccurate, no one denies the burden of caring for the Arabs, whatever their exact numbers. Only a very few refugees have found their way in the larger Arab world, and only a very few more in the camps are self-supporting. The vast majority wait out their lives on the dole. Approximately 70 percent of the funds to maintain the refugees' minimal standard of living has come from United States contributions. Increasingly, there has been a reluctance by the United States to continue these contributions at the same level. Not only have the refugees shown little gratitude, assuming that the payments are some sort of conscience money for American support of Israel, but also other nations, particularly the Arab states, have not, according to Washington, been sufficiently generous. Washington has pointed out the generally recognized disarray of the refugee rolls, filled as they are with dead, absent, and self-supporting Arabs, whereas some 250,000 children are not included. Many ration cards have changed hands, often accumulating in one man's control. The flow of United Nations funds has, in fact, been diverted into an underground economy generally benefiting both the refugees and their host countries but also particularly benefiting certain individuals who now have vested interests in the system.

The result is a bureaucratic jumble of obsolete statistics, corruption, wasted funds, and unassuaged need. In 1965–1966 the United States reduced its contribution. But the United Nations faces rising costs and increasing numbers of children, which will demand larger, rather than smaller budgets.

In 1959 at the request of the General Assembly to suggest means for the reintegration of the refugees into the economic life of the Middle East by repatriation or resettlement, Dag Hammarskjöld produced an estimate on the cost of reintergration—$1.5 billion. As there was no agreement, even this appalling sum would now be too small. The Arab states have continued to insist that resettlement is out of the question, in view of the refugees' determination to return to Palestine. The passing years have in no way muted the Palestinian Arabs' dream of return.

> "From the hill there I can see my land. I
> burn for it. My son has promised that my
> bones will rest there one day."[11]

In the meantime the Arabs live out their lives, dependent on the uncertain charity of the United Nations. The Israelis, on the other hand, have shown no inclination to allow the massive repatriation desired by the refugees, insisting that there is simply no room in Israel for hundreds of thousands of unskilled, angry, and subversive Arabs. There is no longer a Palestine, only an Israel—foreign to the Arab in tongue, in religion, in customs, and in institutions. For Israel repatriation can be only at a token level.

In 1961, in one more effort to break the deadlock, the Palestine Conciliation Commission asked Dr. Joseph E. Johnson, President of the Carnegie Endowment for International Peace, to make a new study. The resulting Johnson plan was certainly the most feasible solution in 1962. It accepted both the Israeli need for security and Arab aspirations. But the details of the Johnson plan have since become immaterial, lost in the long archives of failures, for, as others had learned before him, neither side wanted a negotiated settlement but only vindication. Israel had steadily grown not more but less compromising. In 1958 and again in 1960 Israel insisted that the correct solution was resettlement outside Israel. In November 1961 the Knesset passed a resolution stating that there could be no return of the Arab refugees to Israel greater than the 100,000 originally offered in 1949. The Johnson plan assumed that the Israelis would soften when presented with a practical proposal. They did not. The Arabs, equally adamant, simply insisted on full repatriation. The refugee problem remains pitiful, expensive, and menacing. For many refugees the only hope for return seemed to lie in violence.

In the Gaza strip in 1955–1956 the refugees had eagerly participated in the Egyptian fedayeen program as a means to achieve immediate vengeance and as a first step toward eventual return to Falastine Arabiyeh. In January 1964 the Arab League supported an effort to form the Palestine Liberation Organization. The Organization, under Ahmed Shukairy, did begin training the Palestine Liberation Army in the Gaza strip and Syria. By 1966 these Palestinian Army units had either been integrated into the Egyptian, Iraqi, and Syrian armies or demobilized into the ranks of the refugees.

More dangerous were the covert terrorist groups. The Syrian-based El Fatah, which carried out sabotage raids, offered ample evidence that, among many Palestinian Arabs, there is no patience with

Arab diplomacy. In Jordan the impact of this impatience has been sufficiently dangerous so that even supporters of the more moderate Palestine Liberation Organization have been arrested, as King Hussein is forced to deny the existence of Palestinians in order to underline the unity of all Jordanians.

Of all the long-lived disputes between Israel and the Arabs after that over the refugees, the question of diversion of the Jordan River water has grown most serious. The Arabs have been particularly agitated about Israeli projects because these projects threaten not only to drain the Jordan basin but also to bring a great increase in Israel's population and an improvement in the Israeli economy. By 1970 Israel will be diverting 320 million cubic meters of water annually to the Negev, supplying a population of 375,000. The Jordanians have shown little interest in provocative interdicting irrigation programs and have concentrated on diverting the waters of the Yarmuk River, a Jordan tributary. Even this effort has given rise to charges by Israel that the Yarmuk project is increasing the salinity of the Jordan. Although the Jordanian projects and perhaps the planned Lebanese schemes are potentially sources of high tension, there is no doubt that Syrian proposals are far more dangerous. The Syrians in particular claim that, as the Arabs control 77 percent of the Jordan's head- waters, Israel should have only 23 percent. The Syrians theoretically have the capacity to enforce this interpretation.

Once the Syrians began work, Israel made it quite clear that, if Syria diverted water in excess of that alloted under the Johnson plan, a casus belli would exist. In January 1965 Premier Levi Eshkol claimed that such diversion "would be an encroachment on our soil. A military confrontation would become inevitable."[12] The Syrians, however, could go ahead with their projects for some time before such a confrontation became likely. The Israelis used the tense border to underline their point. On March 17, 1965, Israeli troops and armor attacked a construction unit near Doka. On August 12, 1965, there was another clash in the demilitarized zone close to the Syrian project. It was not coincidental that the Israeli air strike of July 1966 was conducted against the Syrian canal project; in fact, General Itzhak Rabin, Israeli Chief of Staff, specifically told the press that the choice of target was apt, in that diversion of the Jordan River is the symbol of Arab sabotage against Israel.

By the summer of 1966 the Syrians had completed only about 1 percent of the construction necessary to arrive at a full-fledged confrontation with the Israelis. Even that 1 percent had, however, produced serious concern in Israel.

Although in ten years none of these stresses and provocations had led to open war, both the Israelis and the Arabs believed it essential to be prepared for the eventuality. The result was an armament race that gobbled up development funds, further undermined the shaky stability of the area, and created anxiety rather than security for both competitors. The furor of the Suez crisis had momentarily distracted attention from the 1955 Czech arms deal. In fact, that deal had set off an arms race that made the Israelis choose preventive war. After 1957 the Israelis, although temporarily secure with their victory, their French alliance, and their captured equipment, were far from content and were determined never to be caught so short again.

The major obstacle to a satisfactory arms balance remained the Soviet Union, still delighted to flood friendly Arabs with the latest line of prestige armaments. Not even the small Arab capacity to pay limited the flow. Only the difficulty in absorbing increasingly sophisticated equipment by armed forces that were woefully weak in technical skills moderated to some degree the Soviet influx. As soon as the 1956 crisis had simmered down, Soviet arms again moved into Egypt and Syria. After 1958 similar arrangements were made with the new revolutionary Iraqi government. The British continued to supply their traditional Arab friends, although after 1958 British arms shipments waned. Increasingly America took up the slack in supplying the Arab kings. The Israelis did not think that one-for-one parity in weapons was necessary, but they were anxious that their operational weapons, even though far fewer for their smaller army, be comparable to those of the Arabs.

To match the Soviet equipment, the Israelis continued to pin their hopes on the French. Even after the collapse of the Fourth Republic in the midst of the Algerian war and the advent of Charles de Gaulle's Fifth Republic, Israeli-French relations remained intimate. Nor did France's post-Algerian concern with Islamic Africa have a noticeable impact on its relations with Israel. When France finally reestablished diplomatic relations with Egypt in 1963, Nasser was informed that the Israeli relationship would continue. In view of the new French posture of isolated grandeur, Israeli access to the secret places of the state remained remarkable. Only Israel had a special army mission attached to the French Defense Ministry and a permanent mission attached to the most secretive of all French agencies, the Atomic Energy Commission. The bulk of Israeli aircraft and several of the new generation of tactical missiles used by the Israelis were French.

Outside Paris the Israelis pushed their plea for weapons parity in Washington. Generally, the United States took a dim view of arms sales to anyone in the Middle East, but the necessity for aiding the more stable anticommunist states with military equipment to match the prestige equipment given the various republican regimes had been accepted. Israel insisted that this approach was unfair and dangerous. Reviewing Israel's vulnerability, Washington reluctantly agreed on occasion to the sale of special weapons to the Israelis, in order to prevent a completely lopsided balance. When the Egyptian air force began to acquire the new Russian TU-16 bombers to replace the old IL-28s, Washington sold an estimated $25 million worth of Hawk antiaircraft missiles to Israel. In 1966 Israel, as well as Jordan, was quietly allowed to purchase Patton medium tanks with 90-millimeter guns. The Israelis also bought an unknown number of A-4 Skyhawk bombers. They were thus assured of being no more than one or two steps behind the Arabs.

Another and most unlikely avenue of military and technical assistance for Israel gradually developed after the signing of the West German reparations agreement. Although Israeli-German relations were troubled by guilt and recriminations, the Germans possessed vast technical resources and a tradition of military skills. Sometime, probably, in 1963, Israeli-German contacts began. The extent of military cooperation is still unknown although some Israelis had been trained in Germany. The Germans had their own problems in recreating a military force in an atmosphere of domestic distaste and international suspicion; but the Israelis established a line to Bonn which could prove valuable in the future.

The result for Israel was a satisfactory parity. Israel could with almost instant mobilization produce over 200,000 adequately armed, well-trained, highly dedicated soldiers in a few days. No militia-army is as effective as a standing force, but the Israelis created a unique military establishment based on an interchangeable civilian and professional soldier. This tendency had gone far to remove the most obvious dangers of a garrison state dependent on a professional army accumulating power and influence. Obversely, it had increasingly produced a militant society where young and old, male and female, were soldiers pursuing civilian occupations. Israel had not, as the pessimists feared, become a Sparta dedicated to war but a equalitarian Roman Republic where the plow and the sword were interchangeable tools.

The Israeli army was not dependent on swords, however, for much of the infantry, often with only civilian transport, was well armed, many with the Uzzi submachine gun, one of Israel's most valuable export items. There were approximately 600 tanks, including the new Pattons, British Centurions, French AMXs, and American Super-Shermans. The air force of 450 planes included French Mystères, Super-Mystères, Mirages, Vautours, new thirty-passenger troop helicopters, and the American Skyhawks as well as odds and ends including much older propellor-driven craft. The Israelis had begun production of Fougas Magister jet trainers, which were adaptable to other uses. At sea the Israelis had only a scratch fleet with two destroyers and two outmoded submarines supported by a collection of patrol boats. Israel had both the American Hawk antiaircraft missiles and French air-to-air and antitank missiles but none of the strategically vital ground-to-ground missiles. On the other hand, Israeli military intelligence, which directs almost all covert and information-gathering activities, was superior to all but those of the super powers and was in some areas even their peer. In sum, the Israeli military establishment was adequately equipped to meet any or all of the Arab armies in the field; but actually the skill and élan of the troops produced the vital superiority, not the missiles or the Mystères.

Israel's lesser Arab opponents, Syria, Iraq, and Jordan, were more than adequately armed; but in varying degrees. Few of their soldiers had either the skills or the morale to match the Israelis. The Syrians had 50,000 troops, armed almost entirely with Soviet weapons; but very few of these were adequately trained for modern war. Often deeply involved in the shifting seas of Syrian politics, the officer corps had a heritage of inefficiency. The Syrians acquitted themselves far better than had been anticipated in the 1948–1949 Palestine war, so there was reason to suppose that on the defensive at least, the Syrian army might be more effective than many professional analysts assumed.

While the Syrian army had spent the last ten years dabbling in politics and provoking minor border incidents, the 70,000-man Iraqi army had fought a long and frustrating campaign against the Kurds. Such a war was difficult to wage and the experience could not but be helpful. The air force using the late model MIG-21D, and reportedly even better ones, had years of practicing ground-strikes without fear of aerial retaliation.

In Jordan the days of the elite Arab Legion had passed with the influx of new recruits and the decay of the Bedouin spirit. The withdrawal of the British officers in 1956 and the rot inherent in a system of political promotion had undoubtedly undone some of Glubb's work, but Hussein's army was still the equal of any Arab army, which may not be saying very much. Its 30,000 men were divided into nine brigades, three of them armored, and supported by tanks and a small air force.

Despite a total of 250,000 men, heavy armor, and modern aircraft, the three Arab states had not corrected their long-standing military weaknesses nor apparently trained a new generation of professional officers. Even with sufficient warning, their defensive capacities against an Israeli offensive appeared slight. In eighteen years their positions relative to Israel had not changed.

Egypt, however, was not troubled by the repeated coups that disturbed Syria and Iraq or the seething unrest of Hussein's former Palestinian citizens. Egypt more than any other Arab state had the capacity, the desire, and the opportunity to produce a first-rate army. In 1957 the regime had to swallow its first hopes of recreating the army overnight or even in four years. In the next decade the Egyptians still had an army not unlike the one that had been shattered in Sinai, up to a strength of something more than 160,000 men. Nasser had difficulty in recruiting both officers and men. The army, despite the eminence of former majors and colonels, was not an attractive career, particularly since the Yemen campaign. The social schism between the commissioned officers and the other ranks remained.

Egyptian equipment, however, was gorgeous. The air force had twenty squadrons, approximately 500 aircraft, MIG-15s, MIG-19s,

MIG-21Ds, equipped with air-to-air missiles, TU-16 bombers, equipped with air-to-ground missiles, and the older IL-28s. There was a domestic fighter Al Kahira 300, which was not really an operative plane. There were SAM-II, ground-to-air missiles. The army had 1,200 Soviet tanks, some equipped with radar for night fighting, and the very best of Eastern small arms and artillery. The navy had seven destroyers and ten Soviet W-class submarines. With the assistance of 200 West German and Austrian scientists, the Egyptians had produced two ground-to-ground missiles, the Conqueror with a range of 400 miles and the Victorious with a range of 200 miles. Both had been plagued with guidance problems, regularly reported corrected, and both had only conventional explosive warheads. Egyptian equipment, however, seemed to give the army a distinct advantage over the Israelis, a fact that had not gone unnoticed in Jerusalem.

All the MIGs and missiles did not compensate for the quality of the Egyptian soldier and officer. The searing experience of Sinai, glossed over even by those who should know better, had been repeated on a more muted scale in Yemen. After four years and a commitment of 70,000 troops, the Egyptians had not been able to crush an essentially tribal revolt. Like the Kurdish campaign, it was not an easy war to win; but was clearly a lesser challenge than another round with Israel. The Yemen campaign should have added a certain reality to Egyptian military pretensions which, properly channeled, could be advantageous. But in the past reality had too often been interpolated into a vision of the past, and a program for the future recognizable only to those addicted to Arab granduer. In July 1966 Field Marshal Amer insisted that Egypt would "always maintain definite superiority in quality and quantity"[13] over Israel in weapons and combat efficiency.

To some extent, the Arab capacity for self-delusion had gone far toward muting the Middle Eastern arms race. As long as the Arabs were content with a military establishment that looked well on parade while retaining sufficient caution not to use the arms against Israel, then the Israelis were content with less than full parity. In 1966 the ratio on paper was approximately two to one in favor of the Arabs, but in fact even the reverse was a low estimate of Israeli superiority. Perhaps the greatest strain on Israel was the constant drain of the defense budget; for in the growing complexity of weaponry, Israel could not lag too far behind. Even a poor pilot in a MIG-21 with air-to-air missiles was superior to a dedicated, determined Israeli in an obsolete plane. Thus as long as the acquisition of weapons by the Arabs did not tempt them to use their new paraphernalia, nor inspire them to create truly modern armies, the arms race alone did not need to lead to open war as it did in 1956.

One aspect of the arms race can, however, most assuredly change the whole pattern of the Middle Eastern confrontation. If, as is quite possible, and even likely, atomic weapons are introduced into the area, pressure to act violently might override caution and self-interest. The prospect of an independent nuclear capacity in the Middle East is the result of Israeli talent and French sympathy. The French ties, stretching back to 1949, led Shimon Peres in 1955 to push the construction of a nuclear program with French support. Work soon began secretly on a 24,000-kilowatt Dimona reactor in Negev and continued covertly in French and Israeli laboratories and testing sites. The United States, unaware of the secret projects, openly cooperated with the Israelis in the construction of a smaller 1,000-kilowatt reactor near Tel Aviv. In 1960 United States intelligence sources discovered the existence and size of the Dimona reactor. Neither the Israelis nor the French were particularly informative about their joint nuclear projects, although it was known that sophisticated experiments were being carried out in the Negev. The twenty-four megawatt reactor has the capacity to produce sufficient plutonium for two atomic bombs annually. The Israelis have indicated that the reactor is being used only for peaceful purposes, a claim supported by visiting Western scientists.

The gradual revelation of Israel's nuclear capacity had a strong impact in Cairo, where Nasser was dependent on the small Russian-built reactor at Inchass. His German scientists, reputedly working to tip Egyptian rockets with radioactive devices, were no match for the Israelis, much less the French. The specter of permanent impotence in the face of Israeli atomic weapons was fearsome. In the fall of 1965 Nasser reputedly sought an agreement with Russia that would permit the sale of atomic weapons to Egypt if Israel began production. The Russians, no more enthusiastic about nuclear proliferation than the Americans were, refused his request, but Moscow did offer a nuclear guarantee if it became necessary. This Soviet offer to step in after the fact was obviously insufficient for Nasser. In February 1966 he warned, "If Israel proceeds with the production of an atomic bomb, then I believe the only answer to this is a preventive war."[14]

Just how Nasser or anyone else would discover the existence of Israeli atomic weapons was not made clear. If the fearful Arabs were to launch such a preventive war with strikes against the Israeli reactors, the only visible targets at present, the Israeli response, particularly if the weapons did exist, would be likely to be devastating. Until recently only Israel has felt its daily security to be in jeopardy, but, if there were an Israeli nuclear striking force, the Arabs in turn would fear for their very existence. To risk a preventive war in the face of a possible atomic response might be mad, [but to wait might doom the Arabs to slower but just as certain extinction.] To people elsewhere, increasingly anxious over the dangers of nuclear proliferation, the prospect of a Middle Eastern atomic war game, played by violent and often irresponsible men dedicated to mutually exclusive goals was frightening. Having already tried every means of war from terrorism to tanks; having employed economic sanctions, diplomatic quarantines, and competitive aid programs; having, in short, exhausted conventional means of conflict, the Israelis and Arabs appeared on the verge of escalating their long war to the nuclear level.

In 1966, even after twenty years of failure, there remained those who contend that a permanent solution to the Israeli-Arab conflict could be found, in fact, must be found if the Middle East was not to remain forever on the edge of an abyss. There had long been feelings that at one golden moment in the past, a little more wisdom would have produced peace.

What is most remarkable about the irreconcilable clash of aspirations held more firmly than life itself is not that efforts at conciliation have failed but that they have come so close to fruition. Few would have supposed that Emir Abdullah, a proud little Bedouin raised amid desert wars and schooled in fratricidal politics, would come so close to arranging an agreement with his fellow Semites, the Zionists. Even the hesitant overtures of the Egyptian Free Officers to their fellow Anglophobes, the Zionists, between 1952 and 1954 seem improbable in retrospect, and actually contrary to the new men's own best interests. Risking excommunication from the Arab world, Habib Bourguiba of Tunisia actually suggested open negotiations, although on terms that would include cession of 25 percent of Israeli territory, a remarkable overture. On the Israeli side Dr. Judah Manges' Ihud urging reconciliation with Arab aspirations during the hysterical efforts to create a Zionist state was as improbable as was the founding of Semitic Action in 1958 to explore conciliation possibilities. All these maneuvers by the participants, whether motivated by self-interest or idealism, whether representative of tiny minorities or of insecure governments, seem unlikely.

International efforts after Ralph Bunche's temporary success have been equally impressive in that they have often come so close to agreement. Dag Hammarskjöld actually levered open the Suez Canal for a few months. The Palestine Conciliation Commission arranged for the progressive release of Arab bank accounts in Palestinian banks. The various border observers have imposed agreements in the very heat of battle.

The incredible amount of time, energy, and funds spent by all the agencies of the United Nations had monitored the violence, relieved the victims, restrained the militant, and diffused the hatred but had not produced a permanent solution. Without the officially disinterested imposition of the United Nations, without the calming presence of men like Ralph Bunche, Dag Hammarskjöld, E. L. M. Burns, and Odd Bull, without the work of the various relief agencies, the delicate truce in the Middle East could not have been maintained, the helpless refugees fed, the border wars limited. That the United Nations has largely maintained a truce seems accomplishment enough, more than could be expected although far less than perfection.

All those who have sought a solution outside the corridors of the United Nations have also been repulsed. By 1966 practically every possibility had been explored: a Middle Eastern federation, frontier adjustments, refugees settlement in the context of a development scheme, a socialist revolution, an approach to an international tribunal, a one-little-step-at-a-time program to a single, multifaceted, imposed answer. Nothing, no matter how novel and promising on inception had worked or even begun to work. The last, best hope was that time would erode Arab hostility or would permit revolutionary changes in the infrastructure of the Arab world, or would result in the orientalizing, deZionizing of the Israelis. The mere passage of time, however, has in itself had no effect. The most militant proponents of a new jihad to rid the Holy Land of the Zionists are found among the young. The most aggressive Arabs are also the most revolutionary and socialist. The longer Israel remains sealed off from the rest of the Semitic world, the more different, more Zionist, and more Western the Israelis become. In twenty years neither the ingenious schemes of the idealists nor the passage of time itself has had any perceptible impact.

That solutions of sorts do exist, but are at the present forbidden, is also clear. If the Arabs had the military superiority possessed by Israel, there soon would be no Zionist problem—only the expense of absorbing the unexpelled Jews into an Arab Palestine. If the Israelis were to be allowed to use *their* power freely, there would be no problem of Israeli security, but merely a huge Zionist state stretching from Sharm-el-Sheikhon the south to Beirut on the north and inland to the Syrian desert. That these are dreams, good or bad, does not deny that dreams are the stuff out of which wars are made. Zionism was a dream. Falastine Arabiyeh may be a dream *manqué* but it is not dead.[15] In 1966 the clash of aspirations seemed more rather than less dangerous.

Nowhere did renewed violence seem so close as along the Syrian frontier. The creation of El Fatah within Syria contained not the hope of swift redemption but the seeds of disaster. The very efficacy of the *fedayeen* terror raids in 1955–1956 went far to provoke *Kadesh*. The Syrians, who announced that they are responsible for their borders, would increasingly run the risk of massive retaliation. Syria, too, ran the risk of an ultimate showdown if in the still distant future Damascus cut off the tributaries of the Jordan. To do so or perhaps even to have the capacity to do so would certainly result in a preventive campaign limited only by the existing state of Arab unity. At the present rate of Syrian progress, Israel may find other sources of water, particularly through atomic desalination, in the years to come; but in 1966 continued Syrian construction ensured continued tension. The inherent instability of Syria may force an aggressive Israeli policy covering domestic chaos by foreign adventures.

Given the constant Arab threat to Israel's existence, it is difficult to imagine the Israelis denying themselves nuclear weapons. Whether or not Israel actually has an atomic bomb is, perhaps, not as important as whether or not the Arabs believe that it has. Assuming a political maturity in Jerusalem that some do not assume, Israeli atomic weapons would be used only to protect the nation from extermination.[16] If, however, the Arabs had atomic weapons, the Palestine problem could be "solved" in one cataclysmic moment. With the diffusion of the Arab population, the temptation for an irresponsible and insecure Arab government to risk a nuclear solution might be great. The only alternative would be an imposed prohibition on atomic proliferation by the present nuclear powers.

These immediate threats to Middle Eastern stability, the future of Jordan, the proliferation of nuclear weapons, the Jordan water diversion scheme, and El Fatah, were merely the glittering tips of the dragon's teeth. The monster was a chain-reaction war involving the great powers and leading to the impasse of nuclear confrontation. In twenty years the monster had been largely caged by the thicket of resolutions, doctrines, understandings, and restraints originating in New York, London, Washington, and even in Moscow. As the Arabs grew more independent of exterior control, regaining bit by bit their freedom of action, their capacity to act as they think fit also grew. In 1966 their stated aspiration was to irradicate Zionism in the Middle East. In ten years, their own weaknesses, Israel's strength, and exterior controls have limited waging of the war for the liberation of Palestine to peripheral diplomatic and economic campaigns, to brief harassment along the frontier, to provoking disastrous Israeli retaliation. Despite their professed optimism the capacity of the Arabs to do more in the next twenty years was slight, the sudden relaxation of international controls unlikely, and a pronounced decline in Israel's vitality dubious.

The Arabs sullen, humiliated, impotent were waiting out the lean years of the long war confident that their hour would come. The Israelis, having weathered the storms of war and the years of hostility, intended to grow stronger in the face of hate, confident of their historical destiny. In the future as in the past, Israel intended to confound its foes, discredit its critics, and remain the physical symbol of a 2000 year-old dream—impervious to challenge.

NOTES

1. The task of modernization is most difficult in the Arabian peninsula, where in January 1966 the Vice-President of the Islamic University at Medina published an article in two government-controlled newspapers,

which read, in part: "Much publicity has been given . . . to the theory that the earth rotates and the sun is fixed. . . . I thought it my duty to write a brief essay that would guide the reader to proofs of the falsity of this theory and to realization of the truth." *The New York Times,* June 1, 1966.

2. Saadat Hasan, *Introducing The Palestine Liberation Organization* (New York: n.d.), p. 14. This publication is Article 19 of the Palestine National Covenant.

3. Malcolm Kerr, *The Arab Cold War 1958–1964: A Study of Ideology in Politics* (London: 1965), p. 131.

4. *Ibid.,* pp. 131–2.

5. *The New York Times,* June 16, 1966.

6. The Syrian Arab Republic Ministry of Information, *Program of the March 8th Revolution* (approved June 1965 by the Regional Congress of the Arab Baath Socialist Party), (Damascus?: 1965?), p. 21. Typographical errors corrected.

7. *The New York Times,* July 17, 1966.

8. Fayez A. Sayegh, *Zionist Colonialism in Palestine* (Beirut: 1965), pp. 61–2.

9. This statement is what "the Negro presidents had told him in effect," whatever that may mean. Harry B. Ellis, "The Arab-Israeli Conflict Today," in Georgiana G. Stevens, e.d., *The United States and the Middle East* (Englewood Cliffs, N.J.: 1964), p. 113.

10. *The New York Times,* June 5, 1966.

11. *The New York Times,* March 21, 1966.

12. *The New York Times,* July 15, 1966.

13. *The New York Times,* July 24, 1966.

14. *Ibid.*

15. Part of the poem, "Falastine Arabiyeh" by Ethel Mannin, published in *Palestine Issue,* vol. I, no. 2, June/July 1966, p. 4, give some indication of the intensity of the dream.

You who usurped
Our homes and lands, our country,
Driving us into exile,
Displaced and dispossessed,
Know that your days are numbered!
Know that we shall return
As an army, strong and triumphant
To wrest from you what is our own.

(*Falastine Arabiyeh.*
Do you hear us?
Battle-cry of our liberation,
Of our flesh and our blood
And our bone!)

16. It may be recalled that the toughest of all the hawks David Ben-Gurion in 1949 restricted the offensive against Egypt twice and against the Arab Legion once and in 1957 acted as if he intended to keep Sinai for only twenty-four hours, [which, unfortunately for his reputation as a moderate man, was twenty-four hours too long].

Epilogue *
1967

During the year from September 1966 to September 1967 the entire balance of the Middle East appeared to have shifted. Syria's increasingly aggressive border policy goaded Israel to heightened militance and Egypt to a reluctant offensive. Prodded by Arab nationalists and Soviet intelligence reports, Gamal Abdel Nasser felt obligated to undertake an Israeli adventure, in order to recoup his declining prestige in the Middle East, to silence his domestic critics, and to reinforce Egyptian primacy. Once the first step had been taken, the factors driving Nasser to confrontation with Israel became dominant. The only real hope of avoiding open conflict during the accelerating crisis was the open intervention of the major powers. Such intervention did not occur. Without an imposed compromise the Israelis faced an Egyptian fait accompli, the stockade at Tiran, a stunning setback painless for the Arabs and portending future intrusions on the security of Israel. Nasser was incapable of withdrawing, the United Nations of effectively intervening, the major powers of interposing their authority between the two sides. Either Nasser would hold his newly gained high ground while the crisis dribbled off into ineffectual diplomatic posturing, or the Israelis would, as they had in the past, reply to provocation.

Nasser thought, perhaps, that the Israelis would have to tolerate his success, which had been achieved without open aggression. He may have assumed that his bright new army would be able to turn back an Israeli strike long enough for the gods of indignant diplomacy to intervene. More likely, in Cairo as elsewhere, the pace of events moved so swiftly that no one could rationally foresee even the immediate future but could only hope for the best. Ten years of peace and a certain self-induced complacency had dulled Nasser's previously acute antennae. To conduct the erratic orchestra of the Middle East one requires a keen ear and luck. Nasser had always had both. This time he had neither.

Imbued by necessity with a siege mentality, the Israelis had no intention of watching passively while their security was whittled away bit by bit, while their friends (but not allies) solicitously urged patience. For Israel the threat was total and the reaction also total. For ten years the Zahal had been honed for a blitz, an instant war to shatter Arab pretensions once again. Sophisticated weapons had been acquired and modified, men trained and retrained, strategic options analyzed in depth. On paper the military balance may have appeared to favor the Arabs, but in spite of the lopsided ordnance holdings and comparative troop figures, Israel remained the dominant military power. Once the Arab air forces had been shattered on the ground, the outcome of the campaign would be assured. The Egyptian army was incapable of mobility in a conflict in which victory would go to the swift and daring. The intervention of Jordan was a hopeless gesture, the result of King Hussein's impossible alternatives: intervention and disaster or evasion and rebellion. Hussein chose military defeat with honor. Syria, responsible more than any other state for the June war, was foolishly aggressive at much too late a date, giving the Israelis an opportunity to wreak vengeance at the last minute. Even in that dream world of military historians, where the board can be cleared and the pieces rearranged, there is every reason to suppose that the result of the June war would have been the same, though at a greater cost to the Israelis. As it was, in six days the Israelis swept to an almost unequaled series of victories.

On the map the Arabs had been forced back to tolerable distances, from the Israeli point of view. The Egyptians clung in disarray to the far bank of the blocked Suez Canal. Jordan had lost the entire west bank of the Jordan River and Syria the Golan plateau. Any new border incidents could harm only Arab civilians. Any counteroffensives would have to be launched by beaten armies into occupied zones far from the old Israeli boundaries. The Arab armies had disintegrated into shaken and disorganized mobs, their weapons burnt out on the battlefield, their officers discredited, and their morale gone. On paper Israel held all the high cards in any future negotiations.

Israel had the vast Sinai peninsula with its new oil field and dominated both the Strait of Tiran and the Suez Canal. The drain on the limited resources of a nearly bankrupt Egypt had been immense, dimming any prospect of recovery. Without the rich west bank, Jordan was left with a rump desert, devoid of resources and incapable of absorbing a new flood of refugees. Syria had no army, an essential prop to the regime, and no means of masking the existence of an Israeli army a few hours' drive from Damascus. No one could deny that Israel had won the war completely and unequivocally. More significant, for the first time a substantial portion of the international community seemed more willing to accept the Israeli insistence that out of battle must come a lasting peace, that simple withdrawal without guarantees would be only the first step in still another round of war, that aggression in the Middle East could not be defined with simple-minded formulas or prevented by high-minded resolutions.

But no peace came. The Arabs could not deny for long that Israel had won the June war, but they did insist that the long war would still continue. A battle had been lost, certainly, as a result of immoral Israeli aggression and the collusion of the West, but the just war would continue. The Arabs insisted that Egypt and Jordan could go on without accommodation with Israel. Whatever economists, international experts, and informed observers might predict, the Arabs remained adamant: They need not negotiate but would only demand unconditional withdrawal by the aggressor. Even though they could not at the moment make war, they would not make peace. During the long rounds of postwar Arab conferences, the more radical proponents of immediate and terrible war were ever so gradually shifted from the center of the stage by the more practical and prudent leaders. This new moderation, however, applied to tactics not to strategy for, with remarkably few exceptions, the Arab world firmly accepted the principle that Israel would have to be temporarily tolerated but could never be accepted.

A year after the war there were still violent border incidents, although on the new different borders; plans to boycott Israel's commercial friends; bellicose pronouncements about the rapidly re-

400 THE LONG WAR: ISRAEL AND THE ARABS SINCE 1946

fitted Arab armies and a new guerrilla campaign; all the familiar facets
of the long war, muted by defeat but not transformed. That Israel
had assumed a new and almost impregnable position in the Middle
East was immaterial, as long as the Arabs remained dedicated to
eventual victory. Arab unity was more apparent than it had been for
a generation. The running sore of Yemen was, hopefully, to be healed
at last. The oil-rich states were to help those that had been so heavily
penalized by the war. Defeat produced some recriminations, and some
internal divisions remained, but for the first time adversity was being
faced with determination. United, with time on their side, and with a
clear recognition of the limitations of their foreign alliances, the
Arabs intended to persist. That such persistence would beggar hundreds of thousands of Arabs, that all that had been gained in Egypt
and Jordan in the previous decade might be lost, that a stalemate
might benefit Israel and further penalize the Arabs were ignored in
favor of total commitment to eventual victory.

Although the map had changed drastically, the fundamentals of the
conflict had not changed at all. A larger, stronger Israel existed but
still as an alien presence in the Arab Middle East. A weaker, largely
discredited Arab world was still determined to secure the old goals.
The United Nations' presence had once again proved futile. The
aspirations and interventions of the major powers had once again
failed to secure either stability or even specific advantage. Perhaps the
crushing defeat of the Arabs, as was supposed to have been true in
1956, had convinced the men in Cairo or Damascus that Israel could
not in the foreseeable future be defeated on the open field of battle.
Perhaps the Israeli stranglehold on the west bank and Sinai would in
time force the Arabs to come to some sort of temporary accommodation negotiated through intermediaries. Perhaps Washington or Moscow had learned something. Perhaps the United Nations, the last and
best hope for world peace, had finally glimpsed the reality of the
Middle East. [What the Arabs refused to learn was that a lost battle is
a lost war, that the intolerable must be tolerated, that their most
cherished aspirations could not somehow at sometime be achieved.
Yet there was no reason to expect that they would learn a lesson that
no other nation or people has ever absorbed.]

As with all Israeli-Arab clashes, violence had been fermenting for a
great many years. The Syrian border had been troubled since 1949.

The regime in Damascus had grown ever more radical and more committed to an aggressive Palestine policy. Relatively immune to Israeli retaliation because of the near invulnerability of the fortified zone in the Golan highlands, Syria had provoked incidents and had first tolerated and then directed terrorist penetrations into Israel. The ordinary border incidents were gradually overshadowed by these deep penetrations of El-Fatah and similar commando units. By the late summer of 1966 Israeli intelligence estimated that many of the formerly independent and ill-trained groups had been taken in hand by the Syrian army. The level of competence began to rise, formerly inept demolition techniques grew more efficient, crude mines were no longer poorly placed on insignificant targets and left unarmed. The Syrians, like the Egyptians in 1955–1956, seeemd bent on a terror campaign. In the Gaza strip Ahmed Shukairy's Palestine Liberation Army was enthusiastically preparing to follow the example of El Fatah. Unpunished, a growing campaign of terror could erode the security of Israel.

On September 6, 1966, an Israeli was wounded by a mine near the Syrian border. On September 7 Israel appealed to the United Nations Security Council. On September 8 an Israeli patrol killed two Arab infiltrators in upper Galilee. The next day a mine exploded inside Israel and killed three soldiers. Syria denied all responsibility. On September 11 Israel protested to the United Nations. All the ingredients of a minor crisis existed. Few people in the Middle East had great hopes for United Nations intervention, and many anticipated the customary Israeli retaliatory raid. On September 17 Syrian Foreign Minister Ibrāhīm Makhūs announced that any future Israeli aggression would be met with Syrian-Egyptian military action. The terror raids tapered off for several weeks, and conditions seemed about to return to an uneasy normality.

Then on October 8 four Israelis were wounded in three explosions in Jerusalem, and the next day two Israelis were killed and four wounded by a mine explosion south of Lake Tiberias. Israel made use of the Mixed Armistice Commission and asked the United Nations Secretary General U Thant and the President of the Security Council to seek assurances from Syria that Damascus was not pursuing a terror campaign. As in September [the Arabs were outraged that the aggressor should accuse the victim] King Hussein of Jordan, no friend of the Damascus regime, promised to open a Jordanian front if

Israel attacked Syria. The Syrian Premier threatened to turn Israel into a graveyard. This time there was no lessening of tension. Israel again appealed to the United Nations. The Jordanian and Israeli armies engaged in a fire fight on October 12. Syria announced preparations to repel aggression. On October 13 three Israeli soldiers were killed in an El Fatah attack across the Jordanian border. Jordan denied involvement. Eleven Arab states announced their support of Syria.

On October 14 the Security Council met to examine the Israeli list of Syrian provocations but, it is safe to assume, without any sense of urgency. Everyone had been through these maneuvers before; the ploys and gambits were almost ritualized. Hopefully, as long as discussions continued in the United Nations, the Syrians would show some discretion and the Israelis sufficient restraint to prevent another serious incident.

During the remainder of October the raids continued, although most were little more than pinpricks; still, Israelis were being killed and wounded. The sense of frustration and insecurity increased. The United States and Great Britain did suggest that the Security Council ask for peaceful assurances from Syria, but the raids continued. The highly publicized success of El Fatah encouraged others. The Palestine Liberation Army supported further raids and even the Mufti of Jerusalem, Hajj Amin al-Huseini, in exile in Saudi Arabia, organized his own commando group. Eventually, Israeli intelligence identified sixteen groups operating from Gaza, Syria, and the Hebron and Nablus districts of Jordan. The situation was nearly as dangerous as it had been during the Egyptian fedayeen raids a decade before. On November 4 the Soviet Union, as expected, vetoed a mild resolution calling upon Syria and Israel to reduce tension. As usual, United Nations conciliation was crippled by Moscow, always ready to support its Arab protégés. With recourse to diplomatic means largely impossible, the Israelis had to consider their traditional alternative, retaliation. On November 12 an Israeli patrol car hit a mine near the Jordan border. Three men were killed and six wounded. The terrorist campaign had produced seventy incidents and showed no sign of slackening. Israeli patience was exhausted.

At 6:13 on Sunday morning, November 13, an Israeli column of tanks and armored personnel carriers shot up the Rujem Madfa police post in Jordan and moved north toward the village of Samu, long a center of Syrian-sponsored terrorist activities. Arab Legion troops moved up to defend the village, and heavy fighting began. Jordan tried to bring up reinforcements in fifteen trucks but ran directly into Israeli tank fire. At 7:30 A.M. Jordanian Hawker Hunter jets showed up over Samu but were driven off by the Israeli air cover. One Hawker Hunter was shot down. After three hours in Samu the Israelis had blown up the last forty houses and withdrawn, leaving the village a smoking ruin. Jordan admitted to thirteen killed and thirty-four wounded and the Israelis to one killed and ten wounded. Samu was the most serious incident in years. Hardly unexpectedly, the long terrorist provocation had led to retaliation, but, to the consternation of many, the attack had been directed against supposedly reasonable Jordan rather than against obviously guilty Syria.

The Israeli reprisal brought almost universal condemnation. On November 15 Premier Levi Eshkol admitted that the raid had been provoked by Syria but that Samu had been a logical target. But the choice of target, however, "logical," simply added Israeli callousness to Israeli aggression in the minds of many. Not only Soviet Russia but also the United States and Great Britain condemned Israel and demanded Security Council action. The result was a forgone conclusion. On November 25 the Security Council again condemned Israel in what Eshkol insisted was a one-sided decision, taking no account of the original provocation. In any case Israel had learned to live with unpleasant United Nations resolutions. In the past retaliation had paid dividends in declining Arab aggression.

Despite howls of indignation from Damascus, Amman, Cairo, and the headquarters of the Palestine Liberation Army, the incidents, as predicted, did decline. Israel had once more offended the sensibilities of the diplomats, who it seemed produced ill-informed emotional majorities against Israel in the United Nations. But this time the affront to the United Nations did not return much for Israel's investment. At the end of December the raids began again. With Soviet backing and growing public support from all shades of Arab opinion, the Damascus regime refused to be intimidated. All that another Israeli strike could do would be to strengthen the Syrian government and further blacken Israel's international reputation. The raids continued during January. The Israelis appealed to the United Nations. The Syrians charged Israel with aggression. It was very nearly an exact playback of the autumn crisis.

Secretary-General U Thant tried to calm Syria and Israel, urging both to accept the offices of the Mixed Armistice Commission. But incidents continued throughout January, as did several fruitless meetings of the Mixed Armistice Commission. There was no solution in sight. General Odd Bull flew to Damascus on a United Nations mission intended to lessen tension, but with no apparent result. By the end of March more than ninety raids had been attributed to El Fatah. Jordan was under pressure from the Palestine Liberation Organization and the Arab League Defense Council to assume a more militant stance. April began with more incidents.

Finally, as practically everyone had anticipated, one more Syrian straw broke the Israeli camel's back. On April 7 firing broke out along the border. The Syrians dropped more than 200 mortar shells on Kibbutz Gadot. Tanks moved up on both sides. Artillery zeroed in all along the frontier. At 1:30 P.M. the Israeli air force intervened. Mirage jet fighters swept in low and pounded the Syrian gun positions. Fifteen minutes later the Syrian air force appeared, but it was hopelessly outclassed. In a few minutes the Israelis shot down six Syrian MIG-21s. This time Arab outrage at Israeli aggression did not simmer down into smoldering frustration. Instead a variety of factors heightened Arab resentment, which demanded an outlet. This time the masses and the militants wanted something more than excuses, however valid, or oratory, however sincere. This time the prudent and the cautious found their old promises falling due.

On April 8 the Jordanian newspaper *Al Quds* ran a headline reading "What Steps Had Cairo Taken?" In biting words, the editor pointed out that Nasser was willing to fight Arabs in Yemen but not Zionists in Palestine. The muttering against Nasser had been growing. Egypt was hiding behind the glass wall of the United Nations Emergency Force in Sinai, safe from the Israelis and free to criticize King Hussein's moderation. In November he had done nothing during the Israeli retaliation raid on Susu. On April 7 he had once again done nothing. Nasser was ill situated to face the attack. His once soaring prestige of 1956 had been squandered bit by bit, not so much wildly as without visible return. At the beginning of the year, the Egyptian economy was near bankruptcy. Gold reserves in Swiss banks had to be withdrawn to pay short-term loans. Neither new Sinai oil wells nor the opening of the Aswan High Dam would do much more than permit the state not to lose ground from the Egyptian population explosion. Nasser's road to Arab socialism had developed too many potholes. His Yemen war had deeply disturbed many Arabs, even Egyptians, and had totally alienated Arab conservatives. His stature as a leader of the "third world" had dribbled away, and his friends in Africa and Asia had disappeared. He remained the leader of the new Arab world, but *Al Quds* implied that such a position entailed responsibilities. Nasser had to put up or shut up, to stop mocking Jordan's passivity while he maneuvered in safety. At one of his most vulnerable moments, Nasser was challenged.

The challenge did not catch Nasser unprepared or without considered alternatives.[1] He still had sufficient room for manuever as long as the Syrians did not provoke the Israelis too far. It is also likely that a crisis involving the Israelis was not unwelcome. On April 10 General Mohammed Sidky Mahmoud, the commander of the United Arab Republic's air force, left for Damascus for a twelve-day visit. On April 17 Egyptian Prime Minister Mohammed Sidky Suliman arrived in Damascus for five days of conferences. During April Nasser must have settled on his most profitable choices. It is likely that he had no interest in allowing the situation to deteriorate to the point at which only military "solutions" would be possible. As recently as November 24 he had pointed out, in the wake of the Susu incident, that the road back to Palestine would be long and hard, which had been his public position since the debacle in 1956. Some of the more naïve Arabs, impressed by the military hardware accumulated during the subsequent decade, may have believed in 1966 that the balance of power had shifted. Certainly, Egyptian military leaders must have been confident that a considerable improvement had been made in the fighting qualities of the army. The Russians had spent a great deal of time and money on the army: New defense lines had been constructed, new weapons tested, a new generation of officers trained, and hopefully a new spirit instilled in the men. Still, it is doubtful that too many responsible Egyptians felt capable of taking on the Israelis alone. Even with a united Arab effort, the risks would be grave and the prospects for more than a limited offensive minimal. A diplomatic coup of some sort was highly desirable, and some risks could be run—but too open a confrontation could lead to disaster, perhaps not as humiliating as the one in 1956 but a disaster nevertheless.

The Syrians kept up the pressure during early May. El Fatah continued to claim successes inside Israel. On their part the Israelis remained cautious and uneasy. In April Eshkol noted in an interview that he did not think there would be a war but that Israel was preparing for all possibilities. Despite mounting Arab excitement and sporadic raids, Israel continued on this course. On May 11, in a closed Mapai Party meeting, Eshkol discussed the dangers of the Syrian situation. United Press International reported, in a garbled account, that Chief of Staff Itzhak Rabin had called for the overthrow of the Damascus regime. In Jerusalem the next day Eshkol publicly announced that Israel might be forced to take appropriate retaliatory measures if no other way out of the impasse appeared, but, in fact, no such overt or covert measures were actually underway.

An Egyptian parliamentary delegation had flown to Moscow to attend May Day celebrations and had stayed on for discussions. At approximately the same time Soviet spokesmen warned members of the delegation that on May 9 a security commission of the Knesset had decided to attack Syria on May 17. Apparently a similar warning was given to Nasser by General Hafez Assad, the Syrian Defense Minister, on May 13. In any case, this Soviet "intelligence" reached Damascus and Cairo. There was no foundation to the report, and Israel had no intention of attacking Syria between May 17 and 21. In other words, the Russians were either grossly wrong, or they misinformed the Arabs for a purpose. The latter explanation has drawn more support, although the nature of the purpose remains elusive, as such a step was hardly necessary to accelerate Syrian-Egyptian cooperation.

Moscow may have regarded any crisis as to Russian advantage. Perhaps, like the British before them, the Russians had the illusion that Soviet methods and advice would certainly produce an efficient Egyptian army capable of repulsing an Israeli attack, despite all the evidence to the contrary. For whatever motive, the Soviet Union did inform Nasser of the supposed Israeli intentions, and Nasser in turn chose to act on the assumption that the report was accurate. If the Russians had not presented him with such a "fact," he might have had to invent one himself. There was certainly sufficient evidence that the Israelis were tiring of Syrian provocations. The Russians were right in general even if wrong in detail. [Something had to be done to take the heat off Syria and to enhance Nasser's fading prestige.]

On May 15 all the forces of the United Arab Republic were put on full alert. Orders went out to begin the buildup in Sinai, where Egyptian strength had been drained by the Yemen war to a low of 30,000 men. On May 15 Israel's Independence Day parade was held in Jerusalem, despite United Nations protests. To minimize tensions, the Israeli government did decide that no heavy equipment would be displayed. The suspicious assumed that the invisible tanks and artillery were being deployed elsewhere. There were news-agency reports of El Al Airlines planes landing and taking off in Boulogne, France, picking up spare parts before hostilities could interrupt the supply. All the bits and pieces seemed to fit together. Nasser's time margin had narrowed.

Nasser had carefully prepared a most subtle maneuver to seize the initiative and distract the Israelis. At 10:00 on the evening of May 16 the Egyptian Chief of Staff General Fawzy telegraphed the commander of the United Nations Emergency Force, Major General Indar J. T. Rikhye, demanding that his 3,400 men be withdrawn at once from their observation posts inside Egypt's borders. Rikhye replied that only Secretary General U Thant could give such an order, but the details did not interest the Egyptians. The next morning Radio Cairo broadcast the surprise demand. Nasser had adopted a brilliant ploy, for the Israelis would hardly dare to attack the Syrians with a crisis brewing on their own southern front; in the meantime, he could exploit the diplomatic storm caused by his request. This ability had always been his strength: to play by ear, uncertain of the future but sure of his luck.

U Thant was trapped in a nasty corner.[2] According to the provisions of the agreement between Dag Hammarskjöld and Nasser, the United Nations force was not to be withdrawn until its task had been completed but this agreement was not an official United Nations document. Officially the force was there on Egyptian sufferance. Egyptian troops were already moving into the border areas, and to stall might be to risk the United Nations men. U Thant believed not only that he had to comply with Nasser's demand, which was quite legitimate, but also that he could not even delay withdrawal by going before the General Assembly or dithering diplomatically. Technically and practically, withdrawal was the only course open. U Thant did make a hurried effort to find a way out, including asking the Israelis to allow United Nations troops to be stationed on their side of the border.

The Egyptians kept up the pressure and on May 18 ordered the United Nation contingent in Sharm-el-Sheikh to withdraw on fifteen minutes' notice. U Thant saw no alternative but to accept the Egyptian demand. On May 19 he told the General Assembly that, despite serious misgivings, he had ordered the withdrawal of the United Nations Emergency Force. Nasser's coup had come off with almost no real resistance from U Thant. Unfortunately, the coup had come too easily and too swiftly. A prolonged wrangle with U Thant and the United Nations in general might have brought the same results, but they would have been final results. On May 19 the Arab world waited with bated breath to see how Nasser would exploit his triumph. Having taken step one, he would, everyone assumed, soon take step two.

The Israelis thought much the same way. On May 18, at a joint executive meeting of the Mapai and Achduf Avoda Parties, the consensus was that war might be closer than had been thought. The Arab press and radio, dismal sources for those intent on accuracy, were building to a crescendo of bellicosity. The call for a new holy war could be heard loud and clear. On May 20 Egypt called up the reserves, and Israel completed a partial mobilization. Field Marshal Amer toured the Gaza strip, where Egyptian troops were replacing the Palestine Liberation Army along the border. Egyptian troops continued to move into Sinai. On May 21 General Rabin reported the total Arab force in Sinai to be 80,000. Eshkol feared that war was inevitable, but the majority of the government insisted that the diplomatic alternatives had not been exhausted. The key to the crisis was the outpost of Sharm-el-Sheikh overlooking the Strait of Tiran. Egyptian troops on the border were a severe irritant but a tolerable one. Egyptian troops at Sharm-el-Sheikh, however, threatened passage through the Strait of Tiran to Elath, the only visible fruit of the 1956 Sinai victory.

On Monday, May 22, Nasser announced that the Strait of Tiran was closed to Israeli shipping. He had taken his second step, a giant escalation. On paper his plan looked very good. The Israelis would be forced to attack Egypt to redress the situation. The Israelis would be the aggressors, rather than the Egyptians, who were merely occupying their own land and territorial waters: "If Israel threatens us with war, we will reply thus: Go ahead, then."[3] Even if the Israelis did attack, Russian support of the Egyptians was assured, as well as that of an international community conditioned by the events of 1956. Even if the Israelis did attack, the Egyptian army should be capable of holding on until the United Nations intervened. Such a "victory" Nasser had discovered in 1956 could be as profitable as a victory won on the field of battle. In the meantime, in a highly charged atmosphere of renewed faith, the Arab states were drawing together behind Nasser, increasing the odds against his defeat, military or diplomatic. On May 23 Moscow announced that any aggressor against the Arabs would have to answer to Russia. Eshkol announced that the closing of the Strait was an act of aggression. Few Arabs accepted the proposition, legally or emotionally; in the wider world also few accepted such "aggression" as a casus belli.

At that point international opinion anticipated eventual discovery of a diplomatic exit from the impasse. On May 24 U Thant arrived in Cairo to confer with Nasser. Israeli Foreign Minister Abba Eban was on his way to Paris, where he saw President Charles De Gaulle; to London, where he saw Prime Minister Harold Wilson; and to Washington, where he saw President Lyndon B. Johnson. Everyone was vaguely hopeful. No one believed that Nasser wanted war. Johnson had announced the United States' full commitment to the territorial integrity of all Middle Eastern nations; the Strait of Tiran was considered to be international waters. The United Nations Security Council met. Everyone was on top of the situation. Surely, some sort of formula could be devised to keep the Strait open without insulting Nasser. On May 25 U Thant left Cairo without having altered the situation. Eban met with Johnson, Secretary of State Dean Rusk, and Secretary of Defense Robert McNamara, also without altering the situation.

Pledges of Arab support continued to pour into Cairo. Algeria offered uniquivocal backing, as did Tunisia, the only real Arab moderate. Arab generals and premiers began to fly into Cairo to sign military pacts with Nasser. Arab radio stations waxed estatic about the transformation of Arab complacency into a new militance, thanks to the magic of Nasser. On May 25 the Egyptian War Minister was in Moscow, emphasizing that card in Nasser's trump hand. On May 25 the Egyptian Foreign Minister announced that the entry of Israeli ships into the Gulf of 'Aqaba would be treated as an act of aggression. The United States 6th Fleet in the Mediterranean cleared for action, publicly revealing Washington's concern. Reports appeared that ten Soviet ships would pass through the Dardanelles, symbolically matching the American presence. Still no one could believe that the crisis might pass the point of no return. Too often the Middle East had tottered on the brink of some form of self-destruction, only to be snatched back at the last moment.

On May 26 the new United States Ambassador to Egypt, Richard Nolte, who had arrived in Cairo only five days earlier, presented Nasser with Johnson's proposals for a peaceful solution. Little enthusiasm was expressed in Cairo. At the United Nations in New York Great Britain and Canada proposed an international fleet to challenge the boycott but gave up the idea just as the United States vigorously took it up. Then Canada suggested four-power talks. The Russians, who had already accused Israel of exacerbating the crisis, refused to participate. On May 27 U Thant went before the Security Council, but no result was forthcoming. On May 28 Nasser rejected the Anglo-American claim that the Strait was international waters. Bit by bit, almost imperceptibly, Nasser's position seemed to be hardening, eliminating room for the compromise that all the powers believed possible but none could construct.

As May drew to a close, all the signs pointed to a major Egyptian triumph, which would have to be tolerated by the Israelis because of their greater maturity and moderation. The United States, supposedly Israel's advocate, apparently felt no sense of urgency about forcing the Strait. In France De Gaulle announced strict neutrality, as did Chancellor Kurt Georg Kiesinger in Bonn and Premier Amintore Fanfani in Rome. Prime Minister Wilson and his Foreign Secretary, George Brown, did not seem inclined to depart from the general Western mood of modest impartiality. From Africa and Asia Nasser received glowing comments on his battle against neo-imperialism. In this heady atmosphere, his aspirations seem to spiral up.

On May 28 Nasser made still another policy statement unrestrained by prudence: "We plan to open a general assault on Israel. This will be total war. Our basic aim is the destruction of Israel."[4] Wise old Arab watchers knew, of course, that this statement was just rhetoric, but did the Israelis? On May 29 Soviet Premier Alexei Kosygin sent Nasser a message of backing and promised that no outside interference would be allowed. The clever Kremlinologists contended that the message was a pro forma maneuver and not a commitment, but did Nasser believe this interpretation? Practiced diplomats continued to hope for the best, and time was on the side of the compromise.

On May 29 the Algerian Defense Minister announced that troops would be sent to Egypt. Nasser, now insisting that there could be no peace until the Palestine Arabs returned to their homeland, revealed more clearly that he might be considering still another step:

> If we have succeeded in returning the situation to what it was before 1956, there is no doubt that God will help us to return the situation to what it was before 1948. The world is very different from what it was ten days ago. Israel as well is different from what it was ten days ago. Lately we have felt that in entering into a campaign with Israel we will be able with the help of God to be victorious.[5]

On May 30 came the culmination of Nasser's drive. The lone holdout, King Hussein of Jordan, flew to Cairo in his Caravelle jet to sign a military pact with the United Arab Republic. Egyptian General Riadh was to assume command of the Jordanian army; an attack on one Arab state would be an attack on all. Nasser had wiped out the memory of 1956, reunited the Arab world under his aegis, garnered the backing of the "third world," capitalized on the support of Russia, and apparently won a bloodless victory to redress the Middle Eastern balance of power.

All he had to do was to hold onto what he had. The West had sat out the crisis urging moderation. The United States in particular appeared increasingly complacent about Israel's tribulations. By the end of the month it seemed that Israel would have to accept some face-saving formula to end the crisis. Nasser had won a great deal, and it was unlikely that he would risk his winnings by provoking the Israelis to open combat, despite the shrill calls to arms in the Arab press and marketplaces. Israel would have to be reasonable.

Of all the messages and signals sent out during the crisis, the vital one, Eshkol's definition of the blockade as an act of aggression, was largely overlooked by the international community. All the scholarly theories of strategy and tactics, all the long practice in war games and peace games were forgotten in an orgy of wishful thinking. For Israel the key question was whether or not Nasser could be made to loosen his hold on the Strait by diplomatic means. If not, war was inevitable. For a variety of reasons such a war could not be postponed indefinitely while Nasser surrounded Israel with united Arab armies, thus raising the cost of Israeli victory, although not precluding it. For the Israeli doves time was vital. As the days passed, the international communities' sense of urgency seemed to decline in direct proportion to Israel's rising anxiety. Within the government a majority, not including Eshkol, pinned its hopes on a diplomatic solution until the moment that King Hussein flew to Cairo. At that point the scales tipped the other way.[6]

For more than a week there had been complicated negotiations to broaden the government by including leaders of the Rafi Party, in particular Moshe Dayan, Ben-Gurion, or both. The intricate bargaining was related as much to the future politics of Israel as to the actual crisis. Eventually, after nonstop haggling, on the night of June 1 Dayan came into the Cabinet as Minister of Defense, and the old Irgun leader Menachem Begin entered as Minister Without Portfolio. The change did not necessarily represent a decision for war but only an effort to establish a war government satisfactory to the feuding political factions and, most important, to the population. Dayan was immensely popular with both the people and the army, a popularity far different from that accorded to the elderly Eshkol. Begin was a known hawk. Their appointments ended what seemed to outsiders to be a crisis of confidence, a spreading and uninformed opinion that Eshkol lacked not only the proper élan but also the will to fight. To a large extent, the presence of the dynamic and articulate Dayan dispelled the Israeli sense of isolation and unease. With Begin and Dayan in the Cabinet, Israelis could be sure that their government would not accept a contrived compromise endangering the security of the state. With Dayan as Minister of Defense the conduct of the campaign, should war come, would be in the hands of a winner.

Dayan's presence in the Cabinet did not suggest that war was inevitable but only that the time for decision had come. Eban's diplomatic maneuvers seemed unlikely to lead to a swift solution. The military situation on the borders could only deteriorate with the arrival of Egyptian and Iraqi units in Jordan and Algerian aircraft in Egypt. The delay after the original Israeli mobilization had been advantageous, but further delay would penalize the economy unduly, lower the military efficiency of the brigades, and bring no foreseeable benefits. The Israelis shrewdly judged that Washington would tolerate a war and that Moscow would refrain from all but verbal interference. Tensions had begun to decline, and a swift Israeli strike would have the advantage of surprise in a world expecting concessions. If Israel was going to make war, the time had come to act.

On Saturday night, June 3, the Cabinet met in a long secret session. The factors in favor of action had piled up. Egyptian overflights might produce too clear a picture of Israeli intentions. Egyptian commanders in Jordan might force Hussein into war. Time had run out, leaving the stark alternatives of war or a crushing defeat engineered by Nasser, who was determined to eliminate Israel. Early on Sunday morning the last doubts disappeared. Israel would go to war on Monday morning.

The rest of the world had not seen the right signals that weekend. Most people assumed that Israel, diplomatically isolated and unable to attack without violating an international sense of morality and, worse, losing the support of the United States, had missed the boat. The moment for a lightning strike had slipped past. The Arabs were too strong. Even Dayan had said on June 3 that it was "too late to react right away against the blockade and too early to draw any conclusions on the diplomatic handling of the matter."[7] Dayan's time to act came the following morning, Monday, June 4.

At 7:45 Monday morning, the first Israeli Vautour jets began moving down the runways. Air Force Commander General Mordechai Hod had prepared a detailed master plan to wipe out the Egyptian air force in three hours. Although Israeli air defenses had been stripped, the Syrian and Jordanian air forces were to be ignored as the bulk of the jets attacked eleven Egyptian fields. The strikes were timed to come during the brief pause in Egyptian air activity when the morning patrols returned to their bases. If successful, the morning strikes would severely limit Egyptian offensive air capacity, ensuring the safety of the Israeli civilian population and freedom of movement for the Israeli columns moving into Sinai. The pilots had no doubts: Skimming just above ground level to avoid radar sweeps, each had decided independently to come in lower, slower, and harder than originally planned. At 8:00 the radio newscaster of Kol Israel announced, "We are at war." there was no Egyptian reaction.

Surprise was complete. The Israeli Mirages and Vautours swept in almost unnoticed. The Egyptian air force was parked in neat rows along the aprons or in three three-sided bunkers. Very few MIGs were in the air. There was almost no initial antiaircraft fire. Relying basically on cannon fire, the Israeli pilots brought their planes in with wheels down and almost at stalling speed and began to rack up the sitting ducks. The Vautour strike far to the south at Luxor destroyed all thirty TU-16s on the field. In eighty minutes the MIGs parked on the strips along the Suez Canal, at Cairo, and in Sinai were burned out, most on the first strike. Then there was a twenty-minute pause. The Israeli air force could return a plane to the air refueled and rearmed in less than eight minutes. The second eighty-minute wave in the staggered air strike hit the Egyptians long before they had recovered from the first crushing sorties. By 11:00 General Hod realized that the Egyptians had no more bombers and no MIGs within range of Israel. In a little less than three hours, the Israelis estimated that 300 of 340 combat-ready planes had been destroyed. Two-thirds of Nasser's bright, new air force was reduced to burnt-out shells on the pocked aprons of shattered airdromes. The Egyptians were naked from the air.

Before the final results in Egypt were tabulated Israeli planes were already being switched to targets of opportunity in Sinai. At noon a first strike wiped out most of Hussein's small air force, a brutal warning of the dangers of intervention. Another strike took out the Syrian air force. Israeli jets strafed the Iraqi air base at H-3 on the eastern Jordanian border and wiped out a squadron of MIG-21s just after they had set down on the runway. Although sorties against Arab airfields continued throughout the day, the air war had been decided by early afternoon. The Israelis claimed 402 enemy planes destroyed on the ground by only 492 sorties. All told, the Arabs lost 452 planes, only thirty-one in air combat, whereas the Israelis lost twenty-four planes to ground fire and none in dogfights. By late Monday afternoon the Israeli air force was fully committed to ground support. Pilots often flew seven or more sorties a day while maintaining higher target accuracy than anticipated. Except for a few Egyptian sorties over Sinai, the Arab air forces simply were not to be a factor in the war. The last remaining Egyptian jets were too far south, unable to land in the north. Syria and Jordan had neither planes nor runways. The Iraqis were out of range. The Israeli pilots, perfectly secure, had a field day over Sinai, knocking out the vulnerable and highly visible Egyptian armor.

Field Marshal Amer had been in the air during the Israeli strike; when he landed in Cairo, the possibility of defending Sinai for any appreciable length of time had already been lost. In a vast empty amphitheater, the Egyptian armor sat naked. To run would be to attract attention. To sit would be to invite attack. Except for deep, hedgehog defenses, the Egyptian army had not in the past had any staying power. Under constant hammering from the air, the Egyptians, immobile and uncertain, would be unable to respond to the fluid pressure of the Israeli strike columns. In Sinai the Egyptian army was not told of the extent of Israeli success in the air, but, as hour after hour the Mirages and the Fougas Magisters (the Israeli-built jet trainer converted to tank killer) provided unimpeded ground support, desperation grew. Even an elite force can grow uneasy under constant and unopposed air attack, as some Israelis discovered on Monday and Tuesday, but the Egyptians, with at best only fragile staying power began to come apart at the seams. Almost before the Israeli armor came within range, some commanders had conceded defeat. General Hod's jets had assured an Israeli victory in Sinai, but how long it would take and how much it would cost depended on the Israeli columns, which had pushed off at 8:00 Monday morning.

In the ten years since the last Sinai campaign, Israeli strategists had prepared with excruciating care for another round. Israeli commanders, relying on personal experience, detailed air reconnaissance, and superbly accurate intelligence, were far more intimate with the wild terrain of the Sinai than the Egyptians were. Alternatives and possibilities had been considered and reconsidered. Intelligence data had been accumulated in great detail and constantly updated. Yet Chief of Staff General Rabin had produced not a master plan but only a detailed set of alternatives. Israeli commanders had long been trained, in a harsh school, to act under pressure, to initiate operations on present conditions rather than on past instructions. Once the operation began, the ultimate goals and the initial thrust would be the only firm factors. All other plans would be subject to change. Limited only by time and space, the Israeli commanders were expected to exploit their advantages as they occurred. That they would occur no one doubted. All ranks assumed that the Egyptians would not go the distance and that victory was certain. Outside his hedgehog, the Egyptian would be hopeless, and the Israelis would pay little penalty for daring.

The basic plan was to smash through the hardest core south of the Gaza strip around Rafa and to let the armor loose to cut into the middle of Sinai and to link up with the second thrust directly through the Umm Gataf-Abu Agueila complex. Once the hard core had been broken, the columns would dash for the high ground on the west of the peninsula and mop up the Egyptians as they withdrew. As usual, on a command map or a sand table, it seemed impossible that the Israelis could do what they had outlined in the time available; as usual, once in action, they proceeded to do the impossible.

On June 5 the Egyptians began shelling twelve Israeli kibbutzim, thus technically making the first attack but against an Israel already poised to strike. At 8:00 Brigadier General Yeshayahou Gavish, Chief of the Southern Command, gave the order to attack all along the front. In the north Brigadier General Israel Tal's division would move into the base of the Gaza strip against the Egyptian 7th Division and split off one force to clear up Gaza and the Palestine Liberation Army while maintaining momentum westward along the coast to El 'Arîsh. In the center Brigadier General Ariel Sharon's beefed-up division was to drive straight west into the Umm Gataf bloc. Brigadier General Avraham Yoffe's two armored brigades and support units would hook around north through the desert to Umm Gataf and would break into Abu Agueila. In the south an independent brigade would attempt to stall the Egyptian Force Shazali in front of Kuntilla to prevent a breakthrough across Israel into Jordan. Essentially, if Sharon and Tal could drive in their initial wedges, the Israeli armor would be loose.

On the first day, although nothing went as planned, results were highly gratifying. Tal's armored division cut through Khan Yunis, and, despite false starts, confusion, and ignorance of an Egyptian brigade on the southern flank, two armored battalions reached El 'Arîsh. All Monday night Tal fought to clear a road to battalions that had been isolated in El 'Arîsh when the El-Jerardi blocking position closed after them. By dawn on Tuesday, although Tal's point was probing the El 'Arîsh airfield, his division was engaged all the way back to Khan Yunis. By noon his men had breached the Bir Lafham position south of El 'Arîsh and had cleared the city. Tal sent one armored task force along the coast road. It broke through six T-54 tanks thirty miles to the west on Tuesday afternoon and reached the Suez Canal the next morning. Tal's other two brigades sorted themselves out and moved toward Jebel Livni behind Abu Agueila.

On Monday night, after a long day spent clearing the way through outlying positions, Sharon launched his attack on Umm Gataf. Heavily fortified, on Russian advice, the Umm Gataf complex was astride the center axis and supposedly unflankable. Sharon had prepared a complicated assault, which included an infantry flanking movement across loose dunes and an attack by helicopter paratroops on the Egyptian artillery base. Once Umm Gataf's trenches had been infiltrated by the infantry, the way into the center would be open for Israeli armor. Rabin had his doubts, as did Gavish, about managing all these moves at night without air support, but Sharon carried on. By 2:30 Tuesday morning, Israeli armor had begun to filter inside the hedgehog. The confused fighting ended thirty minutes after dawn when the last Egyptian M-54 tank was picked off by the expert Israeli tank gunners. Both Tal and Sharon had their rights of way. Another worry faded when Force Shazali pulled back from the frontier in the south.

Gavish wanted to cut off Force Shazali before it could escape toward the west. He sent Sharon across country to Nakhl to close the door. After a fantastically rugged ride across the desert, Sharon arrived just before the Egyptians. Force Shazali was stretched out for twenty miles, harassed from the rear and ignorant of Sharon's arrival. It drove straight into the ambush. The first salvo, from every vehicle in the Israeli column, blew up ten tanks. The Egyptian armor could not push through, could not turn back, and could not get off the road. It was stuck tight. All during the searing hot afternoon, Sharon plastered the column with shells. Israeli Mystères and Mirages came in low in fours, flying back and forth over the Egyptians and raking the stalled vehicles with gunfire. For hours the tank killing continued, leaving a twisted, black snake of hulks on the Nakhl road. Sharon moved on toward Mitla Pass, but by Thursday night there were no more targets.

Tal had meanwhile moved south to Bir Hama, then west on the central axis to Bir Gafgafa. Fifteen of his light AMX tanks were hit in a laager just before dawn on Thursday by sixty T-54s moving in from the west. Tal opened up with his artillery to cover the AMXs and sent a company of Shermans past the shattered laager. Five more T-54s were hit, and the rest disappeared. A company of Centurions leapfrogged the AMX laager and moved out of radio range. The Centurions ran into thirty more T-54s but knocked out ten, with the loss of only one Centurion. The Egyptians continued to hang on to both sides of the highway, and Tal pushed forward, relying on accurate tank fire to pick off the Egyptian armor. Gradually, as the Israelis kept up the pressure, resistance collapsed. Tal's second spearhead reached Suez Thursday night. Along the way the brigade had destroyed another 100 tanks, including 60 T-54s, bringing the total to 275, against a loss of 50.

Yoffe, between Tal and Sharon, supposedly had a secondary mission: to push Egyptian armor toward the two heavier armored divisions. Instead the reverse occurred. Yoffe's 1st Brigade, under Colonel Ishahar Shadmi, cut across the desert north of Umm Gataf toward the road south of Bir Lafham, as planned. When Shadmi arrived on the road, his column was exposed on several sides. He lost one battalion to Colonel Adra, who wanted to hit Abu Agueila from the rear. Then an hour after dark an Egyptian armor brigade, moving to reinforce El 'Arîsh, blundered into Shadmi's position. The first Israeli salvo knocked out a T-54 and blew up seven trucks. The whole Egyptian brigade was illuminated by the flaming gasoline. The armor pulled back and moved into the El 'Arîsh wadi. Both sides settled down to a blind all-night gun battle. At dawn Shadmi found that he had lost one tank and the Egyptians twenty-four. The road to Jebel Livni was open, and at 11:00 A.M. Shadmi began to push on, meeting only sporadic resistance. All twenty miles of the road were cluttered with Egyptian armor, but the men were fighting without direction, as command control dissolved. At 4:00 on June 6 Shadmi launched the attack on Jebel Livni. A confused tank battle developed in the churning dust. The Egyptians stood and fought for a while and then skipped off to the west under cover of the dust.

Gavish flew in and conferred with Tal and Yoffe at 2:00 on June 7. The two divisions would move west in parallel courses, with Bir Hassna as Yoffe's first objective. At 11:00 that morning Colonel Avraham Bar-Am's battalion of Centurions took Bir Hasne and kept on going south. Creeping along a heavily mined road, Bar-Am took three hours to reach the Bir Tamada crossroads less than four miles south. En route he knocked out twelve T-34s and T-54s and passed fifty-one tanks burned out in air strikes. With his point of nine tanks, Shadmi moved down the Bir Hasne–Bir Tamada road directly in front of a vast, disorganized horde of Egyptian armor, plowing west in search of an exit from Sinai. Backed up by his 2nd Battalion, Shadmi opened fire into the undirected herd. Soft-skinned vehicles began to burn. More than 100 were set on fire before the rest of the Egyptians veered off to the south toward Mitla Pass. Dug in at Bir Tamada, Shadmi spent the night knocking off little bunches of Egyptian vehicles as they trickled through toward the west.

Bar-Am, once more in the lead, had been sent on down to the Parker Memorial and from there was to move into Mitla Pass to plug the last gap out of the Sinai killing ground. His little group of Centurions, some of them under tow, slipped along in the great tide of fleeing Egyptian T-34s and T-54s often driving side by side in the dark. In the Mitla Pass Bar-Am managed to thread his way unrecognized through a monumental traffic jam onto a flat rise. There in a defense laager, he plugged the gap. The pass was already a cauldron of burning trucks, smashed command cars and jeeps, smoldering and blackened tanks. Hundreds of undamaged vehicles were trying to grind their way through the wreckage to safety. This vast burning jam was the last escape route, and all day it had drawn the Israeli jets. With his nine tanks and a battery of 105s, Bar-Am opened up on the massed targets. Twenty-two T-54s charged his laager head-on. Miraculously, Bar-Am's gunners knocked out the T-54s before they could smash into the laager. His tanks were pocked and dented but still solid when the last T-54 blew up. For hours, Bar-Am sat firm in the choking dust, the constant din, the light of burning tanks. Using the bright light of the gasoline fires, his gunners knocked out any

Egyptian vehicles that managed to crawl into range. A few half-tracks squeezed by on side trails, but no tank pushed past the laager. At dawn Bar-Am had lost one man killed and four wounded. With the Israeli jets overhead again, the Egyptians had lost their last chance to escape from Sinai. By Friday morning Yoffe had pushed three columns through the cluttered mountain passes and down to the Canal at Chalufa, Ras Sudar, and the Little Bitter Lake.

By then all the ends had been tidied up. On June 7 Sharm-el-Sheikh had been taken unopposed; the paratroop drop was canceled at the last moment. Flying columns from Sharm-el-Sheikh and Ras Sudar on the Gulf of Suez swept on the western coast of Sinai to meet near Abu Zenima on June 8. The navy had listed two probable submarine kills off Haifa and revealed an underwater frogman attack on Egyptian naval units in Ras El Tin anchorage at Alexandria and in Port Said harbor.[8] By Friday, however, even the stupendous armor victories in Sinai, the incredible wreckage at Mitla Pass, and the long toll of Egyptian losses had paled in the light of totally unexpected events far to the northeast.

One factor in planning for the June war, accepted by all Israelis concerned, was that Jordan and Syria could be ignored. Once the air strike had wiped out their air forces, nothing more than a pro forma artillery barrage or a probe or two would be forthcoming. At most the Israelis might have to push south toward Jenin to protect their major air base near Afuleh, but no real fighting was anticipated. The stripped-down northern command of Brigadier General David Eleazar did expect some sort of Syrian display but no real threat. The central-front commander Brigadier General Uzi Narkis was resigned to waiting out the war watching the Jordanians drop a few shells over the frontier. Not only did no one anticipate action in the east; no one even wanted it when the bulk of the army was tied up deep in Sinai.

On Monday morning, almost as soon as reports on the war in Sinai came in, the Jordanians began dropping artillery and mortar fire on Jerusalem's New City, Mount Scopus, and the border settlements. In the north, Jordanian artillery was zeroing in on the Israeli air base, and the northern command had been authorized to respond. Elsewhere, despite the heavy fire, the Israelis were reluctant to become involved and to provoke Jordan to greater intervention. In Jerusalem Jordanian troops occupied Government House. Narkis wanted permission to counterattack and to move up Colonel Ben-Ari's armor brigade, which was then assembled east of Tel Aviv at Ben Shaman. Despite the risks, it began to look as if King Hussein might be serious about his commitment to Nasser. General Rabin agreed to Narkis' requests. Narkis told Ben-Ari to move up to the Jerusalem corridor and to cut the road between Ramallah and Jerusalem by Tuesday morning at 6:00. A brigade of paratroopers, shifted from a Sinai mission, would move on Mount Scopus and link up with Ben-Ari. By late afternoon, with his plans made, Narkis gradually began to realize what the results might be. He called Mayor Teddy Kolleck: "It has begun; you will be the Mayor of a united Jerusalem."

By 5:30 Ben-Ari's brigade was in place before the fortified Jordanian ridges north of the corridor. At 7:30 his men struck out toward Radar Hill. All night Ben-Ari's columns struggled through the steep hills, filling tank ditches, removing mines, levering tanks over rocks, and forcing Arab positions. At dawn the brigade cut the Ramallah-Jerusalem road and settled into the protecting high ground just in time to meet a counterattack led by twenty Patton tanks. In a three-hour fight, the Israelis knocked out twelve Pattons. The rest pulled back. Ben-Ari moved south to link up with Colonel Mordechai Gur's paratroopers in Jerusalem only to be ordered back to take Ramallah and to link up with still another column coming from Latrun. He sent forty tanks barreling straight ahead on the main road. In Ramallah there was heavy sniper and machine-gunfire from the ridges above the town but no coherent resistance.

The next day Jordanian resistance began to crumble everywhere. Stretched too thin and under constant pounding from the air, Hussein's army began to break up. Ben-Ari sent one battalion north and two east toward Jericho. After a variety of false starts and contradictory orders, at 6:30 Wednesday afternoon Ben-Ari's column broke into Jericho accompanied by blasts of ten trumpets liberated at Ramallah. The push from the north toward Jenin on June 5 had continued on south. On June 7 the Israelis swept into Nablus and branched off to clear the northern half of the west bank up to the Jordan River. The sweep through the west bank, which destroyed the Arab Legion, hardly distracted the attention of most Israelis from the dramatic events taking place in Jerusalem.

On Monday afternoon Colonel Gur's paratroop brigade had been unexpectedly committed to the Jerusalem area instead of to the expected Sinai mission. By then it had become clear that more than a limited response to Jordan was in the cards. Narkis and Gur were still, however, considering not a general attack but a limited assault inside Jerusalem, around the north of the Old City toward the Rockefeller archaeological Museum. This sweep would open up the Old City and the area around Mount Scopus. On Monday evening the brigade began to dribble into Jerusalem still largely ignorant of its mission, unfamiliar with the ground, and without its full gear. Not until 2:15 Tuesday morning could it attack. Fighting continued through the dark hours as the three-pronged attack ran into heavy opposition, accurate artillery fire, and constant sniping. By 9:30 Gur realized that he was taking heavy losses and eased off to let the brigade recover. The situation looked promising. Contact had been made with Ben-Ari to the north, the way was open to Scopus, and his own men were continuing to nibble around the Jerusalem perimeter. At 11:30 in the evening, Gur moved into the second stage, occupying the eastern hills behind Jerusalem and sealing off the Old City. In the darkness missed turns, confused orders, and a blundering air attack seemed to pile up to prevent a clear-cut success; but, as elsewhere, the Jordanian army was ebbing away, tired and discouraged. Gur was winning not by a glittering and elegant rapier strike but by plodding pressure. At 5:00 Narkis was ordered to move in and take the Old City before a cease-fire could snatch away the prize. At 9:45 Gur's troops, moving south, broke through Saint Stephen's Gate on the eastern wall. Resistance broke up into tight pockets and individual snipers. At 9:55 Gur arrived at the Dome of the Rock, where he was joined by Narkis ten minutes later. More than 200 Israelis crowded up to the Wailing Wall while sniper bullets kicked up dust puffs around their heads.

Although the Old City had been "captured" by 10:00, not all the Jerusalem Arabs seemed aware of the situation. Another Israeli column, moving along the walls from the south, had to pull back from the Dung Gate in the face of heavy firing and to move on to Saint Stephen's Gate, which was still being defended. Arab half-tracks were still loose in the narrow streets. Machine-gun fire continued all day. Snipers had to be flushed out one by one. Despite the hazards, all the Israelis who could find a way continued to make their way toward the Wailing Wall. Dayan arrived at 2:00 and slipped a written prayer for peace into a crack in the wall. Eshkol came, Ben-Gurion came, and so did anyone who could filter through into the overcrowded space in front of the wall.

In the New City, west of the wall, the population was swept with rejoicing. The popular song "Jerusalem the Golden" was played endlessly. The transformation from Monday morning, a sober moment of militant determination in the face of adversity, through the almost unbroken series of victories in the air and in Sinai, to the capture of the Old City had been almost more than the spirit could bear. No one, from Eshkol and Dayan on down, had dreamed on Monday morning that Israelis would be standing in front of the Wailing Wall before the week was out. Few could take in the fact that, after 2,000 years, Jerusalem—all of it—had been redeemed. After Jerusalem, everything else was anticlimactic.

After the capture of the Old City and the entire west bank, the only remaining target was Syria. Damascus had provoked the war but escaped the consequences. Despite their little Maginot Line snaking through the Golan plateau, the Syrians presented no insurmountable military challenge but only a considerable diplomatic risk. International reaction to the war had been mixed but, most important, no one abroad seemed able to absorb the rapid pace of events. That war had come at all had been a shock, and the first consideration had been to prevent escalation into a great-power confrontation. Kosygin had made use of the hot line to Washington and had assured Johnson on Monday that Russia was opposed to the war. In public the Russians were less moderate, verbally backing the Arab position to the hilt. The major field of diplomatic battle, as usual, was the corridors and conference rooms of the United Nations in New York. There the Arabs were handicapped by the reluctance of Cairo to admit to the rapid disintegration of the Egyptian army. As the hours passed, the differences between the Arabs' proud posture and the condition of their armies embarrassed their friends and irritated the uncommitted. Egyptian efforts to promote the charge of collusion among the Americans, the British, and the Israelis may have helped Nasser among the Arabs, but it alienated many of the more sophisticated citizens of other nations by its patent falseness. Even the Russians would not go along, though not because of any innate love of the truth. The continuing Arab calls for the destruction of Israel may have been merely baroque Arab language, but almost alone the Arabs had built up a case for Israel. Finally, in contrast to 1956, there was in 1967 widespread support for brave little Israel repelling the Arab hordes. Although De Gaulle moved from a position of neutrality to ill-defined support of Arab arguments, vast crowds of demonstrating Frenchmen did not; although the Communist governments of East Europe condemned Israel, many of their more prominent citizens made it clear that they did not accept the party line. Consequently, as the United Nations diplomats cast about for the proper terms for a cease-fire resolution, the Israelis had some room for maneuver.

A cease-fire resolution was inevitable, of course. The important questions were the timing and the specific terms. The Arabs demanded unconditional withdrawal and used up precious hours trying to put together the necessary majority while Israeli armies continued their advance. Hussein was the first to accept reality and agree to a cease-fire without conditions. The other belligerent Arabs ignored the United Nations resolution or rejected it. Another resolution, again without conditions, was passed by the Security Council. Again only Jordan concurred. Finally, Cairo caved in. On the evening of June 8 U Thant read to the Security Council a message handed him by Ambassador El Kony agreeing to a cease-fire if Israel would also agree. At 4:00 on Friday Syria sent a message to the Israeli-Syrian Mixed Armistice Commission in Damascus declaring that Syria would comply. The message was forwarded to the Security Council, by then adjourned, and passed to U Thant. Technically Syria had complied with the resolution, but word was slow to reach Israel.

The Israelis had all but determined to risk an attack on Thursday, but no action was taken while troops were being massed and the Syrians lulled into a sense of false security. Few in Israel had any doubts that, whatever the Syrians said about observing a cease-fire, Damascus would contradict it in its actions. For four days the fifty-mile border had been the scene of rolling artillery barrages, Israeli airstrikes, and one or two small Syrian thrusts. There had been a brief lull, but Syrian artillery had begun firing again. At 7:00 Friday morning General Rabin ordered Eleazar to take the Golan plateau. Later at a press conference Rabin made it clear that the Syrians should not come out of the June war unpunished. He felt that the

Syrians were the people who brought about the whole war by years of subversive activities, and by dragging Nasser after them.

Pressed for time and facing a tight network of deep fortifications dug into the heights, Eleazar could not prepare a subtle, indirect approach. The main thrust would be directly up the steep slope in front of Kfar Szold into the fortified maze on the northern edge of the heights. There would be a secondary probe in the center and a later end run hooking above the Yarmuk River and making use of helicopter paratroops. Most of the marbles would ride on the northern attack. Once that wedge reached the peaks, strike columns could spread out behind the defenses and connect with the columns moving up from the south.

At 11:45 Friday morning, Colonel Elfrat Yona's Golani Brigade moved out for Tel Fahar, six acres of interconnected trenches, dugouts, and bunkers. The brigade struggled up the slope, protected by a churning tank file. By 3:30 the first infantry had reached the perimeter of Tel Fahar but without its half-tracks, which had all been knocked out or stalled somewhere on the twisting trail below. Despite heavy losses among field commanders and a collapse in communications with the rear, the infantry pushed into Tel Fahar. The Israelis suffered thirty-seven killed and eighty-two wounded in clearing out the Syrians, but by dusk they had broken the linchpin of the Syrian defenses.

Yona moved up reinforcements all night, and at dawn the brigade split, moving north and south behind the Syrians, at times against stubborn but uncoordinated resistance. The heart began to leak out of the Syrians, exhausted by five days of hammering and rumors of collapse. At 2:30 the Israeli point reached El Kuneitra, several hours after Damascus had announced its fall to speed a new cease-fire. From the south the paratroopers reached Boutmiyé an hour later, linking up with the Israelis moving south. Far to the north the last redoubt, Baniyas, on the headwaters of the Jordan, was overrun later that afternoon. The Israelis had lost 115 killed and 322 wounded in shattering the Syrian army. There was nothing to prevent a blitz right on to Damascus, but more important the Golan plateau was clear. Saturday night, standing high over the Jordan Valley, the Golani men could see the twinkle of lights from the kibbutzim, secure from harassment for the first time in twenty years.

In less than six days the June war was over. From the slopes of Mount Hermon in the north to the tip of the Sinai peninsula in the south, from the banks of the Suez Canal in the west to the edge of the River Jordan at the Allenby Bridge in the east the Israelis stood easy. There had seldom been as swift or as final a victory. In the eyes of the unsophisticated, the campaign had been one of blacks and whites, the righteous lightning out of Israel to strike down the boastful. Other analysts emphasized the ease of the Israeli success, not always taking into account the endless preparations, the sweat and tears necessary to such a virtuoso performance. The Arabs had not all been fools or cowards. The ragged Palestine Liberation Army had fought hard and long around Gaza. The Arab Legion, hopelessly outmatched, had fought with spirit and determination although without success. Again it was a case of a dedicated modern nation, familiar with sophisticated weaponry and completely confident of victory, matched against states still dominated by ancient class and economic structures and still unable to produce modern armies. The Egyptian commanders were again, as they had been in 1948 and 1956, appallingly incompetent, whereas the men were often quite capable though usually only in set defenses. The gleaming Soviet weapons had convinced many who should have known better that ten years had wrought great changes. Changes there had been but not sufficient for the Egyptians to wage modern war against a skillful and implacable foe. A righteous cause is not alone the key to victory, nor, as the Arabs pointed out, does victory always go to the righteous.

"The war is over," said Moshe Dayan. "Now the trouble begins."[9] During the next months, the Israelis in particular and the world in general would find a peaceful solution far more elusive than even Dayan could have anticipated. The Arabs without exception opted for a policy of no war, no peace. They would not, perhaps in some cases could not, recognize the legitimacy of Israel. Defeat on the field of battle had to be grudgingly admitted and gradually accepted, but no one seemed willing or able to take the first step toward conciliation. Jordan, without the vital west bank, inundated with a new wave of refugees, economically a disaster area, had in less than a week become a desert displaced persons' camp. Yet King Hussein could not risk open negotiations with the Zionists without triggering revolution. Egypt, once Nasser had been reinstated in a wave of fervent popular enthusiasm, faced a bleak future: The Suez Canal was closed, the cotton crop in jeopardy, the Sinai oil lost, the army destroyed, perhaps the gains of a generation undone as well. Under pressure from all directions, Nasser refused to treat with the Zionists, even to avert economic chaos for his country. Syria, unrepentant under the guns of the Israelis on the Golan plateau, did not even consider peace but only a new guerrilla war. Algeria wanted war. The Iraqis were unreconciled to defeat. Seldom before had the victors sued for peace and the defeated demanded terms.

Solutions to the impasse were plentiful, and perhaps there were Arabs privately willing to consider rationally the consequences of defeat, but no "solution" attracted both sides. In the Middle East capitals moderation meant no more than cessation of provocative attacks on Israel during the diplomatic campaign to force the Zionist aggressors to disgorge conquered territory. Direct negotiations with Israel were out. The Arabs did have some solid assets left: Russian backing, a firm voting bloc in the United Nations, considerable international support, and universal concern at Israeli annexation of Jerusalem and the fate of the new refugees. As the weeks passed, the Arabs remained adamant: Peace had to come on their terms.

The Israelis were equally determined on a peace that would ensure the security of the state. They showed no inclination to compromise in return for paper promises arranged by a third party. For the first time in twenty years, Israel had physical security: The zigzag borders of the state were no longer vulnerable. All the old Arab strangleholds had been broken: The Strait of Tiran was open; the headwaters of the Jordan in Israeli hands; the future of the Suez Canal, of the Golan plateau, of the west bank, of the Gaza strip were not to be determined by distant negotiators or unilateral Arab action. Israel in fact had all the guarantees that security required, even though the Arabs were still inimical to that security. Unless the Arabs could devise a way to pry loose the gains of the June war, Israel could afford to wait, if not forever at least for a very long time. Little could be more advantageous for Israel than the status quo. As the months passed, it became clear that, despite the Jerusalem question, the closing of the Suez Canal, and the west-bank refugees, the international community did not intend to impose a solution and, as usual, could not devise an acceptable compromise.

The stalemate continued. After a series of conferences, meetings, exchanges, and summits, the Arabs emerged more united than even the most dedicated would have believed possible. Nasser accepted a face-saving compromise in Yemen and began to withdraw his troops. The oil states agreed to bankroll Egypt and Jordan, staving off economic chaos in return for toleration of renewed oil sales to the West. King Hussein agreed to hang on without opening negotiations. Nasser refused to consider opening the Suez Canal, although he did accept a token United Nations force to prevent incidents. Syria, supported by Algeria, wanted to go over to the offensive with a Palestine war of national liberation. El Fatah, still determined to strike at the Israelis whatever the wider consequences, began reorganizing on the west bank. Most Arabs sympathized with Syrian militance and El Fatah determination but agreed that the time was hardly ripe for provocation. Despite the predictions of the realists, after six months, at great sacrifice and in the face of deep divisions, the Arabs had still refused to accept the consequences of defeat—its occurrence yes but its implications no.

The Israelis, as euphoria evaporated, faced a massive array of challenges, all less serious than those of May but still imposing. On an international plane the diplomats had to fight a holding action, insisting on a real solution achieved by direct negotiations, rather than a return to insecurity punctured by Arab threats. In the meantime the future of the new territories, excluding Jerusalem, remained vague, although enthusiastic indiscretions and calculated feelers prompted suspicion that there might never be a withdrawal without the pressure of international sanctions. As the months passed, oil was pumped from the Sinai field, irrigation work began on the Jordan north of Galilee, refugees from Gaza were allowed to move to the west bank, the Etzion bloc south of Jerusalem was re-established, and the massive flow of financial contributions was funneled into the economy. The Israelis could sit tight, giving a little on the Suez Canal or on the religious foundations in Jerusalem but basically waiting for the Arabs to open negotiations or to suffer consequences that could only grow more severe with the passage of time.

The prospects for a peaceful and final solution to the long war are no brighter than they have been in the past. As long as the Arabs cannot or will not accept the existence of Israel as final and immutable, the best that can be expected is an uneasy truce maintained by Israeli strength. If the Arabs remain adamant, and there is no reason to assume that they will not, a war of redemption some time in the future, whether or not the Israelis withdraw from Sinai or the Golan plateau, remains a strong possibility. Perhaps the slow erosion of time, a generation of new men, or emotional conversion among the Arab masses can produce a change, but few would pin their hopes for peace on "possibilities" that have in the past proved illusory. Perhaps Israel is now, or will become, so secure, so dominant, that the state is at last invulnerable, but the resulting Arab frustration and humiliation at continuing military inadequacy are more likely to bring violence than peace. In the near future perhaps some interim solution can be found to tidy up the inconvenient aftermath of the June war, but the golden formula that will satisfy all and deny no one is nonexistent.

If in a thousand years the militant nationalists of Europe have been able to find no "solution" to their conflicting aspirations, except occasional mutual exhaustion, there is no compelling reason why the Zionists and the Arabs should deny themselves. The ideal that all human conflicts can be reconciled and all wars avoided remains only an ideal. As long as some men's dearest aspirations contradict the aspirations of others, violence is probable. As long as the cause is more important than life itself, men will fight wars. Perhaps they should not, perhaps in time they will not, but in the Middle East at the moment they do. There the long war has obviously entered a new phase, but, if indeed the past is merely a prologue, the last act is still far off.

NOTES

1. The "orthodox" Egyptian explanation of the war heavily stresses the significance of the Soviet "intelligence" report; there is ample evidence, however, that Nasser had been contemplating a summer crisis of a sort for some time. See Walter Laqueur, "The Hand of Russia," *The Reporter*, 36, No. 13 (June 29, 1967), 18–20. Laqueur intends to publish a study of the background to the war, covering the period from May 10 to June 5. *The Road to Jerusalem: The Origins of the Arab-Israeli Conflict, 1967* (Macmillan, New York, 1968).

2. Sustained attacks on U Thant resulted in a rather unusual step: The Secretary-General produced on June 26, a memorandum explaining his reasons.

3. Randolph S. Churchill and Winston S. Churchill, *The Six Day War* (London: 1967), p. 38.

4. S. L. A. Marshall, *Swift Sword: The Historical Record of Israel's Victory, June 1967* (New York: 1967), p. 19.

5. Claire Sterling, "A Matter of Survival," *The Reporter*, 36, No. 13 (June 29, 1967), 17. Although Nasser's speeches during the last days before the war can be combed for moderate expressions, there is also some evidence that Egypt had planned an attack on Israel for June 5 but that Russia had urged moderation on Nasser. *The New York Times* printed in considerable detail reports from an authoritative diplomatic source in Madrid. Rabin's report on the Sinai campaign includes quotations from captured documents (June 2, 1967) that suggest that there was planning for an Egyptian air strike apparently prepared by Field Marshal Amer. See *Jewish Observer and Middle East Review*, 16, No. 27 (July 7, 1967), 10–4.

6. Isolated in Dublin at the time, I found that the two factors that most impressed me were the Algerian declaration of aid and the report that no Israeli ships had actually used the Strait in months. The latter looked like the first step to force a "compromise" on Israel and the former like a serious upping of the cost of an Israeli victory. Generally, however, the Israelis insist that it was Hussein's arrival in Cairo that tipped the balance, although the cynical could be forgiven for concluding that the Israelis simply sensed their moment and took it.

7. Marshall, *Swift Sword*, p. 19.

8. Leo Heiman, "Naval Action in the Six-Day War," *Jewish Digest*, XII, No. 12 (September 1967), 1–8.

9. The Associated Press, *Lightning out of Israel: The Six-Day War in the Middle East* (New York: 1967), p. 154.

Bibliography

Under conventional circumstances, when a bibliography is not intended for scholars, it is entitled "Supplementary Readings," which clearly implies that the reader will pursue the topic further, an assumption based, in my judgment, on unwarranted idealism. The average "common reader," long may he live, seldom goes beyond the text, almost never refers to the notes, and could not care less about a balanced bibliography. Scholars, on the other hand, ordinarily and often justly think that they have already read more than the author; they automatically look first to see if they themselves have been cited, and second to find the inevitable unpardonable omissions. This particular bibliography is, however, intended for the rare creature who does not already have a working knowledge of the massive corpus of printed works and would like a handy if, alas, fallible guide. It is, in fact, what I would like to have found four years ago to help me avoid the traditional trials of three-by-five cards, unpublished dissertations, and obscure and totally valueless Egyptian periodicals.

In any area of contemporary history, a definitive bibliography must await the eventual application of computer technology; in fact, in some areas even to read tentative bibliographies is a considerable task. In Middle Eastern scholarship there are certain bibliographic and research aids like The Hebrew University's *Selected Bibliography*, the volumes in the Middle East Institute (Washington) *Reports on Current Research on the Middle East*, the Zionist Archives' (New York City) bibliographical series, or issues of the more important periodicals devoted to events in the Middle East (see, for example, Middle East Journal, summer 1965, pp. 354–362). Generally, however, such aids tend to be scattered, incomplete, and not readily available. The general books in the field necessarily have general bibliographies, and there are far too few scholarly works on the more recent period that contain the full bibliographical apparatus. If there were a few more gems like J. S. Hurewitz's awesome, closely set twenty-five-page bibliography in *The Struggle for Palestine*, which up to 1950 apparently contained everything relevant to the late Mandate, then researchers in the field would be happier. Alas, I am not capable of filling the lacuna, only of noting it with regret.

As every source could not be included here, even if I were familiar with all sources (which I am not), this selection is an individual one, limited by the lamentable state of my knowledge of Semitic languages, the available space, and personal predilections. I have tried to include all the vital sources, as well as a few odd bits that I have seldom seen mentioned alsewhere. I have not bothered to include all the sources cited in the rather limited notes, which have been pared to such a point that I am protected from violating copyright laws but little else. By and large, this bibliography is my working bibliography, offered in the hope of saving another tyro time and indicating the hidden scaffolding of the text.

Much of the historiography of the Middle East is the sad tale of ignorant, though enthusiastic, writers clashing in the public print. I cannot easily think of any other subject that has for twenty years inspired more repetitive junk than Israel, the Arabs, and their encounters. Scattered through the welter of journalism, instant memoirs, spotty surveys, open propaganda, and special pleading, are an increasing number of sound, disinterested, balanced works, but they are still too rare. Even the previously most stolid of scholars seems to lose his cool, analytical approach when venturing into the Middle East. No issue seems immune to contention. The various volumes surveying the contemporary world produced by the Royal Institute of International Affairs are invariably recognized as solid, sound, and thorough; yet George Kirk's volumes, on the Middle East in particular, have been harshly attacked as anti-Zionist, anti-French, and anti-American. Whether or not the charges are fully justified, the essential point is that hardly anyone, skilled professionals included, can escape unscathed from the whirling controversy.

As a substantial portion of the sources for a definitive study of any aspect of the Middle East in the last twenty years remains buried in sealed archives or locked in individual minds, there is a wide field for clashing interpretations based on limited evidence. Even crises like that over Suez, which produced mountains of official and unofficial documents, memoirs galore, books, slanted from every angle and for every taste, scholarly articles tucked away in *The Australian Journal of Politics or The Review of Politics*, unexpected journalistic revelations in *France-Observateur*, and significant oral evidence, have not necessarily inspired the desirable definitive volumes. There are, to be sure, many fine books, scholarly monographs, excellent interpretive journalistic reports, and memoirs. Journalists like Hedrick Smith, Thomas F. Brady, and Jon Kimche are invaluable sources of information, where as scholars like J. C. Hurewitz on the Mandate, Walter Z. Laqueur on the Soviet presence, and Don Peretz on the Arabs in Israel have produced highly distinguished work. More than elsewhere, however, in the Middle East a scholarly Gresham's law seems to work with a vengeance.

Documents

Ordinarily, bibliographies begin with documentary sources, but, although in this case documents are legion, the only area where such materials are truly valuable is the work of the United Nations. Elsewhere diplomatic archives are closed, manuscript collections still classified, and private papers usually unopened. All the dependable old faithfuls are available: the State Department *Bulletins*, the Assemblée Nationale *Journal Officiel: Débats*, and the British Command Papers, and the United Nations material in judicious conjunction with other sources, is a mine of information.

THE UNITED NATIONS

Official Records of the General Assembly, Emergency and Ordinary Sessions (1946–1966).

Report of the Special Committee on Palestine (1947).
Report of the Mediator on Palestine (1948).
Reports of the Conciliation Commission for Palestine.
Official Records of the Security Council (1946–1966).
  Reports of the Chief of Staff of the Truce Supervision Organization.
  "Records of the Mixed Armistice Commissions."
  Reports of the Mediator.
  Reports of the Acting Mediator.
  Reports of the Secretary-General.
Annual Reports of the Director of the Relief and Works Agency.

CANADA

The Crisis in the Middle East, October–December 1956 (White Paper).
The Crisis in the Middle East, January–March 1957.
  These two volumes are of interest because of the extensive part played by
  Lester B. Pearson in creating the United Nations Emergency Force.

GREAT BRITAIN

  There is a variety of reports on the Mandate by the British Government to
the League of Nations and to the United Nations. The most helpful is *The
Political History of Palestine under British Mandate* (presented to the United
Nations Special Committee on Palestine in 1947). Among the other official
releases, see also the Foreign Office's "Communique on Palestine with Refer-
ence to the Deportation of the Illegal Immigrants on the Exodus 1947 to the
British Zone in Germany."
Parliamentary Debates, House of Commons, 1946–1966.
Parliamentary Debates, House of Lords, 1946–1966.
  The number of Parliamentary Command Papers is considerable, but the
more interesting are:
Palestine Statement of Policy (The White Paper of May 1939), Cmd. 6019.
Palestine Statement of Information Relating to Acts of Violence (July 1946),
  Cmd. 6873.
The Suez Canal Conference: London, August 2–24, 1956, Cmd. 9853.

ISRAEL

  The Israelis, beside the normal record of debates in the Knesset and similar
traditional releases, have published in English an extensive collection of
White Papers. A most useful handbook of statistics is the annual *Israeli Government Yearbook.*

The Arab refugees. Jerusalem, 1953.
The Defense Department. *The Soviet-Czech Arms Deal with Egypt.* Tel
  Aviv: n.d.

Office of Information. *Israel's Struggle for Peace.* New York: 1960.
———. *Nasser's Pattern of Aggression.* New York: 1956.
———. *Jerusalem and the United Nations.* New York: 1953.
Ministry of Foreign Affairs. *The Arab Refugees: Arab Statements and the Facts.* Jerusalem: 1961.
———. *The Jewish Exodus from the Arab Countries and the Arab Refugees.* Jerusalem: 1961.
———. *Documents Relating to the Agreement Between the Government of the Federal Republic of Germany* (September 10, 1952). Jerusalem: 1953.
———. *Egypt and the Suez Canal, 1948–1956: A Record of Lawlessness.* Jerusalem: 1956.
———. *Gaza Bulletin.* Jerusalem: 1956–1966.
———. *The Gaza Strip: Aggression or Peace?* Jerusalem: 1957.
———. *The Gulf of 'Aqaba: Free Navigation or Piracy?* Jerusalem: 1958.
———. *Israel's Peace Offers to the Arab States, 1948–1958: The Record.* Jerusalem: 1958.
———. *Israel's Peace Offers to the Arab States, 1948–1963: The Record.* Jerusalem: 1963.
———. *The Threat to Israel: Some Egyptian Documents.* Jerusalem: 1957.
It is obvious from the titles of these selected documents that many are not White Papers or "documents" in the accepted sense but "official" propaganda.

The Arab states and the Arab League have prepared similar information releases but not with the regularity or efficient distribution of the Zionists. See, for example:

Trans-Jordan Foreign Affairs Ministry. *The Rising Tide of Terror: or, Three Years of an "Armistice" in the Holy Land.* Amman: 1952.
League of Arab States Information Agency. *Arab Property in Israeli-Controlled Territories.* New York: 1956.

At one time or another all the major powers have been involved with either Israel, the Arabs, or both, as, for that matter, have most of the smaller states. The sources of information on their relations with the Middle East are the traditional ones: from France's Assemblée Nationale, *Journal Officiel: Débats* to the United States' *Congressional Record* or the annual *United States Participation in the United Nations.* Two of the more interesting United States State Department Publications are:

The Suez Canal Problem, July 26–September 22, 1956.
United States Policy in the Middle East, September 1956 to June 1957.

One of the most vital sources for documentation and authoritative commentaries is the series of documents and individual studies issued by the Royal Institute of International Affairs: *Documents on International Affairs* and *Survey of International Affairs.* See also:

British Interests in the Mediterranean and Middle East. London, 1958.
Defense of the Middle East. London: September 1953.
Documents on the Suez Crisis. London: February 1957.
Great Britain and Egypt, 1914–1951. London: 1952.
Great Britain and Palestine, 1915–1941. London: 1946.
The Baghdad Pact: Origins and Political Setting. London: 1956.
The Middle East: A Political and Economic Survey. London: 1958.
The Western Powers and the Middle East. London: 1959.

Much less authoritative but neat and handy are the outline folders edited by A. G. Mezerik and published by International Review Service.

Arab-Israel Conflict and the United Nations. New York: 1962.
Arab Refugees in the Middle East. New York: 1958.
The Crisis in the Middle East. New York: 1958.
The Middle East: Unification Among Arab States. New York: 1958.

Other useful collections are:

Davis, Helen Miller. *Constitutions, Electoral Laws, Treaties of States in the Near and Middle East.* Durham: 1953.
Eayrs, James. *The Commonwealth and Suez: A Documentary Survey.* London: 1964.
Hurewitz, J. C. *Diplomacy in the Near and Middle East,* Vols. I and II. Princeton: 1956.

Newspapers

Newspapers are basic to any study of the contemporary Middle East; the production of monographs and surveys declined after 1958, and instant memoirs are now more written about experiences in Cuba or Vietnam. Almost all the elite newspapers, *The New York Times, Le Monde, Corrier dell Sera, The Times,* keep not only abreast but also at times ahead of events. In Israel the *Jerusalem Post* and the *Jewish Chronicle* are published in English, but in the Arab world newspapers are a kind of institution entirely foreign to Western readers, even those experienced with captive newspapers and the political press. Most of the influential newspapers like Cairo's *Al Ahram* are, of course, in Arabic, but there are some available to Europeans: *Egyptian Gazette, Egyptian Mail, La Bourse Egyptienne, L'Orient* (Beirut), *Commerce du Levant-Beyrout Express.*

Periodicals

Although most of the weekly news magazines—*Vita, Time, L'Express,* and so on—cover the Middle East, they seldom contain more than brief summaries of events. Far more useful to the historian is occasional coverage in *The Economist, Spectator, Commentary, Midstream,* or *The World Today.* As might be expected, there are occasional articles, usually listed in appropriate bibliographies, in scholarly or almost scholarly periodicals like *International Organization, Politique Étrangère, Foreign Affairs,* and the international-law quarterlies. An area of Middle Eastern affairs that is extensively covered is oil in all its ramifications; see *Petroleum Times* (London), *World Petroleum* (New York), *World Oil* (Houston), and the like. Most important are those periodicals that are solely concerned with the Middle East.

Arab Journal (Organ of Arab students in Canada and the United States).
Der Islam (Hamburg).
Egyptian Economic and Political Review.
Egyptian Political Science Review.
L'Égypte Contemporaine.
Israel Academy of Sciences and Humanities Proceedings.
Israel Background (United Jewish Appeal).
Israel Digest of the Press and Events in Israel and the Middle East.
Israel Economic News.
Israeli Economist.
Israel and the Middle East.
Israel Today.
Issues (American Council for Judaism).
Jewish Agency Digest of Press and Events.
Jewish Observer and Middle East Review (London).
Middle Eastern Affairs (Council for Middle Eastern Affairs, New York).
Middle East Forum (The American University, Beirut).
Middle East Journal (Middle East Institute, Washington, D.C.).
Mideast Mirror (Arab News Agency, Cairo).
Muslim World (Hartford, Conn.).
Palestine and Near East Economic Magazine.
Palestine Issue (Palestine Liberation Organization, New York).
Revue du Droit International pour le Moyen Orient.
Revue Égyptienne du Droit International.
New Outlook (Tel Aviv).
Orient (Paris).
Oriente Moderno (Rome).
Zionist Review.

Few of these journals have been published without interruption throughout the period since 1946, others have ceased publication or changed titles, and some make only limited reference to the Israeli-Arab conflict. Special note should be taken of Jon Kimche's *Jewish Observer and Middle East Review,* which regularly contains revelations and insights and is always enlightening though often irritating. *Middle East Forum* often has solid articles with an Arab point of view.

Books and Articles

This section is so massive, including several extensive lists of titles that are not so much definitive as reflecting the flavor and failings of the literature, that a straight alphabetical treatment would be only confusing. On the other hand, the topical sections are at times unwieldy, requiring material to be listed in one section that could as easily go in another. Nor are the topical sections exactly chronological. Still, if the rare reader for whom this bibliography is actually intended will suffer through, I think he will find this approach useful.

THE ARAB WORLD

Scholarship on the Arab world by Arabs has particularly reflected the ideas and ideals of Arab nationalism and unity (see Nabbel Shaath, "The Arab Research Committee: An Introduction," *Arab Journal*, No. 4 (1964), 4–48, which describes thirty Ph.D. dissertations by Arab students in the United States. Other interesting work has been done as well, often by men first trained at The American University, Beirut. A substantial portion of American scholarship in the area has been undertaken by Jews, who have certain linguistic advantages and a built-in interest but far less open prejudice than their Arab counterparts often show. Beside the professional scholars of all nationalities and persuasions who have dedicated their lives to the study of the Middle East, there are others, highly knowledgeable and often enlightening, who have written primarily on the Arabs. The British, scholar and layman alike, seem particularly fascinated by the Arabs, a tendency that antedates T. E. Lawrence.

There is a substantial number of first-rate works on the Arabs in general and Islam in particular, written and revised over the last twenty years by the outstanding scholars in the field: Morroe Berger, Carl Brockelmann, Philip Hitti, Walter Z. Laqueur, Don Peretz, Wilfred C. Smith, and Sir Hamilton Gibb, to mention a few. There are also several more contentious surveys, particularly of recent Arab politics in general.

Atiyah, Edward. *The Arabs*. London: 1955.

Berger, Morroe. *The Arab World Today*. London: 1962.

Berque, Jacques. *The Arabs: Their History and Future*. London: 1964.

Bonne, Alfred. *State and Economics in the Middle East: A Society in Transition*. London: 1955.

Brockelmann, Carl. *History of the Islamic Peoples*. London: 1949. Brookings Institution. *The Security of the Middle East: A Problem Paper*. Washington, D.C.: 1950.

Campbell, John C. *The Defense of the Middle East*. New York: 1960.

Eban, Abba. *The Tide of Nationalism.* New York: 1959.

Europa Publications. *The Middle East* (annual). London: 1948 to date.

Fisher, Sydney Nettleton, ed. *Social Forces in the Middle East.* Ithaca: 1955.

Fisher, W. B. *The Middle East: A Physical, Social, and Regional Geography.* New York: 1950.

Frye, Richard N. *Islam and the West.* The Hague: 1957.

———, ed. *The Near East and the Great Powers.* Cambridge, Massachusetts: 1951.

Gibb, Sir Hamilton. *Modern Trends in Islam.* Chicago: 1947.

Hitti, Philip K. *History of the Arabs.* London: 1946.

Hollingworth, C. *The Arabs and the West.* London: 1952.

Hoskins, Halford. *The Middle East.* New York: 1954.

Ireland, P. W., ed. *The Near East: Problems and Prospects.* Chicago: 1942.

Izzedin, Nejla. *The Arab World.* Chicago: 1953.

Kimche, Jon. *Seven Fallen Pillars, The Middle East from 1945 to 1952.* New York: 1953.

Kirk, George E. *Contemporary Arab Politics.* New York: 1961.

———. *Short History of the Middle East.* New York: 1959.

Laqueur, Walter Z. *Communism and Nationalism in the Middle East.* London: 1959.

———, ed. *The Middle East in Transition.* New York, 1958.

Lewis, Bernard. *The Arabs in History.* London: 1950.

Peretz, Don. *The Middle East Today.* New York: 1963.

Rondot, Pierre. *The Changing Patterns of the Middle East: 1919–1958.* London: 1961.

Smith, Wilfred C. *Islam in Modern History.* New York: 1959.

Thayer, Philip W., ed. *Tensions in the Middle East.* Baltimore: 1958.

Totah, Khalil. *Dynamite in the Middle East.* New York: 1955.

Yale, William. *The Near East.* Ann Arbor: 1958.

This list is, of course, a mixed bag containing Abba Eban's brief assault on the contemporary Arab world and omitting my two favorite books on the Arabs, T. E. Lawrence's *Seven Pillars of Wisdom* and Charles M. Doughty's *Travels in Arabia Deserta,* which may actually tell us more about the English than they do about the Arabs.

ARAB NATIONALISM

I have excluded most of the work on the Arab rebellion, except for Antonius' classic, which sets the stage for contemporary problems.

Antonius, George. *The Arab Awakening.* London: 1938.

Batayneh, Nasir Sa'ad, "Arab Political Thought Between 1945–1962." Ph.D. dissertation, New York University, 1963.

Binder, Leonard. "Nasserism: The Protest Movement in the Middle East." In Morton Kaplan, ed. *The Revolution in World Politics.* New York: 1962.

Dabbas, Hashim Ahmed. "Arab Unity: Prospects and Problems." Ph.D. dissertation, University of Missouri, 1964.
Ghalayini, Khalil A. "A Plan for the Organization of an Arab Federation." Ph.D. dissertation, The American University, 1956.
Grunebaum, G. E. von. *Modern Islam: The Search for Cultural Identity.* Berkeley: 1962.
Haim, Sylvia G., ed. *Arab Nationalism: An Anthology.* Berkeley: 1962.
Khandra, Omar About. "Arab Unity: Trend and International Implications." Ph.D. dissertation, Princeton University, 1949.
Mohamad, Fadhil Zaky. "Prospect for Arab Federation." Ph.D. dissertion, University of Colorado, 1956.
Nuseibh, H. Z. *The Ideas of Arab Nationalism.* Ithaca: 1956.
Qubain, Fahim I. *Inside the Arab Mind.* Arlington, Va.: 1960. This work is a survey of ninety-five Arab books.
Sayegh, Fayez A. *Arab Unity: Hope and Fulfillment.* New York: 1958.
Sharabi, Hisham. "The Transformation of Ideology in the Arab World," *Middle Eastern Review,* 19, No. 4 (Autumn 1965), 471–86.
Wynn, Wilton. "The Latest Revival of Islamic Nationalism," *Muslim World,* No. 38 (January 1948), 11–6.

RECENT ARAB HISTORY

Although all phases of recent Arab history, from a study of the economic development of Iraq to one on the place of women in society, are related, even though distantly, to the Israeli conflict, obviously a total listing is impossible. I have included what I think is a judicious selection of the best and the most useful books, as well as several typical specimens that are neither. Also included are several studies at present available only in Arabic but too significant to ignore.

Alami, Musa. "The Lesson of Palestine," *Middle East Journal,* 3, No. 4 (October 1949), 373–405.
Ata, Mohamed Moustafa. *Egypt Between Two Revolutions.* Cairo: n.d.
Baulin, Jacques. *The Arab Role in Africa.* Harmondsworth, Middlesex: 1962.
Birdwood, Lord. *Nuri as-Said.* London: 1959.
Boutros-Ghali, B. Y. "The Arab League 1945–1955," *International Conciliation,* No. 498 (May 1954), 385–448.
Caractacus (pseud.). *Revolution in Iraq.* London: 1959.
Colombe, Marcel. "L'Egypte et le Nationalisme Arabe de la Ligue des États Arabes à la République Arabe unie (1945–1958)," *Orient,* 2, No. 1 (1958), 113–34.
Cooke, M. L. *Nasser's High Aswan Dam.* Washington, D.C.: n.d.
Cremeans, Charles D. *The Arabs and the World: Nasser's Arab Nationalist Policy.* New York: 1963.
Egyptian Political and Economic Review, *The Armed Forces* (special supplement). Cairo: 1955–1956?

Foudah, Ezz El Din. "Principles of Arab Policy in Twelve Years," *Egyptian Political Science Review*, No. 40 (July 1964), 71–80.

Glubb, John Bagot. *The Story of the Arab Legion*. London: 1958.

———. *War in the Desert*. London: 1960.

Goldner, Werner Ernst. "The Role of Abdullah ibn Husain, King of Jordan in Arab Politics, 1914–1951." Ph.D. dissertation, Stanford University, 1954.

Himadeh, Sa'id B. "Economic Factors Underlying Social Problems in the Arab Middle East," *Middle East Journal*, 5, No. 3 (Summer 1951), 269–83.

Husaini, Ishaq Musa. *The Muslim Brotherhood* (in Arabic). Beirut: 1952.

Hussein. *Uneasy Lies the Head*. London: 1962.

Ingrams, Harold. *The Yemen: Imam, Rulers and Revolutions*. London: 1964.

Ionides, Michael. *Divide and Lose: The Arab Revolt 1955–1958*. London: 1960.

Issawi, Charles. *Egypt in Revolution: An Economic Analysis*. London: 1963.

Kayali, Nizar. "Syria—A Political Study (1926–1950). Ph.D. dissertation, Columbia University, 1951.

Kerr, Malcolm. *The Arab Cold War 1958–1964: A Study in Ideology and Politics*. London: 1965.

Khadduri, Majid. *Independent Iraq: 1932–1958*. London: 1960.

Khalil, Dr. Muham, ed. *The Arab States and the Arab League*. Beirut: 1965.

Kirkbride, Alex. *A Crackle of Thorns*. London: 1956.

Lacouture, Jean, and Simone Lacouture. *Egypt in Transition*. New York: 1958.

Little, Tom. *Egypt*. London: 1958.

Longrigg, Stephen, and Frank Stoakes. *Iraq*. New York: 1958.

Macdonald, Robert. *The League of Arab States*. Princeton: 1965.

Moyal, Maurice. "Post-Mortem on the Arab League," *World Affairs*, 3 (April 1949), 187–95.

Nasser, Gamal Abdel. *Egypt's Liberation: The Philosophy of the Revolution*. Washington, D.C.: 1955–

———. Speeches (1958–1959) 2 vols. Cairo: N.D.

Nassur, Adib. "The Moral Crisis of the Arabs" (in Arabic), *al-Abhath* 3 (June 1950), 153–162.

Neguib, Mohammed. *Egypt's Destiny*. New York: 1955.

Palmer, M. "The United Arab Republic: An Assessment of Its Failure," *Middle East Journal* 20, No. 1 (Winter 1966), 50–67.

Patai, Ralphael. *The Kingdom of Jordan*. Princeton: 1958.

Qubain, Fahim I. *Crisis in Lebanon*. Washington, D.C.: 1961.

Raleigh, J. S. "Ten Years of the Arab League," *Middle East Affairs*, 6, No. 3 (March 1955), 65–77.

Rivlin, Benjamin, and Joseph Szyliowiecz. *The Contemporary Middle East*. New York: 1965.

Royal Institute of International Affairs, *The Baghdad Pact: Origins and Political Setting*. London: 1956.

Sadat, Anwar El. *Revolt on the Nile*. New York: 1957.

Safran, Nadav. "Modern Egypt in Search of an Ideology." Ph.D. dissertation, Harvard University, 1959.

St. John, Robert. *The Boss: The Story of Gamal Abdel Nasser.* New York: 1960.

Schechtman, Joseph B. *The Mufti and the Fuehrer.* New York: 1965.

Seale, Patrick. *The Struggle For Syria: A Study of Post-War Arab Politics.* New York: 1965.

Seton-Williams, M. V. *Britain and the Arab States: A Survey of Anglo-Arab Relations 1920–1948.* London: 1948.

Shwadran, Benjamin. *Jordan: A State of Tension.* New York: 1959.

————. *The Power Struggle in Iraq.* New York: 1960.

Simonhoff, Harry. *Under Strange Skies.* New York: 1953.

Smolanksy, O. M. "The Soviet Union and the Arab East, 1947–1957: A Study in Diplomatic Relations." Ph.D. dissertation, Columbia University, 1959.

Stevens, Georgiana G. ed. *The United States and the Middle East.* Englewood, N.J.: 1964.

Tannous, Afif I. "Land Reform: Key to the Development and Stability of the Arab World," *Middle East Journal,* 5, No. 1 (Winter 1951), 1–20.

Taylor, Edmund. *The Real Case Against Nasser.* Washington, D.C.: 1956.

Torrey, Gordon H. *Syrian Politics and the Military, 1945–1958.* Columbus: 1965.

Vatikiotis, P. J. *The Egyptian Army in Politics.* Bloomington, Ind.: 1961.

Wendell, Cleland. "The League of Arab States After Fifteen Years," *World Affairs,* 123 (Summer 1960), 49–52.

Westfried, Alex H. "The Action and Doctrine of Habib Bourguiba: A Case Study of Arab Nationalism." Ph.D. dissertation, University of Pennsylvania, 1956.

There is another area of recent Arab history, the importance of oil, on which I found little or nothing of interest connected with the Israeli conflict, but another study written from a slightly different angle might find a brief oil bibliography a place to begin.

Chenery, Hollis B. *Arabian Oil: America's Stake in the Middle East.* Chapel Hill: 1949.

Elwell-Sutton, L. P. *Persian Oil: A Study in Power Politics.* London: 1955.

Engler, Robert. *The Politics of Oil.* New York: 1960.

Hartshorn, J. *Oil Companies and Governments.* London: 1962.

Hoskins, Halford L. *Middle East Oil in United States Foreign Policy.* Washington, D.C.: 1950.

Kemp, Norman. *Abadan: A First Hand Account of the Persian Oil Crisis.* London: 1953.

Leeman, W. A. *The Price of Middle East Oil.* London: 1961.

Lenczowski, George. *Oil and State in the Middle East.* Ithaca: 1960.

Longrigg, S. *Oil in the Middle East.* London: 1961.

Shwadran, Benjamin. *The Middle East: Oil and the Great Powers.* New York: 1959.

ZIONISM

Included in this section is the merest fraction of the published materials. Zionism in all its phases does, of course, play a central part in the long war, and I have included several relevant works under other headings. Understanding of one area of Zionism, revisionism, requires more study, particularly its evolution over the past generation, if for no other reason than the response it has engendered among the Arabs.

Cohen, Israel. *The Zionist Movement.* New York: 1946.
Halperin, Samuel. *The Political World of American Zionism.* Detroit: 1961. This title is more neutral than that of his dissertation at Washington University: "American Zionism: The Building of a Political Interest Group."
Halpern, Benjamin. *The Idea of the Jewish State.* Cambridge, Massachusetts: 1961.
Hertzberg, Arthur, ed. *The Zionist Idea.* New York: 1960.
Herzl, Theodor. *The Jewish State: An Attempt at a Modern Solution of the Jewish Question.* London: 1934.
Learsi, Rufus. *Fulfillment: The Epic Story of Zionism.* Cleveland: 1951.
Mallison, W. T. "The Zionist-Israel Juridical Claims to Constitute 'the Jewish People' Nationality Entity and to Confer Membership in It: Appraisal in Public International Law," *The George Washington Law Review,* 22, No. 4 (June 1964), 983–1075.
Rabinowicz, Oskar K. *Fifty Years of Zionism.* London: 1950.
Stevens, Richard Paul. "The Political and Diplomatic Role of American Zionists as a Factor in the Creation of the State of Israel." Ph.D. dissertation, Georgetown University, 1960.
Tartakower, Arieh. "The Making of Jewish Statehood in Palestine," *Jewish Social Studies* (July 1948), 207–22.
Taylor, Allan R. *Prelude to Israel: An Analysis of Zionist Diplomacy, 1897–1947.* New York: 1959.

THE MANDATE

In a very real sense an extended bibliography of the Mandate period, particularly after 1936, has been made unnecessary by J. C. Hurewitz's *The Struggle for Palestine.* There are, of course, new materials since 1950. They include a growing number of memoirs that bear indirectly on the Mandate period, particularly in moments of crisis, for example, those of former President Harry S Truman or Field Marshal Viscount Bernard Montgomery. There are, as well, large heaps, still undigested, of material on Jewish emigration, personal histories, and agency reports. What is given here is a selection of only the best and the most interesting.

Abcarius, M. F. *Palestine Through the Fog of Propaganda.* London: 1946.

Barbour, Neville. *Nisi Dominus.* London: 1946.

Benjamin, Leo. *Martyrs in Cairo: The Trial of the Assassins.* New York: 1953.

Berlin, Isaiah. *Chaim Weizmann.* New York: 1958.

Borisov, J. *Palestine Underground.* New York: 1947.

Crossman, Richard. *Palestine Mission.* London: 1947.

Dickstein, Moishe. *From Palestine to Israel.* Montreal: 1951.

ESCO Foundation for Palestine, Inc. *Palestine: A Study of Jewish, Arab, and British Policies.* 2 vols. New Haven: 1947.

Frank, Gerold. *The Deed.* New York: 1963.

Garcia-Granados, Jorge. *The Birth of Israel: The Drama As I Saw It.* New York: 1948.

Glick, Edward B. "Latin America and the Establishment of Israel," *Middle East Affairs*, 9, No. 1 (January 1958), 11–15.

Gruber, Ruth. *Destination Palestine: The Story of the Haganah Ship Exodus, 1947.* New York: 1948.

Habas, Bracha. *The Gate Breakers.* New York: 1964.

Hanna, Paul L. *British Policy in Palestine.* Washington, D.C.: 1942.

Hurewitz, J. C. *The Struggle for Palestine.* New York, 1950.

Hymson, Albert M. *Palestine Under the Mandate, 1926–1948.* London: 1950.

Joseph, Bernard. *British Rule in Palestine.* Washington, D.C.: 1948.

Klieman, Aaron S. "Harry S Truman and the Recognition of Israel," *The Chicago Jewish Forum*, 23, No. 1 (Fall 1964), 34–39.

Marlowe, John. *The Seat of Pilate.* London: 1959.

Polk, William, David M. Stamler, and Edmund Asford. *Backdrop to Tragedy: The Struggle for Palestine.* Boston: 1957.

Robinson, Jacob. *Palestine and the United Nations: Prelude to a Solution.* Washington, D.C.: 1947.

Roosevelt, Kermit. "The Partition of Palestine: A Lesson in Pressure Politics," *Middle East Journal*, 2, No. 1 (January 1948), 3–16.

Sakran, Frank. *Palestine Dilemma.* Washington, D.C.: 1948.

Schechtman, Joseph B. *The United States and the Jewish State Movement, The Crucial Decade: 1939–1949.* New York: 1966.

Schwarz, Leo W. *The Redeemers.* New York: 1953.

Slotzki, Yehuda. *History of the Haganah.* Jerusalem: 1954.

Stein, Leonard. *The Balfour Declaration.* London: 1961.

Sykes, Christopher. *Crossroad to Israel, 1917–1948.* Cleveland: 1965.

Waters, M. P. *Haganah: The Story of Jewish Self-Defense in Palestine.* London: 1947.

Weizmann, Chaim. *Trial and Error: The Autobiography of Chaim Weizmann.* New York: 1949.

It should be apparent that, from an inexplicable personal predilection, I have not included some books in this section but have hidden them in the previous or following sections. In passing, I note that the Polk, Stamler, and Asford work offers excellent background on the Palestine war and that the ESCO study is a solid collection of articles on the Mandate period comparable to the Royal Institute of International Affairs surveys. Hymson is sympathetic to the Zionist, whereas Marlowe is not.

THE PALESTINE WAR: 1948–1949

The greatest single problem for the curious is the dearth of published material on the Arab side. The Israelis have collected and published in Hebrew in *Be'enei Oyev (Through the Eyes of the Enemy)* (Tel Aviv: 1955) the memoirs of three Arabs. Although in Arabic, there is much available material ranging from the Iraqi commander's report to Parliament and the Egyptian commander's book review (v. General Sadaq's review of Jon Kimche's *Seven Fallen Pillars*, in Akher Sa'a, Cairo), there are simply no disinterested analyses or published memoirs. Glubb's book, which is a memoir and not a history, with all that form entails, is very important, as are some other available scraps. On the Israeli side, Lorch's book, *The Edge of the Sword*, is excellent on the up-one-hill-down-the-other level but vague on command decisions and relevant political questions. The same is true of O'Ballance's work. Jon and David Kimche's *Both Sides of the Hill* is filled with revelations but is often unfootnoted. Jon Kimche does not approve of footnotes with apparently ample evidence. Sachar's *Israel: The Establishment of a State* seems sound but contains no notes at all. Ben-Gurion's memoirs are listed in the section on Israel. There is also a wide variety of materials published in Hebrew, including official histories, military periodicals, memoirs, and newspaper accounts. To a large extent, however, the plain tale of events can best be followed in Lorch and O'Ballance.

Abdullah. *Memoirs of King Abdullah of Transjordan.* New York: 1950.

Avinoam, Reuben, ed. *Such Were Our Fighters.* New York: 1965.

Avneri, Uri. *Los Zorros de Sansón: Diario de la Guerra de Israel.* Buenos Aires: 1951.

Begin, Menachem. *The Revolt: Story of the Irgun.* New York: 1951.

——. *This Is the Resistance: Palestine's Fighting Army of Liberation.* New York: n.d.

Bell, J. Bowyer. *Besieged.* Philadelphia: 1966.

Berkman, Ted. *Cast a Giant Shadow: The Story of Mickey Marcus, Who Died to Save Jerusalem.* New York: 1962.

Bernadotte, Folke. *To Jerusalem.* London: 1951.

Bilby, Kenneth W. *New Star in the Near East.* New York: 1950.

Brodetsky, Selig. *Memoirs: From Ghetto to Israel.* London: 1960.

Burstein, Samuel M. *Rabbi With Wings.* New York: 1965.

Carlson, J. R. *Cairo to Damascus.* New York: 1951.

Childers, Erskine B. "The Other Exodus," *The Spectator*, vol. 206, May 12, 1961. 672–3.

Courtney, David. *Column One*. Tel Aviv: 1953.

Dekel, Efraim. *SHAI: The Exploits of Haganah Intelligence*. New York: 1959.

Farran, Roy. *Winged Dagger: Adventures on Special Service*, London: 1948.

Glubb, John Bagot. *A Soldier with the Arabs*. London: 1957.

Graves, R. M. *Experiment in Anarchy*. London: 1940.

———. *Haganah Becomes an Army: A Brief Account of the Jewish Armed Forces*. Tel Aviv: 1949.

Gurion, Itzhak. *Triumph on the Gallows*. New York: 1950.

Hewins, Ralph. *Count Folke Bernadotte: His Life and Work*. Minneapolis: 1950.

Hyrkanos-Ginzburg, Devora. *Jerusalem War Diary*. Israel: 1950.

Joseph, Dov. *The Faithful City: The Siege of Jerusalem, 1948*. New York: 1960.

Kagan, Colonel Benjamin. *Combat Secret pour Israël*, Loos-lez-Lille: 1963.

Katz, Doris. *The Lady Was a Terrorist*. New York: 1953.

Khalidi, Walid. "The Fall of Haifa," *Middle East Forum*, 35, No. 10 (December 1959), 22–32.

———. "Plan Dalet, the Zionist Blueprint for the Conquest of Palestine," *Middle East Forum*, 37, No. 9 (November 1961), pp. 22–8.

———. "Why did the Palestinians Leave?" *Middle East Forum*, 35, No. 7 (July 1959), 21–4, 35 ff.

Kimche, Jon, and David Kimche. *Both Sides of the Hill*. London: 1960. Published in the United States as *A Clash of Destinies* (New York: 1960).

Knohl, Dov, ed. *Siege in the Hills of Hebron*. New York: 1958.

Koestler, Arthur. *Promise and Fulfillment: Palestine 1917–1949*. New York: 1949.

Larkin, Margaret. *The Six Days of Yad Mordechai*. Jerusalem: 1965.

Lever, Walter. *Jerusalem Is Called Liberty*. Jerusalem: 1951.

Levin, Harry. *Jerusalem Embattled: A Diary of the City Under Siege*. London: 1950. Published in the United States as *I Saw the Battle of Jerusalem* (New York).

Lias, Godfrey. *Glubb's Legion*. London: 1956.

Lorch, Netanel. *The Edge of the Sword: Israel's War of Independence, 1947–1949*. New York: 1961.

Mackworth, Cecily. *The Mouth of the Sword*. London: 1949.

Mardor, Munya M. *Strictly Illegal*. London: 1964. Published in the United States as *Haganah* (New York).

Meinertzhagen, Colonel Richard. *Middle East Diary, 1917–1956*. New York: 1960.

Nasser, Gamal Abdel. *The Truth About the Palestine War*. Cairo: 1956.

O'Ballance, E. *The Arab-Israeli War 1948*. London: 1956.

"A Report on the Final Battle of Kfar Etzion." Stenciled. Israel: n.d.

Reynier, Jacques de. *À Jérusalem un Drapeau Flottait sur la Ligne de Feu.* Neuchâtel: 1950.

Roosevelt, Kermit. "Will the Arabs Fight?" *Saturday Evening Post* (December 27, 1947), pp. 20 ff.

Rose, Patricia. *The Siege of Jerusalem.* London: 1950.

Sachar, Harry. *Israel: The Establishment of a State.* London: 1952.

St. John, Robert. *Shalom Means Peace.* New York: 1949.

Sharef, Zeev. *Three Days.* New York: 1962.

Spicehandler, Daniel. *Let My Right Hand Wither.* New York: 1950.

Wilson, Major R. D. *Cordon and Search with 6th Airborne Division in Palestine.* Aldershot: 1949.

ISRAEL

Despite the appalling number of books entitled *Israel*, there is still no definitive, not even a decent, history of Israel. There are excellent books on politics, the kibbutzim, or governmental administration, but for a total treatment we are dependent on failures. Many of these failures are well-meaning, but few are worth the trouble to read them. In general, surveys fall into two groups: either "I Came, Saw Israel, and was Amazed" or those pasted up from clippings from yearbooks on ten or twelve conventional aspects of the state. To a large extent the contents and the prejudices of the authors can be discerned by looking no farther than the titles. As for Arab authors, they see through a glass darkly.

Beside no general history of Israel, we have no great biography of David Ben-Gurion. At present he is publishing his memoirs in the *Jewish Observer and Middle East Review*, but they neither reveal his personality nor reflect any self-criticism. See *Rebirth and Destiny of Israel* (New York: 1954) and *Israel: Years of Challenge* (New York: 1963). Some of his speeches and notes on Sinai, revealing little, have been published, and Moshe Pearlman has produced *Ben-Gurion Looks Back in Talks with Moshe Pearlman* (London: 1965). Also see

Edelman, Maurice. *David: The Story of David Ben-Gurion.* New York: 1965.

Litvinoff, Barnet. *Ben-Gurion of Israel.* New York: 1954.

Samuels, Gertrude. *Ben-Gurion, Fighter of Goliath: The Story of David Ben-Gurion.* New York: 1961.

David Horowitz's memoirs have been published; some of Moshe Sharett's diary has been published by his son, and more is expected; but there has not yet been a flood of revelations.

Despite my complaints, there are solid books—for example, Bernstein's *The Politics of Israel*, Peretz's *Israel and the Palestine Arabs*, and Patai's *Israel Between East and West*—but to date no Israeli Gibbon has appeared.

Alcambar, José. *Israel e o Mundo Árabe.* Lisbon: 1957.

Bayne, E. A. *Four Ways of Politics.* New York: 1965.

Ben-Jacob, Jeremiah. *The Rise of Israel.* New York: 1949.

Bentwich, Norman. *Israel Resurgent.* New York: 1960.

Berger, Elmer. *The Jewish Dilemma.* New York: 1945.

Bernstein, Marver H. *The Politics of Israel: The First Decade of Statehood.* Princeton: 1957.

Catarivas, David. *Israël.* Paris: 1957.

Chouraqui, André. *L'État d'Israël.* Paris: 1955.

Cooke, Hedley V. *Israel: A Blessing and a Curse.* London: 1960.

Duhamel, Georges. *Israël, Clef de l'Orient.* Paris: 1957.

Dunner, Joseph. *The Republic of Israel: Its History and Its Promise.* New York: 1950.

Elston, D. R. *Israel: the Making of a Nation.* London: 1963.

Elston, Roy. *No Alternative: Israel Observed.* London: 1960.

"L'État d'Israël," *Synthèse, Année* 7, No. 75–76 (August–September 1952), pp. 133–318.

Etzioni, Amitai. "The Israel Army: The Human Factor," *Jewish Frontier,* 26 (November 1959), 4–9; 27 (January 1960), 9–13; 27 (February 1960), 16–20.

Falk, Andre. *Israël, Terre Deux Fois Promise.* Paris: 1954.

Fein, Leonard J. "The Political Worlds of Israel," Ph.D. dissertation, Michigan State University, 1962.

Frischwasser-Ra'anan, H. *The Frontiers of a Nation.* London: 1955.

Gamzey, Robert. *Miracle of Israel.* New York: 1965.

Gaury, Gerald de. *The New State of Israel.* New York: 1952.

Gruber, Ruth. *Israel Without Tears.* New York: 1950.

Haelling, Gaston. *Palestine Israëlienne.* Paris: 1952.

Harman, Zena. "The Assimilation of Immigrants into Israel," *Middle East Journal,* 5, No. 3 (Summer 1951), 303–18.

Heller, Abraham Mayez. *Israel's Odyssey.* New York: 1959.

Hobman, J. B., ed. *Palestine's Economic Future: A Review of Progress and Prospects.* London: 1948.

Horowitz, David. "The Economic Problems of Israel," *Middle Eastern Affairs,* 7, No. 11 (November 1956), 373–4.

Huebner, Theodore, and Carl Herman Voss. *This Is Israel—Palestine: Yesterday, Today, and Tomorrow.* New York: 1956.

Hull, William E. *Fall and Rise of Israel.* Grand Rapids: 1954.

Janowsky, Oscar. "Israel: A Welfare State," *Middle Eastern Affairs,* 9, No. 8–9 (August–September 1959), 270–285.

Kraines, Oscar. *Government and Politics in Israel.* Boston: 1961.

———. *Israel: The Emergence of a New Nation.* Washington, D.C.: 1954.

Lehrman, Hal. *Israel: The Beginning and Tomorrow.* New York: 1951.

Lipschutz, Norman. *Victory Through Darkness and Despair.* New York: 1960.

Lowdermilk, Walter Clay. *Palestine: Land of Promise.* New York: 1944.

McGill, Ralph Emerson. *Israel Revisited.* Atlanta: 1950.

Magil, Abraham. *Israel in Crisis.* New York: 1950.

Magliocco, Vito. *La Strada per Gerusalemme.* Milan: 1958.

Mandlebaum, Bernard, ed. *Assignment in Israel.* New York: 1960.

Marshall, S. L. A. "Why the Israeli Army Wins," *Harper's,* 217 (October 1958), 38–45.

Mikes, George. *Milk and Honey: Israel Explored.* London: 1950.

Miller, Irving. *Israel: The Eternal Ideal.* New York: 1955.

Musard, François. *Israël: Miracle du XXᵉ Siècle.* Paris: 1959.

Pajaud, Henri. *Israël Cet Inconnu.* Algiers: 1956.

Paraf, Pierre. *L'État d'Israël dans le Monde.* Paris: 1958.

Patai, Raphael. *Israel Between East and West: A Study in Human Relations.* Philadelphia: 1953.

Peretz, Don. *Israel and the Palestine Arabs.* Washington, D.C.: 1958.

Plá, José. *Israel en los Presentes Días.* Buenos Aires: 1958.

Ramati, Alexander. *Israel Today.* London: 1962.

Ramírez, Alfonso Francisco. *La Republica de Israël.* Mexico: 1950.

Rivlin, Gershon, ed. *Israel Defense Army, 1948–1949.* New York: 1963.

Roletto, Giorgio B. *Israele.* Milan: 1960.

Rubner, Alex. *The Economy of Israel: A Critical Account of the First Ten Years.* New York: 1960.

Russell, E. F. L. R. *If I Forget Thee: The Story of a Nation's Rebirth.* London: 1960.

Sachar, Howard. *Aliyah: The Peoples of Israel.* Cleveland: 1961.

———. *From the Ends of the Earth: The Peoples of Israel.* Cleveland: 1964.

Samuel, Edwin. "The Government of Israel and Its Problems," *Middle East Journal,* 3, No. 1 (January 1949), 1–16.

———. *Problems of Government in the State of Israel.* Jerusalem: 1956.

Schwarz, Walter. *The Arabs in Israel.* London: 1960.

Shihor, Schmuel. *Hollow Glory: The Last Days of Chaim Weizmann, First President of Israël.* New York: 1960.

Sitton, Shlomo. *Israel: Immigration et Croissance, 1948–1958, Suivi d'un Bref Aperçu de la Période 1956–1961.* Paris: 1963.

Spiro, Melford E. *Kibbutz: Venture in Utopia.* Cambridge, Mass.: 1956.

Stone, I. *This Is Israel.* New York: 1948.

Sugrue, Thomas. *Watch for Morning.* New York: 1950.

Sykes, Christopher. *Cross Roads to Israel.* London: 1965.

Tavener, Laurence Ellis. *The Revival of Israel.* London: 1961.

Van Cleef, Eugene. "The Status of Israel—And a Look Ahead," *Middle East Journal,* 18, No. 2, 306–12.

Van Paassen, Pierre. *Jerusalem Calling!* New York: 1950.

Weinryb, Bernard D. "Arabs in Israel," *Palestine Affairs* (October 1948), 113–5.

Williams, L. F. R. *The State of Israel.* New York: 1957.

Wilson, Edmund. *Red, Black, Blond, and Olive.* New York: 1956.

ISRAEL IN WORLD AFFAIRS

Carnegie Endowment for International Peace. *Israel and the United Nations.* New York: 1956.

Christman, Henry M., ed. *This Is Our Strength: The Selected Papers of Golda Meir.* New York: 1962.

Dixon, Fred. "United States–Israel Relations During the Decade 1948–1958." Ph.D. dissertation, University of Virginia, 1960.

Elath, Eliahu. *Israel and Her Neighbors.* London: 1956.

———. "Israel's Relations with the Emerging States in Asia," *Royal Central Central Conference of American Rabbis Yearbook,* 71 (New York: 1961), 248–63.

———. ":Israel's Relations with the Emerging States in Asia," *Royal Central Asian Journal,* 50 (January 1963), 21–9.

Ellis, Harry B. *Israel and the Middle East.* New York: 1957.

Eytan, Walter. *The First Ten Years: A Diplomatic History of Israel.* New York: 1958.

———. "Israel's Foreign Policy and International Relations," *Middle Eastern Affairs,* 11, No. 5 (May 1951), 155–60.

Gal, Alon. "Israel and Iran Draw Closer," *New Outlook,* 7, No. 8 (October 1964), 18–25.

Giniewski, Paul. *Israël Devant l'Afrique et l'Asie.* Paris: 1958. Preface by Jacques Soustelle.

Golding, David. "The United States Foreign Policy in Palestine and Israel, 1945–1949." Ph.D. dissertation, New York University, 1961.

Grossman, Kurt R. *Germany and Israel.* New York: 1958.

Hebrew University, The. *Israel and the United Nations.* New York: 1956.

Howard, Harry. "The United States and Israel: Conflict of Interest and Policy," *Arab Journal,* 2, No. 2 (Spring 1965), 13–24. Cf. *Issues,* 18, No. 4 (Summer 1964), 14–27.

Kahn, Y. Leo. "Israel and the New Nation States of Asia and Africa," *Annals of the American Academy of Political and Social Science,* 324 (July 1959), 96–102.

Kozicki, Richard J. "Burma and Israel: A Study in Friendly Asian Relations," *Middle Eastern Affairs,* 10, No. 3 (March 1959), 109–16.

Kreinin, Mordechai. *Israel and Africa: A study in Technical Cooperation.* New York: 1964.

Lilienthal, Alfred. *The Other Side of the Coin: An American Perspective of the Arab-Israeli Conflict.* New York: 1965.

———. *There Goes the Middle East.* New York: 1957.

———. *What Price Israel?* Chicago: 1953.

Lorch, Netanel. "Israel and Africa," *World Today,* 19 (August 1963), 358–68.

McDonald, James. *My Mission in Israel.* New York: 1951.

Manuel, Frank. *The Realities of American-Palestine Relations.* Washington, D.C.: 1949.

Nanet, Jacques. *Les Juifs et les Nations.* Paris: 1957.

Nikitina, G. S. "The Expansion of Israel into Africa and Neo-Colonialism" (in Russian), *Narody Azii i a Friki,* No. 3 (1963), pp. 36–44.

Peretz, Don. "Israel and the Arab Nations," *Journal of International Affairs,* 19, No. 1 (January 1965), 100–10.

Plotkin, Arieh Leopold. "Israel's Role in the United Nations: An Analytical Study." Ph.D. dissertation, Princeton University, 1955.

Rabinowicz, Oskar K. *Winston Churchill on Jewish Relations: A Half-Century Survey.* London: 1956.

Reich, Bernard. "Israel's Policy in Africa," *Middle East Journal,* 18, No. 1 (Winter 1964), 14–26.

Rivkin, Arnold. "Israel and the Afro-Asian World," *Foreign Affairs,* 37, No. 3 (April 1959), 486–95.

Rondot, Pierre. "L'Opinion Musulmane et l'Incident Irano-Arabe au Sujet d'Israël," *Orient,* No. 3 (1960), 95–101.

Rosenblatt, Bernard Abraham. *The American Bridge to the Israel Commonwealth.* New York: 1959.

Safran, Nadav. *The United States and Israel.* Cambridge, Massachusetts: 1963.

Samuel, Edwin. "Israel and the Arab States," *Political Quarterly* (London), 28 (April–June 1957), 179–87.

———. "Israel and the Arab World," *Political Quarterly* (London), 17 (October–December 1956), 398–410.

Sayegh, Fayez A. *Zionist Colonialism in Palestine.* Beirut: 1965.

Syrkin, Marie. *Golda Meir: Woman with a Cause.* New York: 1963.

Voss, Carl Herman. *The Palestine Problem Today: Israel and Its Neighbors.* Boston: 1953.

Zionist Organization, Great Britain. *Israel, the United Nations and the Arabs: A Guide for Zionist Keyworkers.* London: 1957.

ISRAELI-ARAB CONFLICT: GENERAL

There are a few interesting works in Arabic and Hebrew that have not yet been translated, like Yigal Alon's *A Curtain of Sand* (Israel: 1959), Israel Baer's *In the Orbit of Security Problems* (Tel Aviv: 1957), and Abdullah el-Tell's polemical *The Dangers of World Jewry to Islam and Christianity.* There are also inumerable pamphlets, news releases, and "studies" that add little light. Scholarly studies are rare. Earl Berger's *The Covenant and the Sword* is most useful for the 1948–1956 period, [although it is written within the context of the United Nations]. One of the strongest proponents of the Arab view has himself become a topic of the conflict; *see* Morris Gerschlick, *Erskine Childers and Israel* (Israel: 1965).

Abdel-Kader, A. Razak. *Le Conflict Judéo-Arabe: Juifs et Arabes Face à l'Avenir.* Paris: 1961.

Alon, Yigal. "Israel at Bay," *Midstream,* 11 (Spring 1956), 5–11.

American Zionist Council. *Israel and the Arab States.* New York: 1951.

————. *Israel and the Arab States*. New York: 1956.

Assaf, M. "The Revenge Complex in the Arab World," *Hamizrah Hehadash*, 1 (April 1950), 185–9. In Hebrew with a summary in English.

Beatty, Ilene. *Arab and Jew in the Land of Canaan*. Chicago: 1957.

Berger, Earl. *The Covenant and the Sword: Arab-Israeli Relations 1948–1956*. Toronto: 1965.

Bloomfield, Lincoln M. *Egypt, Israel and the Gulf of 'Aqaba in International Law*. Toronto: 1957.

Brook, David. *Preface to Peace: The United Nations and the Arab-Israel Armistice System*. Washington, D.C.: 1964.

Childers, Erskine. "Palestine: The Broken Triangle," *Journal of International Affairs*, 19, No. 1 (January 1965), 87–99.

Davis, John H. "Arab-Israeli Conflict: A Challenge to Leadership," *Arab Journal*, 2, No. 3 (Summer 1965), 28–32.

Ereli, Eliezer. "The *Bat Galim* Case Before the Security Council," *Middle Eastern Affairs*, 6, No. 4 (April 1955), 108–16.

Frye, W. *A United Nations Peace Force*. New York: 1957.

Ghubashy, Omar A. "Israel and the Suez Canal," *The Egyptian Economic and Political Review*, 6, No. 4 (April–May 1960), 9–13.

————. "Tiran and 'Aqaba," *The Egyptian Economic and Political Review*, 5, No. 2 (January 1959), 18–25.

Hadawi, Sam. *Palestine: Loss of a Heritage*. San Antonio: 1963.

Harkavi, Yehushafat. "The Arab-Israel Confrontation," *Midstream*, 12, No. 3 (March 1966), 3–12.

Hasan, Saadat. "Why the Palestine Liberation Organization," *Arab Journal*, 2, No. 3 (Summer 1965), 3–7.

Hurewitz, J. C. "Arab-Israel Tensions," *Academy of Political Science: Proceedings*, 24 (January 1952), 513–21.

————. *Middle East Dilemmas*. New York: 1953.

————. "The United Nations Concilation Commission for Palestine: Establishment and Definition of Function," *International Organization*, 7 (1955), 482–97.

Institute for Strategic Studies, *The Military Balance*. London.

Katz, Franz Josef. *Witness to Fullfillment: Israel Under the Truce*. New York: 1949.

Mehdi, Muhammad T. *The Question of Palestine*. New York: 1961.

Mohn, Paul. "Jerusalem and the United Nations," *International Conciliation* (October 1950), pp. 421–71.

Naufal, Sayyid. "A Short History of the Arab Opposition to Zionism and Israel," *Islamic Review*, 53, No. 2 (February 1965), 4–8; 53, No. 3 (March 1965), 11–4.

Peretz, Don. "Arab Blocked Bank Accounts in Israel," *Jewish Social Studies*, 18 (January 1956), 25–40.

Rosenne, Shabtai. *Israel's Armistice Agreements with the Arab States*. Tel Aviv: 1951.

Sahwell, Aziz S. *Exodus: A Distortion of Truth.* New York: 1960.
Sayegh, Fayez A. *Arab-Israeli Conflict.* New York: 1964.
————. *The Record of Israel at the United Nations.* New York: 1957.
Sharett, Moshe. "Israel's Position and Problems," *Middle Eastern Affairs*, 3, No. 5 (May 1952), 137–9.
Shimoni, Yaacov. "Israel in the Pattern of Middle East Politics," *Middle East Journal*, 4, No. 3 (July 1950), 277–95.
Shwadran, Benjamin. "Jordan Annexes Arab Palestine," *Middle Eastern Affairs*, 1, No. 4 (April 1950), 99–111.
Simpson, Dwight J. "Israel: The State of Siege," *Current History*, 48, No. 285, 263 ff.
Tannous, Izzat. *The Enraging Story of Palestine and Its People.* New York: 1965.
————. *A Picture of the Palestine Problem in the United Nations, 1947-1965.* New York: 1965.
Weems, Miner. "The Propaganda Struggle in the Middle East 1955-1958: A Comparative Study of the Role of Propaganda as a Legitimate Tool of Government in the Cold War." Ph.D. dissertation, Georgetown University, 1962.
Weigert, Gideon. "Arab Writers Look at Israel," *World Today*, 15 (December 1959), 501–8.
Weinberger, Siegbert J. "The Suez Canal Issue 1956," *Middle Eastern Affairs*, 8, No. 2 (February 1957), 46–56.
World Jewish Congress. *Evidence of the Arab War in Peacetime Against Israel.* Tel Aviv: 1957.

ISRAEL–ARAB CONFLICT: BORDER TENSION

Armstrong, Hamilton Fish. "The United Nations Experience in Gaza," *Foreign Affairs*, 35 (July 1957), 600–19.
Brilliant, Moshe. "Israel's Policy of Reprisals," *Harper's* (March 1955), 68–72.
Burns, E. L. M. *Between Arab and Israeli.* Toronto: 1962.
Byford-Jones, W. *Forbidden Frontiers.* London: 1958.
Cohen, Maxwell. "The United Nations Emergency Force: A Preliminary View," *International Journal*, 12, No. 2 (Spring 1957).
Dayan, Moshe. "Israel's Borders and Security Problems," *Foreign Affairs*, 33 (January 1955), 250–67.
Glubb, John Bagot. "Violence on the Jordan-Israel Border," *Foreign Affairs*, 32 (July 1954), 552–62.
Goodrich, Leland M., and Gabriella E. Rosner. "The United Nations Emergency Force," *International Organization*, 11 (Summer 1957), 413–30.
Hurewitz, J. C. "The Israeli-Syrian Crisis in the Light of the Arab-Israel Armistice System," *International Organization*, 5 (August 1951), 459–79.
Hutchison, E. H. *Violent Truce.* London: 1956.

Khouri, Fred J. "Friction and Conflict on the Israeli-Syrian Front," *Middle East Journal*, 17, No. 1 (Winter–Spring 1963), 14–34.

Nicholas, Herbert. "United Nations Peace Forces and the Changing Globe— The Lessons of Suez and Congo," *International Organization*, 17, No. 2 (Spring 1963), 321–37.

Rolf, W. "Guerilla gegen Israel," *Diskussion*, 6, No. 17 (1965), 10–2.

Shwadran, Benjamin. "Isreal-Jordan Border Tension," *Middle Eastern Affairs*, 6, No. 12 (December 1953), 385–401.

Young, Peter. *Bedouin Command*. London: 1956.

ISRAELI-ARAB CONFLICT: JORDAN RIVER

Doherty, Kathryn B. "Jordan Waters Conflict," *International Conciliation*, No. 553 (May 1965).

Goichon, A. M. *L'Eau: Problème vital de la région du Jourdain*. Brussels: 1964.

Hacohen, Mordecai. "The Administrative Aspects of a Proposed Jordan Valley Development Project for Israel." Ph.D. dissertation, the New School for Social Research, 1957.

Hayes, James Buchanan, and A. E. Barrekette. *T.V.A. on the Jordan*. Washington, D.C.: 1948.

Rizk, Edward. *The River Jordan*. New York: 1964.

Stevens, Georgiana G. *Jordan River Partition* (Stanford: 1965); cf. *International Conciliation*, No. 506.

ISRAELI-ARAB CONFLICT: ARAB REFUGEES

Aggiouri, René. "Le Plan Hammarskjoeld et les Arabes," *Orient*, 111, No. 3 (1959), 41–50.

Bentwich, Norman. "The Arab Refugees," *Contemporary Review*, No. 1006 (August 1949), pp. 79–82.

Bruhns, Fred C. "A Study of Arab Refugees' Attitudes," *Middle East Journal*, 9, No. 2 (Spring 1955), 130–8.

Comay, Michael. *Resettling the Arab Refugees*. Jerusalem: 1957.

Eban, Abba. *The Arab Refugee Problem: Need for Candor*. Jerusalem: n.d.

Gabbay, Rony E. *A Political Study of the Arab-Jewish Conflict: The Arab Refugee Problem (A Case Study)*. Geneva: 1959.

Harvey, Mary Frances. "The Palestine Refugee Problem: Element of a Solution," *Orbis*, 3 (Summer 1959), 193–207.

Mannin, Ethel. *A Lance for the Arabs*. London: 1963.

Peretz, Don. "The Arab Refugee Dilemma," *Foreign Affairs*, 33 (October 1954), 134–48.

———. "The Arab Refugees: A Changing Problem," *Foreign Affairs* (April 1963), pp. 558–70.

———. "Detente in the Arab Refugee Dilemma," *Orbis*, 5 (Fall 1961), 306–9.

———. "Problems of Arab Refugee Compensation," *Middle East Journal*, 8 (Autumn 1954), 403–16.

Pinner, Walter. *How Many Arab Refugees?*, London: 1959.

Rabinowicz, Oskar K. "The Jews and the Arab Refugees," *Jewish Social Studies*, 21 (October 1959), 238–45.

Richardson, Channing B. "The United Nations and Arab Refugee Relief, 1948–1950: A Case Study in International Organization and Administration." Ph.D. dissertation, Columbia University, 1951.

St. Aubin, W. de. "Peace and Refugees in the Middle East," *Middle East Journal*, 3, No. 3 (July 1949), 249–59.

Stevens, Georgiana G. "Arab Refugees, 1948–1952," *Middle East Journal*, 6 (Summer 1952), 287–98.

Syrkin, Marie. "The Arab Refugees: A Zionist View," *Commentary*, 40, No. 1 (January 1966), 23–30.

Thicknesse, S. C. *Arab Refugees: A Survey of Resettlement Possibilities* (London: 1949).

Tibawi, A. L. "Visions of the Return: The Palestine Arab Refugees in Arabic Poetry and Art," *Middle East Journal*, 17, No. 5 (Late Autumn 1963), 507–26.

ISRAELI-ARAB CONFLICT: SINAI CAMPAIGN

With one or two exceptions, which are the result of a paucity of Egyptian sources, the purely military events of Operation Kadesh are well known. Robert Henriques rushed his book out a wee bit early, but S. L. A. Marshall's *Sinai Victory*, Edgar O'Ballance's *The Sinai Campaign 1956*, and the Lt. Colonel Ben-Zion Tehan's official *The Sinai Campaign* chronicle the operation in detail. Moshe Dayan's diary is a most helpful corrective, for it shows that the campaign was not perfect everywhere at every time. Erskine Childers' works tend to overcorrect in the Arabs' favor. There are several volumes still available only in Hebrew: Ben-Gurion's *The Sinai Campaign*, Shlomo Dov Gepner's *The Book of the Sinai War*, Měnahem Talmī's *Thus We Fought in Sinai*, and Shabtay Tevet, *The Campaign of the Israeli Defense Army in Sinai*. But none, not even Ben-Gurion's, adds anything vital.

Barer, Shlomo. *The Weekend War*. London: 1959.

Bar-Zohar, Michel. *Suez Ultra Secret*. Paris: 1964.

Childers, Erskine B. "The Sinai War, 1956," *Arab Journal*, No. 2–3 (1964), 68–82.

———. "The Sinai War, 1956," *Middle East Forum*. 37, No. 2 (February 1961), 20–8.

Comay, Joan. *The Six Days of the Sinai Campaign*. Israel: 1957.

Dayan, Major General Moshe. *Diary of the Sinai Campaign*. New York: 1966.

"Hagiography for a Zionist War," *Egyptian Economic and Political Review*, 6, No. 6 (May 1958), 25–8.

Henriques, Robert. *A Hundred Hours to Suez.* New York: 1957. See the review, "Hagiography," and revisions by Henriques in *The Daily Telegraph* (May 3, 1957).

Lev, Amos. *With Plowshare and Sword: Life in the Army of Israel.* New York: 1961.

Marshall, S. L. A. *Sinai Victory.* New York: 1958.

O'Ballance, Edgar. *The Sinai Campaign 1956.* London: 1959.

Stocks, Ernest. "Israel on the Road to Sinai: A Small State in a Test of Power." Ph.D. dissertation, Columbia University, 1964.

Tehan, Lieutenant Colonel Ben Zion. *The Sinai Campaign.* Israel: n.d.

ISRAELI-ARAB CONFLICT: SUEZ CRISIS

The major problem in compiling a bibliography of the Suez Crisis is that, for most participants and many subsequent writers, Israel's involvement was only a side show, except for the problems of collusion and to a lesser degree withdrawal from Sinai. Once Kadesh had been completed, the conflict was less between the Arabs and Israel than between Israel cum France and nearly everyone else. Even then the great body of material is largely tangential to Israel. I have been reluctant to include all the biographies of John Foster Dulles or his own articles, his collected speeches, his dissertations on his "moral thought" or his brother Allen's passing references to Suez. The same is true for Dwight D. Eisenhower and Hammarskjöld *et al.* This bibliography will not serve as a basis for a diplomatic history of the Suez crisis, or the United States role, or the impact on the Commonwealth, although selected listings for each topic are included, in order to reveal the extent of the existing materials that have almost no bearing on Israel or the Arabs.

There are also many sources on the military aspects of the expedition tucked away in regimental journals, army reviews, the reports of participants, and the standard reviews concerned with tactical problems. One other point, which by this time should be superfluous, is that almost without exception everyone who wrote on Suez had an ox to gore or an ax to whet or a point to prove. Herman Finer, for example, an American scholar of splendid repute, has written an extensive analysis, *Dulles Over Suez,* that is most enlightening and most contentious. See also "Communications," *American Political Science Review,* 60, No. 2 (June 1966), 392-3, in which he takes exception to John H. Millett's rather harsh review of his book. Millett replies, "The thrust of my review of Professor Finer's most recent work was that is was part of the events themselves, rather than an analysis of them." To a greater or lesser extent, this statement applies to all work on the crisis, from Robertson's praise of Pearson to Eden's curiously unrevealing memoirs. *Caveat emptor.*

Ball, W. Macmahon. "The Australian Reaction to the Suez Canal," *The Australian Journal of Politics and History,* 2 No. 2 (May 1957).

Barker, A. J. *Suez: Seven Day War.* London: 1964.

Bar-Zohar, Michael. *Suez Ultra Secret.* Paris: 1964.

Beloff, Max. "Suez and the British Conscience," *Commentary,* 23, No. 4 (April 1957), 309–15.

Bentwicht, Norman. "Israel After Suez," *Royal Central Asian Journal,* 48 (April 1961), 160–7.

Bromberger, H., and S. Bromberger. *Les Secrets de l'Expedition d'Egypte.* Paris: 1957. Revised and published in Great Britain as *Secrets of Suez.* London, 1957.

Childers, Erskine B. *The Road to Suez.* London: 1962.

Churchill, Randolph S. *The Rise and Fall of Sir Anthony Eden.* London: 1959.

Clark, D. M. J. *Suez Touchdown.* London: 1964.

Dougherty, James E. "The Aswan Decision in Perspective," *Political Science Quarterly* (March 1949), 21–45.

Drummond, Roscoe, and Gaston Coblentz. *Duel at the Brink.* New York: 1960.

Eayrs, James. "Suez, Britain, and the Canadian Conscience," *Canada in World Affairs, 1955–1957.* Toronto: 1959.

Eden, Anthony. *Full Circle: The Memoirs of Anthony Eden.* Boston: 1960.

Epstein, Leon D. *British Politics in the Suez Crisis.* Urbana: 1964.

———. "Partisan Foreign Policy: Britain in the Suez Crisis," *World Politics,* 12 (January 1960), 201–24.

Feis, Herbert. "Suez Scenario: A Lamentable Tale," *Foreign Affairs,* 38 (July 1960), 598–612.

Finer, Herman. *Dulles Over Suez: The Theory and Practice of His Diplomacy.* Chicago: 1964.

Fitzsimmons, M. A. "The Suez Crisis and the Containment Policy," *Review of Politics,* 19 (October 1957), 419–45.

Foot, Michael, and Mervyn Jones. *Guilty Men, 1957: Suez and Cyprus.* New York: 1957.

G. L. "Suez and Its Consequences: The Israeli View," *World Today,* 13 (April 1957), 152–61.

Halpern, Manfred. "Dulles in the Suez Crisis: Response to Law, Aggression, and Revolution," *Worldview,* 7, No. 10 (October 1964), 12–5.

Hourani, A. H. "The Middle East and the Crisis of 1956," *Middle Eastern Affairs,* No. 1 (London: 1958).

Johnson, Paul. *The Suez War.* London: 1957.

Keightley, General Charles F. "Dispatch on Suez Operations, June 10, 1957," *Supplement, London Gazette* (September 10, 1957).

Kline, Earl Oliver. "The Suez Crisis: Anglo-American Relations and the United Nations." Ph.D. dissertation, Princeton University, 1961.

Lawrence, E. V. *Egypt and the West: Salient Facts Behind the Suez Crisis.* New York: 1956.

Longgood, William F. *Suez Story: Key to the Middle East.* New York: 1957.

Mahan, Jitendra. "South Africa and the Suez Crisis," *International Journal,* 16, No. 4 (Autumn 1961).

Makleu, Ismail S. "The Suez Crisis: A Perspective Analysis." Ph.D. dissertation, University of Pittsburgh, 1964.
Malone, Joseph J. "Germany and the Suez Crisis," *Middle East Journal*, 20, No. 1 (Winter 1966), 20–30.
Nutting, Anthony. *I Saw for Myself: The Aftermath of Suez*. New York: 1958.
Robertson, Terrence. *Crisis: The Inside Story of the Suez Conspiracy*. Toronto: 1964.
Schonfield, Hugh J. *The Suez Canal in World Affairs*. New York: 1953.
Smolansky, O. M. "Moscow and the Suez Crisis, 1956: A Reappraisal," *Political Science Quarterly*, 80, No. 4 (December 1965), 581–605.
Speier, Hans. "Soviet Atomic Blackmail," *World Politics*, 9 (April 1957), 307–28.
Spry, Graham. "Canada, the United Nations Emergency Force, and the Commonwealth," *International Affairs*, 33, No. 3 (July 1957), 289–300.
Stewart, James. "The Suez Operation," *United States Naval Institute Proceedings*, 90, No. 4 (April 1964), 37–47.
Tournous, J.-R. *Secrets d'État*. Paris: 1960.
Wint, Guy, and Peter Calvocoressi. *Middle East Crisis*. London: 1957.

ISRAELI-ARAB CONFLICT: SOLUTIONS

With few exceptions, all books, articles, and other materials dealing with the Arab-Israeli confrontation suggest solutions, however modest. I may have missed genocide as a modest proposal, but it is about the only approach not advocated in print.

Alon, Yigal. "The Arab-Israel Conflict: Some Suggested Solutions," *International Affairs*, 60, No. 2 (April 1964), 205–18.
Aminadav, D. *The Israeli-Arab Conflict: To the International Court* (in Hebrew). Tel Aviv: 1956.
Eban, Aubrey S. "The Future of Arab-Jewish Relations," *Commentary*, 6 (September 1948), 199–206.
Hadawi, Sami. "Israel's Sham Peace Offers," *Middle East Forum*, 60, No. 2 (February–March 1964), 27–9.
Howard, Harry N. "The Bourguiba Proposals: Time's Erosion of the Arab-Israel Conflict," *Issues*, 19, No. 2 (Summer 1965), 5–17.
Johnson, Joseph E. "Arab vs. Israeli: A Persistant Challenge," *Middle East Journal*, 18, No. 1 (Winter 1964), 1–13.
Kerr, Malcolm H. "Israel, the Arabs, and the Blueprint Illusion," *Issues*, 15, No. 1 (Winter 1961), 9–17.
Laqueur, Walter Z. "Israel and the Arab Blocs," *Commentary*, 24 (September 1957), 185–91.
Thomas, Norman. *The Prerequisites for Peace*. New York: 1959.
Wells, Frederick. "Federalism, A Radical Proposal: Could Merger Reconcile Israel and Her Neighbors?" *Issues*, 19 (Summer 1965), 29–31.

Epilogue: 1967

During 1966 several most useful books appeared on various aspects of the Arab-Israeli confrontation, particularly the Suez-Sinai crisis. Hugh Thomas has produced a solid study of Suez (*The Suez Affair*, London: 1967), but, alas, with too many notes reading "Evidence of a Cabinet Minister." One authority Anthony Nutting, has spoken out clearly (*No End of a Lesson: The Story of Suez*, London: 1967). See also

Abi-Mershed, Walid. *Israeli Withdrawal From Sinai.* Beirut: 1966.
Aldrich, W. W. "The Suez Crisis," *Foreign Affairs*, 45, No. 3 (April 1967), 541–2.
Calvocoressi, Peter. *Suez: Ten Years After.* London: 1967.
Mathews, R. O. "The Suez Canal Dispute: A Case Study in Peaceful Settlement," *International Organization*, 21, No. 1 (1967), 79–101.

Ernest Stock's *Israel on the Road to Sinai* (Ithaca: 1967) has a final chapter that takes into account the events of June 1967. Several other new and useful books are

Abu Jaber, Kamel. *The Arab Baath Socialist Party.* Syracuse: 1966.
Horn, General Carl von. *Soldiering for Peace.* London: 1966.
Schechtman, Joseph B. *The United States and the Jewish State Movement, The Crucial Decade: 1939–1949.* New York: 1966.
Vatikiotis, P. J. *Politics and the Military in Jordan: A Study of the Arab Legion, 1921–1957.* New York: 1967.

In the case of the six-day war, never have so many written so much and revealed so little. The vast outpouring of instant history, potted analysis, firsthand reports, and artificial books staggers the imagination. The Zionist Archives in New York has already accumulated numerous huge boxes of clippings and extracts in most known languages. Nearly every publishing house and periodical has added to the flood. Some journals (*Commentary* for one) published special issues, often containing much reasonable analysis. The January 1968 issue of *Foreign Affairs* has three solid, though not novel, articles by Charles W. Yost, Bernard Lewis, and Don Peretz. Most of the "material" has not been quite as solid. Some major newspapers (the *Sunday London Times* is something of an exception), wire services (see The Associated Press, *Lightning Out of Israel: The Six-Day War in the Middle East*, New York: 1967), and several private entrepreneurs (see *Israel's Finest Day*, West Pittston, Pa., 1967) turned out clip-and-paste books for the masses in record time. There were, however, some good though hasty surveys of the military compaign, like those by S. L. A. Marshall and Winston S. Churchill, whereas Shmuel Segev, military correspondent of *Ma'ariv*, produced the first Hebrew account of the campaign.

Anner, Zeev, and Yoseph Alkone, eds. *The War 1967*. Tel Aviv: 1967.

Benson, Alex, ed. *The 49 Hour War: The Arab-Israeli Conflict*. New York: 1967.

Churchill, Randolph S., and Winston S. Churchill. *The Six Day War*. London: 1967.

Curtis, David, and Stephen G. Crane. *Dayan*. New York: 1967.

Dayan, Yaël. *Israel Journal: June, 1967*. New York: 1967.

Donovan, Robert J. *Six Days in June: Israel's Fight for Survival*. New York: 1967.

Fuldheim, Dorothy. *Where Were the Arabs?* Cleveland: 1967.

Gervasi, Frank. *The Case for Israel*. New York: 1967.

Glubb, Sir John Bagot. *The Middle East Crisis*. London: 1967.

MacLeish, Roderick. *The Sun Stood Still*. New York: 1967.

Marshall, S. L. A. *Swift Sword: The Historical Record of Israel's Victory, June 1967*. New York: 1967.

Stevenson, William. *Israeli Victory*. London: 1967.

This list by no means exhausts the new "books" but gives some indication of the technology if not the taste of the publishing industry. Marshall and Churchill and Churchill will probably last for some time, as it is unlikely that the Egyptians will be forthcoming with new material and the security-conscious Israelis probably think existing accounts are already too detailed. Walter Laqueur proposes to publish an account of the background of the crisis in the spring of 1968, and on that subject A. S. Khalidi's "An Appraisal of the Arab-Israeli Military Balance," *Middle East Forum*, 42, No. 3 (1966), 55–6, reveals Arab optimism before the crisis all too clearly.

Index

Sukarno, 269
Suliman, Mohammed Sidky, 405

Tabenkin, Yosef, 125
Taft, Robert, 66
Taha, Sayid (Black Tiger), 209, 213–14
Tal, Brig. Gen. Israel, 416–19
Tell, Col. Abdullah el-, 217, 228, 230–31, 245
Ten-day war (July 6–16, 1948), 181–96
Terrorism
  in 1945, 12–13, 16, 20
  in 1946, 21–23, 25–27, 32
  in 1947, 38, 41–43, 69
  in 1966, 401, 402
  refugees involved in, 382–83
Thomas, Abel, 289, 291, 300
Tito, Marshal, 284
Tolkovsky, 289
Tripartite Declaration (1950), 267, 269, 270
Truman, Harry S, 15, 23
  concessions demanded by, 240
  Israel recognized by, 123, 232
  Israel supported by, 64–65, 162
Tsarapkin, Semen K., 55

U Kyaw Nyein, 378
U Nu, 269
U Thant, 401, 404, 407–8, 424
United Nations, Israel's admission to (May 11, 1949), 232
Underground organizations, see Haganah; Irgun; Lechi

War
  of attrition (1949–56), 237–77; see also

Border war; June war; Palestine war; Sinai war
Weizmann, Chaim, 6, 7, 13, 15, 31
Westlake, Peter, 298
Wilson, Harold, 410

Yadin, Gen. Yigal, 117, 118, 123, 124, 172
  Ben-Gurion opposed by, 168–69
  counter-offensive in Jerusalem and (May 1948), 152–54
  offensive on Jerusalem and (July 1948), 194
  Operation Avak and (Aug. 1948), 198
  Operation Shin-Tav-Shin and (Feb.–Mar. 1949), 227, 228
  Operation Ten Plagues and (Oct. 1948), 202–5, 207
  Operation Ayin (Dec. 1948–Jan. 1949) and, 218–23
  ten-day war and, 182
Yoffe, Brig. Gen. Avraham, 330–35, 416–20
Yona, Col. Elfrat, 425

Zahal
  equipment of (by 1966), 384–86
  elimination of Irgun and, 170–72
  formation of (May 1948), 167
  in June war (1967), 397–430
  Operation Dekel (July 1948) and, 185–86
  remolded by Dayan, 302
  strength of (fall 1948), 199
  ten-day war and, 181–96
Zayen, Yussef, 375
Zionism, first Congress of (1897), 5–6